Introduction to
Employee Benefits Law

Introduction to Employee Benefits Law

Kathryn J. Kennedy
PROFESSOR OF LAW
DIRECTOR OF THE LL.M TAX PROGRAM
DIRECTOR OF THE LL.M EMPLOYEE BENEFITS PROGRAM
DIRECTOR OF THE LL.M. ESTATE PLANNING PROGRAM
UIC JOHN MARSHALL LAW SCHOOL

CAROLINA ACADEMIC PRESS
Durham, North Carolina

Library of Congress Cataloging-in-Publication Data

Names: Kennedy, Kathryn J., 1952- author.
Title: Introduction to employee benefits law / by Kathryn J. Kennedy.
Description: Durham, North Carolina : Carolina Academic Press, LLC, 2020.
Identifiers: LCCN 2020035643 | ISBN 9781531018276 (paperback) | ISBN
   9781531018283 (ebook)
Subjects: LCSH: Pension trusts--Law and legislation--United States. |
   United States. Employee Retirement Income Security Act of 1974. |
   Employee fringe benefits--Law and legislation--United States.
Classification: LCC KF3512 .K465 2020 | DDC 344.7301/252--dc23
LC record available at https://lccn.loc.gov/2020035643

Carolina Academic Press
700 Kent Street
Durham, North Carolina 27701
Telephone (919) 489-7486
Fax (919) 493-5668
www.cap-press.com

Printed in the United States of America

For my father, Mark J. Jennings, whose passion for integrity and justice propelled me into the pursuit of law, and to my mother, Doris M. Jennings, whose passion for education propelled me into teaching, and for my husband, Brian A. Kennedy, whose insights and constant support allowed me to pursue my dreams.

Contents

Section IV · Other Employee Benefits Plans

Table of Cases

Cases in bold font indicate primary cases in Materials.

Table of Authorities

Pages with tables are indicated by a "t" following the page number.

xl   TABLE OF AUTHORITIES

Preface

For the past ten years, I have relied on Barry Kozak's textbook *Employee Benefit Plans*, from Carolina Academic Press, published in 2010, in teaching an introductory course in employee benefits law. It has been an excellent resource for such a course. However, significant changes have been made to the law since 2010. New rules emerged from the Tax Cuts and Jobs Act (TCJA)[1] passed in 2017, which was the most significant overhaul of the tax rules in more than three decades, and from the Setting Every Community Up For Retirement Enhancement of 2019 (SECURE),[2] which made significant changes to the employee benefit rules promulgated by ERISA. Thus, an update to Kozak's textbook was necessary to make it more current. This textbook is outlined similarly to the Kozak textbook, concentrating more on the rules applicable to retirement plans, but also covering the general ERISA rules to all employee benefit plans, and other types of employee benefit plans (e.g., executive compensation, health and welfare plans, and IRAs). Like the Kozak's textbook, this textbook does not presume the student has any prior knowledge about employee benefits law.

This book is written for M.J. (Masters Jurisprudence) and LL.M. (Masters in Legal Letter) students who are new to the field of employee benefits, as well as for J.D. students. It may also be beneficial to tax students in understanding the tax implications of employee fringe benefits.

This book is organized in four sections. Section I is an introduction to employee benefits—why employers offer them, the tax advantages of such plans, and the federal law that governs employee benefits, which is the Employee Retirement Income Security Act of 1974 (ERISA). Back in 1974, retirement benefits were the main focus of employee benefits law—thus most of the substantive rules in ERISA revolve around retirement benefits. Section II explains those substantive rules both in Title I (ERISA's labor provisions) and in Title II (the Code's qualification provisions). Legal protections, fiduciary concerns, plan termination rules, and reporting provisions are set forth in Section III and are applicable not only to retirement plans, but also to health and welfare benefit plans. There are three federal agencies that regulate ERISA include the U.S. Department of Treasury and the Internal Revenue Service, the U.S. Department of Labor, and the Pension Benefit Guaranty Corporation. Section IV

---

1. Pub. L. No. 115-97, 131 Stat. 2054 (Dec. 22, 2017).
2. The Act is part of the Further Consolidated appropriations Act, 2020, H.R. 1865, No. 116-94, Division O (Dec. 20, 2019).

focuses on other types of employee benefit plans—namely executive compensation plans, health and welfare benefit plans, and Individual Retirement Accounts.

Each chapter begins with a reading assignment, which should be done before reading the text of the chapter. All of the reading assignments direct the student to read the applicable provisions in the ERISA statute. There are class discussion questions set forth, which the student should be able to answer after reading the chapter. The Overview, which appears at the beginning of each chapter, should be read *after the text* of the chapter, as it is designed to be a *review* of that material. There are footnotes within the text, simply to direct the student to the source of the statement for further information. Examples are provided within the chapter so that the student apply a given rule to a set of facts.

The materials in this textbook is designed to provide an overall guide to learning employee benefits law. It can be overwhelming as there is so much content within Titles I, II, III and IV of ERISA. I look forward to introducing and teaching you this fascinating area of law, as it impacts so many other areas of the law, such as corporate law, securities law, family law, and tax law.

Acknowledgments

I would like to acknowledge my colleague Barry Kozak for the use of his "Overview Sections," that appear at the beginning of each of my chapters. These originally appeared in Barry Kozak's book entitled *Employee Benefit Plans*, published by Carolina Academic Press. I used them mostly verbatim, as they served as a excellent review of the materials discussed in the text of the chapter. I have Barry Kozak's permission, as well as Carolina Academic Press's approval, to replicate them in my textbook. I would like to acknowledge my colleague Christopher Condeluci for his insights, especially with respect to the chapter on welfare benefits. Also my thanks to my research assistants who worked diligently to assist me in finalizing this book: Gabrielle Neace and Aldridge Maurer.

Section I

Preliminary Concerns

Before tackling the complicated rules that govern employee benefit plans, especially qualified retirement plans, this section introduces the reader to why an employer would provide employee benefits, the favorable tax rules afforded to employee benefits, and the rationale by which the federal law of Employee Retirement Income Security Act (ERISA) of 1974 was passed.

Chapter 1 discusses what types of employee benefits are offered through employers, along with the metaphor of a "three legged stool" to describe sources of retirement benefits. As most employer-provided employee benefits can only be offered to employees (as opposed to independent contractors and non-working family members), the text discusses who qualifies as an employee as ERISA's definition is not helpful.

Chapter 2 discusses basic tax concepts for the reader to better appreciate the tax preferential rules extended to certain employee benefits. As compensation for an employee's services (including fringe benefits) are included in the employee's gross income in the tax year in which the services were rendered, the reader is introduced to the Internal Revenue Code's sections that provide a total or partial exclusion from gross income; a deferral of the timeframe in which gross income is recognized; and tax credits extended.

Chapter 3 introduces the reader to the rationale for which ERISA was passed and why there are four Titles to ERISA, which are regulated through various federal agencies. The chapter concludes with the roles of various professionals that interact with employee benefits plans, such as attorneys, accountants, Enrolled Actuaries, and other benefits professionals.

Section 1

Preliminary Concerns

Chapter 1

Employee Benefits Offered to Employees by Employers

Reading Assignment:	Skim Title I, II, III and IV of ERISA
	Sigman v. Rudolph Wurlitzer Co., 11 N.E.2d 878 (Ohio Ct. App. 1937)
	Nationwide Mutual Ins. Co. v. Darden, 503 U.S. 318 (1992)
	Rev. Rul. 87-41
Class Discussion Questions:	Explain the statement that the "U.S. private pension system can be described by the following three distinguishing characteristics — employment based, voluntary, and tax deferred."
	Why does the government use the tax code as leverage for employers in the delivery of employee benefits?
	What are the various types of employee benefits?
	What is the three-legged stool describing an employee's sources of income for retirement?
	How is an employer contractually liable for employee benefits?
	Who is a "common law employee" as opposed to an independent contractor?

Overview

Why would employers offer employee benefits in addition to cash wages?

- to attract, retain, and reward good employees
- to distinguish the employer from its competitors
- for income tax advantages to both the employer and employee
- paternalistic feelings of the employer to protect the health, well-being, and financial security of its workforce (while they are employed and after retirement)

What are the general categories of employee benefits?

- compensation
- paid time off
- health benefits (either the employer pays the premiums to an insurance company or the employer directly reimburses the employee for certain medical expenses)
- welfare benefits (either fringe benefits to make the employee's life easier so that the employee is more productive or benefits like reimbursement of their legal expenses or their children's day care expenses)
- retirement benefits (the employer voluntarily provides some replacement income during retirement after the employee stops earning a salary as an active employee)
- severance benefits (the employer continues to pay a portion of the employee's salary for a transition period after the employee is terminated for good cause but before a successor job is secured)
- death benefits (the employer pays a certain multiple of the employee's base salary to the beneficiary or estate of the employee who dies while still an active employee)
- equity ownership (the corporate employer either gives shares of stock or the option to purchase stock at a discount; the LLC entity does the same for membership units) to transfer ownership of the employer business to employees (either for a sense of profit sharing or for true equity and succession planning)

What is the "three-legged stool" theory for sources of income during retirement?

- individual savings (including equity in the home, credit worthiness, and individual retirement accounts)
- governmental pensions (through Social Security)
- employer-provided retirement benefits

Who can employers promise the employee benefits to?

- qualified retirement plans: only common-law employees of the employer can be participants in a qualified retirement plan
- health and welfare benefit plans: only common-law employees of the employer can enroll in the health and welfare plans, and the employer can then allow spouses, children, and dependents to also enroll (where the cost of the coverage for these family members is excluded from the employee's taxable income, as discussed in Chapter 2), and the employer can further allow other family members, such as a sibling (but the cost for these non-traditional family members will be imputed into the employee's taxable income)
- executive compensation plans: can be offered to individuals other than common-law employees, such as independent contractors, consultants and business advisors, and members of the board of directors, as long as the individual receives remuneration for services performed

What are the four Titles of ERISA?

- Title I prescribes minimum standards for both employee pension plans and profit sharing plans
- Title II amended provisions of the Internal Revenue Code relating to employee pension and profit sharing plans that were "qualified" under the Code
- Title III provided jurisdictional authority to the Department of Labor, Employee Benefits Security Administration, and the Internal Revenue Service, Employee Plans group of the Tax Exempt/Government Entities Operating Division
- Title IV created a new federal corporation, the Pension Benefit Guaranty Corporation and provided for compulsory termination insurance coverage for covered defined benefit plans

What is a common-law employee?

- it is determined based on facts and circumstances, such as the level of control the employer has over the worker (such as setting hours and deadlines, providing office space and tools, paying professional dues), and who owns the worker's creative work product
- the U.S. Supreme Court adopted the general rules for purposes of employee benefit plans
- sometimes a leased employee might be considered as a common-law employee
- by default, any worker who is not a common-law employee is considered to be an independent contractor
- although limited for other purposes, self-employed individuals (such as partners of a partnership, owners of an S corporation, and sole proprietors) are considered common-law employees for purposes of participating in an employee benefit plan

A. Employee Benefits in General

1. Why Offer Benefits?

When an employee renders services to an employer, he or she is paid cash compensation on an hourly, weekly, bi-weekly, or monthly basis by the employer, and that compensation is included in the employee's income when paid pursuant to the federal income tax code. Employee benefits generally refer to non-cash compensation afforded to employees by their employers in exchange for compensation for services. But they can also refer to certain cash compensation afforded to employees through a tax-sheltered vehicle which renders that compensation nonincludable or partially includable in the employee's income for tax purposes. Employee benefits came into vogue after World War II when there had been a freeze on any increases in cash compensation; thus, employee benefits were a means to increase compensation without the payment of additional cash.[1] Back then, employers had a paternalistic feeling toward employees and wanted to protect their health, well-being, and financial security. But the real appeal for employee benefits is the tax preferential nature extended to these benefits through the federal income tax code (to be discussed in Chapter 2). As they result in little or even no additional federal income tax to an employee, they are both favorable to the employee as well as to the employer who can deduct them, just as they do cash compensation for services rendered.[2] This means employers generally must offer them in order to attract, retain, and reward a talented work force. Union employees also bargain for employee benefits, which are then provided under their collectively bargained agreements.

2. Various Categories of Employee Benefits

There are a variety of ways in which an employer can compensate an employee for services rendered. The following list highlights the most frequent types of compensation:

Compensation: An employer is generally free to determine the level of compensation payable to an employee, consistent with federal and state minimum wage laws, for services actually rendered. In the union context, an employer may be subject to a compensation table, agreed upon under the collectively bargained agreement. The employer may also decide to compensate employees for a set amount of sick days, vacation days, sabbaticals, and certain leaves of absences. These types of paid time off may vary by the employee's length of service. For example, a newly hired employee may receive three sick days and 10 vacation days for the first year of employment, whereas an employee with 10 years of employment may receive the same three sick days, but 20 vacation days. While federal law (such as the Family and Medical Leave Act of 1993[3] and the Uniformed Services Employment and Reemployment Rights Act of 1994[4]) may require an employer to grant leaves of absences for family medical reasons, the birth or adoption of a child, death of a family member, or recruitment to active military service or jury duty, the employer is not required by federal law to compensate the employee for these types of leaves; however, many employers do so voluntarily.

Paid time off: Many employers provide paid time off for sickness, vacation days, sabbaticals, and other leaves of absence. While the Family Medical and Leave Act (FMLA) requires certain employers to provide leaves of absence (12 weeks in a 12-month period)

---

1. Mark Berger, *The Contingent Employee Benefits Problem*, 32 Ind. L. Rev. 301, 317 (1999) (citing Alicia Haydock Munnell, The Economics of Private Pensions 7–12 (1982), *reprinted* in Mark A. Rothstein & Lance Liebman, Employment Law 1169 (4th ed. 1998)).

2. Under the federal income tax code, an employer pays tax only on *net* income—meaning it can deduct the expenses associated with generating the income from the gross income. For many employers, deductions under I.R.C. § 162(a)(1) for employees' salaries and fringe benefits can be sizeable.

3. Pub. L. No. 103-3, 107 Stat. 6 (Feb. 5, 1993).

4. Pub. L. No. 103-353, 108 Stat. 3149 (Oct. 13, 1994).

for certain family and medical reasons, along with continuation of group health insurance coverage, such leaves of absence do not have to be paid time off.[5]

Health benefits: Until the advent of the Patient Protection and Affordable Care Act of 2010, large employers were not required to provide health benefits (in the form of paying premiums to an insurance company or directly reimbursing the employee for such costs).[6] Many did so because the federal income tax code did not tax employees for such benefits, either due to an exclusion from the premiums paid to an insurance company or from the benefits themselves when reimbursed by the employer.

Welfare benefits: These benefits are those designed for the "welfare" of the employee, so as to make them more productive. They can include such benefits as reimbursement of day care expenses for the employee's child, which are excludable from the employee's federal income up to a maximum of $5,000 per year (or $2,500 per year if married filing separately).[7] Such benefits must be provided through a flexible spending account (otherwise referred to as an employer sponsored cafeteria plan).[8] Other miscellaneous fringe benefits that may be provided include employee achievement awards (e.g., an award for length or service or safety achievement); on-premise gyms or athletic facilities; de minimis benefits (e.g., meal money or transportation expenses for working overtime); employee discounts on property or services that the employer otherwise offers to customers in the ordinary course of business (e.g., 20% discount on the purchase of the employer's products); and meals and/or lodging provided by the employer to the employee on its business premises; moving expense reimbursements for newly hired employees; no additional cost services (e.g., allowing a pilot to fly free in an airline's empty seat); and working condition fringe benefits (e.g., reimbursement for uniforms worn on the employer's business premises). Many employers extend certain welfare benefits just to their executives (e.g., use of a corporate jet; payment of country club dues; use and maintenance of cell phones), but such benefits may not be granted preferential federal income tax treatment. Despite that, executives nevertheless negotiate for such benefits in their employment packages.

Retirement benefits: An employer may voluntarily provide a percentage of an employee's pre-retirement salary in the form of a retirement benefit as an incentive for the employee to retire, making room for younger employees to replace the older

---

5. 29 U.S.C. § 2614(a)(1) (family and medical reasons include caring for a new child or a seriously ill family member or recovering from a serious illness). Due to the 2020 COVID-19 pandemic, Congress expanded FMLA protections to include paid and unpaid leave for certain employees unable to work to care for a child, applicable to employers with fewer than 500 employees. FFCRA, Division C, § 3102. It also requires those employers to provide up to 80 hours of emergency paid sick leave related to certain specified coronavirus events. FFCRA, Division E. Both provisions expire on December 31, 2020.

6. ACA § 1513, amending I.R.C. § 4980H.

7. I.R.C. § 129.

8. A flexible spending account offered through a cafeteria plan is regulated by I.R.C. § 125. These accounts provide the employee with the choice of receiving cash or electing to receive certain welfare benefits. If cash is not elected, the welfare benefits are excluded from gross income. Such accounts can also be funded with employee pre-tax deferrals.

worker. As of March 31, 2018, the total U.S. retirement assets (excluding Social Security) were $29.2 trillion, three times the size of the amount accumulated at the end of 2000.[9] In the past, the typical type of plan was a defined benefit plan — similar to that provided by Social Security. Under a defined benefit plan, the plan would pay a percentage of the employee's pre-retirement salary (averaged over his or her career or over the last few years pre-retirement) as a monthly benefit, beginning at a given retirement age, for the employee's life, or if the employee were married, over the joint lives of the employee and his or her spouse. For example, an employer would promise to pay 70% of the employee's pre-retirement salary, beginning at age 65 when the employee retired from his or her job, for the remainder of the employee's life or the joint lives of the employee and his or her spouse. The value of the defined benefit model is that the mortality and investment risk of outliving one's income is shifted to the employer and away from the employee and/or his or her spouse. For small employers that would not underwrite such costs, they could provide such benefits through a defined benefit plan that was guaranteed by an insurance company. Over the past 30 to 40 years, especially due to the volatility of the investment risk that the employer undertook through this model, employers began to shift to a defined contribution model, especially one that used an I.R.C. § 401(k) feature. Under a defined contribution plan, the employer promises to make an annual employer contribution to the plan (usually a percentage of the employee's compensation) but does not guarantee the rate of interest on the underlying investments. As the employee's benefit is based solely on the amount in his or her account as of retirement, the employer does not underwrite the mortality risk; hence, the employee is not assured that such account balance will not be exhausted over his or her lifetime, nor the lifetime of his or her spouse.

If the defined benefit or defined contribution benefits are structured properly in a "qualified" retirement plan, there are substantial tax benefits afforded to both the employer and its employees. Chapter 4 will discuss the type of employer sponsoring retirement benefits, contrasting for-profit employers that sponsor qualified retirement benefits as opposed to non-profit employers (such as state and local governments, churches, public schools, and tax-exempt entities) that sponsor other types of non-qualified retirement plans that nevertheless extend favorable tax treatment to employees. As the rules governing qualified retirement plans have historically been more onerous than non-qualified retirement plans, Chapters 4 through 11 of this text will focus on the rules applicable to qualified plans. In addition, when an employer provides retirement only to certain highly paid employees, officers, directors, and other individuals, those executive compensation plans are subject to an alternative set of rules, summarized in Chapter 18.

---

9. *See* Marlene Satter, *Retirement Assets Hit $29.2T: ICI Report*, https://www.thinkadvisor.com/ 2018/12/27/retirement-assets-hit-29-2t-ici-report/ (with $9.5 trillion in Individual Retirement Accounts and $8.1 trillion in private sector defined contribution plans) and Mark Nolan, *For Third Quarter of 2019 Retirement Assets Total $29.2 Trillion*, MySolo401kFinancial, https://www.mysolo401k.net/for-third-quarter-of-2018-retirement-assets-total-29-2-trillion/.

Severance benefits: These benefits are sometimes extended by an employer to an employee as a result of an involuntary termination of service, (e.g., layoff of employees at a given location). They generally are a number of weeks or months of continued salary, even though the employee is no longer working for the employer. In the context of a corporate takeover, the new employer may contract to pay severance benefits to certain employees who will no longer be retained by the new employer. This could be because the employee is terminated for redundancy or relegated to a lower position on the employer's organization chain of command. Severance pay and golden parachute arrangements as part of an executive's employment package will be discussed in Chapter 18.

Death benefits: These are benefits payable upon the employee's death while an active employee, as a given multiple of the employee's salary (e.g., one times pay) to a named beneficiary or the estate of an employee. Such benefits may also be provided through an employer's retirement plan.

Equity ownership: For executives, the most common type of equity ownership (i.e., obtaining ownership interest in the employer) is the granting of common stock or the option to purchase the stock (usually at below-market prices). These types of grants will be discussed in Chapter 18. For rank-and-file employees, ownership in the employer can be obtained through the employer's use of an employee stock ownership plan (ESOP) as a form of retirement savings. In lieu of making employer cash contributions to a defined contribution plan, the employer makes awards of employer stock to the plan to be allocated to individual participants.

3. The "Three-Legged Stool" Used to Visualize Retirement Savings in the United States

Historically, retirement savings for the typical employee in the United States has been explained through the use of a "three-legged stool."[10] The first leg stood for governmental savings, achieved by the Social Security Administration (SSA). Most employees are subject to SSA whereby both the employee and the employer are required to pay a federal payroll tax (referred to as the FICA tax) on cash compensation at the time services are rendered—presently 7.65% of an employee's salary—6.2% of an employee's salary up to a given dollar limitation (in 2020, the dollar limitation was $137,700), plus 1.45% of an employee's salary not subject to a dollar limitation; the employee may pay an additional .9% of salary in excess of $200,000 (for individuals) or $250,000 (for joint filers). The 6.2% tax funds Social Security benefits, and the 1.45% tax funds Medicare (i.e., medical benefits) for employees who have reached a given retirement age. The second leg of the stool was employer's savings through a retirement plan. While that plan had been a traditional defined benefit savings plan,

---

10. The three-legged stool was a metaphor used by the post-World War II generation when planning for retirement. It is often attributed to Franklin Delano Roosevelt, who originated the Social Security System, but he never used the term. It may have begun with Reinhard Hohaus, an actuary, who used the phrase during a 1949 speech on the Social Security program.

it has now evolved into a defined contribution savings plan, making more uncertain whether such savings will be sufficient to last an employee and his or her spouse through their retirement. The third leg of the stool was the employee's individual savings, outside of his or her employer's retirement plan. That leg has been delinquently underfunded in recent years as the typical employee has more debt than savings, especially for retirement purposes.[11] Auto loans have been up by 40% in the last decade, and over the past 30 years, health care spending is up 276%, housing prices are up 188%, and tuition at public four-year colleges is up 549%, but household income is only up 135%.[12] Thus, it's no wonder that the middle-class is not saving enough given the costs of health care, housing, cars, and education.

Using the visual of a three-legged stool was meant to assist a typical employee in understanding the various sources of income that would be relied upon for an adequate retirement.

As the second and third legs of the stool have clearly become less reliable for employees, the first leg of the stool has become even more important. Yet we've heard from the experts in recent years that Social Security will become "bankrupt"—meaning that the flow of FICA taxes to SSA can no longer support the flow of benefits from SSA due to the change in the demographics of the U.S. workforce. That topic could be its own chapter in this textbook!

The General Accounting Office issued a report in 2019, providing a comprehensive reevaluation of the United States to rethink its retirement savings system due to changes that have occurred since the 1970s.[13] It reported that fundamental changes over the past 40 years have shifted the three main pillars upon which the U.S. retirement system had relied. Those changes include:

- The Social Security pillar will be sufficient to pay only 77% of scheduled benefits by 2034 due to the aging of the U.S. population;

- The employer-provided plan pillar has experienced a major shift away from defined benefit plans to defined contribution account-based plans, particularly 401(k) plans. There are numerous reasons for this, but defined contribution plans have proven to be less expensive and complex to manage, as compared to defined benefit plans. While defined contributions have led to better portability for a mobile workforce, they also require individuals to assume more responsi-

---

11. Steven Hill, Expand Social Security Now!: How to Ensure Americans Get the Retirement They Deserve 42–43 (2016); Stephen F. Befort, *The Perfect Storm of Retirement Insecurity: Fixing the Three-Legged Stool of Social Security, Pensions, and Personal Savings*, 91 Minn. L. Rev. 938, 960–62 (2007).

12. AnnaMaria Andriotis, Ken Brown & Shane Shifflett, *Families Go Deep in Debt to Stay in the Middle Class*, Wall St. J. (Aug. 1, 2019), https://www.wsj.com/articles/families-go-deep-in-debt-to-stay-in-the-middle-class-11564673734.

13. U.S. Gov't Accountability Office, GAO-190342T, *The Nation's Retirement System: A Comprehensive Re-evaluation Needed to Better Promote Future Retirement Security* (Feb. 6, 2019), https://www.gao.gov/assets/700/696766.pdf.

bility for planning and managing their savings. And while such plans can provide meaningful retirement security, especially for the highly paid, the lower earners have little or no savings in their accounts. For the remaining defined benefit plans, the PBGC, which insures most private sector defined benefit plans, estimates a greater than 90% chance the multiemployer program will be insolvent by 2025; and

• The individual's savings pillar has been constrained by trends such as low real wage growth and growing out-of-pocket health care costs.[14]

The report concludes that these challenges put individuals at greater risk of outliving their savings and fiscal pressures on government programs will continue to mount.

B. Employees as the Recipients of Employee Benefits

1. Only Employees Can Be Promised Benefits

Congress passed the Employee Retirement Income Security Act (ERISA) of 1974,[15] which resulted in sweeping changes for all employee benefit plans. The legislative history indicates that ERISA was passed in order to protect participants' rights under employee benefit plans, and to provide employers with a uniform set of requirements regarding standards of conduct, responsibility, and obligations under such plans.[16] Because employee benefits conferred preferential tax treatment for employers and employees (as will be explained in Chapter 2), ERISA was not only a labor statute (impacting the payment of compensation, and therefore amending section 29 of the U.S.C.), but also a tax statute which imposed new tax requirements on tax-preferred employee benefit plans (therefore, amending section 26 of the U.S.C). But the benefits protected under ERISA are those afforded to employees, in contrast with independent contractors.

There are four titles under ERISA:[17]

---

14. *Id.*

15. Pub. L. No. 93-406, 88 Stat. 829 (1974), codified as amended in various sections of 26 and 29 of the United States Code (U.S.C.), effective January 1, 1976.

16. *See* S. Rep. No. 93-127, at 35 (1973), *reprinted in* 1974 U.S.C.C.A.N. 4838, 4871 (describing Senate version of enforcement provisions as intended to "provide both the Secretary and participants and beneficiaries with broad remedies for redressing or preventing violations of [ERISA]"); H.R. Rep. No. 93-533, at 17 (1973) *reprinted in* 1974 U.S.C.C.A.N. 4639 ("describing House version in identical terms," as quoted by the Supreme Court in *Variety Corp. v. Howe*, 516 U.S. 489, 512 (1996)). For a detailed history of the events leading up to the passage of ERISA, see James A. Wooten, "*The Most Glorious Story of Failure in the Business: The Studebaker-Packard Corporation and the Origins of ERISA*," 49 Buffalo L. Rev. 683 (2001).

17. ERISA's labor provisions were codified in Title 29 of the U.S.C., whereas the related tax provisions of the Internal Revenue Code were codified in Title 26 of the U.S.C.

- *Title I prescribes minimum standards for both employee pension plans and welfare plans.* Reporting requirements to various governmental agencies and disclosure requirements for participants and beneficiaries are set forth for the various types of plans. Title I prescribes minimum participation, vesting, accrual, and funding standards for pension and profit sharing plans. Fiduciary standards and prohibited transactions are set forth for plans in general. And the civil enforcement causes of action and remedies for violations under the plan or against ERISA are prescribed.

- *Title II amended provisions of the Internal Revenue Code relating to employee pension and profit sharing plans that were "qualified" under the Code.* Some of these substantive requirements were duplicative of the requirements set forth under Title I; others were more restrictive than those posed under Title I. For this reason, ERISA is regarded as tax law as well as labor law.

- *Title III provided jurisdictional authority to the Department of Labor (DOL), Employee Benefits Security Administration (EBSA), and the Internal Revenue Service (IRS), IRS Employee Plans group of the Tax Exempt/Government Entities operating division.* While Title I was generally under the DOL's domain and Title II was definitely under the IRS's domain, conflict was inevitable if the two regulatory agencies deviated in their interpretation of the provisions under Title I and II. The ERISA Reorganization Plan of 1978[18] assigned responsibility by subject matter to either the DOL or IRS to avoid such conflict in interpretations.

- *Title IV created a new federal corporation, the Pension Benefit Guaranty Corporation (PBGC), and provided for compulsory termination insurance coverage for covered defined benefit plans.* Since coverage under Title IV was designed as a mixture of social and private insurance coverage, there has been significant legislation under this Title as the goals of dual coverage often collide and conflict.

Numerous legislative changes had been made to ERISA during its first 40 years. A list of the applicable federal laws amending ERISA and the Code has been provided in the Material section of this chapter. As retirement and health benefits represent the two largest tax expenditures in the federal income tax code, they are easy targets to "chip away" if Congress is in need of additional tax revenue. A tax expenditure is a phrase used to describe a tax break or a tax loophole. It occurs when the government collects less revenue (either by excluding income, allowing an exemption, permitting a deduction for an expense, providing a tax credit, using a preferential tax rate, or

---

18. ERISA Reorganization Plan No. 4 of 1978, Executive Order No. 12, 108, 44 Fed. Reg. 1065 (Dec. 28, 1978). The DOL has primary jurisdiction over the reporting and disclosure provision, fiduciary rules (and the related prohibited transaction rules), and the administrative and enforcement provisions under Title I; whereas the IRS has primary jurisdiction over the requirements under Parts 2 and 3 of Title I and the independent requirements under the Code for qualified retirement plans.

granting a deferral of a tax liability) than under its normal tax rules. The U.S. Department of the Treasury provides a 10-year estimate of the amount of tax expenditures: for 2020–2029, it estimates a tax expenditure for the exclusion of employer contributions for medical insurance premiums and medical care to be $3,104,400 million and a tax expenditure for defined contribution employer-provided plans of $1,296,880 million.[19]

As benefits under employee benefit plans are *voluntary* in nature, a delicate balance had to be struck between the plan sponsor's ability to draft, amend, and terminate such plans, and the protections to be afforded to participants and beneficiaries once benefits had been promised. ERISA sets forth appropriate causes of action, remedies, and sanctions; provides access to the federal courts to enforce such actions; and preempts state legislation and regulations that relate to such plans.[20] Although ERISA's preemption clause is drafted broadly, it "saved" from preemption state legislation over insurance, banking, and securities businesses though its "savings clause."[21] To prevent a state from deeming an employee benefit plan as an "insurance company or other insurer, bank, trust company, or investment company" and therefore subject to state regulation, ERISA's "deemer clause" limits the states' rights to so act.[22]

Although ERISA regulates the delivery of both pension and welfare benefits, and the Code provides for the tax preferential treatment of such benefits from an employer to its employees, the bulk of ERISA's and the Code's substantive requirements are applicable only to pension and profit sharing plans. Thus, Part I of this book is devoted to examining those requirements. Part II of this book examines the remaining ERISA provisions that are applicable to all employee benefit plans, including pension and profit sharing plans.

Prior to ERISA's protection through various causes of action, an employer's promise to pay a retirement benefit to its employees was not always honored. An employee's recourse was to sue in state court for either breach of contract or as a tort action. At

---

19. *See* U.S. Dep't of Treasury, https://home.treasury.gov/policy-issues/tax-policy/tax-expenditures.

20. *See* ERISA §§ 502(a) and 514(a).

21. *See* ERISA § 502(b) (referred to as ERISA's "savings clause"). ERISA § 514(a) states that "[e]xcept as provided in subsection (b) of this section, Title I and IV preempt all state laws that relate to an employee benefit plans." Hence subsection (b) is an exception to the preemption and carves out state insurance, banking, or securities law; thus those types of state laws are said to be "saved" from ERISA's preemption clause in subsection (a).

22. ERISA § 514(b)(2)(B) (referred to as ERISA's "deemer clause"). As ERISA § 514(b) saves certain state laws from ERISA's preemption, subsection (b) goes on to say that an employee benefit plan or trust established under a plan will not be deemed to be an insurance company or bank or investment company for purposes of the saved state insurance, banking, and securities laws. Hence, a state law cannot deem an employee benefit plan or its trust to be an insurance company, a bank, or an investment company in order to attempt to regulate it.

this stage of the reading, read the *Sigman v. Rudolph Wurlitzer Co.* case in the Materials section of this chapter.

Consider whether this case proves this point, focusing on the employer's terms "when old age overtakes them" instead of the words "retirement" and whether the employer was allowed under federal and state laws to interpret the terms of its agreement for its benefit and not for the benefit of its employees.

2. Who Is an Employee?

Title I defines an "employee" as an individual employed by an employer, whereas Title II does not define the term "employee" for purposes of the qualification rules.[23]

Read the *Nationwide Mutual Ins. Co. v. Darden* case in the Materials section of this chapter. In that case, the U.S. Supreme Court early on applied a common-law test for determining who is an "employee" for purposes of ERISA § 3(6).[24] The factors considered by the court in categorizing a service provider as an "employee" included the following: "the skill required; the source of the instrumentalities and tools; the location of the work; the duration of the relationship between the parties; whether the hiring party has the right to assign additional projects to the hired party; the extent of the hiring party's discretion over when and how long to work; the method of payment; the hiring party's role in hiring and paying assistants; whether the work is part of the regular business of the hiring party; whether the hiring party is in business; the provision of employee benefits; and the tax treatment of the hired party."[25]

In that case, the court rejected its earlier purposive approach set forth in *NLRB v. Hearst Publications, Inc.*,[26] and *United States v. Silk*,[27] in order to promote greater certainty and predictability.[28] In contrast, the Internal Revenue Service (IRS) has its own set of factors in determining whether an employer-employee relationship exists. Beginning with Rev. Rul. 87-41, the IRS developed a list of 20 factors, the weight of each varying depending on the occupation and the factual context in which the services are performed, which include: instructions, training, integration of the services into the business operations, services rendered personally, hiring, supervising, and paying assistants, continuing relationship, set hours of work, full time required, doing work on the employer's premises, order or sequence set, oral or written reports, payment by hour, week, or month, payment of business and/or traveling expenses, furnishing of tools and materials, significant investment in the facilities, realization

---

23. ERISA § 3(6) for Title I purposes; see I.R.C. § 414 for the definition of terms used under the qualification rules of I.R.C. § 401(a).
24. *See* Nationwide Mutual Insurance Co. v. Darden, 503 U.S. 318 (1992).
25. *Id.* at 323.
26. 322 U.S. 111 (1944).
27. 331 U.S. 704 (1947).
28. *Id.* at 324–27.

of profit or loss, working for more than one firm at a time, making service available to the general public, right to discharge, and right to terminate.[29]

More recently, the IRS has used three categories of evidence to determine whether the requisite control exists under the common-law test: (1) behavioral control, (2) financial control, and (3) relationship of the parties.[30] But it states these categories, in addition to the 20 factors, must be considered, noting that the weight of the factors varies based on the facts, that the relevant factors may change with time, and that all facts must be considered.[31]

However, for purposes of the current federal law for employee benefits, self-employed individuals, partners of a partnership, shareholders in an LLC or LLP, or leased employees (unless covered by their leasing organization) can also be covered as "owner-employees." The term "owner-employee" is defined as an individual who owns the entire interest in an unincorporated trade or business, or in the case of a partnership, a partner who owns more than 10% of either the capital interest or the profits interest in the partnership.[32] Thus, the individual who owns the entire interest in an unincorporated trade or business is both the employer and the employee; in the partnership, the partnership is the employer of each partner who is an employee.

A leased employee can also be a common-law employee. Generally, a "leased employee" is a common-law employee of the leasing organization, but can be treated as an employee of the recipient of his or her services.[33] A leased employee will be an employee of the recipient of his or her services if: (1) the services are provided pursuant to an agreement between the recipient and the leasing organization, (2) the person has performed these services for the recipient (or related persons) on a substantially full-time basis for a period of at least one year, and (3) such services are performed under the primary direction or control of the recipient.[34] However, the law provides a safe harbor if the leased employee is presently covered by the leasing organization's pension plan, such that he or she need not be covered under the recipient employer's plan.[35]

If a worker does not qualify as a common-law employee or owner-employee, then he or she is deemed to be an independent contractor. As such, individuals are not eligible to participate under an employer-sponsored employee benefit plan.

---

29. Rev. Rul. 87-41.
30. U.S. Dep't of Treasury, IRS, *Independent Contractor or Employee?*, Training Materials, Training 3320-102 (10-96) TPDS 84238I, at 2-7, https://www.irs.gov/pub/irs-utl/emporind.pdf.
31. *Id.* at 2-3 through 2-7.
32. I.R.C. §401(c)(3)(A)–(B).
33. I.R.C. §414(n)(2).
34. I.R.C. §414(n)(2)(A)–(C).
35. I.R.C. §414(n)(5) (requiring the leasing organization's plan to be a money purchase pension plan with an employer contribution of at least 10% of compensation, with full and immediate vesting, and immediate participation).

C. Materials
Sigman v. Rudolph Wurlitzer Co.
11 N.E.2d 878 (Ohio Ct. App. 1937)

Harmon, Colston, Goldsmith & Hoadly and Henry B. Street, all of Cincinnati, for appellant.

Roy Manogue and J. Lewis Homer, both of Cincinnati, for appellee.

TATGENHORST, Presiding Judge.

This is an appeal on questions of law from the court of common pleas of Hamilton county.

Suit was instituted by the appellee, Thurse Sigman, to recover from the appellant, the Rudolph Wurlitzer Company, the amount of a pension claimed to be due him by reason of his compliance with the terms of the pension requirements.

The appellant was engaged in the business of manufacture and sale of musical instruments. The appellee had been in the employ of the appellant for more than twenty-seven years, when he was discharged because it had no further employment to which he was suited. He had served appellant as order clerk, salesman on the road, manager of its Victrola department, wholesale and retail, and manager in charge of its wholesale radio department.

From time to time during his employment, the appellant issued booklets containing various declarations covering the institution of a pension system, applicable to its employees and including the appellee. That such program was calculated to and did induce continued service in the corporation there can be no question. It constituted a continuing offer on the part of the company, which was continuously accepted by the employees who preserved their status with the company. We quote from the booklet:

'He who serves best receives most.

'Rules for Your Success

'And the policy outlined for your welfare

'The Rudolph Wurlitzer Co.

'Chicago, Cincinnati, New York, and all principal cities

'For You

'This booklet was written for you. It was written for your interest and the attention of every employee thruout the enormous organization of The Rudolph Wurlitzer Co.

'There is something on every page of this booklet that should be of vital importance to you, that is, of course, if you desire to become successful with the vast amount of opportunities before you. The employees who shoulder the greatest responsibilities and have become most successful in our organization today are only those who have strictly adhered to and closely observed the simple but necessary rules and policies.

'After all, the important part of any rule is the spirit of it. This is gained by understanding the wisdom and necessity of the rule, and not by mere obedience because it is a rule. No rule seems hard when you see that it is wise — worked out from experience — made necessary by existing conditions.

'Every possible method has been outlined for your welfare and protection while in our employ. Your saving, bonus, compensation for promptness and efficiency, protection during sickness, pension and insurance has all been thoroughly explained in this booklet.

'All that we ask is that you kindly read every page and feel that you are a part of an organization which is doing everything within its power for your success and welfare.

'The Rudolph Wurlitzer Co.

'Pension System

'In order to take care of our loyal and trustworthy employees when old age overtakes them, we have put in this pension system: We will pay 2% on the entire amount you have earned each year, which will be paid to you in monthly instalments, and as long as you live. The largest pension we pay any one is $100.00 per month, or $1,200.00 a year. For example, we will take an employee that has earned $900.00 per year:

'Worked 10 years at $900.00 a year — $9,000.00. Pension, $15.00 per month.

'Worked 15 years at $900.00 a year — $13,500.00. Pension, $22.50 per month.

'Worked 20 years at $900.00 a year — $18,000.00. Pension, $30.00 per month.

'Worked 25 years at $900.00 a year — $22,500.00. Pension, $37.50 per month.

'Worked 30 years at $900.00 a year — $27,000.00. Pension, $45.00 per month.

'From the above table you can easily figure what your pension would amount to.

It pays to be loyal. A rolling stone gathers no moss.'

At the bottom of the pages of the booklet are interesting statements designed apparently to encourage industry, faithfulness, loyalty, and continued service with the company. Among them, appears the following:

'No man in this world ever rightfully receives more than he gives. — Adams.

'A man with push can get there, but it takes a man with character to stay there. — Shepherd.

'Forget the past. Success lies in the future.

'No one can cheat you of final success but yourself.'

There is much good advice contained in the pamphlet, and the whole effect is to produce a feeling of confidence in the fairness and sincere concern of the company for the welfare of the employee.

[1] It is a little difficult for the court to reconcile the present attitude of appellant with the many assurances of concern for the benefit of the employees contained in the pamphlet. As previously stated, in considering another pamphlet issued by this company (Wilson v. Rudolph Wurlitzer Co., 48 Ohio App. 450, 194 N.E. 441), fraud is never presumed, and where two constructions are possible, one of which requires

a finding of fraudulent intent, and the other permits a conclusion of good faith, courts never hesitate in giving effect to the latter interpretation.

[2] The inducement having been accepted by the appellee, the writing of appellant must be construed also most strongly against it, for it could have restricted the existing implications by proper words of limitation. The appellee is entitled to the benefit of all reasonable inferences applicable to the words used.

[3] The appellant places great reliance, in denying to the 52 year old appellee the benefits of its pension system, upon the words 'when old age overtakes you.' Now it must be observed that these words appear only in a clause addressed to a statement of the motivating impulse prompting the initiation and continuance of the pension system. It is further a matter of common knowledge that there is an industrial old age and what may be styled a social old age, an economic human obsolescence, entirely distinct from the evening of life.

It is apparent also that according to the schedule there is an implication that an employee may be paid a pension after only ten years' service. The service of appellee is within two and one-half years of the maximum service stated in the illustration table. We are aware that neither of the extremes are limits of liability, but the appellee is entitled to the value of the natural import of what was presented to him.

[4] It is to be noted also that the pension is payable during life, and would, therefore, naturally be a protection against destitution in old age. We consider the words used do not require an exhibition of senile decrepitude before the pension becomes payable any more than mere incapacity caused by accident or disease, however disastrous to the employee, would invoke the operation of the pension. The age at which men and women cease to be effective employees varies materially in the various industries and professions.

From what the record shows it can be easily concluded that the particular business carried on by appellant was of such a nature that mature youth would be at a premium, and that the appellee had reached a point where a younger man would serve the appellant much more satisfactorily. When it becomes apparent that longer employment will be a detriment to efficient service and that the alternative is a pension, a discharge is a most effective severance of the Gordian knot. While effective and most serviceable to the appellant, it results in a complete abrogation of the security upon which the appellee for twenty-seven and one-half years relied and had a right to rely.

Not one word of criticism is made of such service for this long period.

The federal pension system is mentioned. If age 65 was in the mind of appellant, why was not this or some other age specified, so that the employee could have been permitted to govern himself accordingly with all the facts before him. The illustrative table again is most forceful in its implication of ages of retirement much below the federal age.

The court charged in part as follows: 'Now, this pension system, or contract, or agreement, which has been set forth in the amended petition and shown, in Exhibit No. 1 uses the expression 'When old age overtakes them,' or overtakes him, applying to the plaintiff. I say to you that this means the age at which the average man performing the same or similar duties would ordinarily find himself unable to further perform such duties, or, to find similar employment elsewhere, and therefore I say to you if you find from a preponderance of evidence that the plaintiff at the time his services with the defendant were discontinued then was at that age at which the average man performing the same or similar services would ordinarily find himself unable to further perform such services, or, to find similar employment elsewhere, then the plaintiff is entitled to a verdict, calculated according to the table prescribed in said Exhibit No. 1.'

If there is any criticism of this charge, it is that it states too severe a rule against the appellee. Nothing is said in the pension prospectus as to incapacity. This could have been made the criterion. It was not specified.

[5] The appellee had earned while in the service of the appellant more than $54,000. During these years he was led to believe that 2 per cent of his earnings would be paid him when the company considered him more favorably in the position of a pensioner than as an employee receiving a full salary or wage. The appellant has made its election. It has concluded that he has reached the point of industrial old age. It is to its interest to discontinue the payment of the full wage. The employee must bow to the appellant's opinion and edict. He, however, cannot be in good faith and justice denied the alternative held out by the employer as an inducement, for more than a quarter of a century, to continue service with the appellant.

The judgment is affirmed.

Judgment affirmed.

ROSS and HAMILTON, JJ.,

Nationwide Mut. Ins. Co. v. Darden

503 U.S. 318 (1992)

Opinion

Justice SOUTER delivered the opinion of the Court.

In this case we construe the term "employee" as it appears in § 3(6) of the Employee Retirement Income Security Act of 1974 (ERISA), 88 Stat. 834, 29 U.S.C. § 1002(6), and read it to incorporate traditional agency law criteria for identifying master-servant relationships.

I

From 1962 through 1980, respondent Robert Darden operated an insurance agency according to the terms of several contracts he signed with petitioners Nationwide Mutual Insurance Co. et al. Darden promised to sell only Nationwide insurance policies, and, in exchange, Nationwide agreed to pay him commissions on his sales and enroll him in a company retirement scheme called the "Agent's Security Compensation Plan" (Plan). The Plan consisted of two different programs: the "Deferred Compensation Incentive Credit Plan," under which Nationwide annually credited an agent's retirement account with a sum based on his business performance, and the "Extended Earnings Plan," under which Nationwide paid an agent, upon retirement or termination, a sum equal to the total of his policy renewal fees for the previous 12 months.

Such were the contractual terms, however, that Darden would forfeit his entitlement to the Plan's benefits if, within a year of his termination and 25 miles of his prior business location, he sold insurance for Nationwide's competitors. The contracts also disqualified him from receiving those benefits if, after he stopped representing Nationwide, he ever induced a Nationwide policyholder to cancel one of its policies.

In November 1980, Nationwide exercised its contractual right to end its relationship with Darden. A month later, Darden became an independent insurance agent and, doing business from his old office, sold insurance policies for several of Nationwide's competitors. The company reacted with the charge that his new business activities disqualified him from receiving the Plan benefits to which he would have been entitled otherwise. Darden then sued for the benefits, which he claimed were nonforfeitable because already vested under the terms of ERISA. 29 U.S.C. § 1053(a).

Darden brought his action under 29 U.S.C. § 1132(a), which enables a benefit plan "participant" to enforce the substantive provisions of ERISA. The Act elsewhere defines "participant" as "any employee or former employee of an employer ... who is or may become eligible to receive a benefit of any type from an employee benefit plan...." § 1002(7). Thus, Darden's ERISA claim can succeed only if he was Nationwide's "employee," a term the Act defines as "any individual employed by an employer." § 1002(6).

It was on this point that the District Court granted summary judgment to Nationwide. After applying common-law agency principles and, to an extent unspecified, our decision in *United States v. Silk*, 331 U.S. 704, 67 S. Ct. 1463, 91 L. Ed. 1757 (1947), the court found that "'the total factual context' of Mr. Darden's relationship with Nationwide shows that he was an independent contractor and not an employee." App. to Pet. for Cert. 47a, 50a, quoting *NLRB v. United Ins. Co. of America*, 390 U.S. 254, 88 S. Ct. 988, 19 L. Ed. 2d 1083 (1968).

The United States Court of Appeals for the Fourth Circuit vacated. *Darden v. Nationwide Mutual Ins. Co.*, 796 F.2d 701 (1986). After observing that "Darden most probably would not qualify as an employee" under traditional principles of agency law, *id.*, at 705, it found the traditional definition inconsistent with the "'declared policy and purposes'" of ERISA, *id.*, at 706, quoting *Silk, supra,* 331 U.S., at 713, 67 S. Ct., at 1468, and *NLRB v. Hearst Publications, Inc.*, 322 U.S. 111, 131–132, 64 S. Ct. 851, 861–862, 88 L. Ed. 1170 (1944), and specifically with the congressional statement of purpose found in § 2 of the Act, 29 U.S.C. § 1001. It therefore held that an ERISA plaintiff can qualify as an "employee" simply by showing "(1) that he had a reasonable expectation that he would receive [pension] benefits, (2) that he relied on this expectation, and (3) that he lacked the economic bargaining power to contract out of [benefit plan] forfeiture provisions." 922 F.2d 203, 205 (CA4 1991) (summarizing 796 F.2d 701). The court remanded the case to the District Court, which then found that Darden had been Nationwide's "employee" under the standard set by the Court of Appeals. 717 F. Supp. 388 (EDNC 1989). The Court of Appeals affirmed. 922 F.2d 203 (1991). In due course, Nationwide filed a petition for certiorari, which we granted on October 15, 1991. 502 U.S. 905, 112 S. Ct. 294, 116 L. Ed. 2d 239. We now reverse.

II

We have often been asked to construe the meaning of "employee" where the statute containing the term does not helpfully define it. Most recently we confronted this problem in *Community for Creative Non-Violence v. Reid*, 490 U.S. 730, 109 S. Ct. 2166, 104 L. Ed. 2d 811 (1989), a case in which a sculptor and a nonprofit group each claimed copyright ownership in a statue the group had commissioned from the artist. The dispute ultimately turned on whether, by the terms of § 101 of the Copyright Act of 1976, 17 U.S.C. § 101, the statue had been "prepared by an employee within the scope of his or her employment." Because the Copyright Act nowhere defined the term "employee," we unanimously applied the "well established" principle that

> "[w]here Congress uses terms that have accumulated settled meaning under ... the common law, a court must infer, unless the statute otherwise dictates, that Congress means to incorporate the established meaning of these terms.... In the past, when Congress has used the term 'employee' without defining it, we have concluded that Congress intended to describe the conventional master-servant relationship as understood by common-law agency doctrine. *See, e.g., Kelley v. Southern Pacific Co.*, 419 U.S. 318, 322– 323 [95 S. Ct. 472, 475–476, 42 L. Ed. 2d 498] (1974); *Baker v. Texas & Pacific R. Co.*,359 U.S. 227, 228 [79 S. Ct. 664, 665, 3 L. Ed. 2d 756] (1959) *(per curiam); Robinson v. Baltimore & Ohio R. Co.*, 237 U.S. 84, 94 [35 S. Ct. 491, 494, 59 L. Ed. 849] (1915)." 490 U.S., at 739–740, 109 S. Ct., at 2172 (internal quotation marks omitted).

While we supported this reading of the Copyright Act with other observations, the general rule stood as independent authority for the decision.

So too should it stand here. ERISA's nominal definition of "employee" as "any individual employed by an employer," 29 U.S.C. § 1002(6), is completely circular and explains nothing. As for the rest of the Act, Darden does not cite, and we do not find, any provision either giving specific guidance on the term's meaning or suggesting that construing it to incorporate traditional agency law principles would thwart the congressional design or lead to absurd results. Thus, we adopt a common-law test for determining who qualifies as an "employee" under ERISA, a test we most recently summarized in *Reid:*

> "In determining whether a hired party is an employee under the general common law of agency, we consider the hiring party's right to control the manner and means by which the product is accomplished. Among the other factors relevant to this inquiry are the skill required; the source of the instrumentalities and tools; the location of the work; the duration of the relationship between

the parties; whether the hiring party has the right to assign additional projects to the hired party; the extent of the hired party's discretion over when and how long to work; the method of payment; the hired party's role in hiring and paying assistants; whether the work is part of the regular business of the hiring party; whether the hiring party is in business; the provision of employee benefits; and the tax treatment of the hired party." 490 U.S., at 751–752, 109 S. Ct., at 2178–2179 (footnotes omitted).

Cf. Restatement (Second) of Agency § 220(2) (1958) (listing nonexhaustive criteria for identifying master-servant relationship); Rev. Rul. 87-41, 1987-1 Cum. Bull. 296, 298–299 (setting forth 20 factors as guides in determining whether an individual qualifies as a common-law "employee" in various tax law contexts). Since the common-law test contains "no shorthand formula or magic phrase that can be applied to find the answer, ... all of the incidents of the relationship must be assessed and weighed with no one factor being decisive." *NLRB v. United Ins. Co. of America,* 390 U.S., at 258, 88 S. Ct., at 991.

In taking its different tack, the Court of Appeals cited *NLRB v. Hearst Publications, Inc.,* 322 U.S., at 120–129, 64 S. Ct., at 855–856, and *United States v. Silk,* 331 U.S., at 713, 67 S. Ct., at 1468, for the proposition that "the content of the term 'employee' in the context of a particular federal statute is 'to be construed "in the light of the mischief to be corrected and the end to be attained."'" *Darden,* 796 F.2d, at 706, quoting *Silk, supra,* 331 U.S., at 713, 67 S. Ct., at 1468, in turn quoting *Hearst, supra,* 322 U.S., at 124, 64 S. Ct., at 857. But *Hearst* and *Silk,* which interpreted "employee" for purposes of the National Labor Relations Act and Social Security Act, respectively, are feeble precedents for unmooring the term from the common law. In each case, the Court read "employee," which neither statute helpfully defined, to imply something broader than the common-law definition; after each opinion, Congress amended the statute so construed to demonstrate that the usual common-law principles were the keys to meaning. *See United Ins. Co., supra,* 390 U.S., at 256, 88 S. Ct., at 989 ("Congressional reaction to [*Hearst*] was adverse and Congress passed an amendment ... [t]he obvious purpose of [which] was to have the ... courts apply general agency principles in distinguishing between employees and independent contractors under the Act"); Social Security Act of 1948, ch. 468, § 2(a), 62 Stat. 438 (1948) (amending statute to provide that term "employee" "does not include ... any individual who, under the *usual common-law rules* applicable in determining the employer-employee relationship, has the status of an independent contractor") (emphasis added); *see also United States v. W.M. Webb, Inc.,* 397 U.S. 179, 183–188, 90 S. Ct. 850, 852–855, 25 L. Ed. 2d 207 (1970) (discussing congressional reaction to *Silk*).

To be sure, Congress did not, strictly speaking, "overrule" our interpretation of those statutes, since the Constitution invests the Judiciary, not the Legislature, with the final power to construe the law. But a principle of statutory construction can endure just so many legislative revisitations, and *Reid's* presumption that Congress means an agency law definition for "employee" unless it clearly indicates otherwise signaled our abandonment of *Silk's* emphasis on construing that term " 'in the light of the mischief to be corrected and the end to be attained.'" *Silk, supra,* 331 U.S., at 713, 67 S. Ct., at 1468, quoting *Hearst, supra,* 322 U.S., at 124, 64 S. Ct., at 857.

At oral argument, Darden tried to subordinate *Reid* to *Rutherford Food Corp. v. McComb,* 331 U.S. 722, 67 S. Ct. 1473, 91 L. Ed. 1772 (1947), which adopted a broad reading of "employee" under the Fair Labor Standards Act (FLSA). And *amicus* United States, while rejecting Darden's position, also relied on *Rutherford Food* for the proposition that, when enacting ERISA, Congress must have intended a modified common-law definition of "employee" that would advance, in a way not defined, the Act's "remedial purposes." Brief for United States as *Amicus Curiae* 15–21. But *Rutherford Food* supports neither position. The definition of "employee" in the FLSA evidently derives from the child labor statutes, *see Rutherford Food, supra,* at 728, 67 S. Ct., at 1475, and, on its face, goes beyond its ERISA counterpart. While the FLSA, like ERISA, defines an "employee" to include "any individual employed by an employer," it defines the verb "employ" expansively to mean "suffer or permit to work." 52 Stat. 1060, § 3, codified at 29 U.S.C. §§ 203(e), (g). This latter definition, whose striking breadth we have previously noted, *Rutherford Food, supra,* at 728, 67 S. Ct., at 1475, stretches the meaning of "employee" to cover some parties who might not qualify as such under a strict application of traditional agency law principles. ERISA lacks any such provision, however, and the textual asymmetry between the two statutes precludes reliance on FLSA cases when construing ERISA's concept of "employee."

Quite apart from its inconsistency with our precedents, the Fourth Circuit's analysis reveals an approach infected with circularity and unable to furnish predictable results. Applying the first element of its test, which ostensibly enquires into an employee's "expectations," the Court of Appeals concluded that Nationwide had "created a reasonable expectation on the 'employees' part that benefits would be paid to them in the future," *Darden,* 796 F.2d, at 706, by establishing "a comprehensive retirement benefits program for its insurance agents," *id.,* at 707. The court thought it was simply irrelevant that the forfeiture clause in Darden's contract "limited" his expectation of receiving pension benefits, since "it is precisely that sort of employer-imposed condition on the *employee's* anticipations that Congress intended to outlaw with the enactment of ERISA." *Id.,* at 707, n. 7 (emphasis added). Thus, the Fourth Circuit's test would turn not on a claimant's actual "expectations," which the court effectively deemed inconsequential, *ibid.,* but on his statutory entitlement to relief, which itself depends on his very status as an "employee." This begs the question.

This circularity infects the test's second prong as well, which considers the extent to which a claimant has relied on his "expectation" of benefits by "remaining for 'long years,' or a substantial period of time, in the 'employer's' service, and by foregoing other significant means of providing for [his] retirement." *Id.,* at 706. While this enquiry is ostensibly factual, we have seen already that one of its objects may not be: to the extent that actual "expectations" are (as in Darden's case) unnecessary to relief, the nature of a claimant's required "reliance" is left unclear. Moreover, any enquiry into "reliance," whatever it might entail, could apparently lead to different results for claimants holding identical jobs and enrolled in identical plans. Because, for example,

Darden failed to make much independent provision for his retirement, he satisfied the "reliance" prong of the Fourth Circuit's test, *see* 922 F.2d, at 206, whereas a more provident colleague who signed exactly the same contracts, but saved for a rainy day, might not.

Any such approach would severely compromise the capacity of companies like Nationwide to figure out who their "employees" are and what, by extension, their pension-fund obligations will be. To be sure, the traditional agency law criteria offer no paradigm of determinacy. But their application generally turns on factual variables within an employer's knowledge, thus permitting categorical judgments about the "employee" status of claimants with similar job descriptions. Agency law principles comport, moreover, with our recent precedents and with the common understanding, reflected in those precedents, of the difference between an employee and an independent contractor.

III

While the Court of Appeals noted that "Darden most probably would not qualify as an employee" under traditional agency law principles, *Darden, supra,* at 705, it did not actually decide that issue. We therefore reverse the judgment and remand the case to that court for proceedings consistent with this opinion.

So ordered.

D. List of Legislation Affecting Employee Benefit Plans

1. Public Health Safety Act (PHSA)
   Pub. L. No. 78-410, 58 Stat. 682 (May 23, 1944)
2. ADEA: Age Discrimination in Employment Act of 1967
   Pub. L. No. 90-202, 81 Stat. 602 (Dec. 15, 1967)
3. ERISA: Employee Retirement Income Security Act of 1974
   Pub. L. No. 93-406, 88 Stat. 829 (Sept. 2, 1974)
4. TRA '76: Tax Reform Act of 1976
   Pub. L. No. 94-455, 88 Stat. 832 (Oct. 4, 1976)
5. Revenue Act of 1978
   Pub. L. No. 95-600, 92 Stat. 2810 (Nov. 6, 1978)
6. MPPAA: Multiemployer Pension Plan Amendments Act
   Pub. L. No. 96-364, 94 Stat. 1210 (1980)
7. Miscellaneous Revenue Act of 1980
   Pub. L. No. 96-605, 94 Stat. 3521 (Dec. 28, 1980)

8. ERTA: Economic Recovery Act of 1981
   Pub. L. No. 97-34, 95 Stat. 172 (Aug. 13, 1981)

9. TEFRA: Tax Equity and Fiscal Responsibility Act of 1982
   Pub. L. No. 97-248, 96 Stat. 324 (Sept. 3, 1982)

10. DRA: Deficit Reduction Act of 1984
    Pub. L. No. 98-369, 98 Stat. 494 (Jul. 19, 1984)

11. REA: Retirement Equity Act of 1984
    Pub. L. No. 98-397, 98 Stat. 1426 (Aug. 23, 1984)

12. COBRA '85: Consolidated Omnibus Budget Reconciliation Act
    Pub. L. No. 99-272, 100 Stat. 222 (Apr. 7, 1985)

13. SEPPAA: Single-Employer Pension Plan Amendments Act of 1986
    Pub. L. No. 99-272, 100 Stat. 237 (Apr. 7, 1986)

14. OBRA '86: Omnibus Budget Reconciliation Act of 1986
    Pub. L. No. 99-509, 100 Stat. 1874 (Oct. 21, 1986)

15. TRA '86: Tax Reform Act of 1986
    Pub. L. No. 99-514, 100 Stat. 2085 (Oct. 22, 1986)

16. Pension Protection Act of 1987, Subtitle D of Title IX of OBRA '87:
    Omnibus Budget Reconciliation Act of 1987 (OBRA '87)
    Pub. L. No. 100-203, 101 Stat. 1330 (1987)

17. TAMRA: Technical and Miscellaneous Revenue Act of 1988
    Pub. L. No. 100-647, 102 Stat. 3342 (Nov. 10, 1988)

18. DEFRA: Debt Limitation Extension Act of 1989
    Pub. L. No. 101-140, 103 Stat. 830 (Nov. 8, 1989)

19. American Disabilities Act of 1990 (ADA)
    Pub. L. No. 101-336, 104 Stat. 327 (July 26, 1990)

20. OBRA '89: Omnibus Budget Reconciliation Act of 1989
    Pub. L. No. 101-239, 103 Stat. 2106 (Dec. 19, 1989)

21. OWBPA: Older Workers Benefits Protection Act of 1990
    Pub. L. No. 101-433, 104 Stat. 978 (Oct. 16, 1990)

22. OBRA '90: Omnibus Budget Reconciliation Act of 1990
    Pub. L. No. 101-508, 104 Stat. 1388 (Nov. 5, 1990)

23. UCA: Unemployment Compensation Amendments of 1992
    Pub. L. No. 102-318, 106 Stat. 290 (Jul. 31, 1992)

24. FMLA: Family and Medical Leave Act of 1993

Pub. L. No. 103-3, 107 Stat. 6 (Feb. 5, 1993)

25. OBRA '93: Omnibus Budget Reconciliation Act of 1993

Pub. L. No. 103-66, 107 Stat. 312 (Aug. 10, 1993)

26. USERRA: Uniformed Services Employment and Reemployment Rights Act of 1994

Pub. L. No. 103-353, 108 Stat. 3149 (Oct. 13, 1994)

27. PAPA: Pension Annuitants Protection Act of 1994

Pub. L. No. 103-401, 108 Stat. 4172 (Oct. 22, 1994)

28. RPA: Retirement Protection Act of 1994

Pub. L. No. 103-465, 108 Stat. 4809 (Dec. 8, 1994)

29. SBJPA: Small Business Job Protection Act of 1996

Pub. L. No. 104-188, 110 Stat. 1755 (Aug. 20, 1996)

30. HIPAA: Health Insurance Portability and Accountability Act of 1996

Pub. L. No. 104-191, 110 Stat. 1936 (Aug. 21, 1996)

31. NMHPA: Newborns' and Mothers' Health Protection Act of 1996

Pub. L. No. 104-204, 110 Stat. 2935 (Sept. 26, 1996)

32. TRA '97: Taxpayer Relief Act of 1997

Pub. L. No. 105-34, 111 Stat. 788 (Aug. 5, 1997)

33. IRS Restructuring and Reform Act of 1998

Pub. L. No. 105-206, 112 Stat. 685 (Jul. 22, 1998)

34. WHCRA: Women's Health and Cancer Rights Act

Pub. L. No. 105-277, 112, Stat. 2681 (Oct. 21, 1998)

35. EGTRRA '01: Economic Growth and Tax Relief Reconciliation Act of 2001

Pub. L. No. 107-16, 115 Stat. 38 (Jun.7, 2000)

36. JCWAA '02: Job Creation and Worker Assistance Act of 2002

Pub. L. No. 107-147, 116 Stat. 21 (Mar. 9, 2002)

37. SOX: Sarbanes-Oxley Act of 2002

Pub. L. No. 107-204, 116 Stat. 745 (Jul. 30, 2002)

38. JGTRRA: Jobs and Growth Tax Relief Reconciliation Act of 2003

Pub. L. No. 108-27, 117 Stat. 752 (May 28, 2003)

39. PFEA '04: Pension Funding Equity Act of 2004

Pub. L. No. 108-218, 118 Stat. 596 (Apr. 10, 2004)

40. AJCA '04: American Jobs Creations Act of 2004

Pub. L. No. 108-357, 118 Stat. 1418, Oct. 22, 2004)

41. DRA '05: Deficit Reduction Act of 2005
    Pub. L. No. 109-171, 120 Stat. 4 (Feb. 8, 2006)

42. PPA '06: Pension Protection Act of 2006
    Pub. L. No. 109-280, 120 Stat. 780, Aug. 17, 2006)

43. GINA: Genetic Information Nondiscrimination Act of 2008
    Pub. L. No. 110-233, 122 Stat. 881 (May 21, 2008)

44. HEART: Heroes Earning Assistance and Relief Act of 2008
    Pub. L. No. 110-245, 122 Stat. 1624 (June 17, 2008)

45. MHPAEA: Mental Health Parity and Addictions Equity Act
    Pub. L. No. 110-343, 122 Stat. 3765 (Oct. 3, 2008)

46. EESA: Emergency Economic Stabilization Act of 2008
    Pub. L. No. 110-343, 122 Stat. 3806 (Oct. 3, 2008)

47. WRERA: Worker, Retiree, and Employer Recovery Act of 2008
    Pub. L. No. 110-458, 122 Stat. 5092 (Dec. 23, 2008)

48. ARRA: American Recovery and Reinvestment Act of 2009
    Pub. L. No. 111-5, 123 Stat. 115 (Feb. 17, 2009)

49. ACA: Patient Protection and Affordable Care Act
    Pub. L. No. 111-148, 124 Stat. 119 (March 23, 2010), as modified by
    Pub. L. No. 111-152, 124 Stat. 1029 March 30, 2010)

50. PRA '10: Preservation of Access to Care for Medicare Beneficiaries and Pension Relief Act of 2010
    Pub. L. No. 111-192, 124 Stat. 1280 (June 25, 2010)

51. Dodd-Frank: Dodd-Frank Wall Street Reform and Consumer Protection Act
    Pub. L. No. 111-203, 124 Stat. 1376 (July 21, 2010)

52. SBJA: The Small Business Jobs Act of 2010
    Pub. L. No. 111-240, 124 Stat. 2504 (Sept. 27, 2010)

53. MAP-21: Moving Ahead for Progress in the 21st Century Act of 2012
    Pub. L. No. 112-141, 126 Stat. 405 (July 6, 2012)

54. BBA '13: Bipartisan Budget Act of 2013
    Pub. L. No. 113-67, 127 Stat. 1165 (Dec. 26, 2013)

55. CSEC Pension Flexibility Act of 2013
    Pub. L. No. 113-97, 128 Stat. 1101 (Apr. 7, 2014)

56. HAFTA: Highway and Transportation Funding Act of 2014
    Pub. L. No. 113-159, 128 Stat. 1839 (Aug. 8, 2014)

57. Consolidated and Further Continuing Appropriations Act
    Pub. L. No. 113-235, 128 stat. 2130 (Dec. 16, 2014)

58. BBA '15: Bipartisan Budget Act of 2015
    Pub. L. No. 114-74, 129 Stat. 584 (Nov. 2, 2015)

59. 2015 PATH Act: Protecting Americans From Tax Hikes of 2015
    Pub. L. No. 114-113, 129 Stat. 2242 (Dec. 18, 2015)

60. The Consolidated Appropriations Act of 2016
    Pub. L. No. 114-150, 130 Stat. 266 (Apr. 29, 2016)

61. Cures Act: 21st Century Cures Act
    Pub. L. No. 114-255, 130 Stat. 1033 (Dec. 13, 2016)

62. TJCA '17: Tax Cuts & Jobs Act of 2017
    Pub. L. No. 115-97, 131 Stat. 2054 (Dec. 22, 2017)

63. BBA '18: Bipartisan Budget Act of 2018
    Pub. L. No. 115-123, 132 Stat. 112 (Feb. 9, 2018)

64. Further Consolidated Appropriations Act, 2020
    Pub. L. No. 116-94, 133 Stat. 2534 (Dec. 20, 2019)

    Division N, Health and Human Services Extenders, Pub. L. No. 116-94, 133 Stat. 3095

    Division M, Bipartisan American Miners Act of 2019, Pub. L. No. 116-94, 133 Stat. 3091

    Division O, Setting Every Community Up for Retirement Enhancement of 2019 (SECURE '19), Pub. L. No. 116-94, 133 Stat. 3137

65. FFCRA: Families First Coronavirus Response Act
    Pub. L. No. 116-127, 134 Stat. 178 (March 18, 2020)

66. CARES: The Coronavirus Aid, Relief, and Economic Security Act of 2020
    Pub. L. No. 116-136, 134 Stat. 281 (March 27, 2020)

Upcoming footnotes in the remaining chapters will reference the name of the federal law and the section number, instead of the public law number and statute.

Chapter 2

Basic Tax Concepts

Reading Assignment: I.R.C. §§ 61, 104–106, 132, 402

Comm'r v. Glenshaw Glass Co., 348 U.S. 426 (1955)

Class Discussion Questions: What are the general income tax rules that govern employee benefits?

What are the tax preferential rules applicable to retirement benefits from a qualified plan?

What are the tax preferential rules applicable to health and welfare benefit plans?

Why do executives take advantage of nonqualified deferred compensation plans?

Overview

What are the general income tax rules to understand?

- According to the Internal Revenue Code (and the Form 1040):

  ◦ gross income

  ◦ less deductions (all above-the-line deductions, the greater of the individual's itemized deductions or standard deduction, and all exemptions)

  ◦ equals taxable income

  ◦ multiply by tax rate (although under current law, certain long-term capital gains and dividends are taxed at a different rate)

  ◦ equals income tax

  ◦ tax is greater of income tax or alternative minimum tax (AMT)

  ◦ less credits (most credits reduce tax to zero, but refundable credits actually allow the tax to be negative, meaning that the government owes the individual money)

  ◦ equals income tax liability

  ◦ less advance payments (like withholding)

  ◦ plus other taxes (like self-employment tax or penalty taxes for premature distributions from IRAs or retirement plans)

- ○ equals income taxes owed for the year (if negative, then the IRS owes the individual a refund)

- ○ all salary and the value of the employee benefits received in exchange for services rendered as an employee are included in the individual's gross income in the tax year paid or accrued, unless there is a specific Code provision excluding or deferring such income

- ○ therefore, the true tax advantage that Congress can provide to a taxpayer is to specifically allow income to be permanently excluded from gross income or at least deferred and included in a future year's gross income, or Congress can allow certain expenses actually paid by the taxpayer to be a deduction against gross income to lower the calculated tax or allow certain expenses to be a credit against the tax to lower the actual taxes owed

- ○ a corporate taxpayer makes a similar calculation, but is allowed to deduct salary paid to employees (which, as discussed throughout this textbook, includes contributions to certain employee benefit plans which are set up to comply with whatever rules Congress requires)

What are the income tax advantages of retirement benefits from a qualified plan?

- if structured properly, deferred compensation provided to plan participants will not be included in their individual gross income until the tax year in which it is paid

- the employer gets an immediate deduction in the year that the retirement promises are deposited into a qualified retirement trust

- since the assets are invested in a tax-exempt retirement trust, no one will pay income taxes on all fund earnings along the way

What are the income tax advantages of health and welfare benefits?

- if structured properly, the value of the health and welfare benefits provided to them as employees and also provided to their traditional family members (such as spouses, children, and dependents) will never be included in their individual gross income

- the employer gets an immediate deduction in the year that the health and welfare benefits are funded or paid to a third-party insurer

- as long as the amounts to fund the health and welfare benefits are part of the employer's general assets, the employer will pay income taxes on all fund earnings along the way

What are the income tax advantages of non-qualified deferred compensation?

- if structured properly, deferred compensation provided to the favored employees and executives will not be included in their individual gross income until the tax year in which there is no longer a "substantial risk of forfeiture"

- the employer gets a corresponding deduction in that same future tax year

- since the assets are always considered part of the employer's general assets until paid, the employer will pay income taxes on all fund earnings along the way

A. Computation of Income Tax Liability

1. Hierarchy of Tax Computation

There is a tax hierarchy one must follow in computing an employee's final federal tax liability. It begins with an employee's gross income which is defined in I.R.C. §61 as "all income from whatever source derived, including ... compensation for services, including fees, commissions, fringe benefits, and similar items."[1] Certainly gross income would include amounts an employee received from his or her employer for compensation for services. For most common-law employees, the employer reports these amounts on the Form W-2, which reports total taxable compensation for the calendar year (also noting payroll taxes paid to fund Social Security and Medicare, unemployment insurance and worker's compensation, income taxes withheld by the employer and paid to the IRS on the employee's behalf, and other voluntary payroll deductions). In contrast, independent contractors receive a Form 1099 from a service provider indicating renumeration paid. Partners in a partnership receive a Form K-1, denoting his or her share of the profits or losses. Sole proprietors and self-employment individuals utilize Schedule B to the Form 1040, denoting his or her business income (referred to as "earned income").

Gross income also includes the taxable portions of individual retirement accounts (IRAs) and retirement plan distributions, the taxable portion of Social Security distributions (which depend on an individual's gross income for the calendar year), and unemployment compensation. Other income, unless specifically excluded under one of the provisions of the tax code, includes gambling winnings, monies from illegal activities, jury duty pay, and cancelled debts. The Code used to include alimony as gross income for the payee (along with a deduction for the payor), but the TCJA of '19 eliminated this rule by repealing sections 71 and 215 of the Code, effective January 1, 2019, with respect to divorce and separation instruments executed on or after that date.

The term "gross income" has been interpreted broadly by the IRS and the courts. At this point in the textbook, read the case *Comm'r v. Glenshaw Glass Co.* in the Materials section of this chapter, where the Supreme Court defines gross income to be the "undeniable accessions to wealth, clearly realized, and over which the taxpayers have complete dominion."[2]

---

1. I.R.C. §61(a).
2. Comm'r v. Glenshaw Glass Co., 348 U.S. 426, 431 (1955).

2. Doctrines Used to Determine What, When, and Who

There are three common doctrines that the IRS has used over the years to determine the what (i.e., how much), when (i.e., what tax year), and who (i.e., what person) for purposes of calculating gross income:

- For determining *what* to include in gross income, the economic benefit doctrine is used. This doctrine applies to cash basis taxpayers who receive property as compensation for services. Let's say the employee performs services but defers receipt of the property. The employee will not be taxed until he or she has the absolute right to receive the property in the future, and the amount is fixed and not otherwise subject to the employer's creditors.

- For determining *when* to include the amount in gross income, the constructive receipt doctrine is used. Clearly if a taxpayer is in actual receipt of income, he or she is taxed on such income. But an item is said to be "constructively received" and therefore taxable, when it is credited to the taxpayer's account or otherwise available to him or her and there are no substantial restrictions on his or her control.[3]

- For determining *who* must include the amount in gross income, the transfer of property doctrine is used. This doctrine is applied when the employee receives property, instead of cash, for the performance of services. Generally, the fair market value of the property will be includable in the employee's income in the year of services. But an important exception applies if the property is subject to a substantial risk of forfeiture. If it is, taxation is deferred until the substantial risk of forfeiture has lapsed.

Most employees are cash method taxpayers, which means they report their gross income when actually or constructively received.[4] This method applies regardless of whether the amounts received are in the form of property or services.[5] What if the employee is paid *by check* from the employer — is it income when the employee receives the check or after it is cashed? The IRS has used the doctrine of cash equivalence to hold that receipt of a check that is otherwise readily negotiable at or near its face value is treated the same as the receipt of cash and, therefore, the check is income upon receipt, not when it is cashed.[6] Similarly, the economic benefit doctrine would say that a cash method taxpayer has income when he receives the economic benefit of the proceeds, regardless of whether he has actual or constructive receipt or the receipt of a cash equivalent.[7] To illustrate this doctrine, let's say that the employer gave its employee an IOU for $5,000 payable in six months' time, instead of a check. Here, the Service is more inclined to say payment has not occurred under the cash

---

3. *See* Treas. Reg. § 1.451-2(a).
4. *See* Treas. Reg. § 1.451-1(a).
5. *See* Treas. Reg. § 1.446-1(c)(1)(i).
6. *See* Kahler v. Comm'r, 18 T.C. 31 (1952).
7. *See* Sproull v. Comm'r, 194 F.2d 541 (6th Cir. 1952).

method of accounting as no significant economic benefit was given to the employee. That would certainly be the case if there was a substantial risk of non-payment by the employer (e.g., an employer facing bankruptcy) or if no third party was willing to buy the IOU at its face value of $5,000 (or the present value of $5,000 payable six months from now).

In contrast, the doctrine of constructive receipt states that an item is assumed to be income if it is credited or otherwise set aside for the taxpayer and there are no substantial restrictions on his or her control over the monies.[8] This doctrine prevents the taxpayer from deciding in which tax year to include the amounts. For example, if the employer would have otherwise given the employee his or her check on December 31 of year 1, can the employee request the check be paid in year 2? The doctrine of constructive receipt would require the employee to report the amounts as income in year 1 as he or she had notice and control over the receipt of the income.

The transfer of property doctrine comes into play when property (i.e., not cash or check) is transferred to an employee in connection with the performance of services. Normally the excess of the fair market value of the property over the amount (if any) paid for the property would be included in the gross income of the employee performing services in the first calendar year in which the rights of the employee having the beneficial interest in such property are transferred.[9] However, an exception to that rule applies if the rights to the beneficial interest are subject to a substantial risk of forfeiture. For example, if the employee is granted a nonstatutory stock option with no readily ascertainable fair market value as of the date of the grant, the employee has not received income; the general rule would apply to the property received upon the employee's exercise of the option.

I.R.C. § 61 is written with an introductory clause that states "except as otherwise provided…," which means Congress has determined that gross income may have some exclusions (i.e., meaning it is never taxed) or deferrals of income until subsequent years (i.e., meaning it is income in a later tax year). That's where employee benefits fit in, as certain welfare benefits enjoy a full exclusion from gross income, whereas certain retirement benefits enjoy a deferral from gross income until the benefits are actually received by the recipient.

3. Adjustments to Gross Income

There are six steps involved in computing a taxpayer's final federal tax liability. The first step is to determine **gross income** which is the *net* of pre-exclusion gross income amounts less permitted statutory exclusions. The second step is to reduce this gross income number by "above the line" deductions which are set forth in I.R.C. § 62(a). Examples of above the line deductions would be contributions to Health

8. *See* Treas. Reg. § 1.451-2(a).
9. *See* I.R.C. § 83(a).

Savings Accounts and to individual retirement accounts.[10] The net of gross income less above the line deductions is referred to as **adjusted gross income,** which in turn may be used to determine whether certain below the line deductions may be taken.[11] The third step is to reduce adjusted gross income by either the standard deduction or the taxpayer's itemized deductions (the latter referred to as "below the line deductions"), in determining **taxable income.** Popular itemized deductions included charitable deductions, state income and property taxes, certain unreimbursed medical expenses, and home mortgage interest. TCJA made substantial changes in this regard. It more than doubled the standard deduction, making it more attractive than the itemized deductions, while reducing the amount that could be taken for certain itemized deductions (e.g., state income and property taxes are now limited to a maximum deduction of $10,000).[12] TCJA also modified the fourth step which would be to reduce taxable income by personal and dependency exemptions allowed to the taxpayers by lowering these exemptions to zero for tax years 2018 through 2025.[13] The fifth step involves applying the applicable tax rates (e.g., individual, married filing jointly, married filing separately, or head of household) to taxable income, to produce the **pre-credit tax liability.** The final step involves deducting any tax credits to determine the taxpayer's **final tax liability or refund.** For some taxpayers, the alternative minimum tax may be applied.

Unlike deductions (above or below the line deductions), nonrefundable credits reduce the taxpayer's final tax liability on a dollar-for-dollar basis, but usually not below $0. However, there are some credits, referred to as refundable credits, that can actually result in the IRS owing a low-income taxpayer money. Popular tax credits include the dependent care tax credit, the child tax credit, two higher education credits, the withholding tax credit, and the earned income credit; only the latter two are refundable credits.

The TCJA modified the seven income tax brackets by lowering some of them from 10%, 15%, 25%, 28%, 33%, 35% and 39.6% to 10%, 12%, 22%, 24%, 32%, 35%, and 37%.[14] Section 1 of the Internal Revenue Code provides the tax rates that apply to individuals (single individuals, married couples filing jointly, married couples filing separately, and heads of household). The tax brackets which applied to each of these seven income tax rates were also revised and indexed for inflation. The tax system is progressive or graduated, which means that as a taxpayer's income increases, the tax rate increases. The tax rate at each bracket of taxable income is referred to as

---

10. *See* I.R.C. §§ 62(a)(19) and (7). Note the deduction for alimony and certain moving expenses were repealed or substantially altered by the TCJA.

11. For example, medical expenses permitted under I.R.C. § 213 are permitted only to the extent they exceed 7.5% of the taxpayer's Adjusted Gross Income.

12. *See* I.R.C. §§ 63(c) and 164(b)(6).

13. *See* I.R.C. § 151(d)(5). For example, in 2017, a married couple with three children could have claimed five exemptions of $4,050 each on the joint tax return, for a deduction of $20,250. For 2018, the couple claims $0 deductions.

14. I.R.C. § 1(j)(2)(A)–(D), effective for taxable years 2018 through 2025.

the marginal rate tax. For example, for a single individual in 2018 making $40,000 of taxable income, his or her tax would be calculated as follows:

> Using the individual table (labeled Unmarried Individuals Other Than Surviving Spouses and Heads of Households) in I.R.C. § 1(j)(2)(C), 10% of the first $9,525 + 12% of the excess of $40,000 over $9,525 = $952.50 + $3.657 = $4,609.50.

> This taxpayer's marginal tax rate is 12% as that is the highest tax bracket his or her $40,000 is subject to, and the taxpayer's effective tax rate is **11.5%** (or $4,609.50 ÷ $40,000). Unless the taxpayer is in the first tax bracket, his or her effective tax rate will always be less than his or her marginal tax rate.

The qualification rules applicable to retirement plans have nondiscrimination requirements that must be satisfied. The reason for these rules is that highly compensated employees find qualified retirement plans of more value than lower compensated employees because they are subject to a higher marginal tax rate. Let's take an example of two individual taxpayers—Employee A making $50,000 and Employee B making $100,000. Let's say each one of them wants to defer $10,000 of his or her compensation as an elective contribution to a 401(k) plan. For Employee A, a reduction of $10,000 of his or her compensation is a savings of 22% of $10,000 or $2,200, as A is in the 22% marginal tax bracket, whereas for Employee B, a reduction of $10,000 of his or her compensation is a savings of 24% of $10,000 or $2,400, as B is in the 24% marginal tax bracket. Thus the 401(k) feature allows B to save more in taxes than A, making it more valuable to B than A. In addition, the lower Employee A's income, the more difficult it is to defer any of his or her compensation as it is needed for current personal expenses (e.g., rent, transportation, food).

Once the income tax liability is calculated, the taxpayer owes that amount. However, employees generally have income taxes withheld by the employer paycheck to paycheck, whereas self-employed individuals use pre-paid quarterly payments to pay self-employment taxes. To the extent more taxes have been withheld than necessary, the taxpayer receives a refund from the IRS, without interest. Thus, it serves the employee well to have the proper amount, and not too much, withheld in taxes from his or her paycheck.

4. Income Tax Policy

While there has been a movement around for years to simplify the Internal Revenue Code, Congress has failed to succeed in that goal. One of the essential features of the United States' tax system is that the government should assess taxes commensurately with the taxpayer's ability to pay those taxes. The issue of whether an income tax or consumption tax is the best way to extract taxes is central to any tax debate. An income tax taxes a taxpayer's income earned in a tax year (i.e., how much the taxpayer added to the economy), whereas a consumption tax taxes the purchase of a good or service (i.e., how much the taxpayer consumes or spends during the tax year). The heart of the issue is what is the base, meaning what is income and what is consumption. Income equals one's earnings plus any increase in net worth over the tax year, whereas consumption equals one's use of one's net worth over the tax year. The difference is that a consumption tax does not tax savings, thereby encouraging savings. Our tax system is an income tax, and the federal government gets the most of its revenue from the income tax.

In an ideal tax system, there are three principles to be achieved: fairness, efficiency, and neutrality. Fairness requires similarly situated taxpayers to be treated similarly and differently situated taxpayers be treated differently. This would lead to a tax code where two equal taxpayers earning $50,000 in income pay the same amount in income tax, while two taxpayers—one earning $50,000 in income and another earning $100,000 in income—pay different amounts. The next goal is efficiency, meaning that collecting the tax revenue shouldn't burden the economy by stifling economic activity. To the extent collecting the tax becomes burdensome on the economy, it is not achieving this goal. Finally, the tax system should be neutral, which means it shouldn't unnecessarily shape economic behavior. However, we know that isn't the case in the context of employee benefits, where employers extend such benefits to their employees because of their tax preferential treatment.

The term "tax expenditure" is one that you'll see in the press. It is also referred to as a tax break or tax loophole. It refers to an exclusion, a deduction, a reduced tax rate, or a tax credit granted under the tax code that results in the IRS collecting less tax than it could otherwise. For example, an employer's payment of an employee's health care premium in a calendar year is an exclusion from gross income because of an exclusion permitted under the Internal Revenue Code. That exclusion is a tax expenditure, as such an exclusion should have been included in an employee's gross income, just as if the employer had paid the employee's annual car insurance premium. Why does Congress grant tax expenditures? The answer is that it is trying to alter the taxpayer's behavior; for example, by excluding from gross income the cost of employee's health care premiums, Congress is encouraging employers to offer group health care coverage. For 2017, the largest tax expenditures were exclusions from workers' taxable income for employers' contributions for health care costs, deferral of employer contributions for retirement benefits, preferential tax rates on dividends and long-term capital gains, deferral for profits earned abroad, and the itemized deduction for state and local taxes.[15]

5. Corporate Income Tax

There are four main types of business structures in the United States, each with different tax, income, and liability implications for their owners and their companies:

- A corporation (or a C corp), which is a separate legal entity from its owners, is subject to tax and can be held legally liable. The owners of the corporation are

---

15. *See* Joshua Shakin, *Tax Expenditures*, Cong. Budget Office (Mar. 17, 2017), https://www.cbo.gov/publication/52493.

not personally liable for the debts of the corporation. As the corporation is a separate legal entity, if a shareholder leaves the corporation or sells his or her shares, the corporation continues to do business. The profits of a corporation are taxed twice, as they are taxed on the corporate level and again when dividends are paid to the shareholders, as dividends are income to the shareholders. A limited liability corporation (LLC) is a type of corporation where the owner's personal assets are protected as the owner has limited liability; it can elect to be taxed like an S corp instead of a C corp. It is a common form for small businesses.

- An S corporation (S corp) is a special type of corporation, designed to avoid the double taxation drawback of a corporation. S corps cannot have more than 100 shareholders and all shareholders must be U.S. citizens. The S corp's profits and some losses are passed through directly to the owner's personal income and are not subject to corporate rates.

- A partnership is a business in which two or more individuals are the owners. There are two types of partnerships:

  ◦ (1) a limited partnership (LP) has only one general partner (with unlimited personal liability) and all other partners have limited liability (i.e., protection from the debts of the partnership). Profits pass through to the partners to report income on their personal tax returns; the general partner must also pay self-employment taxes.

  ◦ (2) A limited liability partnership (LLP) which is similar to an LP but gives limited liability to every owner.

- A sole proprietorship occurs when an individual engages in a business and does not register as any other type of business. The owner retains personal liability for the debts of the business and pays personal tax on the business' net income.

A corporate employer is treated as a separate taxpayer that owes income taxes under the federal income tax code. Its taxes on gross income are based on corporate tax rates, which were considerably reduced by TCJA from 35% to a flat 21%, for tax years beginning after January 1, 2018.[16] These rates also apply to LLC entities who elect to be treated as corporations for tax purposes but not to S corporations. Corporate taxpayers use a Form 1120 in lieu of a Form 1040. Corporate taxpayers are allowed to deduct reasonable business expenses, including a reasonable allowance for salaries or other compensation for personal services rendered; traveling expenses while away from home in the pursuit of a trade or business; and rentals and other payments required to be made as a condition to the continued use or possession, for purposes of the trade or business, of property to which the taxpayer has not taken nor owns.[17] In addition, corporate taxpayers may deduct the cost of providing or funding certain employee benefits. An example will illustrate the importance of these deductions. If ABC Corporation sells $1,000,000 in products in 2019, it would report

---

16. TCJA § 13001(a), for tax years beginning after December 31, 2017.
17. I.R.C. § 162(a)(1)–(3).

gross income of $1,000,000 on its corporate tax return and pay 21% × $1,000,000 = $210,000 in corporate taxes. Instead, what if ABC pays $600,000 in 2019 to employees as compensation and contributions to various employee benefits plans (we're assuming the compensation is reasonable and that the employee benefit plans comply with the requirements of the Code). Its net corporate gross income is now $400,000 and it would pay 21% × $400,000 = $84,000 in corporate taxes. The ABC Corporation now has $126,000 in tax savings which can be reinvested in the company or paid in dividends to its shareholders.

In contrast, partnerships, LLC entities treated as partnerships, S corporations, and sole proprietorships are not deemed to be separate taxpayers under the federal income tax code. All the tax attributes of the business "pass though" or "flow through" to the owners instead of being taxed at the business level. While the businesses may file reports to the IRS and prepare tax schedules for the managing individuals, they do not pay taxes. Tax-exempt organizations, government agencies, Indian tribes, and certain public entities may have special income tax rules governing them.

B. Income Tax Advantages of Employee Benefit Plans

1. Tax Advantages of Qualified Retirement Plans

If an employer offers a retirement plan that complies with all the applicable qualification rules set forth in I.R.C. §401(a), the following favorable tax benefits flow to the employer sponsoring the plan and the employees covered under the plan:

- The employer's contribution to the plan will be deductible at the time of contributions according to I.R.C. §404(a), within certain limits;

- The participating employee will not be taxed on his or her vested and secured benefits under the plan according to I.R.C. §402(b), until they are actually distributed to him or her upon retirement or termination of employment. For example, if the employer makes a contribution of $10,000 which is allocated to the participating employee's account and the participant is vested in such amount, it is not taxable to him or her. Thus, the tax system provides an immediate tax deduction on the employer for its contributions and a deferral of income to the employee on such funds until actual receipt. This means the employer contributions made on the employee's behalf, and any corresponding cumulative interest, are not taxed until they are ultimately distributed to the employee in the form of a benefit. To the extent an employee makes elective employee contributions under I.R.C. §401(k), these may be currently taxable to the employee if he or she elects to treat them as Roth 401(k) contributions. I.R.C. §408A allows 401(k) employee elective deferrals to be paid with after-tax dollars, referred to as Roth contributions. The value of maintaining a Roth 401(k) account is that **both** the contributions themselves and any corresponding accumulated interest escape tax upon subsequent distribution, provided the distributions occur more than five years after establishing the account and after the beneficiary has reached age 59½.

Example: An employee at age 35 makes an after-tax Roth contribution of $20,000. Due to the compounding of interest (at a rate of 10% interest), that amount will equal $562,048 at age 70. Since the original contribution was a Roth contribution, the entire amount of the interest growth ($562,048 – $20,000) will escape taxation.

The earnings on plan assets accumulate free of federal and state income taxes until the earnings are distributed to the participant. Due to the effect of compounding of interest, this can be a huge tax savings for the employee. When the employer establishes a qualified plan, it must also establish a separate legal entity to hold the plan assets, known as a tax-exempt trust pursuant to I.R.C. § 501(a). All fund earnings under this tax-exempt trust accumulate tax-free unless there is any incidence of unrelated business income tax[18] and thus escape tax for both the employer and the employees.

Example: If an employer were to contribute $20,000 annually to an employee's account beginning at age 35 at a 10% interest rate, those annual amounts will accumulate and total at age 70 to $5,420,487.

To the extent an employee is in a lower income tax bracket during retirement, the amounts distributed from the qualified plan and includable in the retiree's gross income may result in a lower tax liability. And generally, for payroll tax purposes, employer contributions to fund retirement plan promises (other than elective employee deferrals in a 401(k) plan) are not subject to Federal Insurance Contribution Act (FICA) and Federal Unemployment Tax Act (FUTA) taxes to fund Social Security, Medicare, and unemployment benefits.

2. Income Tax Advantages of Health and Welfare Benefit Plans

Various welfare benefits have special tax treatment under the Code; however, the term "qualification" does not apply to such welfare benefits. To qualify for special tax treatment, there are applicable rules to be satisfied under specified Code sections (e.g., group term insurance provides specific tax treatment if the rules of I.R.C. § 79 are met). These special tax treatments may apply to the employee, as well as certain family members. I.R.C. §§ 101 through 140 set forth items that are specifically excluded from gross income. For welfare benefits, there is no one single Code provision relied upon for exclusion, but there are instead of variety of Code provisions that may or may not provide nondiscrimination tests. If properly structured to avoid full or partial federal income taxes, most or all employer contributions or reimbursements will not be taxable to the employee and his or her spouse and dependents, and the employer may claim an immediate deduction for such expenses or reimbursements.

---

18. I.R.C. § 512.

I.R.C. § 79 provides a partial exemption from gross income for employer-provided group term life insurance. If the requirements of I.R.C. § 79 are met, the cost of the first $50,000 of group term life insurance is excluded from taxation. If the coverage exceeds $50,000 of group term life insurance, the cost of the coverage in excess of $50,000 is taxable as a fringe benefit at the greater of (1) the cost under the uniform premium tables contained in the regulations, or (2) the employer's actual cost.[19]

I.R.C. §§ 105 and 106 provide an exclusion from the employee's gross income amounts paid by the employer for either premiums paid for or amounts received through health coverage, whether the coverage is extended to the employee, his or her spouse, and/or his or her dependents. Prior to the legendary Supreme Court decisions in *United States v. Windsor*[20] and *Obergefell v. Hodges*,[21] spouses covered under an employer-provided group health plan referred to opposite-sex spouses. The *Windsor* decision struck down the constitutionality of Section 3 of the Defense of Marriage Act (DOMA) which defined a marriage and spouse for federal law purposes to include only a union between one man and one woman, excluding same sex couples. It directed the federal agencies to look to state law in determining whether there was a marriage and who was a spouse.[22] Thereafter, the IRS took the position that for federal tax purposes, the state of celebration approach would govern (e.g., if the couple had a valid same-sex marriage in the state of celebration, they were married and spouses for federal tax purposes).[23] In the *Obergefell* decision, the Supreme Court struck down the states' bans on same-sex marriages and their nonrecognition of same-sex marriages lawfully licensed and performed out of state.[24] Thus, it is clear for I.R.C. §§ 105 and 106 purposes that same-sex spouses may be covered under the employee's employer-provided group health coverage without any income tax consequences. However, the *Obergefell* decision did not create federal recognition for unmarried partners or same-sex or opposite-sex partners in civil unions or domestic partnerships.

I.R.C. § 125 provides employers with the ability to provide a flexible benefit plan (sometimes referred to as a cafeteria plan). Such plans provide the employee with the choice of receiving cash or electing to receive certain non-taxable welfare benefits (hence, the term "cafeteria" used to reflect that the employee can choose between a variety of welfare benefits). If cash is not elected, the value of the welfare benefits may then be excluded from gross income.[25] Such plans can be used by employees to pay employee contributions to employer-provided health insurance coverage with pre-tax dollars, as well as to cover medical expenses not covered by the employer's plan (e.g., portion of benefits not paid due to the plan's deductible or co-insurance limits).

---

19. Treas. Reg. § 1.79-3(d). There are applicable nondiscrimination rules that must be satisfied to assure that the benefits are not being provided primarily for key employees or discriminatory employees.

20. 133 S. Ct. 2675 (2013).

21. 135 S. Ct. 2584 (2015).

22. 133 S. Ct. 2675, 2692 (2013).

23. Rev. Rul. 2013-17.

24. 135 S. Ct. 2584 (2015).

25. I.R.C. § 125(a).

I.R.C. § 132 provides a variety of miscellaneous fringe benefits that are afforded a full or partial exclusion from gross income. They include the following:

- Achievement awards, defined to be tangible personal property (e.g., plaque) given to an employee as an award for either length of service or safety achievement;[26]

- Use of an athletic facility on the employer' premises or an athletic facility that the employer operates if substantially all of the use of the facility is by the employees and their spouse and children;[27]

- *De minimis* benefits, defined as any property or service provided by the employer to the employee that has so little value that accounting for it would be unreasonable or impracticable (e.g., use of the employer's photocopying machine for personal use);[28]

- Employee discounts, which are price reductions given by an employer to an employee on property or services offered to customers in the ordinary course of the employer's business (e.g., 15% reduction on the price of the employer's goods);[29]

- Moving expense reimbursements, which are expenses associated with moving household goods and personal effects from the former home to the new home due to employment with an employer;[30]

- No additional cost services, which include services provided by the employer to the employee if such service is offered for sale to customers in the employer's ordinary course of business and the employer incurs no substantial additional cost in providing the service to the employee (e.g., free flight for the airline's pilot on an empty airplane);[31]

- Qualified transportation reimbursements, which include reimbursement for expense incurred in commuting to and from work;[32] and

- Working condition fringe benefits, which are property or services provided by an employer to an employee so that the employee can perform his job (e.g., uniforms for the employer's janitorial staff).[33]

For the employer, health, welfare, and fringe benefits provided to employees are treated as immediate deductible trade or business expenses for salary or other compensation for services rendered.[34] However, such contributions may not be entitled to a business deduction if the employer is a partnership, S corporation, LLC, or LLP,

---

26. I.R.C. § 74(c).

27. I.R.C. § 132(j)(4).

28. I.R.C. § 132(e).

29. I.R.C. § 132(c).

30. I.R.C. § 132(g) (limited by TJCA to moving expenses for Armed Forces personnel only, *see* I.R.C. § 132(g)(2) for taxable years 2018 through 2025).

31. I.R.C. § 132(b).

32. I.R.C. § 132(f).

33. I.R.C. § 132(d).

34. I.R.C. § 162(a)(1).

or a sole proprietorship. Thus, when deciding the type of business entity to form, managing individuals need to be aware of the difference in deduction for various employees benefit plans. If the employer wishes the employee to pay for some of these benefits, a separate funding vehicle such as a health savings account, a cafeteria plan, or flexible spending arrangement may need to be established to allow the employees to fund such vehicles with pre-tax dollars.

3. Income Tax Advantages of Non-Qualified Deferred Compensation Arrangements

Corporations and executives have legitimate business reasons for wanting a portion of an *executive's* compensation to be deferred in lieu of current cash compensation. While a typical rank-and-file employee (i.e., not an executive) would shudder at the concept of deferring a substantial part of his or her current compensation to a subsequent year, especially if the payment was contingent upon subsequent job performance or forfeited upon subsequent employment with a competitor, it is common practice for employers to condition the payment of current compensation upon future events. Such a practice benefits the corporation's shareholders as it conditions the executive's future compensation upon performance, and a portion of that compensation may be forfeited by the executive if the executive later works for a competitor. While arrangements between an executive and his or her employer can be made pursuant to an individual employment agreement, deferred compensation arrangements available to a "select group of management or highly compensated employees" may be subject to the rules of ERISA[35] but exempt them from many of its requirements. These plans are referred to a "top hat" plans and the exemption accounts for the variety of different types of these plans that are presently being used.

Qualified retirement plans available to both the rank-and-file and executives of the employer are limited by the Internal Revenue Code by maximum limitations on the amount of benefits or annual deferrals that may be accumulated. For example, if an employer maintains a qualified defined benefit plan replacing 75% of the employee's pre-retirement income, the maximum limit on the amount of annual pension that may be paid to a 65-year-old executive for 2020 is $230,000, beginning at age 65 for life. If the executive was making a pre-retirement salary of $500,000, the maximum amount from the qualified plan of $230,000 annually would be woefully inadequate to replace the executive's pre-retirement income level of $500,000. Thus, the employer may have a nonqualified defined benefit "sit on top" of the qualified

---

35. ERISA § 3(2)(A) subjects any employee pension benefit plan which provides retirement income to employees or results in a deferral of income by employees for periods extending to the termination of covered employment or beyond to its rules. ERISA § 4 exempts excess benefit plans (which are plans designed solely for the purpose of providing benefits for certain employees in excess of the maximum limitations on contributions or benefits imposed by I.R.C. § 415 from coverage), whereas ERISA §§ 201, 301, and 401 exempt from coverage plans that are unfunded and maintained by the employer primarily for the purpose of providing deferred compensation for a select group of management or highly compensated employees.

defined benefit plan such that the nonqualified defined benefit plan pays $145,000 annually, beginning at age 65 for life. Together, the nonqualified and qualified defined benefit plans would disperse $375,000 annually, giving the executive 75% replacement income during retirement. Such nonqualified defined benefit plans could be funded either through employer contributions or a combination of employer and employee contributions. These plans are generally referred to as Supplemental Executive Retirement Plans or SERPs.

In addition, ERISA's and the Code's vesting schedules do not allow an employer to "handcuff" an employee for a sizable amount of time, nor do they permit an employee to forfeit his or her benefit as a result of a subsequent employment with a competitor. Executive deferred compensation can impose such "handcuffs" or more onerous vesting schedules as a way to limit the payment. The cumulative legislative changes made to the maximum limitations applicable to qualified defined benefit and defined contribution plans, the reductions in the statutory vesting schedules, and the more restrictive nondiscrimination tests imposed on qualified plans have led to more pressure on employers to establish and maintain executive deferred compensation plans. Their growth has expanded exponentially in the past years.[36]

The Code generally utilizes a general "matching" principle with respect to employee deferred compensation such that the employer receives a deduction for the payment of the compensation when the executive reports the deferral as income.[37] Exception exists of course if the deferred compensation is pursuant to a qualified retirement plan—granting an employer an immediate deduction even though the employee's inclusion into gross income is deferred until he or she actually receives the payment much later. Such preferential tax treatment is granted to qualified retirement plans in order to promote their coverage. Code section 401(k) provides an additional tax feature whereby an employee may make a pre-tax contribution from his or her current compensation into a qualified profit sharing plan, delaying the payment of tax on the contribution as well as its income until later actual distribution.

For compensation deferrals made under a nonqualified plan, for tax purposes, the monies must remain with the employer and thus continue to be taxed at corporate tax rates; any interest accrued on the deferrals will also be taxed to the employer as they are the employer's monies. If properly designed, the executive's taxation on the deferrals may be deferred until actual receipt of the payment if the deferrals are unavailable to the executive, or if otherwise available, are subject to a substantial risk of loss or forfeiture.[38]

In reaction to the collapse of Enron in which corporate executives were allowed access to their deferred compensation subject to a "haircut" (i.e., a portion of the payment was forfeited in order to access the compensation currently), Congress

---

36. *See 2019 Non-Qualified Deferred Compensation Plan Survey*, Plan Sponsor Council of Am. (PCSA), https://www.psca.org/research/nqdc/2019AR.

37. I.R.C. §404(a)(5). *See also* Albertson's Inc. v. C.I.R, 42 F.3d 537, 541 (9th Cir. 1994).

38. Treas. Reg. §1.451-2(a).

reacted with the passage of I.R.C. § 409A. Under the new rules, if an executive wished to defer current compensation to a subsequent year, the initial deferral election had to be made in the tax year prior to the year the services were performed (or within 30 days of initial eligibility), and any subsequent elections to delay the time of or change the form of the distribution could not take effect until 12 months after the election and must defer payment for at least five years after original election (exceptions granted in the case of death, disability, or unforeseeable emergency).[39] The amount deferred may only be distributed upon separation of employment, or in the case of a key employee, six months after separation, death, disability, a specified time or fixed schedule set forth in the plan at the date of deferral, change of control of the employer, or an unforeseeable emergency.[40] Plans may not permit acceleration of the time or schedule of any distribution.[41] Failure to comply with the new rules results in current income tax as well as a 20% penalty tax.

Because ERISA's rules may not cover all types of executive deferred compensation arrangements, those amounts remain subject to the employer's general creditors if the employer were to become bankrupt. Early on, employers sought to *fund* such non-qualified deferred compensation promises through trusts, referred to as "rabbi trusts."[42] A rabbi trust is simply an irrevocable grantor trust providing executives with protection in the event the employer has a later change of heart or protection in the event of a change of control such that the new owner would not honor the prior commitment. The intent behind the trust was to provide security to the executives that funds would be available to pay the promised deferred compensation in the event of a change of control whereby a new employer would not honor the prior commitment. To be exempt from taxation, the assets of the rabbi trust could be set aside or segregated for the purpose of only providing deferred compensation, provided such funds were available to the employer's creditors in the event of bankruptcy or insolvency.[43] For tax

---

39. I.R.C. § 409A(a)(4).

40. I.R.C. § 409A(a)(2). The deferred compensation rules contained in I.R.C. § 409A(a)(2) impose special rules for distributions to key employees. A key employee is defined in I.R.C. § 416(i), which contains the top-heavy rules. Generally, key employees are certain owners and officers of the business. This term will be defined in Chapter 7.

41. I.R.C. § 409A(a)(3).

42. *See* Priv. Ltr. Rul. 81-13-107 (Dec. 31, 1980). The term "rabbi trust" was coined by the first IRS private letter ruling that addressed such funding vehicles. The private letter ruling was requested by a congregation seeking to set aside or segregate funds for the express purpose of satisfying its obligation to the rabbi under a deferred compensation plan. Employers cannot formally fund nonqualified deferred compensation arrangements without putting the executive's benefit at risk for taxation.

43. Although funds set aside in a rabbi trust must be available to the employer's general creditors, the trust tends to afford executives a larger share of assets in bankruptcy or insolvency proceedings. *See* M Benefit Solutions, White Paper: Why Companies Use Rabbi Trusts 4 ("M Benefit Solutions has had several clients go through a bankruptcy and the existence of a rabbi trust, we believe, helped executives there to obtain payment of all or a large percentage of their nonqualified deferred compensation benefits. Whether they would have been able to obtain this result without an asset already set aside to make the benefit payments is difficult to say, but is likely.").

purposes, the rabbi trust was deemed to be an employer grantor trust, and its income, losses, and deductions flowed back to the employer.[44]

I.R.C. §409A curbed some abuses surrounding rabbi trusts by requiring all assets of the trust be held within the jurisdiction of the federal U.S. courts.[45] Congress also added a new Code section, I.R.C. §457A, which created limitations on foreign corporations from promising nonqualified deferred compensation to U.S. executive in hopes of circumventing the rules of I.R.C. §409A.

C. Materials

Commissioner v. Glenshaw Glass Co.

348 U.S. 426 (1955)

Mr. Chief Justice WARREN delivered the opinion of the Court.

This litigation involves two cases with independent factual backgrounds yet presenting the identical issue. The two cases were consolidated for argument before the Court of Appeals for the Third Circuit and were heard en banc. The common question is whether money received as exemplary damages for fraud or as the punitive two-thirds portion of a treble-damage antitrust recovery must be reported by a taxpayer as gross income under s 22(a) of the Internal Revenue Code of 1939. In a single opinion, 211 F.2d 928, the Court of Appeals affirmed the Tax Court's separate rulings in favor of the taxpayers. 18 T.C. 860; 19 T.C. 637. Because of the frequent recurrence of the question and differing interpretations by the lower courts of this Court's decisions bearing upon the problem, we granted the Commissioner of Internal Revenue's ensuing petition for certiorari. 348 U.S. 813, 75 S. Ct. 50.

The facts of the cases were largely stipulated and are not in dispute. So far as pertinent they are as follows:

Commissioner v. Glenshaw Glass Co.—The Glenshaw Glass Company, a Pennsylvania corporation, manufactures glass bottles and containers. It was engaged in protracted litigation with the Hartford-Empire Company, which manufactures machinery of a character used by Glenshaw. Among the claims advanced by Glenshaw were demands for exemplary damages for fraud and treble damages for injury to its business by reason of Hartford's violation of the federal antitrust laws. In December, 1947, the parties concluded a settlement of all pending litigation, by which Hartford paid Glenshaw approximately $800,000. Through a method of allocation which was approved by the Tax Court, 18 T.C. 860, 870–872, and which is no longer in issue, it was ultimately determined that, of the total settlement, $324,529.94 represented payment of punitive damages for fraud and antitrust violations. Glenshaw did not report this portion of the settlement as income for the tax year involved. The Com-

---

44. I.R.C. §§671–77.
45. I.R.C. §409A(b)(1).

missioner determined a deficiency claiming as taxable the entire sum less only deductible legal fees. As previously noted, the Tax Court and the Court of Appeals upheld the taxpayer.

Commissioner v. William Goldman Theatres, Inc. — William Goldman Theatres, Inc., a Delaware corporation operating motion picture houses in Pennsylvania, sued Loew's, Inc., alleging a violation of the federal antitrust laws and seeking treble damages. After a holding that a violation had occurred, William Goldman Theatres, Inc., v. Loew's Inc., 3 Cir., 150 F.2d 738, the case was remanded to the trial court for a determination of damages. It was found that Goldman had suffered a loss of profits equal to $125,000 and was entitled to treble damages in the sum of $375,000. William Goldman Theatres, Inc., v. Loew's, Inc., D.C., 69 F. Supp. 103, affirmed 3 Cir., 164 F.2d 1021, certiorari denied 334 U.S. 811, 68 S. Ct. 1016, 92 L. Ed. 1742. Goldman reported only $125,000 of the recovery as gross income and claimed that the $250,000 balance constituted punitive damages and as such was not taxable. The Tax Court agreed, 19 T.C. 637, and the Court of Appeals, hearing this with the Glenshaw case, affirmed. 211 F.2d 928.

It is conceded by the respondents that there is no constitutional barrier to the imposition of a tax on punitive damages. Our question is one of statutory construction: are these payments comprehended by s 22(a)?

The sweeping scope of the controverted statute is readily apparent:

's 22. Gross income

'(a) General definition. 'Gross income' includes gains, profits, and income derived from salaries, wages, or compensation for personal service * * * of whatever kind and in whatever form paid, or from professions, vocations, trades, businesses, commerce, or sales, or dealings in property, whether real or personal, growing out of the ownership or use of or interest in such property; also from interest, rent, dividends, securities, or the transaction of any business carried on for gain or profit, or gains or profits and income derived from any source whatever. * * *' (Emphasis added.)

This Court has frequently stated that this language was used by Congress to exert in this field 'the full measure of its taxing power.' Helvering v. Clifford, 309 U.S. 331, 334, 60 S. Ct. 554, 556, 84 L. Ed. 788; Helvering v. Midland Mutual Life Ins. Co., 300 U.S. 216, 223, 57 S. Ct. 423, 425, 81 L. Ed. 612; Douglas v. Willcuts, 296 U.S. 1, 9, 56 S. Ct. 59, 62, 80 L. Ed. 3; Irwin v. Gavit, 268 U.S. 161, 166, 45 S. Ct. 475, 69 L. Ed. 897. Respondents contend that punitive damages, characterized as 'windfalls' flowing from the culpable conduct of third parties, are not within the scope of the section. But Congress applied no limitations as to the source of taxable receipts, nor restrictive labels as to their nature. And the Court has given a liberal construction to this broad phraseology in recognition of the intention of Congress to tax all gains except those specifically exempted. Commissioner v. Jacobson, 336 U.S. 28, 49, 69 S. Ct. 358, 369, 93 L. Ed. 477; Helvering v. Stockholms Enskilda Bank, 293 U.S. 84, 87–91, 55 S. Ct. 50, 51–53, 79 L. Ed. 211. Thus, the fortuitous gain accruing to a lessor by reason of the forfeiture of a lessee's improvements on the rented property was taxed in Helvering v. Bruun, 309 U.S. 461, 60 S. Ct. 631, 84 L. Ed. 864. *Cf.* Robertson v. United States, 343 U.S. 711, 72 S. Ct. 994, 96 L. Ed. 1237; Rutkin v. United States, 343 U.S. 130, 72 S. Ct. 571, 96 L. Ed. 833; United States v. Kirby Lumber Co., 284 U.S. 1, 52 S. Ct. 4, 76 L. Ed. 131. Such decisions demonstrate that we cannot but ascribe content to the catchall provision of s 22(a), 'gains or profits and income derived from any source whatever.' The importance of that phrase has been too frequently recognized since its first appearance in the Revenue Act of 19135 to say now that it adds nothing to the meaning of 'gross income.'

Nor can we accept respondents' contention that a narrower reading of s 22(a) is required by the Court's characterization of income in Eisner v. Macomber, 252 U.S. 189, 207, 40 S. Ct. 189, 193, 64 L. Ed. 521, as "the gain derived from capital, from labor, or from both combined." The Court was there endeavoring to determine whether the distribution of a corporate stock dividend constituted a realized gain to the shareholder, or changed 'only the form, not the essence,' of his capital investment. *Id.*, 252 U.S. at page 210, 40 S. Ct. at page 194. It was held that the taxpayer had 'received nothing out of the company's assets for his separate use and benefit.' *Id.*, 252 U.S. at page 211, 40 S. Ct. at page 194. The distribution, therefore, was held not a taxable event. In that context — distinguishing gain from capital — the definition served a useful purpose. But it was not meant to provide a touchstone to all future gross income questions. Helvering v. Bruun, *supra*, 309 U.S. at pages 468–469, 60 S. Ct. at page 634; United States v. Kirby Lumber Co., *supra*, 284 U.S. at page 3, 52 S. Ct. 4.

Here we have instances of undeniable accessions to wealth, clearly realized, and over which the taxpayers have complete dominion. The mere fact that the payments were extracted from the wrongdoers as punishment for unlawful conduct cannot detract from their character as taxable income to the recipients. Respondents concede, as they must, that the recoveries are taxable to the extent that they compensate for damages actually incurred. It would be an anomaly that could not be justified in the absence of clear congressional intent to say that a recovery for actual damages is taxable but not the additional amount extracted as punishment for the same conduct which caused the injury. And we find no such evidence of intent to exempt these payments.

It is urged that re-enactment of s 22(a) without change since the Board of Tax Appeals held punitive damages nontaxable in Highland Farms Corp., 42 B.T.A. 1314, indicates congressional satisfaction with that holding. Re-enactment — particularly without the slightest affirmative indication that Congress ever had the Highland Farms decision before it — is an unreliable indicium at best. Helvering v. Wilshire Oil Co., 308 U.S. 90, 100–101, 60 S. Ct. 18, 24, 84 L. Ed. 101; Koshland v. Helvering, 298 U.S. 441, 447, 56 S. Ct. 767, 770, 80 L. Ed. 1268. Moreover, the Commissioner promptly published his non-acquiescence in this portion of the Highland Farms holding and has, before and since, consistently maintained the position that these receipts are taxable. It therefore cannot be said with certitude that Congress intended to carve an exception out of s 22(a)'s pervasive coverage. Nor does the 1954 Code's legislative history, with its reiteration of the proposition that statutory gross income is 'all-inclusive,' give support to respondents' position. The definition of gross income has been simplified, but no effect upon its present broad scope was intended. Certainly punitive damages cannot reasonably be classified as gifts, *cf.* Commissioner v. Jacobson, 336 U.S. 28, 47–52, 69 S. Ct. 358, 368–370, 93 L. Ed. 477, nor do they come under any other exemption provision in the Code. We would do violence to the plain meaning of the statute and restrict a clear legislative attempt to bring the taxing power to bear upon all receipts constitutionally taxable were we to say that the payments in question here are not gross income. *See* Helvering v. Midland Mutual Life Ins. Co., *supra*, 300 U.S. at page 223, 57 S. Ct. at page 425, 81 L. Ed. 612.

Reversed.

Chapter 3

Introduction to Employee Retirement Income Security Act of 1974 (ERISA)

Reading Assignment: Skim the four titles of ERISA

           Message of the President regarding the Reorganization Plan of 1978

Class Discussion Questions: Why did Congress pass ERISA?

           What protection does ERISA extend to employees regarding promised employee benefits?

           If ERISA is a labor statute, why are there corresponding income tax provisions contained in ERISA?

           What are the three agencies that regulate ERISA, and what are each of their roles?

           What roles and duties must an employer undertake when voluntarily deciding to establish and maintain an employee benefit plan? If the employer cannot fulfill these roles and duties, who must be hired?

Overview

Does an employer need to provide employee benefits?

- no
- but, if the employer voluntarily makes a promise to employees, then they must deliver them through a plan that might be subject to governance under the Employee Retirement Income Security Act of 1974 (ERISA)

What is ERISA and why was it enacted?

- in 1974, there were perceived and actual abuses in retirement plans, such as
  - broken promises by the employers
  - improper use of plan assets

- ○ inadequate advance funding
- ○ failure to cover a fair cross-section of lower paid employees
- Congress enacted ERISA primarily to provide rights to the employees being promised employee benefits
- ERISA governs the requirements for employer-sponsored retirement plans and health and welfare benefit plans
- almost all the rules and penalties under ERISA are for acts or non-acts of the employer, not for the acts of the individual employees or their beneficiaries

What protections does ERISA provide to employees promised employee benefits?

- every ERISA plan imposes certain reporting requirements to the federal government and certain disclosure requirements to the plan participants and beneficiaries (Title I, Subtitle B, Part 1 of ERISA)
- certain retirement plans (discussed throughout this textbook as "qualified retirement plans") have minimum vesting and advance funding rules (Title I, Subtitle B, Parts 2 and 3 of ERISA)
- qualified retirement plans and certain group health plans impose specific fiduciary duties on the individuals who have management control over plan assets (Title I, Subtitle B, Part 4 of ERISA)
- every ERISA plan (and individuals associated with the plan) is subject to the criminal and civil causes of action and remedies specifically stated in the statute, and are therefore preempted from state-level causes of action (Title I, Subtitle B, Part 5 of ERISA)
- certain group health plans are subject to continuation requirements under COBRA and portability and accountability under requirements HIPAA (Title I, Subtitle B, Parts 6 and 7 of ERISA)
- certain qualified retirement plans must pay premiums to a federal agency (the Pension Benefit Guaranty Corporation), which acts as the insurer for employer sponsors that go bankrupt before fully funding the retirement promises, and other qualified retirement plans common to a group of union employees can impose a withdrawal liability on employers that wish to stop contributing to the common collectively bargained union fund (Title IV of ERISA)

What are the corresponding income tax provisions of ERISA?

- in addition to the "labor" rights and protections under Titles I and IV of ERISA, Title II of ERISA provides the corresponding provisions under the Internal Revenue Code which allows properly drafted and operated plans to provide the income tax advantages to employees and employers

What are the main agencies that regulate ERISA-governed employee benefit plans?

- The U.S. Department of Labor (DOL), through the Employee Benefits Security Administration (EBSA)

- The U.S. Department of the Treasury, through the Employee Plans group of the Internal Revenue Service (IRS), Tax Exempt and Governmental Entities operating division (IRS EP)

- The Pension Benefit Guaranty Corporation (PBGC)

How do federal agencies generally work?

- they are staffed with experts

- they perform audits and examinations to make sure plans are compliant with the rules under ERISA and the Internal Revenue Code (IRC)

- they attempt to educate employers that sponsor employee benefit plans and individuals promised benefits from the plans

- they provide interpretation of the Congressional statutes where needed

- the highest form of guidance is a regulation, which, when published in final form, either has the effect of law, if Congress specifically asked them to draft regulations, or is presumed to be correct, if Congress does not specifically ask for the regulations

- a proposed regulation has no legal effect but signals how the agency would like to eventually interpret a statute and allows a period of several months where the members of the public can provide comments

- lesser guidance (such as Revenue Rulings or Notices from the IRS or Advisory Opinions from the EBSA) just sets forth an agency's position, but can be challenged by the plan if the plan sponsor has a different interpretation of the statute

Which agencies have jurisdiction to regulate the different aspects of ERISA?

- the original division of jurisdiction between the Departments of the Treasury and Labor were in Title III of ERISA

- after a few years of experience, President Carter reorganized the division of jurisdiction

Is ERISA actively amended?

- yes, almost every year since its enactment in 1974, ERISA has been amended (sometimes in a very minor manner, and sometimes in a major manner)

- think about the public policy between changes:

- is it an amendment to the labor provisions?

  ○ if yes, then were more protections provided to plan participants and beneficiaries (thus favoring the participants), or were the rules relaxed somewhat (thus favoring the employer sponsor)?

- or is it an amendment to the income tax provisions?

  ○ if yes, then is it expanding the income tax benefits to employer or participant (thus costing the government tax revenue in additional subsidies) or is it restricting the income tax benefits (thus increasing expected tax revenues, which is likely just the simplest mechanism available to Congress to pay for some other law they have enacted)?

When an employer voluntarily chooses to sponsor an ERISA plan, then what roles and obligations must it fulfill?

- once the promises are made through a plan, then the employer must actually administer the plan so that all promises are delivered properly and timely and so that the regulatory agencies have a contact for audits and questions
- if there are plan assets, then at least one individual must be named as the plan fiduciary, and then that individual can delegate and transfer fiduciary duties to others

If the employer does not employ internal staff with an expertise in the governance of the employee benefit plan, then who are the other employee benefits professionals it can work with?

- attorneys to draft the plan documents, provide legal advice, and represent its interests in litigation
- accountants to tie deductions and financial accounting of the employee benefit plans with other matters of the business, and to provide independent audits of plan assets
- actuaries to perform required valuations for certain qualified retirement plans and to provide other statistical and financial forecasts as needed or desired
- insurance advisors to provide proper and adequate forms of insurance to fund, or simply be part of, the plan assets
- investment advisors to help diversify plan assets in accordance with modern portfolio theory
- recordkeepers to assist the employer's payroll and human resources departments in keeping specific employee data organized in order to determine the level of benefits that were promised to the employees
- third-party administrators to step in the shoes of the employer and run the day-to-day operations of the employee benefit plan
- enrolled retirement plan agents (ERPAs) to represent the employer's qualified retirement plan in front of the IRS (because the only individuals allowed to receive power of attorney from the employer sponsor and represent the plan in front of the IRS are ERPAs, attorneys, accountants, actuaries, and enrolled agents)

A. Reasons for ERISA's Passage

1. Voluntary Nature of Promised Employee Benefits

When an employer hires an employee, it generally needs to offer competitive compensation packages, which includes cash compensation as well employee benefits. As mentioned earlier, by offering employee benefits as part of the package, the employer and employee both save money as a result of the tax treatment of these benefits. Due to the pooling of risk, employers can deliver the employee benefits at a cheaper rate than what the employee could find in the marketplace. For example, an employer with 1,000 employees can ensure health coverage for its employees at a cheaper rate than if the employees purchased health insurance coverage in the marketplace. When promising cash compensation and employee benefits in exchange for services rendered, the employer must comply with federal and state minimum wage laws, family medical and leave laws, and other relevant labor laws that govern compensation.[1] Until the passage of the Affordable Care Act (ACA), employee benefits were regarded as *voluntary* benefits that an employer offered to employees. The ACA mandated large employers offer certain minimum valued health insurance coverage to employees, assessing an excise tax on the employer if it failed to comply.[2]

As employee benefits were regarded as voluntary benefits offered by the employer, there were no federal or state laws protecting those promises. In the context of retirement benefits, defined benefit plans were more common than defined contribution plans, and there were no federal laws mandating the funding of those benefits during the employees' working lifetime nor any federal guarantee of the payment of such benefits should the unfunded defined benefit plan terminate. Section 2 of Title I of ERISA enumerates the following reasons why ERISA was passed:

- The growth in size, scope, and number of employee benefit plans has been rapid and substantial;

- The fact that the operational scope and economic impact of such plans is becoming increasingly interstate;

---

1. See the Dep't of Labor's Wage and Hour Division site for all minimum wage issues, available at http://www.dol.gov/esa/whd.

2. Pub. L. No. 111-148, the Patient Protection and Affordable Care Act (PPACA) was signed into law. Days later, the President signed Pub. L. No. 111-152, the Health Care and Education Reconciliation Act (HCERA), amending PPACA. HCERA made amendments to PPACA to secure passage by both Houses of Congress. The ACA made a number of market reforms including: prohibition on preexisting condition exclusions; development of wellness programs; 90-day waiting period limitations; prohibition on lifetime/restricted annual limits; prohibition on rescissions; coverage of preventative health services; extension of dependent coverage; summary of benefits and coverage; and internal claims and external review. I.R.C. § 4980D, as amended by PPACA, § 1563(f) (PPACA), imposes an excise tax on large employer who fails to meet the employer mandate.

- The lack of employee information and adequate safeguards with respect to the establishment, operation, and administration of employee benefit plans;
- The goal of providing minimum standards to assure the equitable character of such plans and their financial soundness; and
- Despite the enormous growth in such plans, many employees with long years of employment are losing retirement benefits due to the lack of vesting provisions and minimum funding standards.

As a result, ERISA was enacted and signed into law on Labor Day in 1974, which resulted in sweeping changes for all employee benefit plans. Its goal was to protect participants' rights under employee benefit plans, and to provide a uniform set of federal requirements regarding standards of conduct, responsibility, and obligations under such plans. As many of these benefits are promised by the employer on a voluntary basis, ERISA presumes that the employer who offers such benefits has affirmatively agreed to comply with its requirements. Thus, most of its requirements subject the employer to penalties for noncompliance, not the individual employees or their beneficiaries. As noted above, the lack of employee information and lack of funding safeguards were important legislative goals for the act. But back in the early 1970s, the realm of health benefit promises and delivery were entirely different than they are today. In a last-minute compromise, the act was amended to extend many of ERISA's protections to those benefits, along with other welfare benefits.

2. Other Important ERISA Protections

Employee Communication of Benefits: As noted in the legislative history, the lack of employee information regarding the promised benefits was a main motivator of passage. Thus, in general, all covered employee benefit plans are subject to ERISA's reporting and disclosure requirements. Plan administrators who are responsible for the day-to-day administration of the plan in operation must regularly prepare and filed reports with the responsible federal government agencies. In addition to annual reports, employers can be required to submit reports and to make additional disclosures following certain plan events (e.g., amendment to the plan document, change in benefits, plan distributions, and plan terminations). Likewise, covered employees must be notified of their rights and obligations under the plan through a summary plan description (SPD), and if the plan is later materially modified, employees must be informed about the changes. All documents relied upon by the plan administrator in operating the plan (e.g., plan document, trust agreement, plan amendments) must be made available to the participants and beneficiaries. Chapter 16 of the textbook will describe these reporting and disclosure requirements.

Minimum Vesting: Prior to the passage of ERISA, employers could impose onerous vesting schedules (i.e., a requirement that an employee work a minimum number of years, such as 20 years) in order to receive retirement benefits. While ERISA initially permitted between 10 and 15 years of employment in the plan's vesting schedule, Congress continues to reduce the minimum number of years such that it now ranges between 3 to 6 years. Chapter 7 of the textbook will describe the current vesting schedules as well as benefit accrual rules to determine the amount of a participant's benefit if he or she terminates employment prior to retirement.

Advance Funding: Prior to the passage of ERISA, there was no federal mandate as to whether the employer had to advance fund promised defined benefit plans — meaning funding the cost of such benefits over the employees' active work life — as opposed to paying it on a pay-as-you-go basis. ERISA now prescribes the funding requirements for defined benefit plans and for certain defined contribution plans. Chapter 10 of the textbook will examine those funding rules.

Fiduciary Duties: While the decision to establish an employee benefit plan is regarded as a settlor function, once the employer has established such a plan, it has fiduciary standards imposed by ERISA as to how it should act with respect to such plans. Other individuals hired by the employer to perform certain duties under the plan (e.g., a plan administrator to operate the plan, a plan trustee to invest the plan assets) are subject to these fiduciary standards. Chapter 13 of the textbook will review the standards and the consequences of failing to abide by them.

Civil Enforcement and ERISA Preemption Clause: As ERISA provided for various federal causes of action on behalf of plan participants and beneficiaries, it also established that ERISA would preempt any state law that "relates to" an employee benefit plan, with some exceptions. This was designed to provide consistency for employers operating over multiple state lines. Due to the generality in which the preemption clause was written, it has been subject to a number of interpretations, even at the level of the Supreme Court. Chapter 14 of the textbook will discuss the current state of ERISA litigation.

Continuation Coverage and Portability of Group Health Insurance Plans: The Consolidated Omnibus Budget and Reconciliation Act of 1985 (COBRA) was passed to allow employees to continue coverage under their employer's group health plan, at their own expense, when certain qualifying events occur that otherwise would cause them to lose coverage under the plan (e.g., termination of employment). In 1996, the Health Information Portability and Accountability Act (HIPAA) was passed to prohibit group health plans from discriminating against participants and beneficiaries based on health factors (e.g., medical history) as well as safeguarding the privacy of personal health information. Chapter 19 of the textbook will discuss the laws that govern group health plans provided through employers.

Termination of Defined Benefit Plans: Along with requiring advance funding of covered defined benefit plans, ERISA created a new federal entity, the Pension Benefit Guaranty Corporation (PBGC) to provide federal insurance, guaranteeing the payment of benefits from underfunded defined benefit plans, through Title IV of ERISA.[3] Un-

---

3. ERISA § 4002 created the Pension Benefit Guaranty Corporation which guarantees certain benefits to be paid even if a terminating defined benefit plan is unfunded (i.e., plan assets are not sufficient to pay all current plan liabilities).

fortunately, Title IV was not originally conceived in terms of purse insurance and risk and reward concepts. For example, the original premium was assessed against a covered plan on a per capita basis, not on the basis of its financial health. Thus, Congress has amended Title IV numerous times to provide more funding for the PBGC in order to make good on its insured promise. Chapter 15 of the textbook reviews how a single-employer defined benefit plan is terminated and the PBGC's role in such termination.

3. Income Tax Provisions

While many of the employee benefits offer preferential tax treatment under the federal income tax code pre-ERISA, Congress wanted to extend the changes being made to the federal labor statute under Title I of ERISA to the tax code. Thus, Title II of ERISA makes changes to the federal tax code corresponding to the Title I changes such that the employer must comply with such changes to continue to enjoy the preferential tax treatment of such employee benefits afforded to employers and employees. By 1998, through the IRS Restructuring and Reform Act of 1998, the IRS itself had a separate operating division—known as the Tax Exempt/Government Entities Division—to regulate employee benefit plans. That division was recently revamped, effective January 1, 2019, and renamed Employee Benefits, Exempt Organizations, and Employment Taxes (EEE).

B. Role of the Federal Agencies

1. Federal Agencies Overseeing ERISA

There are three federal agencies overseeing ERISA:

- Because Title I amends 29 U.S.C. (labor statute), those provisions are regulated by the Department of Labor, Employee Benefits Security Administration (EBSA) (formally the Pension and Welfare Benefits Administration);
- Because Title II amends 26 U.S.C. (federal tax code), those provisions are regulated by the Department of the Treasury, through the IRS;
- Because Title IV creates new federal insurance protection, Congress created a new federal entity, the PBGC, to regulate those provisions. The Board of Directors of the PBGC consists of the Secretaries of Labor, Commerce, and the Treasury, and its executive director is appointed by the president.

As will be discussed in Chapter 11, the IRS, through the Employee Benefits segment of its TE/GE division, is charged with providing top-quality service in understanding the tax laws and in protecting the public interest for its three customer bases: retirement plans, IRAs, and related trusts; plan participants and beneficiaries; and employer sponsors of retirement plans. In discharging this mission, it issues rulings and agreements to assure up-front compliance with the law; conducts examinations of plans through audits to identify and address non-compliance; offers education and communication to assist customers in understanding their tax responsibilities; offers customer account services to provide taxpayers with efficient tax filings and accurate and timely responses to questions; and provides coordination with other IRS divisions and oversight entities, including the Department of the Treasury, DOL, PBGC, congressional committees, and state governments.[4] At the DOL, the EBSA's mission is to educate and assist plan participants, retirees, and their families covered under private retirement plans, health plans, and other welfare benefits plans, as well as plan sponsors, by balancing proactive enforcement with compliance assistance. Employees, retirees, and beneficiaries of employee benefit plans can file consumer complaints with EBSA as well as request plan documents. EBSA also renders rulings and opinions, through regulation; interpretative guidance; and advisory opinions or information letters. Unlike the Department of the Treasury or the DOL, the PBGC is a federally chartered corporation created by ERISA and designed to promote the continuation and maintenance of voluntary private defined benefit pension plans, to provide timely and uninterrupted payment of pension benefits, and to keep pension insurance premiums at the lowest level necessary to fulfill its mission. The PBGC is not funded by general tax revenues; instead, its funds derive from four sources: insurance premiums paid by sponsors of defined benefit plans, assets held by the pension plans it takes over, recoveries of unfunded pension liabilities from the plan sponsors' bankruptcy estates, and investment income.

With the advent of the ACA, other government agencies have also become relevant, such as the Department of Health and Human Services (HHS), and in the collective bargaining/union context, the National Labor Relations Board (NLRB). Lastly, employee benefits professionals may need to be knowledgeable in various state laws and agencies that tangentially regulate employee benefit plans, such as state agencies that oversee insurance companies, banks and financial institutions, and labor and employment issues over and above those mandated by federal law.

2. Overview of the Federal Agencies

For the Department of the Treasury (and through the IRS), the primary source of the law comes from the Internal Revenue Code, which is at Title 26 of the United States Code. The "section" is the basic unit used in the Code. Sections are divided into subsections; subsections into paragraphs; paragraphs into subparagraphs; subparagraphs into clauses and even subclauses. But when we're referring to a given section we cite it as I.R.C. § 401(a)(9)(A)(i), instead of saying "clause i of subparagraph A of paragraph 9 of subsection a of section 401." Congress grants either general authority or specific rule-making authority to the Department of the Treasury to promulgate regulations which interpret the Code.[5] In either event, Treasury regulations

4. A list of the current leadership team for the IRS' TEGE Division is available at https://www.irs.gov/government-entities/tax-exempt-government-entities-division-at-a-glance.

5. *See* I.R.C. §7805(a), for Congress' grants of general authority to the Department of the Treasury, or I.R.C. §25A, for grants of specific rulemaking authority. When Congress grants specific rulemaking

have the effect of law. In the recent case of *Mayo Foundation v. United States*, the Supreme Court applied the *Chevron* standard to a Treasury Department regulation.[6] Under the *Chevron* standard, there is a two-step analysis: step one asks whether the statute was ambiguous in defining the question at issue, and if so, step two asks whether the agency's interpretation was "arbitrary or capricious in substance, or manifestly contrary to the statute."[7] If the agency's interpretation is not arbitrary or capricious nor manifestly contrary to the statute, deference will be given to the agency's interpretation of the ambiguous statute.[8] The *Chevron* standard applies regardless of whether Congress' delegation of authority was general or specific.[9]

Regulations are generally issued as proposed regulations and published in the Federal Register for public comment. After reviewing the comments, Treasury can then issue the regulations in final form. Occasionally, Treasury issues the proposed regulations as temporary regulations, which are then authoritative when issued. While proposed regulations are normally not authoritative when issued, they may be relevant, as Treasury has the ability to apply final regulations retroactively to the date they first appeared as proposed regulations. Regulations are numbered in a similar fashion to the Code section to which they relate but generally are preceded by a numerical prefix. For example, the numerical prefix for income tax provisions is "1", and thus the regulations under I.R.C. § 401(a)(9)(A)(i) would be labeled Treas. Reg. § 1.401(a)(9)(A)(i). Likewise, the DOL issues regulations under Title I of ERISA which are also extended *Chevron* deference by the courts.[10]

Both agencies also issue rulings, procedures, notices, and announcements. To the extent a plan or individual taxpayer is audited and assessed penalties for noncompliance, ERISA requires all causes of action that relate to an employee benefit plan be litigated in federal district court.[11] In tax litigation, three trial courts have original jurisdiction: the U.S. District Court, the U.S. Claims Court, and the U.S. Tax Court. To litigate in the first two tax forums, the taxpayer must pay the tax deficiency and then file an administrative claim for refund. When the refund is then denied, the taxpayer can petition either the federal district court or the claims court for a refund. The taxpayer need not refuse to pay the IRS' deficiency in order to proceed with a cause of action in tax court. For all Title I ERISA causes of action, the litigation proceeds through federal district court. If the taxpayer is not granted relief at the trial level, he or she can appeal to the federal circuit courts of appeal. If the taxpayer is

---

authority, it will use such language as "The Secretary may prescribe such regulations as may be necessary or appropriate to carry out this section …"

6. 562 U.S. 44 (2011).

7. *Id.* at 60.

8. *Id.* at 55.

9. *Id.* at 56.

10. *See* Long Island Care at Home, Ltd. v. Coke, 551 U.S. 158, 162 (2007).

11. ERISA § 502(e)–(f) vests exclusive jurisdiction for ERISA causes of action with the federal courts, regardless of the amount in controversy or the citizenship of the parties. There are two exceptions whereby the state courts have concurrent jurisdiction: causes of action for benefit denial cases under ERISA § 502(a)(1)(B) and for QMCSO compliance under ERISA § 502(a)(7).

not successful at the appellate level, he or she can petition the U.S. Supreme Court to grant certiorari. While the U.S. Supreme Court has been developing federal "common law" for some ERISA cases, it relies on principles from contract, labor, and trust common law principles.[12]

3. Overlapping Jurisdiction between Treasury Department and Labor Department

Prior to ERISA, the IRS had exclusive jurisdiction in determining the qualification of plans, whereas the Department of Labor (DOL) played no role. ERISA made sweeping changes to the law governing the delivery of employee benefit plans and reorganized the jurisdiction of such plans. ERISA envisions the division of administration and enforcement of its requirements among three regulatory agencies: the IRS, the DOL, and the newly created corporation, PBGC.[13]

ERISA is divided into four titles. Title I contains the substantive provisions applicable to retirement and profit sharing plans, imposes reporting and disclosure requirements on all covered employee benefit plans, requires fiduciaries for plan administration and holding of plan assets and sets forth fiduciary standards for judging conduct, and provides causes of action for participants and beneficiaries under covered employee benefit plans. Initially, the primary responsibility for implementing Title I was through the DOL. Title II of ERISA made substantive amendments to the Code's qualification standards, many of which duplicated Title I requirements, while others provided additional requirements for Code purposes only. Responsibility for implementing Title II provisions is through the IRS.

Sections under Title I and Title II of ERISA that are identical and reflect dual jurisdiction include:

---

12. *See* Firestone Tire and Rubber Co. v. Bruch, 489 U.S. 101, 110 (1989) (using trust law to fashion the appropriate standard of judicial review in adjudicating ERISA benefit claim cases).

13. ERISA, Title III and § 4002.

	Title I of ERISA	Code Provisions
Minimum participation standards	202	410(a)
Minimum vesting requirements	203	411
Joint & survivor annuity requirements	205	401(a)(11) & 417
Commencement of benefit rules	206(a)	401(a)(14)
Reduction in benefits due to increase in Social Security Benefits	206(b)	401(a)(15)
Spendthrift clause requirements	206(d)	401(a)(13)
Early retirement	206(a)	401(a)(14)
No forfeiture on withdrawal of employee contributions	206(c)	401(a)(19)
Merger and consolidation rules	208	401(a)(12) & 414(l)
Benefit restrictions	206(g)	436
Diversification rights	204(j)	401(a)(35)
Limitations on certain distributions while plan has liquidity shortfall	206(e)	401(a)(32)
Prohibition on benefit increases in bankruptcy	204(i)	401(a)(33)

Code sections that have no Title I counterparts include:

Permanency	401(a)(1)
Incidental death benefit rules	401(a)(9)
Minimum coverage tests	401(a)(3) & 410(b)
Nondiscrimination tests	401(a)(4), (5)
Full vesting upon plan termination	411
Maximum benefits/contribution limitations	401(a)(16) & 415
Top-heavy rules	416

Title III of ERISA speaks to the division of jurisdiction, administration, and enforcement of Titles I and II between the IRS and the DOL. Due to the overlap of jurisdiction, President Carter submitted to Congress for passage the Reorganization Plan for 1978, dividing up responsibility between the IRS and the DOL for topics that overlapped ERISA and the Code. Read that message in the Materials section of this chapter. Now the IRS has authority for minimum funding standards, coverage, and vesting standards, whereas the DOL has authority for minimum participation and fiduciary standards. Both agencies retain enforcement authority created under ERISA.

4. Amendments to ERISA and the Code

As noted earlier, ERISA and the Code have been amended over 50 times since ERISA's enactment. Due to the enormous tax expenditures afforded to employee benefit plans, they are a rich source of tax revenue for Congress if it wishes to balance the influx of tax revenue with a totally unrelated tax drain on revenue.

The following is a brief history lesson as to how bills originate in Congress. We'll use the recent SECURE act as an example. A bill can originate in the House of Representatives or the Senate, but appropriation bills (e.g., those that raise tax revenue) must originate in the House. SECURE was part of a year-end appropriation bill and thus originated in the House. Normally, two legislators introduce the bill, hopefully one Democrat and one Republican, to show bipartisan support for the legislation. In the House, Rep. Richard Neal, a Democrat from Massachusetts, introduced H.R. 1994 to the 116th Congress in March of 2019. As the bill had both labor and tax components, it was reviewed by the House Ways and Means Committee (with tax jurisdiction) and the Education and Labor Committee (with labor jurisdiction). After passage by the House as a whole, the bill moves to the Senate and is reviewed by its respective committees—the Senate Finance Committee (with tax jurisdiction) and the Health, Education, Labor, and Pension (HELP) Committee. There is a staff of non-partisan experts at the Joint Committee on Taxation which assists the House Ways and Means Committee and the Senate Finance Committee in analyzing the proposed legislation and its economic impact. Once the bill is passed by the Senate, it moves to a conference committee to analyze and reconcile the differences between the House's version and the Senate's version. A "Chairman's Markup" is then voted upon by both houses, and if both approve, the legislation is sent to the president for approval or veto. Once approved by the president, it becomes law and is assigned an official and unique Public Law number. SECURE was assigned Pub. L. No. 116-94, which means it is the 94th public law enacted by the 116th Session of Congress.

C. Various Roles of the Employer and Other Benefits Professionals

1. Some of the Roles the Employer Must Take On or Contract Out

An employer who establishes and maintains an employee benefit plan is responsible for satisfying all ERISA requirements. This entails: assuring that the plan document is correct and timely amended with legislative changes and operated in accordance with the terms of the plan, ensuring that a trust document is established so as to hold plan assets, complying with the reporting and disclosure requirements, and timely processing benefits claims with accurate employee records. Failure to satisfy the Code's requirements may lead to the employer's loss of a corporate tax deduction and inclusion of income for covered plan participants as well as any applicable excise or penalty taxes. As fiduciary to the plan, the employer may be personally liable for any losses to the plan or disgorgement of profits from the plan. Many small- to medium-size employers do not have the expertise to fulfill all these roles. Thus, they turn to employee benefit professionals to accomplish them.

Plan Administrator: The plan sponsor is by default the plan administrator, which is responsible for the day-to-day administration of the plan in accordance with its terms.[14] Should the plan sponsor feel it cannot undertake such duties, it has a fiduciary duty to appoint a plan administrator and to monitor such appointment going forward to assure it is prudent.[15] Financial institutions (e.g., Fidelity, Dreyfuss) may sell a retirement plan to a small employer and agree to act as the plan administrator and recordkeeper. It is important for the small employer to understand what responsibilities the plan administrator is undertaking and to document that agreement. If a medium or large employer decides to delegate some but not all responsibilities to an outside plan administrator, it should have a written set of administrative procedures as to who has what responsibilities. For example, the outside plan administrator may make the initial determination as to whether a claim for benefits should be granted, leaving the ultimate review of such determination in the hands of the plan sponsor.

Fiduciary Over Plan Assets: ERISA requires every employee benefit plan to be established and maintained pursuant to a written instrument, which names one or more fiduciaries who jointly or severally have authority to control and manage the operation and administration of the plan.[16] The named fiduciary is either the person/entity named in the plan instrument, or who, pursuant to plan procedures, is identified as a fiduciary by the employer or employee organization with respect to the plan or by the employer and employee organization acting jointly.[17] ERISA imposes very high standards for fiduciaries—duties of prudence and due diligence, duties of expertise, diversification of plan assets if the fiduciary is responsible for investing plan assets, and duties to act in accordance with the plan and other instruments consistent with the requirements of ERISA. Should a fiduciary breach his or her duty, he or she can be subject to personal liability. Therefore, plan sponsors of an employee benefit plan should be clear as to who is plan fiduciary and for what purpose, and if the sponsor has delegated such responsibility, it must continue to monitor such delegation for its continued prudence. Generally, outside professionals who assist a plan

---

14. ERISA § 3(16)(A).

15. As will be discussed in a later chapter, ERISA imposes a prudence standard of care whereby the plan sponsor is to act "with the care, skill, prudence, and diligence under the circumstances then prevailing that a prudent man acting in a like capacity and familiar with such matters would use in the conduct of an enterprise of a like character and with like aims" in fulfilling its responsibilities in establishing and maintaining an employee benefit plan. *See* ERISA § 404(a)(1)(B).

16. ERISA § 402(a)(1).

17. ERISA § 402(a)(2).

sponsor with the establishment or maintenance of a plan (e.g., attorneys, accountants, and actuaries) are not plan fiduciaries. But officers of the employers who select and delegate such powers to outside professionals may be fiduciaries.

2. Other Professionals the Employer May Rely Upon

When establishing and maintaining an employee benefit plan, the employer should know that there are a variety of different costs associated with the plan. Many of these costs are associated with hiring professionals to assist the employer. Start-up costs include drafting the plan document (or selecting the choices on a preapproved plan document), IRS filings, employee communications, and internal and external administrative costs. The ongoing costs may include the services of a plan actuary to compute the funding costs of a defined benefit plan, reporting and disclosure costs associated with filings with governmental agencies and employee communications, and recordkeeping and administrative costs associated with running the plan. The following are the types of professionals an employer may hire in connection with the start-up or ongoing maintenance of an employee benefit plan:

- An attorney may assist in drafting the plan document and representing the employer in a filing with the IRS for a determination letter (i.e., review of the initial terms of the document to see if it meets the Code's qualification rules). As the Code's qualification rules are amended, the attorney can assist with drafting necessary plan amendments to comply with the new law. Due to the complexities of ERISA, the employer should hire an attorney who has the expertise necessary to practice in this area of law.

- An accountant is necessary for large plans as their plan assets are required to be audited on an annual basis. The accountant also must compute the costs associated with the employee benefit plan as they may be included in the corporate financial statements. Each state administers its own set of exams to certify public accountants (referred to as Certified Public Accountants).

- An enrolled actuary's services will be necessary in computing the annual costs of a defined benefit plan. He or she is also necessary in computing the variable portion of the PBGC annual premium as it is dependent on the amount of the plan's unfunded vested benefits. An enrolled actuary is someone who has completed the set of exams administered by the federal Joint Board for the Enrollment of Actuaries, and thus competent to make the necessary actuarial computations required for a defined benefit plan.

- An insurance advisor will be necessary if the retirement plan is to be invested in insurance products, provided the plan primarily offers retirement benefits. On the health and welfare side, if the benefits are to be insured, an insurance advisor can assist in choosing the type of insurance product. Even if the benefits are self-insured (i.e., the employer will take on the insurance risk), a portion of the benefits may have stop-loss insurance to limit the employer's total exposure.

- An investment advisor should be hired to assist in the management and investment of the trust funds. Such an advisor generally makes investment recommendations for the plan assets or does securities analysis, for a fee.

- Recordkeepers do the general bookkeeping for a plan, especially defined contribution plans where individual account balances are maintained for plan participants and beneficiaries.

- Third-party administrators and ERPAs are professionals who have expertise in employee benefit matters but do not necessarily have professional licenses. If the employer does not wish to assume the role of plan administrator, it will have to hire an outside third-party plan administrator who will assume that role. Under the rules of the IRS (i.e., Circular 230), initially only attorneys, enrolled actuaries, enrolled agents (federally licensed tax practitioners authorized to represent taxpayers before the IRS on collections, audits, and appeals), and certified public accountants were allowed to represent clients before the IRS. In 2007, Circular 230 was amended to expand this universe with a new professional designation: enrolled retirement plan agents (ERPAs). After demonstrating their expertise through passing certain exams, an ERPA is allowed to represent the employee benefit plan sponsor before the IRS for the following matters: the Employee Plans Determination Letter program, the Employee Plans Compliance Resolution System, the Employee Plans Preapproved Program, and the representation of taxpayers with respect to IRS forms under the 5300 and 5500 series which are filed by retirement plans and their sponsors (excluding actuarial forms and schedules).

D. Materials

Message of the President

5 U.S.C.A. App. 1, Reorg. Plan No. 4 of 1978

To the Congress of the United States:

Today I am submitting to the Congress my fourth Reorganization Plan for 1978. This proposal is designed to simplify and improve the unnecessarily complex administrative requirements of the Employee Retirement Income Security Act of 1974 (ERISA) [see Short Title note set out under section 1001 of Title 29, Labor]. The new plan will eliminate overlap and duplication in the administration of ERISA and help us achieve our goal of well regulated private pension plans.

ERISA was an essential step in the protection of worker pension rights. Its administrative provisions, however, have resulted in bureaucratic confusion and have been justifiably criticized by employers and unions alike. The biggest problem has been overlapping jurisdictional authority. Under current ERISA provisions, the Departments of Treasury and Labor both have authority to issue regulations and decisions.

This dual jurisdiction has delayed a good many important rulings and, more importantly, produced bureaucratic runarounds and burdensome reporting requirements.

The new plan will significantly reduce these problems. In addition, both Departments are trying to cut red tape and paperwork, to eliminate unnecessary reporting requirements, and to streamline forms wherever possible.

Both Departments have already made considerable progress, and both will continue the effort to simplify their rules and their forms.

The Reorganization Plan is the most significant result of their joint effort to modify and simplify ERISA. It will eliminate most of the jurisdictional overlap between Treasury and Labor by making the following changes:

1) Treasury will have statutory authority for minimum standards. The new plan puts all responsibility for funding, participation, and vesting of benefit rights in the Department of Treasury. These standards are necessary to ensure that employee benefit plans are adequately funded and that all beneficiary rights are protected. Treasury is the most appropriate Department to administer these provisions; however, Labor will continue to have veto power over Treasury decisions that significantly affect collectively bargained plans.

2) Labor will have statutory authority for fiduciary obligations. ERISA prohibits transactions in which self-interest or conflict of interest could occur, but allows certain exemptions from these prohibitions. Labor will be responsible for overseeing fiduciary conduct under these provisions.

3) Both Departments will retain enforcement powers. The Reorganization Plan will continue Treasury's authority to audit plans and levy tax penalties for any deviation from standards. The plan will also continue Labor's authority to bring civil action against plans and fiduciaries. These provisions are retained in order to keep the special expertise of each Department available. New coordination between the Departments will eliminate duplicative investigations of alleged violations.

This reorganization will make an immediate improvement in ERISA's administration. It will eliminate almost all of the dual and overlapping authority in the two departments and dramatically cut the time required to process applications for exemptions from prohibited transactions.

This plan is an interim arrangement. After the Departments have had a chance to administer ERISA under this new plan, the Office of Management and Budget and the Departments will jointly evaluate that experience. Based on that evaluation, early in 1980, the Administration will make appropriate legislative proposals to establish a long-term administrative structure for ERISA.

Each provision in this reorganization will accomplish one or more of the purposes in Title 5 of U.S.C. 901(a). There will be no change in expenditure or personnel levels, although a small number of people will be transferred from the Department of Treasury to the Department of Labor.

We all recognize that the administration of ERISA has been unduly burdensome. I am confident that this reorganization will significantly relieve much of that burden.

This plan is the culmination of our effort to streamline ERISA. It provides an administrative arrangement that will work.

ERISA has been a symbol of unnecessarily complex government regulation. I hope this new step will become equally symbolic of my Administration's commitment to making government more effective and less intrusive in the lives of our people.

JIMMY CARTER.

THE WHITE HOUSE, August 10, 1978.

Section II

Qualified Retirement Plans

The focus of this textbook is retirement plans, as opposed to health and welfare plans and executive compensation plans. For-profit employers sponsor retirement plans qualified under IRC § 401(a) in order to generate deductions for the employers and deferral of income for the employees; other employers, such as governmental employers, church employers, public school employers, and not-for-profit employers sponsor other types of plans. The rules for qualified plans are the most complicated, and thus, by learning those rules, a practitioner can become familiar with the rules for other types of retirement plans if their clients are governmental employers, etc.

Chapter 4 discusses the nomenclature used in Titles I and II to classify retirement plans, such as defined contribution plans versus defined benefit plans, profit sharing plans versus pension plans, and individual account plans versus plans that are not individual account plans. The text then discusses the difference between defined contribution plans and defined benefit plans, and the variety of different kinds of these plans.

Chapter 5 outlines the Code's qualification rules applicable to retirement plans and related ERISA rules. These rules are extremely complex and at times difficult to understand, but they are designed to ensure that the rank-and-file employees enjoy these benefits, not just the highly paid employees. Each of the subsequent chapters in Section II explain each of the different qualification rules. As many of the rules in Titles I and II at times overlap, Congress had to assign jurisdiction between the agencies by topic; for example, the prohibited transaction rules appear in both Title I and Title II, but the Department of Labor has jurisdiction in interpreting both sets of rules.

Chapter 6 discusses the minimum participation rules and the minimum coverage tests. The minimum participation rules focus on the plan's eligibility standards (i.e., who can and cannot participate in the plan). The minimum coverage tests demonstrate that the plan's eligibility standards do not discriminate in favor of the highly paid employees.

Chapter 7 reviews the applicable vesting schedules that may be used under a qualified retirement plan, the accrual rules applicable to defined benefit plans, the top heavy rules applicable to all qualified plans, and the maximum limitations as to benefits or contributions. The numerous changes made over the past decades to the maximum limitations demonstrate the large tax expenditures afforded to qualified retirement plans.

Chapter 8 provides an overview of the nondiscrimination rules applicable to qualified retirement plans and the special nondiscrimination rules for IRC § 401(k) plans. Unless the plan's formula is designed to meet one of the safe harbors, there are numeric tests that must be performed annually to assure that the plan is not discriminatory.

Chapter 9 discusses the forms of payment that amounts are distributed from retirement plans and how those payments are taxed. To assure that benefits are taxed during the participant's lifetime, there are minimum distribution rules applicable to qualified retirement plans and IRAs. The recent SECURE Act made several significant changes to the minimum distribution rules.

Chapter 10 sets forth the minimum funding rules applicable to pension plans and the deductibility rules that limit the amount an employer can contribute and deduct to a qualified retirement plan. While large employers offer employee benefit plans to be competitive and to attract relevant talent, small employers seeking to maximize their deductions are limited by the Code's deductible ceilings.

Chapter 11 reviews the role of the Internal Revenue Service (IRS) in regulating qualified plans. This will then complete Section II of this book.

Chapter 4

Differences between Defined Benefit Plans and Defined Contribution Plans

Reading Assignment: ERISA §§ 2(a), 3(1), 3(3)

I.R.C. §§ 408(p), 414(i), 414(j)

Class Discussion Questions: Why have most employers shifted away from defined benefit plans and toward I.R.C. § 401(k) plans?

What are the types of defined contribution plans to choose from?

Who has the investment risk and the longevity risk in a defined benefit plan—the employer or the employee?

What considerations would a small business take into account in choosing between a defined benefit or a defined contribution plan?

Overview

What are the legal definitions of defined contribution plans and defined benefit plans?

- a defined contribution plan has

  ○ individual accounts; and

  ○ the benefits at retirement are based solely on the accumulation of contributions and fund earnings

- a defined benefit plan is any qualified retirement plan that is not a defined contribution plan

- over the years, hybrid designs have been developed, such as target benefit plans (which are defined contribution plans with some of the attributes of a defined benefit plan) and statutory hybrid plans with a cash balance design (which are defined benefit plans with some of the attributes of a defined contribution plan)

What are the main differences between defined contribution and defined benefit plans?

- a defined contribution plan is one in which the annual contribution may be defined in the plan document, but where the contribution is subject to certain minimum and maximum allocations
    - the benefit that an individual will receive upon retirement consists entirely of the accumulation of contributions and fund earnings
    - the benefit is usually paid out in a single lump sum
    - each year, the participant receives a statement reconciling the preceding year's account balance with the current year's balance
- A defined benefit plan is entirely different because it is the promised benefit at retirement that is defined in the plan document, and the benefit is subject to certain minimum and maximum accrual rules
    - the plan document defines the benefit the employee will receive at retirement, usually as an annuity starting at retirement and continuing for the life of the employee, the joint lives of an employee and his or her chosen beneficiary, a term certain, or any combination thereof
    - the employer accumulates assets in a common pool and simply pays liabilities as they come due to retired or terminated employees
    - by statutory mandate, every qualified defined benefit plan must annually use an enrolled actuary (defined in Chapter 3) to value the future expected liabilities, compare them to accumulated assets, make certain actuarial assumptions, and then ultimately determine the contribution needed for that year which will properly fund the plan if all assumptions and expected future contributions are met
    - almost all defined benefit plans (except those that only cover owner-employees or those sponsored by a professional corporation (P.C.) with fewer than 25 employees) must pay annual premiums into the Pension Benefit Guaranty Corporation as insurance for government protection of certain benefits guaranteed to participants pursuant to ERISA
    - each year, the participant receives a statement showing the deferred retirement annuity accrued to date and the deferred annuity promised by the plan if the employee were to continue working until reaching his or her normal retirement age

Who bears the investment risk in defined contribution and defined benefit plans?

- In a defined contribution plan,
    - the employer is either responsible for making a certain mandatory contribution for each employee who participates in the plan (i.e., a money purchase plan), or the employer is responsible for allocating a discretionary contribution among all accounts in any year in which a contribution is actually made (i.e., a profit sharing plan)

- as long as the employer sponsoring the plan invests the plan assets prudently and in the best interest of plan participants and beneficiaries (as those terms are defined in ERISA's fiduciary rules), then the employer is not liable for losses to the accounts and the investment risk is thus shifted to the employee
- in a 401(k) plan, with some additional steps, the plan can allow the individuals to make their own investment decisions (referred to as a self-directed plan)
- In a defined benefit plan,
  - the enrolled actuary determines the optimal funding pattern, so there should always be adequate assets in the common pool to pay the promised benefits for each individual as they come due
  - if assets earn a lower-than-expected rate of return, the enrolled actuary will calculate a higher-than-expected contribution which, under current law, must be contributed by the employer (this means that the employer bears the investment risk, not the individual employee)

Which plans are better for younger (or older) participants?

- because of the special plan qualification rules (including limits on contributions into defined contribution plans and limits on benefits paid from defined benefit plans):
  - younger employees will generally have larger accounts at age 65 (or any other reasonable retirement age) from a defined contribution plan than the equivalent lump sum of any benefit that can be provided under a defined benefit plan—primarily due to the impact of compound interest over long periods of time
  - older employees will generally accrue larger benefits at age 65 (or any other reasonable retirement age) from a defined benefit plan than any account that can be accumulated under a defined contribution plan—due to the large funding that is allowed over short periods of time
- these general statements assume that an individual would either get the greatest allocations allowed under a defined contribution plan each and every year, or that the individual would receive the greatest benefit allowed at retirement from a defined benefit plan

What is a money purchase plan?

- the plan document defines exactly what amount will be contributed for each plan participant (such as a certain percentage of salary)
- the employer must contribute the amount promised

What is a profit sharing plan?

- the plan document defines exactly how any contribution will be divided and allocated among the participant's accounts, which can be based on:
  - salary

- ° permitted disparity (those with salaries in excess of the Social Security taxable wage base will be favored)
- ° a combination of age, service, and/or salary (those who are older or have been employed longer are favored)
- ° cross testing to pass the nondiscrimination tests (as will be discussed in Chapter 8) (those who are highly compensated employees are favored)
- the employer determines each year what contribution it would like to make to the plan (the employer does not need to actually show a profit on its corporate returns to make a contribution)
- there are rules that if an employer goes too many years without making a substantial contribution, then the IRS may deem the plan terminated based on facts and circumstances

What is a traditional 401(k) plan?

- each year, the participant determines how much salary is not needed for current living expenses, and elects the amount he or she would like to be deferred into the plan
- the employer must honor the election (as long as it does not exceed statutory limits) and take the elective deferral out of the employee's paycheck and timely deposit it into the plan
- salary deferrals into a traditional 401(k) plan are excluded from the employee's Gross Income until a future year when distributed (but the deferral is subject to payroll taxes in the year earned)
- the employer can voluntarily match all or a portion of salary deferrals (referred to as the employer match)

What is a Roth 401(k) plan?

- most of the basic rules of a traditional 401(k) plan are applicable to Roth 401(k) plans (or Roth-designated accounts within a traditional 401(k) plan)
- each year, the participant determines how much salary is not needed for current living expenses, and elects the amount he or she would like to be contributed into the plan
- the employer must honor the election (as long as it does not exceed statutory limits) and take the designated Roth contribution out of the employee's paycheck and timely deposit it into the plan
- designated Roth contributions into a 401(k) plan are included in the employee's Gross Income in the year earned (and are subject to payroll taxes in the year earned), but will not be included in the individual's Gross Income when distributed in a future year (if the account was established for at least five years and distributions occur after the individual has attained age 59½)
- the employer can voluntarily match all or a portion of designated Roth contributions

What is an automatic enrollment feature in a 401(k) plan?

- Congress has accepted the psychological phenomenon of inertia, and now allows employers sponsoring a 401(k) plan to automatically enroll eligible employees on the day of hire, but permits them to opt out later
- in a plan without an automatic enrollment feature, the new employee receives tons of paperwork and information on the date of hire, including election forms and information about the 401(k) plan, and then must take an affirmative step in deciding how much salary to defer, most likely decide how the deferrals will be invested, and then go to the payroll or human resources department and submit the completed forms
- in a plan with an automatic enrollment feature, the new employee will receive notices and information about being automatically enrolled in the 401(k) plan on the date of hire, and if he or she decides that the salary deferral election should be stopped, decreased, or increased, or if the investment mix should be changed from the default, then he or she must take an affirmative step and go to the payroll or human resources department and submit the completed forms
    - ○ if the employee affirmatively contacts the plan administrator of a 401(k) plan with an automatic enrollment feature within 90 days of automatic enrollment, then he or she can request an immediate distribution of all deferrals, plus interest (after 90 days, all he or she can do is stop future deferrals, but most likely cannot get an in-service distribution while still an employee)
    - ○ there are two levels of automatic enrollment features:
        - in an eligible automatic enrollment contribution arrangement (EACA), the employer simply has assurance that the feature will not violate any state law
        - the default percentage of salary must be uniform for all employees
        - the plan sponsor selects a reasonable and prudent default investment
        - sufficient notice and communications must be provided to employees when hired and each year thereafter
    - ○ in a qualified automatic contribution arrangement (QACA), the plan will automatically pass the nondiscrimination and top heavy tests (as described in Chapter 8)
        - meets all requirements of an EACA
        - escalating deferrals (at least 3% of salary in first year of employment, at least 4% of salary in the second year, at least 5% of salary in third year, and at least 6% of salary in successive years—but never to exceed 15% of salary unless the participant affirmatively elects to defer an amount higher than 15% of salary)
        - the employer agrees to either match 100% of the first 1% of salary deferred and 50% of the next 5% of salary deferred, or agrees to make a money-pur-

chase type contribution of 3% of salary for every eligible employee (even those that elect to make no salary deferrals)

- additional information must be included in the notices
- because of the income tax implications, an automatic enrollment feature does not make sense in a Roth 401(k) plan

What are defined benefit plans?

- any plan that is not a plan with individual accounts (usually a pool of assets) and/or where the benefits are not based solely on the accumulation of contributions and fund earnings (usually some component of the benefit is guaranteed)
- they can be based on:
  - ○ a flat benefit (a flat dollar amount multiplied by the number of years worked with the employer)
  - ○ a fixed benefit (an income replacement percentage multiplied by the participant's average salary)
  - ○ a unit benefit (a unit income replacement percentage multiplied by the participant's average salary and the number of years worked with the employer)

What is a statutory hybrid plan (such as a cash balance plan)?

- although a defined benefit plan, subject to minimum funding under the direction of an enrolled actuary and annual premiums to the PBGC, each participant's retirement benefit is calculated and communicated as a current (hypothetical) account
- unlike a defined contribution plan, which is simply invested and the accounts increase at whatever actual rate of return is realized, interest credits are guaranteed in a hybrid defined benefit plan, and the employer contributions will fluctuate in order to fund those guaranteed promises
- Congress had made cash balance designs going forward absolutely legal and proper, but there was some litigation in the federal courts on purported age discrimination and other issues with conversions to cash balance plans before Congress added the statutory provisions

What is a combined DB/401(k) plan?

- until 2010, pre-tax elective salary deferrals could only be deposited into a 401(k) plan that was part of a defined contribution plan
- starting in 2010, certain small employers can allow pre-tax elective salary deferrals into a 401(k) plan that is part of a defined benefit plan if:
  - ○ in the defined benefit portion of the plan, which will most likely be a cash balance type hybrid design, the pay credit is at least
    - 2% of salary for any participant who has not attained age 30
    - 4% of salary for any participant who is between 31 and 40
    - 6% of salary for any participant who is between 41 and 50

- 8% of salary for any participant who has attained age 51
- in the 401(k) portion of the plan
  - the automatic enrollment rules apply
  - the employer must match at least 50% of deferrals of up to 4% of salary

A. Distinguishing between Defined Benefit Plans and Defined Contribution Plans

1. Nomenclature Used under ERISA versus the Code

Although Title I and II were written at the same time, they do not use the same nomenclature in discussing types of retirement plans, which can be very confusing to an employee benefits novice. Title I of ERISA uses the terms "employee pension benefit plan" or "pension plan" to refer to any plan that provides retirement income to employees or results in the deferral of income by employees until termination of employment.[1] Under that umbrella of "employee pension benefit plan" or "pension plan," there are two types of plans: individual account plans or defined contribution plans versus defined benefit plans. Defined contribution plans are defined by ERISA § 3(34) as pension plans which provide for an individual account for each participant and for benefits based solely upon the amount contributed to the participant's account, and any income, expenses, gains or losses, and forfeitures of accounts from other participants.[2] In contrast, defined benefit plans are defined by ERISA § 3(35) as pension plans other than individual account plans.[3] For example, a defined contribution plan can provide for employer and employee contributions, which are allocated to a participant's account; the account grows with either interest or gains/losses and may be assessed an investment expense or administrative expense. Whatever is the total amount in the account balance at the participant's retirement or termination is what he or she is entitled to under the plan. Forfeitures refer to amounts forfeited by participants who terminate employment before becoming fully vested under the plan. Such forfeitures can be allocated to other participants' accounts or be used to reduce employer contributions.

Remember: when reading Title I, pension plan means either a defined contribution plan or defined benefit plan.

Title II of ERISA (i.e., the Code's provisions) uses the terms "stock bonus, pension, or profit-sharing plan" to refer to all retirement savings, making the distinction between pension or profit sharing plans, as there are more substantive rules applicable to pension plans than for profit sharing plans. Prior to ERISA's passage, the Code

---

1. ERISA § 3(2)(A).
2. ERISA § 3(34).
3. ERISA § 3(35).

extended favorable income tax treatment to qualified retirement plans and the prior Treasury regulations separated retirement plans into pension plans, profit-sharing plans, and stock bonus plans, which accounts for the continued use of that phrase under I.R.C. § 401(a) when ERISA was passed. Pension plans consist of defined benefit plans, money purchase defined contribution plans, and target benefit defined contribution plans. All defined contribution plans focus on input (i.e., contributions to the plan, whether made through employer and/or employee contributions). In contrast, defined benefit plans focus on output. For example, a defined benefit plan may pay $1,000/month beginning at age 65 for the participant's life. There are three components to a benefit under a defined benefit plan: the formula determining the amount of the benefit, the normal retirement age, and the form of payment (e.g., annuity).

I.R.C. § 414(i) defines a defined contribution plan as follows: "[f]or purposes of this part, the term 'defined contribution plan' means a plan which provides for an individual account for each participant and for benefits based solely on the amount contributed to the participant's account, and any income, expenses, gains and losses, and any forfeitures of accounts of other participants which may be allocated to such participant's account."[4] What does the phrase "for purposes for this part" mean? Let's go back to our lesson in Chapter 2. Title 26 of the United States Code is divided into nine subtitles—we're interested in Subtitle A, which contains all the income tax provisions and includes I.R.C. §§ 1 through 1563. Each subtitle is divided into chapters, each chapter into subchapters, and each subchapter into parts. Chapter 1 of Subtitle A is Normal Taxes and Surtaxes and includes I.R.C. §§ 1 through 1400U-3. Subchapter D in Chapter 1 is Deferred Compensation and includes I.R.C. §§ 401 through 436. Part 1 of Subchapter D is Pension, Profit-Sharing, and Stock Bonus Plans, etc. and includes I.R.C. §§ 401 through 420. Thus, the definition of a defined contribution plan as contained in I.R.C. § 414(i) applies for purposes of interpreting I.R.C. §§ 401 through 420, which include the qualification rules.

I.R.C. § 414(j) defines a defined benefit plan as follows: "[f]or purposes of this part, the term 'defined benefit plan' means any plan which is not a defined contribution plan."[5] Hence, any retirement plan that does not satisfy the definition of a defined contribution plan is by definition a defined benefit plan for purposes of interpreting I.R.C. §§ 401 through 420, which include the qualification rules.

Remember: when reading Title II (the Code), it distinguishes between profit sharing and pension plan, where pension plan means a subset of defined contribution plans (i.e., money purchase and target benefit plans) and all defined benefit plans. Unlike Title I, pension plan does not mean all defined contribution plans and all defined benefit plans.

Employers have shifted away from defined benefit plans toward defined contribution plans in order to control costs. While annual contributions do not necessarily have to be fixed under a defined contribution plan, the employer's liability is limited solely to

---

4. I.R.C. § 414(i).
5. I.R.C. § 414(j).

its obligation to timely remit any promised employer contributions to the plan. Benefits from a defined contribution plan are based solely upon the participant's account balance at retirement, which may or may not adequately fund a participant's retirement income needs. For example, a $1,000,000 nest egg at age 65 will provide $5,660/month at age 65 for a male's life or $5,440/month at age 65 for a female's life.[6] That monthly amount may be more than sufficient for most people in retirement; the problem is most participants in defined contribution plans do not have anywhere near $1,000,000 in their account balances.[7] Thus, the participant bears the investment and mortality risk with a defined contribution plan — meaning, if the plan does not earn an expected interest rate, the participant will receive a lower benefit, and the participant may outlive the distributions from the account balance. For this reason, policy makers have been focusing on making defined contribution participants more cognizant of these risks. The SECURE Act calls for plan administrators of defined contribution plans to make lifetime-income disclosures on the benefit statements. The benefit statements now have to show the monthly payments that a participant's current account balance could generate in retirement if he or she were to purchase various types of annuities, at prescribed actuarial assumptions.

While all defined benefit plans are pension plans, defined contribution plans can be either pension plans or profit sharing plans. The IRS has identified four different types of defined contribution plans — profit sharing, money purchase, stock bonus, and target benefit — profit sharing being the most popular, particularly the I.R.C. § 401(k) profit sharing plan, because it allows employees to make pre-tax contributions to the plan. While each of the four types vary in how the plan sponsor defines the level of annual contributions it makes to the plan (i.e., employer contribution formula), all defined contribution plans must specify how such contributions are allocated among eligible participants (i.e., employee allocation formula).

A defined benefit plan shifts the investment risk and the longevity risk (also, referred to as mortality risk) to the employer as the promised benefit is described as a formula for the benefits, payable at the plan's normal retirement age, as a life only or joint and survivor annuity. Thus, the employer's contributions made during the employee's working lifetime are expected to grow with interest or gains and be sufficient to pay benefits over the employee's lifetime (after retirement) or joint lifetime of the employee and his or her spouse (after retirement). If the interest or gains are not sufficient to fund the full benefit, the employer must contribute more; likewise, if the employee lives into his or her 90s, the employer must still pay the benefit. In

---

6. *See* Walter Updegrave, *How much retirement income will $1,000,000 generate?*, CNN Money, https://money.cnn.com/2015/07/22/retirement/retirement-income/index.html. Women have a longer life expectancy than men and thus $1,000,000 doesn't buy as much in retirement income for a female as compared to a male.

7. See Arielle O'Shea, *The Average 401(k) Balance by Age*, NerdWallet (May 9, 2019), https://money.cnn.com/2015/07/22/retirement/retirement-income/index.html, indicating that a seven-figure 401(k) balance is the exception and not the rule. According to Fidelity which holds 16.2 million 401(k) accounts, the average 401(k) balance was $103,700 as of March 2019.

contrast, a defined contribution plan shifts the investment risk and mortality risk to the employee. If the growth of the plan assets in the employee's account is less than he or she hoped for, the account will not be sufficient for retirement; likewise, the employee may outlive the account balance if he or she takes out too much.

The accepted wisdom is that defined contribution plans favor younger employees as they have a longer working lifetime for the allocations to accumulate. Conversely, defined benefit plans favor older employees as they received the promised benefit sooner than a younger employee.

> **Example:** If a defined contribution plan allocates 5% of two employees' compensation, each with compensation of $50,000 (e.g., 5% × $40,000 = $2,000), the employee who is age 35 will have that $2,000 grow until age 65 to $8,643 (due to the compounding of interest at a rate of 5%), whereas the employee who is age 55 will have that $2,000 grow until age 65 to only $3,257. Thus, the younger employee is better off than the older employee.

> Conversely, if we promised both the 35-year-old and the 55-year-old the same annual benefit of $2,000 beginning at age 65 for life, the cost of that benefit would be $61,406 for the 55-year-old employee but only $23,140 for the 35-year-old employee — showing that the benefit is more valuable for the older employee than the younger employee.

B. Types of Defined Contribution Plans

1. Money Purchase Plan

Money pension plans are defined contribution plans that were intended to be retirement-type vehicles, and thus the employer contribution formula was fixed under the plan and pre-determinable.[8] As a result, the employer allocation formula and the employee allocation formula are both fixed and set forth under the terms of the plan. Initially, the employer's deductibility limits were larger for money purchase plans than for profit sharing plans in order to encourage their growth, but EGTRRA '01 eliminated this difference and so the deductibility limits are now the same.[9]

Due to the requirement that the employer must contribute the annual contribution fixed under the plan, it may couple the money purchase plan (e.g., contribution and allocation of 10% of salary) with a profit sharing plan with discretionary employer contributions (i.e., optional contributions that the employer may determine to make on a year to year basis).

> **Example:** A 10% money purchase plan may state that the employer will make a contribution of 10% of covered payroll every year, and each eligible participant with a year of service as of the end of the plan year will receive an

---

8. Rev. Rul. 73-379.
9. EGTRRA '01 §616(a)(1)(A), replacing the 15% ceiling with a 25% ceiling.

allocation of 10% of his or her annual salary. Thus, Employee A making $50,000 will receive an allocation of $5,000 for the year, whereas Employee B making $100,000 will receive an allocation of $10,000. Such an allocation formula reflects the fact that Employee B needs a larger allocation than A as his or her salary is twice as large. If Employee B is a more valuable employee, and hence compensated accordingly, his or her allocation formula should also reflect that fact.

Since the primary purpose of this kind of plan was to defer compensation until retirement or termination of employment, in-service distributions of employer contributions are prohibited.[10] If the money purchase plan is to be qualified, the plan must provide for a "systematic payment of benefits" to the participant after retirement.[11] This means that the plan must describe when and how benefits are to be paid. Usually benefits are paid for a period of years (e.g., the life of the participant or the joint lives of the participant and his or her spouse). But a pension plan may not provide that a lump sum distribution is the sole form of distribution.[12] If benefits are distributable in any form of a life annuity, then qualified joint and survivor annuity must be provided. Due to changes made by TRA '86, forfeitures from the plan may now be used either to increase participants' benefits or to reduce employer contributions.[13]

2. Profit Sharing Plans

Profit sharing plans originally limited employer contributions to current or accumulated profits, but now they may be unrelated to the employer's profits on the corporate return due to I.R.C. §401(a)(27).[14] The employer contribution formula may be stated in the plan (e.g., 5% of the participants' salaries) or determined annually by the employer (i.e., referred to as a discretionary formula). But regardless of the type of contribution formula used, the allocation formula (how the contribution is to be allocated to each eligible participant) must be set forth and fixed in the plan document. If the contributions are discretionary, they must be substantial and recurring in order for the plan to remain qualified.[15] The primary purpose of these types of plans is to simply defer compensation (not to necessarily provide retirement benefits) for a minimum period of time. Thus, distributions of a participant's account balance are not restricted solely to retirement, death, or termination of employment. In fact, in-service distributions may be made according to the following parameters:

- a "fixed period of years" (e.g., two years, unless the employee has been a participant for five years, then anytime),
- attainment of a stated age (e.g., retirement age, or age 55), or

---

10. Treas. Reg. §1.401-1(b)(1).
11. *Id.*
12. Rev. Rul. 62-195.
13. TRA '86 §1119(a), amending I.R.C. §401(a)(8).
14. I.R.C. §401(a)(27).
15. Treas. Reg. §1.401-1(b)(1)(i) and (ii).

• prior occurrence of a specified event (e.g., death, disability, layoff, or other termination of employment).[16]

When ERISA was passed, there were no I.R.C. §401(k) participant-direct profit sharing plans, although they are now the most popular form of retirement savings today offered by employers. Section 401(k) is probably the only Code section the average participant knows about! These types of plans permit employees to make pre-tax employee contributions, that may or may not be matched by employer contributions, and to select the types of investments for their accounts. For example, the plan may permit eligible employees to contribute up to 10% of their annual salary, with the employer matching those contributions at a 50%, 75%, or 100% rate. To the extent the lower paid employees do not make employee contributions, the employer may nevertheless contribute a uniform 3% of all employees' pay, referred to as the employer's nonelective contribution (as it is not dependent on what the employee contributed). Thus, there could be three types of contributions under these plans—employee elective contributions, employer matching contributions (which are dependent upon what the employee contributed), and employer nonelective contributions (which are not dependent upon what the employee contributes). Employers favor I.R.C. §401(k) profit sharing plans because the employees participate in funding their own retirement, and, if the requirements of ERISA §404(c) are met, shelter the plan trustees from fiduciary liability for the participants' selection of their investments.

Unlike employer contributions allocated to participants' accounts, employee elective deferrals under an I.R.C. §401(k) plan may not be distributed earlier than:

• participant's separation from service, death, or disability;

• participant's attainment of age 59½; or

• termination of the plan without the establishment or maintenance of a successor plan.[17]

Despite this list, the statute does allow employee elective deferrals to be distributed because of hardship.[18] The needs that may qualify for a hardship distribution include certain medical expenses of the employee, spouse, or dependent; post-secondary education tuition payments for the employee, spouse, children, or dependents of the employee; purchase costs or a principal residence of the employee; expenses for the repair of damage to the employee's principal residence that would qualify for a casualty deduction (not limited to casualties that are declared to be federally declared disasters); payments for burial or funeral expenses for the employee's deceased parent, spouse, children, or dependents; amounts needed to prevent eviction from or foreclosure on the employee's principal residence; and expenses and losses (including loss of income) incurred by an employee on account of a FEMA-designated disaster, if the employee's principal residence or principal place of employment at the time of the disaster is in

---

16. *Id.*
17. I.R.C. §401(k)(2)(B)(i)(I)–(III).
18. I.R.C. §401(k)(2)(B)(i)(IV).

the FEMA-designated disaster zone.[19] A hardship distribution needs to satisfy an "immediate and heavy financial need" of the participant, but the employer may rely on the employee's representation as to such need.[20]

a. Allocations Based on Salary

If the profit sharing plan does not offer a 401(k) elective deferral feature for employees, the employer must decide upon an allocation formula (i.e., how each participant will share in the employer contribution that may be made annually). This formula must be set forth in the plan document and must be nondiscriminatory. Generally, the allocation formula is based on the participant's compensation, which could also consider permitted disparity with social security; the participant's compensation and service; or any other manner provided under the plan.

By far, the most popular allocation formula is for each of the eligible participants to receive the same proportion that their respective salary bears to the total of all eligible participants' salaries. For example, if the employer's contribution is determined to be $1,000,000 for the plan year and the total of all eligible participants' salaries is $10,000,000, each participant's share of the contribution is 10% ($1,000,000 ÷ $10,000,000); hence, a participant with a $50,000 salary would receive an allocation of 10% × $50,000 = $5,000, and a participant with a $100,000 salary would receive an allocation of 10% × $100,000 = $10,000.

b. Allocations Based on Permitted Disparity
(previously referred to as Social Security Integration)

Employer and employee contributions (each at a rate of 6.2% since 1990, referred to as the OASDI) to pay for Social Security benefits are applied only up to a maximum Social Security wage base (SSWB) (e.g., for 2020, the SSWB is $137,700); in contrast, employer and employee contributions (each at a rate of 1.45%) to pay for Medicare benefits are applied to all wages, not just those up to the SSWB. Since employer contributions for Social Security benefits are applied only up to the SSWB, employers do not make any contributions for an employee's wages in excess of the SSWB. [As an aside, Social Security benefits are determined only using an employee's wages up to the SSWB, even if the employee's wages are over the SSWB amount.] Under the original nondiscrimination rules, employer contributions under an employer-provided plan were deemed nondiscriminatory if they were a uniform percentage of the employee's total wages (e.g., 10% × employee's wages). The original permitted disparity rules (referred to as integration rules) permitted the employer to make contributions for participants based *solely* on their wages in excess of the SSWB (up to the maximum OASDI rate), such that when added to their contributions to Social Security (on wages up to the SSWB), they resulted in a uniform percentage of the employee's total wages. For example, if the employer contribution rate to Social Security in a given

---

19. Treas. Reg. § 1.401(k)-1(d)(3)(iii)(B).
20. Treas. Reg. § 1.401(k)-1(d)(3)(i).

year was 5.7% and the SSWB was $42,000, the employer's contribution to the employer-provided plan could be 5.7% on the participant's wages *in excess* of $42,000 and 0% on the participant's wages less than or equal to the SSWB of $42,000. Many employers took advantage of these integration rules in order to reduce employer contributions under the employer-provided plan.

Congress radically altered the rules in 1986, codifying them with the permitted disparity rules of I.R.C. § 401(l).[21] As a result, a participant's wages less than or equal to the SSWB could no longer be ignored; instead, Congress enacted a "two-for-one" comparison between the allocation rate applied to wages at or below the SSWB and the allocation rate applied to wages above the SSWB. For example, if the employer contribution to the employer-provided plan was 1% on wages at or below the SSWB, then the additional employer contribution to the employer-provided plan could be 2% on wages above the SSWB (i.e., the 2% rate could only be twice the 1% rate). As a result, if the SSWB was $55,500 (the 1992 SSWB) and an eligible participant earned $70,000, the employer contribution under the employer-provided plan could be [1% × $55,500 + 2% × ($70,000 − $55,500)] = $555 + $290 = $845 (1.2% allocation rate). Back in 1986, the OASDI rate was 5.7% (lower than the current 6.2%). Thus, the only way for an employer to achieve the prior 5.7% spread was to contribute 5.7% on wages at or below the SSWB and 11.4% on wages above the SSWB. Since this required an additional 5.7% contribution on wages at or below the SSWB, the permitted disparity rules resulted in a dramatic increase in employer contributions to achieve the pre-TRA '86 results, and thus were not enthusiastically received by employers.

Obviously, due to the complexity of a permitted disparity allocation formula under the employer-provided plan, communications to plan participants became more challenging, leaving the employer to balance the savings costs with the communication challenges.

c. Allocations Based on Age and Service Weightings

While more challenging than basing allocations solely on salary, the employer may also wish to have the allocation take into account the participant's age or service. Generally, this is accomplished through a uniform points formula. Let's do an example. Plan A wishes to grant each eligible participant 10 points for each year of service and 1 point for each $100 of compensation. The employer's contributions will then be allocated based on the following formula: each employee's allocation is equal to (i) the total amount of all allocations for the plan year multiplied by (ii) the ratio of the employee's points for the plan year to the sum of all participants' points for the plan year. Thus, for the current plan year, there are total allocation points for all participants of 8,120 and the employer contribution is to be $81,200 (meaning each point is worth $10). Participant A with 10 years of service and salary of $100,000

---

21. TRA '86 § 1111(a), adding I.R.C. § 401(l) to the Code, effective for plan years beginning after December 31, 1988.

has $[10 \times 10 + 1 \times (\$100,000 \div \$100)] = 100 + 1,000 = 1100$ points. A's allocation $= [81,200 \times (1,100 \div 8,120)] = \$11,000$. A's allocation rate is $\$11,000 \div \$100,000 = 11\%$. In contrast, Participant B with 1 year of service and salary of $50,000 has $[10 \times 1 + 1 \times (\$50,000 \div \$100)] = 10 + 500 = 510$ points. B's allocation $= [81,200 \times (510 \div 8,120)] = \$5,100$. B's allocation rate is $\$5,100 \div \$50,000 = 10.2\%$. By using a points allocation formula, the employer is able to provide different allocation rates to the participants, with those having more years of service getting a larger allocation rate than those with fewer years of service.

d. Comparison of the Above Types of Formulas

The following example can help you visualize why an employer (especially a small employer) may wish to consider all three types of allocation formulas.

A consultant has approached a small business and proposed the establishment of a qualified profit sharing plan in order to shelter income by increasing deductions. Upon discussion, the small business owner indicates that an ongoing annual employer contribution of $50,000 to $60,000 would not be burdensome, given that its profits are consistently in the $100,000 to $300,000 range. As a result, the consultant proposes three different allocation formulas (all of them using an employee's total compensation):

- Pro rata allocation formula using the participant's total plan year compensation;

- A uniform point system with x points for each year of service and y points for each $100 of the participant's total plan year compensation; and

- An integrated formula of 7% of the participant's total plan year compensation + 6.2% of the participant's total plan year compensation in excess of the SSWB.

The consultant estimates the following allocation rates for business owners A and B, and for its five other employees for the first applicable plan year under each of the proposed formulae:

Name	PY Compensation	Pro Rata Allocation %	Points Formula Allocation %	Integrated Formula Allocation %
A	$200,000	10%	10.5%	10.6%
B	200,000	10%	10.5%	10.6%
C	60,000	10%	9.3%	7%
D	35,000	10%	1.4%	7%
E	25,000	10%	1.8%	7%
F	25,000	10%	1%	7%
G	15,000	10%	12%	7%
	$560,000	$56,000	$50,000	$53,472

This chart visualizes for the two owners A and B that the first type of formula is the costliest, to the tune of $56,000, as it provides 10% for everyone. In contrast, the second formula is the least costly, but it still provides A and B with at least 10% (in fact 10.5% for A and B), while providing a considerably lesser percentage for everyone else (except G). The third formula comes in the middle at $53,472, providing A and B with 10.6% but a greater percentage for everyone else (except G) when compared to the second formula.

e. Allocations Based on Cross Testing

Under the cross-testing nondiscrimination rules, an employer can provide a variety of different allocation rates based on a table that is contained in the plan document. However, the plan must show on an annual basis that the different allocation rates do not discriminate in favor of the highly paid employees.[22] Usually an enrolled actuary assists the employer in determining what the table is, whereas the plan's attorney will amend the plan on an annual basis to insert the applicable table. For example, one table may state participant A (who is a highly compensated employee (HCE)[23]) will receive an allocation rate of 40%, where all other participants (who are all non-highly compensated employees (NHCEs)) will receive an allocation rate of 6.25%. Normally, one would think that such disparity between the HCE's allocation rate of 40% and the NHCEs' allocation rate of 6.25% would be discriminatory, and it is when viewed under a defined contribution plan. But the IRS allows the employer to convert the allocation rate into a benefit accrual rate (i.e., what would that allocation amount purchase as an accrual rate on a defined benefit basis),[24] and then apply the benefit accrual rate to the nondiscrimination rules. If there is a wide disparity in ages between the non-highly paid and the highly paid, a small allocation amount buys a much larger accrual rate as there is more time for the allocation amount to accumulate (e.g., from age 35 to age 65). Hence an allocation rate of 6.25% for a younger non-highly paid employee versus an allocation rate of 40% for an older highly paid employee may buy the same accrual rate at age 65 for life, which would be nondiscriminatory from a defined benefit perspective.

Since accrual rates for a defined benefit plan are tied to the participant's current age (whereas allocation rates under defined contribution plans are generally not tied to the participant's current age), the cross-testing rules provide an alternative testing device, especially for small employers. In our example, the IRS regulations impose a "toll charge" which requires each NHCE's allocation rate to be at least the lesser of 5% or one-third of the allocation rate of the HCE with the highest rate. Since the NHCEs' allocation rates are all 6.25%, that satisfies the requirement that they must be at least the lesser of [5%, $\frac{1}{3} \times 40\% = 13.33\%$] = 5%.

---

22. I.R.C. §401(a)(4).

23. A highly compensated employee (HCE) is a defined term under I.R.C. §414(q) which includes certain owner-employees and certain highly paid employees. Any employee who is not an HCE is by definition a nonhighly compensated employee (NHCE).

24. Treas. Reg. §1.401-(a)(4)-8.

3. Stock Ownership Plans

a. Stock Bonus Plans

Stock bonus plans are really a subset of defined contribution profit sharing plans. They have all the same features as a profit sharing plan except that benefits from the plan may be distributed in the form of employer stock or in cash. They are qualified retirement plans and thus are subject to the standard rules of retirement plans. Their contributions can be discretionary but must be substantial and recurring. By having the plan's investments be employer securities, these plans are designed to increase the employees' vested interest in the employer's continued economic success. The disadvantage of such plans for employees is that a disproportionate share of their retirement savings is tied up in a single investment — the employer securities — which means they are not diversified.

Under the Code's requirements, a stock bonus plan must:

- Allow participants the right to have their benefits distributed in the form of employer securities; if the securities are not readily tradable on an established market, the participants must have the right to require the employer to repurchase such securities at a fair market value;[25]
- Provide that if the participant and, if applicable, with the consent of the participant's spouse, elects a distribution of the participant's account balance, such distribution must commence no later than (i) one year after the close of the plan year in which the participant separates service due to attainment of the normal retirement age, disability, or death, or (ii) the fifth plan year following the year in which the participant separates from service (unless the participant is reemployed before such time).[26] There is a limited distribution period whereby the plan must provide that unless the participant elects otherwise, distributions will be in substantially equal periodic payments over a period not longer than the greater of (i) five years or, (ii) if the participant has an account balance in excess of $800,000, five years plus one additional year (but no more than five additional years) for each $160,000 or fraction thereof by which the account balance exceeds $800,000.[27]

b. Employee Stock Ownership Plans (ESOPs)

An employee stock ownership plan (ESOP) is an I.R.C. § 401(a) qualified defined contribution plan that is either a stock bonus plan or a stock bonus/money purchase plan. It must be designed to invest *primarily* in employer securities as defined by I.R.C. § 4975(e)(8).[28] Thus, ESOPs have a greater concentration of employer securities than the garden-variety stock bonus plan.

---

25. I.R.C. § 401(a)(23), cross referencing the requirements of I.R.C. § 409(h).
26. I.R.C. § 401(a)(23), cross referencing I.R.C. § 409(o).
27. I.R.C. § 409(o)(1)(C).
28. SECURE '19, § 203(a)(3).

Just like the requirements for stock bonus plans, ESOPs must allow participants the right to demand that benefits be distributed in employer securities and must abide by the distribution rules applicable to stock bonus plans.[29] But the employer securities invested within the ESOP must be registered with the Securities and Exchange Commission (if the employer is public) and thus, the participants may have certain voting rights.[30] Provided the ESOP does not offer a cash or deferred 401(k) arrangement and is separate and apart from all other employer plans, it does not have to satisfy the diversification requirements of I.R.C. §401(a)(35) for defined contribution plans.[31]

4. Target Benefit Plans

A target benefit plan is a defined contribution plan that tries to mimic the advantages of a defined benefit plan while providing the security of a given level of retirement income. The employer contributions are determined and contributed based on a "targeted" benefit formula. If the assumptions used in the determination are actually realized, the participant's account balance should be sufficient to pay the "targeted" benefits; but if the assumptions are not realized, benefits will be paid solely based on what the participant's account balance can buy in a benefit at retirement. The Services defines a target benefit plans as:

- A money-purchase pension plan,
- Formulated to meet a targeted benefit as of a designated normal retirement date,
- Funded with employer contributions necessary to meet the targeted benefit, which were computed according to actuarial assumptions,
- With forfeitures being used to decrease employer contributions,
- With separate accounts maintained for each participant, to which allocable employer contributions and trust earnings are made, and
- From which plan benefits are provided.[32]

These plans were designed to look like defined benefit plans but avoid some of the disadvantages of such plans (e.g., PBGC premiums and coverage).

5. Cash or Deferred Arrangements (CODA) (otherwise known as §401(k) Plans)

A §401(k) plan is a defined contribution plan (either a profit sharing or a stock bonus plan) that offers a participant the ability to elect to defer a portion of his or her compensation on a pre-tax basis in lieu of receiving that compensation in cash, pursuant to the rules of I.R.C. §401(k).[33] Beginning in 2006, participants were given

---

29. I.R.C. §409(h).
30. I.R.C. §409(e).
31. I.R.C. §401(a)(35)(E)(ii).
32. Treas. Reg. §1.401(a)(4)-8(b)(3)(i).
33. I.R.C. §401(k).

the opportunity to make these deferrals on an after-tax basis (referred to as "designated Roth contributions") pursuant to I.R.C. § 402A. Employer contributions to a § 401(k) plan may be either or both matching contributions (i.e., matching some percentage of the employee's deferral) or nonelective contributions (i.e., employer contributions made irrespective of the employee's deferral). To the extent the employer contributions are matching, the IRS deems these contributions are made to a separate § 401(m) plan. Special nondiscrimination rules are then applied to the employees' deferrals, the employer's matching contributions, and the employer's nonelective contributions. To avoid these rules, the plan can be designed as a safe harbor or compliant automatic enrollment feature plan. And as mentioned earlier, the § 401(k) is designed to be a retirement savings plan and thus distributions of the employees' deferrals are generally restricted while the employee is employed, except that hardship distributions may be made.

a. Traditional § 401(k) Plans

A traditional § 401(k) plan permits participants to make pre-tax salary deferrals. Distributions are limited while the participant is employed, but hardship distributions are allowed. The advantage of such a plan is that it is the only qualified plan vehicle that permits an employee to make pre-tax salary deferrals to save for retirement.[34] The maximum amount an employee can defer is limited by a maximum annual amount set forth in I.R.C. § 402(g) (e.g., $19,500 for 2020, with an additional $6,500 catch-up limit for those age 50 and older).[35] The earnings on the salary deferrals in a § 401(k) plan accumulate tax-free until the time of distribution, similar to the earnings accumulation of employer contributions under a qualified plan. However, since the pre-tax deferrals have not been taxed as earned while the participant is employed, the entire amount of the benefit payment is taxable upon actual distribution.

b. Roth § 401(k) Plans

Congress revised the statutory rules by adding I.R.C. § 402A, beginning in 2006, such that the elective salary deferrals could be made on an after-tax basis, and designated as Roth contributions.[36] These plans are designed like traditional § 401(k) plans and may include employer matching contributions. The advantage to the participant is that the earnings on the after-tax deferrals are tax-free if taken after the participant attains age 59½ and provided the deferrals remain invested in the plan for a minimum of five years. Let's look at an example. In a traditional § 401(k) plan, Participant A with annual compensation of $50,000 makes a pre-tax deferral of 10% (or $5,000). Thus, A takes home $45,000 in take-home pay (which is includable in gross income) and defers $5,000 in the plan which will accumulate at a gross amount of $5,000 until retirement. Upon distribution, A is taxed on the entire amount (principal plus earn-

---

34. I.R.C. § 401(k), with the exception of the new combined defined benefit/401(k) plans for small businesses.

35. I.R.C. § 402(g).

36. I.R.C. § 402A (named for Senator William Roth who pioneered the idea).

ings). In contrast, if A makes a $5,000 Roth deferral, A is taxed on the entire $50,000 ($45,000 take-home pay + $5,000 Roth deferral), but upon later distribution, neither the Roth deferral nor the earnings on the Roth deferral are subject to tax. Some argue that those participants making Roth deferrals contribute less as they must currently pay the tax on such deferrals, leaving less available for retirement savings.

c. Automatic Enrollment Features in § 401(k) Plans

ERISA prohibits the attachment of an employee's benefit, except in certain circumstances.[37] Hence, if an employer attempted to withhold salary deferrals from an employee's wages without the employee's consent, it could violate this anti-attachment protection. Thus, Congress amended ERISA to promote automatic enrollment of employees in a CODA, and thus automatic withholding of salary deferrals, as it has shown to increase participation and savings. As a result of PPA '06, a CODA may be designed so as to automatically enroll a participant in the plan unless he or she affirmatively elects otherwise.[38] There are two ways to automatically enroll participants, either through an eligible automatic enrollment arrangement (EACA), codified in I.R.C. § 414(w), or a qualified automatic contribution arrangement (QACA), codified in I.R.C. § 401(k)(13)).

EACA acts accordingly:

- The plan provides participants with a cash or deferred arrangement in which they choose between cash or salary deferrals into the plan;
- The default elective contribution is a uniform percentage of compensation until the participant specifically elects not to have such contribution made or elects to change the contribution percentage;
- The employer may select a default investment option for a participant in the absence of a participant's affirmative election;
- The participants have been given notice of their rights and obligations under such an arrangement, written in a manner readily understood by a participant, as well as notice as to how their contributions will be invested in absence of their affirmative election.[39]

An employer may choose between an EACA (described above) or a QACA. EACA has simpler requirements than QACAs, but the latter relieves the employer of the nondiscrimination rules applicable to I.R.C. § 401(k) plans and the top-heavy requirements.[40] A QACA satisfies the following:

- It meets all the requirements applicable to an EACA;
- Participants must have the ability to opt out;[41]

---

37. ERISA § 514.
38. PPA '06 § 902(f)(1), adding a new subsection (e) to ERISA § 514.
39. I.R.C. § 414(w)(3)–(4).
40. I.R.C. § 401(k)(13)(A).
41. PPA '06 § 902(a), adding a new subparagraph (C)(ii) to paragraph (13) at the end of I.R.C. § 401(k).

- At a minimum, the percentage of compensation withheld automatically for an eligible participant must be 3% in the initial and second year, 4% in the third year, 5% in the fourth year, and 6% in the fifth and later years; the maximum percentage could not exceed 10% in any one year.[42] However, the SECURE Act amended the 10% maximum limit, increasing it to 15%, effective for plan years beginning after December 31, 2019.[43]

- Employer contributions may be either matching contributions (of 100% of the first 1% of compensation plus 50% of the next 5% of compensation for any non-highly compensated employee) or nonelective contributions (of 3% of compensation for any non-highly compensated employee), and such contributions are subject to a vesting schedule of up to two years;[44]

- Annual notices must be given to participants, informing them of their rights and responsibilities under the arrangement, including their right to opt out, and how contributions will be invested in the absence of an election.[45]

As will be discussed in Chapter 13, plans that provide individually directed investments may continue to rely on the fiduciary protections afforded by ERISA § 404(c) if the automatic contribution deferrals are invested in "qualified default investment alternatives."[46]

An EACA must offer the participants the right to withdraw any salary deferrals within an initial 90-day window during which the automatic deferrals were first made (these are referred to as "erroneous automatic contributions").[47] For the participant, the amount of the withdrawal will be includible in his or her gross income for the tax year in which the distribution is made, but there is no penalty tax for early distribution. For the employer, any employer matching contribution will be forfeited.

6. SEPs, SIMPLEs, and Payroll Deduction IRAs

To encourage small employers to adopt retirement plans, the Code extends a variety of defined contribution plans to these employers with less administrative burdens but with more universal coverage.

a. Payroll Deduction IRAs

Whether or not covered by an employer-provided retirement plan, individual workers may be able to make pre-tax or Roth contributions to an IRA, which is a defined contribution plan designed only for the benefit of a particular taxpayer.[48]

---

42. I.R.C. § 401(k)(13)(C)(iii).
43. SECURE '19 § 102, amending I.R.C. § 401(k)(13)(C)(iii). The new limit is not available for the participant's first year, which remains at 10%.
44. I.R.C. § 401(k)(13)(D).
45. I.R.C. § 401(k)(13)(E).
46. PPA '06 § 624(a), adding a new paragraph (5) to ERISA § 404(c).
47. I.R.C. § 414(w)(2).
48. I.R.C. §§ 408 and 408A.

Such individual plans are exempt from Title I of ERISA.[49] However, employers may wish to facilitate an employee's funding of an IRA through payroll deductions, making it easier for the employee to save. The DOL has provided a "safe harbor" in its regulation whereby an IRA payroll deduction program maintained by an employer or employee organization will not be deemed to be an employee benefit plan for purposes of Title I.[50] To qualify for the safe harbor, the payroll deduction program must satisfy the following:

- No employer or employee association contributions may be made other than the payroll deductions;

- Participation in the program must be completely voluntary for employees or members;

- The sole involvement of the employer or employee organization is without endorsement to permit the sponsor to publicize the program to employees or members, to collect contributions through payroll deductions, and to remit them to the sponsor; and

- The employer or employee organization receives no consideration in the form of cash or otherwise, other than reasonable compensation for services rendered in connection with the payroll deduction.[51]

In a later Interpretive Bulletin 99-1,[52] he DOL clarified the application of the IRA safe harbor with respect to employer communications. It noted that the employer should remain neutral with respect to an IRA sponsor in its communications with employees so as not to appear to endorse the IRA payroll deduction program. The employer may encourage employees to save for retirement and explain the advantages of contributing to an IRA, as long as it is clear that its involvement is limited to collecting the contributions and remitting them to the IRA sponsor.

President Obama made several legislative proposals to make retirement savings easier for lower and middle income workers without an employer-provided plan, but his efforts were largely unsuccessful.[53] Under an Executive Directive, the Treasury Department created "MyRA" savings accounts (referred to as "My Retirement Account") for workers not covered under an employer-provided plan.[54] The model was a Roth IRA, backed by a government guarantee. As it did not require automatic en-

---

49. ERISA § 101(a), as Title I is applicable only to employee benefit plans.
50. Labor Reg. § 2510.3-2(d)(1).
51. *Id.*
52. Labor Reg. § 2509.99-1.
53. The White House, Office of the Press Secretary, *FACT SHEET: Opportunity for All: Securing a Dignified Retirement for All Americans* (Jan. 29, 2014), https://obamawhitehouse.archives.gov/the-press-office/2014/01/29/fact-sheet-opportunity-all-securing-dignified-retirement-all-americans.
54. *myRA: A Simple, Safe, Affordable Retirement Savings Account*, U.S. Dep't of Treasury, https://www.treasury.gov/connect/blog/Documents/FINAL%20myRA%20Fact%20Sheet.pdf ("myRAs will be Roth IRA accounts available to anyone who has an annual income of less than $129,000 a year for individuals and $191,000 for couples.").

rollment, it was not popular among workers, leading the Treasury to cease taking contributions after 2017.[55]

In the meantime, a number of states or state political subdivisions adopted or considered adopting legislation to force employers with no employer-provided retirement plans to deduct amounts from their employees' pay and remit such amounts to state- or state political subdivision IRAs.[56] These programs generally relied upon an automatic enrollment feature whereby employees would be deemed to participate unless they affirmatively opted out from participation. But the looming issue for these plans was whether the creation or administration of such a program created an ERISA-covered plan on the part of the employer. To address this concern, the DOL released two pieces of regulatory guidance—a set of proposed regulations to exempt certain state mandated payroll deduction IRA plans from ERISA and an interpretive bulletin that permitted certain state mandated traditional retirement plans to be covered under ERISA.[57] These forms of guidance were later nullified by joint resolution by Congress and then revoked by the DOL.[58]

b. SEPs

A simplified employee pension plan (SEP) was introduced in 1979 under I.R.C. §408(k) for small employers as an alternative to a qualified profit-sharing plan—one that would be simpler and less expensive.[59] The employer is expected to select a bank or financial institution to which it will remit contributions directly to each employee's IRA or individual retirement annuity. The employer's contribution is to be determined as a uniform percentage of compensation, made available to all eligible employees. Initially the maximum employer contribution under an SEP was less than what was available under a qualified profit sharing plan, limited by the lesser of 15% of the employee's compensation or the applicable I.R.C. §415(c) limit. The Job Cre-

---

55. Press Release, U.S. Dep't of Treasury, *Treasury Announces Steps to Wind Down myRA Program* (July 28, 2017), https://www.treasury.gov/press-center/press-releases/Pages/sm0135.aspx.

56. *See* Illinois Secure Choice Savings Program (ISCSP) (S.B. 2758) (2015), §500 (adding 30 Ill. Comp. Stat. §105/5.855); California Secure Choice Retirement Savings Trust Act (S.B. 1234) (2012), §3 (adding 21 Calif. Gov't Code §100000–§100044); Oregon 2015 Session Laws, ch. 557 (H.B. 2960) (establishing the Oregon Retirement Savings Board to develop a defined contribution retirement plan called the Oregon Retirement Savings Plan); Maryland Small Business Retirement Savings Program Act, ch. 324 (H.B. 1378) (2016). For a description of the various models used by the states and local government, see Kathryn J. Kennedy, IRAs, BNA Tax Mgmt. Portfolio 367.

57. Proposed rule on Savings Arrangements Established by States for Non-Governmental Employees, Prop. DOL Regs. §2510.3(h), (Nov. 18, 2015). RIN 1210-AB71, Savings Arrangements Established by States for Non-Governmental Employees, (Aug. 30, 2016), modifying DOL Reg. §2510.3-2(a), and adding new DOL Reg. §2510.3-2(h) (effective Oct. 31, 2016). *See also* DOL Interpretive Bull. 2015-02, Interpretive Bulletin Relating to State Savings Programs That Sponsor or Facilitate Plans Covered by the Employee Retirement Income Security Act of 1974, 80 Fed. Reg. 71936 (Nov. 18, 2015).

58. H.J. Res. 66, Pub. L. No. 115-35; H.J. Res. 67, Pub. L. No. 115-24; RIN 1210-AB76 (June 28, 2017).

59. Revenue Act of 1978, §152(b), adding I.R.C. §408(k), to be effective for taxable years beginning after December 31, 1978.

ation and Workers Assistance Act of 2002 later increased the 15% limit to 25%, effective beginning in 2002.[60]

Originally, SEPs could also permit employee salary deferrals (referred to as "SARSEPs"), permitting employees to make pre-tax salary deferrals to an SEP. However, the Small Business Job Protection Act of 1996 eliminated the use of salary reduction provisions in an SEP, except for SARSEP arrangements already in effect as of December 31, 1996.[61] Employers wanting to adopt a simplified plan after 1996 with salary deferrals were directed to adopt a SIMPLE plan in lieu of an SEP.

SEP IRAs must satisfy the following requirements:

- The SEP must be an IRA or an individual retirement annuity;

- The employer must make contributions for all employees (with limited exceptions) who have attained age 21, worked at least three of the preceding five years with the employer, and have received at least $450 in compensation from the employer for the year;

- The employer contributions may not be discriminatory in favor of the highly paid;

- Employees must be able to withdraw employer contributions without penalty; and

- The employer's contributions must be allocated among the employees per a written formula set forth in the SEP.[62]

Adoption of an SEP relieves the employer from ERISA's reporting and disclosure requirements if the SEP is established using IRS Form 5305-SEP or if certain information is given to employees.[63] Use of the IRS Form 5305-SEP relieves the employer of the need to draft a plan and trust document. Given that the contribution and deduction ceilings for SEPs are now on par with that of qualified profit sharing plans, SEPs are the preferred retirement vehicle for small employers due to their simplicity and ease of adoption. The main disadvantage is that employee salary deferrals are no longer allowed, except for grandfathered SARSEPs.

c. SIMPLEs

The Small Business Job Protection Act of 1996 created the Savings Incentive Match Plan for Employees under I.R.C. § 408(p), better known as a SIMPLE plan.[64] This type of plan is available only to small employers, defined to be employers that have no more than 100 employees who earned $5,000 or more in compensation during the preceding calendar year.[65] There is a two-year grace period for which the employer may continue the plan for two more calendar years if it satisfied the 100-employee

---

60. JCWAA '02 §411(l)(3), amending I.R.C. §402(h)(2).
61. SBJPA §1421(c), amending I.R.C. §408(k)(6)(H).
62. I.R.C. §408(k)(1)–(5).
63. *See* Prop. Reg. §1.408-9.
64. SBJPA §1421, effective for tax years beginning after December 31, 1996.
65. I.R.C. §408(p)(2)(A) and (C)(i)(I) (defining "eligible employer").

limit, established the plan, and then failed the limit in a subsequent year.[66] The "no other plan rule" applies, which states that the employer cannot make a contribution to a SIMPLE plan for a given calendar year if it or a predecessor employer maintains another qualified plan under which any of its employees receive an allocation or an accrual for any plan year beginning or ending in that calendar year.[67]

These types of plans provide an alternate retirement plan for small employers who wish to avoid the top-heavy and nondiscrimination rules applicable to qualified plans and the other administrative burdens associated with such plans. There are two types of SIMPLE plans—SIMPLE IRA and SIMPLE §401(k).

With a SIMPLE IRA, the employer selects a bank or financial institution in which it will make contributions directly to each employee's IRA or individual retirement annuity. The plan may exclude from eligibility those employees who do not have at least $5,000 in compensation with the employer during any of the two preceding calendar years and who are not reasonably expected to have $5,000 during the current calendar year.[68] The plan must be in writing, but the IRS has model documents relating to SIMPLE IRA arrangements.

Participants in the SIMPLE IRA are provided with a salary reduction option in which they choose between cash or contributions to the plan.[69] There is a maximum salary deferral amount (e.g., $13,500 for 2020) with a catch-up limit (e.g., $3,000 for 2020) for participants age 50 or older.[70] The employer then makes either an employer matching contribution of 100% (subject to a maximum of 3% of an employee's compensation) or a 2% nonelective contribution.[71] Employer contributions are required to be fully vested.[72] Salary reduction contributions are required to be sent by the employer to the employee's SIMPLE IRA no later than 30 days following the last day on which those amounts would otherwise have been paid to the employee, whereas employer contributions must be made no later than the due date for filing its tax return, including extensions.[73]

SIMPLE 401(k) plans may be established provided they meet the mandated eligibility, contribution, and similar requirements applicable to SIMPLE plans. A SIMPLE 401(k) plan is a qualified defined contribution, subject to the applicable qualification rules, but the plan does not need to perform the annual nondiscrimination tests nor the top-heavy tests. It is subject to ERISA's reporting and disclosure requirements. In comparing a SIMPLE 401(k) plan to a traditional 401(k) plan, the maximum amount that an employee can contribute and the maximum amount that an employer can contribute are much lower than the applicable amounts under a 401(k) plan.

66. I.R.C. §408(p)(2)(C)(i)(II).
67. I.R.C. §408(p)(2)(D).
68. I.R.C. §408(p)(4)(A).
69. I.R.C. §408(p)(2)(A)(i).
70. I.R.C. §408(p)(2)(E).
71. I.R.C. §408(p)(2)(A)–(B).
72. I.R.C. §408(p)(3).
73. I.R.C. §408(p)(5)(A); Notice 98-4, Q&A G-5, G-6.

C. Defined Benefit Plans

1. Type of Formula

As mentioned earlier, defined benefit plans focus on *output*, i.e., the benefits payable from the plan. Thus, such plans must expressly formulate the ultimate benefit to be paid to a participant—in terms of the amount, a normal retirement age, and form of payment (e.g., annuity). For example, the normal retirement benefit (NRB) can be designed to be a percentage of the employee's pre-retirement salary (tied or not tied to his or her service with the employer), payable at a given normal retirement age (NRA), for a period of time (e.g., life annuity for an unmarried participant, joint and survivor annuity for a married participant). If the amount of benefit is tied to the employee's pre-retirement salary, the employer must decide whether to use the employee's career average salary (CAE) (which may be considerably less than his salary immediately before retirement) or a final average salary (FSA) (which provides greater protection that such amount is adequate for retirement).

Form 5300 identifies four different kinds of defined benefit plans (fixed benefit, flat benefit, unit benefit, and variable benefit); however, these differences refer *only* to the type of benefit formula used, not the other characteristics of defined benefit plans. "Fixed benefit" refers to a plan formula that provides a participant with a fixed percentage of his or her compensation at retirement (e.g., 70% of compensation at retirement). "Flat benefit" refers to a plan formula that provides a definite amount at retirement regardless of the participant's compensation or years of service (e.g., $1,000/month at retirement). "Unit benefit" refers to a plan formula that provides a participant with a certain unit of pension for each year of credit service (e.g., 2% times compensation times years of service). "Variable" or "equity" refers to a plan formula where the initial participant benefit is determined at retirement to be fixed, flat, or unit benefit type, but then once determined, is adjusted periodically after retirement according to a recognized cost-of-living index.

Let's provide some more concrete examples of NRB formulae:

Legend: CAE = career average earnings; FAE = final average earnings; yos = years of service; life only = single life annuity for unmarried participants; J&S = joint and survivor annuity for married participants

NRB = 80% × CAE/65/life only or J&S

NRB =[2% × yos] × FAE/60/life only or J&S

NRB = [2⅓% × yos (for years 1–10) + 3% × yos (for years 11–20) + 4% × yos (for all years over 20)]/62/life or J&S

NRB = $1,000/month/65/life only or J&S

Which of these formulae provides the greatest benefit and which is the most expensive? The answer is: it depends on the demographic of the employer's workforce and what the employer is trying to accomplish.

- First, let's look at the formula used to define the amount of the benefit. The last one—$1,000/month—is unrelated to salary or service and thus may not be very motivating to an employee who wishes to stay with an employer. The first one—80% of career average pay—provides a generous replacement income level of 80%, but those employees who have been with the employer longest will have a lower CAE than recent hires of the employer. The formula is also very generous for older new hires (e.g., someone hired at age 55).The second one— 2% for each year of service—rewards based on service, but will only provide a replacement income level of 80% for those employees with 40 years of service. To the extent the employer doesn't have employees with lengthy years of service, this formula may not be motivating. The third one—graduated from 2⅓% to 4% based on service—is trying to reward employees with more years of service by crediting those years with a greater accrual rate. Finally, the fourth one is unrelated to salary and thus may not be motivating to employees.

- Second, let's look at the NRA. One thinks of the typical retirement age as age 65, but even Social Security has moved up its normal retirement age to ages 67 to 70, depending on one's year of birth. Obviously the earlier the age used for NRA, the more valuable the benefit and the more costly the benefit for the employer to fund. Large-size employers have little incentive to move the NRA down below age 60, but some small employers may be tempted to move the NRA down to make succession planning easier for young stars to move up the ranks and take the place of the retirees.

- Third, our form of distribution is constant in all four of the formulae. We'll discuss the rationales for various forms of payment in Chapter 9.

Given the promise of a certain benefit, the investment risk of a defined benefit must then rest with the employer (meaning, if the investment results are poorer than expected, the employer must increase plan contributions to meet the promised benefit). A qualified defined benefit plan must make the joint life annuity form of payment the automatic form for married participants. As a result, the employer must hire an actuary to compute expected contribution levels for the promised benefits. We'll discuss those funding concerns in Chapter 10.

2. Career Average versus Final Average Formulae

For employers with a benefit formula dependent on the participant's compensation, the employer must decide whether to use the participant's career average of earnings (CAE) or his or her final average of earnings (FAE). For most participants working for an employer, salaries are lower at the beginning of one's career compared to salaries at the end of one's career. Thus, using a career average salary generally reduces the level of salary that the accrual is based upon.

Example: Participant A had the following salary history with the employer: $40,000 for the first 10 years, $50,000 for the next 10 years, $60,000 for the next 10 years, and finally $70,000 for the final 10 years. Using a CAE for purposes of benefit accrual results in a CAE of $55,000. Thus, if the NRB formula was 70% of CAE, the final benefit would be 70% × $55,000 = $38,500, which is only 55% of the participant's actual pre-retirement salary of $70,000.

In contrast, using FAE disregards the participant's lower salary years and focuses on the salaries in the immediate pre-retirement years. Employers consider various descriptions of FAC: highest three years over the last five years; highest three consecutive years over the last 10 years; highest three years over the last 10 years. In our example above, if the NRB formula was 70% of FAE, the final benefit would be 70% × $70,000 = $49,000, which is 70% of the participant's actual pre-retirement salary of $70,000. As will be discussed in Chapter 7, every defined benefit plan must have an accrual formula which defines how the participant earns the NRB formula over time, in the event he or she terminates employment prior to retirement. In our example, say the accrual benefit (AB) formula related to the NRB formula was [3% × yos (cap at 23⅓) × FAE]/65/life only or J&S. After the first 10 years of accrual, the participant has an AB = [3% × 10 × $40,000]/65/life only or J&S = $12,000/65/life only or J&S. During the next 10 years of accrual, his or her FAE is now $50,000, which means the AB from the first 10 years of benefit accrual is retroactively increased to [3% × 10 × $50,000]/65/life only or J&S = $15,000/65/life only or J&S, to take into account that his new FAE is now at $50,000 instead of the prior $40,000. As a result, the employer's actuary must make assumptions as to the growth of the participants' salaries in order to be funding an adequate accrual.

As a result, FAE results in a more realistic replacement income level for the employee but is more costly for the employer.

3. Defined Benefit Plans with Permitted Disparity

The integration rules originally applicable to defined benefit plans were more complex than those applicable to defined contribution plans. Those rules used three defining terms; the integration rate which was the OASDI rate for the year; the integration level which was the SSWB for the year; and covered compensation (CC) which was the average of the SSWB over time. The original integration rules for defined benefit plans took one of two approaches: either the excess benefit approach or the offset approach. Under the excess benefit approach, the accrued benefit and the normal retirement benefit formula was permitted to provide a specified percentage only for a participant's wages in excess of the integration level. For example, AB = NRB = [1% × yos × (FAE − CC)]/65/life only or J&S—providing a benefit only on wages in excess of the CC.

In contrast, the offset approach provided the same accrued benefit and normal retirement benefit for all participants but then subtracted from such benefit a certain percentage of the employee's actual Social Security benefits (i.e., the portion that was assumed purchased by the employer's FICA contributions). For example, AB = NRB = [(2% × yos × FAE) − 50% of Social Security benefit]/65/life only or J&S.

These rules were drastically altered by TRA '86, narrowing the spread between benefits provided for participants whose wages exceeded the current integration level and those whose wages were at or below the current integration level. The new rules made the offset and excess defined benefit plans operate in a similar fashion by requiring three key elements:[74]

- The maximum annual offset or the maximum spread between the benefit levels is now .75% per year of service, with a cap at 35 years;

- The two-for-one rule applies (for offset plans, the offset rate cannot be more than one-half the rate used to determine the gross benefits; for excess plans, the benefit rate above the integration level cannot be more than twice the base benefit rate below the integration level); and

- The standard integration level is covered compensation.

Thus, after the changes, a sample accrued benefit and normal retirement benefit formula could be [(.5% × compensation up to the integration level + 1.0% × compensation in excess of the integration level) × yos (capped at 35 years)]/65/life only or J&S.

Due to the complexity of these new integration rules, only small- and medium-size employers consider using them as they must weigh their complexity against the cost savings.

4. Pension Plans

Because all defined benefit plans are designed as retirement vehicles, they are pension plans. Thus, many of the same requirements applicable to money purchase pension plans (as discussed above) apply equally here:

- A defined benefit plan must provide a definite and predetermined formula (or stated amount) used to determine the ultimate benefit payable to the participant.

- Employer contributions may not be contingent upon the employer's profits. Since benefits are projected as of some future point in time, the employer must use the services of an actuary to ascertain the proper level of employer contributions necessary to fund the plan's benefit formula.

- The *primary purpose* of defined benefit plans is to provide retirement benefits. Thus, other benefits such as death and disability benefits may be provided as long as they are "incidental." And distributions generally may not be made to an employee prior to termination of employment or plan termination.

- Qualified defined benefit plans are subject to the "systematic payment of benefits" rule; hence, annuity forms must be made available as a form of payment for the promised retirement benefits. In the event the participant is married, joint life annuities must be provided automatically.

---

74. I.R.C. § 401(l)(3), as amended by TRA '86 § 1111(a).

• Forfeitures may not be used to increase participants' benefits, but rather to reduce employer contributions.

D. Choice between a Defined Contribution Plan or a Defined Benefit Plan

In deciding whether to provide a defined contribution plan or defined benefit plan to a select group of employees, an employer must carefully consider the cost of a given plan. Generally, defined contribution plans afford employers the ability to control costs by fixing the level of contributions either through plan design or annual impositions on funding levels. From the employee's perspective, such fixed costs may or may not provide adequate retirement income replacement, depending on his or her years of plan participation. Due the long-term tax-free compounding of interest, these plans generally favor younger employees who have the ability to accumulate deferrals. In contrast, defined benefit plans are usually designed to provide an adequate level of retirement income replacement for retirees, but for a given level of benefits, costs under defined benefit plans will differ dramatically depending on the average age of the employer's workforce. Defined benefit plans also subject employers to minimum annual funding requirements which make them not as flexible as defined contribution plans.

Example: A defined contribution plan provides an annual allocation of 5% of the employee's compensation. In contrast, a defined benefit plan provides an annual accrued benefit of 5% of the employee's compensation for each year of plan participation. Which plan is more generous?

Answer: From the perspective of the plan participant, the choice between a 5% allocation or a 5% benefit accrued is about equivalent if the participant is age 42. If the plan participant is younger than age 42, the 5% allocation under a defined contribution plan will generally provide a greater accumulation than an annual benefit accrual of 5% of compensation at the plan's retirement age of 65; if the plan participant is older than age 42, the defined benefit accrual provides a greater benefit than the defined contribution allocation.

For an employee of a medium- to large-size employer, the employer dictates the type of plan offered and the participant does not have much input. In the case of a small-size employer, the employer's choice of plan will depend on what the employer is trying to accomplish — the establishment of a defined benefit plan so that the owner of the small business can retire, or a defined contribution plan so that the employees can make pre-tax contributions to save for retirement. While it was said earlier that defined benefit plans have fallen out of favor with employers, small employers are very much interested in establishing and maintaining them in order for the owner to retire with a sizeable retirement benefit and to maximize deductions by maintaining both a defined benefit and defined contribution plan.

E. Miscellaneous Kinds of Plans

1. Excess Benefit Plans

These plans are defined in ERISA as benefit plans maintained solely for the purpose of providing benefits for certain employees in excess of the maximum limitations on contributions and benefits imposed by I.R.C. § 415.[75] Such plans are exempt from Title I's rules on eligibility, participation, vesting, minimum funding, benefit accrual, and qualified joint and survivor annuity requirements; an *unfunded* excess benefit plan is exempt from all of ERISA Title I, including the fiduciary rules, enforcement, claims procedure, and reporting and disclosure.[76]

Due to these maximum limitations, many employers offer nonqualified deferred compensation plans for executives which were designed to satisfy ERISA's "excess benefit plan" definition. However, when Congress later imposed a maximum compensation ceiling under I.R.C. § 401(a)(17) to limit the benefit and allocations that could be offered, it did not foresee that employers' nonqualified plans would supplement the benefits/allocations limited by both the Code's §§ 415 and 401(a)(17) limitations and did not amend ERISA's "excess benefit plan" definition. As a result, the typical nonqualified plan does not satisfy ERISA's definition of an excess benefit plan.

2. Top Hat Plans

This is a term of art that refers to unfunded plans established and maintained for a "select group of management or highly paid employees." Simplified reporting and disclosure requirements are applicable. While such plans are exempt from the coverage provisions of Parts 2, 3 and 4 of Title I of ERISA, there is no specific definition in ERISA as to what constitutes a top hat plan.[77] Historically, the DOL has given little guidance as to what constitutes a top hat plan. Nonqualified plans that could not have met ERISA's definition of an excess benefit plan have nevertheless relied on this exemption.

3. Cash Balance or Statutory Hybrid Plans

These terms refer to a defined benefit plan arrangement where participants' accrued benefits are referred to in terms of balances in hypothetical individual accounts. With this type of plan, employers credit employees annually with a percentage of their yearly compensation as "earnings" or "pay" credit and then with "interest" or "earnings" credits at a predetermined rate on the entire balance of their hypothetical account. This plan functions much like a profit sharing plan; however, the earnings credits

---

75. See ERISA § 3(36).
76. ERISA § 4(b)(5).
77. ERISA §§ 201(2), 301(a)(3), and 401(a)(1), respectively.

are determined by formula and no actual account exists, and thus these plans are not defined contribution plans despite their appearance as such.

This type of arrangement has suffered through many years of regulatory disfavor and has exposed employers to liability because of extreme difficulty in conforming the plan terms to the rigid requirements of ERISA and the Code respecting age discrimination in benefit accruals (and other minor issues). Older participants to these plans sued under the theory that, when the effect of future compounding interest credits is taken into account, the pay credits made in a given year will prove far more valuable for younger workers, who will obviously receive more future interest credits than their older counterparts when the accrued benefit is expressed as an annuity commencing at retirement.[78] While many of the U.S. appeals courts which have dealt with this issue head-on have rejected the theory that this violates ERISA,[79] some circuit courts have embraced it and have not been overruled.[80] However, PPA '06 endorses this plan type as non-age discrimination going forward from June 29, 2005,[81] and thus only retroactive litigation remains, and the plan type is likely to see a resurgence in the future.

4. DB(k) Plans, Beginning in 2010

This is a second plan design which has become permitted by the PPA '06, but unlike cash balance plans, this type of arrangement did not exist prior to the statute. Since 2010, employers with fewer than 500 employees are permitted to set up a plan which has both a qualified 401(k) aspect as well as a separate PBGC-guaranteed defined benefit portion, while treating the plan(s) as one for Form 5500 reporting and

---

78. Specifically, plaintiff participants under this type of plan brought suit claiming that this plan type violates the provisions of the Code and ERISA which prohibit a participant's "benefit accrual" from being reduced "because of the attainment of any age." I.R.C. §411(b)(1)(H)(i); ERISA §204(b)(1)(H)(i); *see also* Edward A. Zelinsky, *The Cash Balance Controversy Revisited: Age Discrimination and Fidelity to Statutory Text*, 20 VA. TAX. REV. 557 (2001).

79. Cooper v. IBM Personal Pension Plan, 457 F.3d 636 (7th Cir. 2006), *cert. denied* 127 S. Ct. 1143 (2007); Register v. PNC Financial Services Group, Inc., 477 F.3d 56 (3d Cir. 2007); Drutis v. Rand McNally & Co., 499 F.3d 56 (3d Cir. 2007); Hirt v. Equitable Ret. Plan for Employees, Managers and Agents, 533 F.3d 102 (2d Cir. 2008); Hurlic v. Southern Cal. Gas Co., 539 F.3d 1024 (9 th Cir. 2008). For an analysis of the cash balance litigation post-Cooper and Register, see Barry Kozak & Joshua Waldbeser, *Much Ado About the Meaning of "Benefit Accrual": The Issue of Age Discrimination in Hybrid Cash Balance Plan Qualification is Dying but Not Yet Dead*, 40 JOHN MARSHALL. REV. 867 (2007).

80. *See In re* JP Morgan Cash Balance Litigation, 460 F. Supp. 2d 479, 489 (S.D.N.Y. 2006) (holding that the black and white statutory requirements of ERISA mandate that all defined benefit plans provide non-discriminatory benefit accruals as based on additions to the size of annuity payments received in retirement); *In re* Citigroup Pension Plan ERISA Litigation, 470 F. Supp. 2d 323 S.D.N.Y. 2006). However, these cases have been since overruled. *See* Vaughn v. Air Lines Pilots Ass'n, Int'l, 395 B.R. 520, 2008 U.S. Dist. LEXIS 56741 (E.D.N.Y. 2008).

81. *See generally* Pub. L. No. 109-280, § 701 (PPA '06), amending ERISA §§ 203 and 204, and IRC § 411, to permit "applicable defined benefit plans" (cash balance plans) to define benefit accruals as additions to hypothetical accounts, thus permitting this plan type to pass non-discrimination muster.

participant disclosure purposes.[82] This plan is also exempt from the top-heavy rules usually applicable to defined benefit plans and from the ADP/ACP nondiscrimination testing required of most 401(k) plans.[83] This is permitted for smaller employers in order to encourage them to provide both types of benefits to employees, which may have been too expensive or burdensome to provide individually.

The plan's 401(k) portion must utilize an automatic enrollment arrangement with a minimum deferral rate of 4% and must provide an immediately vested 50% employer match on the 4% contribution.[84] The defined benefit portion must have a three-year maximum vesting period and satisfy one of the two benefit accrual standards: either provide at least 1% of the highest average compensation (averaging a period no longer than 5 years) per year of service, capped at no less than 20 years[86] (or 20% of the highest average compensation), or utilize a "cash balance" approach with a minimum pay credit that is indexed upward as participants get older.[87] Under the cash balance approach, the minimum pay credit is 2% if the participant's age at the beginning of the year is 30 or less; 4% if age 31 to 40; 6% if age 41 to 50; and 8% if older than age 50.

5. Multiemployer Plans

These refer to plans to which more than one employer is required to contribute, maintained pursuant to a collective bargaining agreement, which meet other requirements set forth by the DOL.[88] This term was redefined by the Multiemployer Pension Plan Amendments Act of 1980 (MEPPA), which changed the withdrawal and termination rules for such plans. These plans have historically been defined benefit plans, requiring fixed contributions by participating employers.

---

82. *See* generally Pub. L. No. 109-280, § 903 (PPA '06), amending ERISA § 210 and IRC § 414 to permit this type of combined plan.

83. *See* IRC § 414(x)(4), added by Pub. L. No. 109-280, § 903 (PPA '06) (stating that the defined benefit portion of an eligible combined plan will satisfy the top-heavy requirements of IRC § 416).

84. *See* IRC § 414(x)(3)(A), (B), added by Pub. L. No. 109-280, § 903 (PPA '06) (stating that the defined contribution portion of an eligible combined plan will satisfy the testing requirements of IRC § 401(k)(3)(A)(ii) and § 401(m)(11). *See also* Treas. Reg. §§ 1.401(k)-1(b)(2), 1.401(m)-1(b). The terms ADP and ACP (testing) refer to "Actual Deferral Percentage" and "Actual Contribution Percentage," respectively, and refer to the special non-discrimination requirements applicable to 401(k) plans.

85. IRC § 414(x)(2)(C&D), added by Pub. L. No. 109-280, § 903 (PPA '06).

86. IRC § 414(x)(2)(B)(ii), added by Pub. L. No. 109-280, § 903 (PPA '06).

87. IRC § 414(x)(2)(B)(iii), added by Pub. L. No. 109-280, § 903 (PPA '06).

88. ERISA § 3(37)(A).

Chapter 5

ERISA and Qualification Rules Applicable to Retirement Plans

Reading Assignment:	ERISA §§ 3(33)
	I.R.C. §§ 170(b)(1)(A)(ii), 401(a), 402(a), 403(b), 457(a), 457(b), 457(f), 414(d), 414(e)
	Advocate Health Care Network v. Stapleton, 137 S. Ct. 1652 (2017)
Class Discussion Questions:	Why do different types of employers sponsor different types of retirement plans under the Code?
	Why did the Supreme Court opine in the recent case involving church plans? Was there a split in the circuits?
	What types of failures may cause a plan to become disqualified?
	How can an employer avoid disqualification of a plan?
	What are the requirements for a written plan document?
	What is the difference between a preapproved plan document and an individually designed plan document? What types of employers favor each type?

Overview

What types of employer-sponsored retirement plans are there?

- qualified retirement plans, as described in Internal Revenue Code (I.R.C.) § 401(a), which is the major focus of Section II of this text
- qualified annuity plans, as described in I.R.C. § 403(b)
- other employer-purchased annuity plans, as described in I.R.C. § 403(a)
- eligible deferred compensation plans, as described in I.R.C. § 457(b)
- non-eligible deferred compensation plans, as described in I.R.C. § 457(f)

What types of employers cannot deliver retirement benefits through a qualified retirement plan?

- governmental employers
- church employers
- public schools
- non-profit corporations

What is a governmental employer?

- the actual federal, state, or local government unit that employs individuals
- it then also includes political subdivisions which, based on facts and circumstances, are under the control of elected officials and statutes or ordinances (like local fire departments or transit agencies)

What type of retirement plans can a governmental employer sponsor for its workforce?

- eligible deferred compensation plans, as described in I.R.C. § 457(b)
- non-eligible deferred compensation plans, as described in I.R.C. § 457(f)

What is a church employer?

- a church or covenant
- a convention or association of churches
- also includes related trades or businesses which, based on facts and circumstances, are under the control of the church (like a church-run hospital)

What types of retirement plans can a church employer sponsor for its workforce?

- qualified annuity plans, as described in I.R.C. § 403(b)
- other employer-purchased annuity plans, as described in I.R.C. § 403(a)
- eligible deferred compensation plans, as described in I.R.C. § 457(b)
- non-eligible deferred compensation plans, as described in I.R.C. § 457(f)
- qualified retirement plans, as described in I.R.C. § 401(a), but only if the church makes a certain election

What is a public school?

- an educational organization which normally maintains a regular faculty and curriculum and normally has a regularly enrolled body of pupils or students in attendance at the place where its educational activities are regularly carried on

What type of retirement plans can a public school sponsor for its workforce?

- qualified annuity plans, as described in I.R.C. § 403(b)

What is a non-profit organization or charity?

- one that is approved by the IRS and exempt from income tax under I.R.C. § 501(c)(3)

What type of retirement plans can a non-profit organization or charity sponsor for its workforce?

- qualified annuity plans, as described in I.R.C. §403(b)
- eligible deferred compensation plans, as described in I.R.C. §457(b)

What are the requirements for a retirement plan to be considered a qualified retirement plan?

- there are a variety of requirements at I.R.C. §401(a)
- the most important ones include:
  - the plan must be for the exclusive purpose of providing retirement benefits to plan participants and their beneficiaries
  - the plan must benefit at least a certain number of lower-paid employees (but not necessarily all of them)
  - the benefits, rights, and features of the plan cannot discriminate in favor of the higher-paid employees
  - the plan must provide minimum vesting and accruals
  - regardless of whether the individual wants it or not, the plan must generally start paying retirement benefits to individuals once they attain age 70½ (recently changed to age 72)
  - the plan can cover self-employed individuals, but must use earned income to determine benefits rather than salary
  - the plan must not favor high-paid owners and officers
  - if the participant is married, then certain death benefits must go to the spouse unless the spouse waives the rights to those benefits
  - the retirement benefits for any individual may not be alienated from the plan to pay any of the individual's creditors or the employer's creditors
  - unless the participant consents otherwise, payments from the plan must start at the latest of the normal retirement age, 10 years of plan participation, or termination of employment
  - the plan must limit benefits and contributions, and must limit the compensation used to determine plan benefits

How can a retirement plan lose its qualified income tax status?

- an improper type of employer sponsors a §401(a) qualified plan
- the written plan document does not comply with the laws
- the written plan document complies with the laws, but the plan is not operated and administered in accordance with its terms
- the plan demographics change, and it violates the minimum coverage, nondiscrimination, or other annual tests

How can a plan avoid disqualification?

- The IRS allows three methods:

- ◦ self-correction of insignificant operational failures, which requires no fees to the IRS and no IRS approval;
- ◦ voluntary-correction of significant operational failures or other failures requiring a plan amendment, which requires fees paid to the IRS and their approval of the correction methodology; or
- ◦ audit-cap, which requires higher fees and penalties since the error was discovered

What are the income tax advantages of qualified retirement plans for employers?

- • if all the rules are complied with, then within certain limits, the amount deposited in any year to fund the qualified retirement plan can be deducted on the employer's corporate income tax return (or business reporting form if the business is a pass-through entity, like a partnership, S corporation, or LLC)

What are the income tax advantages of qualified retirement plans for employees?

- • if all the rules are complied with, then the retirement benefits promised by the employer are not included in the individual's gross income until the year they are actually paid

What issues does an employer need to be concerned with when drafting a qualified retirement plan document?

- • the law is frequently changed by Congress, as are its enforcement guidance by federal agencies and interpretations by federal courts
- • therefore, plan documents need to be amended from time to time to remain in compliance
- • generally, there is a remedial amendment period (RAP) which Congress allows between the time the law changes and the need for the plan document to be amended (even though the plan must operate in accordance with the new law during that RAP)

What is a master and prototype plan or a volume submitter plan document (now called a Preapproved plan)?

- • a bank or financial institution, or a law firm, prepares a basic plan document for any employer that chooses to invest the plan assets with them
- • they provide very little flexibility in plan design
- • while the employer might receive some level of legal advice, many things the law allows cannot be incorporated into the plan because that might cause it to be materially modified

What is an individually designed plan document?

- • either an attorney affirmatively drafts a document to include all the business goals and desires for that specific employer, or a preapproved plan document is amended so much that it loses its umbrella protection
- • the high level of attention and legal advice comes at the price of paying attorneys at their hourly billable rates

When can a plan document be amended?

- generally, any future promises that have not accrued (*see* Chapter 7) can be reduced or eliminated

- for minimum funding purposes (*see* Chapter 10), an amendment adopted within 2½ months of the plan year end can have a retroactive effect to the first day of the plan year at issue but cannot reduce benefits already accrued

Why does a qualified retirement plan also need a separate trust document?

- one of the requirements of a qualified plan is that all plan assets are segregated into a separate tax-exempt trust that is not part of the employer's general assets

- the trust provisions can either be part of a separate legal document or can constitute a stand-alone document

A. Retirement Plans Sponsored by Type of Employer

1. How Not-for-Profit Employers Deliver Retirement Benefits to Employees

While Section I of this textbook discusses "qualified retirement plans," there are also other types of retirement plans that are not qualified but nevertheless extend income tax advantages to employees if they comply with various sections of the Code, even though the employer does not need a tax deduction. The term "qualified retirement plan" refers to a profit sharing or pension plan that satisfies the applicable qualification rules set forth in I.R.C. §401(a). For-profit businesses can sponsor a qualified retirement plan, whereas other types of employers (e.g., government employers, church employers, public schools, and other non-profit and charitable organizations) will sponsor other types of retirement plans that are not qualified.

a. Governmental Employers

A governmental employer extends tax preferential retirement benefits pursuant to I.R.C. §457(b) (an eligible deferred compensation plan) or I.R.C. §457(f) (non-eligible deferred compensation plan). Generally, these plans are not governed by either Title I or IV of ERISA.[1] A governmental plan is defined in both I.R.C. §414(d) and ERISA §3(32) as "a plan established or maintained for its employees by the Government of the United States, by the government of any State or political subdivision thereof, or by any agency or instrumentality of any of the foregoing ... [and also] includes a plan which is established or maintained by an Indian tribal government..., a subdivision of an Indian tribal government..., or an agency or instrumentality of either, and all of the participants of which are employees of such entity substantially

---

1. ERISA §4(b)(1).

all of whose services as such an employee are in the performance of essential governmental functions but not in the performance of commercial activities (whether or not an essential government function)."[2]

As the IRS, DOL, and PBGC share almost identical definitions of the term "governmental plan," these agencies have historically tried to coordinate their rulings and opinion letters to achieve some level of uniformity among governmental plan determinations. Due to the agencies' perception that there was a growing number of requests for governmental plan determinations from plan sponsors (especially if their relationship to the government entity was remote), the IRS, in consultation with the DOL and PBGC, issued two advance notices of proposed rulemaking in 2011 relating to the determination of "governmental plan" under I.R.C. §414(d).[3] These have yet to be finalized. They illustrate the difficulty in determining whether an activity is a governmental or commercial activity (e.g., operations involving a hotel, casino, or marina) for purposes of covering employees, as their services must involve the performance of essential governmental functions and not commercial activities.

Governmental employers may offer eligible deferred compensation as defined under I.R.C. §457(b) which require:

- Only individuals who perform services for the employer may become participants;

- There is a maximum dollar amount which may be deferred under the plan for the taxable year that may not exceed an applicable dollar amount or 100% of the participant's compensation;

- Compensation may be deferred for any calendar month only if the deferral agreement has been entered into before the beginning of such month;

- Distributions from the plan may not be available earlier than the calendar year in which the participant attains age 70½, when the participant severs employment with the employer, or when the participant is faced with an unforeseeable emergency; and

- All amounts deferred under the plan, including income on such amounts, remain solely the property and right of the employer, subject only to the claims of the employer's general credits, until they are made available to the participant or beneficiary.[4]

For plans that fail to comply with the requirements of I.R.C. §457(b), the governmental employer will be deemed to be offering a non-eligible plan, which according to the terms of I.R.C. §457(f) results in the participants under the plan being taxed on compensation and retirement benefits in the year in which there is no longer a substantial risk of forfeiture, instead of the year in which the benefits are actually

---

2. I.R.C. §414(d) and ERISA §3(32).
3. ANPRM REG-157714-06 (filed Nov. 7, 2011). relating to governmental plans generally, and ANPRM REG-133223-08 (filed Nov. 7, 2011), relating to Indian tribal government plans.
4. I.R.C. §457(b)(1)–(6), §457(d).

distributed from the plan.[5] There are numerous exceptions under the rules of I.R.C. § 457(f)(2), one of which applies to "employment retention plans" that permits local educational agencies or education associations to retain or reward employees for their service.[6]

b. Church Employers

The Code allows church employers to provide tax preferential retirement benefits to their employees pursuant to I.R.C. § 403(b) or § 457(b), or if they make a special election, a qualified plan pursuant to I.R.C. § 401(a). ERISA exempts church plans with respect to which no election under I.R.C. § 410(d) has been made from Title I. A church plan is defined as "a plan established or maintained ... for its employees (or their beneficiaries) by a church or by a convention or association of churches which is exempt from tax under section 501."[7] It does not include plans established or maintained primarily for the benefit of employees (or their beneficiaries) of such church or convention or association of churches who are employed in connection with one or more unrelated trades or businesses.[8] Six years after ERISA was passed, it amended the definition of church plan to cover "a plan established and maintained ... by a church or by a convention or association of churches includ[ing] *a plan maintained by an organization, whether a civil law corporation or otherwise, the principal purpose or function of which is the administration or funding of a plan or program for the provision of retirement benefits or welfare benefits, or both,* for employees of a church or a convention or association of churches, if such organization is controlled by or associated with a church or a convention or association of churches,"[9] referred to by the courts as "principal-purpose organizations."

In recent years, there has been considerable litigation whereby employees in federal lawsuits are suing large healthcare companies which claim their pension plans are "church plans" and therefore exempt from ERISA.[10] These healthcare companies are non-profit corporations that are religiously affiliated with a church but themselves are not churches. In 2017, the Supreme Court in *Advocate Health Care Network v. Stapleton,* held that a special type of "church plan" was exempt from Title I even though it was not "established" by a church or a convention or association of churches.[11] According to the Court, a plan maintained by a principal-purpose organization as defined in ERISA § 3(33)(C)(i) qualifies as a "church plan," regardless

---

5. I.R.C. § 457(f)(1).

6. I.R.C. § 457(f)(4).

7. I.R.C. § 414(e)(1). ERISA § 3(33)(A) defines a "church plan" as a plan established or maintained ... for its employees (or their beneficiaries) by a church or by a convention of association of churches which is exempt from tax under I.R.C. § 501.

8. I.R.C. § 414(e)(2).

9. ERISA § 3(33)(C)(i) (emphasis added).

10. *See Church Plan ERISA Litigation Resource Center,* KELLER ROHRBACK L.L.P., https://krcomplexlit.com/church-plans-erisa-litigation/.

11. Advocate Health Care Network v. Stapleton, 137 S. Ct. 1652, 1658 (2017).

of who established it.[12] There are several unanswered questions in the opinion, including what is necessary for an organization to "maintain" such a church plan.

Read the case of *Advocate Health Care Network v. Stapleton* in the Materials section of this chapter to discern how the courts determine whether an employer is eligible to maintain a church plan for purposes of ERISA's exemption.

c. Public Schools

Public school employers generally can provide retirement benefits pursuant to I.R.C. § 403(b) plans. These plans are subject to ERISA, as there is no exemption, particularly if the employer makes contributions. Under the Code, a public school is "an educational organization which normally maintains a regular faculty and curriculum and normally has a regularly enrolled body of pupils or students in attendance at the place where its educational activities are regularly carried on."[13] There are three types of funding arrangements to which I.R.C. § 403(b) apply: annuity contracts issued by an insurance company, custodial accounts invested solely in mutual funds, and retirement income accounts (for church employees and certain ministers).[14] The requirements of I.R.C. § 403(b) necessitate the annuity plan to include the following:

- The employee's rights under the contract must be nonforfeitable (except for failure to pay future premiums), regardless of the type of contribution used to buy the plan;[15]

- Any contracts purchased under a salary reduction agreement must fulfill the requirements that relate to limitations on elective salary deferrals;[16]

- All contributions under the plan are expressed as annual additions, limited by I.R.C. § 415;[17]

- All 403(b) contracts purchased on behalf of an individual by an employer are treated as purchased under a single contract;[18]

- All elective deferrals permitted under the contract must be available to all employees on a nondiscriminatory basis (i.e., the universal availability rule, which means all other public school employees must be eligible to make elective salary deferrals);[19] and

- All 403(b) contracts satisfy the minimum distribution requirements, the incidental benefit requirements, and the rollover distribution rules.[20]

---

12. *Id.*
13. I.R.C. § 170(b)(1)(A)(ii).
14. I.R.C. § 403(b).
15. I.R.C. § 403(b)(1)(C).
16. I.R.C. § 403(b)(1)(E).
17. I.R.C. § 403(b)(1).
18. I.R.C. § 403(b)(5).
19. I.R.C. § 403(b)(12).
20. I.R.C. § 403(b)(10).

d. Non-Profit Organizations and Charities

For tax purposes, non-profit and charitable organizations (defined by I.R.C. §501(c)(3)) may offer tax preferential retirement benefits through I.R.C. §403(b) or I.R.C. §457(b) plans. They are subject to ERISA as there is no given exemption.

2. How For-Profit Employers Deliver Retirement Savings

a. Fundamental Requirements of a Qualified Plan

For-profit employers may take advantage of the tax preferential savings of a retirement plan only if the plan satisfies the qualification rules of I.R.C. §401(a) and if the trust that holds the plan assets satisfies the tax exempt rules of I.R.C. §501(a). As such, the employer will be able to take an immediate deduction for contributions it makes to the plan, and employees may defer taxation on those contributions, and their interest, until actual distribution. There are four fundamental requirements of qualification. First, the plan must be established by the employer even if all the contributions are being made by the employees.[21] Thus, employees on their own cannot establish a qualified plan; employees without an employer-provided plan only have the use of an individual retirement account (IRA) for tax-deferred retirement savings.[22]   Second, the plan must be for the exclusive benefit of the employees of the employer and/or their beneficiaries.[23] This requirement does not prevent an employer from receiving incidental benefits from the plan (e.g., good will, enhanced productivity by employees). However, this standard serves as the litmus test as to whether an employer's action or conduct is for the exclusive benefit of the employees covered under the plan or for the employer's benefit.[24] Qualified plans are permitted to benefit beneficiaries as well as employees. For this purpose, a "beneficiary" of an employee may include the employee's estate, spouse, or dependents of the employee, persons who are the natural object of the employee's bounty, and any person designated by the employee to share in benefits after the death of the employee.[25] An employer may not be the beneficiary, as this would violate the exclusive benefit rule.

Third, the plan must be established with the intent that it is to be permanent.[26] Although the employer may reserve the right to change or terminate the plan, or to discontinue contributions, abandonment of the plan for any reason other than business necessity within a few years after its inception will not be regarded as a bona

---

21. I.R.C. §401(a)(1); Treas. Reg. §1.401-1(a)(2).

22. For 2020, the maximum IRA dollar amount is $6,000, in contrast with the maximum defined contribution dollar amount of $57,000. Thus, qualified retirement plans allow for greater deferrals than IRAs.

23. I.R.C. §401(a)(2); Treas. Reg. §1.401.-1(b)(3)(ii). *See also* ERISA §403(c).

24. See Donovan v. Bierwirth, 680 F.2d 263 (2d Cir. 1982), *cert. denied*, 459 U.S. 1069 (1982), where the Second Circuit affirmed the incidental benefit to the fiduciary on account of his or her action provided the action was prudent and made in the best interests of the plan participants and beneficiaries.

25. Treas. Reg. §1.401-1(b)(4).

26. Treas. Reg. §1.401-1(b)(2).

fide program for the exclusive benefit of employees.[27] The IRS uses a facts and circumstances test in determining the permanency requirement; for example, legitimate business reasons such as bankruptcy, discontinuance of the business, sale of the business, or financial difficulties are sufficient.

Finally, as qualified plan assets are premised on the assumption such assets will be used for employees' retirement savings, any reversion of such plan assets to the employer is severely limited.[28] Assets of a qualified plan must be held either in a trust or an annuity contract. Both instruments must prohibit the diversion of plan assets for purposes other than the exclusive benefit of the employees or beneficiaries. Limited exceptions to this general rule are permitted. In the trust context, these exceptions include:

- Employer contributions that are contingent upon the plan's initial qualification may be returned to the employer if the newly established plan fails to meet the qualification requirements and the employer is not willing to amend the plan to comply;[29]

- Employer contributions that were contingent upon deductibility under I.R.C. § 404(a) but later denied full deduction may be returned;[30] and

- Employer contributions made due to a mistake of fact may be returned.[31]

Return on employer contributions must be made within one year of the mistaken contribution, denial of qualification, or disallowance of the deduction. But earnings attributable to the amounts returned are not returnable, while investment losses of the plan assets must be allocated on the amounts returned on a pro rata basis.[32]

There is a fourth exception limited to certain defined benefit plans. The Code permits a reversion of plan assets upon a plan termination provided all liabilities with respect to the employees and their beneficiaries have been satisfied.[33] As a result, surplus assets due to "actuarial error" (meaning that the actuary's assumptions were too conservative) may be returned to the employer.

b. Formal Requirements for Plan Qualification

The Plan Must Be in Effect: This rule requires that the plan be formally adopted by the employer and that any trust instruments be executed by the end of the employer's tax year for which the deduction is claimed.[34] A corporation acts through its board of

---

27. Id.

28. Treas. Reg. § 1.401-2(a)(1), requiring the terms of the trust instrument to make it impossible to divert plan assets before the satisfaction of all liabilities to the employees or their beneficiaries from the plan.

29. ERISA § 403(c)(2)(B); Rev. Rul. 60-276.

30. ERISA § 403(c)(2)(C).

31. Examples of a mistake of fact leading to an overcontributed amount include a misplaced decimal point, an incorrectly written check, or an error in doing a calculation. Priv. Ltr. Rul. 91-44-041.

32. ERISA § 403(c)(2)(A)(ii).

33. I.R.C. § 401(a)(2).

34. I.R.C. § 404(a)(1). There is an excise tax applicable to the reversion.

directors and thus, a formal board resolution would have to exist establishing the plan. As to the execution of the trust, the tax year in which it is executed will determine the tax year for which the employer can claim the deduction. For example, if the employer is a calendar year taxpayer, it will need to execute the trust instrument by December 31, 2020, to claim a 2020 deduction on its return. If it executes the document on January 1, 2021, the deduction cannot be claimed until the 2021 return.

This rule also assumes that the plan and trust documents were in total compliance to conform with the Code's qualification rules. Due to the complexity of the qualification rules, employers are permitted, but not required, to request a determination letter from the IRS regarding the form of the plan and trust documents. To the extent plan amendments may be necessary to bring the plan into formal compliance, the Code provides a retroactive remedial amendment period for those plans that take advantage of the determination letter process.

If a trust is used, the trust document may be a separate document or consolidated with the plan as a single document. If it is a separate document, it must, on its face, prohibit the diversion of plan assets as discussed previously. Since the plan and trust exist concurrently, the trust must be executed at the same time as the plan document.[35] The trust must be recognized as valid under local trust law. In order to be valid, all state trust laws require that there be:

- Property, which is subject to the trust;
- Trustee(s) who so qualify under state law; and
- Beneficiaries of the trust.

The Service permits the use of a trust without corpus as long as the initial contribution is made by the due date for filing the employer's tax return.[36] Custodial accounts may be used if they satisfy the qualification requirements of I.R.C. § 401(a), and the trustee is either a bank or a person who has received IRS approval. Annuity contracts issued by an insurance company may be used by a plan in lieu of a trust.

Written Document: In order to be qualified, a plan must be documented as a formal written plan.[37] ERISA also requires every employee benefit plan to be written and to spell out the following terms: procedure for implementing the plan's funding policy, including any procedures for allocating fiduciary responsibilities; plan procedures for allocating administrative duties; and a procedure for amending the plan and identifying who may amend the plan, and the basis on which benefits are distributed from the plan.[38]

---

35. *But see* Dejay Stores, Inc. v. Ryan, 229 F.2d 867 (2d Cir. 1956) (holding there is no need to execute the trust document before the close of the tax year).

36. Rev. Rul. 81-114.

37. ERISA § 403(a); Treas. Reg. § 1.401-1(a)(2).

38. ERISA §§ 402(b), 403, respectively. *See also* Curtiss-Wright Corp. v. Schoonejongen, 514 U.S. 73 (1995) (a seminal case in determining whether a plan document's amendment language was sufficient to comply with ERISA § 402(b)(3)).

Communicated to Employees: The qualification of the plan is dependent upon it being communicated to the employees.[39] Thus, a timely communication is important in the first year of the plan's establishment.[40] A copy of the plan or notice of its salient features (given by written communication to each employee or company bulletin board) constitutes sufficient communication.[41] Note that such communication can be limited to covered employees only.[42] ERISA requires a summary plan description (SPD) to be furnished to participants (not all employees) within the later of 120 days after the plan is established or 90 days after an individual becomes a participant.[43] Updated plan descriptions must also be provided to participants every five years where there have been plan amendments, or every 10 years if there were no plan changes. Also, notice of material modifications to the plan must be made within 210 days after the end of any plan year in which a material change occurs. Documents must be made available for examination by participants or beneficiaries at the principal office of the plan administrator and other such places as are necessary to provide reasonable access.

c. Substantive Qualification Requirements of I.R.C. § 401(a)

I.R.C. § 401(a) provides the overall outline of the substantive requirements applicable to all qualified plans — some may be applicable to a given type of plan (e.g., defined benefit plans), others may not be applicable. Some of the qualification rules are summarized within the subparagraphs of I.R.C. § 401(a), whereas other rules are cross-referenced to other Code sections within the 400 series.

A basic breakdown of I.R.C. § 401(a) provisions is as follows:

I.R.C. § 401(a)(3):

A plan that restricts participation based on age, service, or other criteria must satisfy minimum participation standards as set forth in I.R.C. § 410. Section 401(a)(6) requires a plan to satisfy the coverage standards on one day in each quarter of the plan year.

I.R.C. §§ 401(a)(4)–(5):

Contributions to or benefits under the plan must not discriminate in favor of highly compensated employees within the meaning of I.R.C. § 414(q). Contributions or benefits that are integrated with Social Security contributions or benefits are subject to special nondiscrimination rules, known as permitted disparity rules.

I.R.C. § 401(a)(7):

A plan that imposes vesting requirements must satisfy minimum vesting standards as set forth in I.R.C. § 411. Defined benefit plans must comply with minimum accrual standards as set forth in section 411(b) of the Code.

---

39. Treas. Reg. § 1.401-1(a)(2).
40. Rev. Rul. 72-509.
41. Rev. Rul. 71-90.
42. Rev. Rul. 73-78.
43. *See* ERISA § 102(b) for required contents of the summary plan description.

I.R.C. § 401(a)(8):

A defined benefit plan may not provide that forfeitures be applied to increase the benefits an employee would otherwise receive under the plan.

I.R.C. § 401(a)(9):

A plan must meet required distribution standards concerning the commencement of benefit distributions by April 1 of the calendar year following the calendar year in which the employee reaches age 70½ (now age 72) or retirement (but note that 5% owners are not given the benefit of a later retirement age).

I.R.C. § 401(a)(10):

A plan which is or may become "top heavy" must satisfy additional requirements as set forth in § 416, concerning vesting, minimum contribution or benefits and adjustments to the § 415 limits.

I.R.C. § 401(a)(11):

A plan which provides for the payment of benefits in the form of an annuity must also provide for the payment of benefits in the form of a qualified joint and survivor annuity (QJSA). If a plan provides for the payment of benefits before normal retirement age in the form of a life annuity, it must permit each participant to elect to have a benefit in the form of a life annuity payable to the participant's spouse in the event the participant dies in active service with the employer after the attainment of the qualified early retirement age and prior to the attainment of normal retirement age (QPSA). These are referred to as the QJSA rules and the QPSA rules.

I.R.C. § 401(a)(12):

A plan must provide that on merger or consolidation of a plan, each participant shall be entitled to a benefit after the merger that is no less than his/her benefit before the merger.

I.R.C. § 401(a)(13):

A plan must provide that benefits under the plan may not be assigned or alienated except in limited circumstances (e.g., qualified domestic relations orders, referred to as "QDROs").

I.R.C. § 401(a)(14):

A plan must provide that benefits shall commence, unless the participant elects otherwise, at the latest of normal retirement age, 10 years of plan participation, or termination of service.

I.R.C. § 401(a)(16):

Benefits under a defined benefit plan must not exceed certain maximum benefit limitations which are defined in terms of maximum dollar limits and percentage of compensation limits. Allocations under a defined contribution plan must not exceed certain maximum contribution limitations which are also defined in terms of maximum dollar limits and percentage of compensation limits. Prior to 2000, there was a combined plan limitation if a participant was covered under both a defined benefit and defined contribution plan maintained by the same employer.

I.R.C. § 401(a)(17):

Compensation for a participant has been limited to $200,000 (as adjusted for inflation after 2002, for example, the limit for 2020 is $285,000) under all provisions of the plan.[44]

I.R.C. § 401(a)(22):

A stock bonus plan must meet the requirements of I.R.C. §§ 409(h) and (o) with certain qualifications.

I.R.C. § 401(a)(25):

A defined benefit plan will not be treated as providing definitely determinable benefits unless actuarial assumptions are set forth in the plan which will be used to determine benefits.

I.R.C. § 401(a)(26):

Additional coverage requirements must be met by defined benefit plans, which require the plan to cover the lesser of 50 employees or 40% of all employees.

I.R.C. § 401(a)(29):

A defined benefit plan must restrict the level and distribution of benefits in accordance with the rules of I.R.C. § 436.

I.R.C. § 411(b)(3):

A plan must provide that upon termination and in certain cases, on a discontinuance of contributions, the rights of plan participants shall vest.

d. Plan Disqualification

There are four typical ways in which a retirement plan can become disqualified:

Employer Eligibility Failure: As noted earlier, governmental entities, non-electing church employers, not-for-profit entities, and educational institutions are not permitted to sponsor a 401(a) qualified plan. If they were to sponsor one, the plan would later have to be rendered null and void.

Plan Document Failure: A disqualifying provision (or the absence of a qualifying provision) in a new plan or a plan amendment can cause the plan to become disqualified. That is why the typical employer applies with the IRS for a determination letter so that the IRS has a chance to review the plan's initial terms and approve its qualification. Likewise, if legislative changes mandate plan amendments, employers would then amend their plans and resubmit them for a determination letter. Due to a lack of resources, the IRS discontinued the determination letter program for use

---

44. *See* EGTRRA '01, amending I.R.C. § 401(a)(17), effective 2002 until 2010. For 2020, the maximum dollar compensation limit is $285,000.

by sponsors of individually designed plans on their plan amendments.[45] As will be discussed in Chapter 11, an employer generally has until the end of the remedial amendment period to make plan amendments, provided the plan operates in good faith compliance with the changes.

Operational Failures: Even if the plan document is in compliance with ERISA, it needs to be operated in accordance with its terms. Failure to comply with the plan terms is known as an operational failure. Chapter 11 will discuss the IRS' voluntary compliance program known as Employee Plans Compliance Resolution System (EPCRS) which assures continued and ongoing qualification of plans.

Demographic Failures: A qualified plan may be able to bypass certain nondiscrimination testing by complying with certain safe harbors. If the plan doesn't rely on those safe harbors, it is required to test annually for nondiscrimination, minimum coverage, minimum participation, and top heaviness. Failure to meet these tests is referred to as a demographic failure and can result in the plan's disqualification.

e. Ways to Avoid Disqualification

The Secretary of the Treasury may disqualify a retirement plan, but if it involves a violation of the exclusive benefit rule under I.R.C. § 401(a)(2), it must notify the-DOL.[46] Treasury has delegated its enforcement power to the IRS, which the IRS will utilize either upon its review of a new plan submitted for a determination letter or as a result of a plan audit. The Service may retroactively disqualify a plan for any "open year" (i.e., tax years for which the statute of limitations has not yet run).[47] Generally, the statute of limitations runs three years after the tax return filing date; however, it may be six years after the employer files its return if the exclusion from income exceeds 25% of the total gross income claimed.[48]

When a retirement plan is disqualified, the plan's trust loses its tax-exempt status and becomes a nonexempt trust. The disqualification affects three groups: the employees, the employer, and the plan's trust. Let's use an example to see the impact of plan disqualification:

> P is a participant in the ABC profit sharing plan. The plan calls for immediate vesting of all employer contributions. In calendar year 1, the employer contributes $3,000 to the trust under the plan on P's behalf; in calendar year 2, the employer contributes $4,000 to the trust on P's behalf. In calendar year 2, the IRS disqualifies the plan retroactively to the beginning of calendar year 1.

---

45. *See* Announcement 2015-9, in which the IRS eliminated the staggered five-year remedial amendment cycle for individually designed plans.

46. ERISA Reorganization Plan, § 103; Executive Order No. 12108, 44 Fed. Reg. 1065 (Dec. 28, 1978), which affords the DOL the opportunity to certify that it has no objection to the disqualification or to fail to respond.

47. I.R.C. § 7805(b).

48. I.R.C. § 6501(a), (e); Treas. Reg. § 301.6501(a)-1, (e)-1.

Consequence 1: The general rule is that the employee must now include employer contributions made to the trust on his or her behalf in the calendar years in which the plan is disqualified to the extent he or she is vested in those contributions.[49] So, in our example, P would have to include $3,000 as income in calendar year 1 and $4,000 as income in calendar 2, as P is fully vested in those contributions. There is an exception to this general rule: if the plan is disqualified for failure to satisfy the minimum coverage tests, then only the highly compensated employee will include any previously untaxed amount of their entire vested account balance in income.[50]

Consequence 2: In contrast to the rules for contributions to a trust under a qualified plan, if the employer contributes to a nonexempt employees' trust, it cannot deduct the contribution until the contribution is includible in the employee's gross.[51] If the employer and employee are both calendar year taxpayers, then the employer's deduction is delayed until the calendar year in which the contribution amount is includible in the employee's gross income. If their tax years are different, the employer cannot take a deduction for its contribution until its first tax year that ends after the last day of the employee's tax year in which the amount in includible in the employee's income. So, in our example, if the employer and P are both calendar year taxpayers, the employer's $3,000 deduction for calendar year 1 and $4,000 in calendar year 2 remain unchanged as P includes those amounts in his or her income for those years. If the employer's tax year ends September 30 and P is a calendar year taxpayer, the employer's contribution is includible in P's income for the tax year that ends on December 31 of year 1, and the employer cannot take a deduction for that contribution until its tax year that ends on September 30 of year 2.

Consequence 3: The Trust Owes Income Tax on the Trust Earnings. The trust for the ABC profit sharing plan is a separate legal entity. Thus, when the plan is disqualified, the trust loses its tax-exempt status and must pay income tax on its trust earnings.[52]

Consequence 4: Rollovers Are Disallowed. A distribution from a disqualified plan is not an eligible rollover distribution and cannot be rolled over to another eligible retirement plan or to an IRA rollover account. When a disqualified plan distributes the benefits, they are subject to taxation.

To encourage plans to correct failures as they arise, the IRS continues to update and revise EPCRS:[53]

Self-Correction Program (SCP): This part of the program allows employers to self-correct significant operational failures within a two-year window period; insignificant operational failures may be cured within any time period. It also provides limited

---

49. I.R.C. §402(b)(1).

50. I.R.C. §402(b)(4) (the grounds for disqualification must be either failure to meet the minimum participation rule of I.R.C. §401(a)(26) or the minimum coverage rules of I.R.C. §401(b)).

51. I.R.C. §404(a)(5).

52. *See* Rev. 74-299, as amplified by Rev. Rul. 2007-48 (noting that the trust must file Form 1041).

53. The current revenue procedure outlining EPCRS is Rev. Proc. 2019-19. For a description of the rules under this revenue procedure, see Kathryn J. Kennedy, *A Current Update of EPCRS Through Rev. Proc. 2019-19*, 47 Tax Mgmt. Comp. Planning J. 12 (Dec. 6, 2019).

use of correction for operational failures that require retroactive plan amendments to conform the terms of the plan to its prior operations. There is no IRS compliance fee assessed in SCP. The cost of correction is the cost it takes to apply the corrective method to the affected participants and beneficiaries.

Voluntary Correction Program (VCP): This part of the program allows employers to correct plan document failures, demographic failures, employer eligibility failures, and significant operational failures that were not cured within the two-year window. There is a modest fee assessed by the IRS for correction. There are special rules applicable for anonymous (John Doe) and group submissions.

Correction on Audit (Audit CAP): This last part of the program allows employers to correct disqualifying defects that are found once the plan is "under examination" by an IRS agent. All types of qualification failures may be cured (except defects relating to the misuse or diversion of plan assets and abusive tax avoidance transactions (ATATs)). There is a sanction imposed equal to a percentage of the maximum payment amount that the IRS could assess if the plan were disqualified.

With the passage of PPA '06, Congress affirmed the Secretary of the Treasury's authority and power to establish and implement the EPCRS program, as well as any other employee plans correction programs, including the power to waive income, excise, and other taxes.[54] Thus, the IRS continues to expand EPCRS.

3. Multiemployer Plans

A multiemployer plan refers to a plan in which more than one unrelated employer is required to contribute, as it is maintained pursuant to a collective bargaining agreement. Such plans exist as the union worker may work for multiple employers during his or her career. For example, employers employing union workers of Local 101 of the Plumber's Union will all contribute fixed contributions (e.g. $2.10 per hour worked by the union member) to a multiemployer plan. As these plans are generally defined benefit plans, if the plan were to terminate unfunded (e.g., assets are insufficient to cover liabilities), Title IV of ERISA does not wish to penalize only the employers participating in the plan at the time of plan termination. Thus, under the rules of Title IV, when an employer withdraws from an ongoing multiemployer plan that is not fully funded, a withdrawal liability may be assessed against that employer.[55]

4. Single-Employer Plans

A single-employer plan is one that has been created and maintained by a single employer or by multiple employers who are *related to one another* (e.g., parent corporation and a subsidiary corporation). For example, parent corporation P and its subsidiary corporation S jointly adopt the same qualified defined contribution plan.

---

54. PPA '06 § 1101.
55. ERISA § 4201.

The plan is regarded as a single-employer plan even though there are two participating employers.

5. Multiple-Employer Plans

A multiple-employer retirement plan (referred to as a MEP) is a plan maintained by one or more employers that is not a multiemployer plan and is not a single-employer plan.[56] For purposes of ERISA, the term "employer" means "any person acting directly as an employer, or indirectly in the interest of an employer, in relation to an employee benefit plan; and includes a group or association of employers acting for an employer in such capacity."[57] As ERISA did not explain what it meant for an entity to act "directly as an employer," or act "indirectly in the interest of an employer," or what is a "group or association of employers," the courts have grabbled with trying to interpret such phrases.[58] The DOL's long-standing position distinguishes between two types of MEPs—one that is a single ERISA plan and one that is not:

- A closed MEP (i.e., a single plan) must meet certain DOL criteria whereby members of a "bona fide association" could establish and maintain a single ERISA plan (with a single Form 5500, a single audit and one bond).[59] Under these criteria, the DOL required the group or association to have a sufficiently close economic or representational nexus to the employers and employees unrelated to the provision of benefits (referred to as commonality).[60] Due to the criteria necessary to meet a "bona fide association," not many groups qualified as an employer to sponsor a closed MEP.

- An open MEP (i.e., a multiple plan), sometimes referred to as a pooled employer plan (PEP), allowed multiple employers to join together and establish and maintain a plan, regardless of whether they had any nexus with the other employers (i.e., without any commonality), but this was not considered by the DOL to be a single ERISA plan, and thus *each* employer had to satisfy ERISA reporting, audit, and bonding requirements.

As a result of President Trump's Executive Order 13847 to expand circumstances in which small- and mid-size business could sponsor an association retirement plan (ARP) so as to reduce administrative costs through economies of scale and strengthen their negotiating power with financial institutions and other service providers, the DOL issued a final regulation in 2019 expanding access to more groups to form a

---

56. Instructions to 2019 IRS Form 5500, Line A—Box for Multiple-Employer Plans.

57. ERISA § 3(5).

58. *See* Meredith v. Time Ins. Co., 980 F.2d 352, 356 (5th Cir. 1993); Mass. Laborers' Health & Welfare Fund v. Starrett Paving Corp., 845 F.2d 23, 24 (1st Cir. 1988); MD Physicians & Assocs. v. State Bd. of Ind., 957 F.2d 178, 184 (5th Cir. 1992).

59. DOL Adv. Op. 20008-07A; DOL Adv. Op. 2003-17A; DOL Adv. Op. 2001-04A.

60. DOL Adv. Op. 2012-04A; DOL Adv. Op. 1983-21A; DOL Adv. Op. 1983-15A; DOL Adv. Op. 1981-44A.

closed MEP.[61] The SECURE Act went beyond these rules to encourage open MEPs (now called pooled employer plans or PEPs) by allowing them to be treated as a single ERISA Plan.[62] Such PEPs can be sponsored by a service provider (e.g., third party administrator or financial service company). To maintain qualification under the Code and to be regarded as a single ERISA plan, the PEP must be run by a pooled plan provider (PPP) who is identified as the named fiduciary in the plan document, the PPP must acknowledge its fiduciary status in writing, specific rules must be set forth for allocating responsibilities in the plan document, and the participating employers must retain a fiduciary duty to monitor the PPP and for decisions regarding investment options.[63] The qualification rules now provide that one employer's qualification problem will not lead to the disqualification of the entire PEP.

B. Income Tax Advantages of Retirement Plans

1. For Employers

Generally, for-profit employers receive a deduction under I.R.C. § 162 against gross income for ordinary and necessary expenses paid or incurred during its tax year in carrying on a trade or business, including a reasonable allowance for salaries, traveling expenses while away from home in pursuit of a trade or business, and rentals and other payments made as a condition to the continued use of property.[64] If part of an employee's salary is contributed to a qualified retirement plan, then the employer contribution must meet the specific rules of I.R.C. § 404(s) in order to deduct such contributions. Not-for-profit entities such as churches, governmental employers, public schools, or charitable organizations do not pay income taxes and thus a deduction is not necessary.

2. For Employees

Contributions by a for-profit employer to a qualified retirement plan are excluded from the gross income of the employee for the tax year for which they are contributed; instead they will be includable in the employee's or beneficiary's gross income in the year they are distributed.[65] Contributions by a public school or charitable organization to a compliant I.R.C. § 403(b) annuity plan are excluded from the gross income of the employee for the tax year for which they are contributed, and taxable when dis-

---

61. Labor Reg. § 2510.3-55 (July 31, 2019), effective September 30, 2019. As a result, groups such as local chambers of commerce, members of the same trade or line of business, professional employer associations, and businesses in the same state or city can form closed MEPs.

62. SECURE § 101.

63. *Id.*, effective for plan years beginning after December 31, 2020.

64. I.R.C. § 162(a).

65. I.R.C. § 402(a).

tributed.[66] Contributions by a state or local entity or a tax-exempt organization to an I.R.C. §457(b) eligible deferred compensation plan are similarly excluded from the employee's gross income and taxable upon distribution.[67]

C. Choices of Written Retirement Plan Documents

1. Types of Written Plan Documents for Qualified Plans

I.R.C. §401(b) requires the qualified retirement plan to be in writing, and the terms of the plan must be in compliance with all applicable federal laws. In addition, ERISA §402(a) requires every employee benefit plan to be established and maintained pursuant to a written instrument, which provides for one or more named fiduciaries who are responsible for controlling and managing the operation and administration of the plan. ERISA §402(b) outlines the provisions that must be in every plan document:

- A procedure for establishing and carrying out a funding policy (i.e., how the employer is going to pay for the benefits);
- A procedure for allocating responsibilities for the operation and administration of the plan;
- A procedure for amending the plan, including the persons who are authorized to amend the plan; and
- The basis on which payments are made to and from the plan.

ERISA §402(c) outlines optional provisions for a plan document:

- A provision that any person or group of persons may serve in more than one fiduciary capacity with respect to the plan (e.g., an entity may be both plan trustee and plan administrator);
- A provision that allows a named fiduciary to employ persons to render advice with regard to his or her responsibilities under the plan (e.g., the employer as fiduciary may employ a plan administrator); and
- A provision that allows a named fiduciary to appoint an investment manager to manage plan assets.

There are two ways for an employer to satisfy the written plan document requirement: preapproved plans and individually designed plans. Small and medium-size employers utilize a standardized master or prototype plan or a volume submitter

---

66. I.R.C. §403(b)(1)(E).
67. I.R.C. §457(a).

plan, which the IRS now simply refers to as preapproved plans.[68] These are generally sold through financial institutions, stock brokerage firms, or insurance companies, which are responsible for the initial drafting of the documents and for making timely amendments. A preapproved plan consists of two documents—the prototype plan document and an adoption agreement. The prototype plan document contains the provisions of the plan applicable to all adopting employers, which comply with the requirements of I.R.C. §401(a). The adoption agreement provides choices for the employer regarding various plan design features (e.g., which vesting schedule to choose from, eligibility requirements). The financial institution will also provide the employer copies of these documents, along with applicable summary plan descriptions. A master plan provides a single funding medium for all adopting employers, whereas a prototype plan provides a separate funding medium for each adopting employer.

The institution will approach the IRS for a determination letter on a given preapproved plan. If the IRS affirms that the terms of the plan satisfy the requirements of I.R.C. §401(a), it will issue an opinion letter to the institutional sponsor. The institution will then relay a copy of the opinion letter to each adopting employer for reliance. The institution is then responsible to make timely plan amendments to keep the preapproved plan in compliance.

In contrast, large employers utilize an individually designed plan which is unique to the employer. These plans are drafted and timely amended by the employer's inhouse or outside counsel. These plans have individually designed summary plan descriptions, outlining the terms of the plan. The attorney responsible for drafting the document is generally the individual who approaches the IRS for a determination letter on the plan. These plans entail specific legal services inherent in drafting a customized plan document and thus are generally not used by small- and medium-size employers.

2. Establishment of a Trust Document

As noted earlier, retirement assets associated with a qualified plan must be held in trust or in insurance policies. While the plan document lists the plan features such as eligibility, vesting schedules, plan benefits, distribution options, etc., if a trust is being used, there will generally be a separate trust document. The trust document spells out the responsibilities of the trustee, powers of delegation, any limitations on the investment of assets, and how benefits are to be distributed by the trustee. This trust is a tax-exempt trust and thus is a separate legal entity that needs a taxpayer identification number (TIN).

Adopters of preapproved master and prototype plans generally utilize the trust document offered by the sponsoring institution.

---

68. Rev. Proc. 2017-41. The term "volume submitter" plan refers to documents prepared by an employee benefits consultant (e.g., an attorney or law firm).

D. Materials
Advocate Health Care Network v. Stapleton
137 S. Ct. 1652 (2017)

Opinion

Judge: Justice KAGAN delivered the opinion of the Court.

The Employee Retirement Income Security Act of 1974 (ERISA) exempts "church plan[s]" from its otherwise-comprehensive regulation of employee benefit plans. 88 Stat. 840, as amended, 29 U.S.C. § 1003(b)(2) Under the statute, certain plans for the employees of churches or church-affiliated nonprofits count as "church plans" even though not actually administered by a church. See § 1002(33)(C)(i). The question presented here is whether a church must have originally *established* such a plan for it to so qualify. ERISA, we hold, does not impose that requirement.

Petitioners identify themselves as three church-affiliated nonprofits that run hospitals and other healthcare facilities (collectively, hospitals). They offer defined-benefit pension plans to their employees. Those plans were established by the hospitals themselves—not by a church—and are managed by internal employee-benefits committees.

ERISA generally obligates private employers offering pension plans to adhere to an array of rules designed to ensure plan solvency and protect plan participants. See generally *New York State Conference of Blue Cross & Blue Shield Plans v. Travelers Ins. Co.*, 514 U.S. 645, 651, 115 S. Ct. 1671, 131 L. Ed. 2d 695 (1995) (cataloguing ERISA's "reporting and disclosure mandates," "participation and vesting requirements," and "funding standards"). But in enacting the statute, Congress made an important exception. "[C]hurch plan[s]" have never had to comply with ERISA's requirements. § 1003(b)(2).

The statutory definition of "church plan" came in two distinct phases. From the beginning, ERISA provided that "[t]he term "church plan" means a plan established and maintained ... for its employees ... by a church or by a convention or association of churches." § 1002(33)(A). Then, in 1980, Congress amended the statute to expand that definition by deeming additional plans to fall within it. The amendment specified that for purposes of the church-plan definition, an "employee of a church" would include an employee of a church-affiliated organization (like the hospitals here). § 1002(33)(C)(ii)(II). And it added the provision whose effect is at issue in these cases:

> A plan established and maintained for its employees ... by a church or by a convention or association of churches includes a plan maintained by an organization ... the principal purpose or function of which is the administration or funding of a plan or program for the provision of retirement benefits or welfare benefits, or both, for the employees of a church or a convention or association of churches, if such organization is controlled by or associated with a church or a convention or association of churches. § 1002(33)(C)(i).

That is a mouthful, for lawyers and non-lawyers alike; to digest it more easily, note that everything after the word "organization" in the third line is just a (long-winded) description of a particular kind of church-associated entity—which this opinion will call a "principal-purpose organization." The main job of such an entity, as the statute explains, is to fund or manage a benefit plan for the employees of churches or (per the 1980 amendment's other part) of church affiliates.

The three federal agencies responsible for administering ERISA have long read those provisions, when taken together, to exempt plans like the hospitals' from the statute's mandates. (The relevant agencies are the Internal Revenue Service, Department of Labor, and Pension Benefit Guaranty Corporation.) The original definitional provision—§ 1002(33)(A), or paragraph (A) for short—defines a "church plan" as one "established and maintained ... by a church"—not by a church-affiliated non-profit. But according to the agencies, the later (block-quoted) provision—§ 1002(33)(C)(i), or just subparagraph (C)(i)—expands that definition to include any plan maintained by a principal-purpose organization, regardless of whether a church initially established the plan. And, the agencies believe, the internal benefits committee of a church-affiliated nonprofit counts as such an organization. See, *e.g.,* IRS General Counsel Memorandum No. 39007 (Nov. 2, 1982), App. 636–637. That interpretation has appeared in hundreds of private letter rulings and opinion letters issued since 1982, including several provided to the hospitals here. See App. 57–69, 379–386, 668–715.

The three cases before us are part of a recent wave of litigation challenging the agencies' view. Respondents, current and former employees of the hospitals, filed class actions alleging that their employers' pension plans do not fall within ERISA's church-plan exemption (and thus must satisfy the statute's requirements). That is so, the employees claim, because those plans were not established by a church—and ERISA, even as amended, demands that all "church plans" have such an origin. According to the employees, the addition of subparagraph (C)(i) allowed principal-purpose organizations to *maintain* such plans in lieu of churches; but that provision kept as-is paragraph (A)'s insistence that churches themselves *establish* "church plans." See *id.,* at 265–268, 435–437, 783–785. The District Courts handling the cases agreed with the employees' position, and therefore held that the hospitals' plans must comply with ERISA.

The Courts of Appeals for the Third, Seventh, and Ninth Circuits affirmed those decisions. The Third Circuit ruled first, concluding that ERISA's "plain text" requires that a pension plan be established by a church to qualify for the church-plan exemption. *Kaplan v. Saint Peter's Healthcare System,* 810 F.3d 175, 177 (2015). In the court's view, paragraph (A) set out "two requirements" for the exemption—"establishment and maintenance"—and "only the latter is expanded by the use of "includes'" in subparagraph (C)(i). *Id.,* at 181. The Seventh and Ninth Circuits relied on similar reasoning to decide in the employees' favor. See *Stapleton v. Advocate Health Care Network,* 817 F.3d 517, 523 (C.A.7 2016); *Rollins v. Dignity Health,* 830 F.3d 900, 906 (C.A.9 2016).

In light of the importance of the issue, this Court granted certiorari. 579 U.S. ___, 137 S. Ct. 546, 547, 196 L. Ed. 2d 442 (2016)

II

The dispute in these cases about what counts as a "church plan" hinges on the combined meaning of paragraph (A) and subparagraph (C)(i). Interpretive purists may refer back as needed to the provisions as quoted above. See *supra,* at 1656–1657. But for those who prefer their statutes in (comparatively) user-friendly form, those provisions go as follows:

> Under paragraph (A), a ""church plan" means a plan established and maintained ... by a church."

> Under subparagraph (C)(i), "[a] plan established and maintained ... by a church ... includes a plan maintained by [a principal-purpose] organization."

The parties agree that under those provisions, a "church plan" need not be maintained by a church; it may instead be maintained by a principal-purpose organization. But the parties differ as to whether a plan maintained by that kind of organization must still have been established by a church to qualify for the church-plan exemption. The hospitals say no: The effect of subparagraph (C)(i) was to bring within the church-plan definition all pension plans maintained by a principal-purpose organization, regardless of who first established them. The employees say yes: Subparagraph (C)(i) altered only the requirement that a pension plan be maintained by a church, while leaving intact the church-establishment condition. We conclude that the hospitals have the better of the argument.

Start, as we always do, with the statutory language—here, a new definitional phrase piggy-backing on the one already existing. The term "church plan," as just stated, initially "mean[t]" only "a plan established and maintained ... by a church." But subparagraph (C)(i) provides that the original definitional phrase will now "include" another—"a plan maintained by [a principal-purpose] organization." That use of the word "include" is not literal—any more than when Congress says something like "a State 'includes' Puerto Rico and the District of Columbia." See, *e.g.,* 29 U.S.C. § 1002(10). Rather, it tells readers that a *different* type of plan should receive the same treatment (*i.e.,* an exemption) as the type described in the old definition. And those newly favored plans, once again, are simply those "maintained by a principal-purpose organization"—irrespective of their origins. In effect, Congress provided that the new phrase can stand in for the old one as follows: "The term "church plan" means a plan established and maintained by a church [a plan maintained by a principal-purpose organization]." The church-establishment condition thus drops out of the picture.

Consider the same point in the form of a simple logic problem, with paragraph (A) and subparagraph (C)(i) as its first two steps:

Premise 1: A plan established and maintained by a church is an exempt church plan.

Premise 2: A plan established and maintained by a church includes a plan maintained by a principal-purpose organization.

Deduction: A plan maintained by a principal-purpose organization is an exempt church plan.

Or, as one court put the point without any of the ERISA terminology: "[I]f A is exempt, and A includes C, then C is exempt." *Overall v. Ascension,* 23 F. Supp. 3d 816, 828 (E.D. Mich. 2014). Just so. Because Congress deemed the category of plans "established and maintained by a church" to "include" plans "maintained by" principal-purpose organizations, those plans—and *all* those plans—are exempt from ERISA's requirements.

Congress wanted, as the employees contend, to alter only the maintenance requirement, it had an easy way to do so—differing by only two words from the language it chose, but with an altogether different meaning. Suppose Congress had provided that "a plan maintained by a church includes a plan maintained by" a principal-purpose organization, leaving out the words "established and" from the first part of the sentence. That amendment would have accomplished exactly what the employees argue Congress intended: The language, that is, would have enabled a principal-purpose organization to take on the maintenance of a "church plan," but left untouched the requirement that a church establish the plan in the first place. But Congress did not adopt that ready alternative. Instead, it added language whose most natural reading is to enable a plan "maintained" by a principal-purpose organization to substitute for a plan both "established" and "maintained" by a church. That drafting decision indicates that Congress did not in fact want what the employees claim. See, e.g., *Lozano v. Montoya Alvarez,* 572 U.S. 1, ___–___, 134 S. Ct. 1224, 1235, 188 L. Ed. 2d 200 (2014) (When legislators did not adopt "obvious alternative" language, "the natural implication is that they did not intend" the alternative).

A corollary to this point is that the employees' construction runs aground on the so-called surplusage canon—the presumption that each word Congress uses is there for a reason. See generally A. Scalia & B. Garner, Reading Law: The Interpretation of Legal Texts 174–179 (2012). As just explained, the employees urge us to read subparagraph (C)(i) as if it were missing the two words "established and." The employees themselves do not contest that point: They offer no account of what function that language would serve on their proposed interpretation. See Brief for Respondents 34–35. In essence, the employees ask us to treat those words as stray marks on a page-notations that Congress regrettably made but did not really intend. Our practice, however, is to "give effect, if possible, to every clause and word of a statute." *Williams v. Taylor,* 529 U.S. 362, 404, 120 S. Ct. 1495, 146 L. Ed. 2d 389 (2000) (internal quotation marks omitted). And here, that means construing the words "established and" in subparagraph (C)(i) as removing, for plans run by principal-purpose organizations, paragraph (A)'s church-establishment condition.

The employees' primary argument to the contrary takes the form of a supposed interpretive principle: "[I]f a definition or rule has two criteria, and a further provision expressly modifies only one of them, that provision is understood to affect only the criterion it expands or modifies." Brief for Respondents 22. Applied here, the employees explain, that principle requires us to read subparagraph (C)(i) as "modify[ing] only the criterion" in paragraph (A) that "it expressly expands ('maintained'), while leaving the other criterion ('established') unchanged." *Id.*, at 14. The employees cite no precedent or other authority to back up their proposed rule of construction, but they offer a thought-provoking hypothetical to demonstrate its good sense. *Id.*, at 22. Imagine, they say, that a statute provides free insurance to a "person who is disabled and a veteran," and an amendment then states that "a person who is disabled and a veteran includes a person who served in the National Guard." *Ibid.* (quoting 810 F.3d, at 181). Would a non-disabled member of the National Guard be entitled to the insurance benefit? Surely not, the employees answer: All of us would understand the "includes" provision to expand (or clarify) only the meaning of "veteran"—leaving unchanged the requirement of a disability. And the same goes here, the employees claim.

But one good example does not a general rule make. Consider a variant of the employees' hypothetical: A statute offers free insurance to a "person who enlisted and served in the active Armed Forces," with a later amendment providing that "a person who enlisted and served in the active Armed Forces includes a person who served in the National Guard." Would a person who served in the National Guard be ineligible for benefits unless she had also enlisted in the active Armed Forces—say, the regular Army or Navy? Of course not. Two hypotheticals with similar grammatical constructions, two different results. In the employees' example, the mind rebels against reading the statute literally, in line with the logical and canonical principles described above. In the variant, by contrast, the statute's literal meaning and its most natural meaning cohere: Satisfaction of the amendment's single eligibility criterion—service in the National Guard—is indeed enough. What might account for that divergence? And what does such an explanation suggest for ERISA?

Two features of the employees' hypothetical, when taken in combination, make it effective. First, the criteria there—veteran-status and disability—are relatively distinct from one another. (Compare enlistment and service, which address similar matters and tend to travel in tandem, the one preceding the other.) The more independent the specified variables, the more likely that they were designed to have standalone relevance. Second and yet more crucial, the employees' example trades on our background understanding that a given interpretation is simply implausible—that it could not possibly have been what Congress wanted. Congress, we feel sure, would not have intended *all* National Guardsmen to get a benefit that is otherwise reserved for disabled veterans. (Compare that to our sense of whether Congress would have meant to hinge benefits to Guardsmen on their enlistment in a different service.) That sense of inconceivability does most of the work in the employees' example, urging readers to discard usual rules of interpreting text because they will lead to a "must be wrong" outcome.

But subparagraph (C)(i) possesses neither of those characteristics. For starters, the criteria at issue—establishment and maintenance—are not unrelated. The former serves as a necessary precondition of the latter, and both describe an aspect of an entity's involvement with a benefit plan. Indeed, for various purposes, ERISA treats the terms "establish" and "maintain" interchangeably. See, *e.g.*, § 1002(16)(B) (defining the "sponsor" of a plan as the organization that "establishe[s] or maintain[s]" the plan). So an amendment altering the one requirement could naturally alter the other too. What's more, nothing we know about the way ERISA is designed to operate makes that an utterly untenable result. Whereas the disability condition is central to the statutory scheme in the employees' hypothetical, the church-establishment condition, taken on its own, has limited functional significance. Establishment of a plan, after all, is a one-time, historical event; it is the entity *maintaining* the plan that has the primary ongoing responsibility (and potential liability) to plan participants. See Brief for United States as *Amicus Curiae* 31; *Rose v. Long Island R.R. Pension Plan*, 828 F.2d 910, 920 (C.A.2 1987), cert. denied, 485 U.S. 936, 108 S. Ct. 1112, 99 L. Ed. 2d 273 (1988) ("[T]he status of the entity which currently maintains a particular pension plan bears more relation to Congress' goals in enacting ERISA and its various exemptions[ ] than does the status of the entity which established the plan"). So removing the establishment condition for plans run by principal-purpose organizations has none of the contextual implausibility — the "Congress could not possibly have meant that" quality — on which the employees' example principally rides.

To the contrary, everything we can tell from extra-statutory sources about Congress's purpose in enacting subparagraph (C)(i) supports our reading of its text. We say "everything we can tell" because in fact we cannot tell all that much. The legislative materials in these cases consist almost wholly of excerpts from committee hearings and scattered floor statements by individual lawmakers — the sort of stuff we have called "among the least illuminating forms of legislative history." *NLRB v. SW General, Inc.*, 580 U.S. ___, ___, 137 S. Ct. 929, 943, 197 L. Ed. 2d 263 (2017). And even those lowly sources speak at best indirectly to the precise question here: None, that is, comments in so many words on whether subparagraph (C)(i) altered paragraph (A)'s church-establishment condition. Still, both the hospitals and the employees have constructed narratives from those bits and pieces about Congress's goals in amending paragraph (A). And our review of their accounts — the employees' nearly as much as the hospitals' — tends to confirm our conviction that plans maintained by principal-purpose organizations are eligible for ERISA's "church plan" exemption, whatever their origins.

According to the hospitals, Congress wanted to eliminate any distinction between churches and church-affiliated organizations under ERISA. See Brief for Petitioners 18, 33–35. The impetus behind the 1980 amendment, they claim, was an IRS decision holding that pension plans established by orders of Catholic Sisters (to benefit their hospitals' employees) did not qualify as "church plans" because the orders were not "carrying out [the Church's] religious functions." IRS General Counsel Memorandum No. 37266, 1977 WL 46200, (Sept. 22, 1977). Many religious groups protested that ruling, criticizing the IRS for "attempting to define what is and what is not [a] "church" and how the mission of the church is to be carried out." 125 Cong. Rec. 10054 (1979) (letter to Sen. Talmadge from the Lutheran Church-Missouri Synod); see *id.*, at 10054–10058 (similar letters). And that anger, the hospitals maintain, was what prompted ERISA's amendment: Congress, they say, designed the new provision to ensure that, however categorized, all groups associated with church activities would receive comparable treatment. See Brief for Petitioners 35.

If that is so, our construction of the text fits Congress's objective to a T. A church-establishment requirement necessarily puts the IRS in the business of deciding just what a church is and is not—for example (as in the IRS's ruling about the Sisters), whether a particular Catholic religious order should count as one. And that requirement, by definition, disfavors plans created by church affiliates, as compared to those established by (whatever the IRS has decided are) churches. It thus makes key to the "church plan" exemption the very line that, on the hospitals' account, Congress intended to erase.

The employees tell a different story about the origins of subparagraph (C)(i)—focusing on the pension boards that congregational denominations often used. See Brief for Respondents 14, 38–42; see also Brief for United States as *Amicus Curiae* 19–22. In line with their non-hierarchical nature, those denominations typically relied on separately incorporated local boards—rather than entities integrated into a national church structure—to administer benefits for their ministers and lay workers. According to the employees, subparagraph (C)(i)'s main goal was to bring those local pension boards within the church-plan exemption, so as to ensure that congregational and hierarchical churches would receive the same treatment. In support of their view, the employees cite several floor statements in which the amendment's sponsors addressed that objective. See Brief for Respondents 38. Senator Talmadge, for example, stated that under the amendment, a "plan or program funded or administered through a pension board ... will be considered a church plan." 124 Cong. Rec. 16523; see also 124 Cong. Rec. 12107 (remarks of Rep. Conable).

But that account of subparagraph (C)(i)'s primary purpose cuts against, not in favor of, the employees' position. See Brief for United States as *Amicus Curiae* 21 (accepting the employees' narrative, but arguing that it buttresses the opposite conclusion). That is because, as hearing testimony disclosed, plans run by church-affiliated pension boards came in different varieties: Some were created by church congregations, but others were established by the boards themselves. See, *e.g.,* Hearings on S. 1090 et al. before the Subcommittee on Private Pension Plans and Employee Fringe Benefits of the Senate Committee on Finance, 96th Cong., 1st Sess., 400–401, 415–417 (1979). And still others were sufficiently old that their provenance could have become the subject of dispute. See *id.,* at 411; 125 Cong. Rec. 10052 (remarks of Sen. Talmadge) ("The average age of a church plan is at least 40 years"). So keeping the church-establishment requirement would have prevented some plans run by pension boards— the very entities the employees say Congress most wanted to benefit from qualifying as "church plans" under ERISA. No argument the employees have offered here supports that goal-defying (much less that text-defying) statutory construction.

III

ERISA provides (1) that a "church plan" means a "plan established and maintained ... by a church" and (2) that a "plan established and maintained ... by a church" is to "include[ ] a plan maintained by" a principal-purpose organization. Under the best reading of the statute, a plan maintained by a principal-purpose organization therefore qualifies as a "church plan," regardless of who established it. We accordingly reverse the judgments of the Courts of Appeals.

It is so ordered.

Justice GORSUCH took no part in the consideration or decision of these cases.

Justice SOTOMAYOR, concurring.

Chapter 6

Minimum Participation Rules and Minimum Coverage Tests

Reading Assignment: ERISA § 202(a)

I.R.C. §§ 401(a)(26), 410(a)–(b), 414(q)

Class Discussion Questions: Generally, a plan may condition eligibility upon the attainment of age 21 and a one-year waiting period. In what situation may a plan condition eligibility upon a two-year waiting period?

How is the first year of service measured for eligibility purposes?

In what circumstances can the plan switch to a plan year for eligibility purposes?

How is the test group determined for purposes of the Code's coverage test in I.R.C. § 410(b)?

When may plans be aggregated for purposes of the Code's coverage tests?

Overview

What are the eligibility rules applicable to all qualified retirement plans?

- Congress prohibits a qualified retirement plan from excluding employees who are age 21 or older and employees who have completed one year of service; certain tax-exempt educational institutions can exclude employees who are younger than age 26

  ○ one year of service is the first 12-month period for each employee, beginning on his or her hire date, in which the employee attains 1,000 hours of service (new rules for part-timers)

  ○ for employees who fail to meet 1,000 hours of service within the first year of service, the plan can switch the eligibility measurement period to the plan year

- for plans utilizing entry dates for eligibility purposes, employees who satisfy 1,000 hours of service within the eligibility measurement period must enter the plan within six months of satisfying the requirement

Why do legally separate employers need to be aggregated for purposes of annual testing in a qualified retirement plan?

- Congress put forth the minimum coverage tests to ensure enough lower-paid employees are benefitting under a qualified retirement plan and the nondiscrimination tests to ensure that the retirement plan does not excessively discriminate in favor of the higher-paid employees

- Congress requires that employers do not "play games" with the establishment of separate business entities (although legal for tax purposes and for liability purposes) simply to avoid these rules

- for purposes of annual testing in a qualified retirement plan, all employees within a controlled group of corporations (or businesses), or all employees within an affiliated service group, are considered to be eligible to participate in every qualified plan sponsored by any member of the controlled group or affiliated service group (and whether they are benefitting or not will determine the results of the test)

- controlled groups of corporations (or other businesses)

  ○ whether planned (such as through a corporate merger) or unplanned (such as having ownership in a business through inheritance or marriage),

  ○ a "parent-subsidiary controlled group" is one or more of a chain of corporations where the parent owns at least 80% of the stock of a subsidiary, and

  ○ a "brother-sister controlled group" is where five or fewer persons (individuals, estates, or trusts) have actual ownership of at least 80% and effective control of at least 50% of one or more corporations

  ○ for purposes of annual testing in a qualified retirement plan, all employees within the controlled group of corporations or businesses are considered to be eligible to participate in every qualified plan sponsored by any member of the controlled group (and whether they are benefitting or not will determine the results of the test)

- affiliated service groups

  ○ whether planned or unplanned, based on facts and circumstances, an affiliated service group consists of a service organization and one or more of the following:

    - any service organization which is a shareholder or partner in the first organization that regularly performs services for the first organization or is regularly associated with the first organization in performing services for third persons, and

    - any other organization if a significant portion of the business of such organization is the performance of services of a type historically performed in such service field by employees, and 10% or more of the interests in such organization is held by persons who are highly compensated employees of the first organization

Who are the highly compensated (HCE) employees?

- by default, every employee who is not classified as an HCE is classified as a non-highly compensated employee (NHCE)

- since salaries and ownership can change from one year to the next, the plan administrator must annually go through the roster of employees and classify each and every eligible employee as either an HCE or NHCE

- there are three ways that an employee can be classified as a highly compensated employee in a given year:

    ○ an employee had at least a 5% ownership in the sponsoring employer this year or last year,

    ○ an employee earned compensation in excess of the annual threshold of $80,000 (as adjusted for inflation) last year, or

    ○ an employee was an HCE at any time after attaining age 55

- there are two rules available under the compensation criteria for determining HCEs:

    ○ if the top-paid group comprises more than 20% of the employees and they are paid in excess of $80,000 (as adjusted for inflation), such as in law firms, the employer limits the HCEs to the top 20%, and

    ○ the calendar year data election, where the plan year is not a calendar year plan, but the employer chooses to determine salaries based on the calendar year, since that is how payroll records are maintained

Which annual tests compare the HCEs to the NHCEs?

- the minimum coverage test determines if enough NHCEs are benefitting in the plan when compared to the percentage of HCEs benefitting in the plan

- the minimum participation test determines if enough NHCEs are benefitting in a defined benefit plan when compared to the percentage of HCEs benefitting in that defined benefit plan

- the nondiscrimination test determines if enough NHCEs are getting comparable benefits, rights, and features in the plan as compared to the HCEs

- the nondiscrimination tests in 401(k) plans determine if enough NHCEs are deferring percentages of their salaries and receiving employer contributions (when expressed as percentages of their salaries) as compared to the HCEs

How can a qualified retirement plan prove it meets the minimum coverage tests each year?

- if the plan document only excludes participants who have not yet attained age 21 or who have not yet been credited with a year of service, then the plan passes every year

- however, if any other eligible employees are specifically excluded by plan design, then the mathematical tests will need to be performed every year

- preliminary issues

- the following common law employees can be eliminated from the testing group:
- employees who are younger than age 21
  - employees who have not yet completed a year of service
  - employees who are members of a union where retirement benefits are part of the collective bargaining negotiations
  - employees who are non-resident aliens
  - and certain employees in the aviation and railroad industries
- all other common law employees are considered "eligible" employees, and are classified as either:
  - current employee or former employee
  - HCE or NHCE and
  - benefitting in the plan or not benefitting in the plan
- the Plan's ratio percentage is calculated as a top fraction divided by a bottom fraction, where
  - the top fraction is a fraction whose numerator is the number of NHCEs benefitting in the plan and the denominator is the number of NHCEs eligible to benefit in the plan
  - the bottom fraction is a fraction whose numerator is the number of HCEs benefitting in the plan and the denominator is the number of HCEs eligible to benefit in the plan
- each year, the plan only needs to pass any one of the following tests:
  - *70% test:* the plan benefits at least 70 percent of employees who are NHCEs
  - *ratio percentage test:* the plan's ratio percentage is at least 70%, or
  - *average benefit percentage test:*
    - based on all the facts and circumstances, the classification of eligible employees who are covered by the plan is reasonable and is established under objective business criteria,
    - based on a table in the regulations, the plan's ratio percentage, although lower than 70%, is greater than or equal to the plan's "safe harbor percentage" for that year, or is greater than the plan's "unsafe harbor percentage" and the IRS approves an affirmative request for determination, and
    - the average benefit percentages for NHCEs divided by the average benefit percentages for HCEs is at least 70% (for a defined contribution plan, the average benefit percentage is basically each participant's annual addition divided by his salary, and for a defined benefit plan, the average benefit percentage is calculated by the plan's enrolled actuary as the normal accrual rate)
- if the plan fails to meet any of the three mathematical tests in any year, then

- ○ the plan must satisfy such minimum coverage rules on at least one day in each quarter, so the plan administrator can try to find "better" dates for testing

- ○ if the employer maintains more than one plan, then they may be aggregated for minimum coverage testing purposes (but they will need to be aggregated for nondiscrimination testing as well)

- ○ otherwise, the plan must be amended to allow enough excluded employees to be covered under the plan

A. Eligibility Standards

1. Statutory Coverage

As the establishment and maintenance of a retirement plan has been voluntary on the part of any employer, Congress has permitted employers to decide which employees will benefit under a given plan. But for the plan to be tax-qualified, Congress has always required that the plan not discriminate in favor of a certain class of employees. Historically, this group was known as the "prohibited group" (i.e., those employees who were officers, shareholders, or highly compensated). Prior to ERISA's passage, Congress recognized that most retirement plans used an age and/or service requirement to limit participation in the plan. Such requirements generally reflected the employer's experience that younger employees and high-turnover employees (regardless of age) were not interested in retirement benefits. Thus, pre-ERISA, a typical retirement plan had a requirement of age 25 and three years of service before becoming eligible to participate in the employer's plan. However, many employers used a third participation limitation for a variety of reasons. For example, if an employer had both salaried and hourly workers and the hourly workers were covered under a multiemployer plan through a collectively bargained agreement, the employer would be required under federal labor law to contribute to a multiemployer plan maintained for those unionized hourly workers. Thus, it would wish to have a separate retirement plan solely for its salaried workers.

When ERISA was passed, Congress implemented two sets of participation standards under the Code (the first of which were duplicated under Title I):

- The first set refers to age and service requirements that could limit individual employee participation in the plan, set forth in I.R.C. § 410(a) and ERISA § 202(a); and

- The second set permits the employer to use any rational third criteria for participation (e.g., eligibility limited to salaried employees, as opposed to hourly employees). Given the flexibility permitted in choosing this criterion, Congress then imposed a set of nondiscriminatory coverage tests in I.R.C. § 410(b) to ensure the limitation was not being used for discriminatory purposes.

2. Covered Plans

These two sets of participation standards are set forth in I.R.C. §§ 410(a) and (b) and apply to all qualified retirement plans (defined benefit and defined contribution) except for the following plans:

- Governmental plans as defined in I.R.C. § 414(d);
- Church plans as defined in I.R.C. § 414(e);
- Plans which have not at any time after September 2, 1974, provided for employer contributions; and
- Plans maintained by a fraternal society or voluntary employee beneficiary association with no part of the contribution under the plan coming from the employer.[1]

Note that the participation requirements of Title I of ERISA overlap with the participation requirements of the Code.[2] Since the DOL was given jurisdiction under the Reorganization Act of 1978 over participation, we will be referring to DOL regulations in analyzing the Code's and Title I's minimum participation standards.

Use of Age: A plan is not required to use an age requirement, but if the employer wishes to exclude employees from participation based on a minimum age, that minimum age cannot be greater than age 21.[3] [Note the original House bill allowed an exclusion on account of age to be age 25, whereas the Senate bill used age 30; the final version of ERISA settled on age 21 to expand coverage for younger employees.] Hence, an employee who has attained age 21 must be permitted to participate in a qualified retirement plan provided all other requirements for plan participation have been met.[4] There is one exception to the minimum age 21 rule: if a plan is willing to provide for full vesting after just two years of service, the plan may delay an employee's participation until the later of the date he or she attains age 21 or completes two years of service.[5]

Initially, defined benefit plans were permitted to impose a maximum age limitation due to funding problems for aged hires. However, subsequent age discrimination legislation precluded the use of such a limitation.[6] OBRA '86 amended I.R.C. §§ 410 and 411, requiring the elimination of plan provisions that exclude from participation employees on the basis of the attainment of any age or cause the cessation or re-

---

1. I.R.C. § 401(c)(1).

2. ERISA § 202(a)(1)(A).

3. *See* I.R.C. § 410(a)(1)(A)(i). Originally, there was a permissible minimum age of 25, but § 202(a)(1) of the Retirement Equity Act of 1984 lowered the minimum age to 21 for plan years beginning after December 31, 1984.

4. Plans for employees of educational institutions can use a minimum age of 26 if vesting is 100% after one year of service.

5. *See* I.R.C. § 410(a)(1)(B)(i). Originally, there was a permissible three-year delay if full vesting was provided.

6. *See* I.R.C. § 411(b)(1)(G), effective for plan years beginning after December 31, 1987. Prior to this change, defined benefit and target benefit plans could exclude from participation those employees who were hired at an age that was within five years of the plan's normal retirement age.

duction of benefit accruals or allocations of participants on the basis of the attainment of any age.[7]

Use of Service: An employer may impose a waiting period for participation, known as the service requirement. The rationale for the waiting period was to exclude employees who had high turnover. However, the maximum waiting period is "one year of service."[8] For eligibility purposes, this is defined by the Code as the 12-month period, beginning on the date of employment, during which the employee has completed at least 1,000 "hours of service."[9] An employee who satisfies the one-year waiting requirement is credited with a service year at the *end* of the applicable period. This definition provides a minimum standard; however, employers are free to be more generous.

> **Example:** Employee A is hired on January 1, 2020 as a part-time worker and has only 490 hours as of December 31, 2020. A does not have "one year of service" and can be excluded from participation.

To promote greater participation of part-time employees, SECURE requires I.R.C. § 401(k) plans to allow participation by long-term, part-time employees who work at least 500 hours in three consecutive 12-month periods (and have reached age 21).[10] The 12-month periods are to be determined as the same as a "year of service" as defined by the minimum participation rules.[11]

a. Definitions of Year of Service and Hours of Service

As the "year of service" is determined using "hours of service," such terms are defined by ERISA and the Code. As a general rule, an employee must be credited with all hours of service for each:

- hour for which he or she is directly or indirectly paid for the performance of services for the employer ("hours worked");
- hour for which he or she is directly or indirectly paid for periods in which no services are performed due to vacation, holiday, illness, incapacity, layoff, jury duty, military duty or authorized leave of absence; and
- hour of back pay awarded or agreed to by the employer (and credited in the year to which the back pay relates versus paid).[12]

---

7. OBRA '86, §§ 9203(a)(2) and 9202(b)(1)(A)–(B).

8. *See* I.R.C. § 410(a)(1)(a)(ii) (a two-year waiting period is permitted if the plan provides for full vesting upon eligibility).

9. *See* I.R.C. § 410(a)(3)(A). Note: this term "year of service" is defined in three different contexts under the Code and ERISA — referring to service for eligibility purposes, vesting purposes, and years of participation for accrual purposes — measuring different 12-month periods.

10. SECURE § 112, amending I.R.C. § 401(k)(2)(D), generally effective for plan years beginning after December 31, 2020.

11. *Id.* at § 112(a)(2)(D).

12. *See* Labor Reg. § 2530.200b-2. As some employers find it difficult to keep track of exact hours, the regulations permit crediting of service based on worked hours (e.g., the plan counts only 750 regular time hours and those are treated as equal to 1,000 hours). Alternatively, the plan may credit

In the case where a plan is being newly adopted, the plan sponsor does not have discretion as to whether to count prior plan service in determining eligibility. If the employee fails to work the required 1,000 hours within the initial 12-month period, the plan may switch the eligibility computation period from the employee's anniversary year to the plan year.[13] In that case, the first plan year used for eligibility computation purposes includes the plan year which contains the employee's first anniversary of employment. For eligibility purposes, service with a related employer must also be counted even if the related employer has not adopted the sponsoring employer's plan.[14]

For subsequent eligibility computation periods, the regulations permit employers to adopt a universal eligibility computation period so that all employees have the same subsequent eligibility computation period.[15] This alternative subsequent eligibility computation period is first plan year beginning after the employee's employment commencement date. For example, an employee is hired on 3/1/16 as a full-time employee in a calendar plan year. While the first eligibility computation period runs from 3/1/16 through 2/28/17, the subsequent eligibility computation periods will be measured on a calendar plan year, beginning with the 2017 plan year. Thus, between 1/1/17 and 2/28/17, the first and second computation periods overlap.

Some employers attempted to usurp the one-year service rule by excluding "part-time employees," "temporary employees," or "employees whose customary employment is less than 20 hours per week or 5 months in a year." The Service views such criteria as "disguised service" limitations and thus prohibits them.[16]

b. Entry Dates

In the early days of ERISA, employers used common entry dates for participation under the plan (e.g., an initial quarterly, semiannual, or annual date), as the tracking of eligibility was done manually. ERISA and the Code both permit the use of an entry date system. Once an employee satisfies the plan's age and service requirements and is otherwise entitled to participation in the plan, the plan may actually delay commencement of participation in the plan to the earlier of:

- the first day of the plan year after he or she meets those requirements, or
- within six months after the date the plan requirements were met.[17]

Typically plans use semi-annual entry dates (the beginning date of the plan year and the half-way point) for entry into the plan.

---

service on the basis of days of employment instead of hours of service (e.g., one day employed is credited with 10 hours of service).

13. *See* I.R.C. §410(a)(3)(A). *See also* Labor Reg. §2530.202-2(b)(2).

14. *See* I.R.C. §414(b), 414(c), 414(m)(4), 414(n)(4) and 414(o).

15. *See* Labor Reg. §2530.202-2(b)(2).

16. *See* Treas. Reg. §1.410(a)-3(e), Example 3.

17. *See* I.R.C. §410(a)(4)(A),(B); Treas. Reg. §1.410(a)-4(b)(1).

Example: When does Participant A enter the plan if he or she satisfied the 1,000 hours as of 2/28/17, in a plan with a calendar plan year and dual entry dates of 1/1 or 7/1? The plan may delay A's entry until 7/1/17, but not until 1/1/18 (as that would exceed six months from 2/28/17). An exception to this rule exists if the employee completes the 1,000 hours as of his or her "year of service," but separates from service prior to the anticipated entry date. In such case, the plan must permit such employee to participate immediately upon reemployment (not the next re-entry date), unless the break-in-service rules (to be discussed next) disregard his or her prior service.[18]

Example: Participant A satisfied the 1,000 hours as of 2/28/17 but separates service on 4/1/17 and is later reemployed on 9/1/17. Participant A's entry date would be 9/1/17, not 1/1/18 (the next entry date). Clearly Participant A's entry date could not be 7/1/17 as he or she is not an employee as of the entry date.

c. Break-in-Service Rules

For employees who had attained a year of service but subsequently terminated employment, a question arose as to whether such previously credited years of service could be later forfeited. For example, Participant A satisfied the one year of service and became a participant. Later, A terminates employment but is later reemployed by the employer. Does A have to satisfy the one year of service requirement again? The tension existed between the employee's attainment of the required years of service and the employer's recordkeeping requirements regarding previously hired employees. Congress compromised with the "break-in-service" forfeiture rules for years of service and provided them to those employers who elected them under the plan. For employers deciding to utilize these rules, previously earned years of service may be later forfeited if the employee incurs a sufficiently long break in service.

A plan may ignore certain years of service if an employee severs employment sufficiently enough to incur a break in service.[19] A "one-year break in service" is defined as a 12-month period during which the employee has 500 or less hours of service.[20] If the employee is credited with 501 or more hours of service, he or she has not incurred a break in service. Hence, if an employee were to experience a drastic cut in his or her hours of service during a given year, he or she would experience a break in service. The same standards for measuring years of service are used in determining whether there is a break in service. If the plan continues to use the employee's employment anniversary years in the case where an employee does not complete 1,000 hours in the first eligibility computation period, then year of service for the break-in-service computation begins with the 12-month period beginning on the employee's reemployment date and if applicable, subsequent periods are measured on the sub-

---

18. *See* Treas. Reg. § 1.410(a)-4(b)(1).
19. *See* I.R.C. § 410(a)(5).
20. *See* I.R.C. § 411(a)(6)(A); Labor Reg. § 2530.200b-4(a).

sequent anniversaries of the reemployment date.[21] Where the plan switches to the plan year to measure subsequent eligibility computation periods, the year of service for the break-in-service computation begins at the 12-month period beginning on the employee's employment date and if applicable, subsequent periods are measured beginning with the plan year that includes the first anniversary of the employee's reemployment date.[22]

There are three notable exceptions that must be complied with if the plan utilizes the break-in-service rules:

- *Maternity/Paternity Leave*: Employees on "qualified" maternity/paternity leave must continue to be credited with "hours of service," during their leaves, up to 501 hours in a given 12-month period.[23]

- *Family and Medical Leave*: FMLA requires employers to provide up to 12 weeks of unpaid leave for certain authorized family and medical reasons.[24] Such periods of unpaid leave may not be counted in determining a break-in-service.[25]

- *Military Leave*: Employers must count a reemployed veteran's period of military service as service with the employer for purposes of avoiding a break in service.[26] SBJPA '96 added subsection (u) to I.R.C. § 414 which applies this USERRA requirement to qualified retirement plans.[27]

d. Requirement of Employment Status

The qualified rules of I.R.C. § 401(a) permit plans to cover eligible employees of the employer.[28] Hence, an employer that includes an individual as a participant by misclassifying him or her as an employee instead of an independent contractor thereby violates this statutory eligibility rule.[29] However, the criteria used in distinguishing employees from independent contractors are not set forth in the Code's qualification rules.[30] The Code has been amended to permit partners and self-employed individuals to be covered under qualified plans, defining their status as "owner employees." To avoid covering an individual originally classified as an independent contractor but later found to be an "employee," employers of individually designed plans now insert

---

21. *See* Labor Reg. § 2530.200b-4(b)(1)(i).

22. *See* Labor Reg. § 2530.200b-4(b)(1)(ii).

23. 4 *See* I.R.C. § 410(a)(5)(E).

24. *See* FMLA § 2601.

25. *See* Labor Reg. § 825.215(d)(4).

26. *See* I.R.C. § 414(u)(8)(A).

27. *See* SBJPA '96 § 1704(n)(1).

28. For the common law definition of an employee, see *Donovan v. DialAmerica Marketing, Inc.*, 757 F.2d 1376 (3d Cir. 1985), and *U.S. v. Silk*, 331 U.S. 704, 67 S. Ct. 1463, 91 L. Ed. 1757 (1947).

29. *See Vizcaino v. Microsoft Corporation*, 97 F. 3d 1187 (9th Cir. 1996).

30. *See* I.R.C. § 401 et seq. *See also* Revenue Act of 1978 § 530; Miscellaneous Revenue Act of 1980 §§ 9(d)(1) and 9(d)(2); Tax Treatment Act of 1980 §§ 1(a) and (b); TEFRA '82 § 269(c)(2); TRA '86 § 170(a); and SBJPA '96 § 1122(a).

plan language to explicitly exclude such misclassified individuals to avoid coverage issues (to be discussed next).

B. Coverage Requirements of I.R.C. § 410(b)

1. Preliminary Matters

As mentioned earlier, the qualified plan document may use a second set of participation criteria that is unique to the employer. For example, the plan may say "this covers all salaried employees, but not hourly," "this covers hourly employees who are not unionized and covered by a collectively bargained agreement," "this plan covers only those employees employed at the Illinois facility," or "this plan covers only those employees employed at the headquarters location." By inserting this second set of participation criteria, the plan will need to be tested under I.R.C. § 410(b) to see if the coverage of eligible participants is nondiscriminatory. Congress does not want *only* the highly paid employees covered under the plan, leaving rank-and-file employees excluded.

In order to apply the coverage tests, the total group of employees of the employer has to be counted. Here, the term "employee" is defined to be a common law employee or a self-employed individual.[31] This total number of employees may later be subject to certain exclusions. Since the choice of business entity (e.g., corporation) is governed by state law, the federal Code aggregates certain "related employers" for purposes of the coverage tests. Congress does not want employers to "play games" by establishing separate business identities (which is lawful under state law) in order to circumvent the federal nondiscrimination laws.

> **Example:** An employer has 100 employees—75 rank-and-file and 25 highly paid employees. The employer forms two corporations—Corporation A employs all 75 rank-and-file employees but offers no plan, while Corporation B employs all 25 highly paid employees and covers all of them under a qualified plan. That would be discriminatory. So, for Code purposes, Corporations A and B are related and their combined employee population will be aggregated when doing the coverage tests.

Employers who are members of the same controlled group as determined under I.R.C. § 414(b) and affiliated service groups as determined under I.R.C. § 414(m) may be aggregated; leased employees of related employers as determined under I.R.C. § 414(n) may also have to be counted as employees of the employer which is maintaining the plan for purposes of the coverage test. The Tax Reform Act of 1986 created two exceptions to the application of the related employer rule for testing minimum

---

31. *See* Treas. Reg. § 1.410(b)-9, where "employee" is defined in the context of a common law employee of an employer, or a self-employed individual treated as an employee, or certain leased employees.

coverage.[32] First, coverage testing may be performed by the employer for each separate line of business.[33] Second, there is a grace period for meeting the new rules if there has been an acquisition or divestiture of a related employer.[34]

Under the controlled group rules, there are two types of controlled groups:

- A "parent-subsidiary controlled group" which consists of one or more of a chain of corporations where the parent entity owns at least 80% of a subsidiary;

Example: Corporation A has a wholly owned subsidiary, Corporation B. A and B comprise a parent-subsidiary controlled group.

- A "brother-sister controlled group" in which five or fewer persons (individuals, estates, or trusts) have actual ownership of at least 80% of related entities and effective control of at least 50% of related entities.[35]

Example: Person C owns 50% of Corporation A and 30% of Corporation B, whereas Person D owns 30% of Corporation A and 50% of Corporation B. Although Corporations A and B do not have ownership interests in each other, Persons C and D collectively own 80% of Corporations A and B, and when you take the smallest percentage interest Persons C and D have in the two corporations (30% + 30%), they have a majority effective control. Thus, Corporations A and B are brother-sister corporations because of Persons C's and D's ownership interests.

For purposes of the affiliated service groups, there are generally two types of affiliated service groups:

- An "FSO" and an "A org" in which there are at least two organizations: the FSO whose principal business is performing services and an A org that is a service organization, partner, or shareholder of the FSO, and regularly performs services for the FSO or with the FSO for others;

Example: Partnership P is a law partnership. Corporation C is a partner in the law firm. Corporation C provides paralegal services for the attorneys in the law partnership. P and C comprise an affiliated service group.

- An "FSO" and a "B org" in which there are at least two organizations: the FSO whose principal business is performing services and a B org that is a service organization, 10% or more of the equity interest of the B org are held in the aggregate by persons who are HCEs of the FSO, and a significant portion of B's business is the performance of services for the FSO or A orgs of the FSO.[36]

Example: Partnership A is a law partnership, with 11 partners, who are all HCEs of the Partnership. Each partner owns 1% interest in the stock of Corporation B. Corporation B provides services to Partnership A of the type

32. TRA '86 §§ 1112(a) and 1115(a).
33. I.R.C. § 414(r).
34. TRA '86 § 1112(a), amending I.R.C. § 410(b)(6)(C).
35. I.R.C. § 414(b).
36. I.R.C. § 414(m).

historically performed by employees in the legal field. A significant portion of Corporation B's business consists of providing services to Partnership A. Corporation B and Partnership A comprise an affiliated service group.

Once the related employers have been identified, the total number of employees employed by such employers must be aggregated. Then, there are permitted exclusions that may be made from the coverage's computation testing group used for coverage and nondiscrimination purposes. These exclusions include:

- employees who have not yet met the plan's minimum age and service requirements;[37]

- employees who are not included in the plan and are a part of a collective bargaining unit where retirement benefits have been the subject of good faith bargaining;[38]

- certain airline pilots;[39]

- non-resident alien employees whose compensation is not from U.S. sources (even if they are covered under the plan, they may be excluded from computation under the tests);[40] and

- terminated employees with not more than 500 hours of credited service (the IRS regulations permit an exclusion for employees who terminate with no more than 500 hours of service and do not accrue a benefit because of the plan's service requirement, provided this exclusion applies to all such employees for the plan year).[41]

Example: Employer ABC has 100 employees, 50 are union employees and 50 are non-union employees (of these 50, 10 are either younger than 21 or have less than a year of service). ABC wants to establish a plan where eligibility = age 21 + 1 yos + nonunion status. The plan's test group of nonexcludable employees = $[100 - (50 + 10)] = 40$ employees, as 60 were excludable employees.

This concept of *excludable* versus *nonexcludable* employees is crucial in the initial determination of who is to be counted for coverage and nondiscrimination purposes. Once an employee is deemed excludable for a given plan year, that employee is not counted for coverage and nondiscrimination purposes.

The IRS regulations prescribe situations in which plans are deemed to have satisfied the minimum coverage requirements of I.R.C. § 410(b).[42] They include:

---

37. TRA '86 § 1112(a), amending I.R.C. § 410(b)(4), permitting such exclusion only if the rules are applied uniformly to all eligible employees. For example: if the plan routinely waives the one-year service requirements for employees hired after age 40, it cannot exclude any employees who have not satisfied the plan's service requirement.

38. I.R.C. § 410(b)(3).

39. *Id.*

40. *Id.*

41. *See* Treas. Reg. §§ 1.410(b)-6(f)(1)(v) and (vi).

42. *See* Treas. Reg. § 1.410(b)-2(b)(5)–(7).

- Plans that cover all nonexcludable employees;
- Plans that benefit only NHCEs in a given plan year;
- Plans maintained by an employer that has only HCE employees; and
- Plans benefiting collectively bargained employees.

While each plan is generally tested individually under the coverage tests, a plan that could not satisfy the minimum coverage rules of I.R.C. §410(b) on its own may nevertheless be aggregated with one or more other plans for purposes of testing.[43] If an employer permissively aggregates plans to meet the coverage rules, the combined plans must also meet the I.R.C. §401(a)(4) nondiscrimination tests on a combined basis. Beginning in 1990, plans must have the same plan year to be permissively aggregated.[44] If two plans are aggregated for purposes of the coverage tests, but their eligibility requirements are different (e.g., 21 and older or 18 and older and one-year-waiting period), the test group for purposes of the aggregated plans is determined using the least restrictive eligibility requirements (e.g., 18 and older).[45] This means more employees will be included in the test group, making it harder to satisfy the coverage tests.

The coverage tests compare the group of employees "benefiting" under the plan for a given plan year to the test group of employees.[46] For purposes of this rule, an employee benefits under a plan only if, for that plan year, the employee receives an allocation of contributions or forfeitures (in the case of a defined contribution plan) or accrues a benefit (in the case of a defined benefit plan).[47] Under I.R.C. §§401(k) and 401(m) arrangements, employees who are eligible to make elective deferrals or who are eligible to make employee contributions or receive matching contributions are treated as benefiting under the plan for purposes of this rule, regardless of whether such contributions are made or received.[48] Employees who are unable to receive an allocation or an accrual because of the application of the I.R.C. §415 limits are also treated as benefiting for the plan year if they are otherwise eligible to receive an allocation or accrual.[49]

> **Example:** The plan's test group = 40 nonexcludable employees, 30 of which are NHCEs, and 10 of which are HCEs. This is a 401(k) plan with salary electives and employer matching contributions. Of the eligible 30 NHCEs, only 20 NHCEs make elective salary deferrals and receive an employer match. Of the eligible 10 HCEs, all 10 HCEs make elective salary deferrals and receive

43. I.R.C. §410(b)(6)(B) and Treas. Reg. §1.410(b)-7(d)(1). Note Treas. Reg. §1.410(b)-7(d)(2) provides that certain plans cannot be aggregated for this purpose (e.g., 401(k) plans with non-401(k) plans; 401(m) plans with non-401(m) plans; ESOPs with non-ESOPs; plans covering collective bargained employees with non-collectively bargained employees).
44. *See* Treas. Reg. §1.410(b)-7(d)(5).
45. *See* Treas. Reg. §1.410(b)-6(b)(2).
46. I.R.C. §410(b)(1), using the phrase "the plan *benefits* ..." (italics added).
47. *See* Treas. Reg. §1.410(b)-3(a), with examples provided in Treas. Reg. §1.410(b)-3(a)(3).
48. I.R.C. §410(b)(6)(E); Treas. Reg. §1.410(b)-3(a)(2)(i).
49. *See* Treas. Reg. §1.410(b)-3(a)(2)(ii).

an employer match. Of the 10 NHCEs who do not make any salary deferrals, their deferrals percentage is 0%.

The coverage tests must be satisfied for a plan year as of the "testing date."[50] The regulations provide three testing date options: daily testing, quarterly testing, or annual testing.[51]

2. Definition of Highly Compensated Employee in I.R.C. § 414(q)

When Congress modified the coverage tests in 1986, it explicitly redefined the prohibited group as any "highly compensated employee" (HCE) satisfying the requirements of I.R.C. § 414(q).[52] An employee is considered an HCE if he or she has a given ownership interest in the employer and/or earns a salary at or in excess of a dollar limit (that fluctuates year to year). As ownership and salaries change from year to year, the determination of who is an HCE must also be made annually. By default, if an employee does not satisfy the current year's HCE requirements, he or she is a nonhighly compensated employee ("NHCE") for purposes of the coverage tests.

Congress has simplified the definition of HCE to include an employee who:

- was a 5% owner (which really means has ownership **over** 5%) for the current year or preceding year;[53] or

- is paid over $80,000 (as of 1997, subject to indexing; for 2020, this number is $130,000 and for 2019, it was $125,000) in the **preceding** year.[54]

---

50. *See* Treas. Reg. § 1.410(b)(8).

51. Daily testing takes into account only those employees who are employees on that date; quarterly testing applies the coverage test on one day in each quarter of the plan year and takes into account only those employees who are employees on that date; annual testing is done as of the last day of the plan year and takes into account all employees who were employees on any day during the plan year. The annual testing option must be used when testing for coverage under a § 401(k) plan, § 401(m) plan, or when using the average benefits test of I.R.C. § 410(b)(2). Whatever testing option is utilized by the employer for coverage purposes must be the same option utilized for nondiscrimination testing.

52. TRA '86, § 1114(a).

53. I.R.C. § 414(q)(2), cross-referencing the definition of a 5% owner under I.R.C. § 416(i)(1), which means an owner with more than 5% ownership (using the attribution rules of I.R.C. § 318, which are highly expansive). With respect to stock ownership, an employee is a 5% owner if he or she owns more than 5% of all stock or more than 5% of the voting stock. If the employer is not a corporation, a 5% owner must own more than 5% of the capital or profits interest of the employer. The attribution rules treat family members as separate HCEs, but measure whether an individual is an HCE through stock ownership of a family member.

54. I.R.C. § 414(q)(1)(B). Initially this prong of the test provided an option to the employer to elect to include only those employees with compensation in excess of $80,000 that were also within the top 20% paid group. Such an elective feature was eliminated by EGTRRA '01 § 663(a), beginning in 2002. The legislative history reflects that the repeal of this election was to close a loophole created by TRA '86 for the benefit of an employer with one employee or a small group of employees. The IRS' previously issued regulations regarding "highly compensated employees," published in 1988 were amended in 1994, but never updated nor revoked to reflect the statutory changes made in 1996. *See*

A former employee is treated as an HCE if

- He or she was an HCE upon separation of employment or

- He or she was an HCE at any time after attaining age 55.[55]

Ownership Interest: An employee is an HCE for the current year if he or she has **more than** a 5% ownership interest in the employer for the current year or for the prior year. Ownership is determined by stock ownership if the employer is a corporation or by capital or profit interests if the employer is a partnership or other type of business. As a result of this definition, once an employee attains a minimum ownership in excess of 5% in the employer, he or she becomes an HCE for the current year and the subsequent year, even if such ownership interest falls below the 5% level in the subsequent year. The family attribution rules of I.R.C. §318 apply such that an individual is deemed to own the stock owned by his or her spouse, children, grandchildren, and parents.[56] For example, if an employee owns 10% of the employer, he or she cannot avoid the HCE status by giving his or her 10% ownership to their spouse. The determination of a 5% owner (for both HCE and key employee definitions) is made on a per company basis, *not* on the basis of ownership in a controlled or affiliated service group basis.[57]

Compensation Level: In order to identify those employees who are HCEs for the current year, the second prong of the HCE test asks whether the employee earned compensation *in the prior year* from the employer in excess of the applicable dollar ceiling. (For example, in 2020, an employee would have had to earn $125,000 or more in 2019 to be considered an HCE as of the 2020 determination date.) Such a determination allows the employer to identify at the beginning of the year who satisfies the HCE compensation level, providing greater certainty in applying the coverage tests as the group of HCEs (at least by compensation level) will not change during the year. An employee's compensation for purposes of the second prong of the test is defined by I.R.C. §415(c)(3);[58] however, cafeteria contributions under I.R.C. §125, elective deferrals under I.R.C. §§401(k) and 403(b), and SEPs are not to be taken into account in defining compensation.[59] For example, Participant A has 5% ownership in the employer and Participant B's salary was over $125,000 during 2019. As Participant A does not have more than a 5% ownership, he or she is not an HCE for 2020, but as Participant B made over the 2019 dollar maximum during 2019, he or she is an HCE for 2020.

In recognition of the fact that large employers may pay a substantial portion of their workforce in excess of the I.R.C. §414(q) compensation threshold, there is a

---

IRS Notice 97-455, 1997-2 C.B. 296 (Aug. 1, 1997), for a discussion of the new rules for determining HCEs after 1996.

55. I.R.C. §414(q)(6).
56. Treas. Reg. §1.416-1, Q&A T-18.
57. I.R.C. §416(i)(1)(C).
58. I.R.C. §414(q)(4), cross-referencing the definition of compensation as used in I.R.C. §415(c)(3).
59. SBJPA '96 §1434(b)(1), amending I.R.C. §414(q)(4).

20% top-paid group limit for employers. It limits the group of HCEs to the top 20% of employees (when ranked by compensation). The end-result excludes employees who would have otherwise satisfied the compensation threshold for the prior year but are not within the top-paid 20% group. For example, if the employer had 25% of its employees paid in excess of the applicable compensation limit, the HCE group would be limited to the top 20% group of employees, instead of 25%.

3. First Three Coverage Tests of I.R.C. § 410(b)

The coverage tests of I.R.C. § 410(b) are automatically met if the employer uses only the first set of age/service eligibility criteria, as it is covering all nonexcludable employees; so an employer needs to perform coverage tests if the employer uses a second set of other eligibility criteria. The coverage tests then begin with the determination of the potential pool of NHCEs and HCEs that could have been covered under the plan had it not used a second set of eligibility criteria—referred to as the NHCE test group and the HCE test group. Both of these groups are obviously greater than the pool of NHCEs and HCEs actually covered under the plan because the plan used a second set of eligibility criteria. The tests will being doing a comparison— how many NHCEs are benefiting relative to the pool of NHCEs that could have been covered as compared to how many HCEs are benefiting relative to the pool of HCEs that could have been covered. The tests are purely a head count comparison.

a. Percentage Test

The first test under I.R.C. § 410(b) is referred to as the percentage test. This test **presumes** that the plan's eligibility criteria results in 100% coverage of all HCEs. The test requires the plan to cover at least 70% of all nonhighly compensated employees (NHCEs) in order to satisfy it.[60] This is a very high hurdle for most plans to meet and therefore not one readily relied upon. For example, the plan's eligibility criteria results in 10/10 = 100% coverage of all 10 HCEs. Thus, the number of NHCEs that must benefit under the plan relative to the potential eligible NHCE group of 100 would be 70 (i.e., 70% × 100). If the plan benefits 70 NHCEs, it satisfies this test.

b. Ratio Percentage Test

The second test, referred to as the ratio percentage test, **requires that the percentage of covered NHCEs be at least 70% of the percentage of covered HCEs.**[61] Unlike the

---

60. I.R.C. § 410(b)(1)(A).

61. I.R.C. § 410(b)(1)(B). Note that a plan which satisfies the percentage test of I.R.C. § 410(b)(1)(A) will also satisfy the ratio percentage test of I.R.C. § 410(b)(1)(B), hence the percentage test is really not needed. *See* Treas. Reg. §§ 1.410(b)-2(b)(2)(i). The percentage test checks to see if total coverage amounts to 70% of the NHCE test group; in contrast, the ratio percentage test only requires that the coverage of the NHCE test group be proportionate to the coverage of the HCE group. The percentage test presumes coverage of the HCE group to be 100% and thus requires coverage of the NHCE group to be 70% to achieve the 70% proportionality.

percentage test, coverage of the NHCE does not have to be a firm 70%; instead, coverage of the NHCEs is measured relative to the coverage of the HCEs. Note the percentage test need not have been created, because if the coverage of the NHCE is a firm 70%, it automatically will meet the ratio percentage test.

Here, the relative percentages of coverage of the two groups is relevant. Thus, in determining the plan's ratio percentage for this test, two percentages must be compared:

- the percentage of NHCEs benefiting = NHCEs benefiting under the plan ÷ NHCE Test Group
- the percentage of HCE benefiting = HCEs benefiting under the plan ÷ HCE Test Group

The plan's ratio percentage is then the percentage of NHCE benefiting ÷ the percentage of HCE benefiting, and the ratio percentage test requires this ratio to be at least 70% for the plan to pass.

> **Example:** If a plan benefits 40% of the employer's NHCE test group and 60% of the employer's HCE test group, then the plan's ratio percentage is 66⅔% (40/60) which is less than the required 70%. Another way to understand the test is to look at the coverage of the HCE group (here, it is 60%), which means the coverage of the NHCE group must be at least 70% of 60% or 42%. Since the plan benefits only 40% of the NHCE group, it fails the test.

Plans are only required to pass one of the coverage tests to be qualified. The ratio percentage test is more liberal and provides the employer with more flexibility. However, the percentage test is useful since it requires fewer calculations and therefore leaves less room for error and subsequent coverage problems. The IRS regulations also prescribe situations in which plans may automatically satisfy the minimum coverage requirement.[62] These include plans that benefit only NHCEs, plans maintained by employers that have only HCE employees, and collectively bargained plans or portions of plans (including governmental plans described in I.R.C. § 414(d)).

c. Third Coverage Test of I.R.C. § 410(b)

The third coverage test is the average benefit percentage test, which has both a head count comparison as well as a comparison of benefits being received by the benefiting NHCEs and HCEs. Changes made to the coverage tests in I.R.C. § 410(b) were in response to the public's concern that the IRS' coverage tests were too subjective; thus, the IRS in its regulations wanted to make the rules more concrete. This test has two components:

---

62. Treas. Reg. §§ 1.410(b)-2(b)(5)–(7).

- The classification test, which actually is comprised of two parts; and
- The average benefits percentage test, whereby the average employer-provided benefit received by the NHCEs must be at least 70% of the average employer-provided benefit received by the HCEs, under *all plans* maintained by the employer.[63]

The first prong of the classification test as defined under the Treasury Regulations has two parts:

- A reasonable classification test, which tests whether the eligibility criteria used satisfies "reasonable business criteria."[64] For example, using an eligibility criterion of "salaried" employee is deemed to be reasonable.

- A nondiscriminatory classification test, which applies a modified reduced ratio percentage test to the plan's coverage (i.e., reducing the 70% to a smaller percentage).[65] Although the statute does not set forth a specified amount for this modified reduced ratio percentage test, the Treasury Regulations have designed a table which sets forth a safe harbor and unsafe harbor reduced ratio percentages.[66] Again, the IRS was trying to make the test more transparent and concrete. The intent of the table was to afford certainty for employers in applying this portion of the test and to extend greater leeway to employers whose test group consisted predominately of NHCEs (meaning, the more NHCEs in the test group, the lower the modified ratio percentage could drop). If the plan's actual ratio percentage is at or above the table's safe harbor percentage, the first prong of the average benefits test is deemed met.[67] Similarly, if the plan's coverage is at or below the unsafe harbor percentage, the first prong of the average benefits test is not met.[68] And if the plan's coverage falls in between the safe and unsafe harbors, relevant facts and circumstances can be presented to the IRS to establish that the eligibility classification is nondiscriminatory.[69]

---

63. I.R.C. § 410(b)(1)(C).

64. *See* Treas. Reg. § 1.410(b)-4(b). Reasonable classifications generally include specified job categories (e.g., sales associates, engineers, architects), nature of compensation (e.g., salaried or hourly), geographical location (e.g., Chicago versus New York), and similar *bona fide* business criteria. Listing of eligible employees by name is not considered a reasonable classification.

65. *See* Treas. Reg. § 1.410(b)-4(c).

66. *See* Teas. Reg. § 1.410(b)-4(c)(4)(iv).

67. *See* Treas. Reg. § 1.410(b)-4(c)(2).

68. *See* Treas. Reg. § 1.410(b)-4(c)(3).

69. *Id.*

The following table provides the appropriate safe and unsafe harbor percentages:

NHCE concentration %[70]	Safe Harbor %	Unsafe Harbor %
0–60%	50.00%	40.00%
61	49.25	39.25
62	48.50	38.50
63	47.75	37.75
64	47.00	37.00
65	46.25	36.25
66	45.50	35.50
67	44.75	34.75
68	44.00	34.00
69	43.25	33.25
70	42.50	32.50
71	41.00	31.00
72	41.75	31.75
73	41.00	31.00
74	40.25	30.25
75	39.50	29.50
76	38.75	28.75
77	37.25	27.25
78	36.50	26.50
79	35.75	25.75
80	35.00	25.00
81	34.25	24.25
82	33.50	23.50
83	32.75	22.75
84	32.00	22.00
85	31.25	21.25
86	30.50	20.50
87	29.75	20.00
88	29.00	20.00
89	28.25	20.00
90	27.50	20.00
91	26.75	20.00
92	26.00	20.00
93	25.25	20.00
94	24.50	20.00
95	23.75	20.00
96	23.00	20.00
97	22.25	20.00
98	21.50	20.00
99	20.75	20.00

By setting forth this range of safe and unsafe harbor percentages, the Service has attempted to add some certainty to this nondiscriminatory classification test by setting forth a range of safe and unsafe harbor percentages. The safe and unsafe harbor percentages drop significantly below the 70% requirement of the ratio percentage test,

---

70. The NHCE concentration percentage is determined by dividing the number of NHCEs by the total number of employees in the test group. For example, if the test group consists of 100 NHCEs and 10 HCEs, the nonhighly compensated employee concentration percentage is $100 \div 110 = 91\%$. *See* Treas. Reg. § 1.410(b)-4(c)(4)(iii).

depending on how significant the NHCE group is relative to the total test group of employees (this is referred to as the NHCE concentration ratio). The larger percentage presumes that the NHCEs will be better able to protect their own interest than would be the case where the NHCEs were an insignificant percentage of the workforce. For example, if the NHCE concentration ratio is 99%, the plan's overall coverage of NHCEs compared to HCEs can drop to 20.75% (significantly below the 70% in the ratio percentage test) and may even drop to 20% if relevant facts and circumstances can be shown to justify the classification used.

Because the second prong of the average benefits test is dependent upon the amount of benefits actually provided or contributions actually made under the plan, the IRS has linked the coverage of I.R.C. § 410(b) with the nondiscrimination rules of I.R.C. § 401(a)(4).[71] The benefit percentages used in this calculation will be determined under the I.R.C. § 401(a)(4) regulations as the normal accrual rate or allocation rate, expressed either as a percentage of annual average compensation or a dollar amount.[72] Since the statute determines the average benefit percentage for **all plans** in the testing group, all non-excludable employees (both NHCEs and HCEs) are counted. Thus, if a non-excludable NHCE or HCE does not benefit under the plan, his or her benefit percentage is 0% and computed in part of the calculation.[73] While this may help in satisfying the second of the first two coverage tests of I.R.C. § 410(b), those individuals receiving $0 benefits under such plan reduce the overall benefit percentage received by the group as a whole.

> **Example:** A sample employer has 1,000 employees, 100 of whom are union employees covered under a multi-employer plan. For the remaining 900 employees, there is a qualified plan, but only for salaried employees who are age 21 and have one year of service. Thus, hourly employees who are not covered under the multi-employer plan are not covered under any plan.
>
> Test Group of Nonexcludable Employees = 1,000 total employees – permitted exclusions (100 union employees) = 900 employees. Out of the test group of 900 employees, 800 are NHCEs and 100 are HCEs. Hence, the NHCE test group is 800 and the HCE test group is 100. These will be the two denominators for our ratio percentage comparisons.
>
> Plan Benefits = Salaried Status + age 21 + one-year wait → results in 400 employees benefiting, of whom 300 are NHCEs and 100 are HCEs. Note the hourly nonunion employees are not being considered as they do not benefit under the plan.

---

71. *See* Treas. Reg. § 1.401(a)(4)-0 through -13. These regulations were initially proposed in 1990 and finalized in September 1991. Changes were proposed and then finalized to these rules in 1993, with a 1994 effective date. A reasonably good faith standard applied to prior years. *See* Treas. Reg. §§ 1.401(a)(4)-13 and 1.410(b)-10.

72. *See* Treas. Reg. § 1.410(b)-5(d)(5).

73. *See* Treas. Reg. § 1.410(b)-5(d)(3).

Percentage Test:

Does the plan benefit at least 70% × 800 (NHCE Test Group) = 560 NHCEs? No, since coverage of NHCEs under the plan is only 300, which is less than 560.

Ratio Percentage Test:

Comparison of ratios:

NHCE ratio = 300 NHCEs benefiting ÷ 800 NHCEs in Test Group = 37.5%

HCE ratio = 100 HCEs benefiting ÷ 100 HCEs in Test Group = 100%

Plan's Ratio Percentage = 37.5% ÷ 100% = 37.5%, which is less than the 70% required by the ratio percentage test.

Average Benefits Test:

(1) Is the plan's classification of "salaried status" reasonable? According to the regulations, it is.
(2) Apply a modified ratio percentage test. Going back to the test group of 900, 800 of which are NHCEs, we have an NHCE concentration percentage of 800/900 = 89%.

For an NHCE concentration percentage of 89%, the table provides a modified ratio percentage test within the 28.25% to 20% range. Since the plan's actual ratio percentage is 37.5% and above the safe harbor percentage, this prong of the test has been satisfied.

(3) The final prong of the average benefits test would necessitate computing a benefit percentage for all non-excludable employees (i.e., the 900 employees in the test group). Since hourly employees are included in the test group but not covered under any qualified plan, their benefit percentage will be 0% and will obviously reduce the average overall NHCE benefit percentage. Is the average benefit percentage for the NHCEs under all plans of this employer at least 70% of the average benefit percentage for the HCEs under all plans of this employer? The plans' actuary would answer this question.

d. Additional Coverage Test of I.R.C. § 401(a)(26)

TRA '86 added a separate coverage test which was designed to limit the aggregation of plans by an employer. Under these new rules, each defined benefit plan must itself "benefit" at least 50 employees, or if less, 40% of the test group.[74] This new test applies

---

74. TRA '86 § 1112(a), adding subsection (a)(26) to I.R.C. § 401, effective beginning in 1989. In 1989, the Service released lengthy and complex proposed regulations under I.R.C. § 401(a)(26), which attempted to subject the test to each separate benefit structure within a plan. These proposed regulations were later withdrawn and replaced with shorter and simpler rules. *See* Treas. Reg. § 1.401(a)(26)-3.

separately to each plan of the employer. Thus, an employer may not aggregate plans for purposes of meeting this test, even where the plans are identical in all respects or where the plans are treated as a single plan for purposes of I.R.C. §§ 401(a)(4) and 410(b).[75] The intent of the rule was to prevent employers from avoiding the IRS anti-discrimination rules by creating multiple plans covering small numbers of employees.[76]

Later, this additional coverage test was restricted to defined benefit plans only and the IRS revised the test such that each defined benefit plan must benefit the lesser of (1) 50 employees or (2) the greater of 40% of all employees of the employer or two employees (unless there is only one employee, then one). In addition, the extra minimum participation rule may be applied separately to each line of business, even if the line of business has fewer than 50 employees.[77]

> **Example:** If the Test Group = 110 and the plan actually benefits 10 HCEs and 40 NHCEs, this test requires the plan to cover the lesser of [50 employees, 40% × 110 Test Group (or 2)] = 44 employees. Since our plan benefits 50 employees (10 HCEs and 40 NHCEs), it satisfies this test.

While the penalty for failing to meet either the minimum coverage requirements or the specific coverage rules of I.R.C. § 401(a)(26) had been disqualification, Congress modified the sanction to penalize the HCEs, not all participants under the plan.[78] Hence, if the plan fails to meet either of the minimum coverage tests, current and former highly compensated employees will be taxed on their entire amount of vested benefits.[79]

e. Checklist for Applying the Coverage Tests of I.R.C. § 401(b) and 401(a)(26)

- Identify the employer offering the plan. Related employers within the controlled group and affiliated employers need to be aggregated. Leased employees may have to be aggregated subject to the rules of I.R.C. § 414(n).

- Identify all common law employees and identify which employees are "excludable" employees for coverage testing purposes. Be mindful of individuals who have been identified by the employer as "independent contractors" but may later be classified as "common law employees," which would mean the prior coverage tests were performed inaccurately.

- Identify prior plan year compensation for all employees and ownership percentage interest (prior plan year and current plan year) of the employer for all employees in order to perform the HCE determination and possible ABT testing.

---

75. *See* Treas. Reg. § 1.401(a)(26)-1(b)(ii).
76. *See* Conf. Report H.R. 3838 (9/18/86), II-422 and 423.
77. SBJPA '96 § 432(a), effective after 1996.
78. TAMRA '88 § 1011(h)(3), adding subparagraph (G) to I.R.C. § 401(a)(16).
79. I.R.C. § 402(b)(4).

- Key to the coverage test is to separate employees into two groups—NHCEs and HCEs. We'll call these the NHCE test group and the HCE test group.
- Identify qualified plans to be tested. I.R.C. §410(b) prohibits the aggregation of certain plans; otherwise. plans could be aggregated for purposes of satisfying the coverage test of I.R.C. §410(b).
- Under each plan, identify employees who are eligible versus benefiting under the plan ("benefiting" means participating, except for 401(k) plans where benefiting means eligible to participate even if the employee elects not to reduce pay).
- Perform the coverage tests of I.R.C. §410(b), which should be applied in the following order:
  - *Percentage Test (PT):* See if participation is large enough to benefit 70% of the NHCE test group. If not, go to the next test.
  - *Ratio Percentage Test (RPT):* Compare the percentage of NHCEs benefiting under the plan to the percentage of HCEs benefiting under the plan relative to their unique test groups and see whether this comparison is at least 70%. If not, go to the next test.
  - *Average Benefits Test (ABT):* Two prongs: the nondiscriminatory classification test and the average benefits percentage test. The nondiscriminatory classification test has two parts: (1) is the classification reasonable, and (2) does the plan's ratio percentage satisfy a modified ratio percentage test? The average benefits percentage test requires the valuing of benefits/allocations under all qualified plans maintained by the employer as a percentage of each employee's compensation, and then a comparison of whether the typical NHCE benefit percentage is at least 70% of the typical HCE benefit percentage.
- If the plan is a defined benefit plan, the coverage rule of I.R.C. §401(a)(26) must be satisfied for each plan separately (no aggregation is allowed here).

Chapter 7

Vesting Schedules, Accrual Rules, Top-Heavy Rules, and Maximum Limitations

---

Reading Assignment: ERISA §§ 201, 203, 204

I.R.C. §§ 401(a)(7), 401(a)(8), 401(a)(16), 401(a)(17), 401(a)(19), 401(a)(25), 411(a), 411(b), 415, and 416

Class Discussion Questions: Can you explain how the vesting and accrual rules work together?

What are the differences between each of the three computation periods used for eligibility, vesting, and accrual?

What is the intent of the anti-cutback rule? What are some examples of plan features that are not protected under this rule?

What are the consequences if a plan is determined to be top heavy?

Why do the I.R.C. § 415 limitations apply on a limitation year basis, instead of on a plan year basis?

Overview

What is the general concept of vesting of benefits?

- vesting is a result of ERISA's classification of benefits as property rights rather than merely gifts since vesting cuts down the benefit entitlements for short service employees
- the plan document specifies each participant's vested right to benefits depending on the number of years the individual has been employed by the sponsoring employer
- if an employee terminates employment, he or she is entitled to the vested portion of his or her accrued benefits and the non-vested portion, if any, then becomes a forfeiture

- upon attaining the Code's definition of "normal retirement age," the participant is 100% vested in his or her accrued benefit

How are years of service for vesting determined?

- an employee must be credited with one year of vesting service in any 12-month period (defined in the plan document) in which he or she is credited with at least 1,000 hours of service
- generally, an hour of service must be credited to an employee
  - for each hour he or she is paid or entitled to payment for the performance of duties for the employer during the computation period
  - for certain periods of non-work (such as vacation, holiday, illness, incapacity, disability, layoff, jury duty, military leave, other approved leaves of absence, or back pay awards)
- to determine the number of hours of service during a computation period, the employer has the option of:
  - counting each hour for each employee,
  - establishing a table which credits a certain number of hours for each unit of time worked (such as 45 hours of service credited for each weekly paycheck, regardless of actual hours worked)

What is normal retirement age for the plan?

- normal retirement age (for purposes of becoming 100% vested) is defined by the Code as the **earlier** of the date provided for in the plan document, or the later of age 65 or the fifth anniversary of plan participation (this allows employers to hire individuals over age 60 without the plan needing to immediately vest and accrue their benefits)

How long can an employer make a plan participant wait before becoming vested in his or her employee contributions in a defined contribution plan?

- all employee contributions, such as elective salary deferrals, and after-tax Roth contributions, must always be 100% vested (i.e., non-forfeitable)

How long can an employer make a plan participant wait before becoming vested in his or her employer contributions in a qualified retirement plan?

- in a defined contribution plan, all employer contributions, such as matching contributions or profit sharing and money purchase plan allocations, must always be vested at least as quickly as the following:
  - if cliff vesting, then 100% after three years of service
  - if graded vesting, then 20% after two years of service, 40% after three years, 60% after four years, 80% after five years, and 100% after six years of service
- slightly different minimum vesting rules apply to defined benefit plans
- there are several situations (such as plan termination) when a participant is automatically 100% vested, regardless of the schedule contained in the plan document

What is the general concept of benefit accruals?

- accrual rights are different than vesting rights—however, both accruals and vesting serve to limit the benefits to employees who do not continue working with the employer until retirement (or death or disability)

- accruals are a concept on how a plan participant is hired without any retirement benefits (i.e., a zero accrued benefit) and at retirement has something, and the accrued benefit is what he or she is entitled to if employment is severed (death, disability, quitting, being fired) or the plan is terminated along the way

- once a benefit, right, or feature has accrued, it cannot be eliminated through a plan amendment

- however, a plan amendment may reduce or eliminate a benefit, right, or feature for *future* promises that have not yet accrued

- although the plan can have a different 12-month period for a year of service for purposes of accruals than for vesting, the definitions and rules of 1,000 hours of service are the same

- at any point in time

  ○ in a defined contribution plan, the accrued benefit is the participant's account balance (i.e., the accumulation of contributions, forfeitures, and fund earnings)

  ○ in a defined benefit plan, the accrued benefit is whatever life annuity is payable starting upon attainment of his or her normal retirement date (or possibly upon his or her early retirement date, if the plan allows for an early retirement benefit)

How does a qualified retirement plan satisfy the definitely determinable benefits rule?

- in a defined contribution plan, the plan document will clearly indicate how allocations will be made to each participant's individual account

  ○ in a profit sharing plan, the formula that will divide the single discretionary contribution

  ○ in a money purchase plan, the exact dollar or amount or percentage of compensation

  ○ in a § 401(k) plan, how participants can make, revise, or revoke elections to make salary deferrals or designated Roth contributions, and if the employer has a mandatory or discretionary match

- in a defined benefit plan, the plan's actuary will convert one form of benefit to another based on the plan's actuarial equivalences, which must be stated in the plan document in a way that precludes any employer discretion

What are the maximum benefit accruals in any year for a qualified retirement plan?

- in a defined contribution plan,

  ○ the annual addition is the sum of employee contributions, employer contributions, and the reallocation of forfeitures

- ○ in any year, the annual addition cannot be more than the lesser of
  - • $40,000 (as adjusted for inflation), or
  - • the participant's annual compensation
- • in a defined benefit plan,
  - ○ in any year, the total benefit paid from the plan cannot be more than the lesser of
    - • $160,000 (as adjusted for inflation, and as adjusted for other reasons), or
    - • the participant's average annual compensation (the average for the highest three consecutive years)

Who are the key employees?

- • a different statutory provision defines a key employee differently than an HCE (although, oftentimes the same individual plan participant is classified as both an HCE and a key employee)
- • by default, every employee who is not classified as a key employee is classified as a non-key employee
- • a key employee is defined as an employee who, during the plan year, is:
  - ○ an officer with compensation greater than $130,000 (as adjusted for inflation),
  - ○ a 5% owner of the employer, or
  - ○ a 1% owner of the employer with compensation greater than $150,000 (not adjusted)

Which annual tests compare the key employees to the non-key employees?

- • only the top-heavy test

When is a plan considered to be top heavy?

- • to determine whether a plan is top heavy for the current year, the determination date is the last day of the preceding year
- • a defined benefit plan is top heavy if at least 60% of the plan's present value of accrued benefits is attributable to <u>key employees</u>
- • similarly, a defined contribution plan is top heavy if at least 60% of the plan's accounts balances are allocated to key employees
- • there is no plan design that automatically satisfies the top-heavy test each year
- • however, if a plan document always provides benefits equal to or greater than the minimum required benefits for a top-heavy defined benefit plan or annual additions equal to or greater than the minimum required annual additions for a top-heavy defined contribution plan, and it also provides a vesting schedule which is at least as rapid as the minimum required top-heavy vesting schedule, then it is irrelevant whether the plan is, in fact, top heavy for any year—although the plan still must run the tests and report the accurate results to the federal government

If the plan is top heavy in any given year, then what are the minimum vesting and accrual rules?

- in a defined contribution plan,
  - all non-key employees must generally receive at least 3% of his or her compensation
  - under current rules, no special vesting rules supersede in top-heavy years
- in a defined benefit plan,
  - all non-key employees must generally receive at least 2% of his or her average compensation (the average for the highest five consecutive years), but after the tenth year of top-heavy minimum accruals, the plan does not need to provide any further minimum benefit accruals
  - a slightly accelerated minimum vesting schedule supersedes in top-heavy years

A. Minimum Vesting Schedules

1. Introduction

Employers were initially interested in providing retirement benefits **only** to those employees who terminated employment as of the plan's designated retirement age, thereby excluding employees who had worked for the employer but terminated prior to the plan's retirement age (for example, the plan provided for retirement benefits only for employees retiring at age 65). Such a plan could certainly be abused by employers who terminate employees immediately prior to the retirement age in order to avoid paying such benefits. To prevent such abuse, ERISA required retirement plans to define and pay a retirement benefit for terminated employees—coining the term "accrued benefit" for terminating employees (the plan would have to provide retirement benefits for participants whether or not they retired under the plan's retirement provisions). Such benefit remained a retirement benefit and therefore was generally limited to payment until the plan's retirement age. However, the determination of accrued benefit would be meaningless if the plan could subject benefits to a 0% vesting schedule (i.e., if an employee leaves before the plan's retirement age, he or she is 0% vested in the accrued benefit). While ERISA acknowledged that an employee's accrued benefit is a property right (and not a nonbinding gift), it did permit employers to use a vesting schedule to cut back on this property right for short service employees. If a plan imposes a vesting schedule, it must satisfy one of the requirements of I.R.C. § 411 and ERISA § 203. Again, because these vesting rules overlap between Title I and II, the DOL has jurisdiction over them through the Reorganization Act of 1978. Of course, a plan does not have to have a vesting schedule, or it could impose a schedule more favorable than the minimum ones set forth in the law.

While an employee's accrued benefit refers to the *amount* of benefit that an employee has earned prior to retirement, "vesting" or "nonforfeitable" refers to the percentage that the employee owns or is entitled to if he or she terminates prematurely. In a defined contribution plan, an employee's accrued benefit is his or her account balance at any point in time. In a defined benefit plan, it is defined as the employee's pension earned to date, payable at the plan's normal retirement age, as an annuity. The *vested* portion of an employee's benefit means the portion of the accrued plan benefit to which an employee is entitled if he or she leaves prior to the plan's normal retirement date.

> **Example:** A participant has $10,000 in his or her account balance as of the date of termination at age 50; he or she may be entitled to only 40% of that amount (i.e., $4,000). The remaining 60% (i.e., $6,000) is a forfeiture.

Although an employer can define the plan's normal retirement age, the Code imposes a 100% vesting requirement as of a "normal retirement age," which is a defined term under the Code.[1] For this purpose, "normal retirement age" means the **earlier of**:

(i) The age stated in the plan as normal retirement age; or

(ii) The *later* of: age 65 or the fifth anniversary of the date the employee became a participant.[2]

The purpose of this rule is to prevent the employer from using a very late normal retirement age.

> **Example:** If the plan's normal retirement age were 80, this 100% vesting rule would require full vesting at the **earlier of** (i) age 80 (the plan's NRA) or (ii) the later of age 65 or five years of participation. The earlier of the two is (ii) the later of age 65 or five years of participation. Thus, a participant who becomes a participant at age 59 will get full vesting at the (ii) **later** of age 65 or 64 (i.e., age 64 is the age when the participant has five years of participation), which is age 65. Thus, we disregard the plan's normal retirement age of 80, as it is not earlier than (ii).

> **Example:** However, if the plan uses an early normal retirement age (e.g., age 60), "normal retirement age" for full vesting is defined as the **earlier of** (i) age 60 (the plan's NRA) or (ii) the later of age 65 or the fifth anniversary of participation. The earlier of the two is (i) age 60. Thus, a participant who becomes a participant at age 60 will get full vesting at 60, as it is the earlier (i) age 60.

The Code's 100% vesting rule as described above applies to the portion of the employee's accrued benefit that is attributable to employer contributions. Any portion of an employee's accrued benefit derived from his or her own contributions must always be 100% vested (i.e., nonforfeitable) regardless of whether the contributions are mandatory for participation or voluntary.[3] Thus, all employee contributions, such as elective salary deferrals, after-tax Roth, and pre-tax (non-Roth) contributions, must always be 100% vested.

---

1. I.R.C. §411.
2. I.R.C. §411(a)(8); Treas. Reg. §1.411(a)-7(b).
3. I.R.C. §411(a)(1).

2. Permissible Vesting Schedules

If a plan uses a vesting schedule to forfeit a portion of the employee's accrued benefit attributable to employer contributions, such schedule must be at least as generous as one of the alternative minimum vesting schedules listed in I.R.C. §411(a).[4] The Tax Reform Act of 1986 (TRA '86) made major changes to the Code's vesting rules, effective for plan years beginning after December 31, 1988. Vesting service before the effective date of the change in law must be taken into account in determining current vesting. The current permissible vesting schedules, the faster vesting schedules imposed by EGTRRA '01 and PPA '06, and exceptions to the permissible vesting schedules are as follows:

- For **defined benefit plans,** one of two vesting schedules applies:

  ○ *Five-Year Cliff Schedule:* A plan satisfies this schedule if an employee after five years of vesting service receives a 100% nonforfeitable right to his or her accrued benefit. This is a cliff schedule—meaning, if you leave before having five years of vesting service, you forfeit 100%; once you have five vesting years, you forfeit nothing when leaving employment.

  ○ *Three- to Seven-Year Graded Schedule:* A plan satisfies this schedule if an employee is 20% vested after three years of vesting service and earns 20% per year of vesting service after three years until 100% after seven years.[5] This formula allows you to earn 20% each year, once you have three years of vesting, and then incrementally after that, until you have achieved 100% after 7 years.

  For example, under the three- to seven-year graded schedule, a participant with five years of vesting service has [20% after 3 years + 20% for the 4th year + 20% for the 5th year] = 60% vesting percentage.

- For **defined contribution plans,** one of two vesting schedules applies:

  ○ *Three-Year Cliff Schedule:* A plan satisfies this schedule if an employee after three years of vesting service receives a 100% nonforfeitable right to his or her accrued benefit.

  ○ *Two- to Six-Year Graded Schedule:* A plan satisfies this schedule if an employee is 20% vested after two years and earns 20% per year of vesting service until 100% after six years.[6]

  For example, under the two- to six-year graded schedule, a participant with five years of vesting service has [20% after 2 years + 20% for the 3rd year + 20% for the 4th year + 20% for the 5th year] = 80% vesting percentage.

Of course, an employer may use a vesting schedule that is more generous to the employee as long as it also vests the employee's accrued benefit at least as quickly as one of the prescribed schedules.

---

4. I.R.C. §411(a).
5. I.R.C. §411(a)(2)(A); ERISA §203(a)(2)(A)(i).
6. I.R.C. §411(a)(2)(B); ERISA §203(a)(2)(B).

There are *two exceptions* to the Code § 411(a) vesting schedules:

- If a plan requires two years of service as a minimum participation requirement, vesting must be 100% upon participation.[7]
- If there is a pattern of abuse, or the IRS has reason to believe that a plan's vesting schedule will discriminate in favor of highly compensated employees ("HCEs") as defined in I.R.C. § 414(q), the IRS may require more rapid vesting than under the two schedules.[8]

3. Vesting Schedule Amendments and Plan Terminations

Under the rules of I.R.C. § 411(a)(10), the vesting schedule of a plan may be changed prospectively as long as it leaves nonforfeitable any accrued benefit that became nonforfeitable under the plan's vesting schedule before the amendment *and* as long as each employee with three or more years of vesting service has the option of remaining under the plan's prior vesting schedule.[9]

While Congress permits the voluntary termination of pension plans and/or the discontinuance of contributions under profit sharing plans, it does require that benefits of all affected employees become 100% nonforfeitable upon such events.[10] Full vesting will impact the funding status of benefits under a defined benefit plan. There may also be situations in which a "partial plan termination" has occurred, thereby triggering 100% vesting for affected participants.

4. Years of Service for Vesting Purposes

As the vesting schedules are determined using "years of service," the Code and ERISA define what years must be counted as vesting years. Generally, *all* of an employee's years of service with an employer are to be taken into account for purposes of vesting.[11] There are certain exceptions:

- Vesting service is measured using years of service. The vesting computation period may be the calendar year, the plan year, the employee's employment anniversary year, or any other 12-consecutive month period *designated by the plan*.[12] Normally, an employee must be credited with one year of vesting service for each year that he or she completes 1,000 hours of service.[13] Most plans use the **plan year** as the vesting computation period; most § 401(k) plans use the calendar year as the plan year and vesting year. When an employer is first establishing a

7. I.R.C. § 410(a)(1)(B)(i).
8. Treas. Reg. § 1.401(a)(4)-11(c).
9. I.R.C. § 411(a)(10).
10. I.R.C. § 411(d)(3).
11. I.R.C. § 411(a)(5); Treas. Reg. § 1.411(a)-5(a).
12. I.R.C. § 411(a)(5)(B); ERISA § 203(b)(2)(A).
13. I.R.C. § 411(a)(5)(B); ERISA § 203(b)(2)(A).

plan, it is given the discretion to begin vesting credit as of the effective date of the plan or to provide retroactive vesting credit for prior years of service (i.e., time during which there was no plan in existence). Note that a vesting year of service is not the same 12-month period used for eligibility (which needs to be the first employment year). SECURE requires that I.R.C. § 401(k) plans permit participation by long-term, part-time employees who work at least 500 hours in three consecutive 12-month periods (and have attained age 21). For vesting purposes for these employees, a vesting year is the 12-month period during which the part-time employee earns at least 500 hours of service.[14]

- Normally, an employee must be credited with one year of vesting service for each year that he or she completes 1,000 hours of service. The "hours of service" are basically all hours for which an employee is compensated or entitled to compensation for services performed for the employer and for reasons other than the performance of services (e.g., vacation pay, payment for sick leave).[15] The same definition of "hours" used for minimum participation and benefit accrual purposes applies for vesting purposes. Remember from the prior chapter that if the employer does not count hours of service, it may use a table which credits a certain number of hours for each unit of time worked (e.g., 45 hours of service credited for each *week* employed). Once the employee completes the required number of hours during the vesting computation period, the employee must be given a year of vesting service whether or not he or she is still employed by the employer at the end of the year.

A plan *may* exclude certain years of service for purposes of determining "years of service" under the plan's vesting schedule:[16]

- Years of service prior to age 18;
- Years of service completed by an employee under a plan which requires mandatory contributions provided that the employee does not participate for such year solely due to failure to make all mandatory contributions;[17]
- Years during which the plan or a predecessor plan was not maintained by the employer;
- Service prior to the effective date of I.R.C. § 411 if such service would have been disregarded under the plan's pre-ERISA break-in-service rules;
- Service prior to 1/1/71 (unless the employee has had at least three years of service after 12/31/70); or
- Service during any vesting computation period in which the employee fails to complete a year of service and service that is *not* required to be counted because of the break-in-service rules.[18]

---

14. SECURE § 112, effective for plan years beginning after December 31, 2020.

15. I.R.C. § 411(a)(5)(B); ERISA § 203(b)(2)(B).

16. I.R.C. § 411(a)(4).

17. Treas. Reg. § 1.411(a)-5(b)(2) (if the employee contributes any part of the mandatory contribution for a plan year, such year may not be excluded under this rule).

18. *Id.*

Just as in the case of the eligibility rules, an employer may impose break-in-service criteria so that employees may lose prior credited years because of subsequent intermittent service or reduction in hours worked. The break-in-service rules are optional in nature and are generally used by employers to reduce recordkeeping.

If a participant is credited with less than 501 hours of service within the plan's computation period, the participant has incurred a "break in service."[19] The same definition that was used to describe the applicable break-in-service rules for eligibility purposes are applied equally for vesting. REA added special rules for periods of absences due to maternity or paternity leave.[20] Such periods of absences must be counted as service with the employer in determining whether a break in service has occurred. A maximum of 501 hours for one year is counted under this rule.

5. Permissible Forfeitures of Vested Rights

Vested rights can be forfeited even if a participant has the requisite number of vesting years of service to be guaranteed a certain portion of his or her benefits.[21] These exceptions are not mandatory; however, plans that utilize these exceptions will not be treated as having violated the vesting rules simply because of the provisions. These exceptions recognize that previously vested pension benefits may nevertheless be subsequently forfeited.

Death Before Retirement: A plan does not have to provide for death benefits; hence, a plan may provide for a forfeiture of vested benefits upon death. This exception applies only to employer derived benefits.[22] Also, I.R.C. §401(a)(11) requires certain survivor annuities for the participant's spouse be made payable from the plan; this death benefit forfeiture rule does *not* apply to such survivor annuity.

Suspension of Benefits upon Reemployment of Retiree: To prevent an employee from retiring but later returning to work for the same employer and receiving a salary plus retirement benefits, the plan may provide that payment of his or her benefits is temporarily suspended until the employee actually retires.[23] These are referred to as the suspension of benefit rules. The regulations set forth rules as to what constitutes "reemployment" for this purpose and the procedural guidelines that must be complied with in order to suspend benefits in this context.[24]

Retroactive Amendments: The Code recognizes that certain plan amendments may be made retroactively without being considered as depriving participants of nonforfeitable benefits.[25] Governmental approval of such amendments is required.

---

19. I.R.C. §411(a)(6)(A).
20. REA '84 §202(e)(2), adding I.R.C. §411(a)(6)(E).
21. I.R.C. §411(a)(3).
22. I.R.C. §411(a)(3)(A).
23. I.R.C. §411(a)(3)(B).
24. Labor Reg. §2530.203; 29 C.F.R. §2530.203.
25. I.R.C. §412(c)(8).

Withdrawal of Mandatory Contributions: A plan may provide that a participant who is not yet 50% vested in his or her employer-derived accrued benefit will forfeit such benefit upon withdrawal of any amount of the employee's mandatory contributions.[26] The plan must contain a repayment provision whereby the participant may repay the amount of the distributions (plus interest if the plan is a defined benefit plan) and thereby have his or her employer-derived accrued benefit restored.[27]

Lost Beneficiary: Benefits may be forfeited if the employee or the beneficiary cannot be located. However, such plan must provide for reinstatement of the benefit if a claim is later made by the participant or beneficiary.[28]

Limitations on 25 Highest Paid: In the case of a defined benefit plan that prematurely terminates (i.e., within the first 10 years of establishment or 10 years of a plan amendment to increase benefits), benefits of the 25 most highly compensated individuals may not exceed certain limits even if such employees might lose a portion of their vested accrued benefits.[29]

Forfeitures for Cause (or "Bad Boy" Clauses): Prior to ERISA, a plan could provide that an employee forfeits his or her benefit because of "misconduct" or "dishonesty." While forfeiture for cause is not expressly provided for under I.R.C. §411, the IRS Regulations state that to the extent a plan's vesting schedule is more liberal than the minimum schedules of I.R.C. §411, the employee may forfeit a portion of his or her vested benefit upon the occurrence of certain events (e.g., working for a competitor). Given the further limitations imposed on what constitutes a permissible vesting schedule, such forfeiture clauses are no longer prevalent.[30]

6. Forfeiture Allocations

Those participants who terminate without becoming fully vested forfeit the remaining benefit. For example, Participant A, with five years of vesting service under a two- to six-year graded schedule, will retain 80% of his accrued benefit associated with employer contributions, but forfeit the remaining 20%. The 20% portion is known as a forfeiture. So if Participant A has an account balance of $50,000 attributable to employer contribution, upon termination, A takes $40,000 (80% × $50,000) and forfeits $10,000 (20% × $50,000).

As will be discussed in Part B below, qualified retirement plans are subject to a rule known as the "definitely determinable" rule.[31] For profit sharing and stock bonus plans, forfeitures of nonvested interests from terminating participants can be used *either* to increase other participants' accounts or reduce employer contributions or pay administrative expenses under the plan. But for pension plans (including defined

---

26. I.R.C. §411(a)(B)(D)(i).
27. I.R.C. §411(a)(3)(D)(ii).
28. Treas. Reg. §1.411(a)-4(b)(5).
29. Treas. Reg. §1.401(a)(4)-5(b).
30. *See* Rev. Rul. 85-31, 1985-1 C.B. 153.
31. Treas. Reg. §1.401-1(b)(1).

benefit plans), benefits must be determined in accordance with a stipulated formula, and thus cannot be increased with forfeitures.[32] Qualified pension plans must use forfeitures to reduce employer contributions or to pay administrative expenses under the plan, not to increase benefits.[33]

B. Benefit Accrual Rules

1. Introduction

ERISA established the concept of an "accrued benefit" to work in harmony with its vesting standards. Employees who had otherwise satisfied the plan's eligibility requirements would not be eligible to receive retirement benefits from the plan, even if he or she terminated employment prior to the plan's retirement age.

> **Example:** Participant P becomes a participant at age 45 but leaves employment at age 55, prior to the plan's NRA. Participant P is not eligible for the NRB formula, as he or she is not retiring at the plan's NRA (e.g., age 65). Nevertheless, Participant P has been accruing a benefit during his or her 10 years of plan participation, to which he or she will be entitled to the vested portion of that accrued benefit. But that accrued benefit is still a retirement benefit, to be paid at the plan's NRA, unless the plan permits the participant to take a lump sum payment earlier.

Defined contribution plans were required to ascribe to a fixed allocation rate for all eligible participants in a given plan year, and the vesting standards were designed to protect such benefits if the participant participated for a minimal number of years; the two requirements were easy to understand and to formulate. However, in the context of defined benefit plans, Congress affirmed the employer's ability to formulate the accrued benefit formula, just as it specified the normal retirement formula. Just as the NRB formula has three components—the benefits' formula, the NRA, and the form of payment, the AB formula will have similar components.

> **Example:** If the NRB formula was [80% × FAE]/65/life only or J&S, the employer still had to decide how that benefit was going to be earned over the employee's working lifetime. It could decide to provide faster accruals, say AB = [8% × FAE × years of service]/65/life only or J&S, or slower accruals, say AB =[4% × FAE × years of service]/65/life only or J&S.

Given that the choice remained with the employer (as in the case of coverage), specific tests were imposed under the Code to assure nondiscrimination of benefits in favor of the highly paid (who were assumed to have the maximum years of participation and to be of older age).

---

32. Treas. Reg. § 1.401-1(b)(1)(i).
33. Treas. Reg. § 1.401-7(a).

TRA '86 added I.R.C. §401(a)(17) which provides an annual compensation limit for each employee under a qualified plan.[34] As such, a defined contribution plan may not base allocations on compensation in excess of the annual compensation limit and a defined benefit plan may not base benefit accruals on compensation in excess of the annual compensation limit. For example, for 2020, the annual compensation limit is $285,000; thus, a defined contribution with a contribution and allocation formula of 10% of a participant's total compensation could not allocate any contributions for the participant's compensation in excess of $285,000 for 2020.

> **Example:** If the AB formula = [2% × Pay × yos]/65/life only or J&S and a participant's pay was $300,000 during 2020, his or her accrual for the year would be only [2% × $285,000]/65/life only or J&S.

2. Definition of Accrued Benefit versus Accrual Rate

A participant's accrued benefit is defined as follows:

- In the case of a defined benefit plan, the employee's accrued benefit is to be determined under the plan and expressed in the form of an annual benefit commencing at normal retirement date (if the plan defines accrued benefit in this manner). Thus, just like the NRB has three components to it, the accrued benefit (AB) has three components—the amount of the benefit, when it is payable (NRA), and the form of benefit (e.g., life only or J&S).

- In the case of a defined contribution plan, the employee's accrued benefit is the balance in the employee's account.[35]

An *accrual rate* is different from the accrued benefit, as the former represents the annual rate at which a participant accrues in the plan's normal retirement benefit and must satisfy one of the statutory minimum accrual requirements set forth in I.R.C. §411(b). Generally, one must refer to the plan's accrued benefit formula to ascertain each year's accrual rate. In contrast, a participant's accrued benefit under a defined benefit plan represents the cumulative value of those accruals, to be valued at the plan's retirement age and expressed as an annuity benefit at that age. For a defined benefit plan, the employer is free to use a fixed level to determine the normal retirement benefit formula (e.g., 80% x FAE), but the accrued benefit is inherently a unit-type formula, as the participant generally accrues a benefit for each year of participation (e.g., 4% x FAE x years of service). For example, if the NRB = [80% × FAE]/65/life only or J&S and the AB = [4% × FAE × years of service (cap at 20)]/65/life only or J&S, the accrual rate is 4%, but, for a participant with 15 years of service, his or her AB = [4% × FAE × 15]/65/life only or J&S = 60% × FAE/65/life only or J&S.

---

34. TRA '86 §1106(d)(1), adding paragraph 17 to I.R.C. §401(a).
35. I.R.C. §411(a)(7).

For a defined contribution plan, a participant's accrued benefit represents the cumulative value of allocations made to his or her account balance, plus interest and/or capital gains or losses. The participant's allocation rate or accrual rate is defined in the plan and determines how the participant shares in any given employer contribution.

Accrued benefits should be contrasted with vesting. An employee's accrued benefit describes his or her benefit under the plan, whereas vesting describes how much of that benefit is nonforfeitable or forfeitable.

3. The Accrual Computation Period

An employee generally accrues a benefit based upon participation in the plan and the crediting of one or more years of participation. A year of participation is measured by counting an employee's hours of service during a specified 12-consecutive-month period and will only start counting when the employee becomes a participant under the plan. This third 12-month period is referred to as the accrual computation period, as opposed to the eligibility computation period or the vesting computation period.

Although benefits generally are only earned while the employee is a participant under the plan, the employer of a defined benefit plan may credit benefits based on service rendered prior to the effective date of the plan. Such benefits are then granted as "past service" benefits. Likewise, an employer adopting an increased benefit formula through a plan amendment may increase prior participation years with the increased formula, thereby granting a "past service" benefit.

A plan may designate any 12-consecutive-month period as the accrual computation period, except that the period so designated must apply equally to all participants.[36] The accrual computation period is generally the **plan year**, which is the same 12-month period as the vesting year. A plan may require an employee to earn 1,000 hours of service during the accrual computation period in order to be credited participation.[37] Consequently, an employee must be credited with at least a partial year of participation if he or she earns at least 1,000 hours of service. A plan may require more than 1,000 hours of service to earn a full year of participation, but then must credit the employee with a partial year of participation if he or she earns at least 1,000 hours of service.[38] An employee's period of service for benefit accrual purposes commences when he or she commences participation in the plan.[39] His or her period of service ends when he or she severs from service.[40] An employee's severance from service is the earlier of:

---

36. Labor Reg. § 2530.204-2(a).
37. I.R.C. § 410(b)(4)(C).
38. Labor Reg. § 2530.204(c).
39. Treas. Reg. § 1.410(a)-7(b)(2).
40. Treas. Reg. § 1.410(a)-7(a)(2)(iv), -7(a)(3)(iv), and -7(e)(1).

- The date he or she quits, retires, is discharged, or dies; or

- The first anniversary of the first date of a period in which he or she remains absent from service (with or without pay) for any reason other than the ones mentioned above.[41]

The regulations provide special rules for determining an employee's severance of service due to maternity leave/paternity leave and for military leave.[42] Periods of severance, even if less than 12 months, can be disregarded for benefit accrual purposes.[43]

If the participant enters on a valid entry date which is not the same as the beginning of the plan year, retroactive credit for all hours of service since the beginning of the applicable plan year must be given. For example, if the plan year is the same as the calendar year, but Participant A enters the plan on 7/1/20, his or her service for the entire plan year must be counted.

Consistent with the rules applicable for eligibility and vesting, an employee must be credited with all hours of service for each:

- Hour for which he or she is directly or indirectly paid for the performance of services for the employer ("hours worked");

- Hour for which he or she is directly or indirectly paid for periods in which no services are performed due to vacation, holiday, illness, incapacity, payoff, jury duty, military duty, or authorized leave of absence;[44] and

- Hour of back pay awarded or agreed to by the employer (and credited in the year to which the back pay relates vs. paid).[45]

Similar to the eligibility rules, equivalencies may be used if the employer does not count hours (e.g., an employee is credited with 10 hours for each day worked).[46]

By now, we've identified three computation periods:

- The eligibility computation period, which requires 1,000 hours beginning on the employee's date of hire (i.e., first hour of service) and ending 12 months later (with a new exception for long-term part-time employees). This is the employee's first employment year, not the plan year. If the employee does not attain the requisite number of hours, the employer can continue to use the employee's employment year or switch to the plan year.

- The vesting computation period, which requires 1,000 hours to be earned during the 12-month plan year. Vesting starts to compute when the employee is first hired even though he or she is not yet a participant.

---

41. Treas. Reg. § 1.401(a)-7(b)(2).
42. Treas. Reg. § 1.410(a)-9.
43. Treas. Reg. § 1.410(a)-7(e)(1).
44. Labor Reg. § 2530.200b-2(a)(2).
45. *Id.*
46. *See* Treas. Reg. § 1.410(a)-7(a)(3).

- The accrual computation period, which may require more than 1,000 hours to be earned during the 12-month plan year (with a pro rata credit if the employee has at least 1,000 hours). Accrual does not start until the employee becomes a participant, but all hours of service earned during the plan year will count once the employee becomes a participant if the plan uses entry dates.

4. Defined Contribution Plans

While employer contributions may be discretionary and are more flexible under a defined contribution plan as compared to a defined benefit plan, the Code requires the defined contribution benefits to be definitely determinable. In the context of a profit sharing and stock bonus plan, definitely determinable means that "[t]he plan [document] must provide a definite predetermined formula for allocating the contributions made to the plan among the participants and for distributing the funds accumulated under the plan after a fixed number of years, the attainment of a stated age, or upon the prior occurrence of some event such as layoff, illness, disability, retirement, death, or severance of employment. A formula for allocating the contributions among the participants is definite if, for example it provides for an allocation in proportion to the basic compensation of each participant."[47] Thus, the employer contribution formula may be discretionary, but the allocation formula must be set forth in the plan document so as to predetermine how any employer contributions when made will be allocated.

> **Example:** If the employer contribution is discretionary but the allocation formula is based on salary (i.e., the allocation is to be the same proportion that the participant's salary bears to the total of all participants' salaries), for a participant with $50,000 sharing in an employer contribution of $125,000, where total participants' salaries are $500,000, that participant's allocation would be $125,000 (total contributions) × [$50,000 ÷ $500,000] (the participant's pay divided all participants' pay) = $12,500, which provides for an allocation rate of 25% = ($12,500 ÷ $50,000).

For §401(k) plans, the plan document must state the level of any employer match (e.g., 50% or 100% of the employee's salary deferral contribution) and/or the level of any nonelective employer contributions (e.g., 3% of the participant's compensation).

In the context of defined contribution pension plans (e.g., money purchase and target benefit plans), definitely determinable means that "[t]he determination of the amount of retirement benefits and the contributions to provide such benefits are not dependent upon profits. Benefits are not definitely determinable if funds arising from forfeitures on termination of service, or other reason, may be used to provide increased benefits for the remaining participants."[48] Here, the employer contribution formula and the employee allocation formula are linked. For example, if the money purchase

---

47. Treas. Reg. §1.401-1(b)(1)(ii) and (iii).
48. Treas. Reg. §1.401-1(b)(1)(i).

plan calls for an annual employer contribution equal to 10% of total participants' salaries, the allocation formula for each participant will be 10% of his or her salary.

An employee's accrued benefit under a defined contribution plan is simply the balance in his or her account. A defined contribution plan must separately account for each employee's accrued benefit.[49] A plan is not required to separately account for employer contributions and employee contributions contributed under the same plan. As a practical matter, most if not all plans maintain separate accounts for both employer and employee contributions and separately allocate income, gains, and losses between both accounts. If the plan does not separately account for employer contributions, the portion of an employee's account balance derived from his or her own contributions is determined by multiplying the account balance by a fraction, the numerator of which is the aggregate employee contributions (less withdrawals) and the denominator of which is the sum of the employer's and employee's contributions (both less withdrawals). The numerator and denominator of the fraction exclude income, gains, and losses earned on the contributions.[50]

> **Example:** If only one account is maintained for each participant and the participant contributes 5% of his or her pay, and the employer contributes 10% of his or her pay, the fraction of $[5\% \div (5\% + 10\%)] = 1/3$ is used to determine the portion of the account attributable to the employee's contributions, and 2/3 is used to determine the portion of the account attributable to the employer's contributions.

An employee accrues a benefit for an accrual computation period (generally the plan year) if his or her account is credited with an allocation of employer contributions (including forfeitures) or with employee contributions for that year. Whether an employee accrues a benefit for a plan year generally has no impact on whether he or she accrues a benefit for any other plan year.

A defined contribution plan may require an employee to earn 1,000 hours of service and be employed on the last day of the plan year in order to receive an allocation for the plan year. This last day employment requirement is generally referred to as an "active participant rule" and is closely scrutinized by the IRS to see if it is discriminatory.

Generally, the level of annual allocations under a defined contribution plan is based on the participant's present compensation, and therefore unrelated to the participant's age. Such allocations present no accrued benefit problems. However, the Code prohibits the annual allocations to an employee's account from ceasing or the rate of allocation from being reduced based upon the attainment of any age.[51] Such prohibition is required to be reconciled with the Code's nondiscrimination, coverage, and maximum limitations provisions.[52] Under the final IRS regulations relating to

---

49. I.R.C. §411(b)(3)(B).
50. I.R.C. §411(3)(B).
51. I.R.C. §411(b)(2)(A).
52. I.R.C. §411(b)(2)(C).

coverage and nondiscrimination, the IRS affirmed the use of age-weighted allocation formulas for defined contribution plans, consistent with the nondiscrimination standard of the Code.[53] Such age-weighted formulas increase the rate of allocation on account of age rather than reduce the annual rate of allocation. In the context of target benefit plans, Congress has authorized the IRS to prescribe regulations consistent with its intent regarding all defined contribution plans.[54]

5. Defined Benefit Plans

In the context of defined benefit plans, the definitely determinable requirement specifies that the benefits for each participant must be computed in accordance with an express formula contained in the plan and cannot be subject to the discretion of the employer.[55]

For participants who do not retire with the employer but terminate employment and subsequently attain the plan's retirement age, a defined benefit plan must provide for a portion of the ultimate normal retirement benefit that has been accrued over his or her years of plan participation.[56] Such a formula is referred to as the "accrued benefit formula" and must be described as an annual benefit commencing at the plan's normal retirement age under a normal form of payment (e.g., life only), or the actuarial equivalent of such a benefit if the plan determines the accrued benefit in a form other than an annual benefit commencing at normal retirement date.[57] A plan may delay credit of the accrued benefit of an employee until the employee completes two continuous years of service (used for participation purposes).[58]

In general, the term "accrued benefit" refers exclusively to pension or retirement benefits. Ancillary benefits such as medical expenses (or premiums for such expenses), disability benefits not in excess of an employee's normal retirement benefit, life insurance benefits, incidental death benefits, or the current portion of life insurance protection are not considered part of an employee's accrued benefit.[59] However, optional forms of benefits (e.g., lump sum payment, distribution in-kind) are considered accrued benefits for some purposes.

An employee's accrued benefit derived from his or her own contributions is the employee's aggregate contributions (less withdrawals) expressed as an *annual* benefit commencing at normal retirement date, using an interest rate determined under I.R.C. § 417(e).[60] As a practical matter, very few defined benefit plans permit employee contributions.

---

53. Treas. Reg. § 1.410(a)(4)-2(b)(3).
54. I.R.C. § 411(b)(2)(B).
55. Treas. Reg. § 1.401-1(b)(1)(i).
56. Treas. Reg. § 1.411(b)-1(a).
57. I.R.C. § 411(c)(3). To satisfy the definitely determinable requirement, such actuarial assumptions must be determined in a manner that precludes employer discretion. *See* I.R.C. § 401(a)(25).
58. I.R.C. § 411(b)(1)(E); Treas. Reg. § 1.411(b)-1(d)(1).
59. Treas. Reg. § 1.411(a)-7(a)(1); I.R.C § 411(d)(6)(B)(ii).
60. I.R.C. § 411(c)(2)(B).

As discussed earlier, the plan's NRB formula is described as either flat, fixed, unit, or variable—generally, fixed or unit are the two most popular types used. If the NRB is fixed (e.g., NRB = [80% × FAE]/65/life only or J&S), the employer must determine a separate AB formula to determine how the 80% is being earned from entry into the plan until retirement. In contrast, if NRB is unit (e.g., NRB = [2% × years of service × FAE]/65/life only or J&S), the AB is the same as the NRB formula.

The Code is concerned with excessive backloading of the accrued benefit formula—meaning that the participant accrues very little in the early years of participation and then accrues most of the benefit closer to retirement. This also dovetails with the vesting rules, as minimum vesting requirements are not meaningful if the benefit is essentially very little in the early years. Thus, the determination of an employee's accrued benefit must satisfy one of three alternative tests found in I.R.C. §411(b)(1) to assure that there is not excessive backloading in the AB formula:

- The 3% method;
- The 133⅓% rule; or
- The fractional rule.[61]

The purpose of these rules is to test the annual accrual rate in terms of how fast or slow an employee is accruing the ultimate normal retirement benefit. Normally, an employer will not design the accrual rate to be front-loaded (i.e., provide greater accruals in the early years of participation), as such a formula does not reward seniority. However, an employer may be tempted to back-load the formula (i.e., provide greater accruals in the later years of participation). The goal of the I.R.C. §411(b) tests is to prevent *excessive* backloading. Excessive backloading is a technique used to accrue minimal benefits in the early years of participation and richer benefits in the later years of participation. If allowed, the accrued benefit formula could be used to circumvent the vesting schedule limitations.

> **Example:** The employer uses a five-year cliff vesting schedule in a defined benefit plan, but the accrual rates are 0% for the first 10 years of plan participation, and then 5% × compensation for each year after 10 years. The vesting schedule is meaningless as the participant vests in 100% of 0% per year accruals.

The 3% method basically requires that 3% of the NRB benefit must be accrued over each of the participant's years of participation until the plan's normal retirement age. Obviously, the AB formula would have to cap years of service at 33⅓ years as [3% × 33⅓] = 100%, and the AB formula will never result in a number greater than the NRB. For example, if the NRB formula had a benefit of [80% × FAE], the annual accrual rate in the AB formula must be at least 3% of 80% = 2.4%, which will accomplish earning the benefit over a period of 33⅓ years. Thus designing an AB formula of [3% × years of service (cap 26⅔) × FAE]/65/life only or J&S would satisfy

---

61. I.R.C. §411(b).

this test, whereas a formula of [2% × years of service (cap 40) × FAE]/65/life only or J&S would not, as the annual accrual rate is not at least 2.4%.

The 133⅓ method is designed to test an AB formula that varies the accrual percentages applied to various years of participation. Remember that the incentive is for the employer to want to provide very low accrual in the early years of participation, whereas greater accruals would occur in the later years of participation. This test checks to see if the increases from earlier accrual rates to later accrual rates exceeds increases of over 133⅓%. For example, if the NRB and AB formula = [2% × 1st 10 years of service × FAE + 3% × 2nd 10 years of service × FAE + 4% × years of service over 20 × FAE]/65/life only or J&S, the AB formula would fail the 133⅓ test as the jump from 2% to 3% is 150% and the jump from 2% to 4% is 200%.

The fractional method is a default whereby the AB formula can be drafted to be the fractional rule. Basically, the AB under the fractional rule has each participant accruing the NRB ratably over one's years of participation until normal retirement age. The accrual rate will depend on the age at which the employee became a participant, and thus, will vary employee by employee.

> **Example:** If the NRB formula was [80% × FAE], a participant entering the plan at age 35 with an NRA of 65 (thus having a span of 30 years until NRA) would have an AB = [1/30 × 80% × years of service × FAE]/65/life only or J&S = [2⅔% × years of service × FAE]/65/life only or J&S. start here

> **Example:** In contrast, a participant entering the plan at age 50 with an NRA of 65 (thus having a span of only 15 years until NRA) would have an AB = [1/15 × 80% × years of service × FAE]/65/life only or J&S = [5⅓% × years of service × FAE]/65/life only or J&S. Each participant then has a different accrual rate based on the age at which he or she comes into the plan, making the AB formula expensive for older hires.

Consistent with these rules, the Code also prohibits the accrued benefit from decreasing on account of age or service.[62] However, a plan may limit the number of years of service that may be taken into account for determining the amount of, or the rate at which, benefits accrued under the accrued benefit formula.[63]

Caveat: The rules of I.R.C. § 411(b) are testing the *rate* at which the participant's accrued benefit is changing over his or her years of participation. Thus, defined benefit plans using final average earnings (abbreviated FAE), as opposed to career average earnings (abbreviated CAE), as the basis for the accrued benefit and normal retirement benefit formulae are inherently providing richer accruals in all years of participation as compensation is increasing. Such increase in compensation is not what is being tested under I.R.C. § 411(b).

---

62. I.R.C. § 411(b)(1)(G); however, reductions due to Social Security benefits or the commencement of Social Security benefits are not to be considered. *See also* I.R.C. § 411(b)(2).
63. Prop. Treas. Reg. § 1.411(b)-2(c)(2)(i).

OBRA '86 added the requirement to defined benefit plans that accruals may not cease nor be reduced, in the event that the participant remains employed after the normal retirement age and is otherwise eligible for an accrual.[64] Thus, benefits available upon actual retirement must be the greater of the normal retirement benefit formula using all years of participation (including those after normal retirement age) or the actuarial equivalent of the participant's normal retirement benefit computed as of normal retirement age. Defined contribution plans are also prohibited from ceasing allocations, or reducing the rate of allocation, to an employee's account simply because the employee has attained a given age.[65]

C. Top-Heavy Rules

Plans that benefit one or more "owner-employees" must satisfy the requirements of I.R.C. § 401(a)(10)(B), and except to the extent provided in the regulations, they must satisfy the top-heavy requirements of I.R.C. § 416.[66] This is solely a qualification requirement and not a Title I requirement.

The top-heavy requirements hinge on who is a "key employee" of the employer, which is defined as an employee who at any time during the plan year meets any one of the following tests:

- An officer (e.g., president, vice president, treasurer, secretary) of the employer with annual compensation in excess of $130,000 (which is indexed; for 2020, this number was $185,000); or

- A 5% owner of the employer (determined similarly as a 5% owner for HCE purposes), or

- A 1% owner of the employer (determined similarly as a 5% owner for HCE purposes but with 1% substituted for 5%) with annual compensation in excess of $150,000 (which is not indexed).[67]

The determination date for the plan year is defined as the last day of the preceding plan year or the last day of the first plan year (for new plans).[68] "Under the EGTRRA '01 changes, an employee is a key employee, if during the preceding plan year, the employee met one of the above criteria.[69]

---

64. OBRA '86 §§ 9202(b)(1)(A)–(B), adding subparagraph (H) to I.R.C. § 411(b)(1).

65. I.R.C. § 411(b)(2).

66. When Congress permitted partners and sole proprietors to be covered under a qualified plan as "owner employees," it imposed what were referred to as the Keogh provisions to guarantee that the non-owner employees would be sufficiently protected. The Keogh provisions were introduced by Congressman Eugene Keogh.

67. I.R.C. § 416(i)(1)(A).

68. I.R.C. § 416(g)(4)(C).

69. Treas. Reg. § 1.416-1, T-12. The regulations were promulgated in 1984 and have not been updated for the EGTRRA '01 changes.

For purposes of determining the total number of officers treated as key employees, the statute caps the number at 50, or if less, the greater of [three or 10% of the total number of employees].[70] For example, for a large employer with 10,000 employees, the cap would be at 50 officers to be counted as key employees, whereas for a small employer with 100 employees, the greater of [3, 10% × 100] is 10 employees, which is less than 50, resulting in a cap of 10 officers to be counted as key employees.

Once one can ascertain who is a key employee as of the determination date, the plan can be valued, and it can be determined whether or not it is top heavy. For defined benefit plans, a plan is top heavy if, as of the determination date, the present value of the accrued benefits of the key employees exceeds 60% of the present value of the cumulative accrued benefits under the plan for all employees.[71] For defined contribution plans, a plan is top heavy if, as of the determination date, the aggregate value of the accounts of the key employees exceeds 60% of the aggregate value of the accounts of all employees under the plan.[72]

The consequences of becoming a top-heavy plan include:

- For defined benefit plans, either a three-year cliff schedule or a two- to six-year graded schedule must be used. These are the same schedules presently applicable to all defined contribution plans.

- Minimum required contributions or benefit accruals must be provided to the non-key employees (e.g., for a defined contribution plan, a minimum contribution equal to the lesser of 3% of the participant's compensation or the maximum contribution rate by any key employee); for a defined benefit plan, a minimum benefit of the lesser of [2% × the participant's number of vesting service, 20%] × FAE (using a five-year average of compensation).

- The employer must aggregate all plans in which a key employee is a participant as a single plan for purposes of the minimum coverage rules and the nondiscrimination rules, and test accordingly.[73]

D. Protection of Accrued Benefit (Known as the Anti-Cutback Rule)

The vesting and accrued benefit rules could be rendered meaningless if the employer were able to retroactively reduce an employee's accrued benefits. Thus, ERISA § 204(g) and I.R.C. § 411(d)(6) protect an employee's accrued benefit by prohibiting a reduction through a plan amendment.

While an employer is permitted to amend its plan to reduce or eliminate *prospective* accrual of benefits and/or allocation, it is generally not able to forfeit, or "cut-back,"

---

70. I.R.C. § 416(i)(1).
71. I.R.C. § 416(g)(1)(A)(i).
72. I.R.C. § 416(a)(1)(A)(ii).
73. I.R.C. § 416(g)(2)(A)(i).

participants' benefits that have already accrued.[74] Note that there are notification rules that apply regarding the plan amendments affecting future benefit accruals (referred to as the 402(h) notices), to be discussed in Chapter 16.[75] The Code specifies that a plan may not be amended in a way that would reduce, or "cut-back," the accrued benefit that a participant has earned up to the effective date of the amendment.

In analyzing this protection, we have to ask ourselves three questions: What is considered a *plan amendment* for this purpose? What does it mean to *reduce* a benefit? What is included in an *accrued benefit* for this purpose?

1. What Is a Plan Amendment Reducing Accrued Benefits for Purposes of Code § 411(d)(6)?

The regulations indicate that I.R.C. § 411(d)(6) is not limited to written instruments affecting plan provisions but also extends to other transactions that have similar effects as plan amendments (such as mergers, spinoffs, and transfers).[76] According to the Service, if an employer has the ability to limit the availability of certain optional forms of benefits to certain participants, but not all, that would be impermissible.[77] Such result applies regardless of whether there is a plan amendment to accomplish that.[78] That prohibition extends to the plan administrator, committee, trustee, actuary, fiduciary, or any person other than the participant and/or spouse. For example, the plan administrator cannot decide which participants are eligible for a lump sum distribution. Case law does not necessarily agree that an exercise of employer discretion is subject to I.R.C. § 411(d).[79]

2. What Is Considered a *Reduction* in an Accrued Benefit?

The regulations require all plan provisions be taken into account in determining the computation of the accrued benefits. This includes determination of years of service and break-in-service provisions for determining benefit accruals *and* actuarial factors (interest and mortality) for determining optional and early retirement benefits.[80]

---

74. I.R.C. § 411(d)(6)(A).

75. There are referred to as ERISA § 204(h) notices that must be circulated to affected individuals in a timely fashion. EGTRRA '01 § 659 contains new notification requirements for future cutbacks in defined benefit or money purchase plans.

76. Treas. Reg. § 1.411(d)-4, Q&A 2(a)(3).

77. Treas. Reg. § 1.411(d)-4, Q&A-4(a). In contrast, the legislative history to REA '84 indicates that reduction or elimination of an option as a result of discrimination in favor of employees who are officers, shareholders, or highly compensated is a by-product of I.R.C. § 401(a)(4).

78. Treas. Reg. § 1.411(d)-4, Q&A-4(a).

79. *See* Collignon v. Reporting Serv. Co., 796 F. Supp. 1136 (C.D. Ill. 1992) (stating, "There is no indication that Section VIII of the Plan came about by plan amendment. Where there is no amendment altering the method of payment of benefits, the statute on its face does not apply.").

80. Treas. Reg. § 1.411(d)-3(b).

Plans that use a variable standard (e.g., PBGC interest rate) for computing actuarial equivalence are not subject to the anti-cutback limitations unless the standard used is changed.[81]

3. What Is Included in the Accrued Benefit for Purposes of This Protection?

Initially, the term "accrued benefit" was limited to benefits that began at the normal retirement age. The Retirement Equity Act of 1984 (REA '84) subsequently expanded the definition of "accrued benefit not to be decreased by plan amendment" to include "an early retirement benefit or a retirement-type subsidy" and "an optional form of benefit."[82] Such plan amendment prohibition applied only to service before the amendment and with respect to eligibility for early retirement or the retirement-type subsidy, for participants who satisfied the pre-amendment conditions of the subsidy.

Early retirement benefits included benefits provided under the plan prior to the normal retirement age. As these benefits may have been subsidized to encourage participants to terminate early, such subsidies would now have to be preserved under the accrued benefit rules. Such protection extended not only to early retirement benefits but to retirement-type subsidies (i.e., where the benefit at retirement exceeded the actuarial value of the plan's normal retirement benefit). Optional forms of benefits included alternative distribution options available under the plan (e.g., 10 year certain and life, lump sum), some of which may have been subsidized or not.

REA '84 authorized Treasury to issue regulations regarding the meaning of an optional form and retirement-type subsidy.[83] In 1988, Treasury issued detailed final regulations, interpreting the statute broadly and imposing onerous requirements on plan sponsors, especially in regard to mergers and acquisitions.[84] In March 2000, the Service issued *proposed* regulations, but only with respect to the issue of elimination or reduction of optional forms of benefits.[85] These regulations were criticized as being too restrictive. Final regulations under I.R.C. § 411(d)(6) were issued in September 2000, effective for plan amendments on or after September 6, 2000.[86]

The Code defines "accrued benefit" for purposes of a defined benefit plan as the benefit determined under the plan, expressed in the form of an annual benefit commencing at normal retirement age, and if the accrued benefit is expressed as an amount other than an annual benefit commencing at normal retirement age, then the actuarial equivalent of such benefit.[87] Thus, alternative distribution *forms* (e.g., alternative annuities, installments, lump sum distributions) and alternative distribution

---

81. Rev. Rul. 81-12.
82. REA '84 § 301(a), amended by I.R.C. § 411(d) and ERISA § 204(g).
83. *See* I.R.C. § 411(d)(6)(B); ERISA § 204(g); 29 U.S.C. § 1054(g).
84. Prop. Treas. Reg. § 1.411(d)-4.
85. *Id.*
86. Treas. Reg. § 1.411 (d)-4.
87. I.R.C. § 411(a)(7)(A)(i), 411(c)(3).

ages (e.g., early retirement age) would clearly have to be provided on an actuarial equivalent basis. But the Service's proposed and final 2000 regulations went beyond forms of distributions and ages of distribution and included the payment schedules, medium of distribution, portion of the benefit to which the distribution features apply, and election rights with respect to optional forms of payment as part of the participant's "accrued benefit."[88] The IRS regulations state that distribution alternatives (including normal form) available to participants' accrued benefit, early retirement benefit, or retirement-type subsidies are considered optional forms.[89] Thus, alternate forms under the plan that are paid on substantially the same terms (i.e., relating to timing, medium of distribution, election rights, etc.) may be eliminated.[90] Such interpretation has caused practical problems for employers in the contexts of adopting successor prototype plans and in mergers and transfers.[91]

As the Code defines the accrued benefit as an annual benefit commencing at the normal retirement age, payment of the accrued benefit at a different date (e.g., early retirement date) must be the actuarial equivalent of such benefit.[92]

For plans with age and/or service eligibility criteria for early retirement benefits, all the circuits affirm that such criteria may not be reduced or eliminated once made available to a given group of participants. Hence, if the plan's early retirement benefit (ERB) is contingent upon attainment of age 55 and 20 years of service, a participant age 44 with only 19 years of service must be afforded the opportunity to "grow into" the eligibility for early retirement benefits. The early retirement subsidy may be changed, however, with respect to accruals for future service with the employer. Post-retirement cost of living increases provided under the plan document are considered benefits protected by I.R.C. §411(d)(6).[93]

Examples of plan features that are not considered part of the "accrued benefit" under the regulations and thus may be altered or eliminated from the plan include:

- Social Security supplements;
- Plan loans;
- The right to a particular form of investment or the right to direct investments;

---

88. Prop. Treas. Reg. §1.411(d)-4, Q&A-1(b)(1), and Treas. Reg. §1.411(d)-4, Q&A-1(b).

89. Treas. Reg. §1.401(a)(4)-4(e)(1).

90. *Id.*

91. To illustrate the Service's expansive definition of an "accrued benefit," the Service initially took the position that a participant's minimum required distribution date was a protected optional form of benefit. Thus, in 1996, when the Code modified the minimum distribution requirements so as to permit non-5% owners who had not yet retired to continue deferral of benefits until actual retirement instead of forcing a distribution at age 70½, the Service announced that eliminating such right to a participant to receive a pre-retirement distribution after attaining age 70½ would be a cut-back of benefits. *See* Prop. Treas. Reg. §1.411(d)-4, Q&A-10. The IRS has subsequently withdrawn this position.

92. *See* I.R.C. §411(c)(3); Treas. Reg. §1.411(a)-7(a)(1).

93. *See* Shaw v. I.A.M. Pension Plan, 563 F. Supp. 653 (C.D. Cal. 1983), *aff'd*, 750 F.2d 1458 (9th Cir. 1985); *accord* Hickers v. Chicago Truck Drivers Union, 980 F.2d 465 (7th Cir. 1992). *But see* Priv. Ltr. Rul. 199723053.

- Allocation dates for contributions, forfeitures, and earnings; and
- The right to make pre-tax or after-tax contributions.[94]

The availability and amount of early retirement benefits is also regarded as part of a participant's accrued benefits that is not subject to cut-back, even if the benefit exceeds the actuarial equivalent of the normal retirement benefit. However, early retirement *window* benefits are not regarded as part of the accrued benefit unless there is a pattern of repeated plan amendments with similar window benefits.[95]

EGTRRA '01 directed the Service to issue regulations such that any plan amendment that reduced or eliminated early retirement benefits or retirement-type subsidies or that changed the actuarial factors used to determine optional forms of benefits be allowed unless the amendment adversely affected participants' rights in more than a *de minimis* manner.[96] The result was a complicated set of rules permitting the elimination of protected benefits in two circumstances: (1) the elimination of an optional form of benefit that is deemed to be redundant as compared to other offered optional forms of payment, or (2) the elimination of noncore optional forms, as there are core optional forms of payment otherwise made available.[97]

E. Maximum Limitations on Benefits and Contributions

1. Introduction

I.R.C. § 401(a)(16) provides that a plan shall not be qualified nor its trust exempt unless the plan provides that benefits or contributions will not be in excess of the maximum limitations set forth in I.R.C. § 415. These limitations are designed to affect the highly paid participants by restricting how much they can accumulate under a qualified plan. There are two limitations—one for defined benefit plans and one for defined contribution plans, but each limitation has two components—a dollar limitation and a percentage of compensation limit. The dollar limits generally change year to year (e.g., for 2020, the defined benefit dollar limit was $230,000 and the defined contribution dollar limit was $57,000) with cost of living increases, whereas the percentage of compensation limits are constant.

In an effort to defeat undermining these limitations, the Code requires that all defined contribution plans (maintained by the same employer) must be aggregated, and all defined benefit plans (maintained by the same employer) must be aggregated for purposes of applying the annual tests.[98] As such, if plans with different plan years have to be aggregated, the limitations of I.R.C. § 415 are to be tested on a common

---

94. Treas. Reg. § 1.411(d)-4, Q&A-1(d).
95. Treas. Reg. § 1.411(d)-4, Q&A B1(c)(1).
96. EGTRRA '01 § 645(b)(1), amending I.R.C. § 411(d)(6)(B).
97. Treas. Reg. § 1.411(d)-3(d).
98. I.R.C. § 415(f).

"limitation year" basis. For purposes of Code § 415, "employer" includes not only the employer who sponsors the plan, but all other related employers, whether or not they participate in the plan.[99]

A plan's limitation year is presumed to be the calendar year unless the employer elects an alternate period.[100] Generally, in the case of a single plan, employers will choose the plan's plan year as the limitation year; however, in the case of related plans, the employer may choose a common limitation year for use by all such plans.[101] Parts of the limitations of I.R.C. § 415 are expressed in terms of an employee's "compensation" (these are referred to as the compensation limits). The term "compensation" is defined in I.R.C. § 415 and generally includes all types of compensation received by the employee from the employer within a given limitation year, but such amount is limited by I.R.C. § 401(a)(17).[102] In the context of an I.R.C. § 401(k) plan, compensation includes any elective deferrals made by the participant for the limitation year.[103]

2. Defined Contribution Plans

I.R.C. § 415(c) limits what may be annually "inputted" (referred to as the annual addition) to a participant's account to the lesser of a dollar limit or 100% of the participant's total compensation (which may not exceed the annual limitation of I.R.C. § 401(a)(17)). The term "annual addition" includes the sum of the following for any limitation year:

- Employer contributions allocated to the employee's account;
- Any forfeitures allocated to the employee's account balance; and
- All employee contributions made during the limitation year.[104]

While the elective deferral limitation of I.R.C. § 402(g) (for 2020, the maximum amount is $19,500) applies to the maximum an individual can defer in *all* I.R.C. § 401(k) plans that he or she is eligible to participate in for a given year, the I.R.C. § 415 limits are applicable to a given employer. Thus, someone could participate in two different qualified plans for two different employers in the same year and receive the maximum amounts in each plan.

---

99. I.R.C. § 414(b)–(c), 414(m)(4)(B), 414(n)(3)(B), and 414(o).

100. Treas. Reg. § 1.415-2(b).

101. *Id.* Treas. Reg. § 1.415-2(b)(3); Prop. Treas. Reg. § 1.415(j)-1(c). See Rev. Rul. 79-5, 1979-1 C.B. 165, in which the Service permits different limitation years for the two plans maintained by the same employer.

102. I.R.C. § 415(c)(3).

103. I.R.C. § 415(c)(3)(D).

104. There are certain exclusions permitted: "catch-up" contributions made by participants age 50 and over, employer contributions to restore previously forfeited account balances pursuant to I.R.C. § 411(a)(7)(C) upon the participant's repayment of the prior distribution, restorative payments stemming from plan losses attributable to a breach of fiduciary duty of care, any excess deferrals after being distributed to highly compensated employees, and rollover amounts. *See* Prop. Treas. Reg. § 1.415(c)-1.

If an employer maintains multiple defined contribution plans (e.g., a § 401(k) plan and a money purchase plan), it will document in the appropriate plan where any cutback in benefits should occur so as not to exceed the maximum limitations.

3. Defined Benefit Plans

I.R.C. § 415(b) limits the maximum amount in benefits that a participant can receive to the lesser of a dollar limit (e.g., $230,000 for 2020) or a compensation limit which is 100% of the participant's average total compensation for the highest three consecutive years of service (each subject to the applicable annual maximum limit on compensation from I.R.C. § 401(a)(17)).[105] As both the normal retirement benefit and accrued benefit are defined with three components—the amount of the benefit, when it is payable (e.g., NRA), and the form of distribution (e.g., life only or J&S)—the statute requires the dollar limit to be actuarially adjusted if the benefit is paid any time before age 62 or after age 65, and if the form of distribution is not life only or qualified joint and survivor annuity (if applicable).[106]

> **Example:** If the NRB for a given participant computes to be $285,000/65/life only, the participant could not receive the full $285,000 benefit at age 60. The $285,000 amount would be actuarially reduced to reflect the fact that a benefit is being paid two years earlier. Similarly, if the form of benefit that the participant requests to be paid is not a straight life annuity or qualified joint and survivor annuity (if applicable), the applicable dollar limit must be adjusted actuarially.[107] For example, if the NRB for a given unmarried participant computes to be $285,000/65/life only, he or she will not receive the full $285,000 amount at age 65 in the form of a 10-year certain and life annuity. The maximum dollar limit must also be adjusted pro rata (i.e., proportionately) if the participant has less than 10 years of plan participation.[108] For example, a participant retiring in 2020 with eight years of plan participation would be entitled to 8/10 × $285,000 or $228,000.

I.R.C. § 415(b) provides a de minimis rule whereby a participant may receive an annual benefit (derived from employer contributions) of $10,000 *regardless* of the age at commencement or the form of payment. However, an adjustment is required if the participant has less than 10 years of service (not participation). In order to qualify for this de minimis rule, $10,000 must be the maximum benefit payable to the employee from all defined benefit plans from this employer (for the plan year and any prior plan year) and there must be no defined contribution plan covering such individual from such employer.[109]

---

105. I.R.C. § 414(b)(1).
106. I.R.C. § 415(b)(2)(C)–(D), with a statutory floor of a $75,000 limit imposed at age 55.
107. I.R.C. § 415(b)(2)(B).
108. I.R.C. § 415(b)(5).
109. I.R.C. § 415(b)(4). *See* Treas. Reg. § 1.415-3(f); Prop. Treas. Reg. § 1.415(b)-1G.

Chapter 8

Nondiscrimination Requirements

Reading Assignment:	I.R.C. § 401(a)(4), 401(k)
	Treas. Reg. § 1.401(a)(4)
Class Discussion Questions:	What are the three nondiscrimination tests set forth in Treas. Reg. § 1.401(a)(4)?
	What alternative does an employer have to doing annual testing of its allocation formula or benefit accrual formula?
	What is the general test used to test the plan's allocation formula or benefit accrual formula? Why would one test using rate groups?
	What are some examples of benefits, rights, and features provided under the plan?

Overview

How can a qualified retirement plan prove it meets the nondiscrimination requirements each year?

- the three components of proving nondiscrimination each year are:

   ○ the amount of benefits provided in a defined benefit plan or contributions in a defined contribution plan must be nondiscriminatory—either the plan is designed as a safe harbor or the plan must annually meet the general nondiscrimination test (which is a mathematical test),

   ○ the actual availability of benefits, rights, and features, and the effective availability of BRFs, cannot be discriminatory—there are no plan provisions which can automatically satisfy this requirement, and facts and circumstances must be applied annually, and

   ○ plan amendments and termination cannot have the effect of being discriminatory—there are no plan provisions which can automatically satisfy this requirement, and facts and circumstances must be applied every time the plan is amended or upon plan termination

- former employees who are still participating in the plan need to be tested separately for all three nondiscrimination components

185

- as to benefits and contributions,
  - if the plan document has a uniform contribution allocation for all participants in a defined contribution plan, or a uniform benefit accrual formula in a defined benefit plan, then the plan passes every year
  - however, if there are different allocations or accruals for any participants, then the mathematical tests will need to be performed every year
- preliminary issues
  - the same aggregation of controlled groups and affiliated service groups for minimum coverage testing applies to nondiscrimination testing
  - the same categorization of employees for minimum coverage testing applies to nondiscrimination testing
- the general test is very complicated, and the Treasury Regulations provide many mathematical computations and many legal definitions, exceptions, and exceptions to exceptions
- the general test for nondiscrimination testing is performed as follows:
  - first, an allocation rate is calculated for each participant benefitting under a defined contribution plan, which is his or her allocation divided by salary
  - second, all participants are organized in order of descending allocation rates, where NHCEs are put above HCEs when the rates are equal
  - third, a rate group is created for every HCE benefitting under the plan, which consists of that HCE and every other employee (both HCEs and NHCEs) with an accrual rate equal to or greater than his or hers (there are some conveniences when several HCEs have the same, or similar, allocation rates)
  - fourth, each rate group must satisfy a modified minimum coverage test
- If every rate group satisfies the modified minimum coverage tests, then the plan as a whole passes the nondiscrimination tests (the rationale is that although different allocations are provided to different groups of employees, each allocation goes to enough NHCEs—so instead of sponsoring a single plan with different benefit structures, the employer could have sponsored several stand-alone plans for different segments of the workforce, and each stand-alone plan would pass the minimum coverage tests)
- when testing a defined benefit plan, replace "both the normal accrual rate and most valuable accrual rate" for "allocation rate," but the rest of the general test is the same (the defined benefit plan's Enrolled actuary will calculate the accrual rates)
- if the plan fails the general test in any year, then
  - a plan can be restructured into component parts, or two or more plans sponsored by the same employer may be aggregated by the employer
  - a plan can pass the general test based on "cross testing," where a defined contribution plan will convert contributions to accrued benefits and substitute

accrual rates for allocation rates in its general test, and where a defined benefit plan will convert accrued benefits to allocations and substitute allocation rates for accrual rates in its general test

- otherwise, the plan must be amended to provide greater benefits or allocations to the NHCEs so that the plan passes the general test

- as to rights and features,
  - if the plan has uniform rights and features for all plan participants, then the plan passes this component each year
  - otherwise, under appropriate facts and circumstances, the rights and features of the plan must be currently available and effectively available to enough NHCEs

- as to plan amendments and termination,
  - under appropriate facts and circumstances, the amendments or termination of the plan must not impermissibly discriminate in favor of HCEs

- in addition to the regular nondiscrimination testing required for every qualified plan, 401(k) plans have additional nondiscrimination requirements:
  - if the plan is set up to satisfy the safe harbor requirements, then the 401(k) plan meets the special nondiscrimination rules each year
  - otherwise, the plan must test for salary deferrals and employee contributions and separately test for employer contributions
  - to be a safe harbor 401(k) plan, under Treasury Regulations, the plan must properly and timely provide notice to all employees, and must either:
    - provide every eligible participant with a profit sharing contribution of 3% of salary, or
    - match 100% of the first 3% of salary deferred by every participant who elects to defer plus 50% of the next 2% of salary deferred
  - additionally, a 401(k) plan offering an automatic enrollment can also be structured as a safe harbor plan (satisfying both the ADP and ACP tests), as long as the employer properly and timely provides notices to all eligible employees
  - to test for salary deferrals and contributions in a plan that is not designed as a safe harbor
    - the actual deferral percentage for each individual is basically the total of his or her elective salary deferrals and the designated Roth contributions divided by his or her compensation
    - to pass the test, the average ADP for all HCEs, when compared to the average ADP for all NHCEs, cannot be more than the greater of
      - 125%, or
      - 200%, but only if the difference in ratios is less than 2.0 percentage points
      - to make the testing easier, the employer can choose to use prior year data to determine the average ADP for NHCEs

- to test for employer contributions in a plan that is not designed as a safe harbor
  - the actual contribution percentage for each individual is basically the total of his or her employer matching or other contributions divided by his or her compensation
  - to pass the test, the average ACP for all HCEs, when compared to the average ACP for all NHCEs, cannot be more than the greater of:
    - 125%, or
    - 200%, but only if the difference in ratios is less than 2.0 percentage points
      - to make the testing easier, the employer can choose to use prior year data to determine the average ACP for NHCEs
- if the plan fails the ADP test, then
  - enough qualified nonelective contributions (QNECs) may be allocated to NHCEs so that the plan passes
  - enough excess contributions are distributed
  - or enough elective deferrals may be returned to HCEs as taxable income so that the plan passes ("recharacterization")
  - the plan document must provide for the exact method of correction
  - similar rules apply to plans that fail the ACP tests

A. Introduction

1. Pre-TRA '86 Law

Prior to the Tax Reform Act of '86 (TRA '86), the Service interpreted the rules of Code § 401(a)(4) to prohibit employer contributions under a defined contribution plan and employer-provided accruals of benefits under a defined benefit plan from discriminating in favor of employees who were in the "prohibited group" (i.e., officers, shareholders, and highly compensated employees).[1] For purposes of satisfying this test, the employer could exclude from consideration employees covered under a collective bargaining agreement and non-resident aliens with no U.S. source income (the exclusions outlined in I.R.C. §§ 410(b)(3)(A) and (C)).[2]

For defined contribution plans, all qualified plans must have a definite and predetermined formula for allocating employer contributions, trust earnings, and for-

---

1. The term "prohibited group" was coined by the Service. See Rev. Rul. 68-654, 1968-2 C.B. 179, superseded by Rev. Rul. 84-155, 1984-2 C.B. 95, which was declared obsolete by Rev. Rul. 83-87, 1993-2 C.B. 124.
2. I.R.C. §§ 401(a)(4), 410(b)(3)(A), (C).

feitures.[3] Such formula must not discriminate in favor of the prohibited group. The Code sets forth the general rule that a defined contribution formula (that does not integrate with Social Security) is generally not discriminatory if it bears a uniform relationship to each employee's total compensation.[4] As the general test is in reference to an employee's compensation, the plan's definition of "compensation" for allocation purposes may or may not trigger a qualification test. If the plan definition used is anything other than total compensation, the employer has to demonstrate that the formula does not discriminate in favor of the prohibited group.[5] For example, if the plan's definition of compensation excluded overtime pay, such definition could be discriminatory if rank-and-file employees historically received such pay. For testing under I.R.C. § 401(a)(4), sponsors had to use total compensation, or a definition of compensation that is nondiscriminatory when compared with total compensation.[6]

A defined contribution plan formula that was weighted by compensation and service would be carefully scrutinized by the Service since such plans favored long-term employees and the Service presumed that long-term employees were members of the prohibited group.[7] However, in the post-TRA '86 finalized regulations, the Service affirmed the use of such formula.[8] A defined contribution plan's formula could also be constructed in such a manner to provide greater accrual rates for highly paid employees by integrating the formula with the employer's Social Security contributions. Such rules are now formally contained in I.R.C. § 401(a)(5) and are now referred to as the "permitted disparity" rules. These were discussed in Chapter 4.

For defined benefit plans, all plans must have a definite and predetermined formula for the accrual of benefits under the plan and for the plan's normal retirement benefit.[9] Under the rules of I.R.C. § 401(a)(4), such formula could not discriminate in favor of the prohibited group (subject to permissible integration rules if the plan formula integrates with Social Security benefits). Typically, such formula depended on the participant's career compensation or some average of the participant's compensation in the later, and final, years of employment. In such cases, the definition of compensation used in the plan had to be nondiscriminatory.[10] For testing under I.R.C. § 401(a)(4), sponsors had to use total compensation, or a definition of compensation that is nondiscriminatory when compared to total compensation.[11]

---

3. Treas. Reg. § 1.401-1(b)(i), (ii).

4. I.R.C. § 401(a)(5)(B).

5. See Rev. Rul. 84-74 and 81-74, which was declared obsolete by Rev. Rul. 93-87.

6. Pre-TRA '86, there was no definition of "compensation" in the 400 series of the Code; I.R.C. § 414(s) now provides a nondiscriminatory definition of compensation that is used in determining nondiscrimination of benefits and/or contributions under I.R.C. § 401(a)(4) and (a)(5).

7. See former Rev. Rul. 68-652, former Rev. Rul. 68-653, and former Rev. Rul. 68-659, all superseded by Rev. Rul. 84-155, which was declared obsolete by Rev. Rul. 93-87.

8. Treas. Reg. § 1.401(a)(4)-2(b)(2).

9. Treas. Reg. § 1.401(a)(4)-2(d)(2).

10. Treas. Reg. § 1.401(a)(4)-3(e).

11. Id.

In the past, if an employer aggregated two or more plans together for purposes of the coverage rules, then the two or more plans had to be considered together in determining whether they satisfied the nondiscrimination requirements of I.R.C. §401(a)(4).[12] Thus, the plans, considered together, could not discriminate in favor of the prohibited group. This determination involved a comparison of contributions or benefits under the various plans. As long as the contributions or benefits were "comparable," then the plans could be tested as a whole.[13]

2. TRA '86 Changes

In TRA '86, Congress made several important changes to the nondiscrimination requirements of the Code.[14] First, the Code would now define exactly the group of employees who were in the prohibited group and refer to such employees as "highly compensated." Second, the Code would replace the coverage tests in I.R.C. §410(b) with a new set of tests, one of which (i.e., average benefits test) would depend on the amount of benefits provided or contributions made under all qualified plans. The interpretation of the "classification" and "average benefit percentage" tests under the new coverage rules was left to the Service and the Treasury Department personnel to determine. Although Congress did not amend I.R.C. §401(a)(4) with TRA '86, the legislative history indicates that Congress expected the Service to review its rules in this area,[15] which it did with comprehensive and complex regulations.[16] The regulations view the tests in I.R.C. §§401(a)(4) and 410(b) as interdependent, not separate and distinct. The Service has replaced the qualitative I.R.C. §401(a)(4) nondiscrimination tests with a series of safe harbors and quantitative tests.

Coverage Test: A qualified plan must satisfy one of the coverage tests of I.R.C. §410(b). Assuming it passes the coverage test, it cannot discriminate with respect to benefits or contributions.[17] A group of plans may be aggregated for purposes of the I.R.C. §410(b) coverage tests. Plans that are aggregated for coverage purposes must also pass the I.R.C. §401(a)(4) tests as if they were *one* plan.[18] For example, an employer has two qualified defined contribution plans, one of which cannot satisfy one of the coverage tests. Thus, it must be aggregated with the other plan for both coverage and nondiscrimination. Even if it now satisfies the coverage test, it may not satisfy the nondiscrimination test if, for example, one plan's formula allocates 3% of com-

---

12. See former Rev. Rul. 81-202, made obsolete by Rev. Rul. 93-87.
13. *Id.*
14. These changes are effective for plan years beginning after December 31, 1988.
15. *See* Cong. Rec. H 7705 (Sept. 18, 1986), Confer. Report on H.R. 3838, TRA '86.
16. Treas. Reg. §1.401(a)(4)-0 through 1.401(a)(4)-13.
17. I.R.C. §401(a)(3), (a)(4).
18. Treas. Reg. §1.410(b)(1)(B).

pensation for each eligible participant and the other plan's formula allocates 6% of compensation for each eligible participant (as the allocation rates are not the same).

Benefits/

Allocations Test: Once a plan satisfies the coverage tests, it then must satisfy the nondiscrimination tests of I.R.C. § 401(a)(4) for benefits or contributions. According to the Service regulations, there are three separate tests that apply:

Test 1: The plan must be nondiscriminatory *either* in the amount of benefits provided or contributions made. A plan may satisfy this requirement either through plan design that meets one of the regulations' safe harbors, or through a general test that tests each employee's allocation or accrual rate.[19]

Test 2: Every option, subsidy, or other benefit, right, or feature (i.e., a new term of art, "BRF") must be available to a nondiscriminatory group of employees.[20] A nondiscriminatory group is generally one that satisfies the ratio percentage test or the classification component of the average benefits test, described earlier. Further, based on the facts and circumstances, the group of employees to whom the BRF is "effectively available" must not substantially favor HCEs.[21]

Test 3: Benefits or contributions payable under "special circumstances" (e.g., plan amendment or termination) must be nondiscriminatory.[22]

In applying these three tests:

- Plans are tested on a plan year basis.[23]

- Generally, former employees are tested separately from active employees (for example, if retirees in pay status were to be given cost of living adjustments to their existing benefits, this benefit would be tested only against a retiree group).[24]

- Collectively bargained plans that automatically satisfy I.R.C. § 410(b) are deemed to satisfy I.R.C. § 401(a)(4).[25]

- Employee-provided contributions and benefits are tested separately from employer-provided contributions and benefits.[26]

---

19. Treas. Reg. § 1.401(a)(4)-1(a), -1(b).
20. Treas. Reg. § 1.401(a)(4)-1(b)(3).
21. Treas. Reg. § 1.401(a)(4)-4(b), -4(c).
22. Treas. Reg. § 1.401(a)(4)-1(b)(4).
23. Treas. Reg. § 1.401(a)(4)-1(c)(3).
24. Treas. Reg. § 1.401(a)(4)-1(c)(6).
25. Treas. Reg. § 1.401(a)(4)-1(c)(5).
26. Treas. Reg. § 1.401(a)(4)-1(c)(7).

B. Test 1 —
Amount of Benefits/Contribution

1. Overview and Safe Harbors

The first test is the most important of the three tests under I.R.C. §401(a)(4). Employers have two choices: (1) comply with one of the safe harbors or (2) do annual testing on a plan-by-plan basis. Employers of prototype plans will only be offered safe harbor benefit or allocation formulae so as to automatically comply and avoid testing. Employers of individual designed plans may opt to do annual testing, which is more complex and burdensome.

Varieties of safe harbors are available depending on whether the plan is a defined contribution or a defined benefit plan. The following are the requirements that a plan must comply with before it can rely on one of the safe harbors:[27]

1. The plan's definition of compensation used in the allocation or accrual formula must meet the criteria of I.R.C. §414(s), which cross-references the definition of compensation used under I.R.C. §415(c) (i.e., the definition of compensation used to determine the compensation percentage limits).[28] That definition generally includes all compensation, but allows the employer to exclude employee elective deferrals. The regulations permit employers to use W-2 earnings or several other alternative definitions.[29]

2. The same allocation formula or benefit accrual formula must apply to all participants.

Defined benefit plans also have three other requirements:

3. The plan's normal retirement age must be uniform (e.g., age 65).

4. There must be uniform post-normal retirement age accruals and each subsidized optional form of payment must be available to everyone.

5. There may be no employee contributions.

For defined contribution plans that satisfy the requirements, there are two available safe harbors:[30]

- *Uniform Allocation Formula:* The plan allocates contributions (and forfeitures, if applicable) using the same percentage of compensation (e.g., 5% of each participant's plan year compensation), but the plan's formula may also comply with the permitted disparity rules; or

- *Uniform Points Formula:* The plan allocates contributions by weighting age or service, as well as compensation, through a points formula (which may not be integrated).

---

27. Treas. Reg. §1.401(a)(4)-2(b), -3(b)(2).
28. I.R.C. §414(s), which includes wages, salary, commissions, bonuses, tips, etc.
29. Treas. Reg. §1.414(s)-1(c).
30. Treas. Reg. §1.401(a)(4)-2(b).

Example: each participant is given 10 points for each year of service and one point for each $100 of plan year compensation. Based on the total number of points to be granted (e.g., 8,000), an employer contribution is made (e.g., $80,000) such that each point is worth $10 (8,000 ÷ $80,000). For a participant with $100,000 in salary and 10 years of service, he or she will have 1,100 points. As each point value is $10, his or her allocation will be $11,000 (1,100 × $10), resulting in an allocation rate of 11% ($11,000 ÷ $100,000). Use of this safe harbor requires a simple annual test to demonstrate that the average allocation rate for the HCE group is not more than the average allocation for the NHCE group.

For defined benefit plans that meet the above requirements, there are two available safe harbors that are designed for unit, flat, and fractional defined benefit plans:[31]

- *Unit Credit AB Formula:* This safe harbor defines both the AB and the NRB as a unit credit formula (each year of service is credited) applied to the participant's compensation (an average annual compensation of CAE or FAE can be used), but the formula must satisfy the 133⅓ test.

  Example: NRB = AB = [(3% × 1st 10 yos × FAE) + (4% × all yos after 10 years × FAE)]/65/life or J&S. Since the jump from 3% to 4% is 133⅓%, it meets the 133⅓ test.

- *Fractional Rule:* This safe harbor is available to an NRB formula that is designed as a unit credit formula, but the AB is the fractional rule applied to the NRB. This safe harbor also requires that no participant can accrue at a rate more than 133⅓% of the rate of any other participant.

  Example: NRB = [2% × yos (capped at 25) × CAE]/65/life only or J&S, and AB = fractional rule applied to NRB. All participants with 25 or fewer years of service will accrue at a rate of 2%; but participants with 33 years of service will accrue at a rate of 1.52% (i.e., 1/33 × NRB of [2% × 50%]). Since the 2% rate is not more than one-third larger than the 1.52% rate (as it is only 1.32% larger than 1.52%, not 1.33%), the test is met.

2. General Testing

If the plan does not satisfy one of the safe harbor rules, annual testing with numerical participant-by-participant testing of the plan (referred to as the general test) is required. Under the numerical testing, a plan sponsor is required to develop a *single* number (an allocation rate or accrual rate) for *each* employee, representing total contributions made and/or accruals credited on behalf of that employee for the year, divided by the participant's total compensation.[32] For example, the plan's allocation rate is a uniform 5%, but the plan's definition of compensation excludes over-

---

31. Treas. Reg. § 1.401(a)(4)-3(a)(1).

32. Treas. Reg. § 1.410(b)-5(b). These rates may be adjusted to impute an amount for employer-provided Social Security benefits.

time. Thus, for a participant with total compensation of $50,000, but compensation excluding overtime of $40,000, his or her allocation will be [5% × $40,000]=$2,000 and his or her allocation rate is 4% =[$2,000 ÷ $50,000]. In contrast, for a participant with total compensation of $50,000 and no overtime compensation, his or her allocation is $2,500 = [5% × $50,000] and his or her allocation rate is 5%. This explains why the allocation rates are different depending on the participant.

> **Note:** Just a reminder about the nondiscrimination rules: if a defined benefit plan gives a benefit accrual rate of [5% × compensation × yos]/65/life only or J&S and compensation is defined by I.R.C. §414(s), then the formula is nondiscriminatory because everyone is getting the same 5%, even though the *cost* of that accrual to the employer is much higher for older employees than for younger employees. Conversely, if a defined contribution plan gives an annual allocation of [5% × compensation, where compensation is defined by I.R.C. §414(s)], the formula is nondiscriminatory even though the cost of that allocation to the employer is the same for all employees.

With these individual rates, the *general test* of I.R.C. §401(a)(4) requires that the highest rate for any highly compensated employee (HCE) be no larger than the lowest rate for any nonhighly compensated employee (NHCE)—a very unlikely scenario as it assumes that the rates for the HCEs are at least the same as or less than the rates for the NHCEs. Thus, the regulations go on to permit the plan to be "restructured" into smaller "component plans" so that the allocation rate for any HCE is no more than the allocation rate for any NHCE in the component group.[33] Now, by definition, the smaller unit satisfies the general test of I.R.C. §401(a)(4).[34] However, the employer must now determine that each component part is nondiscriminatory under the I.R.C. §410(b) coverage rules.[35] If proven, the plan as a whole will be nondiscriminatory as to I.R.C. §401(a)(4). The rationale is that although different allocations are provided to different groups of employees, each allocation rate goes to a sufficient number of NHCEs—so instead of sponsoring a single plan with different benefit structures, the employer could have sponsored several stand-alone plans for different segments of the workforce, and each stand-alone plan would pass the minimum coverage test.

3. General Test for Defined Contribution Plans

Under the general test, the employer allocations under a defined contribution plan are not discriminatory if each rate group under the plan satisfies I.R.C. §410 (b). Here the regulations have "restructured" the plan into various rate groups so that the general test can be met at each rate group level. Given this restructuring by rate groups, the plan can be viewed as a pyramid, with a base including the lowest accrual rates under the plan and all employees accruing that rate or a higher rate. Each next level includes the next higher accrual rate and all employees accruing at that or a

---

33. Treas. Reg. §1.401(a)(4)-1(c)(3).
34. Treas. Reg. §1.401(a)(4)-2(c)(3), -3(c)(2).
35. Treas. Reg. §1.401(a)(4)-1(c)(3).

higher rate. Each rate group is then tested as though it were a separate plan currently benefiting the group of employees included in that rate group. If *each* component plan results in nondiscrimination as to amount and coverage, the plan as a whole will be nondiscriminatory.[36]

A rate group exists for each HCE, and includes the HCE and every other employee with an allocation rate greater than or equal to that of the HCE.[37] To pass the general test, each rate group must satisfy I.R.C. §410(b).[38] For purposes of this test, an employee's allocation rate is the sum of all employer contributions and forfeitures allocated to the employee's account, as a percentage of total compensation or as a dollar amount.[39] Allocations of income, expenses, gains, and losses are not included.[40] The regulations permit the employer to ignore small variations between allocation rates by "grouping" rates into ranges and treating all rates within the range as identical.[41] In testing the rate group under I.R.C. §410(b), generally the same rules apply in satisfying any one of the coverage rules.[42] First one checks if the rate group satisfies the ratio percentage test of I.R.C. §410(b); if not, then the rate group must satisfy a modified version of the average benefit test of I.R.C. §410(b).[43] Below is an example illustrating the general test.

> **Example:** An employer has four employees in the test group, all benefiting under the plan, with two NHCEs and two HCEs. The NHCEs have allocation rates of 4% and 5%, and the HCEs have allocation rates of 4% and 5%. Under the general test, since the 5% highest allocation rate for any HCE is greater than the 4% lowest allocation rate for any NHCE, the test fails. We restructure into two groups — one for HCEs with 4% and one for HCEs with 5%.

	NHCE 1	5%
Rate Group #2	HCE 1	5%
	NHCE 2	4%
Rate Group #1	HCE 2	4%

The ratio percentage for Rate Group #1 is [2/2 ÷ 2/2]= 100%

The ratio percentage for Rate Group #2 is [1/2 ÷ 1/2]= 100%

Since both rate groups satisfy the 70% ratio percentage test, test 1 is met.

This example illustrates the rationale for using rate groups. If the employer instead maintained two separate plans — one whose eligibility included only NHCE 1 and HCE 1 with both participants receiving the same 5% and another plan whose eligibility

---

36. Treas. Reg. §1.401(a)(4)-2(c)(1).
37. *Id.*
38. Treas. Reg. §1.401(a)(4)-2(c)(3).
39. Treas. Reg. §1.401(a)(4)-2(c)(2)(i).
40. Treas. Reg. §1.401(a)(4)-2(c)(2)(iii). Permitted disparity under the integration rules may be imputed in determining these rates.
41. Treas. Reg. §1.401(a)(4)-2(c)(2)(v).
42. Treas. Reg. §1.401(a)(4)-1(c)(4).
43. Treas. Reg. §1.401(a)(4)-2(c)(3).

included only NHCE 2 and HCE 2 with both participants receiving the same 4%—why not allow the employer to maintain one plan with different allocation rates of 4% and 5%? Each plan could have satisfied coverage on its own, as each plan's ratio percentage was 100%.

4. General Test for Defined Benefit Plans

Under the general test, the employer-provided benefits under a defined benefit plan are not discriminatory if each rate group under the plan satisfies I.R.C. §410(b).[44] Here the regulations have "restructured" the plan into various rate groups, similar to the general test used for defined contribution plans.[45] A rate group exists for each HCE and consists of that HCE and all other employees who have a normal accrual rate greater than or equal to the HCE's normal accrual rate *and* who also have a most valuable accrual rate greater than or equal to the HCE's most valuable accrual rate.[46] The term "most valuable accrual rate" is a term of art and refers to the most valuable benefit under the plan that could be made available to the participant (e.g., early retirement benefits that are heavily subsidized (to incentivize participants to leave early) are more valuable than the normal retirement benefit).[47] For example, if a participant is currently age 60 with an NRB and a heavily subsidized early retirement benefit (ERB); the ERB is worth more actuarially than the NRB and thus, the ERB should be tested as well as the NRB. However, if a participant is currently age 40 and not yet eligible for early retirement, there is not another benefit that is more valuable than the normal retirement benefit, and thus only the NRB needs to be tested.

Once the rate groups have been identified, each rate group must satisfy I.R.C. §410(b) as if it were a separate plan.[48] Thus, one would check if the rate group met the ratio percentage test of I.R.C. §410(b); if it did not meet this test, the rate group would have to pass a modified average benefits test (similar to the changes noted for the general test used in defined contribution plans).

In the defined contribution context, it is easy to determine the dollar amount allocated to a participant's account, which when divided by the participant's total compensation, produces an allocation rate that can be tested. This is not the case in a defined benefit context. Here, the normal accrual rate is defined as the increase in the employee's accrued benefit during a given measurement period, divided by service, and then expressed as a percentage of average annual compensation.[49] Similarly, the most valuable accrual rate is determined using the subsidized value of the accrued benefit for which the participant is eligible.[50]

---

44. Treas. Reg. §1.401(a)(4)-3(c)(1).
45. *See* Treas. Reg. §1.401(a)(4)-2(c), et seq.
46. Treas. Reg. §1.401(a)(4)-3(c)(1).
47. Treas. Reg. §1.401(a)(4)-3(d)(1)(ii).
48. Treas. Reg. §1.401(a)(4)-3(c)(2).
49. Treas. Reg. §1.401(a)(4)-3(d)(1)(i).
50. Treas. Reg. §1.401(a)(4)-3(d)(1)(ii).

C. Test 2 —
Benefits, Rights, and Features

While I.R.C. § 411(d)(6) assures that "protected benefits" may not be decreased by plan amendments, the Service extended the nondiscrimination protection of I.R.C. § 401(a)(4) (not just the anti-cutback protection) to such protected benefits by means of its regulations.[51] The final regulations required that optional forms of benefits be tested for nondiscrimination based on a two-fold test of "current availability" and "effective availability."[52] The revised final regulations extended the use of these nondiscrimination tests to other plan "rights and features" that are not considered "protected benefits."[53]

"Current availability" requires that the group of employees to whom the optional benefit, right, or feature is made available satisfies the ratio percentage test or the nondiscriminatory classification test (the average benefit percentage test does not apply here). In testing for current availability, most age and service conditions (e.g., age 55 and 20 yos for early retirement) and status conditions (e.g., death, hardship) are disregarded. "Effective availability" is a facts and circumstances test requiring that the group of employees to whom an optional benefit, right, or feature is actually being utilized does not substantially favor HCEs. Generally, if it is impossible for most NHCEs to satisfy the plan conditions that are met by HCEs, this requirement will not be met.[54]

D. Test 3 —
Discrimination in Special Circumstances

Plan amendments that discriminate in favor of highly paid employees will cause the plan to violate I.R.C. § 401(a)(4).[55] The regulations provide a list of "facts and circumstances" to be considered in such a situation to determine if an amendment or the timing of an amendment discriminates "significantly" in favor of the HCEs or former HCEs.[56] Factors to be considered include the relative numbers of HCEs and NHCEs affected by the amendment, the relative length of service of HCEs and NHCEs, the length of time the plan provision being amended has been in effect, and the turnover of employees prior to the plan amendment.[57]

---

51. See the initial nondiscrimination regulations under Treas. Reg. § 1.401(a)(4)-4(a) where optional forms of benefit distributions were protected. I.R.C. § 411(d)(6) assures "protected benefits" (such as optional forms of benefit distribution to the extent accrued) cannot be reduced, eliminated, or subject to the employer's discretion. *See* Treas. Reg. § 1.411(d)(4)-Q&A-1. However, such anti-cutback protection does not afford that such benefits be provided in a nondiscriminatory manner.

52. Treas. Reg. § 1.401(a)(4)-4.

53. Treas. Reg. § 1.401(a)(4)-4(e)(3).

54. Treas. Reg. § 1.401(a)(4)-4(c).

55. Treas. Reg. § 1.401(a)(4)-5.

56. Treas. Reg. § 1.401(a)(4)-5(a)(2).

57. *Id.*

E. Nondiscrimination Requirements for I.R.C. § 401(k) Plans

Cash or deferred arrangements (known as CODAs) (i.e., I.R.C. § 401(k) plans) have additional tests to satisfy. One set is in I.R.C. § 401(k)(3), applicable to traditional elective salary deferrals and Roth deferrals (referred to as the average deferral percentage or ADP test).[58] The second set is in I.R.C. § 401(m)(2), applicable to employer matching contributions and after-tax employee contributions (other than designated Roth § 401(k) contributions) (referred to as the average contribution percentage or ACP test).[59] To avoid these tests, the I.R.C. § 401(k) plan can be designed to satisfy one of two safe harbors (to be discussed later in Section F).

The application of the ADP and ACP tests is similar to the rules under the general test of I.R.C. § 401(a) — an individual deferral percentage is computed for each participant. For the ADP test, the individual percentage is based on the total elective deferrals (excluding catch-up contributions and excluding excess deferrals for the NHCEs) during the year divided by the participant's compensation.[60] For example, for purposes of the ADP test, if an employee had total compensation of $165,000 and elected to defer $16,500, his or her ADP would be 10% ($16,500 ÷ $165,000).[61] CODAs that provide for employer matching contributions or after-tax employee contributions (other than designated Roth deferrals) are subject to the ACP test. The computation of the individual participant's deferral percentage is similar to the above calculation — it is based on the total of employer matching contributions and employee after-tax contributions during the year divided by the participant's compensation.[62] For example, in our prior example, if the plan provided for a 50% employer matching contribution, the participant's ACP would be 5% ($8,250 ÷ $165,000). Note: participants eligible to make elective deferrals but choosing not to do so will have ADP and ACP of 0%.

Once the two percentages (ADP and ACP) are determined for each participant, the ratios are then averaged for the HCEs as a group and the NHCEs as a group.

- The end result is a single HCE ADP and a single NHCE ADP, as well as a single HCE ACP and a single NHCE ACP.

- The ADP for the NHCEs is then compared to the ADP of the HCEs; similarly, the ACP for the NHCEs is compared to the ADP of the HCEs.

- The ADP and ACP tests are parallel.

---

58. I.R.C. § 401(k)(3).

59. I.R.C. § 401(m)(2).

60. I.R.C. § 401(k)(3)(B).

61. I.R.C. § 414(s) compensation must be used as defining compensation for ADP testing, which uses the compensation definition under I.R.C. § 415(c)(3), which in turn includes elective deferrals excluded from gross income under an I.R.C. § 401(k) arrangement and salary reductions under I.R.C. § 125 cafeteria plans. I.R.C. § 401(k)(9).

62. I.R.C. § 401(m)(3).

- The mathematical tests require that the HCE's group ADP (and the HCE's group ACP) cannot exceed the greater of:
  - ○ 125% of the ADP (or the ACP) for the NHCE group, or
  - ○ 200% of the ADP (or the ACP) for the NHCE group plus 2 percentage points.[63]

An easier way to understand the test is to use the following chart:

If the NHCE's ADP/ACP is	Use the following test
0 to 2%	200% test
More than 2 to 8%	within 2% points test
More than 8%	125%

Example: If the NHCE's ADP/ACT is 1.5%, the HCE ADP/ACT cannot be more than [200% × 1.5%] = 3%. Failure to satisfy the ADP/ACP test for the year results in "excess contributions" that must be corrected; otherwise, the plan faces potential disqualification.

Example: If the NHCE ADP/ACT is 4%, the HCE ADP/ACT cannot be more than [4% + 2%] = 6%.

Example: If the NHCE ADP/ACT is 9%, the HCE ADP/ACT cannot be more than [125% × 9%] = 11.25%.

Generally, ADP and ACP testing uses current year data, but the plan document may specify that prior year data be used. The prior year testing method permits the plan sponsor to use NHCE data from the prior plan for purposes of satisfying the current year's ACP and ACP tests.[64]

How does an employer correct ADP failures? There are a variety of ways to correct an ADP failure:

- Depending on the terms of the plan, the employer may be able to recharacterize some of the HCE elective contributions as employee "catch-up" contributions (because the participant is age 50 or older) or as employee after-tax contributions and rerun the ADP test.[65]
- If this is not a possibility, the employer could consider making distributions to members of the HCE group (referred to as "corrective distributions") in order to reduce its overall ADP.[66] Distribution of elective deferrals must be accompanied

---

63. I.R.C. §§ 401(k)(3)(A)(ii), 401(m)(2)(A).

64. Treas. Reg. § 1.401(k)-2(c), 1.401(m)-2(c). The data is taken from the prior plan year based on the group of NHCEs and their deferrals during the prior plan year. The purpose of the prior year testing method is to afford the employer greater predictability in meeting the ADP and ACP tests for the current plan year.

65. Treas. Reg. § 1.401(k)-2(a)(5)(iii). Recharacterization must occur at least 2½ months following the plan year.

66. Treas. Reg. § 1.401(k)-2(b)(2)(i). Corrective distributions must be returned to the HCEs or recharacterized as after-tax employee contributions (with income) within 2½ months after the close of the plan year in which they were contributed and are treated as taxable income for the year of contribution.

with earned income; distribution of matching contributions may be made only if the deferrals are nonvested. For example, if the NHCE ADP rate was 8% and the HCE ADP rate was 11%, it fails the test, as the HCE ADP rate needs to be no more than 10%. If the employer took the extra 1% HCE ADP rate and gave it back to the HCEs, the rate would become 10% and thus, satisfy the test.

- Alternatively, the employer may decide to make additional matching employer contributions (referred to as "qualified matching contributions" or QMACs) or additional nonelective employer contributions (referred to as "qualified non-elective contributions" or QNECs) sufficient to pass the ADP test.[67] These contributions are said to be "qualified," as they must be fully vested and subject to the same distribution restrictions applicable to elective salary deferrals.

If I.R.C. §401(m) contributions made on behalf of the HCEs exceed the permissible amount under the ACP test, the employer has several options:

- It can forfeit nonvested matching contributions made on behalf of the HCEs.[68]
- It can distribute the excess I.R.C. §401(m) contributions (with earnings) to HCEs.[69]
- It can make additional QNECs to NHCEs until the test is met.[70]

F. Safe Harbor Plans to Avoid Nondiscrimination Testing

SBJPA provided safe harbor plans that are designed-based alternatives to the above annual nondiscrimination tests.[71] If the rules are followed, safe harbor plans avoid the ADP test, ACP test, and the top-heavy test. Safe harbor plans include:

- An employer nonelective contribution of at least 3% of compensation for all NHCEs, regardless of whether the employee makes an elective deferral (referred to as the nonelective employer contribution safe harbor plan).[72] There is a "maybe" election attached to this safe harbor whereby the employer may elect to choose to apply the safe harbor provision each year.[73] Special notices had to be given to employees.
- An employer matching contribution of 100% of the first 3% of compensation that an NHCE has deferred plus 50% of the next 2% of compensation that an NHCE has deferred.[74] This represents the minimum safe harbor match formula.

---

67. Treas. Reg. §1.401(d)-2(b)(1)(i).
68. Treas. Reg. §1.401(m)-2(b)(2) (note: recharacterization is not a method for correcting a ACP failure).
69. Treas. Reg. §1.401(m)-2(b)(2)(v).
70. Treas. Reg. §1.401(m)-2(b)(a)(i)(A).
71. SBJPA §1433(a), adding I.R.C. §401(k)(12).
72. I.R.C. §401(k)(12)(C).
73. Treas. Reg. §1.401(k)-3(f)(1).
74. I.R.C. §401(k)(12)(B).

Alternatively, an enhanced employer matching contribution of 100% of the first 4% of compensation that an NHCE has deferred (which may be increased up to 6% without violating the ACP test safe harbor).[75]

The employer contributions under the safe harbor must be fully vested and subject to the same in-service distribution restrictions applicable to employee salary deferrals. The statute imposed an annual safe harbor notice, regardless of the type of safe harbor contribution.[76] The notice had timing and content requirements. The statute also permitted the plan sponsor to adopt a safe harbor with a nonelective employer contribution by the 30th day before the closed of the plan year, provided certain criteria were met.[77] SECURE now allows a plan sponsor to adopt a nonelective employer contribution safe harbor plan (QACA or traditional) without the participant notice requirement.[78] It also allows the nonelective employer contribution safe harbor to be adopted with a plan amendment (1) by the 30th day before the close of the plan year, or (2) if at least a 4% nonelective employer contribution is made for the plan year, then by the last day for distributing excess contributions from the plan year.[79] Previously, safe harbor plans had to distribute an annual notice describing the safe harbor before the beginning of each plan year. By relaxing this requirement, it provides employers with more flexibility, making these plans more attractive.

G. Summation

As this chapter is so complex, a summary of the tests may be helpful:

- To consider a safe harbor allocation or accrued benefit formula, there are possibly five "hoops" that a plan must satisfy: (1) its definition of plan compensation must be nondiscriminatory, and (2) the same formula must apply to everyone. If the plan is a defined benefit plan, the three additional "hoops" require the NRA to be uniform. (3) There must be uniform post-NRA accruals, (4) each subsidized optional form must be available to everyone, and (5) there must be no employee contributions.

- Once the hoops are met, a defined contribution plan's allocation formula should either be uniform for everyone or vary depending on a points formula, but the average allocation rate for the HCE group may not be more than the average allocation rate for the NHCE group, tested annually. A defined benefit plan's accrued benefit formula should either be a uniform credit type of formula or meet the fractional safe harbor set forth in the regulations.

---

75. Treas. Reg. § 1.401(k)-3(c)(3).

76. I.R.C. § 401(k)(12)(D).

77. I.R.C. § 1.401(k)(12)(D).

78. SECURE § 103, by re-designating subparagraph (F) of I.R.C. § 401(k)(12) as subparagraph (G) and by inserting a new subparagraph (F).

79. Id.

- If a safe harbor is not desired, then the employer must perform the general test annually.
  - For each participant, a single number is computed: [total allocations or total increase in accrued benefits credited to the participant] ÷ participant's compensation = allocation or accrual rate.
  - These numbers are averaged for the NHCE group and averaged for the HCE group (for example, if there are three NHCEs with rates of 1%, 2%, and 3%, then the NHCE average = [1% + 2% + 3%] ÷ 3 = 2%; if there are 2 NHCEs with rates of 2% and 4%, then the HCE average = [2% + 4%] ÷ 2 = 3%)
  - The general test requires that the highest HCE rate (in the example, it would be 4%) cannot be larger than the lowest NHCE rate (in the example, it would be 1%), which is not met here as 4% > 1%.
  - Since the test fails, the plan is restructured: (in the example, there are two HCEs with two different rates, thus two rate groups). Restructuring is done by placing everyone with the same or higher rate in the same rate group and then performing the coverage tests on each rate group.
  - In our example, the restructuring into 2 rates groups looks like this:

Rate Group #2	HCE 2	4%
	NHCE 3	3%
	NHCE 2	2%
Rate Group #1	HCE 1	2%

Note: NHCE 1 is not in a rate group as his or her rate is less than 2%.

We fail the coverage rules for Rate Group #2 as there are no NHCEs in that rate group, and thus the ratio of NHCEs benefiting ÷ NHCE Rate Group = 0%

- I.R.C. § 401(k) plans have separate nondiscrimination rules:
  - For each participant, compute their ADP = [total elective deferrals, excluding catch-up] ÷ compensation, with employees electing not to make deferrals having a 0%.
  - Average the ADP for the NHCE group and average the ADP for the HCE group and compare the two using this chart:

If the NHCE's ADP/ACP is	Use the following test
0 to 2%	200% test
More than 2 to 8%	within 2% points test
More than 8%	125%

If the test is met, you're fine. If not, the employer can consider different routes: recharacterize some of the HCE elective contributions as employee "catch-up" contributions or after-tax contributions and rerun the test; make "corrective distributions" to the HCE group to reduce the averaged ADP, sufficient to meet the test; and/or make QMACs or QNECs sufficient to pass the test.

- For each participant, compute their ACP = [total employer matching contributions + after-tax (non-Roth) employee contributions] ÷ compensation, with employees electing not to make deferrals having 0% (as there is no match).

- Average the ACP for the NHCE group and average the ACP for the HCE group and perform the test, identical to the one above.

- If the test is met, you're fine. If not, the employer can consider different routes, for example, making appropriate additional contributions to meet the test or distributing the excess aggregate contributions or forfeiting the nonvested matching contributions for the HCEs.

Chapter 9

Distributions and Taxation of Distributions

Reading Assignment: ERISA §§ 205, 206, 408(b)(1)

I.R.C. §§ 72(a), 72(b), 72(m), 72(p), 72(t), 401(a)(9), 401(a)(11), 401(a)(14), 401(a)(13), 402(b)–(c), 402A(d), 414(p), 417

Class Discussion Questions: What are the policy reasons behind limiting in-service distributions from pension plans?

What penalty taxes are applicable with premature distributions from a retirement plan?

What is the distinction between QPSA and QJSA?

What is the purpose of the minimum distribution rules?

How have the minimum distribution rules changed under the SECURE Act?

Overview

What types of distributions can come from qualified plans?

- *life annuity:* payments from the plan are paid monthly (or annually) to the plan participant starting on his or her normal retirement date and will continue for as long as he or she lives. An unhealthy individual who does not live out his or her full life expectancy will lose all benefits upon death (thus the plan has incurred an actuarial gain), whereas a super-healthy individual who outlives his or her life expectancy will continue getting paid for life (thus the plan has incurred an actuarial loss)

- the law of large numbers suggest that the cumulative gains and losses will cancel each other out from the plan sponsor's point of view (even though individual participants will either suffer losses for premature deaths or enjoy gains for extended lives)

- *10-year certain and life thereafter annuity:* payments from the plan are paid annually (or monthly) to the plan participant starting on his or her normal retirement date and will continue until the later of the date of death or after 10 annual payments have been made (or 120 monthly payments); this is sort of insurance, which obviously costs a premium, and if the participant dies before the 10-year guaranteed term ends, then the premium was worthwhile (any term can be substituted for 10, but 10 is the most common)

- *100% joint and survivor annuity:* payments from the plan are paid annually (or monthly) to the plan participant starting on his or her normal retirement date and will continue until the later of his or her date of death or the date of death of the second life; again, there is a premium, and if the participant dies before the second life, then the premium was worthwhile (any percentage can be substituted for 100%, but 100% is the most common)

- *lump sum (a/k/a single sum distribution):* a single payment today is paid which represents all future expected benefit payments

What is one way to differentiate between annuities and lump sums?

- Annuity = mailbox

  ○ picture a mailbox—with an annuity, every month that the participant is still alive after annuities begin, that retiree can walk down to his or her mailbox and find an annuity check

  ○ if the retiree lives longer than expected and can still receive a monthly check for every month he or she is still alive, then the individual received more benefits than the plan intended

  ○ on the other hand, if the retiree dies sometime before he or she is expected to die, and the life annuity terminates since the he or she is no longer alive, then the individual received less benefits than the plan intended

- Lump sum = piggy bank

  ○ picture a piggy bank—with a lump sum, every month that the participant is still alive, the retiree takes enough out of the bank to pay for that month's living expenses

  ○ if the retiree dies sometime before he or she is expected to die, and assuming the retiree invested the account well while alive and frugally and conservatively withdrew living expenses, there will be a balance that can be bequeathed to his or her estate

  ○ if the retiree lives longer than expected, or invests poorly, or withdrew too much in any given year, etc., and has totally depleted the account, then that individual now has only personal savings and Social Security to pay his or her expenses for the rest of his or her life

How does the enrolled actuary convert the normal form of benefit into an optional form of benefit in a defined benefit plan?

- as a qualification requirement, the defined benefit plan document must provide the tables, exact method of conversion, or an interest rate and mortality table

- this will indicate the premium a participant pays for the choice of an optional form (such as an approximate 10% premium for a 10-year certain and life annuity and an approximate 20% premium for a 100% joint and survivor annuity)

When does the plan need to start making plan distributions?

- as a qualification requirement, unless the participant otherwise elects, the plan must start distributions within 60 days of the later of the participant's
  - ○ normal retirement date
  - ○ 10th anniversary of participation in the plan, or
  - ○ termination of employment

What are the distribution requirements for married participants?

- the pension plan document (i.e., all defined benefit plans and money purchase plans) must provide that the qualified joint and survivor annuity will be the mandatory form of distribution for a married participant unless the spouse agrees with the participant's election for an alternate form of distribution
- the spouse's signature must be notarized or witnessed by the plan administrator
- there are two types of joint and survivor annuities:
  - ○ *qualified pre-retirement survivor annuity (QPSA):* if a married participant dies before retirement, then the surviving spouse must be able to receive at least 50% of the participant's accrued benefit at date of death
  - ○ *qualified joint & survivor annuity (QJSA):* if a participant in a plan subject to these rules has a spouse (as determined in accordance with state law) on his or her benefit commencement date, then the normal form of benefit must be a X% joint and survivor annuity where X is any percentage between 50% and 100% and where the spouse is automatically the second life (every plan must offer a married participant the option to elect a 75% joint and survivor benefit)

What early retirement benefits and subsidies are available under a qualified defined benefit plan?

- the sponsoring employer can give credit for past years of service worked before the plan was adopted, with a predecessor employer, or with an affiliated employer, or can assume future, but yet unearned, years of service
- an early retirement subsidy oftentimes entices older members of the workforce to voluntarily leave
- there are two main types of early retirement subsidies: assume that the annuity payable starting at a younger age is the same benefit payable starting at retirement age and assume that the individual is credited for future years of service he would likely have worked if there was no early retirement subsidy

Under what circumstances can a plan allow in-service distributions (i.e., while the participant is still employed and still receiving a salary)?

- *pension plans (i.e., money purchase plans and defined benefit plans):* no distributions are allowed while the participant is still employed by the employer (other than for death or disability) before age 59½
- *profit sharing plans:* may allow participants who are still employed to withdraw a portion or all of their account balances after the money has been in the plan for a specified number of years (but at least two years)
- *401(k) plan:* for the elective salary deferrals only, only as a hardship distribution
- distributions of an employee's elective salary deferrals can only be withdrawn while the individual is still employed if they meet the "hardship distribution" rules for an immediate and heavy financial need, which include:
  - qualified medical expenses already incurred or about to be incurred for the employee, a spouse, and dependents;
  - the expenses necessary for the employee to purchase a principal residence (or the mortgage amount necessary to prevent foreclosure, but not regular mortgage payments);
  - tuition, related educational fees, and room and board for post-secondary education for the employee, a spouse, children, or dependents for the next year;
  - funds necessary to prevent the eviction of the employee from his or her principal residence;
  - burial or funeral expenses for the employee's deceased spouse, parent, child, or dependent;
  - expenses to repair the participant's primary residence, but only in certain circumstances; or
  - expenses and losses (including loss of income) for FEMA-designated disaster.
  - the employer can only pay an amount equal to the immediate and heavy need, but not greater than the sum of the employee's elective deferrals (less the amount of any previously distributed hardship withdrawal)
  - although exempt from the premature penalty tax, a hardship distribution is included in gross income in the year distributed
  - prior to the Bipartisan Budget Act of 2018, an employee could not elect salary deferrals for at least six months after taking a hardship distribution; beginning in 2020, such a suspension rule is now prohibited
- *Roth 401(k) plan:* any time after the money has been in the participant's account for at least 5 years, and after the participant attains age 59½
- *CARES Act:* — authorizes in-service withdrawals up to $100,000 for 2020 only (similar to relief given in other natural disasters such as Katrina)

- all qualified plans must distribute appropriate benefits to an ex-spouse upon divorce from a plan participant, but only if the parties provide a valid qualified domestic relations order (QDRO)
  - a domestic relations order (DRO) is merely some document that is certified in state court to divide marital property between former spouses upon divorce (a common marital property to be divided might be the benefits one of the spouses has accrued in his or her qualified retirement plan)
  - the benefits of a qualified retirement plan can only be alienated if the domestic relations order is determined, by the plan administrator, to be a qualified domestic relations order
  - the QDRO must provide clear instructions to the plan administrator (drafted specifically for that particular qualified plan) on how and when to pay the "alternate payee" former spouse
  - plans are required to have a QDRO determination procedure which clearly informs all parties what they will look for in a DRO to determine whether it is a QDRO, the time frame in which it will make such determination, and how either party can dispute the plan administrator's determination
  - if a plan administrator is on notice that a QDRO might be forthcoming, then there is a statutory 18-month period where the plan administrator must act in good faith and segregate any benefits which might become distributable to an alternate payee should a valid QDRO be communicated
- a loan is generally not considered a distribution
  - if loans are specifically allowed under the plan document, then each participant who is an employee of the sponsoring employer can take out the lesser of:
    - $50,000, as reduced by the largest outstanding loan balance in the previous 12 months or
    - 50% of the participant's accrued benefits
  - the loan must be paid back within five years (unless it is being used for the purchase of a first home), and must be paid at least quarterly
  - there must be a reasonable interest rate (the rule of thumb is that the IRS will not question rates which are one point above prime on that loan date)
  - if a participant defaults on the loan, then the unpaid balance is deemed a distribution and is included in gross income in the year of default and is subject to the premature penalty tax
  - CARES Act allows for larger loans for 2020 and a one-year suspension of repayments for loans, for impacted participants of the covid-19 health pandemic

How is a normal distribution from a qualified retirement plan taxed?

- if the participant has no basis in his or her plan benefits, then the total amount received in each plan year is included in gross income

- basis generally includes:
  - nondeductible (i.e., after-tax) employee contributions
  - PS-58 costs attributable to insurance included in income as an "economic benefit"
  - employer contributions which have already been taxed and
  - amounts paid by an employee as principal payments on any loans that were treated as "deemed distributions"
- if the participant has a basis in his plan benefits, then the exclusion ratio for annuities paid from qualified retirement plans will use special factors to determine the dollar amount of each distribution excluded from taxation (until the basis is fully recovered)

What are some of the procedural aspects of plan distributions?

- a statement of benefit options and procedures, including a disclosure of the relative values of optional forms of benefits
- a notice explaining all the income tax aspects of a distribution or a rollover
- the plan sponsor must withhold 20% of any distribution and submit that to the federal government as advance income taxes paid by the individual

What is a rollover?

- any portion of a distribution from a qualified retirement plan may be rolled over into a traditional IRA or into another qualified retirement plan which accepts rollover contributions, *unless* the distribution:
  - is a minimum distribution under I.R.C. §401(a)(9), or
  - is a hardship distribution from a §401(k) plan
- if a participant rolls over a distribution, then the participant keeps the same tax advantages (i.e., deferral of taxation of benefits and interest until distributed)
- a distribution of designated Roth contributions, and associated earnings, can be rolled over into a Roth IRA

What is a premature distribution and how is it taxed?

- a 10% penalty is assessed for premature distributions (generally made prior to age 59½)
- Congress decided that anyone who receives money before 59½ is probably not really retired and therefore such individuals are penalized for taking the money too early
- distributions which are excluded from this penalty tax are those which are:
  - paid due to death, disability, or separation of service after attainment of age 55
  - used as qualifying medical expenses
  - paid to an alternate payee pursuant to a QDRO

- ◦ used by unemployed individuals to pay health insurance premiums, or

- ◦ paid for any reason to certain qualified reservists called into active duty, as long as they are repaid within two years after the period of active duty ends

- ◦ distributions of up to $5,000 for the birth or adoption of a child

- ◦ only if paid from a traditional IRA, are used for qualified education or qualified first-time home purchase expenses

- each individual taxpayer is required to indicate premature distributions on his individual tax return and thus pay the penalty

What are the required minimum distributions?

- this provision basically applies to wealthier individuals who have other assets available during retirement, and wish to pass the tax-qualified benefits to their beneficiaries

- a participant must start receiving annual minimum distributions in the year after he or she attains age 70½, or, if not a 5% owner, after retirement if still working at age 70½ (the employee's required beginning date); SECURE increases the age from 70½ to 72, but *only for* individuals turning 70½ after December 31, 2019

- if the plan is a defined contribution plan (or other individual account plan), then the minimum amount that must be distributed (and included in gross income) for the current year equals the account balance as of the last valuation date in the preceding year divided by a life expectancy factor

- if the plan is a defined benefit plan, then certain distribution options automatically meet the minimum distribution rules, whereas other options need to be tested against the minimum distribution incidental benefit rules (where non-spouse beneficiaries, depending on their age, cannot mathematically be expected to receive more benefits after the employee's death than the employee is expected to receive during his lifetime).

- the designated beneficiary is determined on September 30 of the calendar year following the year of the employee's death — which allows accountants and estate planners ample time to fix things for their client since there are certain income tax advantages if the spouse is the sole designated beneficiary and there are income tax disadvantages if the beneficiary is not an individual

- if the employee dies before his required beginning date, then all the benefits from non-defined benefit plans must be distributed either:

- ◦ within 10 years of his or her death;

- ◦ over the life of an eligible designated beneficiary, starting in the year following the year of death; eligible designated beneficiaries include a surviving spouse, child of the employee who has not yet reached majority age, a disabled individual, a chronically ill individual, or an individual not more than 10 years younger than the employee

- the person who fails to receive a distribution upon turning age 70½ (or the new age 72), and not the employer, will pay a 50% penalty tax for failing to take a required minimum distribution

A. Introduction

The terms of the plan generally govern the timing and methods of distribution, subject to applicable limitations under ERISA and the Code. A trust may lose its qualified status if the related plan does not comply with the limitations on distributions contained in I.R.C. §401(a) and the regulations thereunder. While the Code may prescribe distribution options, the sponsor of a qualified plan does not have to extend all the various options to participants.

The issue of distribution is also relevant from the participant's point of view, as it may have income tax consequences. One of the important advantages of a qualified plan is that an employee may have a vested or nonvested property right to an account or benefit under such plan without any immediate income tax consequences. However, when such tax-free accumulations are actually received by the employee-participant, they are then subject to federal income tax. The ability to accelerate payment of benefits either through the timing or form of payment does not subject a participant to immediate taxation because the benefit is funded through a qualified plan.

Many of ERISA's and the Code's distribution requirements applicable to *pension* plans favor the surviving spouse of the participant at the time of death or retirement, which may or may not be the spouse of the participant during the period of time in which the benefits were accrued. In order for former spouses of a participant to protect their rights to benefits under ERISA plans, the state court domestic relations order must comply with ERISA's rules in order to be "qualified" ("QDRO") and therefore enforceable against the plan.

Due to the restrictions against in-service distributions applicable for *pension* plans, plan sponsors may decide to offer loans under the plans. Loans, if properly structured, are not regarded as distributions for Code purposes but do afford access to a participant's account balance. A loan must comply with certain Code requirements to avoid being construed as a distribution and with ERISA requirements to satisfy the statutory exemption for prohibited transactions. Since most defined benefit plans are noncontributory, loans are generally not made available. However, §401(k) plans which provide for employee and employer contributions may provide for loans, as the in-service distribution options are extremely limited.[1]

The focus of this chapter concerns the applicable qualified plan rules that permit or force a distribution from a plan and the federal income tax consequences of such distributions. One way of understanding the distribution rules is from the perspective of three typical participant groups—group one wants its benefits as soon as possible

---

1. I.R.C. §72(p)(b)(2); *See also* I.R.C. §4975(d)(2); ERISA §408(b)(1).

regardless of the negative tax consequences; group two wants its benefits as a retirement annuity when he or she retires, taxable as received; group three doesn't need the income and would prefer to defer the commencement of benefits in perpetuity to avoid any current income tax. Given the diverse interests of these three common groups, ERISA and the Code have responded in a variety of ways.

B. Timing of Distributions

1. Earliest Distribution Date

Pension Plans: All defined benefit and money purchase/target benefit defined contribution plans must restrict in-service distributions (i.e., distributions of benefits while the employee is still employed by the employer), because the primary purpose of such plans is to systematically provide for the payment of benefits over a period of time after retirement.[2] After PPA '06, active participants age 62 and over were permitted to take distributions.[3] SECURE now allows in-service distributions at age 59½ (rather than age 62), effective for plan years beginning after December 31, 2019.[4] SECURE also now permits penalty-free withdrawals of up to $5,000 from their qualified defined contribution, 403(b), and governmental 457(b) plans, and IRAs for expenses related to the birth or adoption of a child for up to one year following the birth or legal adoption.[5]

Defined Benefit Plans: For defined benefit plans that permit a participant to retire earlier than his or her normal retirement age and to begin receiving benefits earlier, the early retirement age will be the distribution date. For example, if the plan's normal retirement age is age 65, it may permit a participant who has attained age 55 and 15 years of service to retire earlier and begin to receive benefits. There are two types of subsidies that the plan can extend to such early retirees:

- The amount of the early retirement benefit is subsidized (i.e., meaning the true actuarial cost for early commencement is not assessed). If a given interest rate

2. *See* Treas. Reg. § 1.401-1(b)(1)(i).
3. I.R.C. § 401(a)(36); ERISA § 3(2)(A).
4. Further Consolidated Appropriations Act, 2020, div. M, § 104, 133 Stat. 3091.
5. Further Consolidated Appropriations Act, 2020, div. O, SECURE '19 § 113, 133 Stat. 3137, effective for distributions after December 31, 2019. As Congress sometimes does in the event of a federally declared disaster, CARES will not apply the 10% early distribution penalty from retirement plans and IRAs under I.R.C. § 72(t) on "coronavirus-related distributions" up to $100,000 per person from the person's retirement plan account. This amount may be re-contributed to the retirement plan, or to another plan, within three years after the date the distribution is received without regard to any plan limit on contribution. Federal income tax withholding is not required on this distribution, and a direct rollover need not be offered. Qualifying individuals for this relief include an individual (1) who is diagnosed with COVID-19 by a CDC-approved test, (2) whose spouse or dependent is diagnosed with COVID-19 by a CDC-approved test, or (3) who "experiences adverse financial consequences as a result of being quarantined, being furloughed, or laid off, or having work hours reduced due to COVID-19," (4) who is unable to work due to COVID-19 child care issues, (5) who has closed or reduced hours in a business owned or operated by the individual due to COVID-19, or (6) who has experienced other factors as determined by the Secretary of the Treasury. CARES § 2202.

and mortality table resulted in a reduction of 6% per year prior to age 65 for early commencing, charging only 3% per year prior to age 65 would result in a subsidized early retirement benefit. For example, if the participant is currently age 55 and has a normal retirement benefit of $1,000/month/65/life only, charging only 3% per year, instead of 6%, would allow the participant to retire early at age 55 with a benefit of $700/month/55/life.

- If the plan's normal retirement formula is a unit credit formula of 1% × FAE × years of service, the plan can credit a participant with future years of service had he or she worked until normal retirement age instead of retiring early. For example, if the participant is currently age 55 and has 25 years of service, the normal retirement formula can credit him or her with an additional 10 years of service for purposes of computing his early retirement benefit.

Profit Sharing Plans: Since the purpose of these plans is to defer compensation, the distribution of employer contributions is not restricted to termination of employment, death, disability, or retirement. Once a participant has a sufficient number of years of participation under the plan, in-service distributions are allowed.

I.R.C. § 401(k) Plans: Elective employee salary deferrals and earnings may not be distributed before termination of employment, death, disability, attainment of age 59½, termination of the plan, but may be made in the event of hardship.[6] Roth 401(k) distributions can be made at any time, but the distribution will be subject to income tax if it is not a qualified distribution (i.e., held in the plan for at least five years and after the individual has attained age 59½.[7]

ESOPs: The payment of benefits under an ESOP must begin no later than one year after the close of the plan year:

- which is the year the participant terminates employment due to attainment of normal retirement age under the plan, disability, or death; or
- which is the fifth plan year following the plan year in which the participant terminates employment.[8]

Employee Election: A plan may not force a distribution before a participant reaches age 62, except that the plan may require distribution upon the employee's termination of employment (without the employee's consent) if the participant's account balance under a defined contribution plan, or the actuarial equivalent of his or her benefit under a defined benefit plan, is $5,000 or less.[9]

CARES Act Temporary Relief: Temporary relief is extended during 2020 for optional coronavirus-related distributions to be exempt from the 10% early withdrawal tax

---

6. I.R.C. § 401(k)(2)(B).
7. I.R.C. § 402A(d)(2).
8. I.R.C. § 409(o)(1)(A).
9. Treas. Reg. § 1.417(e)-1.

and to be eligible for special taxation.[10] This is similar to other qualified disaster distribution reliefs.

2. Normal Distribution Date

I.R.C. § 401(a)(14) provides that, unless the participant otherwise elects, the payment of benefits under the plan to the participant must begin no later than the 60th day after the *latest* of the close of the plan year in which:

- The participant attains the earlier of age 65 or the normal retirement age specified under the plan;
- The 10th anniversary of the year in which the participant commenced participation in the plan; or
- The participant terminates his service with the employer.

The plan may permit a participant to elect that the payment of benefits will commence at a date later than the three dates specified above, except that such election may not have the effect of making any benefits payable upon the participant's death to be more than incidental under Treas. Reg. § 1.401-1(b)(1)(i), and benefits must commence to be paid in accordance with the minimum distribution rules.[11]

If the plan offers an early retirement benefit based on age and years of service, I.R.C. § 401(a)(14) also requires that in the event a participant terminates employment after satisfying the service requirement but before reaching the stated age, then the participant must be entitled upon reaching such age to receive a benefit not less than the benefit to which he or she would be entitled as of normal retirement age, actuarially reduced under the IRS regulations. Note that many defined benefit plans offer a subsidized early retirement benefit contingent upon attaining a given age and service requirement (e.g., attainment of age 60 and 15 years of service).

3. Latest Distribution Date

I.R.C. § 401(a)(9) generally provides that benefits must commence no later than the participant's required beginning date (known as "RBD") and continue in installment fashion over a specified distribution time frame (prescribed by the IRS regu-

---

10. CARES § 2202 permits in-service withdrawals up to $100,000 during 2020 that qualify as "coronavirus-related distributions." These include withdrawals made during 2020 to an individual who is diagnosed with COVID-19; whose spouse or dependent is diagnosed with the virus; who experiences adverse financial consequences as a result of being quarantined, being furloughed, or laid off, or having to work reduced hours due to the virus; or is unable to work due to lack of child care due to the virus; or has experienced reduced or no hours from a business owned or operated by an individual due to the virus. The withdrawal is not subject to the 10% early withdrawal penalty. There is a special tax rule whereby the tax on the distribution can be spread over three years, and it can also be repaid within three years.

11. Treas. Reg. § 1.401(a)-14(b)(3).

lations). The intent is to force distribution of benefits (and resulting taxation of benefits) during the lifetime of the participant and his or her surviving spouse. While plans can permit installment forms of payment, most do not; thus, participants wishing such a form of payment would roll his or her benefits into an IRA which do offer installment payouts. The SECURE Act changed these rules substantially, effective as of January 1, 2020. These changes will be discussed later in this chapter.

C. Methods of Payment

1. Normal and Optional Forms of Payment

The terms of the plan will dictate the method of paying benefits to the participant, or upon his or her death, to his or her beneficiary. Profit sharing plans are generally drafted to offer a lump sum distribution as the sole form of distribution, provided certain death benefits are met.[12] This forces the participant who wishes an installment or annuity form of payment to roll his or her account balance into an IRA, an individual retirement annuity, or another qualified plan that offers installment payments and/or annuities. A lump sum payment is simply the total balance of the participant's account under the plan at the time of distribution—which could be termination of employment, death, disability, or retirement. Such a form of distribution subjects the participant to the investment risk and the longevity risk (sometimes referred to as the mortality risk) of outliving the balance.

Author Barry Kozak used the analogy of a mailbox and a piggy bank to compare an annuity to a lump sum distribution.[13] For a life annuity, picture a mailbox in which the retiree can walk down to the mailbox monthly and find his or her annuity check. As the average male American alive at age 65 has a life expectancy of age 83, if the male retiree dies on his 83rd birthday, he would have received exactly what the employer wanted to provide through the retirement plan.[14] If he survives his 83rd birthday and lives longer, he will continue to receive his monthly check and thus, will have received more benefits than the plan intended. On the other hand, if he were to die before his 83rd birthday, the life annuity will terminate, and he will have received fewer benefits than the plan intended. In contrast, for the lump sum distribution, picture a piggy bank. Every month, the retiree takes enough out of the bank to pay for his monthly living expenses. If this particular retiree dies on his 83rd birth-

---

12. ERISA § 205 and I.R.C. § 401(a)(11)(B) allow profit sharing plans to offer a lump sum distribution as the sole form provided (1) the participant's accrued benefit is payable in full on the death of the participant to the surviving spouse, (2) the participant does not elect the benefit in the form of a life annuity, and (3) the plan is not a direct or indirect transfer of a plan that was a pension plan.

13. *See* BARRY KOZAK, EMPLOYEE BENEFIT PLANS, Ch. 9 (Carolina Academic Press 2010).

14. *See* John Elflein, *Life expectancy for men at the age of 65 years in the U.S. from 1960 to 2017*, Statista (Nov. 27, 2019), https://www.statista.com/statistics/266657/us-life-expectancy-for-men-aat-the-age-of-65-years-since-1960/.

day, assuming he accurately calculated how much to withdraw each month and properly invested the balance, he will withdraw the last dollar from the piggy bank. However, if he survives his 83rd birthday, the piggy bank is likely to be depleted and he will have to turn to his individual savings and Social Security for living expenses. Thus, the mailbox and piggy bank analogy illustrates that the retiree bears the investment risk and longevity risk with a lump sum distribution.

For plans that offer annuity options to retirees, many participants recoil from annuities due to the "all or nothing approach" that they provide. While a lump sum of $1,000,000 can purchase an annuity of $5,660/month at age 65 for a male's life, if the male participant dies at age 67, then he received only two years' worth of the monthly amount of $5,660 for a total of $135,840, leaving nothing for his beneficiaries. Conversely, if the male participant dies at age 90, he has received $1,698,000 in payments. Congress' investigative arm, the Government Accountability Office (GAO), has issued a number of reports addressing the topic of "lifetime income options." As annuities have fallen out of favor with plan sponsors of profit sharing plans, the baby boomers are faced with the cost of purchasing annuities on their own or risk outliving their account balances.[15]

In an effort to promote the use of lifetime income products within a qualified defined contribution plan, the SECURE Act added an optional feature, effective in 2020, whereby a plan that offers lifetime income products as an investment choice may allow a new distribution option (while the participant is still *in-service*) which permits the participant to transfer such product outside the plan without penalty.[16]

Pension plans (e.g., defined benefit plans and money purchase/target benefit plans) must offer as the default form of payment the life annuity for an unmarried participant and a joint and survivor annuity for a married participant.[17] A life annuity is generally monthly payments from the plan to the participant beginning on his or her normal retirement date and continuing for the remainder of his or her lifetime. This is identical to the method of payment for the receipt of Social Security benefits, which thereby guarantees that the recipient will not outlive the stream of payment. This form of payment is then underwritten by the employer (i.e., it must fund the cost of such insurance protection). The joint and survivor annuity form pays a life annuity to the participant and upon his or her death, an annuity to the surviving spouse. The amount paid to the surviving spouse can be the same as that provided to the

---

15. *See* Kathryn J. Kennedy, *How Can Lifetime Income Be Made a Desirable Retirement Plan Distribution Option?*, 2013 N.Y.U. REV. OF EMP. BENEFITS & EXEC. COMP. ch. 1.

16. SECURE § 109, by adding new language to I.R.C. § 401(a)(37), I.R.C. § 401(k)(2)(B)(VI), I.R.C. § 403(b)(D), I.R.C. § 403(b)(7)(i)(VI), and I.R.C. § 457(d)(1)(A)(iv) (an optional provision, effective in 2020, to provide portability for lifetime income investments). This permits the employer to offer lifetime income investments as an investment choice but then later discontinue such an investment choice, making the investment more attractive to the employer. The provision affords the participant the portability to move the lifetime income investment to another tax shelter (e.g., IRA) with a direct trustee-to-trustee transfer.

17. I.R.C. § 401(a)(11); ERISA § 205.

participant (referred to as a J&100%S annuity), or something less (e.g., 50% to the surviving spouse, referred to as a J&50%S annuity). If the spouse predeceases the participant, the participant ends up with a single life annuity. Such joint and survivor benefit is obviously more expensive than a single life annuity, as the J&S annuity is offering annuity protection to two lives. In addition, such benefit's expense depends on the age differential between the participant and spouse — the greater the age difference, the more expensive the benefit as it will be paying the annuity for a greater expected period of time.

Other forms of optional forms of payment include a life annuity with a period certain protection (e.g., five or 10 years). Payments under this form of payment guarantee monthly or annual payments for a period certain (e.g., five or 10 years), and if the participant is still alive at the end of the period certain, he or she receives a life annuity. This assures the participant that his or her beneficiaries will receive something if the participant dies during the period certain. Obviously, this form of payment is more expensive than a single life annuity, as it guarantees payment for a given period of time. However, it softens the "blow" of the single life annuity's "all or nothing approach."

2. Actuarial Equivalence

The IRS regulations prescribe that a defined benefit plan offering the employee's accrued benefit as an amount other than an annual benefit commencing at normal retirement age (i.e., a life annuity) must offer the alternate optional form of benefit as the actuarial equivalent of the life annuity benefit.[18] The cost of the life annuity depends on a variety of factors: age at commencement, mortality table (to project individuals' life expectancy), interest rate, and type of annuity.

> **Example:** In the above example, the $1,000,000 purchased a life annuity of $5,660/month beginning at age 65. Clearly, the $1,000,000 used to purchase a joint and survivor or an annuity with a certain period guarantee would not generate an annuity of $5,660/month, as it is purchasing added protections (i.e., with an associated premium cost) in the form of either a survivor annuity guarantee or a period certain guarantee. Thus, the $5,660/month amount would be adjusted downward to reflect that guarantee.

If the same interest rate and mortality table is used to make the adjustment, the amounts are said to be actuarially equivalent — meaning they are economically the same, as they are based on the same assumptions.

Thus, a defined benefit plan offering optional forms of payment will set forth in the plan the actuarial assumptions to be used to make the conversion. This can be done in a variety of ways: state the interest rate and mortality table to be used; use

---

18. Treas. Reg. § 1.411(c)-1(e).

percentage amounts to approximate the equivalences (e.g., 10-year certain and life annuity costs 10%); or use tables.

3. Qualified Joint and Survivor Annuity and Qualified Preretirement Survivor Annuity

Congress decided to codify protection for the surviving spouse by requiring that pension benefits for married participants be paid in the form of a qualified survivor benefit that meets the requirements under I.R.C. § 417.[19] These rules applied to any plan that was subject to I.R.C. § 412 (i.e., defined benefit plans and money purchase plans (including target benefit plans)), and to any *other* plan *unless* such plan provides certain death benefit protections.

I.R.C. § 417 provides that benefits must be paid in the form a qualified joint and survivor annuity (QJSA). With respect to unmarried participants, the QJSA is a single life annuity or the normal form of annuity under the plan.[20] With respect to married participants, the QJSA is an annuity for the life of the participant with a survivor annuity of not less than 50% and not more than 100% for the life of the participant's surviving spouse, and that is the actuarial equivalent of a single annuity for the participant's life.[21] PPA '06 amended I.R.C. § 417 to require pension plans to offer a "qualified *optional* survivor annuity" of 75% where a plan's QJSA is less than 50%, or 50% where a plan's QJSA is greater than 75%.[22] For example, if the plan's QJSA is 50%, an additional optional J&75% annuity must be offered, or if the plan's QJSA is 100%, an additional optional J&50% annuity must be offered.

I.R.C. § 417 also prescribes that a qualified preretirement survivor annuity (QPSA) must be paid to the surviving spouse of any *vested* participant who dies before payment of his or her retirement benefit has commenced.[23] This protection gives the surviving spouse the same benefit he or she would have received if their spouse-participant had retired immediately prior to death and received benefits under the plan's normal joint and survivor annuity. The QPSA is a survivor annuity for the life of the participant's surviving spouse determined in the following manner: If the participant dies after his or her earliest retirement date (but before benefits have been commenced), the QPSA is determined as if the participant separated from service on the day before his or her death, elected the QJSA, and then died.[24] Without this protection, if a participant died prior to reaching the plan's normal retirement age, the spouse would not have had survivor benefits under the plan even though the participant had accrued significant vested benefits before death.

---

19. I.R.C. § 401(a)(11).
20. I.R.C. § 401(a)(11)(A)(ii); Treas. Reg. § 1.401(a)-20, Q&A-25(a).
21. I.R.C. § 417(b)(1).
22. PPA '06 § 1004(a)(1), adding I.R.C. § 417(a)(1)(A)(ii).
23. I.R.C. § 401(a)(11)(A)(ii).
24. I.R.C. § 417(c)(1)(A)(i).

If the participant dies on or before his or her earliest retirement date, the QPSA is determined as if the participant:

- Terminated service on the date of death;
- Survived until he or she would have attained earliest retirement date but for the fact of death;
- Retired on the earliest retirement date and elected QJSA; and
- Died on the following date.[25]

A participant's "earliest retirement date" is the earliest date on which the participant could elect to commence benefits in accordance with the terms of the plan. If the plan is a defined contribution plan, the QPSA is a survivor annuity for the life of the participant's surviving spouse, the actuarial equivalent of which is not less than 50% of the participant's *vested* account balance as of death.[26]

I.R.C. § 417(e) permits a plan to provide that benefits will be paid in a lump sum without provision for the QJSA or the QPSA if the present value of the participant's vested accrued benefit does not exceed $5,000.[27] The QJSA or QPSA must be provided only with respect to participants and spouses who have been married during the one-year period ending on the *earlier* of the participant's annuity starting date or death. If, however, a participant and his or her surviving spouse have been married for less than one year as of the annuity starting date but have been married for at least one year on or before death, then they are considered to have been married for one year on the annuity starting date.[28] A participant's "annuity starting date" is the date benefits commence to be paid; it need not be the actual date of payment.[29]

A surviving spouse may elect to commence payment of the QPSA beginning not later than the later of:

- In the case of a defined benefit plan, the first day of the month in which occurs the participant's earliest retirement date; or
- In the case of a defined contribution plan, within a reasonable time after the participant's death.[30]

As a result of the *United States v. Windsor*[31] and *Obergefell v. Hodges*[32] decisions, federally mandated benefits provided by ERISA and the qualification rules (e.g., QJSA and QPSA benefits) must be extended to same-sex spouses, but not to domestic partners or individuals in civil unions.

---

25. I.R.C. § 417(c)(1)(A)(ii).
26. I.R.C. § 417(c)(2).
27. TRA '97 § 1071(a)(2)(A) increased the limit on the involuntary cash out of a nonforfeitable benefit in a qualified plan from $3,500 to $5,000.
28. I.R.C. § 417(d).
29. Treas. Reg. § 1.401(a)-20, Q&A-10(b), and Q&A-25(b)(2).
30. Treas. Reg. § 1.401(a)-20, Q&A-12.
31. 570 U.S. 744 (2013).
32. 576 U.S. ___, 135 S. Ct. 2584 (2015).

4. Waiving the QJSA and QPSA

The participant must have the right to waive the QJSA and QPSA unless the plan subsidizes the cost of the survivor benefit.[33] No spousal consent is required to commence payment of benefits. The participant's waiver period begins on the first day of the plan year in which he or she attains age 35 and ends on his or her date of death.[34] For those participants who separate from service prior to age 35, waiver may be made any time after his or her separation date.

Any waiver by the participant is not effective unless the participant's spouse consents to the waiver. Such waiver must be in writing and acknowledge its effect, be notarized or witnessed by a plan representative, and designate an alternative form of benefit and/or an alternative beneficiary.[35] The waiver is revocable by the participant without the spouse's consent, but any new waiver must satisfy the above requirements unless the spouse has irrevocably consented to the waiver.

Within a reasonable time prior to commencement of the participant's benefit, the plan administrator must give a written explanation of the terms and conditions of the QJSA, the right to waivers and their effect, and the right to revoke a waiver and their effect.[36] The participant (with spousal consent) may waive the QJSA during the 90-day period ending on the annuity starting date.[37]

Similarly, the plan administrator must give a written explanation of the QPSA within a period of time defined by statute.[38] The participant (with spousal consent) may waive the QPSA during the period beginning on the first day of the plan year in which the participant attains age 35 and ending on the participant's death.[39]

5. Beneficiary Designation Form

While there is no statutory requirement, most plan administrators provide beneficiary designation forms once an employee becomes eligible to participate in the plan. Thus, should the participant die prior to the normal retirement date, any pre-retirement death benefits can be disbursed to the named beneficiary. The Supreme Court case of *Boggs v. Boggs*[40] (which appears in the Materials section of this chapter) illustrates the importance of keeping these beneficiary designation forms up to date,

---

33. I.R.C. § 417(a)(1).

34. I.R.C. § 417(a)(6)(B).

35. I.R.C. § 417(a)(2). *See* Lasche v. George W. Lasche Profit Sharing Plan, 111 F.3d 863 (11th Cir. 1997) (participant's surviving spouse entitled to her deceased husband's plan benefit, even though she signed document purporting to waive her rights thereto, where section of waiver document providing for witness signatures was left blank). Also note that antenuptial agreements waiving benefits do not satisfy the Code's consent requirements. Treas. Reg. § 1.401(a)-20, Q-28.

36. I.R.C. § 417(a)(3); Treas. Reg. § 1.417(e)-1(b)(2)(i).

37. Treas. Reg. § 1.417(e)-IT(b)(3)(i); *see also* I.R.C. § 417(a)(6)(A).

38. I.R.C. § 417(a)(3)(B). *See* Treas. Reg. § 1.401(a)-20, Q&A-35(a).

39. I.R.C. § 417(a)(6)(B).

40. 520 U.S. 833 (1997).

especially if the participant divorces his or her spouse. In that case, the court held that a Louisiana state law which revoked any beneficiary form that named the ex-spouse as beneficiary was preempted by ERISA. As a result of the participant's failure to file a new beneficiary form upon his divorce, the plan recognized the former spouse as the beneficiary.

D. Qualified Domestic Relations Orders

ERISA has an anti-alienation, assignment, and garnishment provision so that the participants' benefits are guaranteed to be paid.[41] Initially, courts were divided as to whether ERISA's anti-alienation restrictions were applicable in dividing assets between the participant and his or her spouse in a divorce proceeding. As a result, Congress amended ERISA's anti-alienation provision to permit the attachment of domestic relations orders that were "qualified" under I.R.C. § 414(p)(1). The person eligible to receive benefits under this exception was defined as an "alternate payee."

Specific requirements are required to perfect a state domestic relations order, including:[42]

- The creation or recognition of the existence of an alternate payee's right to receive, or assigns to an alternate payee the right to receive all or a portion of the benefits payable with respect to a plan participant; and

- Clearly specifies

  - The name and last known address of the participant and each alternate payee covered under the order;[43]

  - The amount or percent of the participant's benefit to be paid to each alternate payee;

  - The number of payments or duration to which the order pertains;

  - Each plan to which the order pertains;[44]

---

41. ERISA § 206(d)(2); I.R.C. § 401(a)(13). There are three exceptions: (1) voluntary and revocable assignments of 10% or less of any benefit by a participant in pay status, (2) secured loans to participants, and (3) federal tax levies of collection of federal judgments. An anti-alienation provision in a document states that the owner of the property cannot transfer his or her interest to a third party. An anti-assignment provision in a document prevents either party from assigning tasks to a third party without the consent of the nonassigning party. And garnishment is a court order directing property of a third person be seized to satisfy a debt owned by a debtor to a creditor.

42. I.R.C. § 404(p)(4).

43. An "alternate payee" includes any spouse, former spouse, child, or other dependent of a participant who is recognized by a domestic relations order as having the right to receive all, or a portion of, the benefits payable under a plan with respect to such participant. ERISA § 206(d)(3)(k); I.R.C. § 414(p)(8). *See* U.S. Dep't of Labor, *QDROs, The Division of Pensions Through Qualified Domestic Relations Orders,* Q 1-4 (2001).

44. ERISA § 206(d)(3)(c); I.R.C. § 414(p)(2). *See also* U.S. Dep't of Labor, *QDROs, The Division of Pensions Through Qualified Domestic Relations Orders,* Q 1-5 (2001).

○ Does not specify a form of benefit or option that is not available under the plan; and

○ Does not apply to any payments or benefits covered by an earlier QDRO.[45]

There must be a judgment decree order; a marital settlement agreement is not such an order until it is entered with a judgment by the court. The QDRO can designate any or all of the participant's pension benefits to the alternate payee. The DOL rules make clear that there are two (mutually exclusive) approaches to dividing retirement benefits between spouses upon divorce/separation — *shared interest* and *separate interest*.[46] The shared interest approach *has to be* utilized if the participant has already retired and is receiving benefits. Under that approach, an award to the alternate payee of 50% of the participant's benefits upon divorce would mean that the plan would pay 50% to the participant and 50% to the alternate payee, both as an annuity for the remainder of *participant's* life. The alternate payee has no choice over the timing or type of benefit distribution. Unless the QDRO specifies that he or she is to be deemed "the surviving spouse" so as to continue a portion of the participant's benefit upon his or her death, benefits under the shared interest approach cease upon the participant's death.

In contrast, the separate interest approach may be preferable if the participant has not yet retired and the alternate payee wishes to be treated similarly to the participant. Such approach allows the alternate payee to decide when benefits will commence (consistent with choices available to participants under the plan) and how distributions should be paid (consistent with the various forms of benefits payments under the plan). Since this approach splits the present value of benefits between the participant and the alternate payee, it has a radical impact on the valuing of benefits at their different expected retirement ages. For example, let us say John's retirement benefit of $800/month at his age 62 is presently worth $200,000 (at his present age of 45) and let us assume the marital portion of those benefits is 50%. Under the separate interest approach, the entire amount of $200,000 will be split 50% — affording a present value of $100,000 to John and a present value of $100,000 to his former wife, Jane. For John, this present value will provide him with a benefit of $400/month beginning at age 62 as a life annuity. However, for Jane who is 10 years younger than John, her $100,000 will provide a benefit which is considerably less than $400/month at her age 62 as a life annuity. This approach treats Jane as a separate participant and thus she need not be deemed John's surviving spouse for purposes of continuation of his benefits after his death; she will receive benefits over her own lifetime.

---

45. ERISA § 206(d)(3)(i)–(iii); I.R.C. § 414(p)(3)(A)–(C). *See* U.S. Dep't of Labor, *QDROs, The Division of Pensions Through Qualified Domestic Relations Orders*, Q 1-6 (2001), and IRS Notice 97-11, 1997-2 I.R.B. 49 (provides sample language intended to assist domestic relations attorneys, plan participants, spouses and former spouses of participants, and plan administrators in drafting and reviewing a QDRO).

46. *See* U.S. Dep't of Labor, *QDROs, The Division of Pensions Through Qualified Domestic Relations Orders*, Q 3-3 (2001).

What if the plan offers an early retirement benefit that the participant is not presently eligible for? The state domestic relations order can extend to the ex-spouse an interest in the participant's early retirement benefit under I.R.C. § 414(p)(4), provided such benefit (1) begins when the participant has attained the "earliest retirement date" under the plan, (2) considers only benefits actually accrued,[47] and (3) payment is in any form required by the plan (other than a joint and survivor annuity with respect to the alternate payee and his/her spouse).[48] The earliest retirement date means the *earlier* of the date on which the participant is entitled to a plan distribution or the later of:

- the date the participant attains age 50, or
- the earliest date on which the participant could separate from service and commence to receive benefits.[49]

For this purpose, a participant's earliest retirement date is determined by taking into account only the participant's actual years of service at the time of separation from service or death.[50] Thus, if a plan precludes payment of benefits before separation from service, the earliest date on which a QDRO could order benefits paid to an alternate payee is age 50, if the participant does not separate from service.

Plans must establish procedures to determine the qualified status of domestic orders and to notify the participant and each alternate payee when an order is received and how it will be evaluated.[51] During the period in which the plan administrator is evaluating the status of the QDRO, a separate account must be maintained for the amount that would otherwise have been paid to the alternate payee for a maximum of 18 months.[52] This 18-month period provides sufficient time for the plan administrator to review the DRO, and if there are any defects, sufficient time for the alternate payee to perfect those defects.

The DOL regulations have specific rules regarding the timing of when a DRO should be requested and the priority of competing DROs.[53]

E. Hardship Distributions from a § 401(k) Plan

While Congress permitted I.R.C. § 401(k) plans as a statutory exception to the normal constructive receipt rules, it imposed specific limitations on the distribution of these deferrals. Elective deferrals under a § 401(k) plan may not be distributed earlier than:

---

47. I.R.C. § 414(p)(4)(A).
48. I.R.C. § 414(p)(4)(A)(i)–(iii).
49. I.R.C. § 414(p)(4)(B).
50. Conf. Rep. No. 99-841, Vol. II (P.L. 99-574) p. II-518.
51. ERISA § 206(d)(G); I.R.C. § 1.414(p)(6).
52. I.R.C. § 414(p)(7).
53. Labor Reg. § 2530.206(b)–(d).

- The participant's separation from service, death, or disability;
- The participant's attainment of age 59½;
- The termination of the plan without the establishment or maintenance of a successor plan;
- The attainment of a hardship of the employee; or
- The participant's call into active military duty for more than 179 days or indefinitely.[54]

The regulations take a narrow view as to what constitutes hardship. They require an immediate and heavy financial need that can only be satisfied by means of the hardship distribution.[55] The needs that may qualify for a hardship distribution include: medical expenses of the employee, spouse, children, or dependents; post-secondary education tuition payments (for 12-month periods) for the employee, spouse, children, or dependents of the employee; purchase costs for a principal residence of the employees; amounts needed to prevent eviction from or foreclosure on the employee's principal residence; payments for burial or funeral expenses for the employee's deceased parent, spouse, children, or dependent; expenses for the repair of damage to the employee's principal residence that would qualify for the casualty deduction;[56] any expenses and losses, including loss of income, incurred due to a federally declared disaster if the participant's principal residence or principal place of employment is located in an area designated by Federal Emergency Management Agency (FEMA) for individual assistance.[57] The employer may rely upon the employee's representation that he or she qualifies for a hardship unless the employer has actual knowledge to the contrary.[58]

The BBA '18 relaxed certain restrictions on hardship withdrawals for I.R.C. § 401(k) plans by:

- Changing the IRS' hardship distribution regulations to eliminate the existing safe harbor rule prohibiting employees from making elective deferrals for 6 months after a hardship distribution;
- Permitting QNECs, QMACs, and earnings on such contributions to be available for hardship distributions (not just the employee's elective deferrals); and

---

54. I.R.C. § 401(k)(2)(B).

55. Treas. Reg. § 1.401(k)-1(d)(3)(iv)(B).

56. Under the original regulations, the hardship exception for expenses for the repair of damage to the employee's principal residence was limited to situations that qualified for the casualty deduction under I.R.C. § 165, see Treas. Reg. § 1.401(k)-1(d)(3)(iii)(B)(6). TCJA § 11044(a), adding I.R.C. § 165(h)(5), limited the personal casualty deduction under I.R.C. § 165 solely to losses attributable to federally declared disasters in tax years 2018 through 2025, making this hardship exception more difficult to satisfy. As a result, Treasury proposed and finalized this hardship exception in 2019, stating I.R.C. § 165(h)(5) would not be applicable. See Treas. Reg. 1.401(k)-1(d)(3)(iii)(B)(6).

57. Treas. Reg. § 1.401(k)-1(d)(3)(iii)(B).

58. Treas. Reg. § 1.401(k)-1(d)(3)(iv)(C).

- Eliminating the rule that the employee must take out any available plan loans before requesting a hardship distribution.[59]

F. Plan Loans

Since the availability of plan loans increases the administrative costs under a qualified plan, most plan sponsors consider their advantages and disadvantages before deciding to incur their costs. However, § 401(k) plans must severely limit the ability of a participant to make an in-service distribution. Thus, the availability of a loan feature may be the deciding factor for a participant in making § 401(k) contributions, because he or she will know that there is limited access to those funds.

ERISA and the Code provide prohibited transaction exemption rules that must be satisfied if the plan offers loans to participants, including owner-employees. A plan loan made to a married participant must secure the spouse's consent to the portion of the loan being used as collateral for the loan.[60] In addition, the Code has tax rules under § 72(p) that must be satisfied to avoid having a loan treated as a current distribution and potentially taxable to the participant.

ERISA § 406(a)(1)(B) generally prohibits loans between a party and a party-in-interest (which includes an employee of an employer sponsoring the plan).[61] The term "party-in-interest" will be defined in Chapter 13, but basically includes those persons or entities who may have a potential conflict of interest with the plan (e.g., the employer). However, it also provides a statutory exemption for plan loans that satisfy the following criteria:

- At the core of the exemption is the requirement that the plan loan be a bona-fide repayment scheme;[62]

- Loans must be made available to all "parties in interest" on a reasonably equivalent basis;[63]

- Loans must not be made available to highly compensated employees in an amount greater than the amount made available to other employees;[64]

- Loans must be made in accordance with specific plan provisions and disclosed in the plan's summary plan description (SPD);

- Loans must be charged a reasonable rate of interest (e.g., a commercial lending rate charged by a bank under similar circumstances);

---

59. BBA '18 §§ 41113–41114.
60. I.R.C. § 417(e)(4).
61. ERISA § 406(a)(1)(B).
62. ERISA § 408(b)(1); 29 U.S.C. § 1108(b)(1). *See also* I.R.C. § 72(p)(4).
63. ERISA § 408(b)(1)(A); 29 U.S.C. § 1108(b)(1)(A).
64. ERISA § 408(b)(1)(B); 29 U.S.C. § 1108(b)(1)(B).

- Loans must be adequately secured (e.g., using the participant's vested account balance as security for the loan in the event it is not repaid).[65]

I.R.C. § 72(p) presumes that a plan loan is a deemed distribution (and therefore immediately taxable) unless explicit requirements are satisfied.[66] The loan must be written and specify the amount of the loan, date of the loan, and its repayment schedule. Failure to comply with the repayment, level amortization payment, or the enforceability requirements results in a deemed distribution for the entire amount of the loan at the time it was made (i.e., retroactive), whereas failure to comply with the amount requirement results in characterizing only the excess amount as a deemed distribution. Thus, these requirements are as follows:

- The plan loan is required to be repaid within five years, but a loan for the purchase of a principal residence is not subject to a specific time period.

- Repayment of interest and principal on the loan is required to be made on a substantially level amortization schedule over the repayment schedule. These repayments are usually done via payroll deductions.

- The loan must be evidenced by a legally enforceable document (written or obtained through electronic means).

- The maximum amount of the loan is the lesser of (1) (greater of 50% of the participant's vested account balance, $10,000 (a statutory maximum)) or (2) $50,000 (a statutory amount, which is reduced by the highest outstanding loan balance during the prior one-year period).[67]

Example: If the participant has an account balance of $200,000 for which he or she is 60% vested (i.e., $120,000), the maximum dollar amount of the loan for this participant (assuming no prior loans) would be as follows:

Step 1: take the greater of [50% × $120,000, $10,000] = greater of [$60,000, $10,000] = $60,000

Step 2: $50,000 (the statutory limit) − $0 (as there are no prior loan)

Step 3: the maximum dollar amount = lesser of [$60,000, $50,000] = $50,000. If the loan granted was $60,000 (in excess of the maximum $50,000), the excess of $10,000 would be deemed a distribution and immediately taxable to the participant.

---

65. Labor Reg. § 2550.408b-1.

66. I.R.C. § 72(p).

67. I.R.C. § 72(p)(2). CARES relaxed the plan loan rules for any loans from qualified plan to "qualified individuals" that are made during the 180-day period from March 27, 2020, by increasing the $50,000 limit to $100,000 and the 50% limit to 100%. A "qualified individual" is defined similarly to the one used for coronavirus-related in-service distributions rules. The due date for any repayment of such loan is delayed for up to one year, despite the Code's five-year maximum period. Plan administrators may rely on employee certification that he or she qualifies as a "qualified individual." CARES § 2202.

If the plan loan meets these rules, it is not a deemed distribution (i.e., taxable event). However, if the rules are not met, the distribution is a taxable event and may be subject to an additional tax applicable to early distributions.

G. Taxation of Distributions

1. General Rules

Under the federal income tax rules, there are three relevant points to consider in determining when, how, and to whom federal income taxes are due on qualified plan and IRA distributions.[68] The first is that distributions are taxed as ordinary income in the year they are received. The second is that the distribution is taxable to the recipient. And the third is that the form of the distribution (e.g., annuity or lump sum) will determine when the tax is payable. There are several exceptions to these general rules which will be discussed later in the chapter.

The first general federal tax rule for qualified plan[69] and IRA distributions is that the monies will be taxed in the *tax year in which they are distributed*. While funds going into a qualified plan and IRA may be tax-deferred, they are not tax-exempt; hence distributions will be taxed as ordinary income upon receipt. This is true even if the plan or IRA distributes stock to the recipient.[70] It is taxable as ordinary income, but the recipient may elect to defer current taxation of any net unrealized appreciation on employer securities.[71] After-tax employee contributions and a portion of life insurance proceeds distributed from a plan are *exempt* from taxation.[72] Since employee Roth deferrals are not excludable from taxation in the year of deferral, the Roth contributions *and* their earnings are exempt from federal income tax upon distribution provided the applicable requirements have been met and the distribution qualifies as a "qualified distribution."[73] Because the general tax rule includes the distribution as income in the year of receipt, the choice as to *when* the taxpayer is going to receive any or all of the distribution is paramount.

---

68. Because the tax savings on a Roth IRA are so advantageous, we are likely to see a dramatic decline in the traditional deductible and nondeductible IRAs. However, for taxpayers with significant buildups in deductible IRAs, the tax burden of rolling over such an IRA into a Roth IRA may not justify the rollover. Thus, those IRAs will likely continue as nonRoth IRAs. Future contributions should be made to a Roth IRA, even if the contribution is nondeductible, because of the tax-free distribution rules afforded to Roth IRAs. Only taxpayers who are unable to take advantage of the Roth IRAs because of the adjusted gross income phase-outs will be left making future contributions to the nonRoth IRAs.

69. I.R.C. §§ 402 (b)(2), 408(d)(1).

70. I.R.C. § 402(e)(4); Treas. Reg. § 1.402(a)-1(a)(6)(I), -1(b).

71. *Id.*

72. Treas. Reg. § 1.402(a)-1(a)(2).

73. *See* I.R.C. § 402A(d)(2), stating that distributions of "designated Roth contributions" and their earnings are exempt from tax only if made after the end of the five-taxable-year period that begins with the first day of the year in which the participant first made such contribution to the plan.

Secondly, the distribution is taxable to the *recipient* (i.e., the employee, named beneficiary, spouse, or alternate payee).[74] As discussed later, special tax treatments are available *only* to the employee-participant and to his or her spouse, surviving spouse, or former spouse.

Lastly, the *form* of the distribution will dictate the federal income tax consequences to the recipient. For this purpose, there are three different forms of distributions — a lump sum, an annuity distribution, or an installment distribution. A lump sum distribution is ordinarily taxable immediately in the year of receipt. If the qualified plan has permitted after-tax employee contributions (that are not Roth contributions) to the plan (thus, creating a basis for the employee), only a portion of the lump sum distribution will be taxable.[75] The recipient is able to recover tax-free distributions of those after-tax employee monies.[76] Although it is more common now to permit only pre-tax or Roth employee contributions in an I.R.C. § 401(k) plan or employer-only contributed plan, some plans have encouraged the contribution of after-tax (non-Roth) employee monies. While such funds did not enjoy tax-deferral treatment, the earnings on such monies are tax-deferred and monies held in qualified plans are exempt from the claims of the creditors.[77]

If the entire balance of a participant's account or accrued benefit is not distributed in a lump sum, the income tax treatment of the distributions is considerably different and more complicated. The tax treatment will vary as to whether the distribution is an annuity payment versus an installment payment and whether it is made before versus after the annuity starting date.

2. Annuity versus Installments

An annuity payment refers to distributions payable under a contract dependent upon life contingencies (e.g., life only or joint and survivor). If there are no after-tax employee contributions attributable to any of the payments, the ordinary rule prevails, such that each annuity payment is fully taxable in the tax year it is received.[78] However, if there are after-tax employee contributions, the Code permits a certain amount of each separate annuity payment to be attributable to such after-tax contributions, and thus not taxable in the year of receipt.[79] The portion of each annuity payment that is taxable versus non-taxable depends on whether the benefits are paid before *or* after the annuity starting date. The participant chooses the recovery method, not the plan administrator.

The annuity starting date (ASD) is defined as the first date of the first payment under an annuity contract.[80] If the recipient wishes to take monies out of the plan

---

74. I.R.C. § 402(a), (e)(1).
75. I.R.C. § 402(d)(4)(D)(i).
76. *Id.*
77. I.R.C. § 401(a)(13); Treas. Reg. § 1.72-6.
78. Treas. Reg. § 1.401(a)-1(a)(2).
79. Treas. Reg. § 1.72-4(b)(1).
80. I.R.C. § 72(c)(4).

prior to the ASD, the Code uses a rule known to practitioners as the "pro rata recovery" rule in determining what portion of the distribution is taxable.[81] This rule is applied at the time of *each* and *every* payment, and thus, the excludable percentage may vary from payment to payment.[82] The pro rata recovery portion is determined by dividing the sum of all after-tax employee contributions made to the plan by the present value of the annuity payments as of the earlier distribution date.[83] If there are multiple withdrawals before the ASD, this pro rata portion will change since it is recomputed and the denominator is revalued.[84] In addition, as the present value of the annuity payments increases with time, the denominator of the ratio grows bigger and thus the fraction becomes smaller. Hence, a smaller and smaller portion of each distribution is excludable from tax.

If the recipient withdraws any monies *after* the ASD, there are two different ways to compute the taxable portion: the exclusion ratio method or the simplified method.[85] If the taxpayer is not eligible for or does not elect the simplified method, the "exclusion ratio" method is used. The exclusion ratio is equal to the ratio of the total amount of after-tax employee contributions made under the plan divided by the total account balance or the total expected return, determined as of ASD.[86] This fraction computes a fixed percentage, which is applied to each and every subsequent annuity payment.[87]

> **Example:** If the total value of after-tax employee contributions was $36,000 and the account balance as of ASD was $400,000, the exclusion ratio would be [36,000 ÷ 400,000] = 9% for each payment. Thus, 9% of each payment would be recovery of basis (and thus, nontaxable) and the remaining 91% of each payment would be fully taxable.

The simplified method was recently added to the Code as an alternative method. Under this method, the Code provides a table with a fixed number of anticipated payments, which depends on the annuitant's age as of the ASD. For example, using the same numbers above, if the taxpayer was age 55 as of the ASD, the table provides that there are 360 expected monthly annuity payments. The denominator is thereby adjusted to 360, providing that the nontaxable portion of each annuity payment to be $100 (i.e., $36,000 ÷ 360). Later, the Code added a table in the case of joint annuitants.[88] In order to use the simplified method, the primary annuitant must not

---

81. I.R.C. §72(e)(2)(B) to (8)(B).

82. *Id.* See also IRS Notice 87-13, for guidance with respect to basis recovery rules.

83. *Id.,* at Q-18.

84. *See* IRS Notice 87-16, especially Section III.

85. I.R.C. §72(b), (d).

86. I.R.C. §72(b)(1). The present value for the denominator is determined in accordance with Treas. Reg. §1.72-5, and the employee's investment (the numerator) is determined in accordance with Treas. Reg. §1.72-6. Unisex annuity tables are generally used for computations of exclusion ratios for annuity payments after June 30, 1986. There are transitional rules for computations involving after-tax employee contributions made before that date. The expected return multiples from the Tables will have to be altered if annuity payments are made quarterly, semiannually, or annually.

87. I.R.C. §72(b)(1); Treas. Reg. §1.72-4(a)(1)(ii).

88. TRA '97 §1975.

have attained age 75 as of the ASD (unless there are fewer than five years of guaranteed payments under the annuity).[89]

Similar rules apply if the payment stream is installment payments (i.e., payments over time that do not depend on life contingencies) instead of annuity payments.[90] If there are no employee after-tax contributions, each installment payment will be fully taxable in the year of receipt.[91] However, if there are any after-tax employee contributions, then proportions must be computed.[92] The recipient will compute an ASD, which will be the first date on which the installment payments are fixed (this is done even though there is actually no annuity).[93] If installment payments begin as of the ASD, the recipient uses the exclusion ratio method, described above, to compute each portion of the payment that is taxable versus nontaxable.[94] However, if installment payments begin before the ASD, then the rules are different. Here, all installment payments are taxable in full until the taxable portion of the benefits is recovered; only then are the remaining payments treated as nontaxable.[95]

Oftentimes a taxpayer may be deciding whether to take his or her distribution in the form of an annuity or installment payments. Before deciding, it may be worth asking whether there is any significant amount of after-tax money in the plan. If so, the annuity form permits each payment to carry out a portion of the nontaxable monies, whereas the installment form requires the recipient to exhaust the taxable portion before assuming nontaxable monies are being distributed.

3. Exceptions to the General Rules

Rollovers: If the exception applies, the recipient is permitted to defer immediate taxation otherwise due by rolling over the amounts received into an IRA or another qualified plan.[96] The only recipients that may avail themselves of this exception include the participant or IRA owner and his or her spouse.[97] Thus, if the recipient is a child or trust beneficiary, this exception is not available to such beneficiary.

As to the portion of the distribution that can be rolled over, the eligible recipient is permitted to roll over any or all of the distribution that qualifies for an "eligible rollover distribution."[98] The full amount of any *taxable* portion of the distribution may be rolled over, except for:

---

89. I.R.C. § 72(d)(1)(E).
90. Treas. Reg. § 1.72-2(b)(2)(i), (ii).
91. I.R.C. 72(b)(2).
92. I.R.C. § 72(c)(1), (e)(2).
93. Treas. Reg. § 1.72-2(b)(2)(i), (ii).
94. I.R.C. § 72(b).
95. I.R.C. § 72(e)(2)(A).
96. I.R.C. § 402(c)(1), (5).
97. I.R.C. § 402(c)(1), (9). According to Treas. Reg. § 1.402(c)-2, Q&A-12, I.R.C. § 402(c) applies to the distribution in the same manner as if the surviving spouse were the employee.
98. I.R.C. § 402(c)(4).

- Minimum required distribution amounts (discussed later in this chapter);[99]
- One of a series of substantially equal payments in the form of an annuity or installment payments that last for the life of the employee or the joint lives of the employee and his or her beneficiary or for a specified period of 10 years or longer;[100] and
- Certain corrective distributions, loan defaults, and pass-through dividends paid on employer securities.[101]

PPA '06 permits two other provisions relating to rollovers:

- Individuals are permitted to roll over distributions from qualified plans, 403(b) plans, and 457 plans directly into a Roth IRA without having to first roll over the amount into a traditional "conduit" IRA.[102]
- After-tax contributions (and earnings thereon) from a qualified or 403(b) plan may be directly rolled over into another qualified or 403(b) plan, provided the new plan accounts separately for the amounts transferred and any future earnings for purposes of calculating tax liability.[103]

Annuity Contracts: The actual distribution of a nontransferable annuity contract to a recipient is ordinarily not a taxable event.[104] Thus, only as distributions are actually made under the contract are they taxable in accordance with the general rule.

Life Insurance: Life insurance is subject to its own unique set of income tax rules, and these rules are still applicable even if the qualified plan purchases the life insurance on the employee's behalf. Thus, during the period of deferral when the distributions are not taxable to the employee, the employee will be imputed with a term cost of coverage for the insurance product.[105] Such term cost is determined according to the actual insurance cost or tables prescribed by the IRS (known as the "PS-58 costs").[106] For younger employees, this cost is minimal.

Upon distribution, the beneficiary is not taxed on the death benefit portion of the life insurance even though it is a distribution from a qualified plan.[107] Life insurance proceeds enjoy this special tax treatment. The cash value of the life insurance is taxable

---

99. I.R.C. § 402(c)(4)(B).

100. I.R.C. § 402(c)(4)(A).

101. Treas. Reg. § 1.402(c)-2T, Q&A-4.

102. PPA '06 § 824(a), amending I.R.C. § 408A(E) (initially this was limited to individuals with adjusted gross incomes under $100,000, but later that limitation was lifted).

103. PPA '06 § 822(a), amending I.R.C. § 402(c)(2)(A).

104. Treas. Reg. § 1.402(a)-1(a)(2). See also Rev. Rul. 73-124, which provides that the proceeds of an individual annuity contract received by an employee and immediately surrendered to the employer pursuant to a binding agreement with the employer for reinvestment in another annuity contract for the employee with a different insurer are not includible in the gross income of the employee.

105. Treas. Reg. § 1.72-16(b)(4).

106. Rev. Rul. 55-747; Rev. Rul. 66-110.

107. I.R.C. §§ 72(m)(3),101(a). The death benefit portion is the amount of proceeds in excess of cash surrender value and offset by the cumulative PS-58 costs which represent a return of the participant's basis.

under these rules (to the extent it exceeds the amounts previously taxed as PS-58 costs), but the balance of the proceeds are tax-exempt.[108] If the policy has been in existence for a while, the proceeds may far exceed the taxable cash value, thus resulting in a nice tax shelter benefit.

Employer Stock: The last exception to the general income tax rule applies to lump sum distributions from qualified plans that consist of stocks, bonds, and debentures of the employer that sponsors the plan.[109] This exception is available to any recipient of the lump sum distribution, including a beneficiary or the taxpayer's estate.[110] Under this exception, any unrealized appreciation on the employer securities is exempt from tax at the time of distribution.[111] Such tax is deferred until the securities are ultimately sold or disposed of.[112] There are several methods for determining the amount of the net unrealized appreciation.[113]

4. Premature Distributions

Whether or not a distribution can even be made to an individual from a qualified plan or IRA prior to retirement is governed by the terms of the plan and the qualification rules. If the plan or IRA does permit a distribution, such distribution may be subject to an additional 10% penalty tax if made prematurely.[114]

The qualification rules for defined benefit and money purchase pension plans require that distribution not be made prior to normal or early retirement age, death or disability, or earlier termination of employment.[115] However, if the employee takes a distribution on account of separation of service and is not yet age 55, the premature penalty tax may be assessed (unless the distribution is rolled over into another qualified plan or IRA).[116]

Qualified profit sharing and stock bonus plans are permitted more flexibility regarding the in-service withdrawals from the plans. Such plans do not have to take advantage of these more liberal rules, but many do. However, even though the plan may permit a premature distribution, there may nevertheless be an income tax penalty on such distribution. Note: I.R.C. § 401(k) plans *must* impose restrictions on the distribution of elective pre-tax contributions (and nonelective and matching pre-tax contributions that are combined with the elective contributions for purposes of the special nondiscrimination tests).[117]

---

108. *Id.*
109. I.R.C. § 72(m)(3)(C).
110. I.R.C. § 402(a).
111. I.R.C. § 402(d)(4)(D)(ii).
112. Treas. Reg. § 1.402(a)-1(b).
113. Treas. Reg. § 1.402(a)-1(b)(2). The plan trustee will report the amount of net unrealized appreciations to the recipient on Form 1099.
114. I.R.C. § 401(a)(9)(B)(i).
115. I.R.C. § 72(t).
116. I.R.C. § 72(t)(2)(A)(v).
117. I.R.C. § 401(k)(2)(B)(i).

The general rule of I.R.C. § 72(t) imposes a 10% penalty tax on distributions made to the individual prior to age 59½. There are, however, a number of exceptions to this penalty tax.[118] Distributions from IRAs are allowed to take advantage of only some of these exceptions, but qualified plan distributions can take advantage of all of them as listed below.[119]

- Distributions made on account of the individual's attainment of age 59½, his or her death or disability;[120]

- Distributions made as part of a series of substantially equal periodic payments over the life or life expectancy of the individual, or the joint lives or life expectancies of the individual and a designated beneficiary;[121]

- Distributions to unemployed individuals for health insurance premium;[122]

- Distributions made on account of separation of service after the individual attains age 55;[123]

- Distributions that do not exceed the individual's *deductible* medical expenses for the year;[124]

- Distributions of dividends from employee stock ownership plans (ESOPs);[125]

- Distributions to an alternate payee under a qualified domestic relations order (QDRO);[126]

- Distributions to certain qualified reservists called into active duty for at least 180 days or for indefinite duty;[127]

- Distributions of up to $5,000 (determined on a controlled group basis) for expenses related to the birth or adoption of a child for up to one year following the birth of adoption.[128]

The following distributions are excluded from the 10% excise tax from an individual retirement plan (but not from a qualified retirement plan):

- Distributions used for qualified higher education expenses;[129] and

- Distributions used for qualified first time home purchase expenses.[130]

---

118. I.R.C. § 72(t)(2).
119. I.R.C. § 72(t)(3).
120. I.R.C. § 72(t)(2)(A)(ii)–(iii).
121. I.R.C. § 72(t)(2)(A)(iv).
122. I.R.C. § 72(t)(2)(D).
123. I.R.C. § 72(t)(2)(A)(iv)
124. I.R.C. § 72(t)(2)(B).
125. I.R.C. § 72(t)(2)(A)(vi).
126. I.R.C. § 72(t)(2)(C).
127. I.R.C. § 72(t)(2)(G).
128. SECURE § 133, adding subparagraph (H) to I.R.C. § 72(t)(2), effective for distributions after December 31, 2019.
129. I.R.C. § 72(t)(2)(E).
130. I.R.C. § 72(t)(2)(F).

5. Minimum Distribution Rules

The Code has minimum distribution rules devised as a tax penalty provision to prevent employees and their beneficiaries from totally deferring benefits under a qualified plan, IRA, I.R.C. §403(b) plan, or I.R.C. §457 eligible deferred compensation, and thereby transferring them tax free to the next or subsequent generations.[131] The rules are complex and were recently changed by the SECURE Act, which extended the age at which distributions must commence and which altered, for defined contribution plans only, the post-death distribution rules for certain beneficiaries.[132] If the rules are not followed, there is a 50% excise tax on the amount not distributed as required. As I.R.C. §401(k) plans are becoming the dominant plan for retirement savings, individuals should be aware that most employers prefer, for administrative simplicity, the lump sum distribution option for the participant or his or her named beneficiary, in lieu of installment and annuity options. Such choice negates the possibility of extending distributions from the plan. Thus, an individual may have to roll over such distributions into an IRA to take advantage of these deferral rules, as IRAs will permit installment payouts.

These rules require only that the benefits commence being paid, not that they be made in a single lump sum. Also, the distribution time frame may extend beyond one year; however, there are limits to the time frame of payment, so as to prevent distributions over an excessive period of time. Since these rules produce different *annual* distribution amounts, benefits are paid as installments, not as annuities. The regulations prescribe these limitations.[133] To further prolong distribution of benefits, the individual is permitted to designate a beneficiary for continued payment of benefits after the individual's death.[134] Before January 1, 2020, a participant could name a beneficiary to take distributions, upon the participant's death, over the beneficiary's lifetime (referred to as the "stretch" because stretching out the payment of benefits allowed the retirement assets to continue to grow tax free). The SECURE Act drastically changed these rules.

Under the federal income tax rules, there are several relevant points to consider in satisfying the required minimum distribution (RMD) rules. The first is determining the required beginning date (RBD) for the commencement of distributions. The second is ascertaining the distribution period if the employee dies *prior to* his or her required beginning date. If the employee *survives to* the RBD, the third issue is to ascertain the annual amount of the minimum distribution. This determination requires an analysis of (1) the applicable divisor, (2) the relevant account balance, and (3) the named beneficiary in order to ascertain each year's minimum distribution amount.

---

131. I.R.C. §401(a)(9), with the penalty of 50% tax imposed if the minimum amount is not timely distributed.

132. SECURE §§114, 401. Defined contribution plans include IRAs, qualified defined contribution plans, 403(b) plans, and 457(b) eligible deferred compensation plans.

133. Treas. Reg. §1.401(a)(9)-5.

134. Treas. Reg. §1.401(a)(9)-4.

In determining the RBD, a number of factors must be considered. Prior to the SECURE Act, the initial year of distribution was determined using the calendar year in which the participant turned 70½ or if the individual was not a 5% owner, then the calendar year in which he or she retired *if later*.[135] The SECURE Act increases the age from 70½ to 72, but only for individuals turning 70½ after December 31, 2019.[136] Individuals born in January through June turn 70½ in the same calendar year in which they turn 70, whereas individuals born in July through December turn 70½ in the calendar year **after** they turn 70. Thus, individuals born before or on June 30, 1949 must continue to use the prior age 70½ rules, whereas individuals born after June 30, 1949 can use the new age 72 rules.

> **Remember:** Individuals born on or before June 30, 1949, use the age 70½
> rules, and individuals born after June 30, 1949, use the age 72 rules.

Using the new age 72 rules, once an individual attains age 72 (this is the first year of distribution), the actual payment of the first year's benefit need not be made until April 1 of the following calendar year (this April 1 date is known as the RBD).[137] Once the RBD is calculated, distributions must commence for the first year and every year thereafter until death (referred to as the "distribution calendar year").[138] For example, a participant attains age 72 in 2022, but the payment for the first distribution calendar year need not be made until April 1, 2023. For subsequent years' payments (e.g., for the second year in 2023, third year in 2024, etc.), those payments need to be made by December 31 of the respective distribution calendar year. Thus, in the above example, the participant's second distribution for 2023 must be made by December 31, 2023, even though his or her first payment did not have to be made until April 1, 2023.

a. The Participant Dies Prior to His or Her RBD

The rules vary depending on whether the participant dies prior to his or her RBD **or** on or after his or her RBD. If the participant died *prior to* his or her RBD, there was a "five-year rule" that required distributions to be made in full by December 31 of the fifth year following the calendar year of death if the participant did **not** name a designated beneficiary.[139] Since a designated beneficiary must be a natural person, naming one's estate or a charity as the designated beneficiary resulted in the application

---

135. I.R.C. § 401(a)(9)(C). Note that an individual is a 100% owner of his or her IRA and thus cannot take advantage of the calendar year of his or her delayed retirement age.

136. SECURE § 114, amending I.R.C. § 401(a)(9)(C)(i)(I). Much like Congress did back in 2009 in light of the financial downturn in the market, CARES relaxes the minimum distribution rules for 2020 for defined contribution plans (qualified plans, 403(a) and 403(b) plans, governmental 457(b) plans, and IRAs). Minimum distributions with required beginning dates in calendar year 2020 need not be made in 2020. CARES § 2203.

137. I.R.C. § 401(a)(9)(C)(i).

138. Treas. Reg. § 1.401(a)(9)-5, A-1(b).

139. I.R.C. § 401(a)(9)(B)(ii).

of the five-year rule. The SECURE Act did not change this five-year rule for non-designated beneficiaries.

Under the prior rules, if the participant named an individual as the designated beneficiary, more liberal distribution rules were permitted. If a nonspouse was named as beneficiary, distributions could be made over the life expectancy of the beneficiary (referred to as the "stretch"), commencing by December 31 of the calendar year after the calendar year in which the participant died.[140] Thus, if the participant named his or her grandchild as the designated beneficiary (say, age 10), the grandchild could take distributions over his or her lifetime (e.g., 72.8 years)—coining the phrase "a stretch distribution period."

The SECURE Act eliminates this lifetime distribution option for beneficiaries who are **not** "eligible designated beneficiaries."[141] An eligible designated beneficiary includes the participant's surviving spouse, a minor child of the participant who has not reached majority, a disabled person, a chronically ill individual, or an individual who is not more than 10 years younger than the participant (why the latter person was included will be discussed in the next section of this chapter). Note that if a minor child was named, a lifetime distribution option is available only until the child reaches the age of majority, after which the new 10-year rule will apply.[142] For beneficiaries who are not eligible designated beneficiaries, a new 10-year rule applies. This rule requires any post-death distributions to designated beneficiaries to be made by the end of the 10th calendar year following the participant's year of death; these need not be made in annual distributions, but having a single distribution in the 10th year may increase the individual's marginal tax bracket due to the size of the distribution. Thus, the prior lifetime distribution option does not change for the surviving spouse who is named as beneficiary; however, on the death of the surviving spouse, the 10-year rule would apply to the next beneficiary (unless he or she was an "eligible designated beneficiary").

These new rules generally are not applicable to a participant who died before January 1, 2020, as the prior rules continue to apply.[143] However, for pre-2020 deaths, the 10-year rule will apply to any *beneficiary* of an eligible designated beneficiary.[144]

> **Example:** Participant P names his spouse as the designated beneficiary upon death, and the spouse names her grandchild as her designated beneficiary upon her death. Participant dies in 2019. His spouse may take distributions over her life expectancy, but upon her death, the grandchild is subject to the 10-year rule, as he or she does not qualify as an "eligible designated beneficiary," unless he or she was disabled or chronically ill.

---

140. I.R.C. § 401(a)(9)(B)(iii).
141. SECURE § 401(a)(1), adding a new I.R.C. § 401(a)(9)(H).
142. Note that the SECURE Act does not define "age of majority." Presumably, it will be defined in accordance with state law.
143. SECURE § 401(b).
144. SECURE § 401(a)(1), adding a new I.R.C. § 401(a)(9)(H)(iii).

If the participant dies *prior to* his or her RBD but names his or her spouse as the designated beneficiary, not only may the spouse elect to have distributions made over his or her life expectancy (the same as the nonspouse beneficiary), but the spouse can also elect to defer commencement until December 31 of the calendar year in which the participant would have attained age 72 (previously age 70½).[145] Therefore, the Code permits the spouse to step into the shoes of the participant for purposes of taking advantage of the RBD rules. In addition, a spouse beneficiary may roll over any or all of the benefits into an IRA in his or her own name, thereby permitting postponement of commencement until the spouse reaches his or her RBD.[146] SECURE did not change these rules for the participant's spouse.

b. Participant Survives to RBD

If the participant *survives to* RBD, he or she may use the 2002 Uniform Table for Determining Applicable Divisor contained in the regulations to compute the appropriate divisor. It is based on the age of the participant in the calendar year of distribution (and thus it changes as the participant ages), and it presumes that the participant has named his or her spouse as beneficiary and that their ages differ by 10 years.[147] The IRS made this presumption so that a single table could be applied, as opposed to multiple tables based on the actual ages of the participant and his or her named beneficiary. For example, if the participant is age 76 in the calendar year of distribution, the table permits a divisor of 22.0 (the life expectancy of a participant who is age 76 and his or her spouse who is age 66). Thus, the employee can use this table while alive regardless of whether he or she is married and regardless of whether his or her spouse is actually 10 years younger. The account balance to be used as the numerator in the calculation is generally the prior year-end account balance.[148]

Once the participant dies after his or her RBD, the distribution otherwise payable in the year of death must be paid to the participant or his or her estate.[149] Under the prior rules, if a nonspouse beneficiary was named, distributions could then be made based on either the participant's remaining life expectancy at death or the beneficiary's life expectancy (each reduced by one for each subsequent year, referred to as the "nonrecalculation method").[150] Under the new rules, the new 10-year rule applies.[151] Hence, unless the beneficiary is an "eligible designated beneficiary" (as defined above), distributions must be made by the end of the 10th calendar year following the year

---

145. I.R.C. § 401(a)(9)(B)(iv).

146. I.R.C. § 402(c)(9).

147. Treas. Reg. § 1.401(a)(9)-9. In 2019, pursuant to Executive Order 13847, the Service proposed updated Uniform Tables for use in the minimum distribution rules. *See* Prop. Treas. Reg. § 1.401(a)(9)-9, table 2.

148. *Id.* at § 1.401(a)(9)-5, Q&A-3.

149. Treas. Reg. § 1.401(a)(9)-5, Q&A-4(a).

150. Treas. Reg. § 1.401(a)(9)-5, Q&A-5(a)(1).

151. SECURE § 401(a).

of death, and not over the life expectancy of the beneficiary. The 10-year rule does not require the monies to be distributed annually over the 10 years; it simply requires that all monies must be paid out by the end of the 10th year.

> **Note:** One of the beneficiaries that qualifies as an "eligible designated beneficiary" is someone who is not more than 10 years younger than the participant. The 2002 Uniform Table gave the participant a joint life expectancy factor to use for distribution purposes based on a 10-year difference between the participant and his or her beneficiary. This exception under the SECURE Act continues to allow a beneficiary who is no more than 10 years younger the ability to use his or her life expectancy for distribution purposes. For example, if the participant dies at age 73 and the designated beneficiary is his or her sister age 63, the beneficiary may use her life expectancy at age 64 (her age in year following the participant's death), which is 21.8, for purposes of required annual distributions going forward.

Under the rules, if the beneficiary named was the spouse, the spouse could use his or her life expectancy for determining distribution periods but could recalculate life expectancy each year (instead of taking a one-year reduction).[152]

> **Example:** If the participant dies and the spouse is age 72 (in the year following the participant's death), the spouse uses his or her life expectancy of 15.5 for the first year of distribution and his or her life expectancy of 14.8 for the second year of distribution (not 15.5 − 1 = 14.5).[153] The recalculation method allows for a longer distribution period than the nonrecalculation method.

Upon the spouse's later death, the applicable distribution period will be 10 years for the next beneficiary, unless the subsequent beneficiary qualifies as an eligible designated beneficiary.[154]

The IRS regulations allow the designated beneficiary to be determined by September 30 following the calendar year of the employee's death.[155] This flexibility in determining the beneficiary(ies) may be highly beneficial for estate planning purposes, as it permits the *alteration* of the beneficiary designation following the employee's death due to subsequent distributions, division of plan assets, or disclaimer (e.g., the so-called "3-Ds permitted changes" to the beneficiary designation).[156] Hence, a beneficiary may be eliminated from the beneficiary group due to subsequent distribution of benefits, beneficiary designations may be divided in accordance with a division of plan assets, or a beneficiary may disclaim benefits under the plan, constricting the beneficiary

---

152. Treas. Reg. § 1.401(a)(9)-5(c)(2).
153. See single life expectancy tables in Treas. Reg. § 1.401(a)(9)-9.
154. SECURE § 401(a).
155. Treas. Reg. § 1.401(a)(9)-Q&A-4(a).
156. See Preamble to Prop. Treas. Reg. § 1.401(a)(9) (2001).

group for subsequent distribution. This flexibility permits further extension of the remaining payout period based on post-death estate planning recommendations.

> **Example:** Participant P names his spouse as primary beneficiary and his three children as contingent beneficiaries. P dies and his spouse does not financially need a distribution from the plan. The spouse can disclaim the beneficiary designation and allow the three children to take as beneficiaries.

H. Materials

Boggs v. Boggs

520 U.S. 833 (1997)

Justice Breyer dissented and filed an opinion in which Justice O'Connor joined, and in which Chief Justice Rehnquist and Justice Ginsburg joined in part.

We consider whether the Employee Retirement Income Security Act of 1974 (ERISA), 88 Stat. 832, as amended, 29 U.S.C. § 1001 et seq., pre-empts a state law allowing a nonparticipant spouse to transfer by testamentary instrument an interest in undistributed pension plan benefits. Given the pervasive significance of pension plans in the national economy, the congressional mandate for their uniform and comprehensive regulation, and the fundamental importance of community property law in defining the marital partnership in a number of States, the question is of undoubted importance. We hold that ERISA pre-empts the state law.

I

Isaac Boggs worked for South Central Bell from 1949 until his retirement in 1985. Isaac and Dorothy, his first wife, were married when he began working for the company, and they remained husband and wife until Dorothy's death in 1979. They had three sons. Within a year of Dorothy's death, Isaac married Sandra, and they remained married until his death in 1989.

Upon retirement, Isaac received various benefits from his employer's retirement plans. One was a lump-sum distribution from the Bell System Savings Plan for Salaried Employees (Savings Plan) of $151,628.94, which he rolled over into an Individual Retirement Account (IRA). He made no withdrawals and the account was worth $180,778.05 when he died. He also received 96 shares of AT & T stock from the Bell South Employee Stock Ownership Plan (ESOP). In addition, Isaac enjoyed a monthly annuity payment during his retirement of $1,777.67 from the Bell South Service Retirement Program.

The instant dispute over ownership of the benefits is between Sandra (the surviving wife) and the sons of the first marriage. The sons' claim to a portion of the benefits is based on Dorothy's will. Dorothy bequeathed to Isaac one-third of her estate, and a lifetime usufruct in the remaining two-thirds. A lifetime usufruct is the rough equivalent of a common-law life estate. *See* La. Civ. Code Ann., Art. 535 (West 1980). She bequeathed to her sons the naked ownership in the remaining two-thirds, subject to Isaac's usufruct. All agree that, absent pre-emption, Louisiana law controls and that under it Dorothy's will would dispose of her community property interest in Isaac's undistributed pension plan benefits. A Louisiana state court, in a 1980 order entitled "Judgment of Possession," ascribed to Dorothy's estate a community property interest in Isaac's Savings Plan account valued at the time at $21,194.29.

Sandra contests the validity of Dorothy's 1980 testamentary transfer, basing her claim to those benefits on her interest under Isaac's will and 29 U.S.C. § 1055. Isaac bequeathed to Sandra outright certain real property including the family home. His will also gave Sandra a lifetime usufruct in the remainder of his estate, with the naked ownership interest being held by the sons. Sandra argues that the sons' competing claim, since it is based on Dorothy's 1980 purported testamentary transfer of her community property interest in undistributed pension plan benefits, is pre-empted by ERISA. The Bell South Service Retirement Program monthly annuity is now paid to Sandra as the surviving spouse.

After Isaac's death, two of the sons filed an action in state court requesting the appointment of an expert to compute the percentage of the retirement benefits they would be entitled to as a result of Dorothy's attempted testamentary transfer. They further sought a judgment awarding them a portion of: the IRA; the ESOP shares of AT & T stock; the monthly annuity payments received by Isaac during his retirement; and Sandra's survivor annuity payments, both received and payable.

In response, Sandra Boggs filed a complaint in the United States District Court for the Eastern District of Louisiana, seeking a declaratory judgment that ERISA pre-empts the application of Louisiana's community property and succession laws to the extent they recognize the sons' claim to an interest in the disputed retirement benefits. The District Court granted summary judgment against Sandra Boggs. 849 F. Supp. 462 (1994). It found that, under Louisiana community property law, Dorothy had an ownership interest in her husband's pension plan benefits built up during their marriage. The creation of this interest, the court explained, does not violate 29 U.S.C. § 1056(d)(1), which prohibits pension plan benefits from being "assigned" or "alienated," since Congress did not intend to alter traditional familial and support obligations. In the court's view, there was no assignment or alienation because Dorothy's rights in the benefits were acquired by operation of community property law and not by transfer from Isaac. Turning to Dorothy's testamentary transfer, the court found it effective because "[ERISA] does not display any particular interest in preserving maximum benefits to any particular beneficiary." 849 F. Supp., at 465.

A divided panel of the Fifth Circuit affirmed. 82 F.3d 90 (1996). The court stressed that Louisiana law affects only what a plan participant may do with his or her benefits after they are received and not the relationship between the pension plan administrator and the plan beneficiary. Id., at 96. For the reasons given by the District Court, it found ERISA's pension plan anti-alienation provision, § 1056(d)(1), inapplicable to Louisiana's creation of Dorothy Boggs' community property interest in the pension plan benefits. It concluded that the transfer of the interest from Dorothy to her sons was not a prohibited assignment or alienation, as this transfer was "two steps removed from the disbursement of benefits." *Id.*, at 97.

* * *

This case lies at the intersection of ERISA pension law and state community property law. None can dispute the central role community property laws play in the nine community property States. It is more than a property regime. It is a commitment to the equality of husband and wife and reflects the real partnership inherent in the marital relationship. State community property laws, many of ancient lineage, "must have continued to exist through such lengths of time because of their manifold excellences and are not lightly to be abrogated or tossed aside." 1 W. de Funiak, Principles of Community Property 11 (1943). The community property regime in Louisiana dates from 1808 when the territorial legislature of Orleans drafted a civil code which adopted Spanish principles of community property. *Id.*, at 85–89. Louisiana's community property laws, and the community property regimes enacted in other States, implement policies and values lying within the traditional domain of the States. These considerations inform our pre-emption analysis. *See* Hisquierdo v. Hisquierdo, 439 U.S. 572, 581, 99 S. Ct. 802, 808, 59 L. Ed. 2d 1 (1979).

The nine community property States have some 80 million residents, with perhaps $1 trillion in retirement plans. *See* Brief for Estate Planning, Trust and Probate Law Section of the State Bar of California as Amicus Curiae 1. This case involves a community property claim, but our ruling will affect as well the right to make claims or assert interests based on the law of any State, whether or not it recognizes community property. Our ruling must be consistent with the congressional scheme to assure the security of plan participants and their families in every State. In enacting ERISA, Congress noted the importance of pension plans in its findings and declaration of policy, explaining:

> "[T]he growth in size, scope, and numbers of employee benefit plans in recent years has been rapid and substantial; ... the continued well-being and security of millions of employees and their dependents are directly affected by these plans; ... they are affected with a national public interest [and] they have become an important factor affecting the stability of employment and the successful development of industrial relations...." 29 U.S.C. § 1001(a).

ERISA is an intricate, comprehensive statute. Its federal regulatory scheme governs employee benefit plans, which include both pension and welfare plans. All employee benefit plans must conform to various reporting, disclosure, and fiduciary requirements, *see* §§ 1021–1031, 1101–1114, while pension plans must also comply with participation, vesting, and funding requirements, *see* §§ 1051–1086. The surviving spouse annuity and QDRO provisions, central to the dispute here, are part of the statute's mandatory participation and vesting requirements. These provisions provide detailed protections to spouses of plan participants which, in some cases, exceed what their rights would be were community property law the sole measure.

ERISA's express pre-emption clause states that the Act "shall supersede any and all State laws insofar as they may now or hereafter relate to any employee benefit plan...."

§ 1144(a). We can begin, and in this case end, the analysis by simply asking if state law conflicts with the provisions of ERISA or operates to frustrate its objects. We hold that there is a conflict, which suffices to resolve the case. We need not inquire whether the statutory phrase "relate to" provides further and additional support for the pre-emption claim. Nor need we consider the applicability of field pre-emption, *see* Fidelity Fed. Sav. & Loan Assn. v. De la Cuesta, 458 U.S. 141, 153, 102 S. Ct. 3014, 3022, 73 L. Ed. 2d 664 (1982).

We first address the survivor's annuity and then turn to the other pension benefits.

III

[7] Sandra Boggs, as we have observed, asserts that federal law pre-empts and su-persedes state law and requires the surviving spouse annuity to be paid to her as the sole beneficiary. We agree.

The annuity at issue is a qualified joint and survivor annuity mandated by ERISA. Section 1055(a) provides:

"Each pension plan to which this section applies shall provide that —

"(1) in the case of a vested participant who does not die before the annuity starting date, the accrued benefit payable to such participant shall be provided in the form of a qualified joint and survivor annuity."

ERISA requires that every qualified joint and survivor annuity include an annuity payable to a nonparticipant surviving spouse. The survivor's annuity may not be less than 50% of the amount of the annuity which is payable during the joint lives of the participant and spouse. § 1055(d)(1). Provision of the survivor's annuity may not be waived by the participant, absent certain limited circumstances, unless the spouse consents in writing to the designation of another beneficiary, which designation also cannot be changed without further spousal consent, witnessed by a plan representative or notary public. § 1055(c)(2). Sandra Boggs, as the surviving spouse, is entitled to a survivor's annuity under these provisions. She has not waived her right to the survivor's annuity, let alone consented to having the sons designated as the beneficiaries.

Respondents say their state-law claims are consistent with these provisions. Their claims, they argue, affect only the disposition of plan proceeds after they have been disbursed by the Bell South Service Retirement Program, and thus nothing is required of the plan. ERISA's concern for securing national uniformity in the administration of employee benefit plans, in their view, is not implicated. They argue Sandra's com-munity property obligations, after she receives the survivor annuity payments, "fai[l] to implicate the regulatory concerns of ERISA." Fort Halifax Packing Co. v. Coyne, 482 U.S. 1, 15, 107 S. Ct. 2211, 2219, 96 L. Ed. 2d 1 (1987).

[8] We disagree. The statutory object of the qualified joint and survivor annuity provisions, along with the rest of § 1055, is to ensure a stream of income to surviving spouses. Section 1055 mandates a survivor's annuity not only where a participant dies after the annuity starting date but also guarantees one if the participant dies before then. *See* §§ 1055(a)(2), (e). These provisions, enacted as part of the Retirement Equity Act of 1984 (REA), Pub. L. 98-397, 98 Stat. 1426, enlarged ERISA's protection

of surviving spouses in significant respects. Before REA, ERISA only required that pension plans, if they provided for the payment of benefits in the form of an annuity, offer a qualified joint and survivor annuity as an option entirely within a participant's discretion. 29 U.S.C. §§ 1055(a), (e) (1982 ed.). REA modified ERISA to permit participants to designate a beneficiary for the survivor's annuity, other than the nonparticipant spouse, only when the spouse agrees. § 1055(c)(2). Congress' concern for surviving spouses is also evident from the expansive coverage of § 1055, as amended by REA. Section 1055's requirements, as a general matter, apply to all "individual account plans" and "defined benefit plans." § 1055(b)(1). The terms are defined, for § 1055 purposes, so that all pension plans fall within those two categories. *See* § 1002(35). While some individual account plans escape § 1055's surviving spouse annuity requirements under certain conditions, Congress still protects the interests of the surviving spouse by requiring those plans to pay the spouse the nonforfeitable accrued benefits, reduced by certain security interests, in a lump-sum payment. § 1055(b)(1)(C).

ERISA's solicitude for the economic security of surviving spouses would be undermined by allowing a predeceasing spouse's heirs and legatees to have a community property interest in the survivor's annuity. Even a plan participant cannot defeat a nonparticipant surviving spouse's statutory entitlement to an annuity. It would be odd, to say the least, if Congress permitted a predeceasing nonparticipant spouse to do so. Nothing in the language of ERISA supports concluding that Congress made such an inexplicable decision. Testamentary transfers could reduce a surviving spouse's guaranteed annuity below the minimum set by ERISA (defined as 50% of the annuity payable during the joint lives of the participant and spouse). In this case, Sandra's annuity would be reduced by approximately 20%, according to the calculations contained in the sons' state-court filings. There is no reason why testamentary transfers could not reduce a survivor's annuity by an even greater amount. Perhaps even more troubling, the recipient of the testamentary transfer need not be a family member. For instance, a surviving spouse's § 1055 annuity might be substantially reduced so that funds could be diverted to support an unrelated stranger.

In the face of this direct clash between state law and the provisions and objectives of ERISA, the state law cannot stand. Conventional conflict pre-emption principles require pre-emption "where compliance with both federal and state regulations is a physical impossibility, ... or where state law stands as an obstacle to the accomplishment and execution of the full purposes and objectives of Congress." Gade v. National Solid Wastes Management Assn., 505 U.S. 88, 98, 112 S. Ct. 2374, 2383, 120 L. Ed. 2d 73 (1992) (internal quotation marks and citation omitted). It would undermine the purpose of ERISA's mandated survivor's annuity to allow Dorothy, the predeceasing spouse, by her testamentary transfer to defeat in part Sandra's entitlement to the annuity § 1055 guarantees her as the surviving spouse. This cannot be. States are not free to change ERISA's structure and balance.

Louisiana law, to the extent it provides the sons with a right to a portion of Sandra Boggs' § 1055 survivor's annuity, is pre-empted.

* * *

The axis around which ERISA's protections revolve is the concepts of participant and beneficiary. When Congress has chosen to depart from this framework, it has done so in a careful and limited manner. Respondents' claims, if allowed to succeed, would depart from this framework, upsetting the deliberate balance central to ERISA. It does not matter that respondents have sought to enforce their rights only after the retirement benefits have been distributed since their asserted rights are based on the theory that they had an interest in the undistributed pension plan benefits. Their state-law claims are pre-empted. The judgment of the Fifth Circuit is

Reversed.

Chapter 10

Employer Funding and Employer Deductions

Reading Assignment: ERISA § 301, 302

I.R.C. §§ 402(g), 404, 430, 436, 4971

Class Discussion Questions: A client of yours has frozen its defined benefit plan (which is a final pay formula plan), both as to new entrants and future benefit accruals. To freeze a plan in this context, there are no more new entrants, and for existing participants, there are no future benefit accruals. As the plan is not yet fully funded, it cannot terminate the plan. Does it have any funding obligations for the current plan year?

When Congress repealed the combined plan limitations of I.R.C. § 415(e), why did it not repeal the combined plan limitation for deductions under I.R.C. § 404(a)(7)?

Overview

What are the required employer contributions in a qualified retirement plan?

- in a defined contribution plan:

  - *money purchase plan:* the employer must contribute the proper amount so that an allocation can be made to each participant's account in accordance with the amount promised under the plan document

  - *profit sharing plan:* the employer must contribute the amount that it wishes to deduct for the year

  - *401(k) plans:* the employer must contribute the amount that has been promised to the participants as a match to their voluntary pre-tax elective salary deferrals or after-tax designated Roth contributions, and if the plan fails the special 401(k) nondiscrimination tests, then it must deposit the amount determined, if any, to bring the plan into compliance

- in a defined benefit plan

- funding is a moving target, and the true funded status is only determined once all plan liabilities have been paid out
- the enrolled actuary determines how well-funded the defined benefit plan is by comparing the fund assets to the fund liabilities on an annual basis (through statutory controls over minimum required contributions)
- if a plan fails to meet minimum funding requirements, then a penalty tax is imposed
- on the other hand, if the defined benefit plan is overfunded upon termination, then the employer pays a 50% penalty on the amount that is reverted back to the employer
- therefore, the enrolled actuary assists the employer in trying to properly fund the plan over its life
- the enrolled actuary will make a lot of reasonable assumptions to calculate the present value of future benefit promises, and compares that value to the plan's actual current assets to determine the mathematically appropriate minimum required contribution
- Congress hopes each plan is always at least 100% funded on a current basis
  - if the ratio falls below 100% in any year, then the minimum required contribution for that year is larger than expected, and more conservative actuarial assumptions might be required in the following year
  - if the ratio falls below 80% in the current year, then there is a prohibition against plan amendments that in any way increase the benefit accruals, and there are benefit distribution limitations imposed on the plan in the following year
  - if the ratio falls below 60% in the current year, then all future benefit accruals automatically cease, and there are severe restrictions on benefit distributions
- an enrolled actuary charges a fee for his or her professional services, and when added to the PBGC premiums described below, results in higher administrative fees for a defined benefit plan than for a defined contribution plan

What premiums do defined benefit plans pay to the PBGC for the insurance protection it provides?

- almost all single-employer defined benefit plans pay the sum of a flat rate premium ($83 per plan participant for 2020) and a variable rate premium ($45 for each $1,000 (or fraction thereof) for 2020) based on the unfunded vested benefits under the plan as of the close of the preceding pan year (with a maximum cap of $561 per participant for 2020 on the variable premium)

What are the maximum deduction rules for a qualified retirement plan?

- in a defined contribution plan
  - the maximum deduction for all contributions to all defined contribution plans sponsored by the employer is basically limited to 25% of total payroll, where

payroll is the total compensation to all participating employees after limiting each participant's compensation to $200,000 (as adjusted for inflation)

- in a defined benefit plan,
  - ∘ whatever amount is calculated by the enrolled actuary as the minimum required contribution is always required to be deposited and can always be deducted (regardless of its percentage of payroll)
  - ∘ in addition, the employer is generally allowed to contribute some extra money (up to about 50% of the minimum required contribution) in good years to help stave off unexpectedly high contributions in future years
- there is a special deduction limit for certain employers who sponsor both a defined benefit plan and a defined contribution plan that covers the same employee

A. Employer Funding

1. Special Rules for Defined Contribution Plans

As mentioned in a prior chapter, employers generally establish and maintain defined contribution plans because of their flexibility and the ability to forecast employers' costs.

Money Purchase/Target Benefit Plan: These plans require an annual employer contribution for eligible participants. Thus, these plans are subject to the Code's minimum funding requirements and are assessed a 10% penalty tax for failing to meet such standards.[1]

Discretionary Profit Sharing Plan: A profit sharing, stock bonus, or non-leveraged ESOP plan document need only provide the employee allocation formula but may provide that employer contributions are discretionary (i.e., will be determined annually by the employer). This provides the utmost in flexibility for the employer. The employer's contribution no longer has to be dependent on the employer's annual or cumulative profits.

Matching Contributions in a § 401(k) Plan: Safe harbor § 401(k) plans that rely on employer matching contributions must set forth the level of such contributions in the plan document. In other cases, while there is no mandate to make matching contributions, if the employer intends to, it should set forth the level of such contributions in the plan and do so in a manner that does not discriminate in favor of the highly paid.

Salary Deferrals and Roth Deferrals in a § 401(k) Plan: Under the fiduciary rules, the DOL sets forth timetables for the employer to remit employee pre-tax or Roth salary deferrals to the § 401(k) plan. I.R.C. § 402(g) sets forth a $15,000 annual maximum dollar amount (adjusted for inflation, $19,500 for 2020) that an employee can

---

1. I.R.C. § 4971.

defer from his or her salary, plus an additional catch-up amount of $5,000 (adjusted for inflation, $6,500 for 2020) but only for participants age 50 and older.[2] These dollar amounts are the same regardless of whether the salary deferrals are pre-tax deferrals or Roth deferrals.

2. Special Rules for Defined Benefit Plans

When previously describing the advantages of a defined benefit plan, one of the advantages was the ability to provide credit for service that the participant incurred while the plan was not in existence (i.e., referred to as past service credit). Also, if the defined benefit plan has an accrued benefit formula that is later increased, the employer must decide whether to apply the increase retroactively for service already incurred by the participant while a participant. For example, a small business in its 10th year implements a defined benefit when the two owners are ages 35 and 55, with a given NRB = AB = [4% × yos (cap at 20) × FAE]/65/life only or J&S. If the plan grants past service credits, the age 55 owner can retire with an NRB = [4% × 20 years × FAE]/65/life only or J&S, allowing the age 35 owner to take over the business. While such a formula creates an immediate past service liability when the plan is initially created, it provides sufficient replacement income for the age 55 owner to retire in 10 years.

Prior to the passage of ERISA, single-employer defined benefit plans were not required to be prefunded (i.e., contributions made over the employee's active lifetime to assure that the full cost of the benefit was funded at retirement). Instead, the Code required qualified defined benefit plans to fund current accruals and interest only on any past service liability.

With the passage of ERISA, the minimum funding rules would impose minimum limits on what *must* be contributed by the employer to fund not only current costs of the plan, but an amortized value of the plan's past service costs (not just interest only on such liability). For example, if the employer has been in existence for 10 years but established a qualified defined benefit plan in year 11, it must decide whether to grant past service credit for employees working for the employer during the first 10 years. If the employer decides to grant past service credit, it will have an immediate past service liability as of day one of the plan, whereas if it decides not to grant past service, it will have no immediate liability as of the beginning of the plan.

> **Example:** An employer is establishing a plan in year 11 of its existence, and its NRB and AB formulae provide [1% × yos × FAE]/65/life only or J&S. If it decides to grant past service, all employee that have been working for the employer for the past 10 years will have an immediate AB on day one of the plan of AB = [1% × 10 yos × FAE]/65/life only or J&S (assuming they have all worked the entire 10 years).

---

2. I.R.C. § 402(g).

Since there is actuarial discretion involved in deciding *how fast* to fund current and past service costs (referred to the actuarial cost method) and in determining the *amount* of past service costs (referred to as the actuarial assumptions), Congress also imposed limits on the actuary's discretion.[3]

The rules covering minimum funding are found in I.R.C. §§ 412 and 430 (which govern qualified plans) and ERISA §§ 301–306 (which govern certain nonqualified plans as well). This chapter will concentrate on the Code's requirements. Also, minimum funding requirements for multiemployer plans are not discussed. Since the passage of ERISA, Congress has continued to tighten the funding requirements for underfunded plans and limit the ability of employers to delay or avoid funding plan liabilities. The most significant reforms came from PPA '06, which were generally effective as of January 1, 2008.[4] The penalties for noncompliance include: an excise tax; requirement to disclose a "reportable event" to the PBGC; possible adjustments to the maximum the employer can deduct; and a liability to the PBGC if the plan is terminated with any unfunded liability. If the employer terminates an overfunded defined benefit plan, there is the potential for a 50% excise tax on the surplus that reverts to the employer.

As an aside, Congress has loosened the minimum funding rules in light of financial diasters; for example, due to the 2008–09 financial meltdown, it lengthened the time over which an employer could fund its obligations. While it did not do something similar in light of the COVID-19 pandemic, the IRS does allow for a waiver of the minimum funding requirements in the event of a "substantial business hardship."[5]

Note that the term "frozen defined benefit plan" can mean many things. A defined benefit plan is generally frozen when the employer wishes to terminate the plan but cannot as it is not fully funded. So as to prevent liabilities from further accumulating while the employer continues to fund the plan, the employer may consider any or some of the following:

- Freeze the plan for new entrants (i.e., new hires are not eligible to participate);

- Freeze future benefit accruals (i.e., no participant accrues an accrued benefit for any future year of service); and

- Freeze current benefit accruals from further increasing (e.g., if the accrued benefit formula used final average earnings, existing accrued benefits would continue to increase as future salaries increased).

---

3. Dan McGill, *Fulfilling Pension Expectations* (1962).

4. PPA '06 §§ 101(b),111(a).

5. See Rev. Proc. 2004-15 for the process to use to seek a waiver of the minimum funding requirements. The IRS generally looks to the following factors: whether the employer is operating at an economic loss, whether the employer's industry is suffering substantial unemployment or underemployment, whether the employer's industry has depressed sales and profits, and whether the plan will continue only if the waiver is granted.

While freezing a plan does not discontinue the employer's funding obligations, it seeks to minimize the future costs of benefits as the employer continues to fund the plan until it can terminate it.

3. Actuarial Assumptions

The ultimate cost of any defined benefit plan can only be determined *after* the last retired participant dies and all payments have been made. At that time, the ultimate cost will be the sum of the total benefit payments made and total expenses paid *less* any investment income earned on plan assets. Even though the ultimate cost cannot be determined while the plan is ongoing, ERISA and the Code require the employer to engage the services of an enrolled actuary[6] to predict the long-range costs (i.e., the actuary must use actuarial assumptions) and redistribute these costs into a contribution pattern (referred to as an actuarial cost method) that will meet the funding objectives of the employer and comply with minimum funding standards. For example, if you were to buy a house with a mortgage, the lender would use an interest rate, say 3.5% (i.e., an actuarial assumption), and a contribution pattern of monthly payments for a 30-year term (i.e., cost method).

ERISA and the Code regulate the actuarial process by imposing the following requirements:

- Every defined benefit plan must employ an enrolled actuary.[7]

- An actuarial valuation (i.e., a set of actuarial calculations, used to predict long range costs) must be made at least once a year.[8]

- Prior to PPA '06, each covered plan must maintain a funding standard account to assure that the plan is being funded at a minimal level.[9]

- The actuarial assumptions must offer the actuary's best estimate of anticipated experience and *each* assumption must be reasonable (using plan experience).[10] In the alternative, the actuarial assumptions may be reasonable *in the aggregate* provided the resulting contribution is equivalent to the amount determined as if *each* assumption used had been reasonable.[11]

---

6. The actuary's primary function is to mathematically estimate, to the best of his or her ability, the amount needed to be contributed annually to a defined benefit plan so that the plan will meet each and every liability as it comes due to a participant or his beneficiary.

7. I.R.C. § 7701(a)(35); ERISA §§ 3041, 3042, 3043. *Note:* Although the minimum funding standards apply to money purchase and target benefit plans as well, only defined benefit plans require a periodic report by the enrolled actuary which details the requirements of I.R.C. § 412. I.R.C. § 6059. This report is the Schedule B attachment to the Annual Return/Report of Employee Benefit Plan (Form 5500). Treas. Reg. § 301.6059-1.

8. Former I.R.C. § 412(c)(9); ERISA § 302(c)(9).

9. Former I.R.C. § 412(b); ERISA § 302(b).

10. Former I.R.C. § 412(c)(3)(A)(i).

11. *Id.*

- The actuarial cost method used must be acceptable[12] and any change must receive prior approval from the IRS.[13] Now, only the unit credit actuarial cost method may be used.
- There are special rules to be followed in valuing the plan assets for purposes of the actuarial valuation.[14]

Although ERISA requires the enrolled actuary to use his or her best estimate of anticipated experience under the plan,[15] there is no one "correct" set of assumptions.[16] One actuary may use "optimistic" assumptions which produce a lower estimate of true costs and therefore a lower employer contribution; another actuary may use "pessimistic" assumptions which produce a higher estimate and thus a higher employer contribution. Since ultimate costs do not change, the effect of these different assumptions is to have lower costs in some years and higher costs in other years, or vice versa. The result will change the minimum funding standards and maximum deductible ceilings. The following actuarial assumptions may have to be made to predict employer costs:

- *Interest and Fund Earnings:* Since a present value calculation requires a future amount to be discounted to a present cost, the actuary must make an assumption as to the interest rate or rates to be earned on the present contribution. PPA'06 requires this to be a corporate bond yield curve published by the IRS.
- *Mortality Table:* As the distribution of benefits is to be made with either a life only annuity or a joint and survivor annuity, the actuary must make an assumption as to when the participants and beneficiaries are expected to die, based on life expectancies. PPA '06 requires this to be a specific mortality table published by the IRS.
- *Turnover:* For terminating employees, the vesting schedule may not require the full benefit to be paid to the employee and thus, the actuary must make an assumption as to a turnover table, as it need not fund for any expected forfeited benefits (e.g., if 20% of participants leave the employer with only 40% of its benefits vested, the employer does not need to fund for the 60% of the benefits that are forfeited).
- *Disability:* If the plan provides the participant with full benefits upon disability prior to normal retirement, the actuary must make an assumption as to the

---

12. Treas. Reg. § 1.412(c)(1)-1 provides that the term "funding method" has the same meaning as the term "actuarial cost method" as defined in ERISA § 3(31).

13. Former I.R.C. § 412(c)(5). *See also* Rev. Proc. 95-51, 1995-2 C.B. 430.

14. Former I.R.C. § 412(c)(2). Reasonable asset valuation methods must take into account the fair market value of the assets. Treas. Reg. § 1.412(c)(2)-1.

15. I.R.C. § 412(c)(3)(B); ERISA § 302(c)(3)(B).

16. "Congress acknowledged that actuaries are not charged with the responsibility of determining a 'correct' set of assumptions, but with the responsibility of determining assumptions that fall within a range of reasonableness." Citrus Valley Estates, Inc. v. Comm'r, 99 T.C. 379, 401 (citing S. Rep. 93-383 (1973)), 1974-3 C.B. (Supp.) 80, 147, and H. Rept. 93-807 (1974), 1974-3 C.B. (Supp. 262)).

number of participants who will become disabled. These rates would obviously vary by industry, as some involve more physical exertion than others.

- *Salary Increases:* If the plan's formula is based on final average earnings, the actuary must make an assumption as to future salary increases, as such increases will retroactively increase the prior years' accruals.

- *Timing of Payment:* Since the plan may permit benefits to be paid early, at normal retirement, or delay to late retirement, the actuary must estimate when the payments will commence (i.e., an assumed retirement age).

- *Marital Status:* Since the plan must pay benefits to married participants under the joint and survivor form of payment, the actuary must estimate how many participants are married and the age differential between the participant and his or her spouse. Actuarial organizations have statistics as to who in the United States has never been married, is presently married, or is widowed or divorced.

- *Optional Forms of Payment:* If some or all of the optional forms of payment are subsidized and not simply the actuarial equivalent value, the actuary must estimate how many participants will elect an optional form and which optional form will be chosen.

While the interest rate and mortality tables are set by statute, the actuary must determine the other actuarial assumptions and each must be reasonable; alternatively, the actuarial assumptions must be reasonable in the aggregate.

4. Actuarial Cost Method

The purpose of the actuarial cost method is to determine the pattern into which annual employer contributions shall fall (i.e., the cost method allocates to a given year a certain portion of the estimated cost of the benefits to be provided). For example, when you purchase a mortgage to buy a house with a 30-year term, the cost method would require equal periodic monthly payments to be made over the 30-year period.

Initially, the employer had discretion in deciding how best to allocate pension costs. PPA '06 eliminated this discretion and requires the employer to use the unit credit cost method (i.e., the present value of all benefits which are expected to accrue under the plan during the plan year must be funded). This includes benefits attributable to prior years which have increased this year due to participant compensation. For example, if NRB = AB = [1% × yos × FAE]/65/life only or J&S, and Employee A had $20,000 in salary in year 1 and $25,000 in salary in year 2, his or her first year's AB = [1% × 1 year × $20,000]/65/life or J&S = $2,000/65/life or J&S but his or her second year's AB = [1% × 2 years × $22,500]/65/life or J&S = $4,500/65/life or J&S. Because salary increased in the second year to $25,000, FAE in the second year is [$20,000 + $25,000] ÷ 2 = $22,500. As a result, the first year's accrual amount of $2,000 was retroactively increased to $2,250 due to the salary increase in the second year.

PPA '06 defines several new terms of art:

- "Funding target," which is the present value of all benefits accrued under the plan as of the beginning of the plan year. To the extent the plan assets as of the beginning of the year are less than this funding target, there is a "shortfall" which must be amortized.

- "Target normal cost," which is the present value of all benefits that are expected to accrue under the plan *during* the current plan year (including benefits attributable to past years which may now have increased during the current plan year due to compensation increases).

Under the current minimum funding rules, the minimum required contribution for a plan year is defined as the sum of:

- The target normal cost,

- The shortfall amortization charge (if any) for the plan year (which is a seven-year amortization of any unfunded funding target) [Note: Congress allowed for an alternate "two plus seven" amortization or 15-year amortization schedule for the 2008–2011 plan years to grant relief to employers in light of the financial meltdown],

- The waiver amortization charge (if any) for the plan year (which applies if the IRS had *previously* waived part or all of the required contribution).[17]

The goal of the new minimum funding requirements of PPA '06 was to accelerate the process under which underfunded plans must be brought to fully funded status. PPA '06 also created a new status of plans—called "at risk" plans—for which additional requirements relating to funding exist.

5. Funding Targets

While Congress, through PPA '06, wanted to strengthen the funding of single-employer defined benefit plans, it also wanted to prevent underfunded defined benefit plans from becoming even more underfunded by allowing lump sum distributions (referred to as leakage of plan assets) and to halve increased underfunding through plan amendments attempting to increase benefit accruals. The result was the passage of a new Code section—I.R.C. § 436, which was a part of the qualification rules—with parallel rules under Title I of ERISA.[18] For this purpose, the Code coins a new term of art, the adjusted funding target attainment percentage (AFTAP), which gauges the funding status of the plan for purposes of these benefit restrictions. Whether a plan is funded for purposes of these restrictions depends on the AFTAP number.[19]

---

17. PPA '06 §§ 112(a) and 102(a), adding I.R.C. § 430(c)(1) and ERISA § 303(c)(1), respectively.

18. PPA '06 § 113(a)(1)(B), effective for plan years beginning after December 31, 2007.

19. The AFTAP is generally the first day of the applicable plan year. CARES § 3608(b) permits plans with plan years that include calendar year 2020 to use the prior year's AFTAP in light of the recent decline in the financial markets. Using the current year's AFTAP could have triggered funding-related benefit restrictions due to the decline in plan assets.

Under the new limitations, defined benefits are restricted as follows:

- The plan may not pay shutdown benefits and other unpredictable contingent event benefits if the plan is less than 60% funded. For example, the plan may offer subsidized pension benefits to participants who are otherwise laid off due to a plant shutdown even though the participant had not otherwise satisfied the plan's age and service requirements for such a subsidy.

- The plan may not increase benefits, establish new benefits, or change the rate at which benefits become vested through a plan amendment if the plan is less than 80% funded.

- As for distributions from the plan if the plan is less than 60% funded, it may not distribute partial or full lump sum distributions; if it is between 60% and 79.99% funded, partial lump sum distributions are possible; and if the plan is less than 100% funded but the plan sponsor is in bankruptcy proceedings, then the plan must restrict partial and full lump sum distributions.

- If the plan is less than 60% funded, *future* benefit accruals must be frozen (i.e., they must cease).[20]

B. Employer Deductions

1. General Rules of I.R.C. § 404

One of the significant reasons for which an employer adopts a qualified plan is the tax advantages it receives by being able to deduct its contribution, even though the employees do not have any current taxable income. The normal tax matching rule that the employer receives a deduction at the same time the employee takes compensation into income is not applicable because of the rules of I.R.C. § 404. Administrative expenses are investment expenses (e.g., investment manager fees and trustees' fees) that are paid directly by the employer and are deductible under I.R.C. §§ 162 or 212.[21]

In order to claim the full deduction with respect to plan contributions, two criteria must be met:

- The standards of deductibility under I.R.C. § 162 (trade or business) or § 212 (expense for the production of income) must be met.[22] Under the standards of I.R.C. § 162, compensation must be reasonable in order to be deducted. Regarding the issue of reasonable compensation, it is important for students to realize this is more of an issue in the small employer context than the medium or large employer context.

---

20. I.R.C. § 436(b)–(e). CARES allows plans to use the plan's funding status as of December 31, 2019, for purposes of determining whether the benefit restrictions apply in 2020. CARES § 3608.

21. *See* Priv. Ltr. Rul. 93-32-040, Priv. Ltr. Rul. 89-40-013, and Priv. Ltr. Rul. 89-40-014.

22. I.R.C. § 162 generally permits ordinary and necessary expenses incurred in carrying on a trade or business to be deducted by the employer, whereas I.R.C. § 212 permits expenses incurred by the taxpayer which are used for the production of income to be deducted.

Example: If an owner-employee that had been paid in the $50,000 range for the past 10 years then establishes a plan and increases his or her compensation to $100,000 prospectively, query whether his or her compensation is reasonable. It appears that he or she increased compensation so as to boost benefits or allocations under a qualified plan.

As profits may vary dramatically in the small employer arena, compensation paid to the owner-employees may vary accordingly. Factors that the courts consider in determining reasonableness of the compensation level include: (1) the prior year's compensation amount, (2) compensation levels within the industry or within comparable types of employment, (3) hours worked, (4) experience, (5) prestige, (6) value of the employee's name, (7) special knowledge, (8) complexity of business, (9) how the compensation level was determined, (10) whether compensation is determined according to stock holdings, (11) how the employer treats such amounts on its books, (12) whether the compensation is paid equally over the year or in bunched payments, (13) economic conditions, (14) employer's salary policy with respect to all employees, and (15) employer's volume of business.[23]

- The deduction must comply with the specific rules of I.R.C. §404, which is structured to handle pension and annuity plans differently from profit sharing and stock bonus plans.[24] In order to be deductible in the tax year made, the employer's contribution must be to a qualified retirement plan that was in existence no later than the end of the employer's tax year.[25]

Note: Ordinarily, sole proprietors, partnerships, personal service corporations, limited liability companies, and S corporations use the calendar year as their tax year. Large corporations have more flexibility in choosing an alternate fiscal year as their tax year. For example, if the entity's business was seasonal, earning most of the income in the spring and incurring most of the expense in the fall, a tax year ending in July or August may be preferable so as to better align the income with the related expenses.

The employer's tax year need not be the same 12-month period as the plan year. If the employer's tax year is different than the plan's year, it is important to have the plan be established within the tax year that the employer *first* wishes to claim a deduction. For example, if the plan year is the calendar year, and the employer's tax

---

23. *See, e.g.*, Eberl's Claim Service, Inc. v. Comm'r, 249 F.3d 994 (10th Cir. 2001), and Owensby & Kritikos, Inc. v. Comm'r, 819 F.2d 1315 (5th Cir. 1987).

24. I.R.C. §404(a). "In order to be deductible under section 404(a), contributions must be expenses which would be deductible under section 162 (relating to trade or business expenses) or 212 (relating to expenses for production of income) if it were not for the provisions of section 404(a)." Treas. Reg. §1.404(a)-1(b). "Any expenses incurred by the employer in connection with the plan, such as trustee's and actuary's fees, which are not provided for by contributions under the plan are deductible by the employer under section 162 … or 212 … to the extent that they are ordinary and necessary." Treas. Reg. §1.404(a)-3(d).

25. Rev. Rul. 81-114, which supersedes Rev. Rul. 57-419.

year is the fiscal year beginning each April 1, in order to claim a deduction for the fiscal year beginning on April 1, 2019, and ending on March 31, 2020, the plan must be in existence by March 31, 2020, in order to claim a deduction for the plan year that runs from January 1, 2020, to December 31, 2020. If the plan is not in existence by March 31, 2020, the deduction for the first plan year will be delayed until the next fiscal tax year. In addition, an employer contribution to a qualified retirement plan is deductible in the tax year in which the contribution is paid or "deemed" to be paid.[26] An employer contribution is "deemed" to have been made on the last day of the tax year if it is made on account of that tax year and paid no later than the time for filing the employer's tax return plus extensions.[27]

2. Limitation on the Amount of the Deduction

a. Defined Benefit Plans

While I.R.C. §430(a) provides for the *minimum* contribution that must be made to a single-employer defined benefit plan, I.R.C. §404(o), by way of I.R.C. §404(a)(1)(A), provides for the *maximum* deductible contribution for such plans. The same actuarial assumptions used to compute the minimum contribution apply in computing the maximum contribution. PPA '06 set forth new deduction ceilings for single-employer defined benefit plans. The new limit is the greater of (1) the sum of the funding target plus target normal cost plus an applicable cushion, for the plan year, over the value of the plan assets, or (2) the sum of the minimum required contributions determined under I.R.C. §430, for the plan year.[28] The applicable cushion is the sum of 50% of the funding target + an increase in the funding target had the plan taken into account certain increases in expected benefits through increases in compensation or otherwise.[29]

There are applicable special rules:

- For plans that are not at risk, the maximum limit shall not be less than the sum of funding target + the target normal cost, for the plan year, less the value of the plan assets.[30]

- For terminating plans, the maximum deduction allowed is 100% of the amount required to make the plan sufficient for benefit liabilities (as determined under Title IV).[31]

Any contributions in excess of the maximum limits (but otherwise deductible) may be carried over to succeeding tax years and deducted if within the annual limit

---

26. I.R.C. §404(a)(1)(A), 404(a)(2), 404(a)(3)(A)(i).
27. I.R.C. §404(a)(6).
28. I.R.C. §404(o)(1)–(2).
29. I.R.C. §404(o)(3)(A). There are special rules for plans with fewer than 101 participants in the given year.
30. I.R.C. §404(o)(2)(B).
31. I.R.C. §404(o)(5).

applicable for that year.[32] To penalize employers who make excess contributions, there is a 10% excise tax imposed.[33]

While employer contributions generally do not have to be made until the due date plus extensions for filing the employer's tax return, I.R.C. §430(j) has a special rule requiring the minimum required contribution to be made within 8½ months after the end of the plan year.[34] But a plan with a funding shortfall in the prior year must make quarterly payments during the plan year, equal to one-fourth of the lesser of (1) 90% of the current year's minimum required contribution or (2) 100% of the prior year's minimum required contribution.[35]

b. Defined Contribution Plans

For qualified profit sharing, stock bonus, and money purchase plans, the maximum limit on the amount of deductible contributions is 25% of compensation.[36] Compensation for purposes of the limit means all compensation paid or accrued during the tax year (using an I.R.C. §415(c) definition of what is included in compensation) for the participants who are benefiting under the plan, subject to the annual compensation limit of I.R.C. §401(a)(17).[37] However, an employee eligible to participate in an I.R.C. §401(k) plan is treated as benefiting under the plan even if they do not elect to defer.[38] If an employer contributes in excess of the 25% limit, the excess may be carried over and deducted in order of time, subject to a limit (when the carryover is added to current contributions) of 25% of covered compensation or the amount the employer was required to make to the plan trust.[39] The excess is subject to a 10% excise tax.[40]

Employers must make their contributions before the due date for filing their returns for such tax year, including extensions, in order to be "deemed" to have been paid by the last day of the preceding tax year. As the DOL considers employee elective deferrals to be plan assets as soon as the employer can reasonably segregate them from its general assets for purposes of Title I, so it requires such deferrals to be timely remitted to the plan's trust.[41] Generally the remittance must be no later than the 15th

---

32. I.R.C. §404(a)(1)(E); Treas. Reg. §1.404(a)-7.
33. I.R.C. §4972(a).
34. Corporate tax returns are generally due on the 15th day of the third month following the end of the tax year, but the corporation can file for an extension of six months, resulting in a due tax 8½ months after the end of the tax year.
35. I.R.C. §430(j)(3)(C)–(D). CARES provides additional time for employers to meet their funding obligation. Single-employer defined benefit funding requirements for 2020, including quarterly contributions, may be deferred until January 1, 2021 (then paid with interest). CARES §3608(a)(1)–(2).
36. I.R.C. §404(a)(3)(A)(i)(I). For purposes of the maximum deduction limit, employee elective deferral contributions are not considered employer contributions. I.R.C. §404(n). This allows the employer to make larger matching and nonelective contributions to a defined contribution plan.
37. Employee elective salary deferrals are considered part of the employee's compensation in determining the 25% overall limit. I.R.C. §404(a)(12).
38. Treas. Reg. §1.410(b)-3.
39. I.R.C. §404(a)(3)(A)(i)–(ii).
40. I.R.C. §4972(a).
41. Labor Reg. §2510.3-102(a).

business day of the following month, but there is a seven-business-day safe harbor rule for plans with fewer than 100 participants.[42] The latter safe harbor reflects the fact that small businesses may use outside vendors for payroll processing.

c. Combined Deduction Ceiling

Remember that large employers do not create defined benefit or defined contribution plans to maximize their deductions under such plans. They create such plans to be competitive in attracting employees. However, small employers are definitely interested in establishing a defined benefit and a defined contribution in order to maximize their deductions. Thus, the Code has a combined deduction ceiling for those types of employers. Employers not covered by the PBGC (e.g., a professional service employer that does not have more than 25 active participants in the plan or a plan covering only substantial owners) are subject to a combined deduction ceiling. Under the ceiling, the limit on deductions to *both* the defined benefit and the defined contribution plan would be 25% of compensation, if there is at least one participant covered under both plans.[43] However, for purposes of the ceiling, employer contributions to the defined contribution plan are counted only to the extent that those contributions *exceed* 6% of compensation paid during the year.[44] In other words, employer contributions to a simple profit sharing plan will not count against the limit if they are less than 6% of total compensation. Let's do an example: when adding only employer contributions to the defined contribution plan that exceed 6% to the required minimum contribution under the defined benefit plan, the sum exceeds 31% of total compensation. The 6% in excess of the 25% limit is an excess contribution and will be subject to a 10% excise tax.

C. PBGC Premiums for Defined Benefit Plans

Generally, a single employer that sponsors a qualified defined benefit plan will have to pay premiums to the PBGC. This is an additional expense incurred by defined benefit plan sponsors that is deductible as a necessary business expense. ERISA created the federal corporation of the PBGC to ensure that participants and beneficiaries of terminating defined benefit plans that were not fully funded would be paid their benefits. The board of directors that governs the PBGC consists of the Secretaries of Labor (as chair), Commerce, and the Treasury.[45] Pursuant to changes made by PPA '06, the Executive Director of the PBGC is now a presidential appointment, subject to consent by the U.S. Senate.

---

42. Labor Reg. § 2510.3-102(a)(2).
43. I.R.C. § 404(a)(7)(A).
44. I.R.C. § 404(a)(7)(C)(v).
45. ERISA § 4002(d).

Generally, for single-employer plans, there are two parts of the annual premium: a flat dollar amount per participant (for 2020, this was $83) and a variable portion dollar amount per $1,000 of the plan's unfunded vested benefits determined at the end of the preceding plan year, with a maximum cap per participant (for 2020, the variable rate was $45 and the maximum cap per participant was $561).

Plans that are not covered by the PBGC include: defined contribution plans, governmental plans, unfunded deferred compensation plans for highly compensated employees, church plans, and defined benefit plans with 25 or fewer participants that are maintained by a professional service employer (e.g., doctors or lawyers).[46]

---

46. ERISA § 4021(b).

Chapter 11

Role of the IRS

Reading Assignment: I.R.C. § 401(b)

Rev. Proc. 2019-19

Class Discussion Questions: Why would a plan sponsor of a qualified retirement plan seek a determination letter?

What are the consequences if a qualified retirement plan is disqualified?

What correction programs are available to cure disqualifying defects in a retirement plan?

What functions does the Employee Plans group of the IRS perform?

Overview

Which operating division of the IRS has jurisdiction over qualified retirement plans?

- the Tax Exempt/Government Entities division, through its Employee Plans group

What does the Employee Plans group do?

- Rulings and Agreements provides guidance, both in general and to specific plans, on how they can comply with the statutory requirements (including determination letters for compliant plan documents and voluntary compliance submissions)
- Customer Education and Outreach keeps the website ripe with compliance tools, prepares newsletters, and holds live and webcasted programs to communicate the rules to plan sponsors
- examinations agents will go out and audit the plan to ensure compliance.

What is a favorable determination letter and how is an FDL request processed?

- although voluntary, a plan should always apply for a determination letter request upon adoption, upon amendments, and upon plan termination, where the IRS indicates that the plan document complies with the laws, so that if the plan is operated and administered in accordance with the document, then the plan will be deemed to be qualified
- Prior to IRS Announcement 2015-19, individually designed plans used to seek a renewed favorable determination letter every five years, and the cycles are based

on the last digit of the plan's taxpayer identification number (TIN); due to a lack of resources, individually designed plans seek a favorable determination letter upon establishment and termination

- Preapproved plans seek a renewed favorable determination letter every six years

Why would a plan voluntarily perform an audit to find mistakes?

- the IRS clearly signals that if they discover mistakes on audit, the penalties and correction costs will be much more severe than if self-discovered

- the Self-Correction Program (SCP) is available only for insignificant operational failures (as opposed to plan document failures) — if the plan has established compliance practices and procedures, and has received a favorable determination letter, then the plan sponsor may correct operational failures without payment of any fee or sanction, and without any contact whatsoever with the IRS

- the Voluntary Correction Program (VCP) provides general procedures for correction of all qualification failures after paying a fee and making a submission to the IRS

- the Audit Closing Agreement Program (Audit CAP) allows the plan sponsor to correct qualification failures that are discovered by the IRS during an audit but before the audit has concluded

What are some issues with the IRS auditing qualified plan administration and operation?

- the IRS is responsible for ensuring that retirement plans are qualified and, over time, has learned some effective ways to maximize their limited resources, such as:

  ○ focused audits that hit more plans on only the most commonly expected errors and

  ○ team audits on large plans (with agents with different areas of specialty)

- abusive tax avoidance transactions require certain activities, which are outside of the bounds of a reasonable interpretation of the Internal Revenue Code, to be listed, so that the IRS can control the spread of such bad activities

A. Organization of the IRS

As a result of the IRS Restructuring and Reform Act of 1998, the IRS is divided into four operating divisions:

- Wage and Investment Division (e.g., taxpayers who generally pay their taxes through employer withholding);

- Large and Mid-Size Business Division (e.g., C corporations, S corporations, and Partnerships with more than $10 million in assets);

- Small Business and Self-Employed Division (e.g., taxpayers who file Form 1040 or Form 1040-SR and have assets less than $10 million); and

- Tax-Exempt and Governmental Entities Division (e.g., customers that fall into three segments — Employee Plans; Exempt Organizations (e.g., charities); and Government Entities (e.g., federal, state, and local governments, Indian tribal governments, and tax-exempt bonds)).

Employee benefits practitioners are concerned with the Division of Tax-Exempt and Governmental Entities (referred to as TE/GE).

Other principal offices of the IRS include:

- Office of Chief Counsel (which is the chief legal advisor to the Commissioner of the IRS pertaining to interpretation, administration, and enforcement of tax matters). It is the "law firm" within the IRS that renders legal opinions.

- Taxpayer Advocate Service (which is an independent organization within the IRS to assist taxpayers)

- Office of Professional Responsibility (OPR) (which interprets and applies standards of conduct for tax professionals dealing with the IRS)

- Criminal Investigation (which serves the general public by investigating potential criminal violations of the Code)

- Appeals (which is an independent office within the IRS to resolve disputes between the taxpayer and the IRS without litigation)

- Communications and Liaison (which plans, coordinates, and produces Service-wide communications to educate outside stakeholders)

- Whistleblower Office (which receives tips from taxpayers regarding tax problems and concerns)

- Office of Privacy, Information Protection, and Data Security (which protects the privacy of taxpayers and prevents breaches of data security)

In the administration of a qualified plan, employee benefits practitioners generally deal with the attorneys at the Office of Chief Counsel to get a favorable ruling and with Appeals, when there is a dispute between the IRS and the plan sponsor over the operation of the plan. Generally, attorneys, accountants, enrolled actuaries, enrolled agents, and enrolled retirement plan agents can practice before the IRS pursuant to standards of conduct set forth in Circular 230 (and a power of attorney pursuant to Form 2848), and thus are subject to the Office of Professional Responsibility.

B. Employee Plans Group

1. Organization of TE/GE Operating Division

Our focus within TE/GE is the segment known as Employee Plans. Here is a recent excerpt from the IRS' website:

The Employee Plans Office is responsible for ensuring that plan sponsors, individuals and benefits practitioners understand and comply with the tax law governing retirement plans and IRAs. It's part of the Tax Exempt and Government Entities Division of the IRS.

Departments of the Employee Plans Office

- **Determinations** — reviews retirement plan documents and gives assurance to plan sponsors that their documents are written according to the rules
- **Technical** — provides private letter rulings on certain limited topics to individual requestors
- **Voluntary Compliance** — administers IRS programs that allow plan sponsors to correct self-identified problems in plan documents or operations
- **Examinations** — reviews taxpayer books and records to ensure that plans provide the promised benefits and comply with all relevant laws
- **Customer Account Services** — answers account and basic retirement plan-related questions

Administrative responsibility for retirement plans

The Employee Plans Office was created in 1974, following enactment of the Employee Retirement Income Security Act, to help protect the retirement benefits of employees. Under ERISA, jurisdiction over employee benefit plans was divided among the Internal Revenue Service, the Department of Labor and the Pension Benefit Guaranty Corporation.

- The IRS primarily looks at participation, vesting and funding issues.
- The DOL primarily looks at fiduciary responsibility and prohibited transactions.
- The PBGC insures a minimum guaranteed benefit under certain pension plans.

Although jurisdiction is divided among the IRS, DOL and PBGC, ERISA requires them to coordinate their activities."[1]

During 2020, Tammy Ripperda served as Commissioner of TE/GE and Khin Chow served as Acting Director of Employee Plans.

---

1. *What Is the Employee Plans Office?*, IRS (updated Sep. 20, 2019), https://www.irs.gov/retirement-plans/plan-sponsor/what-is-the-employee-plans-office-and-what-does-it-do.

2. Organization of the Employee Plans Business Division

The main website for the Employee Plans Business Division within TE/GE is http://www.irs.gov/retirement-plans. The three major functions within Employee Plans are:

> *Rulings and Agreement:* This function focuses on up-front compliance. Thus, it will issue determination letters on the qualified status of a retirement plan and accept voluntary compliance from plan sponsors who discover errors during the operation of the plan.

> *Customer Education and Outreach (CEO):* This function educates and communicates with customers to help them understand their tax responsibilities. It prepares compliance tools (e.g., 401(k) Fix-it Guide) and newsletters, and hosts live and webcasted programs for plan sponsors and employee benefits practitioners.

> *Examinations:* The function supports IRS agents who identify and address non-compliance discovered when auditing a retirement plan.

The Employee Plans Business Division has five different regional areas, each with an area manager: Northeast Area, Mid-Atlantic Area, Great Lakes Area, Gulf Coast Area, and Pacific Coast Area.

3. Determination Letters for Plan Document

For an individually drafted qualified retirement plan, a determination letter is a written statement issued to the plan sponsor by the IRS' Employee Plans' Ruling and Agreements Office that the terms of the plan document satisfy the qualification requirements of the Code. While it is not required, it is highly recommended as it makes no sense to establish a plan without having the IRS agree to its terms. For pre-approved plans (referred to in the past as master and prototype plans, and volume submitter plans), an advisory or opinion letter is issued to the sponsor of the pre-approved plan as to the acceptability of the form of such plan under the Code and in the case of a master plan, the acceptability of the master trust under I.R.C. § 501(a).

As discussed earlier in this text, ERISA and the Code are amended frequently by Congress. Since every plan must be in compliance with any current changes, it would appear that plans would have to be amended immediately whenever a statutory change is made and becomes effective. But historically, the IRS has grouped successive laws together and set a deadline for a single plan amendment or a total restatement of the terms of the plan to incorporate the changes. This deadline is referred to as the remedial amendment period.[2] However, the plan is expected to operate in accordance with the new law even though it has yet to be amended.

---

2. I.R.C. § 401(b).

The remedial amendment period can also be extended if the plan sponsor files for a determination letter request: "If, on or before the end of a remedial amendment period ... the employer or plan administrator files a request ... for a determination letter with respect to the initial or continuing qualification of the plan, or a trust which is part of such plan, such remedial amendment period shall be extended until the expiration of 91 days after: (i) The date on which notice of the final determination with respect to such request for a determination letter is issued by the Internal Revenue Service...."[3]

The prior iteration of the determination letter request program set forth remedial amendment cycles (RAC) for each plan (i.e., a timeline for submission of initial and subsequent determination letter requests).[4] For individually designed plans, a five-year cycle (Cycle A–E) was established where the determination letter is submitted based on the last digit of the employer's identification number (EIN). For pre-approved plans, there is a six-year cycle (one for defined contribution plans and another for defined benefit plans). For individually designed plans with a five-year RAC, the revenue procedure uniformly extended the remedial amendment period for a qualified plan to the end of the plan sponsor's RAC. But the Service stunned the benefits community in the summer of 2015, when it stated that it would eliminate the five-year RAC for individually designed plans.[5] The Service claimed that it lacked the resources to do ongoing reviews of plan amendments. Thus, effective January 1, 2017, a sponsor of an individually designed plan was permitted to submit a determination letter application for new plans, terminating plans, and certain other limited circumstances.

A favorable determination letter is limited in scope, as it applies to the terms of the plan document and only certain operational (non-form) requirements. It cannot be relied upon with regard to satisfaction of the Code's nondiscrimination requirements, the coverage tests, and the definition of compensation under I.R.C. § 414(s). It also may not be relied upon for any qualification changes that later become effective. The IRS issues a cumulative list every year identifying what changes in the law or regulation affect the plan's qualification requirements.

4. Disqualification of the Retirement Plan

According to the Service, any violation of the qualification rules of Code § 401(a) can result in disqualification of the plan.[6] This affects the various parties at stake for disqualification as follows:

- *For Employer's Tax Return:* The Service may retroactively disqualify a plan for any open year (i.e., tax years for which the statute of limitations has not yet run).[7] Generally, the statute of limitations runs three years after the tax return

---

3. Treas. Reg. § 1.401(b)-1(e)(3).
4. Rev. Proc. 2007-44.
5. IRS Announcement 2015-19.
6. *See* Rev. Proc. 98-22.
7. I.R.C. § 7805(b).

filing date; however, it may be six years after the employer files its return if the exclusion from income exceeds 25% of the total gross income claimed.[8]

- *For the Trust's Tax Return:* The statutory period for taxes against the trust expire three years after the later of (1) filing of the Schedule P of Form 5500 or (2) the last day for filing the trust tax return.

- *For the Trust:* Loss of tax-exempt status subjects the trust to income tax on its earnings for the years in which the plan is disqualified.[9]

- *For Suits Against the Employer:* While ERISA provides a cause of action against plan fiduciaries for violations under ERISA, the courts have held that such causes of action do not apply to violations under the qualification rules that are not reflected under Title I.[10]

- *For the Participants:* Disqualification of the plan has a variety of different consequences depending on whether the participant was vested on the effective date of disqualification, whether the participant was a highly compensated employee, the reason for the disqualification, and whether the plan was a defined benefit or a defined contribution plan.

There are four types of qualification defects:

- Plan document failures (i.e., a plan provision or absence of a plan provision that violates I.R.C. § 401(a)) that cannot be corrected through the determination letter program either because the plan sponsor did not seek a determination letter (referred to as a "nonamender") or because the required retroactive plan amendment was not made within the remedial amendment period (referred to as a "late-amender").

- Operational failures that occur because the terms of the plan were not followed (here, correction could be accomplished either through a retroactive plan amendment or a certain type of correction method).

- Demographic failures in which the coverage and/or participation rules or the nondiscrimination tests rules are not satisfied.

- Employer eligibility failure caused by the employer's inability to establish the type of qualified plan that was adopted (e.g., a governmental entity adopts an I.R.C. § 401(k) plan, or a tax-exempt entity (other than a § 501(c)(3) entity or a public school) adopts an I.R.C. § 403(b) plan).

---

8. I.R.C. § 6501(a), (e); Treas. Reg. § 301.6501(a)-1, (e)-1.
9. I.R.C. § 641.
10. *See* Trenton v. Scott Paper Co., 832 F.2d 806 (3d Cir. 1987).

5. Employee Plans Compliance Resolution System (EPCRS)

In the 1990s, the IRS began a correction program whereby qualification defects could be corrected without disqualification, provided a sanction was assessed against the plan sponsor.[11] Today, the Service's correction program known as Employee Plans Compliance Resolution System (EPCRS) is set forth in revenue procedures.[12] It is administered by the Employee Plans segment of the TEGE Division, through different voluntary compliance (VC) group managers and EP exam area managers, depending on which of the three correction programs is being applied. While the determination letter program assures that the plan sponsor can rely on plan document compliance, the correction program assures plan operational compliance and permits nonamenders to make certain retroactive plan amendments to attain plan document compliance. One may view EPCRS as providing three "doors" of correction; the first two doors are voluntary on the part of the employer and available if the plan is not under examination. The third door may be utilized if errors are discovered upon plan audit. The audit fee schedule penalizes employers who wait to make corrections during an examination.

The first door of correction is the Self-Correction Program (SCP), which neither involves the IRS nor a sanction for the employer. Generally, significant operational failures must be cured within a two-year window to utilize SCP, whereas insignificant operational failures may be cured at any time. In contrast, operational failures that *require* retroactive *plan amendments* to conform the terms of the plan to its prior operations may be cured, but only in certain circumstances. For example, say the plan's eligibility provisions had a one-year service requirement, but in operation, the plan made employees immediately eligible — the plan may be amended retroactively to allow immediate eligibility so that the operation conformed with the plan document. If the first door of correction cannot be used, there is a second door of correction known as the Voluntary Correction Program (VCP). This door involves interaction with the IRS and a sanction fee depending on the amount of plan assets held in the plan. There are model correction methods set forth in the revenue procedures which the employer may rely upon, but the employer can negotiate with the IRS for an alternate correction method.

The final door of correction is known the Audit Closing Agreement Program (Audit CAP), which is available for disqualifying defects discovered upon plan audit. Because

---

11. The Service's original correction program was known as the Closing Agreement Program (CAP), but quickly evolved into an administrative policy known as APRS (Administrative Policy Regarding Sanctions) or the Nonenforcement Policy whereby certain minor operational defects could be corrected without sanction.

12. The most recent revenue procedure setting forth the rules regarding EPCRS is Rev. Proc. 2019-19. For a summary of the rules set forth in that revenue procedure, see Kathryn J. Kennedy, *A Current Update of EPCRS Through Rev. Proc. 2019-19*, 47 Tax Mgm't Comp. Plan. j. No. 12 (Dec. 6, 2019).

the employer did not take advantage of the first two doors of correction, the sanction fee for this correction door is more expensive.

EPCRS continues to evolve, but given its simplified and streamlined nature, it is simply best practice for employers to take advantage of it for the ongoing maintenance of a qualified plan.

According to the IRS' website, the following are the top 10 failures found in VCP:

- Failure to amend the plan for tax law changes by the end of the required period;
- Failure to follow the plan's definition of compensation for determining contributions;
- Failure to include eligible employees in the plan, or the failure to exclude ineligible employees from the plan;
- Plan loans that do not comply with the requirements of I.R.C. § 72(p);
- Impermissible in-service withdrawals;
- Failure to satisfy the I.R.C. § 401(a)(9) minimum distribution rules;
- Employer eligibility failures;
- Failed ADP/ACP nondiscrimination tests under I.R.C. §§ 401(k) and 401(m) not corrected in a timely manner;
- Failure to properly provide the minimum top-heavy benefits or contributions under I.R.C. § 416 to non-key employees; and
- Failure to satisfy the maximum limitations of I.R.C. § 415.[13]

Under PPA '06, Congress affirmed Treasury's authority to establish EPCRS and its successor and to update and improve the correction program as follows: (1) increase the visibility and knowledge of small employers concerning the program; (2) take into account special circumstances that small employers face with respect to compliance and correction of failures; (3) extend the duration of the 2-year window under SCP for significant failures; (4) expand the availability to correct insignificant compliance failures under SCP during plan audit; and (5) assure that any tax, penalty, or sanction imposed by reason of a failure is not excessive and bears a reasonable relationship to the nature, extent, and severity of the failure.[14] Thus, EPCRS continues to remain a top priority in Employee Plans, and subsequent to PPA '06, EPCRS has been updated several times.[15]

6. Examination of Plan Operations

The plan administrator is responsible for administering the plan in accordance with its terms. Thus, the plan documents should always be in conformity with ERISA,

---

13. *See Top Ten Failures Found in Voluntary Correction Program*, IRS (updated Dec. 21, 2019), https://www.irs.gov/retirement-plans/top-ten-failures-found-in-voluntary-correction-program.

14. PPA '06 § 1101(a)–(b).

15. *See* Rev. Proc. 2013-12, 2016-51, 2018-52, 2019-19.

the Code, and all other federal laws (e.g., Age Discrimination in Employment Act (ADEA)). Some ongoing and routine aspects of plan administration may be outsourced to a third party, such as:

- Determining whether and when an employee is eligible to participate;
- Recordkeeping services (e.g., maintenance of participants' account balances to assure timely remittance of 401(k) deferrals and employer contributions are made);
- Processing plan loan applications and timely repayments;
- Performing any annual nondiscrimination testing (e.g., nondiscrimination, special 401(k) testing, minimum coverage, and top-heavy);
- Satisfying all reporting and disclosure obligations;
- Doing benefit determinations and calculations; and
- Computing and remitting minimum required distribution payments.

The plan administrator as a fiduciary has a duty to prudently select such third parties and to continue to monitor their selection. If the plan is audited, the plan administrator will meet with an employee plans (EP) examination agent or will provide the appropriate power of attorney for a benefits professional who will assist in the audit.

EP Examinations is responsible for overseeing compliance with the retirement plan requirements set forth in the Code. It uses a centralized examination case selection and review process to ensure consistency of its enforcement activities and to focus resources on the areas of highest noncompliance. Generally, cases are randomly selected by the IRS, but red flags on the Form 5500 or on targeted compliance questionnaires sent by the IRS can trigger an audit. A list of resources is available on its website.[16] According to IRS Publication 4324, the examination process involves the following:

- A retirement plan is selected for audit, and a letter is sent requesting review of plan records and related documents (e.g., plan document, related trust, Form 5500, and plan loan procedures);[17]
- An appointment date is set between the employer, its attorney[18] or other authorized representative, and the IRS agent;

---

16. *See Examination and Enforcement*, IRS (updated May 15, 2020), https://www.irs.gov/retirement-plans/examinations-and-enforcement.

17. *See EP Examination Process Guide—Section 4—Communications During Examination—Sample Information Document Requests*, IRS (reviewed or updated Mar. 17, 2020), https://www.irs.gov/retirement-plans/ep-examination-process-guide-section-4-communications-during-examination-sample-information-document-requests.

18. Should the employer wish to have an attorney present at the audit, a power of attorney form, Form 2848, Power of Attorney and Declaration of Representative, must be submitted to the IRS agent in advance of the meeting. That person has the power to bind the employer in legal action.

- The IRS agent conducts an on-site audit of the plan, its records, and related documents, generally identifying three areas that will be the focus of the exam;[19]

- If additional information is needed, the employer supplies that content to the agent and there may be a subsequent on-site visit;

- If no additional information is needed, the IRS agent will determine what failures can be cured through SCP (e.g., insignificant failures) versus Audit Cap, and then a sanction will be assessed;

- If the employer and/or its representative believes the agent's findings are unreasonable or inaccurate, it may request to speak with the agent's manager for resolution; and

- The case will be closed, and a closing letter will be issued.[20]

If the employer and/or its representative and the IRS agent are unable to reach an agreement to close the case, there is an appeal process whereby a written protest stating the challenged issues must be made in a timely fashion.[21] If the employer loses at the appeal stage, it can decide whether to litigate the matter in the courts.

Obviously, the goal for any employer is to avoid a plan audit. Benjamin Franklin wisely stated, "an ounce of prevention is worth a pound of cure." If an employer is faced with a plan audit, plan failures may be uncovered, and correction of those failures must be made. One of the goals of EPCRS is to be restitutionary in nature, restoring the participants and beneficiaries to the position they would have been in had the failure not occurred.[22] Thus, avoiding a plan failure is the best alternative, but if one is uncovered, then timely curing it under EPCRS is the next best. To this end, plan sponsors should engage in self-audits of its plans to ensure timely correction of plan failures.

a. Abusive Tax Avoidance Transactions

The IRS has made substantive efforts to curtail abusive tax shelter schemes and transactions and, to this end, has issued regulations on abusive tax shelters. If a taxpayer has engaged in what's known as a "listed transaction," he or she must file a disclosure statement (Form 8886 and instructions) with his or her tax return.[23] A "listed

---

19. *See* Maria T. Hurd, *Employee Plan IRS Examinations*, Legg Mason Global Asset Management (July 2018), https://www.leggmason.com/content/dam/legg-mason/documents/en/insights-and-education/whitepaper/employee-plan-irs-examinations.pdf. The three areas of exam focus are based on the areas that are at higher risk of noncompliance.

20. *See* U.S. Dep't of Treasury, IRS Publication 4324, *Employee Plan Examination Process* (Rev. Nov. 2011), https://www.irs.gov/pub/irs-pdf/p4324.pdf.

21. To review the Employee Plans appeals process, see *EP Examination Process Guide—Section 7—Appeals—Appeals Procedures—Appeals Process*, IRS (updated Mar. 17, 2020), https://www.irs.gov/retirement-plans/ep-examination-process-guide-section-7-appeals-appeals-procedures-appeals-process.

22. *See* Rev. Proc. 2019-19 §6.02(1).

23. *See* *EP Abusive Tax Transactions*, IRS (updated Apr. 21, 2020), https://www.irs.gov/retirement-plans/ep-abusive-tax-transactions. Tax-exempt entities must use Form 8886-T and instructions in disclosing this information.

transaction" is a transaction that is similar to one deemed to be a tax avoidance transaction and identified as such by the IRS. The IRS has identified the following transactions involving employee benefit plans as listed transactions:

- Deduction on excess life insurance in a § 412(i) or other defined benefit plan;
- S corporation ESOP abuses: certain business structures held to violate Code § 409(p);
- S corporation ESOP abuse of delayed effective date for § 409(p);
- Collectively bargained welfare benefit funds under § 419A(f)(5);
- Certain trust arrangements seeking to qualify for exemption from § 419;
- Abusive Roth IRA transactions;
- Abusive transactions that affect availability of programs under EPCRS; and
- Notice 2006-65 (which relates to excise taxes with respect to prohibited tax shelter transactions to which tax-exempt entities are parties and related disclosure requirements).[24]

b. Employee Plans Compliance Unit (EPCU)

The IRS has formed the Employee Plans Compliance Unit (EPCU) which reaches out to plan sponsors with compliance checks that are less burdensome than a full exam or audit. A compliance check is a review by the IRS to determine if an entity is adhering to recordkeeping and information reporting requirements and whether its activities are consistent with its stated tax-exempt purpose, in contrast to an audit that is a review of the entity's books and records. EPCU typically conducts questionnaire projects as a way to understand emerging issues. To date, EPCU has completed 75 projects and conducted over 51,000 compliance checks.[25] Current projects include:

- Asset Mismatch Project;
- Data Analysis Verification Project;
- Final Return with Assets Project;
- Form 5500-EZ First Return Filer and Non-Filer Projects;
- Nonbank Trustees and Custodians;
- Non-Governmental 457(b) Excess Deferrals Project;
- Partial Termination Project; and
- SIMPLE IRA Plans — Eligible Sponsors Project.[26]

---

24. *See id.*

25. *See Employee Plans Compliance Unit (EPCU)*, IRS (updated Mar. 24, 2020), https://www.irs.gov/retirement-plans/employee-plans-compliance-unit-epcu.

26. *Id.*

7. IRS' Advisory Committee (ACT)

The IRS had a number of advisory committees which recently have been consolidated into a single advisory committee. The first advisory committee was established in 1953 as a national policy and/or issue advisory committee and was called the Commissioner's Advisory Group (CAG). It was renamed in 1998 as the Internal Revenue Service Advisory Council (IRSAC) to reflect the agency-wide scope of its focus as an advisory body. Its purpose was to provide an organized public forum to discuss relevant tax administration issues between IRS officials and representatives of the public and to propose changes to the IRS operations.

There is another advisory committee, the Information Reporting Program Advisory Committee (IRPAC), which advises the IRS on information reporting and administration issues of mutual concern to the private sector and the federal government. It works with the IRS Commissioner and other IRS leadership to make recommendations in the area of information reporting.

TE/GE established its own advisory committee known as the Advisory Committee on Tax Exempt and Government Entities (ACT) in 2001 to foster public discussion of issues relevant to the five TE/GE functions: Employee Plans (EP); Exempt Organizations (EO); Federal, State, and Local Governments (FSLG); Indian Tribal Governments (ITG); and Tax Exempt Bonds (TEB). There are 10 members of the ACT; two represent EP, three represent EO, one represents FSLG, two represent ITG, and two represent TEB. The committee members are typically attorneys, actuaries, and consultants who are experts in the field of employee benefits. The ACT has interacted with IRS leadership to address issues affecting TE/GE constituents, representing more than three million customers and entities and approximately $245 billion in federal tax expenditures. For the past 17 years, the ACT has issued reports to the Commissioner which are made available to the general public.[27] These reports contain a wealth of information, as they generally provide history and context regarding the issues that are being addressed. The author of this book was a member of the ACT from 2009 through 2012 when the ACT reported on the following EP topics:

- The 9th Report on EP Analysis and Recommendations Regarding the IRS' Determination Program, presented to the Commissioner and the general public on June 10, 2010;

- The 10th Report on EP Recommendations Regarding Pension Outreach to the Small Business Community, presented to the Commissioner and the general public on June 15, 2011; and

- The 11th Report on EP Analysis and Recommendations Regarding the Scope of the Employee Plans Examination Process.

---

27. A list of the 17 annual ACT reports are available at https://www.irs.gov/pub/irs-pdf/p4344.pdf.

In 2018, the IRS announced that the IRSAC would expand in 2019 to incorporate the two other advisory groups, IRPAC and ACT.[28] The combined group initially numbered 50 members, then consolidated to 36 members with three co-chairs (chairs of IRSAC, IRPAC, and ACT), and then, beginning in 2020, further reduced the number of co-chairs down to one chair of IRSAC. According to the IRS Commissioner Chuck Rettig, "[t]he new committee structure will provide the tax community a bigger, more prominent platform to make recommendations regarding taxpayer service, enhancements in enforcement and utilization of technology."[29]

C. Types of Guidance

The IRS publishes a variety of guidance, each with different authorities:

- *Treasury Regulations:* I.R.C. § 7805(a) grants the Treasury Department general authority to promulgate regulations, which interpret the text of the Code. I.R.C. § 25A grants specific rule-making authority to the Treasury Department in certain Code sections. Treasury regulations have the force and effect of law unless they directly conflict with the Code. The regulations are published in the Internal Revenue Bulletin.

- *Revenue Rulings:* I.R.C. § 7805 empowers the Treasury Department to issue rules. A revenue ruling is guidance from Treasury in response to questions raised by taxpayers that are determined to be important as a whole. They are published in the Internal Revenue Bulletin and then become part of the Cumulative Bulletin (C.B.), which compiles six months' worth of Internal Revenue Bulletins. Each ruling is cited by reference to the Cumulative Bulletin in which it is contained and the page number in which it is published. For example, Rev. Rul. 83-118 was the 118th ruling issued in 1983. Revenue rulings do not have the force and effect of regulations because they can be issued and withdrawn by the Service. Their value is that they let taxpayers know the Service's position relevant to a given fact pattern, which is useful in planning.

- *Acquiescence/Nonacquiescence:* In the Internal Revenue Bulletin, the Service lists its acquiescence (we agree) or its nonacquiescence (we do not agree) to certain opinions of the tax court. An acquiescence is issued when the Service agrees to accept a tax court's holding that was adverse to the Service's position. A nonac-

---

28. *See* IRS News Release IR-2018-212, *IRSAC expands to cover more areas of the IRS; IRPAC and ACT to join centralized advisory committee in 2019* (Nov. 1, 2018) (reviewed or updated Sep. 6, 2019), https://www.irs.gov/newsroom/irsac-expands-to-cover-more-areas-of-the-irs-irpac-and-act-to-join-centralized-advisory-committee-in-2019.

29. *Id.*

quiescence is issued when the Service decides not to abide with an adverse tax court holding. Neither has any effect on the taxpayer whose case the tax court determined, but they tell other taxpayers whether the Service may intend to pursue the same issue it lost in the future.

• *Private Letter Rulings (PLRs):* Here, the Services responds to a taxpayer's inquiry, but only that taxpayer can rely upon the ruling.

• *Other Administrative Pronouncements:* The Service issues revenue procedures (Rev. Proc.) which provide taxpayers with procedures for acquiring rulings or determination letters. It publishes internal revenue notices, which provide guidance to taxpayers on issues such as inflation adjustment factors. It also issues technical advice memorandums (TAMs), which are sent from the Service's national office to a district office when that district office seeks advice in considering a taxpayer's claim for a refund. TAMs are useful in understanding the policies of the Service but do not have precedential value.

Section III

Labor Rights and Protections for ERISA Plans

We've concluded the tax aspects of the Internal Revenue Code applicable to qualified retirement plans. Thus, in Section III, we move to the rights and protections that ERISA provides to employees by virtue of their employers offering an employee benefit plan—regardless of whether the benefits are retirement-related or welfare-related.

Chapter 12 will discuss the requirements for a plan, fund, program or schedule to be covered under ERISA. This will begin with a discussion of what employee benefit plans are subject to ERISA and then elements to be utilized to determine whether a given program is a plan for this purpose. If a given program is a plan and is a covered ERISA plan, there will be a mandated written plan document and a summary plan description for participants and beneficiaries covered under the plan.

Chapter 13 will examine ERISA's definition of a fiduciary and the applicable fiduciary standards of care. In interacting with a plan's assets, a fiduciary may not engage in a prohibited transaction, unless there is a statutory or administrative exemption available. To avoid fiduciary liability under a self-directed defined contribution plan (i.e., a plan in which the participants select the investments for his or her account), the requirements of ERISA § 404(c) must be met. Finally, the fiduciary's liabilities for breaching its fiduciary duties will be discussed.

Chapter 14 will discuss specific ERISA causes of action. We'll begin by explaining ERISA's preemption clause as these ERISA causes of action will become the exclusive remedy for plan participants and beneficiaries. Then we'll discuss the variety of causes of action and the litigation that has surrounded each of them.

Chapter 15 will highlight the reporting and disclosure requirements an employer must comply with, or delegated to a third party, if it decides to establish and sponsor an employee benefit plans. As the reporting and disclosure vary depending on whether the plan is a retirement versus a welfare benefit plans, each will be noted.

Chapter 16 will set forth the requirements under Title IV of ERISA when a single-employer defined benefit plan is being terminated. Even if the defined benefit plan is fully funded, there are still reporting and disclosure requirements that must be satisfied, this time with the PBGC.

Finally, Chapter 17 will explain how the Department of Labor's Employee Benefits Security Administration (EBSA) operates, as well as how the PBGC operates.

Chapter 12

ERISA Plans

Reading Assignment:	ERISA §§ 2, 3(1), 3(3), 104(b), 402(a)(1)
	Labor Reg. §§ 2510.3-2; 2510.3-3, 2520.102-2 through -4
	Donovan v. Dillingham, 688 F.2d 1367 (11th Cir. 1982)
	Firestone Tire & Rubber Co. v. Bruch, 489 U.S. 101 (1989)
Class Discussion Questions:	What is the purpose of Title I of ERISA?
	What is a "plan, fund, or program" for purposes of ERISA?
	What plans are excluded from coverage under ERISA?
	What are the formal requirements of a written plan document?
	What is the purpose of the summary plan description?
	What is the applicable judicial standard of review in a benefits denial case?

Overview

What is a plan for purposes of ERISA?

- the general rule of thumb is that every time an employer promises benefits to employees, ERISA will govern unless a specific statutory or regulatory provision (or binding judicial decree) specifically excludes ERISA coverage

- generally, any scheme, program, or payroll procedure which promises retirement or health and welfare benefits to employees (generally at least two) can be deemed a plan by the DOL or by a court, even if the employer did not intend for the scheme to be a plan

- certain plans are statutorily excluded from ERISA coverage (i.e., plans sponsored by churches and plans sponsored by state and local governments)

- certain plans are excluded from ERISA coverage by regulations (i.e., sick and vacation day plans, certain severance pay plans, and short-term disability plans)

- certain plans are excluded only from certain provisions of ERISA but are subject to others (i.e., top hat nonqualified deferred compensation plans)

What are the drafting requirements for ERISA plan documents?

- although ERISA requires a plan to be in the form of a written document, it does not specify its actual form
- case law has helped somewhat by suggesting the right words to use for certain provisions
- the reason for the requirement of a written plan document is to assure that every employee may, upon examining the plan documents, determine exactly what his or her rights and obligations are under the plan
- the plan's written provisions control and cannot be altered by oral amendments or informal written communications (such as film strips, company newsletters, or letters to employees) — there is a trend, however, of an increasing willingness on the part of many courts to enforce oral amendments to plans under a theory of equitable estoppel
- the term "plan document" is usually comprised of four elements:
  - the plan document, which describes in detail the rules under which the plan operates;
  - the trust agreement, which establishes the trust under which the plan's assets are held (which may be incorporated in the same instrument or may be a separate document);
  - the summary plan description (SPD), which explains the plan's provisions in plain English for the plan participants and beneficiaries; and
  - the ancillary procedures which are adopted by the plan administrator

What is the importance of the summary plan description?

- every employee must be provided with a summary plan description (SPD) once they have met the eligibility requirements of the plan
- although they have the right to request a copy of the actual plan document, the SPD in reality is the only document the employees generally see regarding their benefits and other participant rights
- an SPD may be drafted in a variety of ways, as long as all the required provisions are included and as long as it is written in a manner calculated to be understood by the average plan participant

A. ERISA Plans

1. What Is a Plan?

ERISA was not particularly helpful in defining what is a plan for purposes of ascertaining whether a given plan is an employee welfare benefit plan or an employee pension benefit plan. ERISA § 3(3) simply says "[t]he term 'employee benefit plan' or 'plan' means an employee welfare benefit plan or an employee pension benefit plan or a plan which is both an employee welfare benefit plan and an employee pension benefit plan."[1] The DOL regulations elaborating on ERISA § 3(3) likewise are not helpful, as they define what is *not* a plan: "the term 'employee benefit plan' shall not include any plan, fund, or program, other than an apprenticeship or other training program, under which no employees are participants covered under the plan...." Hence, what is meant by the phrase "any plan, fund, or program" used in ERISA § 3(3) is better understood through caselaw. Read the case of *Donovan v. Dillingham* in the Materials section at the end of this chapter to ascertain the factors in determining whether a plan, fund, or program constitutes an ERISA plan for purposes of ERISA § 3(3). The general rule is that, if an employer promises benefits to its employees, there is a plan, fund, or program, and ERISA will govern unless there is a statutory, caselaw, or regulatory exclusion.

This issue generally arises in the context of a deferred compensation agreement for an executive or a group of executives—is it an employment agreement outside the scope of ERISA or a retirement plan within the scope of ERISA? The issue is important because, if the agreement is a "plan, fund, or program" for ERISA purposes, the remedies for any breach of the agreement are exclusively determined by ERISA and not state law.

2. What Plans Are Covered under ERISA?

Once a plan, fund, or program rises to the level of a plan for purposes of ERISA § 3(3), ERISA then makes the distinction between an "employee welfare benefit plan" for purposes of ERISA § 3(1) or an "employee pension benefit plan" for purposes of ERISA § 3(2)(A). According to the statute, an "employee welfare benefit plan" is a plan, fund, or program that provides, through the purchase of insurance or otherwise, "(A) medical, surgical, or hospital care or benefits, or benefits in the event of sickness, accident, disability, death or unemployment, or vacation benefits, apprenticeship or other training programs, or day care centers, scholarship funds, or prepaid legal services, or (B) any benefit described in section 302(c) of the Labor Management Relations Act."[2] The definition refers to benefits provided through the purchase of insurance or otherwise (i.e., self-insured by the employer), as many of these types of welfare benefits refer to the wellbeing of the participant and/or his or her beneficiary that are outside the control of the individual. Thus, it may be the type of benefit that the employer would prefer to insure with an insurance company (to shift the risk), rather than self-insure and risk having to pay more than anticipated. For example, one purchases car insurance so that in the event of an accident, the insurer pays the cost of the claim instead of the individual; thus, the individual shifts the risk to the insurance company so that he or she does not have to pay the full cost of the claim on his or her own.

---

1. ERISA § 3(3).
2. ERISA § 3(1).

The DOL regulations document what practices may satisfy the above definition of an employee welfare benefit plan but nevertheless will **not** be held as such.[3] These include:

- Payroll practices that pay compensation, including overtime pay, shift premiums, holiday premiums, and weekend premiums;
- On-premises facilities (e.g., dining rooms, recreational areas, sickness stations);
- Holiday gifts (e.g., turkeys or hams during the holidays);
- Sales to employees (e.g., discounted prices for articles the employer offers for sale in the regular course of business);
- Hiring halls;
- Remembrance funds (e.g., flowers for funerals or sickness);
- Strike funds (e.g., payment to union members during strikes);
- Industry advanced programs (i.e., a program maintained by an employer or a group of employers that has no employee participants and does not provide benefits to employees or their dependents);
- Certain group insurance programs; and
- Unfunded scholarship programs (i.e., unfunded means that the payments are made solely from the general assets of an employer or employee organization).[4]

In contrast, an "employee pension benefit plan" is a plan, fund, or program that by its express terms or as a result of surrounding circumstances (meaning that an employer may inadvertently establish such a plan without intending to) provides retirement income to employees or deferred compensation for periods extending to termination of employment or beyond.[5] This term would clearly include all types of qualified retirement plans. For an example of a situation in which the employer had not intended to create an employee pension benefit plan but was found by the court to have established one, see the case of *Musmeci v. Schwegmann Giant Super Markets, Inc.*[6]

ERISA § 3(2)(B) provides an exception whereby the DOL through its regulations can prescribe rules as to when severance pay plans and supplemental retirement income payments (e.g., cost of living increases to pension benefits) may be treated as

---

3. Labor Reg. § 2510.3-1.

4. *Id.*

5. ERISA § 3(2)(A). This is a reminder that ERISA classifies all deferred compensation plans as pension plans, whereas Title II classifies pension plans as defined benefit plans, money purchase plans, or target benefit plans.

6. 332 F.3d 339, 344 (5th Cir. 2003). Due to a sale of the business, the employer discontinued a voucher program established for its retirees so that they could use the vouchers, in lieu of cash, to purchase goods from the employer's stores. The court held that the employer had established an employee benefit plan subject to ERISA. By virtue of the court's finding that the program was an employee pension benefit plan, there was a breach of fiduciary duty, as ERISA's reporting and disclosure rules were not met and the plan was not funded (i.e., assets were not held in trust).

welfare plans rather than pension plans.[7] Under its regulations, the DOL has determined that a severance pay plan that pays no more than 200% of the employee's annual compensation during the year immediately preceding termination of employment for a period no longer than 24 months will not be an employee pension benefit plan.[8] As a result, such a plan would qualify as an employee welfare benefit plan. In addition, the DOL has held that the following will not be considered employee pension benefit plans for purposes of ERISA § 3(2)(B): bonus programs that do not systematically defer compensation for work performed until termination of employment, IRAs, gratuitous payments to former participants (who retired prior to ERISA's passage), and tax-sheltered annuities described in I.R.C. § 403(b) that are completely voluntary for employees and have minimal involvement by the employer.[9]

There are certain plans that are statutorily excluded from ERISA. They include:

- Governmental plans;
- Church plans for which no election has been made to be treated as an ERISA plan;
- Plans maintained solely for the purpose of complying with applicable workers' compensation law or unemployment compensation or disability insurance laws;
- Plans maintained outside the United States primarily for the benefit of persons substantially all of whom are nonresident aliens; and
- Excess benefit plans (defined in ERISA § 3(36)) that are unfunded.[10]

There are certain plans that are covered by ERISA but are excluded from Part 2 of ERISA. They are:

- Welfare benefit plans;
- Unfunded plans maintained by an employer primarily for the purpose of providing deferred compensation for a select group of management or highly compensated employees (referred to as top hat plans);
- An individual retirement account or annuity (IRA); and
- Excess benefit plans.[11]

B. Written Plan Document

1. The Controlling Plan Document

If a given plan, fund, or program is a plan for purposes of ERISA § 3(3), ERISA requires it to be established and maintained pursuant to a written plan document.[12]

---

7. ERISA § 3(2)(B).
8. Labor Reg. § 2510.3-2(b).
9. Labor Reg. § 2510.3-2(b)(2).
10. ERISA § 4(b).
11. ERISA § 201.
12. ERISA § 402(a)(1).

ERISA's Part 4 sets forth its fiduciary duties, one of which is to follow the terms of the plan document;[13] therefore, it makes sense that there be a plan document. The plan document has five elements:

- It must name one or more fiduciaries (referred to as the "named fiduciaries") who are jointly or severally responsible to control and manage the operation and administration of the plan (i.e., it must name those who will determine how the plan will operate);

- It must have a procedure for establishing and carrying out a funding policy (e.g., how are benefits to be funded), consistent with the objectives of the plan and ERISA's funding rules set forth in ERISA §§ 301–305;

- It must describe any procedure under the plan for allocating responsibilities for the administration of the plan (e.g., if the employer wishes to delegate the administrative duties to a third party, how is that to be accomplished);

- It must have a procedure for amending the plan and identifying who has the power to amend the plan (generally, this is the employer);

- It must specify the basis on which payments are made to and from the plan.[14]

Optional provisions that may be provided in the written document include:

- The plan may provide that a person or group of persons may serve in multiple fiduciary capacities under the plan (e.g., be both trustee and plan administrator);

- The plan may allow the named fiduciary (or someone designated by that fiduciary pursuant to a plan procedure) to employ one or more persons to render advice with respect to the fiduciary's duties under the plan; and

- The plan may allow the named fiduciary with control over the management of plan assets to appoint an investment manager to oversee all or a part of the plan assets.[15]

2. *Firestone* Language

The issue of the appropriate judicial standard of review for benefit denial claims had existed even before ERISA's passage in 1974.[16] The question involves when the courts should "second guess" the plan administrator's denial of a benefit claim under an employee benefits plan. ERISA was silent on the applicable judicial standard of review, leaving the courts to decide the issue. The Supreme Court first attempted to answer this question in 1989 in the case of *Firestone Tire & Rubber Co. v. Bruch*.[17] The

---

13. ERISA § 404(a)(1)(D).

14. ERISA §§ 402(a)(2), 402(b).

15. ERISA § 402(c)(1)–(3).

16. *See* Kathryn J. Kennedy, *Judicial Standard of Review in ERISA Benefit Claim Cases*, 50 Amer. U. L. Rev. 1083 (2001); Kathryn J. Kennedy, *Conkright: A Conundrum for Future Courts, An Opportunity for Congress*, 2010 NYU Rev. of Emp. Benefits & Exec. Comp. 16-1.

17. 489 U.S. 101 (1988).

case involved an employer, Firestone Tire & Rubber Co., which maintained and administered a self-insured severance pay plan. Read this case in the Materials section at the end of this chapter.

Under the terms of the plan, severance benefits would be paid "upon a reduction in work force."[18] The plan was an unfunded severance pay plan, which means that it was not pre-funded but instead paid out from the employer's general assets. Upon the sale of one of Firestone's divisions, employees were terminated but then rehired by the new employer. Thus, Firestone Tire & Rubber Co., as plan administrator, determined there was no "reduction in work force" requiring the payment of severance benefits.[19] At issue before the court was the appropriate judicial standard of review in "second guessing" the plan administrator's interpretation of an ambiguous term in the plan document. Here, there was conflict of interest as the employer was also the plan administrator; thus, for every dollar it denied in benefits, it saved by not paying out from its general assets.[20]

The Supreme Court relied on trust law and held that the plan administrator's interpretation of the plan language would be given deferential review (under an abuse of discretion standard), *provided* the plan document reserved discretionary powers to the plan administrator to interpret the plan document.[21] In absence of such discretionary powers, the courts were to use a *de novo* standard of review.[22] If such discretionary powers had been reserved, but the plan administrator was conflicted (as was the case in *Firestone*, as the employer was the plan administrator), such conflict was to be a "factor in determining whether there is an abuse of discretion."[23] Immediately after the decision, plans were amended virtually overnight to provide for the discretionary powers of plan administrators to interpret plan provisions. But litigation ensued as to how to weigh the conflict of interest as a "factor" in applying the abuse of discretion standard.[24]

Due to a conflict among the circuits as to how to "factor" in a plan administrator's conflict of interest into the abuse of discretion standard, the Supreme Court took on this issue a second time in 2008, with the case of *Metropolitan Life Insurance Co. v. Glenn*.[25] The facts in that case involved an employer, Sears, Roebuck and Co., who maintained a long-term disability insurance policy that was insured and administered by Metropolitan Life Insurance Company (MetLife).[26] The plan granted MetLife,

---

18. *Id.* at 105–06.

19. *Id.* at 106.

20. *Id.* Other examples of a conflict of interest would be if the employer insured the benefits with an insurance company and elected the insurer to also administer the plan.

21. *Id.* at 112–15.

22. *Id.* at 115.

23. *Id.*

24. *See* Kathryn J. Kennedy, *Conkright: A Conundrum for Future Courts, An Opportunity for Congress*, 2010 NYU REV. OF EMP. BENEFITS & EXEC. COMP. ch. 16.

25. 554 U.S. 105, 128 S. Ct. 2343 (2008).

26. *Id.* at 2346.

both the insurer and administrator, the necessary discretionary power to ascertain whether a participant met the eligibility requirements for benefits.[27] Although the participant, Wanda Glenn, met the disability standard for the initial 24 months of payment, MetLife held that she did not meet the more strict standard of disability to qualify for long-term disability coverage.[28]

Glenn sued in federal court, claiming MetLife had abused its discretion, but lost; upon appeal to the Sixth Circuit, the court held that MetLife had abused its discretion for a variety of reasons.[29] The U.S. Supreme Court in the *Glenn* decision reaffirmed *Firestone*'s use of trust law to fashion the appropriate judicial standard of review.[30] It then addressed the issue of whether the conflict of interest in question was a *per se* conflict.[31] In the case of an employer who both funds the benefits and evaluates whether to pay the claim, the Court agreed that would be a *per se* conflict of interest.[32] However, under the facts in this case, where MetLife was both the insurer and plan administrator, it was less clear that there was a *per se* conflict.[33] But the Court noted the judicial standard of review was structured in such a fashion so as to permit the insurer to show how they diminish the "significance of severity of the conflict," so as to eliminate the effect of the conflict.[34] The Court then offered a two-step process modifying the *Firestone* standard in the context of a conflict of interest—first, use of a variety of factors, weighing them together,[35] and second, when the factors are closely balanced, consider tiebreaking factors.[36] The Court concluded that the *Firestone* standard did not come with a "detailed set of instructions" and thus it has "not enunciated a precise standard."[37] Chief Justice Robert's dissent criticized the majority opinion, noting that the "Court leaves the law more uncertain, more unpredictable than it found it."[38]

It was no surprise after the *Glenn* decision that the circuits remained conflicted as to how to modify the *Firestone* standard in light of a conflict of interest. This led to

---

27. *Id.*
28. *Id.*
29. *See* Glenn v. MetLife, 461 F.3d 660, 674–75 (6th Cir. 2006) (applying the arbitrary and capricious standard of review and holding that the plan administrator had acted arbitrarily by not engaging in deliberative analysis and by not basing its decision on substantial evidence).
30. *See supra* note 25 at 2347–48.
31. *Id.* at 2348.
32. *Id.*
33. *Id.* at 2349.
34. *Id.* at 2348.
35. *Id.* at 2351 (factors included (1) the extent of the discretion conferred upon the trustee, (2) the purpose of the trust, (3) the nature of the power, (4) the definiteness of any external standard to judge the reasonableness of the trustee's conduct, (5) the motives of the trustee in exercising his or her power, and (6) a conflict of interest with that of the beneficiaries).
36. *Id.* (tiebreaking factors such as whether the insured administrator had a history of bias claims, or whether the administrator had taken proactive steps to diminish bias and improve accuracy).
37. *Id.* at 2352.
38. *Id.* 2354.

the third Supreme Court opinion on the topic, *Conkright v. Frommert*,[39] in 2010, with Chief Justice Roberts writing for the majority. The case involved the Xerox Corporation that maintained a minimum floor offset defined benefit plan, which had a provision whereby prior lump sum distributions that had been made from the plan to a retiree would offset any future retirement benefits if the retiree was rehired (so as to avoid duplicative benefits).[40] Under the terms of the plan, the plan administrator was to be appointed by Xerox's chief executive officer, who in turn, named individual employees as the plan administrator.[41] Thus, using the *Glenn* analysis, there is an assumed per se conflict of interest as the employer is self-funding the retirement plan and administering the plan through its employees.[42] The plan document granted the plan administrator discretion to construe the terms of the plan and trust, including the ability to resolve any ambiguities.[43] Some plan participants sued the plan administrator, claiming that its interpretation of the offset provisions used in the benefits formula violated ERISA (as it resulted in a cut-back in benefits) and thus was an abuse of discretion. The district court affirmed the plan administrator's determination of the offset[44] but the Second Circuit disagreed, as the plan administrator's determination of the offset violated ERISA's anti-cutback rules, and thus the determination was unreasonable under either the arbitrary and capricious standard or the de novo standard of review.[45] The Second Circuit remanded the case to the district court to allow the plan administrator to make a subsequent interpretation of the plan formula.

At issue before the Supreme Court was whether the district court owed deference to the plan administrator's subsequent interpretation of the plan on remand from the Second Circuit's decision. Chief Justice Roberts and Justices Scalia, Kennedy, and Thomas, who had dissented from a portion of the *Glenn* ruling, joined with Justice Alito, and delivered the majority of the *Conkright* decision, whereas Justices Breyer, Stevens, and Ginsburg, from the *Glenn* majority, delivered the dissent.[46] Chief Justice Roberts began the majority opinion with the statements "People make mistakes. Even administrators of ERISA plans."[47] He then wrote that the Second Circuit's remand should have directed the district court to apply a deferential standard of review to the plan administrator's subsequent interpretation of the plan provision.[48] While trust law was not instrumental in determining whether the deferential standard of review should be altered when the plan administrator's previous interpretation violated ERISA, the

---

39. 559 U.S. 506, 130 S. Ct. 1640 (2010).
40. *See* Frommert v. Conkright, 535 F.3d 111, 115 (2d Cir. 2008).
41. *See* Frommert v. Conkright, 328 F. Supp. 2d 420, 428 (W.D.N.Y. 2004).
42. *See* MetLife v. Glenn, 554 U.S. 105, 128 S. Ct. 2343, 2348 (2008).
43. *See* Frommert v. Conkright, 328 F. Supp. 2d at 430.
44. *See id.* at 439.
45. *See* Frommert v. Conkright, 433 F.3d 254, 266, n.11 (2d Cir. 2006).
46. Justice Sotomayor took no part in the decision, as she ruled in a prior decision regarding Xerox's plan.
47. *See* Conkright v. Frommert, 130 S. Ct. at 1644.
48. *Id.* at 1646.

guiding principles of ERISA were.[49] Justice Roberts said the Court should engage in a "'careful balancing' between ensuring fair and prompt enforcement of rights under a plan and the encouragement of the creation of such plan."[50] Thus, in the interest of efficiency, predictability, and uniformity, the Court held that deference to the plan administrator's subsequent plan interpretation does not "suddenly disappear simply because a plan administrator made a single honest mistake."[51] Interestingly, the dissenting justices describe the facts of the case much differently than the majority, noting that a variety of mistakes were made by the plan administrator.[52]

As the *Conkright* decision did not distinguish how lower courts were to reconcile the *Glenn* and *Conkright* decisions, it certainly expanded the *Firestone* deferential standard of review. It makes no mention of *Glenn*'s combination-of-factors approach when factoring in the plan administrator's conflict of interest. But *Conkright* certainly appears to reduce the courts' "second guessing" of the plan administrator's interpretation, as they are to remand benefit claims to the plan administrator for another interpretation of the plan if the initial one involved a fiduciary breach (e.g., not interpreting the plan consistently with ERISA). This is yet another example where the courts attempt to balance the rights of participants and beneficiaries to benefits under the plan with the burden imposed on employers who deliver such benefits *voluntarily*. It appears that in balancing these two goals, the courts are unwilling to interject themselves in the determination of what benefits must be paid from the plan.

C. Summary Plan Description

1. Content of the Summary Plan Description

ERISA requires a summary plan description (SPD) to be furnished to participants (not all employees).[53] An SPD is a summary of the salient plan provisions written in a manner intended to be understood by the average plan participant, such that participants are reasonably apprised of their rights and obligations under the plan.[54] The statute does not define who is the "average plan participant" for this purpose, but the DOL regulations state that the plan administrator should take into account factors such as the levels of compensation and education of the typical participant and the complexity of the plan in drafting the SPD.[55]

The material to be contained in the SPD includes:

---

49. *Id.* at 1643.
50. *Id.* at 1649.
51. *Id.*
52. *Id.* at 1653.
53. ERISA § 102(a).
54. *Id.*
55. Labor Reg. § 2520.102-2(a).

- The name and type of administration of the plan;
- For insured health plans, the name and address of the insurer;
- The name and address of the person designated as agent for the service of legal process if that person is not the plan administrator;
- The name and addresses of the plan administrator, and the name and addresses of any trustees;
- A description of the relevant provisions of any applicable collective bargaining agreement;
- The plan's requirements as to eligibility for participation and benefits;
- The circumstances which may result in disqualification, ineligibility, or denial or loss of benefits;
- The source of financing of the plan and the identity of any organization through which benefits are provided;
- The date of the end of the plan year and whether records are kept on a calendar, policy, or fiscal year basis; and
- The procedures to be followed through which participants and beneficiaries may seek assistance or information regarding their rights.[56]

The plan administrator must furnish to each participant, and each beneficiary receiving benefits under the plan, a copy of the SPD within 90 days after becoming a participant (or for beneficiaries, 90 days after first receiving benefits), or if later, within 120 days after the plan becomes subject to ERISA.[57] Every five years, the plan administrator must provide participants and beneficiaries receiving benefits an updated SPD that includes all plan amendments made within the last five years. If no amendments have been made during this five-year period, an SPD must be furnished every 10 years.

According to the DOL regulations, the format of the SPD must "not have the effect to misleading, misinforming, or failing to inform participants and beneficiaries."[58] As to the issue of whether the SPD must be translated into foreign languages, the DOL regulations set forth the following rules:

- If the plan covers fewer than 100 participants at the beginning of the plan year and 25% or more of all participants are literate only in the same non-English language, the plan administrator must provide these participants with an English-language SPD that displays the notice (in their foreign language) offering them assistance.[59] For example, in the case of a plan with 80 participants at the

---

56. ERISA § 102(b).
57. ERISA § 104(b)(1).
58. Labor Reg. § 2520.102-2(b).
59. Labor Reg. § 2520.102-2(c)(1).

beginning of the plan year of which 40 (i.e., 50%) are literate only in Spanish, an English SPD must be provided to those 40 participants with a notice written in Spanish offering them assistance. Such assistance could take the form of having available a Spanish interpreter with whom the Spanish participants could converse.

- If the plan covers 100 or more participants at the beginning of the plan year and the *lesser* of (1) 500 or more participants or (2) 10% or more of all plan participants are literate only in the same non-English language, the plan administrator must provide these participants with an English-language SPD that displays the notice (in their foreign language) offering them assistance.[60] For example, in the case of a plan with 500 participants at the beginning of the plan year of which 50 (i.e., 10%, which is less than 500 participants) are literate only in Spanish, an English SPD must be provided to those 50 participants with a notice written in Spanish offering them assistance.

If there is a material modification to the SPD, the plan sponsor must describe the change (referred to as a "summary of material modification") within 210 days after the end of the plan year in which the change is adopted to each participant and each beneficiary receiving a benefit.[61]

2. SPDs as Plan Documents

The plan document cannot be altered by the SPD.[62] That was the holding in the Supreme Court's decision in *CIGNA Corp. v. Amara*. In that case, CIGNA had created two separate documents—a plan document and an SPD. The terms of the SPD violated ERISA, and thus the district court reformed the terms of the plan to reflect the SPD.[63] The Supreme Court rejected that approach and enforced the terms of the plan, concluding that SPDs were simply summaries of the plan but not themselves the terms of the plan.[64]

Thus, while the plan's written terms prevail and cannot be altered by oral amendments or informal written communications, some courts have upheld statements made by employers (either orally, through the SPD, or through other company memorandum), even though they were not substantiated under the plan.[65] Those courts invoked the use of equitable estoppel to enforce the employer's statements.

---

60. Labor Reg. § 2520.102-2(c)(2).

61. ERISA § 104(b).

62. *See* CIGNA Corp. v. Amara, 563 U.S. 421 (2011).

63. *See* Amara v. CIGNA Corp., 559 F. Supp. 2d 192 (D. Conn. 2008), *aff'd*, 348 Fed. Appx. 627 (2d Cir. 2009) (unpub. Opin.), *vacated*, 563 U.S. 421 (2011).

64. *See* CIGNA Corp. v. Amara, 563 U.S. at 438.

65. *See* Kane v. Aetna Ins., 893 F.2d 1283, 1285 (11th Cir. 1990), *cert. denied*, 498 U.S. 890 (1990); *but see* Coleman v. Nationwide Life Ins. Co., 969 F.2d 54, 58–59 (4th Cir. 1992); *see also* Trustmark Life Ins. Co. v. University of Chicago Hospitals, 207 F.3d 876, 883 (7th Cir. 1999) (providing that the following four elements must exist in order to prevail on an equitable estoppel claim: (1) a knowing

D. Materials

Donovan v. Dillingham

688 F.2d 1367 (11th Cir. 1982)

Opinion

GODBOLD, Chief Judge:

The Secretary of Labor pursuant to his authority under ERISA s 502(a), 29 U.S.C. s 1132(a), brought this action against the trustees of Union Insurance Trust (UIT) and businesses owned and operated by them, alleging they are fiduciaries subject to the fiduciary responsibility provisions contained in Part 4 of Title I of ERISA, 29 U.S.C. ss 1101 et seq. Fiduciary duties under ERISA, however, arise only if there are employee benefit plans as defined by the Act. The district court held that this case is controlled by Taggart Corp. v. Life & Health Benefits Administration, 617 F.2d 1208 (5th Cir. 1980), cert. denied sub nom. Taggart Corp. v. Efros, 450 U.S. 1030, 101 S. Ct. 1739, 68 L. Ed. 2d 225 (1981), and dismissed for lack of subject matter jurisdiction because there were no employee benefit plans involved. A panel of this court agreed. Donovan v. Dillingham, 668 F.2d 1196 (11th Cir. 1982). Upon reconsideration en banc we find there was subject matter jurisdiction and reverse.

I.

Congress enacted ERISA to protect working men and women from abuses in the administration and investment of private retirement plans and employee welfare plans. Broadly stated, ERISA established minimum standards for vesting of benefits, funding of benefits, carrying out fiduciary responsibilities, reporting to the government and making disclosures to participants. *See generally* H.R. Rep. No. 93-533, 93d Cong. 2d Sess., reprinted in (1974) U.S. Code Cong. & Ad. News 4639.

With a few specific exceptions not pertinent to this decision, Title I of ERISA applies to any "employee benefit plan" if it is established or maintained by any employer or employee organization engaged in commerce or in any industry or activity affecting commerce, or by both an employer and an employee organization. ERISA s 4(a), 29 U.S.C. s 1003(a). "Employee benefit plan" or "plan" means an "employee welfare benefit plan" or an "employee pension benefit plan" or a plan which is both a welfare plan and a pension plan. ERISA s 3(3), 29 U.S.C. s 1002(3).

UIT is a group insurance trust, commonly known as a multiple employer trust ("MET"), whose purpose is to allow employers of small numbers of employees to secure group health insurance coverage for their employees at rates more favorable than offered directly by an insurer. UIT obtained a group health insurance policy from Occidental Life Insurance Company of California to furnish specified insurance benefits. Employers and various employee organizations "subscribe" to UIT to receive the coverage of the blanket Occidental Life policy. Appellees contend that ERISA does

---

misrepresentation (2) made in writing (3) with reasonable reliance by the participant (4) to the participant's detriment).

not apply because there is involved only the "bare purchase of health insurance" and that no employee welfare benefit plans are implicated. The parties have debated whether UIT is a fiduciary and how that status or lack thereof bears on the presence of an employee welfare benefit plan. We agree with the Secretary that whether UIT merely sells insurance or is a fiduciary does not determine whether employee welfare benefit plans exist. Likewise, we agree with appellees that the existence of appellees' management of the trust or their falling within ERISA's fiduciary definition (which they challenge) does not necessarily mandate a finding that employee welfare benefit plans exist.

II.

ERISA s 3(1), 29 U.S.C. s 1002(1), defines "employee welfare benefit plan" or "welfare plan" as any plan, fund, or program which was heretofore or is hereafter established or maintained by an employer or by an employee organization, or by both, to the extent that such plan, fund, or program was established or is maintained for the purpose of providing for its participants or their beneficiaries, through the purchase of insurance or otherwise, (A) medical, surgical, or hospital care or benefits, or benefits in the event of sickness, accident, disability, death or unemployment, or vacation benefits, apprenticeship or other training programs, or day care centers, scholarship funds, or prepaid legal services, or (B) any benefit described in s 302(c) of the Labor Management Relations Act, 1947 (other than pensions on retirement or death, and insurance to provide such pensions).

By definition, then, a welfare plan requires (1) a "plan, fund, or program" (2) established or maintained (3) by an employer or by an employee organization, or by both, (4) for the purpose of providing medical, surgical, hospital care, sickness, accident, disability, death, unemployment or vacation benefits, apprenticeship or other training programs, day care centers, scholarship funds, prepaid legal services or severance benefits (5) to participants or their beneficiaries.

A.

Prerequisites (3), (4) and (5) are either self-explanatory or defined by statute. A plan, fund, or program must be established or maintained "for the purpose of providing for its participants or their beneficiaries, through the purchase of insurance or otherwise," health, accident, disability, death, or unemployment or vacation benefits or apprenticeship or other training programs, day care centers, scholarship funds, prepaid legal services or severance benefits.

The gist of ERISA's definitions of employer, employee organization, participant, and beneficiary is that a plan, fund, or program falls within the ambit of ERISA only if the plan, fund, or program covers ERISA participants because of their employee status in an employment relationship, and an employer or employee organization is the person that establishes or maintains the plan, fund, or program. Thus, plans, funds, or programs under which no union members, employees, or former employees participate are not employee welfare benefit plans under Title I of ERISA. *See* 29 C.F.R. 2510.3-3(b), (c).

An issue in other cases has been whether a multiple employer trust—the enterprise—is itself an employee welfare benefit plan. The courts, congressional committees, and the Secretary uniformly have held they are not. *See, e.g.*, Activity Report of the Comm. on Education and Labor, H.R. Rep. No. 94-1785, H.R. Rep. No. 94-1785, 94th Cong. 2d Sess. 48 (1977); Taggart Corp. v. Life & Health Benefits Administration, Inc., 617 F.2d 1208 (5th Cir. 1980), *cert. denied sub nom.* Taggart Corp. v. Efros, 450 U.S. 1030, 101 S. Ct. 1739, 68 L. Ed. 2d 225 (1981); Wayne Chemical, Inc. v. Columbus Agency Service Corp., 567 F.2d 692 (7th Cir. 1977); Bell v. Employee Security Benefit Ass'n, 437 F. Supp. 382 (D. Kan. 1977). All parties to this appeal agree that UIT is subject to state laws regulating insurance and is not itself an employee welfare benefit plan.

B.

Not so well defined are the first two prerequisites: "plan, fund, or program" and "established or maintained." Commentators and courts define "plan, fund, or program" by synonym-arrangement, scheme, unitary scheme, program of action, method of putting into effect an intention or proposal, design—but do not specify the prerequisites of a "plan, fund, or program." At a minimum, however, a "plan, fund, or program" under ERISA implies the existence of intended benefits, intended beneficiaries, a source of financing, and a procedure to apply for and collect benefits.

"Established or maintained" appears twice in the definition of an employee welfare benefit plan: first, an employer or employee organization or both must establish or maintain a plan, fund, or program, and, second, the plan, fund, or program must be established or maintained for specified purposes. In many instances a plan is established or maintained, or both, in writing. It is obvious that a system of providing benefits pursuant to a written instrument that satisfies ERISA ss 102 and 402, 29 U.S.C. ss 1022 and 1102, would constitute a "plan, fund or program."

ERISA does not, however, require a formal, written plan. ERISA's coverage provision reaches "any employee benefit plan if it is established or maintained" by an employer or an employee organization, or both, who are engaged in any activities or industry affecting commerce. ERISA s 4(a), 29 U.S.C. s 1003(a) (emphasis added). There is no requirement of a formal, written plan in either ERISA's coverage section, ERISA s 4(a), 29 U.S.C. s 1003(a), or its definitions section, ERISA s 3(1), 29 U.S.C. s 1002(1). Once it is determined that ERISA covers a plan, the Act's fiduciary and reporting provisions do require the plan to be established pursuant to a written instrument, ERISA ss 102 and 402, 29 U.S.C. ss 1022 and 1102; but clearly these are only the responsibilities of administrators and fiduciaries of plans covered by ERISA and are not prerequisites to coverage under the Act. Furthermore, because the policy of ERISA is to safeguard the well-being and security of working men and women and to apprise them of their rights and obligations under any employee benefit plan, *see* ERISA s 2, 29 U.S.C. s 1001, it would be incongruous for persons establishing or maintaining informal or unwritten employee benefit plans, or assuming the responsibility of safeguarding plan assets, to circumvent the Act merely because an administrator or other fiduciary failed to satisfy reporting or fiduciary standards. Accord,

Dependahl v. Falstaff Brewing Corp., 491 F. Supp. 1188, 1195 (E.D. Mo. 1980), *aff'd* 653 F.2d 1208 (8th Cir. 1981).

The Secretary contends that "establish" means no more than an ultimate decision by an employer or an employee organization to provide the type of benefits described in ERISA s 3(1), 29 U.S.C. s 1002(1). This sweeps too broadly. A decision to extend benefits is not the establishment of a plan or program. Acts or events that record, exemplify or implement the decision will be direct or circumstantial evidence that the decision has become reality—e.g., financing or arranging to finance or fund the intended benefits, establishing a procedure for disbursing benefits, assuring employees that the plan or program exists—but it is the reality of a plan, fund, or program and not the decision to extend certain benefits that is determinative.

In determining whether a plan, fund, or program (pursuant to a writing or not) is a reality a court must determine whether from the surrounding circumstances a reasonable person could ascertain the intended benefits, beneficiaries, source of financing, and procedures for receiving benefits. Some essentials of a plan, fund, or program can be adopted, explicitly or implicitly, from sources outside the plan, fund, or program—e.g., an insurance company's procedure for processing claims, *cf.* 29 C.F.R. s 2520.102-5 (qualified health maintenance organization)—but no single act in itself necessarily constitutes the establishment of the plan, fund, or program. For example, the purchase of insurance does not conclusively establish a plan, fund, or program, but the purchase is evidence of the establishment of a plan, fund, or program; the purchase of a group policy or multiple policies covering a class of employees offers substantial evidence that a plan, fund, or program has been established.

C.

In summary, a "plan, fund, or program" under ERISA is established if from the surrounding circumstances a reasonable person can ascertain the intended benefits, a class of beneficiaries, the source of financing, and procedures for receiving benefits. To be an employee welfare benefit plan, the intended benefits must be health, accident, death, disability, unemployment or vacation benefits, apprenticeship or other training programs, day care centers, scholarship funds, prepaid legal services or severance benefits; the intended beneficiaries must include union members, employees, former employees, or their beneficiaries; and an employer or employee organization, or both, and not individual employees or entrepreneurial businesses, must establish or maintain the plan, fund, or program.

III.

The record indicates that subscribers to UIT included single-employer, collectively bargained programs, multi-employer health and welfare funds, and union-sponsored funds. For some organizations the subscription to UIT was their initial subscription—e.g., Carpenters Local # 865 (377 members), Rahn's Trucking (4 employees), and Porter Contracting Co., Inc. (8 employees). Most subscribers, however, replaced other METs or carriers with UIT—e.g., Alabama Metal Industries Corp. (5 employees) replaced Blue Cross/Blue Shield, Clean Rental Services, Inc. (35 employees) replaced

Central States Teamster Union, and Atlanta Glaziers Local Union # 1940 Health and Welfare Fund (91 members) replaced Durham Life Insurance Co.

Without inquiring into other assets or purposes of the subscribers, the purpose stated in the Agreement and Declaration of Trust establishing UIT and thus the purpose of those who subscribed to UIT, was "to provide, through policies issued by insurers, life, accident-and-health, sickness-and-health, disability-income, hospital benefits, surgical-benefits, dental-care, and pre-paid-legal-expenses insurance for the use and the benefit of insured employees and of their families and dependents." The group health insurance policy UIT obtained from Occidental Life Insurance Company of California may provide less benefits than those listed in the UIT trust agreement, but clearly employers and employee organizations subscribe to UIT with the intent to provide health insurance, which is covered by ERISA s 3(1), 29 U.S.C. s 1002(1). It is equally clear from participation agreements found in the record that the persons benefiting from the group hospitalization are employees of employers or members of the employee organizations that subscribed to UIT and are financing the participation.

Many of the subscriptions were methods of fulfilling collective bargaining agreements between employers and unions to furnish health insurance benefits to employees. In these situations, the employer or employee organization, or both, were committed to providing benefits to employees or members through the purchase of health insurance on a continuing basis. In some cases, as noted above, unions or employers were already furnishing insurance benefits and merely substituted UIT for other METs or carriers while continuing to furnish health insurance coverage.

Finally, as stipulated in the Articles of Trust of UIT, the subscribers, the beneficiaries, and UIT itself looked to the group health insurance policy and insurer to determine the eligibility requirements to receive benefits and "all other terms, conditions, limitations, restrictions, and provisions applicable to a policy of group insurance." This commonsense approach adequately serves the needs of most employers and unions seeking to provide health insurance to employees at an ascertainable cost; they can agree to furnish only what the insurer contracts to furnish and avoid any unforeseen liability for, or denial of, benefits to employees. For the same reasons employers and unions normally will not require any procedures in addition to those required by the insurer.

Thus, it appears that employers or unions that subscribed to UIT to furnish health insurance for employees or members (either pursuant to an agreement or pursuant to a continuing practice of purchasing the insurance for a class of employees) established employee welfare benefit plans. It also appears that some subscribers that previously had not furnished health insurance to their employees or members, and that did not subscribe to UIT pursuant to an agreement to furnish health benefits, nevertheless did purchase benefits for a substantial percentage of a class of employees or members under circumstances tending to show an anticipated continuing furnishing of such benefits (either through an MET or insurance carrier or otherwise); these subscribers too established employee welfare benefit plans. Thus, it appears that nu-

merous subscribers to UIT established employee welfare benefit plans; with respect
to each of these, ERISA conferred subject matter jurisdiction on the district court.

IV.

The former Fifth Circuit in Taggart Corp. v. Life & Health Benefits Administration,
617 F.2d 1208 (5th Cir. 1980), *cert. denied sub nom.* Taggart Corp. v. Efros, 450 U.S.
1030, 101 S. Ct. 1739, 68 L. Ed. 2d 225 (1981), held that the MET, which was providing group insurance to employers too small to qualify for group rates on their
own, was not itself an employee welfare benefit plan and that Taggart Corporation's
subscription to the MET to furnish insurance coverage to Taggart Corporation's sole
employee did not constitute a "plan, fund, or program" within the meaning of ERISA
s 3(1), 29 U.S.C. s 1002(1).

We agree with the holding and reasoning of the former Fifth that the MET itself
was not an employee welfare benefit plan, *see* Taggart, 617 F.2d at 1210. We also agree
that there was no employee welfare benefit plan in Taggart. Plaintiffs Kansas and Taggart
Corporation alleged that the MET was the welfare plan. Neither party argued that Taggart Corporation had a plan, fund, or program. Taggart, 617 F.2d at 1211. Moreover,
the Taggart district court appeared to agree with the parties that Taggart Corporation
did not have a welfare plan when it found that the MET insured some employees
directly and the "circumstances surrounding the submission of the subscription agreement by Stanley M. Kansas ... simply involve(d) the purchase of insurance by plaintiff,
Stanley M. Kansas, for himself and his family." Taggert [sic] Corporation v. Efros, 475
F. Supp. 124 (S.D. Tex. 1979), *aff'd. sub nom.* Taggart Corp. v. Life & Health Benefits
Administration, 617 F.2d 1208 (5th Cir. 1980), *cert. denied,* 450 U.S. 1030, 101 S. Ct.
1739, 68 L. Ed. 2d 225 (1981). The district court's findings of fact were not clearly er-
roneous, and under those facts the district court was entitled to conclude that Taggart
Corporation's involvement in the transaction was not such that it established or main-
tained a plan, fund, or program. *See also* Hamberlin v. VIP Insurance Trust, 434 F.
Supp. 1196 (D. Ariz. 1977); 29 C.F.R. s 2510.3-1(j); note 13 *supra.*

Although we agree with the holding in Taggart, we find the reasoning of the opinion
that Taggart Corporation did not have a "plan, fund or program" encourages too broad
an interpretation. If Taggart is interpreted to mean ERISA does not regulate purchases
of health insurance when there is no welfare plan, we agree. The purchase of insurance
is only a method of implementing a plan, fund, or program and is evidence of the
existence of a plan but is not itself a plan. If Taggart implies that an employer or employee organization that only purchases a group health insurance policy or subscribes
to a MET to provide health insurance to its employees or members cannot be said to
have established or maintained an employee welfare benefit plan, we disagree. To that
extent Taggart shall no longer be binding in the Eleventh Circuit.

V.

We hold only that the district court had subject matter jurisdiction over this case.
We have not determined how many subscribers established or maintained plans or
if any defendant is a fiduciary to any plan. The judgment of the district court dis-

missing the case is REVERSED and the case is REMANDED for proceedings not inconsistent with this opinion.

Firestone Tire & Rubber Co. v. Bruch
489 U.S. 101 (1989)

Justice O'CONNOR delivered the opinion of the Court.

This case presents two questions concerning the Employee Retirement Income Security Act of 1974 (ERISA), 88 Stat. 829, as amended, 29 U.S.C. § 1001 *et seq.* First, we address the appropriate standard of judicial review of benefit determinations by fiduciaries or plan administrators under ERISA. Second, we determine which persons are "participants" entitled to obtain information about benefit plans covered by ERISA.

I

Late in 1980, petitioner Firestone Tire and Rubber Company (Firestone) sold, as going concerns, the five plants composing its Plastics Division to Occidental Petroleum Company (Occidental). Most of the approximately 500 salaried employees at the five plants were rehired by Occidental and continued in their same positions without interruption and at the same rates of pay. At the time of the sale, Firestone maintained three pension and welfare benefit plans for its employees: a termination pay plan, a retirement plan, and a stock purchase plan. Firestone was the sole source of funding for the plans and had not established separate trust funds out of which to pay the benefits from the plans. All three of the plans were either "employee welfare benefit plans" or "employee pension benefit plans" governed (albeit in different ways) by ERISA. By operation of law, Firestone itself was the administrator, 29 U.S.C. § 1002(16)(A)(ii), and fiduciary, § 1002(21)(A), of each of these "unfunded" plans. At the time of the sale of its Plastics Division, Firestone was not aware that the termination pay plan was governed by ERISA, and therefore had not set up a claims procedure, § 1133, nor complied with ERISA's reporting and disclosure obligations, §§ 1021–1031, with respect to that plan.

Respondents, six Firestone employees who were rehired by Occidental, sought severance benefits from Firestone under the termination pay plan. In relevant part, that plan provides as follows:

> "If your service is discontinued prior to the time you are eligible for pension benefits, you will be given termination pay if released because of a reduction in work force or if you become physically or mentally unable to perform your job.

> "The amount of termination pay you will receive will depend on your period of credited company service."

Several of the respondents also sought information from Firestone regarding their benefits under all three of the plans pursuant to certain ERISA disclosure provisions. *See* §§ 1024(b)(4), 1025(a). Firestone denied respondents severance benefits on the ground that the sale of the Plastics Division to Occidental did not constitute a "reduction in work force" within the meaning of the termination pay plan. In addition, Firestone denied the requests for information concerning benefits under the three plans. Firestone concluded that respondents were not entitled to the information because they were no longer "participants" in the plans.

Respondents then filed a class action on behalf of "former, salaried, non-union employees who worked in the five plants that comprised the Plastics Division of Firestone." Complaint ¶ 9, App. 94. The action was based on § 1132(a)(1), which provides that a "civil action may be brought … by a participant or beneficiary [of a covered plan] … (A) for the relief provided for in [§ 1132(c)], [and] (B) to recover benefits due to him under the terms of his plan." In Count I of their complaint, respondents alleged that they were entitled to severance benefits because Firestone's sale of the Plastics Division to Occidental constituted a "reduction in work force" within the meaning of the termination pay plan. Complaint ¶¶ 23–44, App. 98–104. In Count VII, respondents alleged that they were entitled to damages under § 1132(c) because Firestone had breached its reporting obligations under § 1025(a). Complaint ¶¶ 87–94, App. 104–106.

The District Court granted Firestone's motion for summary judgment. 640 F. Supp. 519 (E.D. Pa. 1986). With respect to Count I, the District Court held that Firestone had satisfied its fiduciary duty under ERISA because its decision not to pay severance benefits to respondents under the termination pay plan was not arbitrary or capricious. *Id.*, at 521–526. With respect to Count VII, the District Court held that, although § 1024(b)(4) imposes a duty on a plan administrator to respond to written requests for information about the plan, that duty extends only to requests by plan participants and beneficiaries. Under ERISA a plan participant is "any employee or former employee … who is or may become eligible to receive a benefit of any type from an employee benefit plan." § 1002(7). A beneficiary is "a person designated by a participant, or by the terms of an employee benefit plan, who is or may become entitled to a benefit thereunder." § 1002(8). The District Court concluded that respondents were not entitled to damages under § 1132(c) because they were not plan "participants" or "beneficiaries" at the time they requested information from Firestone. 640 F. Supp., at 534.

The Court of Appeals reversed the District Court's grant of summary judgment on Counts I and VII. 828 F.2d 134 (CA3 1987). With respect to Count I, the Court of Appeals acknowledged that most federal courts have reviewed the denial of benefits by ERISA fiduciaries and administrators under the arbitrary and capricious standard. *Id.*, at 138 (citing cases). It noted, however, that the arbitrary and capricious standard had been softened in cases where fiduciaries and administrators had some bias or adverse interest. *Id.*, at 138–140. *See, e.g., Jung v. FMC Corp.*, 755 F.2d 708, 711–712 (CA9 1985) (where "the employer's denial of benefits to a class avoids a very considerable outlay [by the employer], the reviewing court should consider that fact in applying the arbitrary and capricious standard of review," and "[l]ess deference should be given to the trustee's decision"). The Court of Appeals held that where an employer is itself the fiduciary and administrator of an unfunded benefit plan, its decision to deny benefits should be subject to *de novo* judicial review. It reasoned that in such situations deference is unwarranted given the lack of assurance of impartiality on the part of the employer. 828 F.2d, at 137–145. With respect to Count VII, the Court of Appeals held that the right to request and receive information about an employee benefit plan "most sensibly extend[s] both to people who are in fact entitled to a benefit under the plan and to those who claim to be but in fact are not." *Id.*, at 153. Because the District Court had applied different legal standards in granting summary judgment in favor of Firestone on Counts I and VII, the Court of Appeals remanded the case for further proceedings consistent with its opinion.

We granted certiorari, 485 U.S. 986, 108 S. Ct. 1288, 99 L. Ed. 2d 498 (1988), to resolve the conflicts among the Courts of Appeals as to the appropriate standard of review in actions under § 1132(a)(1)(B) and the interpretation of the term "participant" in § 1002(7). We now affirm in part, reverse in part, and remand the case for further proceedings.

II

ERISA provides "a panoply of remedial devices" for participants and beneficiaries of benefit plans. *Massachusetts Mutual Life Ins. Co. v. Russell,* 473 U.S. 134, 146, 105 S. Ct. 3085, 3092, 87 L. Ed. 2d 96 (1985). Respondents' action asserting that they were entitled to benefits because the sale of Firestone's Plastics Division constituted a "reduction in work force" within the meaning of the termination pay plan was based on the authority of § 1132(a)(1)(B). That provision allows a suit to recover benefits due under the plan, to enforce rights under the terms of the plan, and to obtain a declaratory judgment of future entitlement to benefits under the provisions of the plan contract. The discussion which follows is limited to the appropriate standard of review in § 1132(a)(1)(B)actions challenging denials of benefits based on plan interpretations. We express no view as to the appropriate standard of review for actions under other remedial provisions of ERISA.

A

Although it is a "comprehensive and reticulated statute," *Nachman Corp. v. Pension Benefit Guaranty Corp.,* 446 U.S. 359, 361, 100 S. Ct. 1723, 1726, 64 L. Ed. 2d 354 (1980), ERISA does not set out the appropriate standard of review for actions under § 1132(a)(1)(B) challenging benefit eligibility determinations. To fill this gap, federal courts have adopted the arbitrary and capricious standard developed under 61 Stat. 157, 29 U.S.C. § 186(c), a provision of the Labor Management Relations Act, 1947 (LMRA). *See, e.g., Struble v. New Jersey Brewery Employees' Welfare Trust Fund,* 732 F.2d 325, 333 (CA3 1984); *Bayles v. Central States, Southeast and Southwest Areas Pension Fund,* 602 F.2d 97, 99–100, and n. 3 (CA5 1979). In light of Congress' general intent to incorporate much of LMRA fiduciary law into ERISA, *see NLRB v. Amax Coal Co.,* 453 U.S. 322, 332, 101 S. Ct. 2789, 2795–2796, 69 L. Ed. 2d 672 (1981), and because ERISA, like the LMRA, imposes a duty of loyalty on fiduciaries and plan administrators, Firestone argues that the LMRA arbitrary and capricious standard should apply to ERISA actions. *See* Brief for Petitioners 13–14. A comparison of the LMRA and ERISA, however, shows that the *wholesale* importation of the arbitrary and capricious standard into ERISA is unwarranted.

In relevant part, 29 U.S.C. § 186(c) authorizes unions and employers to set up pension plans jointly and provides that contributions to such plans be made "for the

sole and exclusive benefit of the employees ... and their families and dependents."
The LMRA does not provide for judicial review of the decisions of LMRA trustees.
Federal courts adopted the arbitrary and capricious standard both as a standard of
review and, more importantly, as a means of asserting jurisdiction over suits under
§ 186(c) by beneficiaries of LMRA plans who were denied benefits by trustees. *See
Van Boxel v. Journal Co. Employees' Pension Trust,* 836 F.2d 1048, 1052 (CA7 1987)
("[W]hen a plan provision as interpreted had the effect of denying an application
for benefits unreasonably, or as it came to be said, arbitrarily and capriciously, courts
would hold that the plan as 'structured' was not for the sole and exclusive benefit of
the employees, so that the denial of benefits violated [§ 186(c)])." *See also* Comment,
The Arbitrary and Capricious Standard Under ERISA: Its Origins and Application, 23
Duquesne L. Rev. 1033, 1037–1039 (1985). Unlike the LMRA, ERISA explicitly authorizes suits against fiduciaries and plan administrators to remedy statutory
violations, including breaches of fiduciary duty and lack of compliance with benefit
plans. *See* 29 U.S.C. §§ 1132(a), 1132(f). *See generally Pilot Life Ins. Co. v. Dedeaux,*
481 U.S. 41, 52–57, 107 S. Ct. 1549, 1555–1558, 95 L. Ed. 2d 39 (1987) (describing
scope of § 1132(a)). Thus, the *raison d'être* for the LMRA arbitrary and capricious
standard — the need for a jurisdictional basis in suits against trustees — is not present
in ERISA. *See Note, Judicial Review of Fiduciary Claim Denials Under ERISA: An Alternative to the Arbitrary and Capricious Test,* 71 Cornell L. Rev. 986, 994, n. 40
(1986). Without this jurisdictional analogy, LMRA principles offer no support for
the adoption of the arbitrary and capricious standard insofar as § 1132(a)(1)(B) is
concerned.

B

ERISA abounds with the language and terminology of trust law. *See, e.g.,* 29 U.S.C.
§§ 1002(7) ("participant"), 1002(8) ("beneficiary"), 1002(21)(A) ("fiduciary"), 1103(a)
("trustee"), 1104 ("fiduciary duties"). ERISA's legislative history confirms that the
Act's fiduciary responsibility provisions, 29 U.S.C. §§ 1101–1114, "codif[y] and mak[e]
applicable to [ERISA] fiduciaries certain principles developed in the evolution of the
law of trusts." H.R. Rep. No. 93-533, p. 11 (1973), U.S. Code Cong. & Admin. News
1974, pp. 4639, 4649. Given this language and history, we have held that courts are
to develop a "federal common law of rights and obligations under ERISA-regulated
plans." *Pilot Life Ins. Co. v. Dedeaux, supra,* at 56, 107 S. Ct., at 1558. *See* also *Franchise
Tax Board v. Construction Laborers Vacation Trust,* 463 U.S. 1, 24, n. 26, 103 S. Ct.
2841, 2854, n. 26, 77 L. Ed. 2d 420 (1983) ("'[A] body of Federal substantive law
will be developed by the courts to deal with issues involving rights and obligations
under private welfare and pension plans'") (quoting 129 Cong. Rec. 29942 (1974)
(remarks of Sen. Javits)). In determining the appropriate standard of review for
actions under § 1132(a)(1)(B), we are guided by principles of trust law. *Central States,
Southeast and Southwest Areas Pension Fund v. Central Transport, Inc.,* 472 U.S. 559,
570, 105 S. Ct. 2833, 2840, 86 L. Ed. 2d 447 (1985).

Trust principles make a deferential standard of review appropriate when a trustee
exercises discretionary powers. *See* Restatement (Second) of Trusts § 187 (1959)

("[w]here discretion is conferred upon the trustee with respect to the exercise of a power, its exercise is not subject to control by the court except to prevent an abuse by the trustee of his discretion"). *See also* G. Bogert & G. Bogert, Law of Trusts and Trustees § 560, pp. 193–208 (2d rev. ed. 1980). A trustee may be given power to construe disputed or doubtful terms, and in such circumstances the trustee's interpretation will not be disturbed if reasonable. *Id.,* § 559, at 169–171. Whether "the exercise of a power is permissive or mandatory depends upon the terms of the trust." 3 W. Fratcher, Scott on Trusts § 187, p. 14 (4th ed. 1988). Hence, over a century ago we remarked that "[w]hen trustees are in existence, and capable of acting, a court of equity will not interfere to control them in the exercise of a *discretion vested in them by the instrument* under which they act." *Nichols v. Eaton,* 91 U.S. 716, 724–725, 23 L. Ed. 254 (1875) (emphasis added). *See also Central States, Southeast and Southwest Areas Pension Fund v. Central Transport, Inc., supra,* 472 U.S., at 568, 105 S. Ct., at 2839 ("The trustees' determination that the trust documents authorize their access to records here in dispute has significant weight, for the trust agreement explicitly provides that 'any construction [of the agreement's provisions] adopted by the Trustees in good faith shall be binding upon the Union, Employees, and Employers'"). Firestone can seek no shelter in these principles of trust law, however, for there is no evidence that under Firestone's termination pay plan the administrator has the power to construe uncertain terms or that eligibility determinations are to be given deference. *See* Brief for Respondents 24–25; Reply Brief for Petitioners 7, n. 2; Brief for United States as *Amicus Curiae* 14–15, n. 11.

Finding no support in the language of its termination pay plan for the arbitrary and capricious standard, Firestone argues that as a matter of trust law the interpretation of the terms of a plan is an inherently discretionary function. But other settled principles of trust law, which point to *de novo* review of benefit eligibility determinations based on plan interpretations, belie this contention. As they do with contractual provisions, courts construe terms in trust agreements without deferring to either party's interpretation. "The extent of the duties and powers of a trustee is determined by the rules of law that are applicable to the situation, and not the rules that the trustee or his attorney believes to be applicable, and by the terms of the trust *as the court may interpret them,* and not as they may be interpreted by the trustee himself or by his attorney." 3 W. Fratcher, Scott on Trusts § 201, at 221 (emphasis added). A trustee who is in doubt as to the interpretation of the instrument can protect himself by obtaining instructions from the court. Bogert & Bogert, *supra,* § 559, at 162–168; Restatement (Second) of Trusts § 201, Comment *b* (1959). *See also United States v. Mason,* 412 U.S. 391, 399, 93 S. Ct. 2202, 2208, 37 L. Ed. 2d 22 (1973). The terms of trusts created by written instruments are "determined by the provisions of the instrument as interpreted in light of all the circumstances and such other evidence of the intention of the settlor with respect to the trust as is not inadmissible." Restatement (Second) of Trusts § 4, Comment *d* (1959).

The trust law *de novo* standard of review is consistent with the judicial interpretation of employee benefit plans prior to the enactment of ERISA. Actions challenging an

employer's denial of benefits before the enactment of ERISA were governed by principles of contract law. If the plan did not give the employer or administrator discretionary or final authority to construe uncertain terms, the court reviewed the
employee's claim as it would have any other contract claim—by looking to the terms
of the plan and other manifestations of the parties' intent. *See, e.g., Conner v. Phoenix
Steel Corp.*, 249 A.2d 866 (Del. 1969); *Atlantic Steel Co. v. Kitchens*, 228 Ga. 708, 187
S.E.2d 824 (1972); *Sigman v. Rudolph Wurlitzer Co.*, 57 Ohio App. 4, 11 N.E.2d 878
(1937).

Despite these principles of trust law pointing to a *de novo* standard of review for
claims like respondents', Firestone would have us read ERISA to require the application
of the arbitrary and capricious standard to such claims. ERISA defines a fiduciary as
one who "exercises any discretionary authority or discretionary control respecting
management of [a] plan or exercises any authority or control respecting management
or disposition of its assets." 29 U.S.C. § 1002(21)(A)(i). A fiduciary has "authority to
control and manage the operation and administration of the plan," § 1102(a)(1), and
must provide a "full and fair review" of claim denials, § 1133(2). From these
provisions, Firestone concludes that an ERISA plan administrator, fiduciary, or trustee
is empowered to exercise *all* his authority in a discretionary manner subject only to
review for arbitrariness and capriciousness. But the provisions relied upon so heavily
by Firestone do not characterize a fiduciary as one who exercises *entirely* discretionary
authority or control. Rather, one is a fiduciary to the extent he exercises *any* discretionary authority or control. *Cf. United Mine Workers of America Health and Retirement
Funds v. Robinson*, 455 U.S. 562, 573–574, 102 S. Ct. 1226, 1232–1233, 71 L. Ed. 2d
419 (1982) (common law of trusts did not alter nondiscretionary obligation of trustees
to enforce eligibility requirements as required by LMRA trust agreement).

ERISA was enacted "to promote the interests of employees and their beneficiaries
in employee benefit plans," *Shaw v. Delta Airlines, Inc.*, 463 U.S. 85, 90, 103 S. Ct.
2890, 2896, 77 L. Ed. 2d 490 (1983), and "to protect contractually defined benefits,"
Massachusetts Mutual Life Ins. Co. v. Russell, 473 U.S., at 148, 105 S. Ct., at 3093. *See
generally* 29 U.S.C. § 1001 (setting forth congressional findings and declarations of
policy regarding ERISA). Adopting Firestone's reading of ERISA would require us to
impose a standard of review that would afford less protection to employees and their
beneficiaries than they enjoyed before ERISA was enacted. Nevertheless, Firestone
maintains that congressional action after the passage of ERISA indicates that Congress
intended ERISA claims to be reviewed under the arbitrary and capricious standard.
At a time when most federal courts had adopted the arbitrary and capricious standard
of review, a bill was introduced in Congress to amend § 1132 by providing *de novo*
review of decisions denying benefits. *See* H.R. 6226, 97th Cong., 2d Sess. (1982),
reprinted in Pension Legislation: Hearings on H.R. 1614 et al. before the Sub-com-
mittee on Labor—Management Relations of the House Committee on Education
and Labor, 97th Cong., 2d Sess., 60 (1983). Because the bill was never enacted, Firestone asserts that we should conclude that Congress was satisfied with the arbitrary
and capricious standard. *See* Brief for Petitioners 19–20. We do not think that this

bit of legislative inaction carries the day for Firestone. Though "instructive," failure to act on the proposed bill is not conclusive of Congress' views on the appropriate standard of review. *Bowsher v. Merck & Co.,* 460 U.S. 824, 837, n. 12, 103 S. Ct. 1587, 1595, n. 12, 75 L. Ed. 2d 580 (1983). The bill's demise may have been the result of events that had nothing to do with Congress' view on the propriety of *de novo* review. Without more, we cannot ascribe to Congress any acquiescence in the arbitrary and capricious standard. "[T]he views of a subsequent Congress form a hazardous basis for inferring the intent of an earlier one." *United States v. Price,* 361 U.S. 304, 313, 80 S. Ct. 326, 332, 4 L. Ed. 2d 334 (1960).

Firestone and its *amici* also assert that a *de novo* standard would contravene the spirit of ERISA because it would impose much higher administrative and litigation costs and therefore discourage employers from creating benefit plans. *See, e.g.,* Brief for American Council of Life Insurance et al. as *Amici Curiae* 10–11. Because even under the arbitrary and capricious standard an employer's denial of benefits could be subject to judicial review, the assumption seems to be that a *de novo* standard would encourage more litigation by employees, participants, and beneficiaries who wish to assert their right to benefits. Neither general principles of trust law nor a concern for impartial decision making, however, forecloses parties from agreeing upon a narrower standard of review. Moreover, as to both funded and unfunded plans, the threat of increased litigation is not sufficient to outweigh the reasons for a *de novo* standard that we have already explained.

As this case aptly demonstrates, the validity of a claim to benefits under an ERISA plan is likely to turn on the interpretation of terms in the plan at issue. Consistent with established principles of trust law, we hold that a denial of benefits challenged under § 1132(a)(1)(B) is to be reviewed under a *de novo* standard unless the benefit plan gives the administrator or fiduciary discretionary authority to determine eligibility for benefits or to construe the terms of the plan. Because we do not rest our decision on the concern for impartiality that guided the Court of Appeals, *see* 828 F.2d, at 143–146, we need not distinguish between types of plans or focus on the motivations of plan administrators and fiduciaries. Thus, for purposes of actions under § 1132(a)(1)(B), the *de novo* standard of review applies regardless of whether the plan at issue is funded or unfunded and regardless of whether the administrator or fiduciary is operating under a possible or actual conflict of interest. Of course, if a benefit plan gives discretion to an administrator or fiduciary who is operating under a conflict of interest, that conflict must be weighed as a "facto[r] in determining whether there is an abuse of discretion." Restatement (Second) of Trusts § 187, Comment *d* (1959).

III

Respondents unsuccessfully sought plan information from Firestone pursuant to 29 U.S.C. § 1024(b)(4), one of ERISA's disclosure provisions. That provision reads as follows:

> "The administrator shall, upon written request of any participant or bene-
> ficiary, furnish a copy of the latest updated summary plan description, plan

description, and the latest annual report, any terminal report, the bargaining agreement, trust agreement, contract, or other instruments under which the plan is established or operated. The administrator may make a reasonable charge to cover the cost of furnishing such complete copies. The Secretary [of Labor] may by regulation prescribe the maximum amount which will constitute a reasonable charge under the preceding sentence."

When Firestone did not comply with their request for information, respondents sought damages under 29 U.S.C. § 1132(c)(1)(B) (1982 ed., Supp. IV), which provides that "[a]ny administrator ... who fails or refuses to comply with a request for any information which such administrator is required by this subchapter to furnish to a participant or beneficiary ... may in the court's discretion be personally liable to such participant or beneficiary in the amount of up to $100 a day."

Respondents have not alleged that they are "beneficiaries" as defined in § 1002(8). *See* Complaint ¶¶ 87–95, App. 104–106. The dispute in this case therefore centers on the definition of the term "participant," which is found in § 1002(7):

"The term 'participant' means any employee or former employee of an employer, or any member or former member of an employee organization, who is or may become eligible to receive a benefit of any type from an employee benefit plan which covers employees of such employer or members of such organization, or whose beneficiaries may be eligible to receive any such benefit."

The Court of Appeals noted that § 1132(a)(1) allows suits for benefits "by a participant or beneficiary." Finding that it would be illogical to say that a person could only bring a claim for benefits if he or she was entitled to benefits, the Court of Appeals reasoned that § 1132(a)(1) should be read to mean that "'a civil action may be brought by *someone who claims to be* a participant or beneficiary.'" 828 F.2d, at 152. It went on to conclude that the same interpretation should apply with respect to § 1024(b)(4): "A provision such as that one, entitling people to information on the extent of their benefits, would most sensibly extend both to people who are in fact entitled to a benefit under the plan and to those who claim to be but in fact are not." *Id.*, at 153.

The Court of Appeals "concede[d] that it is expensive and inefficient to provide people with information about benefits—and to permit them to obtain damages if information is withheld—if they are clearly not entitled to the benefits about which they are informed." *Ibid.* It tried to solve this dilemma by suggesting that courts use discretion and not award damages if the employee's claim for benefits was not colorable or if the employer did not act in bad faith. There is, however, a more fundamental problem with the Court of Appeals' interpretation of the term "participant": it strays far from the statutory language. Congress did not say that all "claimants" could receive information about benefit plans. To say that a "participant" is any person who claims to be one begs the question of who is a "participant" and renders the definition set forth in § 1002(7) superfluous. Indeed, respondents admitted at oral argument that "the words point against [them]." Tr. of Oral Arg. 40.

In our view, the term "participant" is naturally read to mean either "employees in, or reasonably expected to be in, currently covered employment," *Saladino v. I.L.G.W.U. National Retirement Fund,* 754 F.2d 473, 476 (CA2 1985), or former employees who "have ... a reasonable expectation of returning to covered employment" or who have "a colorable claim" to vested benefits, *Kuntz v. Reese,* 785 F.2d 1410, 1411 (CA9) *(per curiam), cert. denied,* 479 U.S. 916, 107 S. Ct. 318, 93 L. Ed. 2d 291 (1986). In order to establish that he or she "may become eligible" for benefits, a claimant must have a colorable claim that (1) he or she will prevail in a suit for benefits, or that (2) eligibility requirements will be fulfilled in the future. "This view attributes conventional meanings to the statutory language since all employees in covered employment and former employees with a colorable claim to vested benefits 'may become eligible.' A former employee who has neither a reasonable expectation of returning to covered employment nor a colorable claim to vested benefits, however, simply does not fit within the [phrase] 'may become eligible.'" *Saladino v. I.L.G.W.U. National Retirement Fund, supra,* at 476.

We do not think Congress' purpose in enacting the ERISA disclosure provisions — ensuring that "the individual participant knows exactly where he stands with respect to the plan," H.R. Rep. No. 93-533, p. 11 (1973), U.S. Code Cong. & Admin. News 1978, p. 4649 — will be thwarted by a natural reading of the term "participant." Faced with the possibility of $100 a day in penalties under § 1132(c)(1)(B), a rational plan administrator or fiduciary would likely opt to provide a claimant with the information requested if there is any doubt as to whether the claimant is a "participant," especially when the reasonable costs of producing the information can be recovered. *See* 29 CFR § 2520.104b-30(b) (1987) (the "charge assessed by the plan administrator to cover the costs of furnishing documents is reasonable if it is equal to the actual cost per page to the plan for the least expensive means of acceptable reproduction, but in no event may such charge exceed 25 cents per page").

The Court of Appeals did not attempt to determine whether respondents were "participants" under § 1002(7). *See* 828 F.2d, at 152–153. We likewise express no views as to whether respondents were "participants" with respect to the benefit plans about which they sought information. Those questions are best left to the Court of Appeals on remand.

For the reasons set forth above, the decision of the Court of Appeals is affirmed in part and reversed in part, and the case is remanded for proceedings consistent with this opinion.

So ordered.

Chapter 13

Fiduciary Rules and Prohibited Transactions

Reading Assignment: ERISA §§ 3(18), 3(21)(A), 3(38), 401, 404, 405, 406, 408, 409, 412

I.R.C. §§ 45E, 4975(e), 4975(f)

Kayes v. Pacific Lumber Co., 51 F.3d 1449 (9th Cir. 1995)

Class Discussion Questions: What is ERISA's definition of who is a fiduciary?

What are the applicable fiduciary standards by which a plan fiduciary is judged?

When must employee salary deferrals under an I.R.C. § 401(k) plan be remitted to the trustee?

What is the purpose of the prohibited transaction rules? Why are they covered in both Title I and Title II?

What are the rules of ERISA § 404(c) in allowing participants to make their own investment decisions?

Overview

Who is a plan fiduciary?

- each plan must name at least one individual as a fiduciary, and the plan document can allow the delegation of duties and assignment of additional fiduciaries

- however, every individual is a fiduciary of the plan to the extent that he or she:

   ○ exercises any authority or control over the management or disposition of the plan assets;

   ○ renders investment advice for a fee regarding plan assets or has authority to do so; or

   ○ has any discretionary authority or responsibility in the administration of the plan

- the DOL takes the view that attorneys, accountants, actuaries, consultants, etc., performing their usual professional duties are not ordinarily considered fiduciaries
- a person may not be a fiduciary of the plan if he or she has been convicted of, or imprisoned for, any of the delineated felonies (such as robbery, bribery, extortion, embezzlement, and fraud)

What are the fiduciary duties and how are they discharged?

- a fiduciary is required to discharge his or her duties:
  - solely in the interest of the plan participants and beneficiaries;
  - for the exclusive purpose of providing benefits to participants and beneficiaries and defraying reasonable plan expenses (i.e., this is the only reason that the plan is set up and a fiduciary cannot have self-concerns);
  - with the skill, care, prudence and diligence under the circumstances then prevailing, that a prudent person would use acting in a like capacity and with like aims (this is stricter than the common law prudent man standard because ERISA presumes a higher degree of expertise for any individual serving as a plan fiduciary);
  - by diversifying the investments of the plan in order to minimize the risk of large losses unless under the circumstances it is clearly prudent not to do so; and
  - in accordance with the documents and instruments governing the plan insofar as such documents and instruments are consistent with the provision of Titles I and IV of ERISA
- in addition, a fiduciary is prohibited from:
  - dealing with plan assets in his or her own personal benefit;
  - involving the plan in any transaction which is adverse to the interests of the plan or to the interests of the participants and beneficiaries; or
  - receiving any consideration for his or her own personal account from any party for a transaction involving the plan assets
- this is an ongoing standard, and therefore, every decision a fiduciary makes is based on this standard, even the decision to delegate certain duties to another individual and the monitoring of such individual to ensure that he or she is properly exercising their delegated fiduciary duties
- the fiduciary is required to maintain the indicia of ownership of all plan assets within the jurisdiction of the district courts of the United States
- any person who is a fiduciary of a plan and who breaches any of the responsibilities, obligations, or duties shall be personally liable to reimburse the plan for losses and to restore any lost profits (however, no fiduciary shall be liable if the breach was committed before he or she became a fiduciary or after he or she ceased to be a fiduciary)

- every fiduciary and every person who handles plan assets must generally be bonded for 10% of the value of the assets he or she specifically is responsible for (up to $500,000)

How can plan assets generally be invested?

- basically, the fiduciaries and trustees can make any investment (i.e., stocks, bonds, real property, futures, artwork, joint ventures) as long as they satisfy the delineated fiduciary duties (discussed above), do not constitute a prohibited transaction (discussed below), and comply with the plan document
- some of the main considerations in plan investments are:
  - whether the aggregate of plan assets is diversified and prudently invested, and whether it is in accordance with the plan's investment policy and short-term liquidity needs
  - if the plan invests in its sponsoring employer's securities, is it limited to the statutory amount of 10% of the aggregate of assets immediately after acquisition and must meet the rules of qualified employer securities (QES, as defined in ERISA § 407(d)(5))
  - if the plan invests in real property, is it limited to the statutory amount of 10% of the aggregate of assets immediately after acquisition and does it meet the rules of Qualified Employer Real Property (QERP, as defined in ERISA § 407(d)(4))

What are the special rules for depositing elective salary deferrals or designated Roth contributions?

- salary deferral contributions must be physically deposited into the plan's trust as of the earliest date on which such contributions can reasonably be segregated from the employer's general assets, but no later than the 15th business day of the month following the month in which the deferrals are withheld or received by the employer

What are prohibited transactions (PTs)?

- a fiduciary shall not cause the plan to engage in a PT if he or she knows (or should know) that such transaction will directly or indirectly constitute a PT
- fiduciaries will be personally liable to make up for any plan losses due to the PT and must restore any personal profits resulting from the PT
- additionally, a court might assess other equitable relief and might remove the fiduciary
- under ERISA, some of the more common transactions prohibited between a plan and a "party in interest" are:
  - a sale, exchange, or lease of any property between the plan and a party in interest;
  - the lending of money or other extensions of credit between the plan and a party in interest;

- the furnishing of goods, services, or facilities between the plan and a party in interest; or

- the transfer of any plan assets to a party in interest, or allowing a party in interest to use or benefit from the use of any plan assets

- the term "party in interest" is defined under ERISA as basically any individual that has an interest in the plan, including employees who are plan participants

- basically, the same transactions are prohibited under the Code as are prohibited under ERISA, but the term used by the Code is "disqualified person" rather than "party in interest"

- A penalty tax is imposed under the Code, whereas civil liability is imposed under ERISA

What transactions are exemptions to the prohibited transactions rules?

- the Secretary of Labor is required to establish a procedure where plans can ask the DOL in advance whether a desired business transaction will be deemed a PT or whether the DOL will issue a private PT exemption letter for the plan

- the following transactions are some of the more important statutory PT exemptions:

  - qualified loans to plan participants;

  - contracting or making reasonable arrangements with a party in interest for office space, or for legal, accounting, or other necessary services to the plan for reasonable compensation;

  - investing assets in a bank or other financial institution which is a fiduciary if certain conditions are met;

  - the purchase of life insurance, health insurance, or annuities with insurers which are fiduciaries if certain conditions are met;

  - the providing of ancillary services by a bank or other financial institution which is a fiduciary if certain conditions are met; and

  - distributions authorized by the fiduciary which comply with the plan provisions and Title IV of ERISA

- although the PT rules seem to bar most transactions, nothing shall be construed to prohibit any fiduciary from:

  - receiving any benefit he or she is entitled to from the plan as a participant of the plan;

  - receiving reasonable compensation for actual services performed and reimbursement for reasonable expenses incurred in the performance of duties; or

  - serving as a fiduciary in addition to being an officer, employee, agent, or other representative of a party in interest

Can participants in a 401(k) plan be allowed to self-direct their accounts?

- if done properly, the true fiduciaries of the plan will not be subject to a breach of fiduciary duty for losses in the participant's respective account balances due to their individual investment choices, but only if:
  - the participants have an opportunity to exercise control, which includes the communication of all information and prospectuses that are necessary for any individual to make an informed decision; and
  - the participants are given a broad range of investment alternatives (they must have at least three alternatives which are diversified, offer materially different risk and return characteristics, aggregately enable each participant to achieve a risk and return level normally appropriate for him or her, and collectively tend to minimize through diversification the overall risk of each participant's portfolio)
- the plan fiduciary is still subject to all fiduciary duties in all actions he or she takes to choose and establish the initial investment alternatives (either through one or several investment companies), monitor their performance, and determine if new or alternative investment choices are necessary
- in choosing the array of investment choices, the plan fiduciary must take into consideration the fees charged to each individual account (currently, one of the top priorities at the DOL, and a growing concern in Congress, is looking at fees charged to plan accounts and determining whether abuses or negligence is rampant)
- there are strict parameters in which plan sponsors can provide individual investment advice to plan participants

What is a blackout period?

- a blackout period occurs when there will be at least a three-day period where participants will not be able to transfer money in or out of an investment vehicle
- the plan sponsor must provide notices to the affected participants at least 30 days prior to the blackout period

What liabilities attach to fiduciaries?

- fiduciaries who breach their duties can be held personally liable for any losses to the plan caused by their action or inaction and can be ordered to disgorge all personal profits

What liabilities attach to co-fiduciaries?

- one fiduciary will be liable for a breach of fiduciary duty by another plan fiduciary if:
  - he or she participates knowingly in, or knowingly undertakes to conceal, an act or omission of another fiduciary, knowing such act or omission is a breach;
  - he or she has enabled the other fiduciary to commit the breach if he or she has failed to comply with the fiduciary duty specifically required for him or her; or

○ he or she has knowledge of a breach by such other fiduciary, unless he or she makes reasonable efforts under the circumstances to remedy the breach

• if the assets are held by two or more trustees, then each trustee shall use reasonable care to prevent a co-trustee from committing a breach and shall jointly control and manage the plan assets and can, by agreement, allocate and limit specific trustee duties

• a trustee will not be subject to liability if he or she merely follows the instructions of the plan fiduciaries, or for the acts or omissions of properly named investment managers

A. Plan Fiduciaries

1. Employee Benefit Plans Subject to ERISA's Fiduciary Rules

All qualified retirement plans (e.g., defined contribution, defined benefit, and hybrid plans) and all non-insured (i.e., self-insured) health and wealth plans are subject to fiduciary rules set forth in ERISA § 404. An unfunded deferred compensation plan maintained by an employer for a select group of management or highly compensated employees is exempt from the fiduciary rules (these are referred to as top hat plans).[1]

2. Who Are Fiduciaries?

The term "fiduciary" has many different meanings under ERISA.

a. Named Fiduciaries

As mentioned earlier, a covered employee benefit plan is required to have a written plan document, name a fiduciary, provide funding procedures, allocate responsibility for the plan's administration, provide for the payment of claims, and provide written notice of the claims procedure.[2] That document must have at least one "named fiduciary" who is either named in the plan document or who, pursuant to a procedure specified in the plan, is identified as a fiduciary by (1) the employer or employee organization with respect to the plan or (2) by an employer or employee organization acting jointly.[3] This named fiduciary (either individually or jointly with one or more other fiduciaries) has the authority to control and manage the operation of the plan. But failure to name a fiduciary under the plan does not enable someone to avoid fiduciary liability under ERISA if they otherwise qualify as a fiduciary.[4] In addition to these formal requirements, the plan may allow the following:

---

1. ERISA § 401(a)(1).
2. ERISA § 402.
3. ERISA § 402(a)(2).
4. *See* Donovan v. Mercer, 747 F.2d 304 (5th Cir. 1984).

- A person or group of persons may serve in more than one fiduciary capacity (e.g., a person or entity could serve as both trustee and plan administrator);
- A named fiduciary or a fiduciary designated by a named fiduciary pursuant to a plan procedure may employ persons to render advice with respect to any responsibility that fiduciary has under the plan (e.g., a plan administrator could employ a recordkeeper); and
- A named fiduciary who has control or management over the assets of the plan may appoint an investment manager to manage (including the power to acquire and dispose of) any assets of the plan.[5]

An employee benefit plan covering employees of a corporation may designate the corporation as the "named fiduciary." If the corporation has been named as fiduciary, the courts are conflicted as to the personal liability of an officer, who in his or her official capacity, acts as a fiduciary on behalf of a corporation.[6]

b. Functional Fiduciary

ERISA §3 sets forth the following definition of a fiduciary that is functional in nature (i.e., if you have or exercise such powers or authority, you become a fiduciary regardless of whether you were named fiduciary) to include a person[7] who:

- Exercises any discretionary authority or control over the management of the plan (e.g., an employer);
- Exercises any discretionary authority or control over the management or disposition of the plan assets (e.g., a trustee);
- Renders investment advice for a fee or otherwise receives monies or property from the plan (referred to as §3(21) investment advice fiduciary); and
- Has discretionary authority or responsibility in the administration of the plan (e.g., a plan administrator, who is referred to as a §3(16) fiduciary).[8]

These are prefaced with the phrase "to the extent" the person performs one of the above functions, which means a person can be a fiduciary for one function but not a fiduciary for another (e.g., the plan administrator has responsibility for plan administration, not for investment of plan assets). Individuals who hold certain positions relative to an employee benefit plan may be a fiduciary because their positions require them to perform one or more of the core fiduciary functions (e.g., the trustee of the plan or the plan administrator).

The determination of whether a person is a fiduciary is generally a factual inquiry and requires one to examine the specific facts and circumstances of each case. Gen-

---

5. ERISA §402(c)(1)–(3).
6. *See* Kayes v. Pacific Lumber Company, 51 F.3d 1449 (9th Cir. 1995); Confer v. Custom Eng'g Co., 952 F.2d 34, 38 n.4 (3d Cir. 1991).
7. ERISA §3(9) defines a "person" to mean an individual, partnership, joint venture, corporation, mutual company, joint-stock company, trust, estate, unincorporated organization, association, or employee organization.
8. ERISA §3(21)(A).

erally, employers will be held to be fiduciaries to some extent due to their discretionary authority over the administration of the plan (e.g., in choosing the plan administrator and adopting plan procedures). Read the case of *Kayes v. Pacific Lumber Co.* in the Materials section of this chapter for an example on how courts determine whether someone is a fiduciary.

c. Plan Administrator

Pursuant to ERISA § 3(16), the plan administrator is the person specifically so designated under the plan document, or if one is not specifically designated, then the plan sponsor.[9] As was noted above in the functional definitions, if the plan administrator has discretionary authority or responsibility in the administration of the plan, he or she becomes a plan fiduciary under ERISA § 3(21).[10] The plan sponsor may name a committee of company officers or employees to serve collectively as the plan administrator, or the plan sponsor may outsource such duties to a third-party administrator (TPA). The DOL's position is that a TPA's administration of the plan can insulate it from fiduciary liability, provided that the plan sponsor has the final decision-making authority under the terms of the plan to interpret the plan and authorize the payment of claims.[11]

d. Plan Trustee

Pursuant to ERISA § 403, all plan assets are to be held in trust by one or more trustees, with certain exceptions for insurance products and custodial accounts.[12] A trustee who has full discretion to manage plan assets is referred to as a discretionary trustee (these are common in defined benefit plans). As such, the trustee makes all investment decisions involving plan assets, including determining the underlying investments and allocating the assets among those vehicles. Alternatively, if the trustee is subject to the direction of a named fiduciary with respect to his or her authority to manage plan assets, he or she is referred to as a directed trustee (these are common in participant-directed 401(k) plans). As such, he or she is responsible for following proper directions (i.e., directions that are not in direct conflict with the terms of the plan, trust, or ERISA). The trust may not permit any reversion of plan assets back to the employer, except in very limited circumstances.

A trustee can be given the power to delegate all or part of plan assets to be managed and invested by a third-party professional fiduciary, provided that professional satisfies

---

9. ERISA § 3(16).

10. ERISA § 3(21).

11. U.S. Dep't of Labor, Emp. Benefits Sec. Admin., *Understanding Your Fiduciary Responsibilities Under a Group Health Plan* (Sep. 2019), https://www.dol.gov/sites/dolgov/files/EBSA/about-ebsa/our-activities/resource-center/publications/understanding-your-fiduciary-responsibilities-under-a-group-health-plan.pdf.

12. ERISA § 403. A custodial account is a savings account held by a financial institution, mutual fund company, or brokerage firm.

the definition of an "investment manager" as defined by ERISA § 3(38).[13] The difference between an investment manager of ERISA § 3(38) and an investment advice fiduciary of ERISA § 3(21) is important as to the liability of the plan trustee. If the trustee has the authority and prudently selects and monitors an investment manager, the trustee will not be liable for the investment decisions made by the investment manager. In contrast, if the trustee hires a § 3(21) investment advice fiduciary, he or she is unable to shift liability to that fiduciary in a comparable way. Due to the shift towards I.R.C. § 401(k) plans, employers and trustees have been increasingly doing more investment monitoring, benchmarking plan fees, and formalizing fiduciary agreements with § 3(21) and § 3(38) individuals.

e. Exceptions to Fiduciary Status

Persons performing ministerial functions in the administration or management of its assets are not considered fiduciaries. Generally, attorneys, actuaries, accountants, and others who render services to the plan (i.e., service providers) are not considered fiduciaries. Persons rendering investment education (as opposed to investment advice) are not considered fiduciaries.

An employer will not be deemed to be acting as a plan fiduciary when performing settlor acts. These involve actions taken by the employer that are considered business decisions, including actions to establish, design, amend, or terminate an employee benefit plan.[14] However, an employer's actions taken in order to implement a settlor decision may well be subject to ERISA's fiduciary standards (e.g., an employer can terminate a plan as a settlor, but its selection of an annuity provider to provide future benefits will be a fiduciary action).

3. Fiduciary Duties

a. General Fiduciary Duties

ERISA § 404 is labeled "Fiduciary duties," which is really a misnomer. "Duties" refers to the jobs and/or tasks that one is obligated to perform in a given role. "Fiduciary duties" as used in ERISA § 404 is really a list of standards of care by which plan fiduciaries will be judged as to whether they sufficiently performed their actual duties. ERISA imposes three standards of care on all fiduciaries of covered employee benefit plans:

- *Exclusive Benefit Rule:* A fiduciary is expected to discharge his or her duties with respect to the plan solely in the interest of the plan participants and beneficiaries

---

13. ERISA § 3(38) defines an investment manager as a fiduciary other than a trustee or named fiduciary who has the power to manage, acquire, or dispose of plan assets; is registered as an investment advisor (under the Investment Advisers Act of 1940) or is a bank or insurance company licensed in more than one state; and has acknowledged in writing to be a fiduciary.

14. *See* Curtiss-Wright Corp. v. Schoonejongen, 514 U.S. 73 (1995).

for the exclusive purpose of providing benefits and defraying reasonable expenses in administering the plan;[15]

- *Prudent Person Rule:* A fiduciary is expected to discharge his or her duties with the care, skill, prudence, and diligence that a prudent person in like capacity and similar circumstances would act;[16] and

- *In Accordance with the Terms of the Plan:* A fiduciary is expected to discharge his or her duties in accordance with the documents and instruments (e.g., the plan document and trust document) that are consistent with ERISA.[17]

A plan trustee has two additional standards of care that are applicable to him or her:

- *Diversification:* A trustee is required to diversify the investments of the plan so as to minimize the risk of large losses (unless under the circumstances it is not prudent to do so). Here there is an exception for employee stock ownership plans; and

- *Indicia of Ownership:* As the federal courts need to have jurisdiction over the plan assets, ERISA requires any indicia of ownership (e.g., a stock certificate) remain within the jurisdiction of the federal district courts.[18] As will be discussed later in this chapter, there is an exception under ERISA § 404(c) for individual direction from participants and for holding employer stock.

As will be discussed later in this chapter, there are a few *prohibited acts* that a fiduciary must avoid:

- Dealing with plan assets in his or her own interest or for his or her own account (e.g., using the plan assets as leverage to receive a discounted mortgage from the bank that holds the plan assets);

- Involving the plan in a transaction whose interests are adverse to the plan's interest or the interests of its participants or beneficiaries (i.e., conflict of interest situations); and

- Receiving any personal consideration from any party entering into a transaction with the plan (e.g., receiving a kickback as a result of the transaction).[19]

b. Investments Permitted in a Qualified Plan

Employer contributions are generally made in cash and then invested by the trustee. In-kind contributions (e.g., transfer of a deed to land) are not permitted for defined

---

15. ERISA § 404(a)(1)(A) (this does not prohibit the employer from deriving "incidental" benefits).

16. ERISA § 404(a)(1)(B). According to the courts, the duties under the prudent person rule are "the highest known to the law," *see* Donovan v. Bierwirth. 538 F. Supp. 463 (E.D.N.Y.), *aff'd as modified*, 680 F.2d 263 (2d Cir. 1981), *cert. denied*, 459 U.S. 1069 (1982).

17. ERISA § 404(a)(1)(D). The Supreme Court has held that the terms of the plan document are paramount and that the statutorily mandated SPD is not a source of the plan's governing terms. *See* CIGNA Corp. v. Amara, 131 S. Ct. 1866, 1878 (2011).

18. ERISA § 404(a)(1)(C), 404(b).

19. ERISA § 406(b)(1)–(3).

benefit or money purchase plans, as this is regarded as a "sale or exchange" under the prohibited transaction rules.[20] The DOL extended that rule to any employer contribution of property used to satisfy a fixed obligation under the plan.[21] Employer cash contributions may be used to purchase any legal investment (e.g., shares of mutual funds, options, etc.), but such investments are subject to annual valuations of their fair market value for purposes of the Form 5500.

If the plan invests in the employer's own securities (e.g., stock), the security must meet the definition of a "qualifying employer security" and cannot encompass more than 10% of the plan's fair market value of assets.[22] Similarly, if the plan invested in the employer's real property (e.g., the employer's manufacturing plant), the real property must meet the definition of an "employer real property" and cannot encompass more than 10% of the plan's fair market value of assets.[23]

While ERISA does not require a plan sponsor of a retirement plan to draft an investment policy statement (IPS), it is considered best practice to do so. An IPS is a document generated to guide the investment committee of the plan in supervising, monitoring, and evaluating the management of the plan, including its investments.[24] The IPS is usually drafted by a plan committee with the assistance of an investment adviser. Even if the plan sponsor delegates investment powers to a fiduciary investment manager, the sponsor is still responsible for its decisions, as it must effectively monitor the manager's decisions. In the context of a participant-directed defined contribution plan (i.e., where the participant chooses his or her investments from the platform made available through the plan), the plan sponsor may wish to consider the employees' demographics and other characteristics (e.g., age, investment sophistication, income range). For example, a law firm may offer a brokerage account as an investment choice, whereas an employer with mostly blue-collar workers would offer investments that participants have a greater chance of using successfully. Plan sponsors should be guided by the prudent person theory in selecting the types of investments and should provide adequate diversification. The IPS usually sets forth the criteria to select, monitor, evaluate, and compare the performance of the plan's investment options, including rate-of-return, fees, and risk characteristics. The IPS should set forth when an investment needs to be removed and replaced. It is recommended that the IPS set forth how fees for the underlying investments are determined and disclosed to participants.[25]

---

20. *See* C.I.R. v. Keystone Consol. Indus., Inc., 508 U.S. 152 (1993).

21. *See* DOL Adv. Op. 81-69A. *See also* DOL Interpretive Bull. 94-3 (Dec. 28, 1994).

22. ERISA § 407(a)(1)(A). A "qualifying employer security" means a security issued by an employer of the employees covered under the plan or by an affiliate of such employer. *See* ERISA § 407(d)(1).

23. ERISA § 407(a)(1)(B). An "employer real property" means real property (and related personal property) which is leased to an employer of employees covered by the plan or to an affiliate of such employer. *See* ERISA § 407(d)(2).

24. *See* 1 STUART D. ZIMBRING ET AL., FUNDAMENTALS OF SPECIAL NEEDS TRUSTS § 7.02[3][D] (2016).

25. *See* Rebecca Moore, *Steps for Creating an Effective IPS*, PLANSPONSOR (Feb. 4, 2020), https://www.plansponsor.com/in-depth/steps-creating-effective-ips/.

In the past, the DOL has opined on the question of whether a plan fiduciary can invest in economically targeted investments (i.e., investments that promote collateral social policy goals in addition to investment return, such as promoting the environment) if such strategy complies with their fiduciary obligations.[26] In its most recent guidance, the DOL reaffirmed its longstanding position that ERISA fiduciaries may not sacrifice investment returns or assume greater investment risks as a means of promoting collateral social policy goals.[27] However, plan fiduciaries can use such collateral considerations as tie-breakers for an investment choice.[28] The DOL also had held that plan fiduciaries may not routinely incur significant plan expenses to pay for the costs of shareholder resolutions or special shareholder meetings, or to initiate or actively sponsor proxy fights on environmental or social issues.[29]

4. Rules for Remittance of Employee Salary Deferrals

Because the DOL views plan assets to include employee elective salary deferrals, it requires such remittance of salary deferrals to be made to the trust at the earliest date on which such contributions can reasonably be segregated from the employer's general assets.[30] It interprets this rule in a variety of ways:

- For large employers, the maximum time period for remittance is no later than the 15th business day of the month following the month in which the participant contributions are withheld or received by the employer (e.g., January deferrals must be remitted no later than February 15).[31] This 15-day period is not a safe harbor (if the employer can remit the deferrals earlier, it should do so). Failure to remit on the earliest date the employer can segregate the deferrals from its general assets will result in a prohibited transaction.

---

26. Labor Reg. § 2509.08-1 (stating that a fiduciary may never subordinate the economic interests of the plan to unrelated objectives and may not select investments on the basis of any factor other than the economic interest of the plan except in very limited circumstances). Generally, investors of economically targeted investments rely on the United Nations Sustainable Development Goals as a guide, see https://www.un.org/sustainabledevelopment/sustainable-development-goals/.

27. See U.S. Dep't of Labor, Field Assistance Bulletin No. 2018-01 (Apr. 23, 2018), https://www. dol.gov/agencies/ebsa/employers-and-advisers/guidance/field-assistance-bulletins/2018-01. See also, Prop. Reg. § 2550.404a, Investment Duties, 85 Fed. Reg. 39113 (June 23, 2020) which were finalized in Treas. Reg. §2550.404a, Investment Duties, Fact Sheet available at https://www.dol.gov/ agencies/ ebsa/about-ebsa/our-activities/resource-center/fact-sheets/final-rule-on-financial-factors-in-selecting-plan-investments (Oct. 30, 2020).

28. See U.S. Dep't of Labor, EBSA, Interpretive Bulletin 2015-01 (IB 2015-01) (Oct. 26, 2015) (noting in the Preamble, "if a fiduciary prudently determines that an investment is appropriate based solely on economic considerations, including those that may derive from environmental, social, and governance [(ESG)] factors, the fiduciary may make the investment without regard to any collateral benefits the investment may also promote").

29. FAS 2018-01, supra note 28.

30. Labor Reg. § 2510.3-102(a)(1).

31. Labor Reg. § 2510.3-102(b) (maximum time period for employee pension benefit plans).

- For plans with fewer than 100 participants, the DOL provides a seven-business-day safe harbor for remitting salary deferrals (i.e., seven business days after the day in which the participant contributions are withheld or received by the employer).[32]

B. Prohibited Transactions and Prohibited Acts

1. Title I's Prohibited Transactions and Prohibited Acts Rules

Title I sets out five specific categories of transactions, direct or indirect, that constitute a prohibited transaction if they occur between the plan and a party in interest. The term "party in interest" includes: any fiduciary, counsel, or employee of the plan; any service provider to the plan; the employer whose employees are covered under the plan; any owner of 50% or more interest in the employer; a union whose members are covered under the plan; certain relatives and owners of the above parties in interest; an employee, officer, director, 10% shareholder, or 10% partner of certain parties in interest mentioned above.[33] The following are five categories of transactions that constitute prohibited transactions if they occur between the plan (through a plan fiduciary) and a party in interest:

- A sale or exchange (or leasing of property);
- Lending of money or other extension of credit;
- Furnishing of goods, services, or facilities;
- The transfer to, or use by or for the benefit of; and
- Acquisition on behalf of the plan of any employer security or employer real property in violation of ERISA § 407.[34]

In addition, ERISA lists the following activities that involve self-dealing and are thus are referred to as prohibited acts:

- The plan fiduciary deals with the plan assets for his or her own personal interest;
- The plan fiduciary receives consideration for his or her own benefit from a party in connection with a transaction involving plan assets; and
- The plan fiduciary is involved in a transaction that deals with plan assets on behalf of a party whose interests are either adverse to the interest of the plan or its plan participants and beneficiaries.[35]

---

32. Labor Reg. § 2510.3-102(a)(2).
33. ERISA § 3(14).
34. ERISA § 406(a)(1).
35. ERISA § 406(b).

2. The Code's Prohibited Transactions

The Code has a similar list of prohibited transactions, but it includes the activities that involve self-dealing on the part of the plan fiduciary as prohibited transactions and not separate prohibited acts.[36] However, the Code's prohibited transaction rules use the term "disqualified persons" (not parties in interest). The term "disqualified person" includes the same list of persons named as parties in interest under Title I, except that all employees are considered to be parties in interest. Only employees earning at least 10% of the employer's payroll are considered disqualified persons under the Code.[37] While engaging in a Title I prohibited transaction or prohibited activity can subject the plan fiduciary to civil penalties, the Code's prohibited transactions subjects the plan fiduciary and/or disqualified person to a tax penalty. The tax penalty is 15% of the amount involved with respect to the prohibited transaction and an additional 100% tax if the prohibited transaction is not timely corrected.[38]

There are also three important distinctions between Title I's prohibited transactions and prohibited acts and Title II's prohibited transactions:

- Title I assumes the plan fiduciary knew or should have known that the transaction was prohibited, whereas Title II does not require knowledge;
- Title I imposes liability on the plan fiduciary, whereas Title II will impose the tax on either the fiduciary or the disqualified person; and
- Title I seeks restitution for the plan, whereas Title II seeks a tax.

Due to the Reorganization Act of 1978, the DOL was given jurisdiction over the prohibited transaction and prohibited act rules.

3. Exemptions from the Prohibited Transactions and Prohibited Acts

Both Title I and Title II provide statutory exemptions such that as long as the parties comply with their requirements, no liability will result. They both provide for administrative exemptions that meet the following general criteria: the potential for abuse is limited, the transaction involves a common business practice such that to prevent the transaction would injure participants and beneficiaries, and the participants and beneficiaries may benefit from the transaction.[39] Some, but not all, of the following are important statutory exemptions:

- Plan loans to plan participants or beneficiaries are allowed, provided (1) plan loans are available to all on a reasonably equivalent basis, (2) loans bear a reasonable rate of interest, (3) loans are adequately secured (e.g., usually secured

---

36. I.R.C. § 4975(c) (which imposes a tax with respect to a prohibited transaction).
37. I.R.C. § 4975(e)(2).
38. I.R.C. § 4975(a)–(b).
39. ERISA § 408(a); I.R.C. § 4975(c)(2).

by the participant's vested account balance), and (4) loans are repaid pursuant to specific plan provisions authorizing such loans.[40]

- Contracting for office space or legal, accounting, or other necessary services is permitted, provided that no more than reasonable compensation is paid for such services and the agreement allows the plan to terminate such services on a reasonably short notice.[41]

- Loans made to an ESOP are allowed provided they bear a reasonable interest rate and are made primarily for the benefit of participants and beneficiaries.[42]

- Purchases of annuity contracts from an insurance company for its own employees covered under the plan, if no more than adequate consideration is paid, or furnishing ancillary services by a bank which is a fiduciary to the plan provided certain safeguards are maintained.[43]

- Paying plan benefits to a party in interest.[44]

- Paying reasonable compensation for services rendered by a party in interest.[45]

- Distribution of plan assets by the fiduciary in the event of a terminated plan, provided the termination complies with Title IV and the reversion of any assets to the employer is allowed.[46]

C. Special Rules for Self-Directed 401(k) Plans

1. Permitting Participants and Beneficiaries to Make Their Own Investment Decisions

ERISA §404(c) provides a limited exception to the general fiduciary liability in the context of individually- or self-directed defined contribution plans (i.e., a plan whereby the participant may direct the investments of his or her account balance). It states that if a defined contribution plan permits a participant or beneficiary to exercise control over the assets in his or her account balance, then (1) such participant or beneficiary will not be regarded to be a fiduciary by reason of such exercise, and (2) other plan fiduciaries will not be liable for any loss, or by reason of any breach, which results from the participant's or beneficiary's exercise of control.[47] Due to DOL

---

40. ERISA §408(b)(1); I.R.C. §4975(d)(1).
41. ERISA §408(b)(2); I.R.C. §4975(d)(2).
42. ERISA §408(b)(3); I.R.C. §4975(d)(2).
43. ERISA §408(b)(5)–(6); I.R.C. §4975(d)(5)–(6).
44. ERISA §408(c)(1); I.R.C. §4975(d)(9).
45. ERISA §408(c)(2); I.R.C. §4975(d)(10).
46. ERISA §408(b)(9); I.R.C. §4975(d)(21).
47. ERISA §404(c).

regulations, there are a number of caveats that must be satisfied to take advantage
of this exemption:

- The plan must be an individual account plan (e.g., profit sharing plan, 401(k)
  plan).[48]

- The plan must offer a "broad range" of investment alternatives such that the
  participant or beneficiary can "materially affect the potential return on amounts
  in his account with respect to which he is permitted to exercise control and
  the degree of risk to which such amounts are subject."[49] This means a minimum
  of three investment options must be offered with different risk and return
  characteristics.

- The plan provides sufficient information to participants and beneficiaries to enable them to make "informed decisions" regarding the investment options.[50]

As PPA '06 permitted the use of automatic enrollment of participants under an
I.R.C. § 401(k) plan, it also directed plans with individually directed investment options
to provide "qualified default investment alternatives" for those participants who were
automatically enrolled but failed to affirmatively elect investments for their accounts.[51]
As a condition to relying on such default investments, the DOL regulations set forth
what investment products are deemed to be permissible, how transfers in and out of
these products are to be made, and specific notice requirements that must be met.[52]

2. Blackout Periods

As part of ERISA's reporting and disclosure requirements, the plan administrator
is required to notify participants and beneficiaries in advance of any blackout period.[53]
A blackout period is defined by statute to mean a period of at least three consecutive
business days when a participant or beneficiary will not be allowed to direct or diversify assets credited to his or her account, to obtain plan loans, or to obtain distributions from the plan.[54] This usually happens when the plan sponsor decides to
transfer plan assets to another financial institution or when there is a change in the
recordkeeper.

To comply with ERISA's requirements, the plan fiduciary must make certain advance notices and implement the blackout period in a fiduciary fashion in order to
avoid liability should a participant's account lose value during the blackout. The
notice must state: the reasons for the blackout period; an identification of the investments and other rights affected; the expected beginning date and length of the blackout

---

48. Labor Reg. § 2550.404c-1(b)(1).
49. Labor Reg. § 2550.404c-1(b)(3)(i)(A).
50. Labor Reg. § 2550.404c-1(b)(2)(B)(1)(vii).
51. ERISA § 404(c)(5).
52. Labor Reg. § 2550.404c-5(c)(1).
53. ERISA § 101(i).
54. ERISA § 101(i)(7).

period; and in the case of investments affected, a statement that the participant or beneficiary should evaluate the appropriateness of their current investment decisions in light of being unable to direct or diversify assets during the blackout period.[55] This notice should be delivered at least 30 days in advance of the beginning date of the blackout period.[56]

D. Liability for Breach of the Fiduciary Duties

1. Personal Liability

ERISA § 409 provides that a fiduciary who has breached his or her fiduciary duty will be personally liable to make good to the plan any losses (i.e., restitutionary relief) and to restore to the plan any profits he or she made through the improper use of plan assets.[57] A breach of fiduciary duty may also result in the removal of a plan fiduciary. But a fiduciary is not liable for any breach of his or her fiduciary duty that occurred before he or she became a fiduciary or after the individual ceased to be a fiduciary. The statute provides a statute of limitations for initiating such a suit, which is normally six years unless the plaintiff has "actual knowledge" of the breach, in which case it would be three years.[58] More recently, fiduciary litigation has been heavy in two areas: (1) fees—namely, in determining whether fees assessed against the plan investments were excessive and, therefore, imprudent and disloyal; and (2) stock drop cases, where an ESOP holds employer securities that are dropping dramatically in value and therefore is imprudent not to sell off the securities.

2. Co-Fiduciary Liability

A plan fiduciary may be held responsible for another plan fiduciary's breach of duty if:

- The fiduciary knowingly participates in the breach or knowingly attempts to conceal the breach;
- The fiduciary's failure to act prudently enables the other fiduciary to commit the breach; or
- The fiduciary has knowledge of the breach and makes no reasonable effort to remedy it.[59]

---

55. ERISA § 101(i)(2)(A).
56. ERISA § 101(i)(2)(B).
57. ERISA § 409.
58. ERISA § 413(a)(2). In a recent Supreme Court case, the court held that "actual knowledge" for purposes of the three-year statute of limitations means that the plaintiff must in fact have been aware of the information contained in disclosures made by the plan fiduciary. *See* Intel Corp. Inv. Pol'y Comm. v. Sulyma, 140 S. Ct. 768 (2020).
59. ERISA § 405.

3. Bonding Requirements

All fiduciaries and other persons (who are not fiduciaries) who handle funds or property of a retirement plan are required to be bonded.[60] The amount of the bond is the greater of $1,000 or 10% of the funds or property handled, but does not have to exceed $500,000.[61] The intent of this requirement is to assure minimal insurance coverage should the plan suffer loss through fraud or dishonesty by a plan official. There are two exceptions to the bonding requirement: (1) where certain plan officials pay benefits only from the general assets of the employer (e.g., in most welfare benefit plan situations), and (2) if the individual involved is a broker-dealer registered under the Securities Exchange Act, subject to bonding by a self-regulatory entity.[62]

4. Exculpatory Clauses

ERISA forbids the use of any provision (i.e., an exculpatory clause) that purports to relieve a fiduciary from responsibility or liability.[63] However, a plan fiduciary is allowed to purchase insurance for his or her own account to protect against fiduciary breaches, including paying the costs of defending an action against the fiduciary. It also permits indemnification provisions whereby another party (e.g., an employer sponsoring the plan) agrees to satisfy any liability incurred by the plan fiduciary.

E. Paying Plan Expenses from Plan Assets

1. Settlor versus Administrator Functions

The employer is both a plan sponsor, making business decisions regarding the establishment, maintenance, or termination of an employee benefit plan (i.e., settlor role), and a plan fiduciary, making decisions regarding the management and operation of the employee benefit plan (i.e., fiduciary role). Expenses for plan administration, fiduciary activities, and plan qualification can generally be paid with plan assets, provided they are reasonable in amount. However, expenses for settlor functions cannot be paid with plan assets.[64] These expenses should be paid out of the employer's general assets and are deductible under I.R.C. § 162(a) as normal and necessary business expenses.

---

60. ERISA § 412(a).
61. ERISA § 412(a)(2)(D); PPA '06 increased the maximum bond level to $1,000,000 for plans holding employer securities.
62. ERISA § 412(a)(1)–(2).
63. ERISA § 410(a).
64. *See* DOL Adv. Op. 2001-01A (Jan. 18, 2001).

2. Special Tax Credits for Small Employers

To encourage small businesses to establish an employee pension benefit plan, the Code provides special tax credits. Under I.R.C. §45E, there is a nonrefundable income tax credit for small businesses in an amount equal to 50% of the qualified startup costs paid or incurred by the business, up to a maximum of $500 per year for each of the first three years of establishment. The tax credit is available to employers with no more than 100 employees who received at least $5,000 of compensation from the employer in the year preceding the establishment of the plan. An eligible employer must adopt a new qualified defined benefit or defined contribution plan (including a §401(k) plan), SIMPLE §401(k), SIMPLE IRA, or SEP. Qualified startup costs include both costs associated with the establishment or administration of the plan and retirement-related education of the employees with respect to the plan. In order to be eligible, the plan must include one employee who is not a highly compensated employee.

The SECURE Act has a number of provisions that encourage small businesses to become plan sponsors. There is an increase in the business tax credit of I.R.C. §38 (which includes the special tax credit of I.R.C. §45E), raising the current amount of $500 to up to $5,000 in certain circumstances.[65] For small businesses that adopt automatic enrollment for new hires, a further $500 in tax credits for three years is now available.[66]

F. Materials

Kayes v. Pacific Lumber Co.

51 F.3d 1449 (9th Cir. 1995)

CHOY, Circuit Judge.

I. FACTUAL AND PROCEDURAL BACKGROUND

This appeal arises out of an action brought by Plaintiffs under the Employee Retirement Income and Security Act ("ERISA"), 29 U.S.C. §1001 et seq., on behalf of beneficiaries and participants of the Pacific Lumber Company Pension Plan ("the Plan"). Plaintiffs are former employees, or eligible spouses of former employees of Pacific Lumber Company ("PLC") or of its subsidiaries. Defendant Charles Hurwitz is principal owner of Maxxam, Inc. ("Maxxam"), which owns Maxxam Group Inc. ("MGI"), which in turn owns PLC. Maxxam and MGI are also defendants. Defendant William Leone is the former President and CEO of PLC, and former director of Maxxam and MGI. Defendants Schwartz and Iaco are present or former executives of Maxxam or MGI.

---

65. SECURE §104(a), effective for taxable years beginning after December 31, 2019.
66. SECURE §105(a), effective for taxable years beginning after December 31, 2019.

This action was filed in response to the termination in 1986 of the Plan, and the subsequent purchase by PLC of a group annuity contract from Executive Life Insurance Company ("ELIC"). The Plan termination followed the successful hostile takeover of PLC by MGI in the fall of 1985. The takeover was financed by $450 million in "junk" bonds, nearly $100 million of which were purchased by ELIC.

Effective March 31, 1986, PLC terminated the Plan. Pursuant to the Plan's terms, the Plan's fiduciaries chose to pay lump sums to Plan participants with less than $3,500 in vested benefits. For the rest of the participants and beneficiaries, PLC initiated a bidding procedure to obtain a group annuity contract to pay vested retirement benefits. ELIC was added to the list of potential bidders at Hurwitz's insistence. On October 1, 1986, despite negative evaluations (the details of which are relevant to the underlying lawsuit, but not to the outcome of this appeal), ELIC was selected to provide the group annuity. ELIC's bid was the lowest offered, $2.7 million lower than the next lowest bid. In accepting this bid, $62 million in "surplus" Plan assets were captured by defendants pursuant to the terms of the Plan.

Plaintiffs filed this suit on September 25, 1989, contending that the above transactions were in violation of the fiduciary duties of ERISA §404, 29 U.S.C. §1104, and constituted prohibited transactions under ERISA §406, 29 U.S.C. §1106.

ELIC was taken over by the State of California on April 11, 1991, due to its precarious financial condition. Payments were suspended for a short time, and resumed at 70% in May. Subsequently, a Stipulated Order was entered on August 14, 1991, under which PLC agreed to make up retroactively and progressively any shortfall in payments due from ELIC, provide Plaintiffs' counsel with 45 days' notice prior to termination of such payments, and notify all Plan participants of pendency of the litigation and of the terms of the agreement. The California conservatorship concluded with the transferring of all of ELIC's "restructured" liabilities to a newly formed Aurora Life Assurance Co. Aurora's financial stability is undetermined at this point.

On June 12, 1991, the Secretary of Labor filed an action against the same defendants alleging violations of ERISA §§404 & 403, 29 U.S.C. §§1104 & 1103, based on the purchase and selection of an annuity. *Reich v. Pacific Lumber Co.*, No. C-91-1812-SBA (N.D. Cal. filed June 12, 1991). The two actions were not formally consolidated, but were treated as related cases and proceeded concurrently pursuant to the same pretrial order.

On March 8, 1993, Defendants moved for summary judgment on the grounds that ERISA's fiduciary duty provisions are inapplicable to the selection of an annuity provider, and that the McCarran-Ferguson Act, 15 U.S.C. §§1011–1015, precludes relief. The district court rejected both these assertions. PLC has filed a cross-appeal solely as to the holding regarding the McCarran-Ferguson Act.

On April 14, 1993, the district court denied Plaintiffs' request for class certification, finding that the action instead had to be maintained as a derivative suit pursuant to Fed. R. Civ. P. 23.1, and ordered Plaintiffs to file an amended complaint. The district court also dismissed certain named plaintiffs as inadequate representatives, and ordered Plaintiffs' counsel to withdraw from representing certain persons and entities with whom it found potential for conflicts of interest. Plaintiffs appeal this order in its entirety.

On May 11, 1993, Defendants moved for summary judgment on the two § 406 prohibited transactions claims. This motion was granted. Plaintiffs appeal this judgment.

On May 17, 1993, the district court held that PLC, Hurwitz, and Leone were fiduciaries as a matter of law, and that summary judgment as to the fiduciary status of the other defendants could not be determined as a matter of law due to unresolved issues of fact. PLC cross-appeals this order. In the same order, the district court held that Plaintiffs were no longer participants or beneficiaries under ERISA because the group annuity purchase provided them with an irrevocable commitment to payment of all vested benefits. Therefore, the district court held that they lacked standing to sue for any breach of fiduciary duty in the choice of the group annuity. On July 17, 1993, this holding was affirmed on reconsideration. Plaintiffs appeal this order.

Plaintiffs made two motions for interim attorneys fees, on June 13, 1992 and on July 26, 1993. Both were denied on the basis that they were premature; the second was also denied for lack of standing. Plaintiffs appeal this holding.

II. DISCUSSION

A. Plaintiffs' Standing

The district court held that Plaintiffs lacked standing to sue within the meaning of 29 U.S.C. § 1132(a)(2) as they were no longer "participants" of a pension plan because the Plan had terminated prior to their commencing this action. Standing is a question of law which we review de novo. *Ellis v. City of La Mesa,* 990 F.2d 1518, 1523 (9th Cir. 1993), *cert. denied,* 512 U.S. 1220, 114 S. Ct. 2707, 129 L. Ed. 2d 834 (1994).

ERISA § 502(a)(2), 29 U.S.C. § 1132(a)(2), provides: "A civil action may be brought — (2) by the Secretary, or by a participant, beneficiary or fiduciary for appropriate relief under section 1109 of this title." A participant is defined as "any employee or former employee of an employer or any member or former member of an employee organization, who is or may become eligible to receive a benefit of any type from an employee benefit plan." ERISA § 3(7), 29 U.S.C. § 1002(7). The district court followed this court's reasoning in *Kuntz v. Reese,* 785 F.2d 1410 (9th Cir.) (per curiam), *cert. denied,* 479 U.S. 916, 107 S. Ct. 318, 93 L. Ed. 2d 291 (1986), which held that former pension plan participants and beneficiaries who had received all of the vested benefits owed to them under the plan no longer had standing to sue on behalf of the terminated plan. The *Kuntz* court reasoned:

> Kuntz plaintiffs are not participants because, as former employees whose vested benefits under the plan have already been distributed in a lump sum, the Kuntz plaintiffs were not "eligible to receive a benefit," and were not likely to become eligible to receive a benefit, at the time that they filed the suit. Because, if successful, the plaintiffs' claim would result in a damage award, not in an increase of vested benefits, they are not plan participants.... any recoverable damages would not be benefits from the plan.

Id. at 1411. The district court declined to apply an exception to the *Kuntz* holding created in *Amalgamated Clothing & Textile Workers Union, AFL-CIO v. Murdock*, 861 F.2d 1406, 1408 (9th Cir. 1988), which permitted former plan participants to pursue the equitable remedy of a constructive trust imposed on the plan fiduciary's ill-gotten profits.

Congress has since directly addressed the ability of former pension plan participants and beneficiaries to bring suit under ERISA. The Pension Annuitants Protection Act of 1994 ("PAPA"), Pub. L. No. 103-401 (Oct. 22, 1994), amends ERISA § 502(a), 29 U.S.C. § 1132(a), to clarify that former participants or beneficiaries of terminated pension plans have standing to seek relief where, as here, a fiduciary breach has occurred involving the purchase of insurance contracts or annuities in connection with their termination as plan participants. Section 2 of PAPA, 29 U.S.C. § 1132(a)(9), provides:

> [(a) A Civil action may be brought ...]
>
> (9) in the event that the purchase of an insurance contract or insurance annuity in connection with the termination of an individual's status as a participant covered under a pension plan with respect to all or any portion of the participant's pension benefit under such plan constitutes a violation of part 4 of this title or the terms of the plan, by the Secretary, *by any individual who was a participant or beneficiary at the time of the alleged violation*, or by a fiduciary, to obtain appropriate relief, including the posting of security if necessary, to assure receipt by the participant or beneficiary of the amounts provided or to be provided by such insurance contract or annuity, plus reasonable prejudgment interest on such amounts.

(emphasis added). PAPA represents, in part, a negative response to the district court's ruling in this case. As Representative Williams asserted:

> S. 1312 does not represent a change from current law, but rather a clarification made necessary because of recent court decisions. The courts have wrongly held that annuitants are not plan participants and therefore lack standing under ERISA to challenge the decision of the plan fiduciary to dispose of plan assets by purchasing annuities ... S. 1312 is designed to overturn this line of specific court cases.

130 Cong. Rec. H 10621 (Oct. 3, 1994).

Accordingly, under ERISA § 502(a)(9), 29 U.S.C. § 1132(a)(9), Plaintiffs have standing to sue for "appropriate relief, including the purchase of a back-up annuity to remedy the breach." 139 Cong. Rec. S 9874, 9874 (July 29, 1993) (Sen. Metzenbaum). We reverse the dismissal of Plaintiffs' suit.

B. The Application of the McCarran-Ferguson Act to ERISA

In its cross-appeal, PLC argues that the district court erred in holding that Plaintiffs' claims are not barred by the McCarran-Ferguson Act. They claim that the McCarran-Ferguson Act prohibits the construction of ERISA upon which Plaintiffs' suit is based. Specifically, Defendants argue that Plaintiffs' construction of ERISA violates

McCarran-Ferguson because it would impose liability for selecting ELIC as an annuity provider even though ELIC is licensed and regulated by California's comprehensive insurance regulatory system. The McCarran-Ferguson Act, in relevant part, states: "No Act of Congress shall be construed to invalidate, impair, or supercede any law enacted by any State for the purpose of regulating the business of insurance ... unless such Act specifically relates to the business of insurance." 15 U.S.C. § 1012(b). The applicability of the McCarran-Ferguson Act to ERISA is a question of law, which we review de novo. *See General Motors Corp. v. California Bd. of Equalization,* 815 F.2d 1305, 1309 (9th Cir. 1987), *cert. denied,* 485 U.S. 941, 108 S. Ct. 1122, 99 L. Ed. 2d 282 (1988); *United States v. McConney,* 728 F.2d 1195, 1201 (9th Cir.) (en banc), *cert. denied,* 469 U.S. 824, 105 S. Ct. 101, 83 L. Ed. 2d 46 (1984).

The McCarran-Ferguson Act, by its own terms, does not preclude a construction of a federal statute that would affect state law if the congressional act "specifically relates to the business of insurance." 15 U.S.C. § 1012(b). Therefore, it must first be determined whether ERISA in general, or the section of ERISA relied upon by Plaintiffs in particular, "specifically relates to the business of insurance." *Id.*

In *Hewlett-Packard Co. v. Barnes,* 571 F.2d 502, 505 (9th Cir.), *cert. denied,* 439 U.S. 831, 99 S. Ct. 108, 58 L. Ed. 2d 125 (1978), we held that California's Knox-Keene Act was preempted by ERISA to the extent that it attempted to regulate ERISA covered employee benefit plans as part of its comprehensive health care service legislation. It was claimed that because the Knox-Keene Act is a state law regulating insurance, construing ERISA to preempt it would violate the McCarran-Ferguson Act. We rejected that argument:

> [A]ppellant's argument not only ignores those ERISA sections that undeniably "specifically relate" to the business of insurance, but also overlooks ERISA's "deemer" clause, which states that an employee benefit plan shall not be deemed to be engaged in the business of insurance for the purposes of state law. If McCarran-Ferguson applies, therefore, ERISA falls within the clause excepting federal laws that "specifically relate" to the business of insurance.

Id. at 505 (citations omitted). PLC asserts that the pronouncement in *Hewlett-Packard* that ERISA falls within the "specifically relates" exception does not indicate that ERISA in its entirety relates to the business of insurance. Rather, it contends that *Hewlett-Packard* holds only that the portion of ERISA which prohibits state laws from regulating employee benefit plans by treating them as insurance companies falls within the "specifically relates" exception.

The resolution of this issue turns on whether ERISA in its entirety "specifically relates" to insurance, or whether only those sections of ERISA which explicitly deal with insurance should be deemed to "specifically relate" to insurance. We find guidance in the Supreme Court's opinion in *John Hancock Mut. Life Ins. Co. v. Harris Trust & Sav. Bank,* 510 U.S. 86, 114 S. Ct. 517, 126 L. Ed. 2d 524 (1993). The issue in *Harris Trust* was whether the contract was a "guaranteed benefit policy" under ERISA § 401(b)(2), 29 U.S.C. § 1101(b)(2). As a preliminary matter, the Supreme Court held that the McCarran-Ferguson Act did not preclude application of ERISA's fiduciary standards to the insured's management of assets held under the contract. "Instead, we hold, ERISA leaves room for complementary or dual federal and state regulation, and calls for federal supremacy when the two regimes cannot be harmonized or accommodated." *Id.* at ___, 114 S. Ct. at 525. In rejecting the McCarran-Ferguson Act preclusion, the Court stated:

> But as the United States points out, "ERISA, both in general and in the guaranteed benefit policy provision in particular, obviously and specifically relates to the business of insurance." Thus, the McCarran-Ferguson Act does not surrender regulation exclusively to the States so as to preclude the application of ERISA to an insurer's actions under a general account contract.

Id. (citation omitted).

PLC contends that just as in *Hewlett-Packard,* the Court's holding in *Harris Trust* is not conclusive on this issue, because the Court was primarily concerned with the scope of ERISA § 401(b)(2), 29 U.S.C. § 1101(b)(2), which specifically refers to the business of insurance. There are two flaws in PLC's argument. First of all, it is refuted by the broad language used by the Supreme Court. The Court states that "*both* in general and ... in particular" ERISA relates to the business of insurance. *Id.* (emphasis added). Secondly, PLC misreads the saving clause in ERISA § 514(b)(2)(A), 29 U.S.C. § 1144(b)(2)(A), to be evidence that the McCarran-Ferguson Act reserves the business of insurance to the states. It is true that this court has held, and the Supreme Court has implied, that the effect of ERISA's saving clause was to preserve the McCarran-Ferguson Act's reservation of insurance regulation to the state. *See General Motors Corp.,* 815 F.2d at 1310; *Metropolitan Life Ins. Co. v. Massachusetts,* 471 U.S. 724, 744 n. 21, 105 S. Ct. 2380, 2391 n. 21, 85 L. Ed. 2d 728 (1985). However, in *Harris Trust* the Court rejected the argument that the saving clause always prevents application of ERISA:

> [W]e discern no basis for believing that Congress, when it designed ERISA, intended fundamentally to alter traditional preemption analysis. State law governing insurance generally is not displaced, but "where [that] law stands as an obstacle to the accomplishment of the full purposes and objectives of Congress," federal preemption occurs.... As the United States recognizes, "dual regulation under ERISA and state law is not an impossibility[;] [m]any requirements are complementary, and in the case of a direct conflict, federal supremacy principles require that state law yield."

510 U.S. at ___, 114 S. Ct. at 526 (citations omitted).

"No decision of this Court has applied the saving clause to supercede a provision of ERISA itself." *Id.* at ___ n. 9, 114 S. Ct. at 526 n. 9. If this court were to accept PLC's argument, it would be the first decision of any court to apply the McCarran-Ferguson Act to supercede a provision of ERISA.

We find that the saving clause was inserted into ERISA specifically because ERISA relates to insurance, and Congress intended to prevent ERISA from preempting state insurance laws. The logical reading of the statutes and the Court's opinion in *Harris Trust* is that ERISA is not subject to the McCarran-Ferguson Act because ERISA relates to insurance. Although the saving clause generally precludes the application of ERISA's broad preemption provision to state insurance laws, that clause does not prevent the application of ERISA's fiduciary standards in areas governed by state insurance laws. Accordingly, the district court was correct in finding that the McCarran-Ferguson Act does not bar the Plaintiffs' claims.

C. Fiduciary Status of the Defendants

On cross-appeal, PLC asserts that the district court erred in ruling that, as a matter of law, defendants Hurwitz and Leone were Plan fiduciaries (thus granting the Secretary of Labor's and arguably Plaintiffs' motion for summary judgment), and that the status of defendants Schwartz, Iaco, MAXXAM and MGI could not be decided as a question of law (thus denying Plaintiffs' motion for summary judgment as well as Defendants' cross-motion for summary judgment).

1. Is the Issue Properly Before This Court?

Before addressing the merits of the district court's fiduciary status holdings, we must determine whether we have jurisdiction to consider the issue. The question of jurisdiction arises because the district court addressed the summary judgment motion of the Plaintiffs in this action as well as that of the Secretary of Labor in the related action, *Reich v. Pacific Lumber*, No. C-91-1812-SBA (N.D. Cal. filed June 12, 1991). The current case and the Secretary's action were treated as related cases, and the two cases proceeded concurrently pursuant to the same pretrial order. On May 11, 1993, the district court heard arguments regarding motions in both actions concerning the fiduciary status of Defendants. However, at the same time, it heard arguments regarding Plaintiffs' standing as "participants" as discussed above. In an order filed on May 17, 1993, the district court held that defendants Hurwitz and Leone were plan fiduciaries and granted summary judgment on this point, but as to the other defendants, summary judgment was denied. At the same time, the district court held that Plaintiffs lacked standing.

Because only Plaintiffs' action is being appealed at this time (the Secretary's action having been stayed pending the outcome of this appeal), it is asserted that the district court did not rule on the fiduciary status of Defendants in the case at bar, but only made the ruling as to the Secretary's action. PLC takes the position that the district court divested itself of jurisdiction over Plaintiffs' action when it ruled that Plaintiffs lacked standing, and so only ruled on the fiduciary duty question in the Secretary's suit.

In the preamble to the district court's May 17 order, the court summarized that at the hearing on May 11, 1993:

> For the reasons stated at oral argument, the court … granted plaintiffs' cross-motions for summary adjudication in both cases regarding the fiduciary status of defendants Charles Hurwitz and William Leone; denied the plaintiffs' cross motion and the defendants' motion for summary adjudication in both

cases regarding the fiduciary status of defendants Maxxam, Inc., Maxxam Group, Inc., Paul Schwartz and James Iaco.

Defendants' motion for summary judgment for lack of standing in the *Kayes* case was taken under submission.

Kayes v. Pacific Lumber Co., Nos. C-89-3500 SBA, C-91-1812 SBA, 1993 WL 187730, at *1, 1993 U.S. Dist. LEXIS 7280, at *1–2 (May 17, 1993). In the body of the Order, the district court held that Plaintiffs lacked standing and dismissed their action. At the conclusion of this Order, the court stated "IT IS HEREBY ORDERED THAT ... (2) The Secretary's motion for summary adjudication of the fiduciary status issue is GRANTED with respect to defendants Pacific Lumber, Charles Hurwitz, and William Leone. With respect to other defendants, the motion and cross-motion for summary adjudication of the fiduciary status is DENIED." *Id.* at *3, 1993 U.S. Dist. LEXIS 7280, at *6–7.

The preamble to the order reveals that the court ruled on the fiduciary status issue in both cases. The court's statement in the written Order, holding that the Secretary's motion is granted in part and denied in part, reflects the fact that the court determined that Plaintiffs lacked standing and therefore dismissed their case. Once it found that Plaintiffs lacked standing, the district court no longer had jurisdiction over their claims and so only had to rule on the Secretary's motion at the conclusion of the Order.

We find that the issue of fiduciary status is properly before this court. The district court ruled orally on the issue as it related to both parties. The fact that it later found that Plaintiffs lacked standing does not change the finality of that order.

2. Fiduciary Status of Hurwitz and Leone as a Matter of Law

PLC argues that the district court erred in finding that, as a matter of law, Hurwitz and Leone were fiduciaries of the Plan. This court reviews the grant of summary judgment de novo, viewing all evidence in the light most favorable to PLC, the non-moving party. *See Wang Laboratories, Inc. v. Kagan*, 990 F.2d 1126, 1128 (9th Cir. 1993). The facts are not in question here; it is purely a question of law that we must determine.

PLC asserts that Hurwitz and Leone were not fiduciaries because they acted solely on behalf of PLC, who was the named fiduciary in the Plan. Under ERISA § 402(a)(1), 29 U.S.C. § 1102(a)(1), every plan must have a named fiduciary with authority to administer the plan. ERISA permits corporations to be fiduciaries. *See* ERISA § 3(9), 29 U.S.C. § 1002(9) (definition of "person" includes corporation, and ERISA § 3(21)(A), 29 U.S.C. § 1002(21)(A) defines fiduciary in terms of a "person"); *Confer v. Custom Eng'g Co.*, 952 F.2d 34, 36 (3d Cir. 1991).

The Plan at issue named the corporation PLC as the Plan fiduciary. Pacific Lumber Company Retirement Plan, § 11(b). It further went on to provide that the Company could delegate fiduciary responsibilities, but that "[t]he Company's duties and responsibilities under the Plan not delegated to other fiduciaries ... shall be carried out by the Company's directors, officers and employees, acting on behalf of and in the name of the Company ... and not as individual fiduciaries." *Id.*, § 11(e).

PLC's proffered ground for error rests on the contention that where a corporation is the named fiduciary, the persons who act on behalf of the corporation do not become individual fiduciaries by virtue of those acts, even under the functional definition of fiduciary set forth in ERISA § 3(21)(A), 29 U.S.C. § 1002(21)(A). PLC's argument lacks merit.

ERISA § 3(21)(A), 29 U.S.C. § 1002(21)(A), provides a functional definition of a fiduciary which depends, in part, upon whether a person "exercises any discretionary authority or discretionary control respecting management of such plan or exercises any authority or control respecting management or disposition of its assets...." The Supreme Court has held that ERISA "defines 'fiduciary' not in terms of formal trusteeship, but in *functional* terms of control and authority over the plan, thus expanding the universe of persons subject to fiduciary duties—and to damages—under § 409(a)." *Mertens v. Hewitt Assocs.*, 508 U.S. 248, ___, 113 S. Ct. 2063, 2071, 124 L. Ed. 2d 161 (1993) (citation omitted).

PLC does not claim that under this functional test Hurwitz and Leone are not fiduciaries. Instead, citing *Confer*, it asserts that because PLC acted solely on behalf of the corporation, only the corporation is a fiduciary, not its officers. In *Confer*, the Third Circuit held that "when an ERISA plan names a corporation as a fiduciary, the officers who exercise discretion on behalf of that corporation are not fiduciaries within the meaning of section 3(21)(A)(iii), unless it can be shown that these officers have *individual* discretionary roles as to plan administration." 952 F.2d at 37.The gist of the Third Circuit's holding is that where a corporation is designated as the plan fiduciary, an officer's actions will not render that officer a fiduciary where those actions are ones with which the designated named fiduciary is chargeable. In other words, when the named fiduciary does not designate the officer, either explicitly or impliedly, as a fiduciary, the officer is shielded from personally becoming a fiduciary, *id.*, so long as he acts within the corporate form. *See id.* at 38 n. 4.

Insofar as *Confer* holds that a corporate officer or director acting on behalf of a corporation is not acting in a fiduciary capacity if the corporation is the named plan fiduciary, we disagree with the Third Circuit's conclusion. The *Confer* holding is undermined by the decision of this court in *Yeseta v. Baima*, 837 F.2d 380 (9th Cir. 1988), the text of ERISA, and the agency interpretations of ERISA. This court has held corporate officers to be liable as fiduciaries on the basis of their conduct and authority with respect to ERISA plans. In *Yeseta* we held that by withdrawing funds from plan assets a corporate officer of a plan sponsor was a fiduciary, whether or not the sponsoring corporation authorized him to make such withdrawals:

> Under § 1002(21), a fiduciary includes a person who "exercises any authority or control respecting management or disposition of [a plan's] assets." Whether Yeseta was authorized to make the $14,200 and the $25,000 withdrawals or not, he did exercise control over and disposed of Plan assets.... On this basis, Yeseta is a fiduciary under § 1002(21) whether or not he individually, or the business as an entity, incurred a benefit from the withdrawal.

Id. at 386. It was irrelevant for the purpose of § 1002(21) whether Yeseta was acting on behalf of the corporation or outside of his authority. Either way, if he met the functional definition of § 1002(21), Yeseta was a fiduciary. Thus, *Yeseta* rejected the distinction relied upon in *Confer,* 952 F.2d at 37, between officers exercising discretion "on behalf of a corporation" and officers "hav[ing] individual discretionary roles."

PLC claims that *Yeseta* is distinguishable from both this case and *Confer,* because unlike the situation in *Confer,* where the corporation was named as the plan fiduciary, in *Yeseta* the corporate employer was not a named fiduciary. Rather, in *Yeseta,* two of the corporate employees were named fiduciaries. Therefore, the argument runs, Yeseta could not claim to have been exercising the fiduciary duty of the corporation, since the corporation was not a named fiduciary. PLC points out that *Confer* is the only case entirely on point in any federal circuit court. No other cases present the analogous situation in which a corporation is the named fiduciary, but the person acting on behalf of the corporation is charged with being a fiduciary.

Even if *Yeseta* were distinguishable on the ground suggested by PLC, the language of ERISA itself undermines the Third Circuit's holding and PLC's contentions. ERISA specifically provides for personal, as well as corporate, liability. 29 U.S.C. § 1109(a) provides that "[a]ny person who is a fiduciary ... who breaches any of the responsibilities, obligations, or duties imposed upon fiduciaries by this subchapter shall be personally liable...." However, "fiduciary" and "named fiduciary" have separate definitions for purposes of the subchapter containing § 1109. The term "fiduciary" is defined "[f]or purposes of this subchapter" at 29 U.S.C. § 1002(21)(A), and it is a functional definition as noted above. In contrast, "named fiduciary" is given a separate and formal definition in 29 U.S.C. § 1102(a)(2):

> For purposes of this subchapter, the term "named fiduciary" means a fiduciary who is named in the plan instrument, or who, pursuant to a procedure specified in the plan, is identified as a fiduciary (A) by a person who is an employer or employee organization with respect to the plan or (B) by such an employer and such an employee organization acting jointly.

There is no indication that an officer of a named fiduciary cannot be a fiduciary and the personal liability provision asserts that all fiduciaries will be held personally liable, without mention of named fiduciaries. 29 U.S.C. § 1109.

Moreover, 29 U.S.C. § 1110 states that "any provision in an agreement or instrument which purports to relieve a fiduciary from responsibility or liability for any responsibility, obligation, or duty under this part shall be void as against public policy." The section goes on to allow insurance of fiduciaries for potential liability, but not to permit relief from liability. *See* 29 C.F.R. § 2509.75-4 (1993) (interpreting the statute in the above manner). Here, PLC relies upon a statement in the Plan itself to establish that the officers of PLC are not acting as fiduciaries, but are acting on behalf of the corporation. Because that statement purports to relieve the officers from fiduciary responsibility or liability, under § 1110 it is void as against public policy. Application of § 1110 requires one to find first that the person in question is a fiduciary. However, the definition of who is a fiduciary under § 1110 is based on the person's functions, not the title conferred by the Plan. If the Plan itself could not define who was or was not a fiduciary, the § 1110 prohibition against relieving fiduciaries from liability would be rendered wholly ineffective. Therefore, we hold that any interpretation of the Plan which prevents individuals acting in a fiduciary capacity from being found liable as fiduciaries is void.

Agency interpretations of ERISA indicate fiduciary status depends on an individual's functional role rather than title. In an ERISA bulletin answering questions, fiduciary status is consistently defined by reference to ERISA § 3(21)(A), 29 U.S.C. § 1002(21)(A):

> D-3 Q: Does a person automatically become a fiduciary with respect to a plan by reason of holding certain positions in the administration of such plans?
>
> A: Some offices or positions of an employee benefit plan by their very nature require persons who hold them to perform one or more of the functions described in section 3(21)(A) of the Act.... Persons who hold such positions will therefore be fiduciaries.
>
> Other offices and positions should be examined to determine whether they involve the performance of any of the functions described in section 3(21)(A) of the Act.

29 C.F.R. § 2509.75-8 (1993) (Department of Labor). *See also id.,* Question D-4 (regarding members of an employer fiduciary's board of directors); *id.,* Question FR-16 (regarding a fiduciary who is not a named fiduciary). The agency interpretations favor finding fiduciary status for discretionary actions and creating personal liability for breach of the fiduciary duties to which those actions necessarily give rise.

Accordingly, we reject the Third Circuit's interpretation in *Confer* that an officer who acts on behalf of a named fiduciary corporation cannot be a fiduciary if he acts within his official capacity and if no fiduciary duties are delegated to him individually. The broadly based liability policy underpinning ERISA and its functional definition of "fiduciary" compel the conclusion that the district court correctly found that Hurwitz and Leone were fiduciaries as a matter of law. As one court noted:

> The legislative history is replete with indications of congressional concern to assure adequate protection for the interests of plan participants and beneficiaries beyond that available under conventional trust law. Applying a restrictive judicial gloss to the term "fiduciary" itself would, in effect, enable trustees to transfer important responsibilities to a largely immunized "administrative" entity.

Eaton v. D'Amato, 581 F. Supp. 743, 746 (D.D.C.1980) (citations omitted). Were we to accept PLC's argument, a corporation would be able to shield its decision-makers from personal liability merely by stating in the plan documents that all their actions are taken on behalf of the company and not in a fiduciary capacity. We find that this was not Congress's intent when it included the "named fiduciary" provision of 29 U.S.C. § 1102(a)(1). We therefore affirm the district court on this point.

3. Maxxam, MGI and Other Individuals' Fiduciary Status

PLC also contends that the district court erred in failing to find that as a matter of law, MAXXAM, MGI, Schwartz and Iaco were not fiduciaries. PLC claims that there has been no showing of direct fiduciary responsibility. This claim lacks merit. Viewed in the light most favorable to the nonmoving party, the district court did not err in finding that a genuine issue of fact exists. While PLC is correct that fiduciary status rests on an objective evaluation of functions performed, and not on an individual's state of mind, such an objective evaluation will be based on questions of fact regarding discretionary duty and control that must be determined at trial.

D. Class Action Certification

1. Class Action or Derivative Suit

Plaintiffs allege that the district court erred in denying their motion for class certification. The district court found that Plaintiffs had alleged only a derivative cause of action and held that under Fed. R. Civ. P. 23 a derivative suit cannot proceed as a class action because the class representatives' claims were not typical of the class claims. The district court reasoned that under *Massachusetts Mut. Life Ins. Co. v. Russell*, 473 U.S. 134, 105 S. Ct. 3085, 87 L. Ed. 2d 96 (1985), "the beneficiaries in the present case do not have a direct claim. Thus, it is impossible for the present plaintiff's [sic] claims to be typical of the claims of the class, because they do not have a claim, rather they bring suit on behalf of the plan's claim." *Kayes v. Pacific Lumber Co.*, C-89-3500 SBA, C-91-1812 SBA, 17 Employee Benefits Cas. 1174 (N.D. Cal. filed April 14, 1993) ("Class Certification Order") at 5. Therefore, the district court held that Plaintiffs' suit had to be brought under Fed. R. Civ. P. 23.1 and ordered Plaintiffs to file a third amended complaint.

Whether or not an ERISA claim may be brought as a class action is a question of first impression in this circuit. This is a question of law which we review de novo. *See generally, United States v. Yacoubian*, 24 F.3d 1, 3 (9th Cir. 1994). We find that the district court erred in holding that an ERISA action must be brought under Rule 23.1 and therefore erroneously concluded that this suit could not be maintained as a class action.

The district court based its holding that an ERISA suit is derivative in nature on the Supreme Court's holding in *Russell* and on this court's interpretation of *Russell* in *Sokol v. Bernstein*, 803 F.2d 532 (9th Cir. 1986). In *Russell*, the Court held that while ERISA §502(a)(2), 29 U.S.C. §1132(a)(2), authorizes a beneficiary to bring an action against a fiduciary under §409 of ERISA, 29 U.S.C. §1109, the recovery available under §502(a)(2) inures to the benefit of the plan as a whole: "A fair contextual reading of the statute makes it abundantly clear that its draftsmen were primarily concerned with the possible misuse of plan assets, and with remedies that would protect the entire plan, rather than with the rights of an individual beneficiary." 473 U.S. at 142, 105 S. Ct. at 3090. The Court held that extra-contractual compensatory or punitive damages based on emotional distress were not available for a breach of fiduciary duty under ERISA due to a delay in processing an individual's benefit claim.

Although the Supreme Court's holding in *Russell* was limited to § 409 of ERISA regarding fiduciaries' personal liability, this court has extended it to embrace § 502(a)(3), 29 U.S.C. § 1132(a)(3), which empowers certain parties to bring an ERISA action. *Sokol,* 803 F.2d at 535–36. In concluding that extra-contractual emotional distress damages were not available to a beneficiary under § 502(a)(3) of ERISA, this court expanded the *Russell* rationale that ERISA protections run to the plan, not to the beneficiaries: "ERISA grants no private right of action by a beneficiary *qua* beneficiary; rather, it accords beneficiaries the right to sue on behalf of the entire plan if a fiduciary breaches the plan's terms." *Id.* at 536.

This rationale was followed in *Horan v. Kaiser Steel Retirement Plan,* 947 F.2d 1412 (9th Cir. 1991), which held that beneficiaries could not maintain an ERISA breach of fiduciary duty claim because they sought a remedy on behalf of themselves rather than on behalf of the ERISA plan. "Under *Russell* and *Sokol,* the plaintiffs fail to present a fiduciary breach claim if the only remedy sought is for their own benefit, rather than for the benefit of the Plan as a whole." *Horan,* 947 F.2d at 1418.

Sokol and *Horan* reveal that this court has interpreted the Supreme Court's *Russell* opinion to prevent any suit under ERISA for extracontractual damages and to require that an ERISA suit cannot be maintained unless the remedy sought inures to the benefit of the plan. On this basis, the district court concluded:

> The logical result of reconciling *Russell* with the plain language of section 1132(a)(2) is that a participant or beneficiary who brings suit for breach of fiduciary duty, does so on behalf of the plan and not in his individual capacity. While the individual has standing to bring suit, and stands to gain if the suit is successful, his benefit is secondary or derivative of the plan's gain.

Class Certification Order at 4–5.

In so concluding, the district court erred in its determination that this action is a "derivative" one which must be brought under Fed. R. Civ. P. 23.1. Although this suit may be characterized as "derivative" in the broad sense, it clearly does not fall within the terms of Rule 23.1. That rule applies only to derivative actions "brought by one or more *shareholders* or *members* to enforce a right of a *corporation* or of an *unincorporated association*" (emphasis added). Plaintiffs here are not suing as "shareholders" or "members" to enforce the right of any "corporation" or "unincorporated association." Rather, they are suing as plan beneficiaries to enforce the right of the plan against its fiduciaries. When a trust beneficiary brings a derivative suit on behalf of a trust, "the specific provisions of Rule 23.1 are not controlling." Charles A. Wright, *Law of Federal Courts* § 73 at 525 (5th ed. 1994).

As the Supreme Court made clear in *Daily Income Fund, Inc. v. Fox,* 464 U.S. 523, 535 n. 11, 104 S. Ct. 831, 838 n. 11, 78 L. Ed. 2d 645 (1984), not every "derivative" action falls under Rule 23.1. Rule 23.1 applies only to a narrow class of derivative suits: those brought by shareholders or members of a corporation or unincorporated association to vindicate a right which may properly be asserted by that corporation or association. *See, e.g., id.* at 535, 104 S. Ct. at 838 (refusing to apply Rule 23.1 where the shareholder plaintiff suing on behalf of the corporation sought to assert a right which could not properly be asserted by the corporation).

The Federal Rules of Civil Procedure single out the specific type of derivative action described in Rule 23.1 because the law has historically been particularly wary of allowing *shareholders* to sue on their *corporation's* behalf. Because of the fear that shareholder derivative suits could subvert the basic principle of management control over corporate operations, courts have generally characterized shareholder derivative suits as "a remedy of last resort." *Renfro v. FDIC*, 773 F.2d 657, 658 (5th Cir. 1985).

Moreover, the law has generally imposed an intracorporate exhaustion requirement on plaintiffs in such cases. *See, e.g., Hawes v. City of Oakland*, 104 U.S. 450, 460–61, 26 L. Ed. 827 (1881). This requirement is reflected in Rule 23.1, which directs the shareholder plaintiff to "allege with particularity the efforts, if any, made by the plaintiff to obtain the action the plaintiff desires from the directors or comparable authority and, if necessary, from the shareholders or members, and the reasons for the plaintiff's failure to obtain the action or for not making the effort."

Neither the text of Rule 23.1 nor the concerns that motivate its separate treatment for shareholder derivative actions apply here, for the plaintiffs are not "shareholders" suing on behalf of a "corporation." Accordingly, we conclude that the district court erred in requiring the plaintiffs to file an amended complaint complying with that rule.

Moreover, the district court erred in concluding that the class representatives' claims were not "typical" under Fed. R. Civ. P. 23(a)(3). Rule 23(a)(3) requires that "the claims or defenses of the representative parties [be] typical of the claims or defenses of the class." There is no doubt that the named plaintiffs' claims are typical of the class claims. Defendants do not suggest that the named plaintiffs are subject to unique defenses or have different claims from those of any other member of the class. They rely only on the fact that Plaintiffs' common claim is a derivative one rather than a direct one. However, Rule 23(a)(3) imposes only the requirement that the class representatives' claims be typical, not that they be direct. Therefore, we reverse the district court's determination that this suit may not be maintained as a class action.

2. Dismissal of Certain Plaintiffs as Inadequate Representatives

The district court dismissed plaintiffs Kayes, G. Kennedy, Lacy, Maurer, L. Reynolds, and Schoenhofer as inadequate class representatives under Fed. R. Civ. P. 23.1 because it found them to be vindictive toward Defendants on the basis of "their long-standing, multiple grievances against the present defendants...." Class Certification Order at 17.

We review the district court's determination regarding adequacy of representation for an abuse of discretion. *Harmsen v. Smith*, 693 F.2d 932, 943 (9th Cir. 1982), *cert. denied*, 464 U.S. 822, 104 S. Ct. 89, 78 L. Ed. 2d 97 (1983).

Vindictiveness is the eighth factor enumerated by this court in *Larson v. Dumke*, 900 F.2d 1363, 1367 (9th Cir.), *cert. denied*, 498 U.S. 1012, 111 S. Ct. 580, 112 L. Ed. 2d 585 (1990), in its consideration of whether certain individuals were adequate class representatives. The district court based its finding that the dismissed plaintiffs were vindictive on three lawsuits filed by Maurer, Lacy, Filby, Kayes, L. Reynolds, and Schoenhofer against Defendants, and on the fact that Maurer campaigned for a seat on the Humbolt County Board of Supervisors based on an "anti-Maxxam platform." Apparently G. Kennedy was considered vindictive because he initiated an Employee Stock Option Plan in an attempt to buy PLC from defendant Maxxam.

The first lawsuit the district court relied upon, *Maurer v. Hurwitz,* Cal. Super. Ct. No. 76564, was a suit brought in state court seeking essentially the same remedy that is being sought in this case—to recover the reversion that PLC received upon the termination of the Plan. That suit was held to be preempted by ERISA, resulting in the present suit. *Maurer v. Hurwitz* shows no more vindictiveness towards Defendants than does the case at bar, but rather indicates a desire to enforce the same rights. The other two suits relied upon by the district court apparently were shareholder derivative suits regarding the leveraged buyout of PLC. While those suits reveal some animosity towards the directors of PLC for allowing the takeover, or towards Maxxam for taking over PLC, they hardly constitute evidence of vindictiveness to such an extent that these plaintiffs cannot adequately represent the class.

Although it was enumerated as a factor in *Larson,* there have been no cases in this circuit in which a plaintiff has been found to be an inadequate class representative on the basis of vindictiveness. The reason we consider vindictiveness as a factor in evaluating adequacy of representation is to render ineligible individuals who possess animus that would preclude the possibility of a suitable settlement. For instance, in *Lim v. Citizens Savings and Loan Ass'n,* 430 F. Supp. 802, 811 (N.D. Cal. 1976), the defendant argued that "plaintiff's professed 'revenge' motive creates clear potential conflicts with the class because, in this frame of mind, plaintiff is likely to by-pass favorable settlement offers." Even in such a situation, however, the court did not find the vengeful plaintiff inadequate: "Indeed, the vengeance of an aggrieved person more often engenders the zealous prosecution essential to a class action than the *over*zealous prosecution which may threaten to strangle a class action." *Id.* at 812.

Viewed in this light, the lawsuits relied on by the district court hardly demonstrate animus that would jeopardize the interests of the class. Rather, they indicate a desire to protect shared financial interests. Similarly, while it is possible that the plaintiffs might try to use the class action as leverage to obtain a settlement in such pending litigation, *see Davis v. Comed, Inc.,* 619 F.2d 588, 593–94 & 97 (6th Cir. 1980), in the case at bar none of the litigation relied upon by the district court was still pending.

This court finds an abuse of discretion when it has a "definite and firm conviction that the court below committed a clear error of judgment in the conclusion it reached upon weighing of the relevant factors. A district court may abuse its discretion if it does not apply the correct law or if it rests its decision on a clearly erroneous finding of material fact." *United States v. Plainbull,* 957 F.2d 724, 725 (9th Cir. 1992) (citations omitted). By giving undue weight to litigation which was neither pending, nor tending to show unusual animus towards Defendants other than a desire to protect named plaintiffs' rights, the district court may have abused its discretion. On the other hand, two other factors mentioned by the district court—the attempt to buy out PLC from Maxxam by Kayes, G. Kennedy, and L. Reynolds, and the anti-Maxxam platform by

Maurer in his campaign—are factors which could properly be considered by the district court in its determination.

It is impossible to determine what weight the district court gave to each of these factors in its determination that the representatives were inadequate, or what standard it used in finding those representatives to be vindictive. Therefore, we remand this issue to the district court to reweigh the evidence, keeping in mind the policy behind considering vindictiveness as a factor in evaluating adequacy of representation.

3. Plaintiffs' Counsel's Potential Conflict of Interest

The district court also found that Plaintiffs' counsel possessed a potential conflict of interest because Plaintiffs' counsel also represents the PL Rescue Fund and named plaintiffs Filby and Lacy with respect to individual annuities not covered by the present suit. Therefore, the district court ruled that Plaintiffs' counsel had to eliminate these potential conflicts by withdrawing from representing the PL Rescue Fund and from representing Filby and Lacy in their individual suits.

Neither side has cited any case in opposition to or in support of the district court's ruling. Plaintiffs' claim of error seems to revolve around the one instance of a conflict cited by the district court regarding an instruction not to answer a question in a deposition. Plaintiffs claim that the district court erroneously perceived this instruction as an example of a conflict; rather, they argue, the instruction not to answer was based on the attorney-client privilege. It is impossible to discover to what instance the district court was referring, as the court provided no citation to the record. Nonetheless, this argument misses the point of the district court's holding. The district court stated that, although there was no evidence that the Plan's representation had been compromised, withdrawal was necessary to eliminate *potential* conflicts. The district court had previously noted that the PL Rescue Fund had a broader mission than did the class, including pressuring Maxxam to sell its interest in Pacific Lumber.

"The responsibility of class counsel to absent class members whose control over their attorneys is limited does not permit even the appearance of divided loyalties of counsel." *Sullivan v. Chase Inv. Servs. of Boston, Inc.*, 79 F.R.D. 246, 258 (N.D. Cal. 1978). Plaintiffs argue that because the conduct of the litigation has shown no manifestation of divided loyalties, requiring withdrawal was improper. Plaintiffs misunderstand the law. The "appearance" of divided loyalties refers to differing and potentially conflicting interests and is not limited to instances manifesting such conflict. In *Sullivan*, the district court ordered withdrawal of counsel under a similar situation where there had as yet been no reason to believe improper influence had resulted from the representation of two parties with conflicting interests. *Id.* We find that the district court did not abuse its discretion in ordering Plaintiffs' counsel to withdraw from conflicting representation.

E. Prohibited Transaction Claims

1. The Purchase of Annuities from ELIC

Plaintiffs next contend that the district court erred in granting Defendants' summary judgment motion on Plaintiffs' claim that certain transactions were "prohibited

transactions" within the meaning of ERISA § 406, 29 U.S.C. § 1106.13 The first transaction at issue involved Defendants' purchase of annuities from ELIC. Plaintiffs asserted that this purchase constituted a prohibited transaction because Defendants
selected ELIC in order to maximize their recovery of surplus plan assets, and therefore
constituted a transfer for the benefit of a party in interest or self-dealing.

This court rejected this same argument in *Waller v. Blue Cross of Cal.,* 32 F.3d 1337,
1346 (9th Cir. 1994):

> [P]urchasing replacement annuities as part of a plan termination even with
> such alleged infirmities is not the kind of transaction § 406 prohibits. As we
> explained in *M & R Inv. Co.:*

> The party in interest prohibitions [under § 406(a)] act to insure arm's-length
> transactions by fiduciaries of funds subject to ERISA. A transaction with a
> party in interest is prohibited under the presumption that it is not arm's-
> length. The result is a broad per se prohibition of transactions ERISA im-
> plicitly defines as not arm's-length.

> 685 F.2d at 287. In other words, the transaction, itself, should communicate
> the breach. ERISA, however, permits the transaction that forms the basis for
> plaintiffs' § 406 claim—the purchase of annuities as part of a plan termina-
> tion. *See* 29 U.S.C. § 1341(b)(3)(A)(i). Plaintiffs do not allege that either Ex-
> ecutive Life or Provident is a party in interest. Absent such an allegation, we
> fail to see how purchasing annuities to terminate plaintiffs' Plan constitutes
> a per se violation of ERISA, even if accomplished through an infirm bidding
> process or for improper purposes. For the same reason, we also reject plain-
> tiffs' § 406(b) claim.

Id. (quoting *M & R Inv. Co., Inc. v. Fitzsimmons,* 685 F.2d 283, 287 (9th Cir. 1982)).
The district court correctly found that the purchase of annuities from ELIC was not
a prohibited transaction under ERISA § 406, 29 U.S.C. § 1106.

2. The Use of Residual Plan Surplus as Collateral

Plaintiffs allege that PLC also engaged in a prohibited transaction in violation of
ERISA § 406, 29 U.S.C. § 1106, in obtaining a bridge loan to finance MGI's takeover
of PLC. In obtaining the loan, PLC pledged as collateral the right to receive the future
residual distributions from the Plan after the Plan's termination, the purchase of annuities, and other required distributions. Plaintiffs asserted below that this transaction
violated the prohibition in § 406 on dealing with a plan asset for the benefit of a party
in interest. The district court dismissed this claim, ruling that the pledge of collateral
was not a prohibited transaction because the collateral pledged was a contingent right
and not an actual plan asset.

Neither Plaintiffs nor Defendants cite any authority addressing whether a contingent
right to receive plan surplus following distribution constitutes a plan asset. Defendants
cite numerous cases supporting the proposition that residual plan assets can legally
revert to the employer after plan termination. However, this point is not disputed
and is inapposite to whether the use of a contingent right of reversion prior to plan

termination constitutes a prohibited transaction. Defendants also cite case law on security interests indicating that the pledge of the right to receive anticipated funds is the pledge of a general intangible, not an interest in the underlying asset.

This court has adopted a broader functional definition of what constitutes an "asset of the plan" for purposes of § 406. In *Acosta v. Pacific Enterprises,* 950 F.2d 611 (9th Cir. 1991), this court stated:

> ERISA's legislative history makes clear that "the crucible of congressional concern was misuse and mismanagement of plan assets by plan administrators and that ERISA was designed to prevent these abuses in the future." In light of Congress' overriding concern with the protection of plan participants and beneficiaries, courts have generally construed the protective provisions of § 406(b) broadly....
>
> Appellees argue that the term "assets of the plan" encompasses only financial contributions received by the plan administrators. We decline to cabin the term in such a restrictive definition. Congress' imposition of a broad duty of loyalty upon fiduciaries of employee benefit plans counsels a more functional approach. To determine whether a particular item constitutes an "asset of the plan," it is necessary to determine whether the item in question may be used to the benefit (financial or otherwise) of the fiduciary at the expense of plan participants or beneficiaries.

Id. at 620 (citations omitted). It is clear from *Acosta* that "assets of the plan" is not defined in strictly financial terms, but rather is determined by examining whether the "item in question may be used to the benefit (financial or otherwise) of the fiduciary at the expense of plan participants or beneficiaries." *Id.* In *Acosta,* the alleged "asset of the plan" was a participant-shareholder list. In *Acosta,* however, we did not reach the question of whether or not this list was a plan asset; rather, we affirmed on the ground that the fiduciaries' use of the list did not constitute self-dealing. *Id.*

Therefore, in this circuit there is a twofold functional test as to whether an item in question constitutes an "asset of the plan": (1) whether the item in question may be used to the benefit (financial or otherwise) of the fiduciary, and (2) whether such use is at the expense of the plan participants or beneficiaries. In this case, it is unquestionable that the contingent interest at issue was used to the benefit of the fiduciary, by helping finance the takeover. The question is whether it was used at the expense of the Plan participants.

PLC correctly points out that the loan transaction did not jeopardize the assets of the Plan, nor did it affect Plaintiffs' vested benefits under the Plan. The loan document cited by Plaintiffs, which indicates that the loan would be in default if the plan incurred liabilities, evidences the bank's concern with its future interest, but it does not in any way indicate that the bank would be able to reach plan assets upon such a default. Therefore, the Plan assets were never at risk by being indirectly put up as collateral.

In enacting ERISA, Congress was concerned about the mismanagement of plan assets to the detriment of the plan and its beneficiaries. Although in this case the

Plan assets themselves were never put at risk, the Plan fiduciary used funds — which were plan assets — as collateral for a purpose which did not benefit the Plan. The purpose and end result of this use was the termination of the Plan. While this did not directly hurt the beneficiaries, since annuities were purchased, it can hardly be argued that it was for the benefit of the Plan.

It is clear from legislative history that in enacting § 406, Congress was not only concerned with deals between the plan and a fiduciary:

> As in other situations, this prohibited transaction may occur even though there has been no transfer of money or property between the trust and any party in interest. For example, securities purchases or sales by the trust in order to manipulate the prices of securities to the advantage of a party in interest constitute "a use by, or for the benefit of, a party in interest of any income or assets of the trust."

S. Rep. No. 383, 93d Cong., 2d Sess. (1974), *reprinted in* 1974 U.S.C.C.A.N. 4890, 4982. The legislative history goes on to indicate a policy against conflicting interests when contemplating termination:

> The bill also treats as a prohibited transaction investment which jeopardize the income or assets of the trust.... Of course, the prohibited transaction provisions do not prevent an employer, on termination of his plan, from recovering assets not needed to pay plan benefits.... If termination is contemplated, it should be clear that investments are not being made or maintained with the interests of potential remaindermen in mind in any case where this is in conflict with the interests of the participants or beneficiaries.

Id. at 4984–85.

In light of the legislative history revealing a policy against self-dealing in plan termination and this court's policy of interpreting the fiduciary duty broadly, we hold that the collateral for the bridge loan was a plan asset. Corporations should not be permitted to rely on their ERISA plan assets to finance takeovers or other risk ventures. One of the reasons § 406 was included in ERISA was that "Congress was apprehensive that exceptions to the common law rules against self-dealing were unduly eroding the underlying principle and included Section 406 as a barrier to such erosion." *Lowen v. Tower Asset Management, Inc.*, 829 F.2d 1209, 1215 (2d Cir. 1987) (citing S. Rep. No. 127, 93d Cong., 2d Sess., *reprinted in* 1974 U.S. Code Cong. & Admin. News 4838, 4865). It is clear that the fiduciaries involved here had in mind only their own interests, or those of a party in interest, when setting up the bridge loan. Such conflicting loyalties should be discouraged. We reverse the district court's dismissal of this prohibited transaction claim.

Chapter 14

ERISA Litigation

Reading Assignment:	ERISA §§ 501, 502, 503, 514
	Gobeille v. Liberty Mut. Ins. Co., 576 U.S. ___, 136 S. Ct. 936 (2015)
Class Discussion Questions:	What are the three parts of ERISA's preemption clause?
	What are the exceptions for the exhaustion of administrative remedies doctrine in order for a claimant to proceed to court?
	What are the factors a court takes into consideration in deciding whether to award attorneys' fees?
	How do the claims procedures differ between retirement plans and group health plans?

Overview

What is ERISA preemption?

- ERISA preempts any state law that purports to govern employee benefit plans, not employee benefits

- the ERISA "preemption clause" has three parts to it:

  - the general preemption clause states that, generally, the provisions of Titles I and IV of ERISA shall supersede any and all state laws insofar as they relate to any employee benefits plan;

  - the savings clause excludes (or saves) insurance, banking, and securities entities from ERISA preemption since the states heavily regulate these industries; and

  - the deemer clause prohibits anything which fits the definition of an employee benefit plan to be deemed an insurance, banking, or securities organization just so it can escape ERISA preemption

- federal courts, including the U.S. Supreme Court, have not always been consistent in determining ERISA preemption (as a very over-simplified observation, during the first 20 years or so of ERISA, courts were continually expanding ERISA preemption to any state law that even minimally related to employee benefit plans; however, the pendulum seems to be swinging back the other way over the past few years, and it appears that courts are now looking at whether the state law at issue substantially relates to employee benefits plans or whether it is so tangential that it does not realistically relate to employee benefits plans)

Who has standing to bring an ERISA cause of action?

- There are four classes of parties who can bring an ERISA action:
  - participants (includes anyone that has a "colorable claim" for benefits, such as alternate payees pursuant to a qualified domestic relations order);
  - beneficiaries;
  - fiduciaries; and
  - the Secretary of Labor (which means the Department of Labor)

What are the common civil causes of actions under ERISA?

- reporting and disclosure failure:
  - *action:* an ERISA § 502(c) action (as cross-referenced under ERISA § 501(a)(1)(A)) is where a participant or beneficiary in an employee benefit plan fails to receive certain mandatory notices or other information required to be disclosed by the plan administrator
  - *remedy:* personal liability to the plaintiffs of up to $100 per day of failure plus any other relief the court deems proper.
- benefits or other rights:
  - *action:* an ERISA § 502(a)(1)(B) action is where a participant or beneficiary in an employee benefit plan wishes to recover benefits or to clarify future benefits due, or to enforce his or her rights under the plan
  - *remedy:* recovery or clarification of such alleged benefits, or availing such alleged rights
- breach of fiduciary duty:
  - *action:* an ERISA § 502(a)(2) action is where the Secretary of Labor, a participant, or a beneficiary seeks appropriate relief
  - *remedy:* individuals who have breached their fiduciary duty shall be personally liable to: (1) make good to such plan any losses to the plan resulting from each breach; (2) restore to the plan any profits made through the use of plan assets; and (3) shall be subject to other equitable or remedial relief as the court may deem appropriate, including the removal of such fiduciary
- equitable relief for actions or inactions (not alleged by the Department of Labor):
  - *action:* an ERISA § 502(a)(3) action is where a participant, beneficiary, or fiduciary seeks to either enjoin any act or practice which violates any provision of ERISA or the terms of the plan, or to obtain other appropriate equitable relief to redress such violations, or to enforce any provision of ERISA or the plan
  - *remedy:* a temporary or permanent restraining order, a court order compelling certain actions, or any other appropriate equitable relief

What are the criminal remedies under ERISA?

- any person who willfully violates any provision of Part 1 of Title I of ERISA (i.e., reporting and disclosure) is criminally liable—
    - if the convicted person is an individual, then the maximum fine is $100,000, and the maximum prison sentence is 10 years
    - if the convicted person is not an individual (i.e., a sponsoring corporation), then the maximum fine is $500,000
    - if a prohibited individual (i.e., a convicted felon) intentionally serves as a plan fiduciary, then such individual can be fined up to $10,000 or imprisoned for up to five years, or both

What attorneys' fees can be awarded in ERISA litigation?

- certain attorneys' fees and costs of action may be awarded to either party (other than for the collection of delinquent contributions)
- courts have developed a five-factor test to determine when attorneys' fees will be awarded:
    - the degree of offending party's culpability or bad faith;
    - the offending party's ability to personally pay the award;
    - whether or not the awarding of attorneys' fees would deter others under similar circumstances;
    - the amount of benefit conferred on participants; and
    - the relative merits of the party's position

What are the required claims procedures?

- every ERISA plan must have a claims procedure which provides adequate notice to a participant or beneficiary that a benefit claim has been denied and which provides a reasonable opportunity, through a formal procedure, for the individual to have a full and fair review by a named fiduciary
- there are timing rules (much quicker turnaround for claims denied in the group health plan than for claims denied in the retirement plan) and procedural rules imposed on the plan sponsor

What is the relevance of a claims procedure in ERISA civil litigation?

- the plaintiff must show that he or she exhausted all administrative remedies before he or she can sue in court; exceptions exist when meaningful access to the review process was unavailable, it would have proved futile, or where there was a danger of irreparable harm
- once a participant gets a final denial, then he or she may proceed to sue in court (but not until then)
- there are two goals of the benefit claims procedure
    - to ferret-out legitimate mistakes or

- ◦ to produce "substantive evidence" for fiduciary decisions
- • if a participant or beneficiary is unhappy after completing the plan's claims procedure, then
  - ◦ if there is *Firestone* language in the plan document (which allows the plan administrator in its sole discretion to interpret the plan document and make all benefit decisions), then the district court's standard of review for the second benefit denial is abuse of discretion
  - ◦ if no *Firestone* language is present, then the district court's standard of review is *de novo*

What is the ERISA statute of limitations?

- • a cause of action for a breach of fiduciary duty must be brought by the earlier of:
  - ◦ six years after the date of the last affirmative act or act of omission on which the fiduciary could have cured the breach; or
  - ◦ three years after the earliest date on which the plaintiff had actual knowledge of the breach
- • in all cases of a fiduciary breach where fraud or concealment is reasonably alleged, the cause of action can be brought up to six years after the discovery of such fraud

A. Federal Preemption of State Laws

By regulating employee benefit plans on a federal level, it was important for Congress to make ERISA's causes of actions, remedies, and access to federal courts universal and not subject to fifty different state laws and state forums. Thus, it mandated the following preemption clause:

§ 514. Other laws

(a) Except as provided in subsection (b) of this section, the provisions of this title and title IV shall supersede any and all State laws insofar as they may now or hereafter relate to any employee benefit plan described in section 4(a) and not exempt under section 4(b) ...

(b)(1) This section shall not apply with respect to any cause of action which arose, or any act or omission which occurred, before January 1, 1975.

(2)(A) Except as provided in subparagraph (B), nothing in this title shall be construed to exempt or relieve any person from any law of any State which regulates insurance, banking, or securities.

(B) Neither an employee benefit plan describe d in section 4(a), which is not exempt under section 4(b) (other than a plan established primarily for the purpose of providing death benefits), nor any trust established under such a plan, shall be deemed to be an insurance company or other insurer, bank, trust company, or investment company or to be engaged in the business of insurance or banking for purposes of any law of any State purporting to regulate insurance companies, insurance contracts, banks, trust companies, or investment companies.

Subsection (a) of ERISA § 514 is the general rule that ERISA supersedes (i.e., preempts) any and all state laws that "relate to" any covered employee benefit plan. We'll return to this subsection later, as the Supreme Court described it as "not a model of legislative drafting."[1]

Subsection (b) of ERISA § 514 recognizes the states' powers in regulating insurance, banking, and securities laws, and thus "saves" those laws from preemption (i.e., the preemption's savings clause). Then, Congress, quite cleverly, remembered to insert a "deemer clause" in order to prohibit state laws from legislating that an employee benefit plan is an insurance company, bank, and/or other financial institution, or trust or investment company. This clause provides that an employee benefit plan may not be deemed to be an insurance company/insurer or a bank, trust company, or investment company for purposes of the state insurance, banking, and securities laws and thus is "saved" from the preemption clause. Other express exceptions to ERISA's preemption clause include causes of action arising before January 1, 1975, other federal laws, and state criminal law.[2]

Thus, when a plaintiff asserts an ERISA cause of action and a state cause of action, solely or in connection with his or her rights under ERISA, the courts must examine ERISA's preemption provision. Hence, the phrase "relates to" in ERISA's preemption clause is highly relevant—if the claim for relief does not "relate to" the employee benefit plan, it is not covered under ERISA and therefore is not preempted under state law, allowing the plaintiff access to state adjudication of his or her claim.

The Supreme Court's interpretations of ERISA's preemption clause have been dramatically different. During the first 20 years following ERISA's enactment, the courts took an expansive view of preemption.[3] But in 1995, the Supreme Court said it was moving to a more nuanced approach in interpreting ERISA's preemption clause.[4] Thus, ERISA should preempt state law only if it explicitly referred to an ERISA covered plan or was in conflict with ERISA.[5] As a result, it has narrowed the application of ERISA preemption to state law. The most recent Supreme Court case on the topic was *Gobeille v. Liberty Mutual Insurance Company*,[6] which appears in the Materials section of this chapter. The Second Circuit had held that ERISA preempted a Vermont health care database law as it applied to a third-party administrator for a self-funded

---

1. *See* Pilot Life Ins. Co. v. Dedeaux, 481 U.S. 41, 46 (1987).
2. ERISA § 514(b)(1), (b)(4), (d).
3. *See* Shaw v. Delta Air Lines, Inc., 463 U.S. 85, 99 (1983).
4. *See* N.Y. State Conf. of Blue Cross & Blue Shield Plans v. Travelers Ins. Co., 514 U.S. 645 (1995).
5. *Id.* at 657.
6. Gobeille v. Liberty Mut. Ins. Co., 746 F.3d 497, 505 (2d Cir. 2009), *cert. granted*, 576 U.S. ___, 135 S. Ct. 2887 (2015).

ERISA plan. Vermont was one of many states that required group health plans to report extensive data regarding medical claims, despite the fact that they were covered by ERISA.[7] The Supreme Court held that ERISA's preemption clause applies to a state law that has an impermissible "connection with" an ERISA plan (i.e., a law that governs, or interferes, with the uniformity of plan administration).[8] Thus, it held that ERISA did preempt Vermont's health care database law, as the DOL had the authority to require data reporting of ERISA covered plans.[9]

B. ERISA Enforcement Scheme

1. ERISA's Causes of Action, Parties with Standing, and Remedies

ERISA has a variety of causes of action, each of which identifies the class of parties with "standing" to bring suit under its enforcement provisions, and each of which has different forms of remedies. Possible classes of parties with standing include plan participants, beneficiaries, fiduciaries, and the Secretary of Labor. The following are ERISA's causes of action and parties with standing:

- *Reporting and Disclosure Failure:* This is known as an ERISA § 502(c) cause of action (cross-referenced under ERISA § 502(a)(1)(A)). It applies when a participant or beneficiary fails to receive mandatory notices or other information required to be furnished by the plan administrator.[10] A participant or beneficiary has standing to bring such a suit. The relief sought under this cause of action is personal liability to the plaintiffs up to $100 per day of failure plus other relief the court deems proper.

- *Recovery for Benefits Due Under an ERISA Plan, Enforcement of Rights Under the Plan, or Clarification of Rights to Future Benefits Under the Plan:* Referred to as an ERISA § 502(a)(1)(B) cause of action, it is by far the one used most prevalently.[11] A participant or beneficiary has standing to bring such a suit. The relief sought under this cause of action is generally monetary relief (i.e., payment of the claim), but injunctive and declaratory relief may also be sought. Remedies such as compensatory damages, consequential damages, and punitive damages are not permitted.

- *Relief Arising from a Breach of Fiduciary Duty:* This is referred to as an ERISA § 502(a)(2) cause of action and is the second most prevalent cause of action. Relief is limited to the remedies described in ERISA § 409 (e.g., personally liable to make good to the plan any losses due to the breach, restoring any

---

7. Gobeille v. Liberty Mut. Ins. Co., 577 U.S. ___, 136 S. Ct. 936, 941 (2016).
8. *Id.* at 942–43.
9. *Id.* at 939–40.
10. ERISA § 502(a)(1)(A).
11. ERISA § 502(a)(1)(B).

profits the fiduciary made through the use of the plan assets because of the breach, and other equitable or remedial relief deemed appropriate by the court, including removal of the fiduciary from office).[12] Such relief is limited for the plan as a whole, not for an individual or group of participants. Participants, beneficiaries, other plan fiduciaries, and the Secretary of Labor have standing to bring such a suit on behalf of the plan. The relief sought under this cause of action is generally monetary, but other equitable or remedial relief may be sought.

• *Injunctive or Other Equitable Relief for Violations Under ERISA and/or Under the Terms of the Plan:* This is known as an ERISA § 502(a)(3) cause of action and is the third most prevalent cause of action.[13] Participants, beneficiaries, and plan fiduciaries have standing to bring such a suit. Defendants may include not only plan fiduciaries but also the plan sponsor, the plan itself, and nonfiduciaries with some involvement with the plan. The Supreme Court has held that "other equitable relief" sought under this cause of action does not include monetary damages.[14] Instead, the types of relief that may be sought are those that were typically available in equity (e.g., injunctions, mandamus, and restitution).[15]

• *Injunctive or Other Equitable Relief for Violations Under ERISA and/or Under the Terms of the Plan Initiated by the Secretary of Labor:* Referred to as an ERISA § 502(a)(5) cause of action, the remedies generally sought here are temporary or permanent restraining orders, court orders compelling certain actions, or any other appropriate equitable relief.

• *Failure by the Plan Administrator to Furnish Individual Statements to Participants and Beneficiaries as Mandated by ERISA § 105(c):* This is referred to as an ERISA § 502(a)(4) cause of action.[16] Under this cause of action, a participant, beneficiary, or the Secretary of Labor has standing to bring suit, and the remedy sought is the furnishing of the statement.

• *Enforcement of Civil Penalties Owed to the DOL for Reporting and Disclosure Failures, Prohibited Transaction Violations, or Any Breach of Fiduciary Duty or Knowing Participation in a Fiduciary Breach by Another Fiduciary:* This is referred to as an ERISA § 502(a)(6) cause of action and the Secretary of Labor has standing to assert such a claim. The remedy is the collection of the owed civil penalty.

• *Violations of a Fiduciary's Duties in Connection with the Purchase of Insurance or an Annuity upon a Former Participant's or Beneficiary's Termination of Service:*[17] This is known as an ERISA § 502(a)(9) cause of action. The former participant/beneficiary, a plan fiduciary, and the Secretary of Labor have standing to bring

---

12. ERISA § 502(a)(2).
13. ERISA § 502(a)(3).
14. *See* Great-West Life & Annuity Ins. Co. v. Knudson, 534 U.S. 204 (2002).
15. *See* Mertens v. Hewitt Assocs., 508 U.S. 248, 256 (1993).
16. ERISA § 502(a)(4).
17. ERISA § 502(a)(9).

this suit and can seek appropriate relief, including the posting of security if needed, to assure receipt by the participant or beneficiary of the amounts provided or to be provided by the insurance contract or annuity, plus prejudgment interest on such amounts.

- A criminal cause of action may be brought against any person who willfully violates ERISA, with a resulting fine of no more than $100,000 or imprisonment of not more than 10 years or both.[18]

2. Subject Matter and Personal Jurisdiction

ERISA § 502(e)–(f) vests exclusive jurisdiction for ERISA causes of action with the federal courts, regardless of the amount in controversy or the citizenship of the parties.[19] There are two exceptions: causes of action for benefit denial cases and for QMCSO compliance.[20] These two exceptions allow state courts to have concurrent jurisdiction, but federal law continues to govern.

3. Venue and Service of Process

Venue refers to the proper or most convenient location for a trial of a case. ERISA § 502(e)(2) sets forth the rules for determining the proper venue for an action, taking into consideration: (1) where the plan is administered, (2) where the fiduciary breach occurred, or (3) where at least one defendant resides or may be found.[21] This is regarded as a liberal venue provision to ensure easy access to the federal courts. As such, it provides plaintiffs with a variety of options that could lead to "forum shopping" depending on the facts of the case and any split of authority on a given ERISA issue. There has been a significant amount of litigation involving the validity of a plan sponsor's mandatory, binding forum selection clause within a plan document, but the consensus of the federal courts is that such forum selection clauses are valid.[22] The DOL in its amicus brief argued to the contrary.[23]

Service of process may be made on a plan trustee, plan administrator, or the Secretary of Labor if the plan has no designated agent for service of process.[24]

---

18. ERISA § 501(a). If the violation is against an entity and not an individual, the fine imposed may be increased, but it must not be more than $500,000.

19. ERISA § 502(e)–(f).

20. ERISA § 502(e) provides exceptions for actions under ERISA § 502(a)(1)(B) (for benefit denial claims) and under ERISA § 502(a)(7) (for state enforcement to comply with a qualified medical child support order (QMCSO)).

21. ERISA § 502(e)(2).

22. *See* Smith v. Aegon Cos. Pension Plan, 769 F.3d 922, 932 (6th Cir. 2014), *cert. denied*, 136 S. Ct. 791 (2016).

23. *Id.*

24. *Id.*

4. Exhaustion of Administrative Remedies

ERISA provides that a claims procedure must be used by the plan in processing claims for benefits.[25] It prescribes a two-fold requirement for the plan's internal claims procedure:

- Adequate written notice must be provided to the participant or beneficiary of the denial of benefits, setting forth the reasons for the denial and written in a reasonable fashion, and

- The participant or beneficiary must be afforded an opportunity for a full and fair review of the benefits denial by a plan fiduciary.[26]

The intent of the claims procedure is to prevent litigation before the plan fiduciary has had full opportunity to review the facts of a clam. While ERISA is silent as to whether a plaintiff must exhaust the claims procedure prior to initiating a lawsuit, the circuits are in agreement that the plaintiff must do so.[27] There are exceptions permitted under this exhaustion doctrine where meaningful access to the review process was unavailable, would prove futile, or where there was a danger of irreparable harm.[28]

5. Statute of Limitations

ERISA sets forth an explicit statute of limitations but only for suits involving the fiduciary standards, the prohibited transactions rules, and other provisions under Part 4 of Title I.[29] The express statute of limitations generally grants a six-year limi-

---

25. ERISA §502(d)(1).

26. ERISA §503.

27. *See* Rodriguez-Abreu v. Chase Manhattan Bank, N.S., 986 F.2d 5880 (1st Cir. 1993); Drinkwater v. Metropolitan Life Ins. Co., 846 F.2d 821, 826, *cert. denied*, 488 U.S. 909, 109 S. Ct. 261 (1988); Kennedy v. Empire Blue Cross & Blue Shield, 989 F.2d 588 (2d Cir. 1993); Berger v. Edgewater Steel Co., 911 F.2d 911, 916 (3d Cir. 1990), *cert. denied*, 499 U.S. 920, 111 S. Ct. 1310 (1991); Barrowclough v. Kidder, Peabody & Co., 752 F.2d 923 (3d Cir. 1985); Hickey v. Digital Equip. Corp., 43 F.3d 941, 945 (4th Cir. 1995); Medina v. Anthem Life Ins. Co., 983 F.2d 29 (5th Cir. 1993), *cert. denied*, 510 U.S. 816, 114 S. Ct. 66 (1993); Denton v. First Nat'l Bank, 765 F.2d 1295 (5th Cir.), *reh'g denied*, 772 F.2d 904 (5th Cir. 1985); Baxter v. C.A. Muer Corp., 941 F.2d 451 (6th Cir. 1991); Filipowicz v. American Stores Benefit Plans, 56 F.3d 807 (7th Cir. 1995) (dicta); Smith v. Blue Cross & Blue Shield United, 959 F.2d 655 (7th Cir. 1992); Layes v. Mead Corp., 132 F.3d 1246, 1252 (8th Cir. 1998); KinKead v. Southwestern Bell Corp. Sickness & Accident Disability Benefit Plan, 111 F.3d 67 (8th Cir. 1997); Sarraf v. Standard Ins. Co., 102 F.3d 991 (9th Cir. 1996); Diaz v. United Agric. Employee Welfare Benefit Plan & Trust, 50 F.3d 1478 (9th Cir. 1995); Amato v. Bernard, 618 F.2d 559 (9th Cir. 1980); McGraw v. Prudential Ins. Co. of Am., 137 F.3d 1253 (10th Cir. 1998); Counts v. American Gen. Life & Accident Ins. Co., (11th Cir. 1997); Communications Workers of Am. v. American Tel. & Tel. Co., 40 F.3d 426 (D.C. Cir. 1994).

28. *See, e.g.*, Denton v. First Nat'l Bank of Waco, 765 F.2d 1295 (5th Cir. 1985); Springer v. Wal-Mart Associates' Group Health Plan, 908 F. 2d 897 (11th Cir. 1990); *but see* Wilczynski v. Lumbermens Mut. Cas. Co., 93 F. 3d 397 (7th Cir. 1996).

29. ERISA §413.

tation from the date of the breach (or in the case of omission, date of possible cure), or three years from the date of actual knowledge of the breach or violation, whichever is earlier. As mentioned earlier, a recent Supreme Court decision held that "actual knowledge" for purposes of the three-year period requires that the plaintiff must in fact have been aware of the information contained in the disclosures made by the plan fiduciary.[30]

For other ERISA causes of actions, the courts use the state statute of limitations which seems most analogous.[31] The Supreme Court in *Heimeshoff v. Hartford Life & Accident Ins. Co.*,[32] upheld the plan's express statute of limitations, provided it is of reasonable length and not contrary to state law.

6. Attorneys' Fees

ERISA § 502(g) grants courts discretion to allow reasonable attorneys' fees and costs of the action to be awarded to either party.[33] Courts have developed the following five-factor test to determine whether attorneys' fees should be awarded, taking into consideration:

"• The degree of the opposing parties' culpability or bad faith;
  • The ability of the opposing parties to pay attorneys' fees;
  • Whether an award of attorneys' fees against the opposing parties could deter other persons acting under similar circumstances;
  • Whether the parties requesting attorneys' fees sought to benefit all participants and beneficiaries of an ERISA plan or to resolve a significant legal question regarding ERISA itself; and
  • The relative merits of the parties' positions."[34]

The award of attorneys' fees under ERISA is certainly not automatic, and thus there is no presumption of such award in favor of the prevailing party.

C. ERISA's Claims Procedures

ERISA's claims procedures are set forth in ERISA § 503. A plan must establish and maintain reasonable procedures governing the filing of benefit claims, notification of benefit determinations (generally done through an explanation of benefits (EOB)

---

30. *See* Intel Corp. Inv. Pol'y Comm. v. Sulyma, 140 S. Ct. 768 (2020).
31. *See, e.g.*, Dameron v. Sinai Hosp. of Baltimore, Inc., 815 F.2d 975 (4th Cir. 1987); Gavalik v. Continental Can Co., 812 F.2d 834 (3d Cir. 1987), *cert. denied*, 484 U.S. 979 (1987); Wang Lab. v. Kagan, 990 F.2d 1126 (9th Cir. 1993).
32. Heimeshoff v. Hartford Life & Accident Ins. Co., 134 S. Ct. 604 (2013).
33. ERISA § 502(g).
34. *See* Leonard v. SW Bell Corp. Disability Income Plan, 408 F.3d 528, 532 (8th Cir. 2005).

form), and appeal of adverse benefit determinations. These procedures must contain administrative processes and safeguards designed to ensure and verify that benefit claim determinations are made in accordance with governing plan documents and that plan provisions have been applied consistently with respect to similarly situated claimants.[35] During the plan's first level of review, the summary plan description (SPD) must describe the plan's claims procedures. The claims procedures must not be administered in a way that unduly inhibits or hampers the initiation or processing of claims (e.g., requirement of a fee as a condition to making a claim would be considered to unduly inhibit the initiation and processing of claims).[36] The claimant must be allowed to have an authorized representative act on his or her behalf.[37]

A claim for benefits is a request for a plan benefit or benefits made by a claimant in accordance with the plan's reasonable procedures for filing benefit claims. If a retirement benefit claim is wholly or partially denied, the plan administrator must notify the claimant of the adverse benefit determination within a reasonable period of time but not later than 90 days after receipt of the claim by the plan, unless the plan administrator determines that special circumstances require an extension of time for processing the claim. If the plan administrator determines that an extension of time for processing is required, written notice of the extension shall be furnished to the claimant prior to the termination of the initial 90-day period.[38]

The plan administrator shall provide a claimant with written or electronic notification of any adverse benefit determination. The notification shall set forth, in a manner calculated to be understood by the claimant, the following:

- The specific reason for the adverse determination;
- The reference to the specific plan provisions on which the determination is based;
- A description of any additional material or information necessary for the claimant to perfect the claim, and an explanation of why such material or information is necessary; and
- A description of the plan's review procedures and time limits applicable to such procedures, including a statement of the claimant's right to bring a civil action under ERISA § 502(a) following an adverse benefit determination on review.[39]

Every employee benefit plan shall establish and maintain procedures by which a claimant shall have a reasonable opportunity to *appeal* an adverse benefit determination to an appropriate named fiduciary of the plan, and under which there will be a full and fair review (i.e., the second level of review) of the claim and the adverse benefit determination.[40] To be considered "full and fair," the review notice must

---

35. ERISA § 503. *See also* Labor Reg. § 2560.503-1(b)(5).
36. Labor Reg. § 2560.503-1(b)(3).
37. Labor Reg. § 2560.503-1(b)(4).
38. *Id.*
39. *Id.*
40. Labor Reg. § 2560.503-1(h)(2).

provide the claimant with at least 60 days to file the appeal. The claimant must have an opportunity to provide written comments, documents, records, or other information. The plan must offer to provide, free of charge, copies of the documents upon which the benefit determination was made. The second level of review should be completed within 60 days. After administrative appeals have been exhausted, the claimant may file suit in federal court to enforce his or her rights. Refer back to Chapter 13 now as to whether the *Firestone* judicial standard of review will be invoked by the court in reviewing a plan administrator's benefits denial.

Due to changes made by the Affordable Care Act, there are different internal claims, appeals, and external review processes that apply to group health plans.[41] The DOL regulations added the following new requirements for group health plans provided through employers:

- A rescission of coverage (i.e., a cancellation or discontinuance of coverage) is now treated as an adverse benefit determination for purposes of the internal appeals processes;[42]

- A notice of urgent care determinations must be decided and communicated to the claimant as soon as possible after receipt of the claim, but in no event later than 72 hours. For pre-service claims, the claimant should be notified of a benefit denial no later than 15 days after receipt of the claim, and for post-service claims, the claimant should be notified no later than 30 days;[43]

- The claimant must be given a full and fair review of the claim, which means that the plan must provide the claimant, free of charge, with any new or additional evidence considered in connection with the claim (e.g., the plan's internal doctor's review of the claim);[44]

- Plans and insurers must avoid conflicts of interest in the appeals process to promote independence and impartiality of the decision maker (e.g., decisions regarding the hiring, compensation, or termination of a medical expert used by the plan should not be based on the likelihood that the expert will deny a claim);[45]

- Notices as to the availability of the internal appeals and external review processes must be provided in a culturally and linguistically appropriate manner;[46]

- If the plan or issuer fails to adhere to the claims procedures, the claimant will be deemed to have exhausted the internal claims and appeals processes, and accordingly, may initiate an external review of the claim.[47]

The appeals procedures for a group health plan have also been modified as follows:

---

41. ACA § 2719.

42. Labor Reg. § 2590.715-2719(a)(2)(i).

43. Labor Reg. § 2590.715-2719(b)(2)(ii)(B). Note for disability claims, the claimant must be notified of a benefit denial within 45 days.

44. Labor Reg. § 2590.715-2719(b)(2)(ii)(C).

45. Labor Reg. § 2590.715-2719(b)(2)(ii)(D).

46. Labor Reg. § 2590.715-2719(b)(2)(ii)(E).

47. Labor Reg. § 2590.715-2719(b)(2)(ii)(F).

- The 60-day period to appeal an adverse benefit determination is extended to 180 days;[48]

- The claims procedures must provide for a review that does not afford deference to the initial adverse benefit determination and that is conducted by an appropriate named fiduciary of the plan who is neither the individual who made the initial adverse benefit determination, nor a subordinate of such individual;[49]

- If the appeal involved is in whole or in part based on a medical judgment, the appropriate named fiduciary shall consult with a health care professional who has the appropriate level of training and expertise to advise on such a matter;[50]

- The plan shall identify the medical or vocational experts whose advice was obtained in connection with the claimant's adverse benefit determination, without regard to whether their advice was relied upon in making the benefit determination;[51]

- The healthcare professional used in the appeals process shall not be the same individual used in the initial adverse benefit claims determination, nor his or her subordinate;[52] and

- If the appeals claim involves a claim regarding urgent care, a request for an expedited review processes may be made orally (e.g., by telephone) or in writing by the claimant.[53]

D. Materials

Gobeille v. Liberty Mut. Ins. Co.

576 U.S. ___, 136 S. Ct. 936 (2015)

Opinion

Justice KENNEDY delivered the opinion of the Court.

This case presents a challenge to the applicability of a state law requiring disclosure of payments relating to health care claims and other information relating to health care services. Vermont enacted the statute so it could maintain an all-inclusive health care database. Vt. Stat. Ann., Tit. 18, § 9410(a)(1) (2015 Cum. Supp.) (V.S.A.). The state law, by its terms, applies to health plans established by employers and regulated by the Employee Retirement Income Security Act of 1974 (ERISA), 88 Stat. 829, as amended, 29 U.S.C. § 1001 *et seq.* The question before the Court is whether ERISA pre-empts the Vermont statute as it applies to ERISA plans.

---

48. Labor Reg. § 2560.503-1(h)(3)(i).
49. Labor Reg. § 2560.503-1(h)(3)(ii).
50. Labor Reg. § 2560.503-1(h)(3)(iii).
51. Labor Reg. § 2560.503-1(h)(3)(iv).
52. Labor Reg. § 2560.503-1(h)(3)(v).
53. Labor Reg. § 2560.503-1(h)(3)(vi).

I

A

Vermont requires certain public and private entities that provide and pay for health care services to report information to a state agency. The reported information is compiled into a database reflecting "all health care utilization, costs, and resources in [Vermont], and health care utilization and costs for services provided to Vermont residents in another state." 18 V.S.A. § 9410(b). A database of this kind is sometimes called an all-payer claims database, for it requires submission of data from all health insurers and other entities that pay for health care services. Almost 20 States have or are implementing similar databases. *See* Brief for State of New York et al. as *Amici Curiae* 1, and n. 1.

Vermont's law requires health insurers, health care providers, health care facilities, and governmental agencies to report any "information relating to health care costs, prices, quality, utilization, or resources required" by the state agency, including data relating to health insurance claims and enrollment. § 9410(c)(3). Health insurers must submit claims data on members, subscribers, and policyholders. § 9410(h). The Vermont law defines health insurer to include a "self-insured ... health care benefit plan," § 9402(8), as well as "any third party administrator" and any "similar entity with claims data, eligibility data, provider files, and other information relating to health care provided to a Vermont resident." § 9410(j)(1)(B). The database must be made "available as a resource for insurers, employers, providers, purchasers of health care, and State agencies to continuously review health care utilization, expenditures, and performance in Vermont." § 9410(h)(3)(B).

Vermont law leaves to a state agency the responsibility to "establish the types of information to be filed under this section, and the time and place and the manner in which such information shall be filed." § 9410(d). The law has been implemented by a regulation creating the Vermont Healthcare Claims Uniform Reporting and Evaluation System. The regulation requires the submission of "medical claims data, pharmacy claims data, member eligibility data, provider data, and other information," Reg. H-2008-01, Code of Vt. Rules 21-040-021, § 4(D) (2016) (CVR), in accordance with specific formatting, coding, and other requirements, § 5. Under the regulation, health insurers must report data about the health care services provided to Vermonters regardless of whether they are treated in Vermont or out-of-state and about non-Vermonters who are treated in Vermont. § 4(D); *see also* § 1. The agency at present does not collect data on denied claims, § 5(A)(8), but the statute would allow it to do so.

Covered entities (reporters) must register with the State and must submit data monthly, quarterly, or annually, depending on the number of individuals that an entity serves. The more people served, the more frequently the reports must be filed. §§ 4, 6(I). Entities with fewer than 200 members need not report at all, *ibid.*, and are termed "voluntary" reporters as distinct from "mandated" reporters, § 3. Reporters can be fined for not complying with the statute or the regulation. § 10; 18 V.S.A. § 9410(g).

B

Respondent Liberty Mutual Insurance Company maintains a health plan (Plan) that provides benefits in all 50 States to over 80,000 individuals, comprising respondent's employees, their families, and former employees. The Plan is self-insured and self-funded, which means that Plan benefits are paid by respondent. The Plan, which qualifies as an "employee welfare benefit plan" under ERISA, 29 U.S.C. § 1002(1), is subject to "ERISA's comprehensive regulation," *New York State Conference of Blue Cross & Blue Shield Plans v. Travelers Ins. Co.,* 514 U.S. 645, 650, 115 S. Ct. 1671, 131 L. Ed. 2d 695 (1995). Respondent, as the Plan sponsor, is both a fiduciary and plan administrator.

The Plan uses Blue Cross Blue Shield of Massachusetts, Inc. (Blue Cross) as a third-party administrator. Blue Cross manages the "processing, review, and payment" of claims for respondent. *Liberty Mut. Ins. Co. v. Donegan,* 746 F.3d 497, 502 (C.A.2 2014) (case below). In its contract with Blue Cross, respondent agreed to "hold [Blue Cross] harmless for any charges, including legal fees, judgments, administrative expenses and benefit payment requirements, ... arising from or in connection with [the Plan] or due to [respondent's] failure to comply with any laws or regulations." App. 82. The Plan is a voluntary reporter under the Vermont regulation because it covers some 137 Vermonters, which is fewer than the 200-person cutoff for mandated reporting. Blue Cross, however, serves several thousand Vermonters, and so it is a mandated reporter. Blue Cross, therefore, must report the information it possesses about the Plan's members in Vermont.

In August 2011, Vermont issued a subpoena ordering Blue Cross to transmit to a state-appointed contractor all the files it possessed on member eligibility, medical claims, and pharmacy claims for Vermont members. *Id.,* at 33. (For clarity, the Court uses "Vermont" to refer not only to the State but also to state officials acting in their official capacity.) The penalty for noncompliance, Vermont threatened, would be a fine of up to $2,000 a day and a suspension of Blue Cross' authorization to operate in Vermont for as long as six months. *Id.,* at 31. Respondent, concerned in part that the disclosure of confidential information regarding its members might violate its fiduciary duties under the Plan, instructed Blue Cross not to comply. Respondent then filed this action in the United States District Court for the District of Vermont. It sought a declaration that ERISA pre-empts application of Vermont's statute and regulation to the Plan and an injunction forbidding Vermont from trying to acquire data about the Plan or its members.

Vermont filed a motion to dismiss, which the District Court treated as one for summary judgment, *see* Fed. Rule Civ. Proc. 12(d), and respondent filed a cross-motion for summary judgment. The District Court granted summary judgment to Vermont. It first held that respondent, despite being a mere voluntary reporter, had standing to sue because it was faced with either allegedly violating its "fiduciary and administrative responsibilities to the Plan" or assuming liability for Blue Cross' withholding of the data from Vermont. *Liberty Mut. Ins. Co. v. Kimbell,* No. 2:11-cv-204, 2012 WL 5471225 (D. Vt., Nov. 9, 2012), p. 12. The District Court then concluded that the State's reporting scheme was not pre-empted. Although that scheme "may have some indirect effect on health benefit plans," the court reasoned that the "effect is so peripheral that the regulation cannot be considered an attempt to interfere with the administration or structure of a welfare benefit plan." *Id.*, at 31–32.

The Court of Appeals for the Second Circuit reversed. The panel was unanimous in concluding that respondent had standing, but it divided on the merits of the pre-emption challenge. The panel majority explained that "one of ERISA's core functions— reporting—[cannot] be laden with burdens, subject to incompatible, multiple and variable demands, and freighted with risk of fines, breach of duty, and legal expense." 746 F.3d, at 510. The Vermont regime, the court held, does just that. *Id.*, at 508–510.

This Court granted certiorari to address the important issue of ERISA pre-emption. 576 U.S. ___, 135 S. Ct. 2887, 192 L. Ed. 2d 923 (2015).

II

The text of ERISA's express pre-emption clause is the necessary starting point. It is terse but comprehensive. ERISA pre-empts

> "any and all State laws insofar as they may now or hereafter relate to any em-
> ployee benefit plan." 29 U.S.C. § 1144(a).

The Court has addressed the potential reach of this clause before. In *Travelers,* the Court observed that "[i]f 'relate to' were taken to extend to the furthest stretch of its indeterminacy, then for all practical purposes pre-emption would never run its course." 514 U.S., at 655, 115 S. Ct. 1671. That is a result "no sensible person could have in-tended." *California Div. of Labor Standards Enforcement v. Dillingham Constr., N.A., Inc.,* 519 U.S. 316, 336, 117 S. Ct. 832, 136 L. Ed. 2d 791 (1997) (SCALIA, J., con-curring). So, the need for workable standards has led the Court to reject "uncritical literalism" in applying the clause. *Travelers,* 514 U.S., at 656, 115 S. Ct. 1671.

Implementing these principles, the Court's case law to date has described two cat-egories of state laws that ERISA pre-empts. First, ERISA pre-empts a state law if it has a "'reference to'" ERISA plans. *Ibid.* To be more precise, "[w]here a State's law acts im-mediately and exclusively upon ERISA plans ... or where the existence of ERISA plans is essential to the law's operation..., that 'reference' will result in pre-emption." *Dilling-ham, supra,* at 325, 117 S. Ct. 832. Second, ERISA pre-empts a state law that has an impermissible "connection with" ERISA plans, meaning a state law that "governs ... a central matter of plan administration" or "interferes with nationally uniform plan ad-ministration." *Egelhoff v. Egelhoff,* 532 U.S. 141, 148, 121 S. Ct. 1322, 149 L. Ed. 2d 264 (2001). A state law also might have an impermissible connection with ERISA plans if "acute, albeit indirect, economic effects" of the state law "force an ERISA plan to adopt a certain scheme of substantive coverage or effectively restrict its choice of in-surers." *Travelers, supra,* at 668, 115 S. Ct. 1671. When considered together, these for-mulations ensure that ERISA's express pre-emption clause receives the broad scope Congress intended while avoiding the clause's susceptibility to limitless application.

III

Respondent contends that Vermont's law falls in the second category of state laws that are pre-empted by ERISA: laws that govern, or interfere with the uniformity of, plan administration and so have an impermissible "'connection with'" ERISA plans. *Egelhoff, supra,* at 148, 121 S. Ct. 1322; *Travelers,* 514 U.S., at 656, 115 S. Ct. 1671. When presented with these contentions in earlier cases, the Court has considered "the objectives of the ERISA statute as a guide to the scope of the state law that Congress understood would survive," *ibid.,* and "the nature of the effect of the state law on ERISA plans," *Dillingham, supra,* at 325, 117 S. Ct. 832. Here, those considerations lead the Court to conclude that Vermont's regime, as applied to ERISA plans, is pre-empted.

A

ERISA does not guarantee substantive benefits. The statute, instead, seeks to make the benefits promised by an employer more secure by mandating certain oversight systems and other standard procedures. *Travelers,* 514 U.S., at 651, 115 S. Ct. 1671. Those systems and procedures are intended to be uniform. *Id.,* at 656, 115 S. Ct. 1671 (ERISA's pre-emption clause "indicates Congress's intent to establish the regulation of employee welfare benefit plans 'as exclusively a federal concern'" (quoting *Alessi v. Raybestos-Manhattan, Inc.,* 451 U.S. 504, 523, 101 S. Ct. 1895, 68 L. Ed. 2d 402 (1981))). "Requiring ERISA administrators to master the relevant laws of 50 States and to contend with litigation would undermine the congressional goal of 'minimiz[ing] the administrative and financial burden[s]' on plan administrators— burdens ultimately borne by the beneficiaries." *Egelhoff, supra,* at 149–150, 121 S. Ct. 1322 (quoting *Ingersoll-Rand Co. v. McClendon,* 498 U.S. 133, 142, 111 S. Ct. 478, 112 L. Ed. 2d 474 (1990)); *see also Fort Halifax Packing Co. v. Coyne,* 482 U.S. 1, 9, 107 S. Ct. 2211, 96 L. Ed. 2d 1 (1987).

ERISA's reporting, disclosure, and recordkeeping requirements for welfare benefit plans are extensive. ERISA plans must present participants with a plan description explaining, among other things, the plan's eligibility requirements and claims-processing procedures. §§ 1021(a)(1), 1022, 1024(b)(1). Plans must notify participants when a claim is denied and state the basis for the denial. § 1133(1). Most important for the pre-emption question presented here, welfare benefit plans governed by ERISA must file an annual report with the Secretary of Labor. The report must include a financial statement listing assets and liabilities for the previous year and, further, receipts and disbursements of funds. §§ 1021(b), 1023(b)(1), 1023(b)(3)(A)–(B), 1024(a). The information on assets and liabilities as well as receipts and disbursements must be provided to plan participants on an annual basis as well. §§ 1021(a)(2), 1023(b)(3)(A)–(B), 1024(b)(3). Because welfare benefit plans are in the business of providing benefits to plan participants, a plan's reporting of data on disbursements by definition incorporates paid claims. *See* Dept. of Labor, Schedule H (Form 5500) Financial Information (2015) (requiring reporting of "[b]enefit claims payable" and "[b]enefit payment and payments to provide benefits"), online at http://www.dol.gov/ebsa/pdf/2015-5500-Schedule-H.pdf (as last visited Feb. 26, 2016).

The Secretary of Labor has authority to establish additional reporting and disclosure requirements for ERISA plans. ERISA permits the Secretary to use the data disclosed by plans "for statistical and research purposes, and [to] compile and publish such studies, analyses, reports, and surveys based thereon as he may deem appropriate." § 1026(a). The Secretary also may, "in connection" with any research, "collect, compile, analyze, and publish data, information, and statistics relating to" plans. § 1143(a)(1); see also § 1143(a)(3) (approving "other studies relating to employee benefit plans, the matters regulated by this subchapter, and the enforcement procedures provided for under this subchapter").

ERISA further permits the Secretary of Labor to "requir[e] any information or data from any [plan] where he finds such data or information is necessary to carry out the purposes of" the statute, § 1024(a)(2)(B), and, when investigating a possible statutory violation, "to require the submission of reports, books, and records, and the filing of data" related to other requisite filings, § 1134(a)(1). The Secretary has the general power to promulgate regulations "necessary or appropriate" to administer the statute, § 1135, and to provide exemptions from any reporting obligations, § 1024(a)(3).

It should come as no surprise, then, that plans must keep detailed records so compliance with ERISA's reporting and disclosure requirements may be "verified, explained, or clarified, and checked for accuracy and completeness." § 1027. The records to be retained must "include vouchers, worksheets, receipts, and applicable resolutions." Ibid.; see also § 1135 (allowing the Secretary to "provide for the keeping of books and records, and for the inspection of such books and records").

These various requirements are not mere formalities. Violation of any one of them may result in both civil and criminal liability. See §§ 1131–1132.

As all this makes plain, reporting, disclosure, and recordkeeping are central to, and an essential part of, the uniform system of plan administration contemplated by ERISA. The Court, in fact, has noted often that these requirements are integral aspects of ERISA. See, e.g., Dillingham, 519 U.S., at 327, 117 S. Ct. 832; Travelers, supra, at 651, 115 S. Ct. 1671; Ingersoll-Rand, supra, at 137, 111 S. Ct. 478; Massachusetts v. Morash, 490 U.S. 107, 113, 115, 109 S. Ct. 1668, 104 L. Ed. 2d 98 (1989); Fort Halifax, supra, at 9, 107 S. Ct. 2211; Metropolitan Life Ins. Co. v. Massachusetts, 471 U.S. 724, 732, 105 S. Ct. 2380, 85 L. Ed. 2d 728 (1985).

Vermont's reporting regime, which compels plans to report detailed information about claims and plan members, both intrudes upon "a central matter of plan administration" and "interferes with nationally uniform plan administration." Egelhoff, 532 U.S., at 148, 121 S. Ct. 1322. The State's law and regulation govern plan reporting, disclosure, and—by necessary implication—recordkeeping. These matters are fundamental components of ERISA's regulation of plan administration. Differing, or even parallel, regulations from multiple jurisdictions could create wasteful administrative costs and threaten to subject plans to wide-ranging liability. See, e.g., 18 V.S.A. § 9410(g) (supplying penalties for violation of Vermont's reporting rules); CVR § 10 (same). Pre-emption is necessary to prevent the States from imposing novel, inconsistent, and burdensome reporting requirements on plans.

The Secretary of Labor, not the States, is authorized to administer the reporting requirements of plans governed by ERISA. He may exempt plans from ERISA reporting requirements altogether. *See* § 1024(a)(3); 29 CFR § 2520.104-44 (2005) (exempting self-insured health plans from the annual financial reporting requirement). And, he may be authorized to require ERISA plans to report data similar to that which Vermont seeks, though that question is not presented here. Either way, the uniform rule design of ERISA makes it clear that these decisions are for federal authorities, not for the separate States.

B

Vermont disputes the pre-emption of its reporting regime on several fronts. The State argues that respondent has not demonstrated that the reporting regime in fact has caused it to suffer economic costs. Brief for Petitioner 52–54. But respondent's challenge is not based on the theory that the State's law must be pre-empted solely because of economic burdens caused by the state law. *See Travelers,* 514 U.S., at 668, 115 S. Ct. 1671. Respondent argues, rather, that Vermont's scheme regulates a central aspect of plan administration and, if the scheme is not pre-empted, plans will face the possibility of a body of disuniform state reporting laws and, even if uniform, the necessity to accommodate multiple governmental agencies. A plan need not wait to bring a pre-emption claim until confronted with numerous inconsistent obligations and encumbered with any ensuing costs.

Vermont contends, furthermore, that ERISA does not pre-empt the state statute and regulation because the state reporting scheme has different objectives. This Court has recognized that "[t]he principal object of [ERISA] is to protect plan participants and beneficiaries." *Boggs v. Boggs,* 520 U.S. 833, 845, 117 S. Ct. 1754, 138 L. Ed. 2d 45 (1997). And "[i]n enacting ERISA, Congress' primary concern was with the mismanagement of funds accumulated to finance employee benefits and the failure to pay employees benefits from accumulated funds." *Morash, supra,* at 115, 109 S. Ct. 1668. The State maintains that its program has nothing to do with the financial solvency of plans or the prudent behavior of fiduciaries. *See* Brief for Petitioner 29. This does not suffice to avoid federal pre-emption.

"[P]re-emption claims turn on Congress's intent." *Travelers,* 514 U.S., at 655, 115 S. Ct. 1671. The purpose of a state law, then, is relevant only as it may relate to the "scope of the state law that Congress understood would survive," *id.,* at 656, 115 S. Ct. 1671 or "the nature of the effect of the state law on ERISA plans," *Dillingham, supra,* at 325, 117 S. Ct. 832. In *Travelers,* for example, the Court noted that "[b]oth the purpose and the effects of" the state law at issue "distinguish[ed] it from" laws that "function as a regulation of an ERISA plan itself." 514 U.S., at 658–659, 115 S. Ct. 1671. The perceived difference here in the objectives of the Vermont law and ERISA does not shield Vermont's reporting regime from pre-emption. Vermont orders health insurers, including ERISA plans, to report detailed information about the administration of benefits in a systematic manner. This is a direct regulation of a fundamental ERISA function. Any difference in purpose does not transform this direct regulation of "a central matter of plan administration," *Egelhoff, supra,* at 148, 121 S. Ct. 1322 into an innocuous and peripheral set of additional rules.

The Vermont regime cannot be saved by invoking the State's traditional power to regulate in the area of public health. The Court in the past has "addressed claims of pre-emption with the starting presumption that Congress does not intend to supplant state law," in particular state laws regulating a subject of traditional state power. *Travelers, supra,* at 654–655, 115 S. Ct. 1671. ERISA, however, "certainly contemplated the pre-emption of substantial areas of traditional state regulation." *Dillingham,* 519 U.S., at 330, 117 S. Ct. 832. ERISA pre-empts a state law that regulates a key facet of plan administration even if the state law exercises a traditional state power. *See Egelhoff,* 532 U.S., at 151–152, 121 S. Ct. 1322. The fact that reporting is a principal and essential feature of ERISA demonstrates that Congress intended to pre-empt state reporting laws like Vermont's, including those that operate with the purpose of furthering public health. The analysis may be different when applied to a state law, such as a tax on hospitals, *see De Buono v. NYSA-ILA Medical and Clinical Services Fund,* 520 U.S. 806, 117 S. Ct. 1747, 138 L. Ed. 2d 21 (1997), the enforcement of which necessitates incidental reporting by ERISA plans; but that is not the law before the Court. Any presumption against pre-emption, whatever its force in other instances, cannot validate a state law that enters a fundamental area of ERISA regulation and thereby counters the federal purpose in the way this state law does.

IV

Respondent suggests that the Patient Protection and Affordable Care Act (ACA), which created new reporting obligations for employer-sponsored health plans and incorporated those requirements into the body of ERISA, further demonstrates that ERISA pre-empts Vermont's reporting regime. *See* 29 U.S.C. § 1185d; 42 U.S.C. §§ 300gg-15a, 17; § 18031(e)(3). The ACA, however, specified that it shall not "be construed to preempt any State law that does not prevent the application of the provisions" of the ACA. 42 U.S.C. § 18041(d). This anti-pre-emption provision might prevent any new ACA-created reporting obligations from pre-empting state reporting regimes like Vermont's, notwithstanding the incorporation of these requirements in the heart of ERISA. *But see* 29 U.S.C. § 1191(a)(2) (providing that the new ACA provisions shall not be construed to affect or modify the ERISA pre-emption clause as applied to group health plans); 42 U.S.C. § 300gg-23(a)(2) (same).

The Court has no need to resolve this issue. ERISA's pre-existing reporting, disclosure, and recordkeeping provisions — upon which the Court's conclusion rests — maintain their pre-emptive force whether or not the new ACA reporting obligations also pre-empt state law.

* * *

ERISA's express pre-emption clause requires invalidation of the Vermont reporting statute as applied to ERISA plans. The state statute imposes duties that are inconsistent with the central design of ERISA, which is to provide a single uniform national scheme for the administration of ERISA plans without interference from laws of the several States even when those laws, to a large extent, impose parallel requirements. The judgment of the Court of Appeals for the Second Circuit is *Affirmed.*

Chapter 15

Plan Termination

Reading Assignment: ERISA §§ 4001, 4002, 4006, 4007, 4021, 4022, 4041, 4042, 4043, 4044, 4048, 4062, 4068

I.R.C. § 411(d)(3)

Class Discussion Questions: Is the PBGC a federal agency?

What is the difference between a standard and a distress plan termination?

What are the consequences under the Code for a full plan termination?

What is a partial plan termination for purposes of the Code?

Why do the multi-employer defined benefit plans have the potential for a withdrawal liability?

Overview

What is the PBGC?

- the Pension Benefit Guaranty Corporation is a "private" corporation established by ERISA and under the federal government's direct control
- basically, the PBGC collects insurance premiums from all defined benefit plans, invests the assets in a trust fund, and will pay certain guaranteed benefits to those terminated defined benefit plans that cannot meet their liabilities
- in cases where the plan itself is so poorly handled or where the sponsoring employer is defunct or in bankruptcy, the PBGC will become trustee of the plan assets

How can a single-employer defined benefit plan be terminated?

- although no employer is required to sponsor a qualified defined benefit plan, those that voluntarily do so must meet certain requirements before the plan can be terminated
- under a "standard termination," the plan has enough assets to pay out all accrued benefit liabilities—here, the plan just communicates certain information to the PBGC about the assets and liabilities, and the plan's enrolled actuary certifies certain aspects of the calculated liabilities (in such case, the defined benefit plan

has paid into the mandatory PBGC insurance system but received absolutely nothing from it)

- under a "distress termination," the plan does not have ample assets to cover its liabilities, and it is apparent that the plan never will because the sponsor is defunct or in bankruptcy (in such case, the plan sponsor asks the PBGC to become the plan trustee, to distribute any remaining plan assets, and then pay the balance of guaranteed benefits to the plan participants from the general PBGC trust fund)

- under a "PBGC initiated termination," the PBGC determines that the plan must terminate and the PBGC immediately becomes the trustee of all plan assets (here, the PBGC has monitored the plan and noted either negligence or willful fiduciary breaches, and the PBGC will try to protect remaining the remaining assets from being mishandled further)

What is withdrawal liability?

- a multi-employer plan is a single plan to which different employers or employee organizations contribute for the benefit of their respective employees

- multi-employer plans are usually a direct result of collectively bargained employees (i.e., union employees), where an individual might have several different employers throughout his or her career, but where each employer is required, through a collectively bargained agreement, to contribute a certain amount to a certain fund

- employers are not required to negotiate collectively bargained agreements, but if they do so for business reasons, then they cannot just withdraw from the fund at any time

- the "withdrawal liability" represents the cost to a sponsoring employer if it wishes to withdraw from the fund (this helps to ensure that promised benefits will actually be funded, and it also serves to prevent a domino effect of several employers withdrawing at once and leaving all liability responsibilities to the remaining employers)

- a withdrawal liability is usually paid over a period of years after the employer withdraws

- a partial withdrawal generally occurs if there is a 70% decline in contributions made by one employer, calculated over a five-year period—here, such employer is only liable for a portion of the withdrawal liability

A. PBGC Rules for Plan Terminations

In reaction to the termination of an unfunded Studebaker plan back in the early 1970s, Congress became concerned that defined benefits plans were not insured, subjecting plan participants and beneficiaries to substantial risk.[1] Thus, Title IV of ERISA was dedicated to such insurance protection—a separate insurance program for single-employer versus multi-employer defined benefit plans. Congress created a new federal entity, known as the Pension Benefit Guaranty Corporation (PBGC).[2] It consists of a board of directors of three individuals—the Secretaries of Labor, Commerce, and Treasury. Title IV sets forth procedures for terminating defined benefit plans, prescribes the coverage and features of the insurance program, and specifies the PBGC's rights against a plan sponsor whose plan termination results in PBGC liability. To finance such an insurance program, an annual premium is assessed against the plan, on a per capita basis.[3]

Plans that are not covered under Title IV include: defined contribution plans; governmental plans; an employee plan funded through I.R.C. §501(c)(9); an unfunded deferred compensation plan for highly compensated employees; defined benefit plans with 25 or fewer participants that are maintained by a professional service employer (e.g., doctors, lawyers); and certain other plans (e.g., church plans).[4]

1. Definition of a Plan Termination

For Title IV purposes, a termination of a single-employer plan extinguishes the employer's funding obligations under the plan, either because the employer is unable or unwilling to continue the funding. Thus, termination ends the employer's obligation to fund the plan after the date of termination.[5] In the multi-employer plan context, employers may be assessed a liability when they withdraw from the plan.[6] Liability is not simply triggered *solely* on the termination of a multi-employer defined benefit plan.

For Code purposes, a termination of a single-employer plan results in *full vesting* of benefits for affected participants.[7] The Code also recognizes that a single-employer plan can be *partially* terminated, resulting in full vesting for just the affected participants (e.g., a plant is sold off and the plant employees are no longer employees of the plan sponsor). Title IV does not recognize a partial termination of a single-employer plan.

---

1. For an excellent description as to why the termination of Studebaker's hourly defined benefit plan, in the aftermath of the shutdown of its South Bend plant, led to the passage of ERISA, see James A. Wooten, *The Most Glorious Story of Failure in the Business: The Studebaker-Packard Corporation and the Origins of ERISA*, 49 Buffalo L. Rev. 683 (2001).

2. ERISA §4002.

3. ERISA §§4002(a)(3), 4006, 4007.

4. ERISA §4021.

5. Prop. Treas. Reg. §1.412(b)-4(a).

6. The plan trustees have the discretion as to whether to assess a withdrawal liability; if the plan is adequately funded, the withdrawing employer may not be assessed any liability. The plan trustees of a multi-employer defined benefit plan consist of several members representing the union, several members representing the contributing employers, and other full-time employees of the fund.

7. I.R.C. §411(d)(3); Treas. Reg. §1.411(d)-2(a)(1).

2. Definition of Terms

As will be discussed, a single-employer plan may be voluntarily terminated if plan assets are sufficient to cover all plan liabilities at the time of the final distribution of assets. For this purpose, the current dollar value of assets must be determined as of a proposed termination date.

The term "total benefit liabilities" includes all benefits promised under the terms of the plan within the meaning of I.R.C. §401(a)(2) for eligible participants and their beneficiaries.[8] A subset of total benefit liabilities encompasses "guaranteed" benefits, which are afforded insurance protection in the event the plan terminates with insufficient assets. In order for a benefit to be guaranteed by the PBGC, it must meet three criteria: (1) it must be nonforfeitable (which does not include those benefits that became nonforfeitable *solely* because of the plan's termination under the Code), (2) it must be a pension benefit, and (3) the participant must have been entitled to the benefit (e.g., if the plan had a subsidized early retirement benefit, only those participants who are eligible for that benefit as of the termination date would be guaranteed that benefit).[9] There is a maximum dollar amount applicable to a participant's guaranteed benefits (e.g., for 2020, $69,750 per year for an individual age 65 as a life annuity), and benefit increases are phased-in over time.[10] The value of early retirement benefits are included as part of the participant's guaranteed benefit, provided he or she had a nonforfeitable right to such benefit before the date of plan termination but had not yet retired.[11]

3. Allocation of Plan Assets

ERISA was initially drafted to permit single employers to voluntarily terminate *underfunded* defined benefit plans. OBRA '87 subsequently changed the rules such that a single employer could only voluntarily terminate its plan if plan assets were sufficient to cover all plan liabilities.[12] As such, it requires plan assets to be allocated by various types of benefit categories (analogous to parceling out corporate assets to various creditors upon a corporation's bankruptcy). If plan assets are insufficient to cover all guaranteed benefits, they are allocated as follows:

- First, assets are allocated to cover benefits attributable to voluntary employee contributions;
- Second, assets are allocated to cover benefits attributable to mandatory employee contributions;
- Third, assets are allocated to cover benefits in pay status to retirees (or that would have been in pay status had the eligible participant actually retired);

---

8. ERISA §4001(a)(16).
9. ERISA §4022(b)(3).
10. *Id.*; PBGC §4022.25.
11. ERISA §4001(a)(16).
12. OBRA '87 §9313(a).

- Fourth, assets are allocated to cover benefits guaranteed by the PBGC;
- Fifth, assets are allocated to cover vested benefits (other than those that vested solely because of the plan termination); and
- Finally, assets are allocated to cover all other benefits under the plan.[13]

For example, if there were $10 million of plan assets sufficient to cover the first four categories of benefits, the PBGC would not need to pay additional benefits as it is limited to the benefits that are guaranteed by the PBGC. The benefits in categories five and six would neither be covered nor paid by the PBGC.

4. Premium Payments

In an effort to simplify the premium structure, the premiums were initially set as a flat per capita amount of $1 per participant. This structure proved to be wholly inadequate, and thus the premium structure has changed to a flat amount per participant (e.g., for 2020, $83 per participant for single-employer plans) plus a variable portion with a maximum dollar cap per participant (e.g., for 2020, $45 per $1,000 of unfunded vested benefits (UVBs) per participant, capped at $561 per participant). There is also a termination premium for certain distress and involuntary pension plan terminations of $1,250 per participant for three years after the plan terminates.

> **Example:** A single-employer defined benefit plan has 1,200 participants, and UVBs = $51,000,000. The flat rate premium cost = [$83 × 1200] = $99,600.
>
> Because the plan has UVBs, the variable rate premium cost = [$45 × 51,000] = $2,295,000. But the variable rate cost is capped at [$561 × 1200] = $673,200, which is less. Hence, the total premium owed = [$99,600 + $673,200] = $772,800. This employer certainly has an incentive to fully fund the plan so as to avoid paying the variable rate premium.

B. How a Single-Employer Plan Terminates under Title IV

There are three ways a single-employer plan can terminate under Title IV. Under a standard termination, plan assets are sufficient to cover all plan liabilities.[14] An enrolled actuary certifies the calculation of the plan liabilities, using mandated interest rates and mortality tables. Satisfaction of such benefit liabilities is usually accomplished by purchasing annuity contracts or distributing immediate lump sum payments. The PBGC incurs no liability but oversees the process through a variety of notices and forms. See the link in the Materials section of this chapter for a timeline that explains when notices, etc., occur in the standard termination context.

---

13. ERISA § 4044(a).
14. ERISA § 4041(b).

The first notice is given to plan participants, beneficiaries, and alternate payees at least 60 days (but no more than 90 days) in advance of the plan termination, by the plan administrator.[15] The second notice, which must be submitted within 180 days of the proposed termination date, requires the plan administrator to send Form 500 with Schedule EA-S to the PBGC, with the actuarial information necessary to process the plan termination, certified by an enrolled actuary.[16] This information allows the PBGC to ascertain the sufficiency of the plan assets in covering all benefit liabilities and to determine whether the standard termination rules have been met. The third notice involves the plan administrator giving to each participant and beneficiary a notice specifying the amount of his or her benefit liability and the form of payment.[17] Any information used to determine the benefit commitment (e.g., age, wages, actuarial assumptions) must be stated in the notice.

After the proper notices have been made, the PBGC has 60 days to issue a Notice of Noncompliance.[18] If the notice is not issued, the plan administrator may close out the plan and distribute the assets.[19] Within 30 days after distribution of plan assets, the plan administrator must submit Form 501 to the PBGC stating that plan assets were distributed in accordance with the PBGC rules on closing out a plan.[20]

Alternatively, if plan assets are insufficient to cover all plan liabilities, but it is apparent that the plan sponsor cannot continue to maintain the plan (e.g., because it has gone into bankruptcy), the plan sponsor will request a distress termination with the PBGC, who then becomes plan trustee. But even if the employer is reorganizing in bankruptcy, the PBGC will continue to work with the employer to fund the pension liabilities; distress termination is a last resort. The plan assets are then transferred to the PBGC trust funds and the PBGC pays all guaranteed benefits (in an annuity form) to retirees and to plan participants when they attain the plan's normal retirement age (i.e., when they become eligible for the benefit sometime in the future).[21] To the extent plan assets are inadequate, the PBGC has a lien for this liability, limited to 30% of the collective net worth of the employer and the controlled group.[22] Similar notices are sent by the plan administrator as is the case in a standard termination, but Forms 600 and 601 with Schedule EA-D are used instead.

---

15. ERISA § 4041(b)(1)(A); PBGC § 4041.23(a).
16. ERISA § 4041(b)(1)(B); PBGC § 4041.24.
17. ERISA § 4041(b)(2)(B); PBGC § 4041.24.
18. Examples of cases where the PBGC would issue a Notice of Noncompliance include an incomplete submission of Form 500 with its schedules or required notices that are deficient or not given in a timely fashion. A Notice of Noncompliance ends the standard termination proceeding, nullifies all actions taken to terminate the plan, and renders the plan an ongoing plan. See PBGC, *Standard Termination Filing Instructions*, https://www.pbgc.gov/documents/500-instructions.pdf.
19. ERISA § 4041(b)(2)(D); PBGC § 4041.26(a)(1).
20. ERISA § 4041(b)(3)(B); PBGC § 4041.29(a).
21. ERISA § 4041(c).
22. ERISA § 4062(b).

Finally, the PBGC can initiate a plan termination and become the trustee of all plan assets.[23] The PBGC may do so in such cases as: the plan failed to meet its minimum funding contributions, the plan cannot pay benefits when due, a certain reportable event has occurred, or the long-run loss to the PBGC with respect to the plan is expected to increase unreasonably if the plan is not immediately terminated.

The PBGC has developed an early warning program to monitor employers with poorly funded defined benefit plans.[24] This may lead to an involuntary plan termination. It also uses its reportable-event regulations to monitor financial problems not only for the pension plans but also for the sponsoring employers.[25]

C. Code Considerations in a Single-Employer Plan Termination

1. Effect of a Code Termination on Vesting

Upon a plan termination, there are Code considerations to be taken into account. These rules are applicable to both defined contribution and defined benefit plans. For a qualified defined benefit plan, if the employer wishes to avoid future minimum funding contributions, it must terminate the plan, and assets must be distributed "as soon as administratively feasible."[26] A determination letter may be requested from the Service regarding the qualified status of the plan to ensure that termination does not retroactively jeopardize the plan or affect the tax status of the distributions made from the plan.[27]

The Code's qualification rules require the plan to provide, that, (1) upon the full or partial termination of the plan, or (2) in the case of profit sharing plans, upon the complete discontinuance of contributions to the plan, all accrued benefits under the plan, to the extent then funded, become fully vested.[28] The complete discontinuance of employer contributions to the plan is a facts and circumstances determination but is contrasted with a suspension of contributions under the plan which is merely a temporary cessation of contributions.[29] Likewise, the determination of a partial plan termination is a facts and circumstances test.[30] But there is a special rule in the context of a defined benefit plan ceasing or decreasing future benefit accruals under the plan. In that case, a partial termination will occur if, as a result of such cessation

---

23. ERISA § 4042.
24. ERISA § 4042(a)(4).
25. ERISA § 4043.
26. *See* Rev. Rul. 89-87.
27. Form 5310-A is the applicable determination letter form for plan terminations.
28. I.R.C. § 411(d)(3). *See also* Treas. Reg. § 1.411(d)-2(a).
29. Treas. Reg. § 1.411(d)-2(d)(1).
30. Treas. Reg. § 1.411(d)-2(b)(1) (providing examples such as the exclusion of a group of employees previously covered under the plan or a plan amendment which adversely affects the rights of employee to vest in benefits under the plan).

or decrease, a potential reversion of plan assets to the employer is created or increased.[31] If no such reversion is created or increased, a partial plan termination shall not occur.[32]

2. Freezing the Plan in Lieu of Full Termination

In lieu of terminating the plan and distributing plan assets, the employer may decide to "freeze" the plan. According to the PBGC, there are four ways to freeze a defined benefit plan:

- Close the plan to new entrants but allow existing participants to continue to accrue benefits;
- Cease benefit accruals for some but not all participants (referred to as partial freeze);
- Cease future benefit accruals for all active participants but permit growth in benefits due to future changes in participants' wages (referred to as a soft freeze). This would apply if the accrued benefit and normal retirement benefit used "final average of earnings" as the definition of "compensation." As a participant's future compensation grows, his or her existing benefit accruals are retroactively increased to take into account the participant's current final average earnings; and
- Cease any new benefit accruals for all participants (whether because of service or compensation) (referred to as a hard freeze).[33]

By freezing the plan, the trust remains intact so that the earnings compound tax-free. No future employer contributions may be envisioned after the freezing date unless the freeze involves allowing some growth in past accruals. But the plan remains subject to the minimum funding standards, such that if any shortfall amortization charge exists for the plan year, it will have to be paid. Frozen plans also must continue to pay PBGC premiums.

Frozen plans must continue to comply with applicable qualification rules. As such, a top-heavy frozen defined benefit plan must continue to provide minimum accruals under I.R.C. § 416(c); however, for a frozen defined contribution plan, no contributions need be made if none are being made for any key employees.[34] Defined benefit plans that have a soft freeze or hard freeze will have trouble complying with the coverage, participation, and/or nondiscrimination rules, as the number of participants will decline or grow older.[35] Failure to satisfy these tests requires the employer to take substantial corrective actions. Since 2013, the IRS has offered limited relief for these

---

31. Treas. Reg. § 1.411(d)-2(b)(2).
32. *Id.*
33. *See* PBGC, *An Analysis of Frozen Defined Benefit Plans* 1, 5 (Dec. 21, 2005), https://www.pbgc.gov/documents/frozen_plans_1205.pdf. In 2002, a new frozen plan question was added to the Form 5500.
34. *See* Treas. Reg. § 1.416-1T-5.
35. Treas. Reg. § 1.401(a)(26)-2(b).

plans, but the SECURE Act now provides expanded relief from the coverage, participation, and nondiscrimination tests in specific circumstances and subject to certain requirements.[36] These new rules provide opportunities whereby a plan under a soft or hard freeze can pass these tests.

3. Partial Plan Terminations

I.R.C. §411(d)(3) also sets forth the rule that full and immediate vesting is required in the case of a *partial* plan termination, but it does not set forth a definition of a partial plan termination.[37] Thus, we look to IRS guidance and case law to determine what constitutes a partial plan termination. The Service has defined two types of partial plan terminations:

- A "vertical plan termination" which is triggered if a significant number of participants under the plan are subsequently excluded from participation.[38] While the Service holds that this is a facts and circumstance test, its rule of thumb is that a 20% exclusion will trigger a partial plan termination for the affected group.[39]

- A "horizontal plan termination" which is triggered if future benefit accruals are permanently decreased or reduced completely or if eligibility or vesting is made more restrictive.[40] The Service refers to this as a curtailment, which will trigger a partial plan termination only if the plan amendment results in a potential for plan asset reversion to the employer or for discrimination.[41]

Read Rev. Rul. 2007-43 in the Materials section of this chapter for discussion of a partial plan termination.

D. PBGC Rules for Multi-Employer Defined Benefit Plans

A multi-employer plan is a single plan to which different employers or different employee organizations contribute for the benefit of their "employees," pursuant to the terms of a collectively bargained agreement. These are plans for union employees where the employees may be members of the same union (e.g., Local Plumbers Union No. 101) but work for different employers throughout their careers as union members. Since there are multiple employers contributing to the same multi-employer plan, Title IV is not only concerned with the termination of such plans but also with a withdrawal by a participating employer while the plan is unfunded. Thus, ERISA §4201 imposes rules that may result in a withdrawal liability when an employer

---

36. SECURE, §205.
37. I.R.C. §411(d)(3).
38. Treas. Reg. §1.411(d)-2(b)(1).
39. *See* Rev. Rul. 73-284; Rev. Rul. 81-27.
40. Treas. Reg. §1.411(d)-2(b)(2).
41. *Id.*

decides that it no longer wishes to contribute to the multi-employer plan. This ensures that the promised benefits will be funded and also serves to deter a number of employers from withdrawing all at once, in an attempt to leave the resulting liabilities in the hands of a few remaining employers.

When an employer withdraws from participation in a multi-employer plan, it may do so either in a complete withdrawal or a partial withdrawal. If the plan has unfunded vested benefits allocable to that employer, the plan will assess a withdrawal liability; the plan determines the amount of the liability, notifies the employer of that amount, and collects it from the employer.

A complete withdrawal occurs when the employer (including all controlled group members) permanently ceases to have an obligation to contribute to the plan or permanently ceases all covered operations under the plan.[42] There are special rules for plans and employers in certain industries (e.g., construction or entertainment). If all or most of the participating employers withdraw completely from the plan, the plan then experiences a mass withdrawal.

A partial withdrawal occurs generally if there is a 70% contribution decline on behalf of one employer, or there is a partial cessation of the employer's contribution obligation.[43] The 70% contribution decline is measured over a five-year period. If a partial withdrawal occurs, only the employer with the contribution decline is responsible for a portion of the withdrawal liability.

If the plan is adequately funded, whether or not the employer involved in a complete or partial withdrawal is assessed any withdrawal liability is at the sole discretion of the plan trustees. Such trustees generally consist of an equal number of individuals elected by the union and elected by the contributing employers.

E. Materials

Review the standard termination timeline on the PBGC's website, available at https://www.pbgc.gov/sites/default/files/legacy/docs/standard_termination_filing_instructions.pdf.

Revenue Ruling 2007-43

ISSUE

Is there a partial termination of a plan under § 411(d)(3) of the Internal Revenue Code under the facts described in this revenue ruling?

FACTS

Employer X maintains Plan A, a defined contribution plan qualified under § 401(a). The plan year for Plan A is the calendar year. The plan participants include both cur-

---

42. ERISA § 4203(a).
43. ERISA § 4205(a).

rent and former employees. Plan A provides that an employee of Employer X has a fully vested and nonforfeitable interest in his or her account balance upon either completion of 3 years of service or attainment of age 65. The plan also provides for each participant to have a fully vested and nonforfeitable right to his or her account balance upon the plan's termination or upon a partial termination of the plan that affects the participant.

Employer X ceases operations at one of its four business locations. As a result, 23 percent of the Plan A participants who are employees of Employer X cease active participation in Plan A due to a severance from employment (excluding any severance from employment that is either on account of death or disability, or retirement on or after normal retirement age) during the plan year. Some of these participants are fully vested due to having completed 3 years of service or having attained age 65. Plan A is not terminated.

Law

Section 411(d)(3) provides in relevant part that a plan will not be qualified unless the plan provides that, upon its partial termination, the rights of all affected employees to benefits accrued to the date of such partial termination, to the extent funded on that date, or the amounts credited to their accounts, are nonforfeitable.

Section 1.411(d)-2(b)(1) of the Income Tax Regulations provides that whether or not a partial termination of a qualified plan occurs (and the time of such event) is determined by the Commissioner with regard to all the facts and circumstances in a particular case. The facts and circumstances include the exclusion, by reason of a plan amendment or severance by the employer, of a group of employees who have previously been covered by the plan, as well as plan amendments that adversely affect the rights of employees to vest in benefits under the plan.

Section 1.411(d)-2(b)(2) provides a special rule with respect to a defined benefit plan that ceases or decreases future benefit accruals under the plan. A partial termination is deemed to occur if a potential reversion to the employer maintaining the plan is created or increased as a result of such cessation or decrease. This special rule does not apply to defined contribution plans.

Section 1.411(d)-2(b)(3) provides that, if a termination occurs, § 411(d)(3) only applies to the part of the plan that is terminated.

In Rev. Rul. 73-284, 1973-2 C.B. 139, an employer established a qualified pension plan that covered all of its 15 employees. The employer later acquired a new business location 100 miles away and closed the original one. All employees were given the opportunity to transfer to the new location and continue to participate in the plan, but only 3 chose to do so. The other 12 employees were discharged and their participation under the plan ended. The employer hired replacements for them at the new location. The revenue ruling concludes that there was a partial termination due to the termination of these employees in connection with the change in business location.

In Rev. Rul. 81-27, 1981-1 C.B. 228, the employer established a qualified defined benefit pension plan that covered employees in the two divisions of its businesses.

The plan covered 165 employees. The employer closed down one division and terminated 95 participants. The revenue ruling concludes that the discharge by the employer of 95 of 165 participants constituted a partial termination.

Weil v. Terson Co. Retirement Plan Administrative Committee, 933 F.2d 106 [67 AFTR 2d 91-1131] (2d Cir. 1991), holds that the turnover rate in both vested and nonvested participants is taken into account in determining whether there has been a reduction in the workforce that constitutes a partial termination for purposes of §411(d)(3). See 933 F.2d at 110.

Matz v. Household International Tax Reduction Investment Plan, 388 F.3d 570 [94 AFTR 2d 2004-6781] (7 Cir. 2004), holds that there is a rebuttable presumption that a 20 percent or greater reduction in plan participants is a partial termination for purposes of §411(d)(3). The court holds that this presumption is rebuttable depending on other facts and circumstances. *See* 388 F.3d at 578. The court, relying on *Weil*, bases the 20 percent calculation on the ratio of those participants who lose coverage, whether or not vested, to all participants, whether or not vested.

ANALYSIS

Based on the foregoing, whether a partial termination of a plan under §411(d)(3) has occurred depends on the facts and circumstances, including the extent to which participating employees have had a severance from employment. If the turnover rate is at least 20 percent, there is a presumption that a partial termination of the plan has occurred. The turnover rate is determined by dividing the number of participating employees who had an employer-initiated severance from employment during the applicable period by the sum of all of the participating employees at the start of the applicable period and the employees who became participants during the applicable period. The applicable period depends on the circumstances: the applicable period is a plan year (or, in the case of a plan year that is less than 12 months, the plan year plus the immediately preceding plan year) or a longer period if there are a series of related severances from employment.

All participating employees are taken into account in calculating the turnover rate, including vested as well as nonvested participating employees. Employer-initiated severance from employment generally includes any severance from employment other than a severance that is on account of death, disability, or retirement on or after normal retirement age. An employee's severance from employment is employer-initiated even if caused by an event outside of the employer's control, such as severance due to depressed economic conditions. In certain situations, the employer may be able to verify that an employee's severance was not employer-initiated. A claim that a severance from employment was purely voluntary can be supported through items such as information from personnel files, employee statements, and other corporate records.

Employees who have had a severance from employment with the employer maintaining the plan on account of a transfer to a different controlled group are not considered as having a severance from employment for purposes of calculating the turnover rate if those employees continue to be covered by a plan that is a continuation of the plan under which they were previously covered (*i.e.*, if a portion of the plan covering those employees was spun off from the plan in accordance with the rules of § 414(l) and will continue to be maintained by the new employer).

Whether or not a partial termination of a qualified plan occurs on account of participant turnover (and the time of such event) depends on all the facts and circumstances in a particular case. Facts and circumstances indicating that the turnover rate for an applicable period is routine for the employer favor a finding that there is no partial termination for that applicable period. For this purpose, information as to the turnover rate in other periods and the extent to which terminated employees were actually replaced, whether the new employees performed the same functions, had the same job classification or title, and received comparable compensation are relevant to determining whether the turnover is routine for the employer. Thus, there are a number of factors that are relevant to determining whether a partial termination has occurred as a result of turnover, both in the case where a partial termination is presumed to have occurred due to the turnover rate being at least 20 percent and in the case where the turnover rate is less than 20 percent.

In the present case, there is a presumption that a partial termination has occurred because the turnover rate is 20 percent or more. The facts and circumstances support the finding of a partial termination because the severances from employment occurred as a result of the shutdown of one of the employer's business locations (and not as a result of routine turnover). Therefore, a partial termination of Plan A has occurred.

If a partial termination occurs on account of turnover during an applicable period, all participating employees who had a severance from employment during the period must be fully vested in their accrued benefits, to the extent funded on that date, or in the amounts credited to their accounts.

A partial termination of a qualified plan can also occur for reasons other than turnover. For example, a partial termination can occur due to plan amendments that adversely affect the rights of employees to vest in benefits under the plan, plan amendments that exclude a group of employees who have previously been covered by the plan, or the reduction or cessation of future benefit accruals resulting in a potential reversion to the employer.

Holding

Under the facts described in this revenue ruling, a partial termination has occurred.

Chapter 16

Reporting and Disclosure Requirements

Reading Assignment: ERISA §§ 4(b), 101, 102, 103, 104, 105, 4010, 4043

Labor Reg. §§ 2510.3, 2510.104

Congressional Findings and Declaration of Policy, ERISA § 2

ACT 2009 Report, https://www.dol.gov/agencies/ebsa/about-ebsa/about-us/erisa-advisory-council/2009-promoting-retirement-literacy-and-security-by-streamlining-disclosures-to-participants-and-beneficiaries

Labor Reg. § 2520.104b-31

Class Discussion Questions: What are the typical communications that participants and beneficiaries receive from the plan?

What is the intent behind Title IV's reportable events rules?

How often must benefit statements be given to plan participants and beneficiaries, and how will those statements change as a result of the SECURE Act?

Overview

What must be reported annually to the government?

- a plan must provide:
  - an annual report (i.e., Form 5500 and attachments); and
  - reports upon plan termination, and any other supplementary reports required by the Secretary of Labor
- there are certain "reportable events" that a qualified defined benefit plan sponsor must communicate with the PBGC to inform them that there is a greater likelihood that they might need to insure unfunded benefits

What must be disclosed to participants of any ERISA covered plan?

- All ERISA plans must provide:

- ○ a summary plan description (SPD);
- ○ a summary of material modifications (SMM) to the SPD when plan amendments materially modify it; and
- ○ a summary annual report (SAR) showing a financial statement and balance sheet for the plan assets
- • a plan must also provide the plan document upon request (but can charge reasonable photocopying expenses)

What are the most common communications that must be disclosed to participants of qualified retirement plans?

- • benefit statements:
  - ○ at least quarterly in a defined contribution plan with self-directed investments;
  - ○ at least annually in other defined contribution plans; and
  - ○ at least every three years in a defined benefit plan
- • in a § 401(k) plan:
  - ○ notice of the advantages of asset portfolio diversification;
  - ○ notice of automatic enrollment (if applicable) and notice of default investments (if applicable);
  - ○ notice of impending blackout periods;
  - ○ notice that the plan intends to comply with a safe harbor design (if applicable), but the SECURE Act eliminates the safe harbor notice requirement with respect to nonelective 401(k) safe harbor plans; and
  - ○ notice indicating fees that will be charged to the participant's account

A. Introduction

As discussed in previous chapters, several government agencies have jurisdiction over the administration and oversight of employee benefit plans, which are subject to ERISA. Administrators of ERISA plans have to comply with all the rules of ERISA and have to know to whom, what, when, where, and how to appropriately report plan information. Failure to report information properly can result in fines, the plan losing its qualified status, and/or subject the plan to termination. At this point, read the Congressional Findings and Declaration of Policy set forth in ERISA § 2 in order to understand the importance of employee disclosure.

This chapter will review the "3 Ws and 1 H" (i.e., what, to whom, when, and how) of reporting for both pension and welfare benefit plans. The first step in reporting is to determine if the plan is subject to ERISA. The second step is to establish what phase the plan is in (e.g., creation, regular reporting, special condition reporting, or termination). The final step is to select the document/form needed to release the necessary information to the correct party in the appropriate time frame.

1. Plans Subject to ERISA Reporting and Disclosure Requirements

In general, all employee benefit plans[1] are subject to the reporting[2] and disclosure[3] requirements of ERISA. Employers with qualified pension benefit plans and welfare benefit plans are required to report information regularly to the agencies responsible for the oversight of the applicable ERISA title. "Employee pension benefit plans" includes any employee benefit plan providing retirement income or income deferral (including profit sharing plans).[4] "Employee welfare benefit plans" includes any employee benefit plan providing any of the following kinds of benefits: medical or surgical care, sickness, accident, disability, unemployment, vacation, apprenticeship, daycare, scholarships, paid legal services, holiday, or severance.[5]

Plan administrators must regularly prepare and file reports with the DOL, IRS, PBGC, and plan participants. In addition to annual reports, employers can be required to submit reports and make additional disclosures following certain plan events, such as amendments to the plan, changes in benefits, plan distributions, and plan termination. Failure to comply with reporting deadlines can result in penalties or in disqualification of the plan.

Even though most pension benefit plans will be required to report annually, there are a number of notable exceptions to customary filing requirements:[6]

- Unfunded excess benefit plans;[7]
- An annuity or custodial account arrangement[8] not established or maintained by an employer;[9]
- "SIMPLE" IRAs;[10]
- Simplified employee pension (SEP) or a salary reduction SEP;[11]
- Church plans not electing coverage under Code;[12]
- Unfunded "top hat" plans;[13]

---

1. See employee benefit plans as defined in ERISA § 3(3).
2. ERISA §§ 103, 104.
3. ERISA §§ 102, 104.
4. ERISA § 3(2); Labor Reg. § 2510.3-2.
5. ERISA § 3(1); Labor Reg. § 2510.3-1.
6. See Form 5500, Instructions, Section 1: Who Must File.
7. See ERISA § 4(b)(5).
8. As defined by I.R.C. § 403(b)(1) or I.R.C. § 403(b)(7).
9. See Labor Reg. § 2510.3-2(f), description of employer.
10. I.R.C. § 408(p), Savings Incentive Match Plan for Employees of Small Employers, "SIMPLE".
11. See I.R.C. § 408(k). See also Labor Reg. §§ 2520.104-48, -49.
12. See I.R.C. § 410(d).
13. See Labor Reg. § 2520.104-23 (pension plans maintained for a select group of management or highly compensated employees, must established via a timely filing of a registration statement with the DOL).

- IRAs or annuities not considered pension plans;[14] and
- Governmental plans.

Welfare plans that are subject to Title I of ERISA are also expected to report annually unless they fall into an exception,[15] such as:

- A plan that covers fewer than 100 participants as of the beginning of the plan year and is unfunded, fully insured, or a combination of insured and unfunded;[16]
- An unfunded or insured "top hat" welfare plan;[17]
- An employee benefit plan maintained only to comply with workers' compensation, unemployment compensation, or disability insurance laws;
- Qualifying church plans;[18] and
- Governmental plans.

2. Annual Reporting Requirements and Forms

ERISA requires the DOL be given an annual report, with comparable requirements under Title II of ERISA requiring the filing of such return with the IRS.[19] For all pension and welfare plans that do not fall into an exception, Form 5500 is the annual reporting vehicle, which represents a combined effort by the DOL and IRS to consolidate certain return information into one form.[20] Plans covered by the PBGC have to file additional forms along with a payment for annual premiums.

Currently, Form 5500 consists of the primary form and 13 attachable schedules, which may be required based on the "size" of the plan or type of information being reported. The three major categories for plan size are small, large, and direct filing entity (DFE). A plan's size is determined by the number of participants covered on the first day of the plan year. A "small plan" covers fewer than 100 while a "large plan" covers 100 or more participants at the beginning of the plan year.[21]

Large plans file the full Form 5500, which must include separate financial statements. An independent, qualified public accountant must audit the financial statements and schedules of such returns and express an opinion on such statements and schedules and on the accounting practices used by the plan.

---

14. *See* Labor Reg. § 2510.3-2(d).
15. *See supra note* 1.
16. *See* Labor Reg. § 2520.104-20.
17. Labor Reg. § 2520.104-24.
18. *See* ERISA § 3(33).
19. ERISA § 101(b)(1); I.R.C. § 6047.
20. *See* Form 5500 Filing Instructions. All Form 5500 and Form 5500-SF are to be filed electronically through the EFAST2 electronic system.
21. *See id.* at Section 4: What to File. (Exception: 80–120 Participant Rule: If a plan covers 80 to 120 participants and filed a Form 5500 in the previous year, then the plan administrator may elect to file the same type of report/return as the prior plan year.) For the instructions for the 2019 Form 5500, refer to https://www.dol.gov/sites/dolgov/files/EBSA/employers-and-advisers/plan-administration-and-compliance/reporting-and-filing/form-5500/2019-instructions.pdf.

Small plans generally file an electronic abbreviated version of the Form 5500 (i.e., Form 5500-SF) and an independent accountant's review is not required regarding the plan's financial statements. One-participant plans with less than $250,000 in assets are not required to file at all.

Generally, a plan must file its annual report, including appropriate schedules, within seven months after the end of the plan year.[22] A plan administrator may request an extension, of up to two and one-half additional months, to file.[23]

Form 5500 offers the following schedules for reporting additional information:[24]

- Schedule A — Insurance Information
- Schedule B — Actuarial Information
- Schedule C — Service Provider Information
- Schedule D — DEF/Participating Plan Information
- Schedule F — Fringe Benefit Plan Annual Information
- Schedule G — Financial Transaction Schedules
- Schedule H — Financial Information
- Schedule I — Financial Information, small plans
- Schedule P — Annual Return of Fiduciary of Employee Benefit Trust
- Schedule R — Retirement Plan Information
- Schedule SSA — Annual Registration Statement Identifying Separated Participants with Deferred Vested Benefits
- Schedule T — Qualified Pension Plan Coverage Information
- Accountant's Report — Required for large plans and DFEs

---

22. *See* Labor Reg. § 2520.104a-5(a)(2); Treas. Reg. § 301.6058-1(d)(4).

23. See Form 5558, requesting an extension to file Form 5500. For DFEs, filing must be no later than nine and one-half months after the end of the DFE year, with no extensions.

24. *See* Form 5500 for a complete list of schedules and information on when and how to complete each.

3. Miscellaneous Reporting and Disclosure

Document	What	To Whom	When	How
Summary plan description (SPD)	A basic summary of a participant's rights and obligations under the plan. It must be easy to understand and accurate in its description of plan function. It must accurately reflect the contents of the plans, no more than 120 days prior to the date it is disclosed.[25]	Plan participants and beneficiaries receiving benefits.[26]	Within 90 days after an employee becomes a participant, or within 120 days after the plan becomes subject to part 1 of title I, or no later than 210 days following the end of the plan year which occurs five years after the last date a change in the information is required to be disclosed.[27]	See DOL Reg. §2520.102-2, for information on suggested format. See DOL Reg. §2520.102-3, for information on required content.
Summary of material modification (SMM)	A summary describing any material modification to the plan or change in plan information that has not yet been included in the summary plan description.[28]	Plan participants and beneficiaries receiving benefits.	Not later than 210 days after the end of the plan year in which the change is adopted.	See DOL Reg. §2520.104b-3.[29]

---

25. Labor Regs. §§2520.102-2, -3.

26. Labor Reg. §2520.102-2(c), sets forth special requirements that if more than a specified number of employees speak a language other than English, guidance must be provided in writing along with the plan document relating to how to obtain assistance or further explanation.

27. Labor Reg. §2520.104b-2. *See also* Labor Reg. §2520.102-3.

28. Labor Reg. §2520.104b-3. *See also* Labor Reg. §2520.104b-3(b) (no separate written SMM is required when a timely SPD is provided with the changes already incorporated.).

29. *See* Labor Reg.§2520.104b-3(d), for special rules for group health plans.

Document	What	To Whom	When	How
Summary annual report (SAR)	Annual report regarding plan finances, based on the information provided in the most recent annual report of the plan.[30]	Plan participants and beneficiaries receiving benefits.	Within nine months after the close of the year; based on plan year for pension plans and fiscal year for welfare plans.[31]	Pension plans: DOL Reg. §2520.104b-10(d)(3). Welfare Plans: DOL Reg. §2520.104b-10(d)(4).[32]
Notification of benefit determination (or "explanation of benefits")	Written notification of plan's adverse determination of a claim for plan benefit(s).	Claimant (plan participants and beneficiaries receiving benefits).	Not later than 90 days after receipt of claim.[33] Expedited notification is required for claims under group health plans and disability plans.	Written or electronic notification according to DOL Reg. §2560.503-1(g).
Plan documents	General term for all documents an administrator must keep and provide to participants or government agency (e.g., SPD, Form 5500, trust agreements, and documents which created the plan or detail how it is to be maintained).	Plan participants and beneficiaries receiving benefits, plan fiduciaries, and Secretary of Labor.[34]	Not later than 30 days after written request.[35]	See individual documents.
Summary of material reduction in covered services or benefits	Explanation of a "material reduction" in covered services or benefits.[36]	Covered participant.	Generally, within days of the material change.[37]	No defined form, see DOL Reg. §2520.104b-3.

---

30. *See* ERISA §104(a)(1), for annual report form and content. Any portion of the SAR form information that is not available in the annual report may be omitted from the SAR, *see also* Labor Reg. §2520.104b-10(d)(1).

31. Labor Reg. §2520.104b-10(c). *See* Labor Reg. §2520.104b-10(c)(2), in the case of an extension, SARs must be filed within two months of the extension grant.

32. *See* Form 5500, additional format information. *See also* Labor Reg.§2520.104b-10(g) (exemptions from filing).

33. *See also* Labor Reg. §2560.503(f). Under special circumstances, if an extension of time is needed to evaluate the claim, the plan administrator must notify the claimant within 90 days of receipt of the claim, indicating the special circumstances and the date by which the plan expects to make a determination.

34. *See* Labor Reg. §2520.104a-8; Labor Reg. 2520.104(a)(1).

35. *See* Labor Reg. §2520.104b-1(b).

36. Labor Reg. §2520.104b-3(d)(3), defines "material reduction" and "reduction in covered services or benefits."

37. *See also* Labor Reg. §2520.104b-3(d)(2) (90-day alternative rule).

Document	What	To Whom	When	How
COBRA notice	Notice explaining a participant's right to purchase a temporary extension of group health insurance coverage when coverage would otherwise terminate due to a "qualifying event."[38]	Covered employees, covered spouses, and qualified dependents.	Initially when group health plan coverage begins and again after a qualifying event occurs.[39]	No set form, content must be sufficient for notice to comply with ERISA §606.
Individual benefit statements for pension and profit sharing plans	Statement, based on the most current information available, indicating total benefits accrued and the nonforfeitable pension benefits, if any, which have accrued, or the earliest date on which benefits will become nonforfeitable.[40]	Plan participants and beneficiaries.	For participant-directed defined contribution plans: quarterly. For non-participant directed defined contribution plans: annually. For defined benefit plans: once every three years, unless upon request if administrator provides annual notice.[41]	No form. Must be in writing, minimum information according to ERISA §105.
Suspension of benefit notice	Notice to employees whose benefits are to be suspended during certain periods of employment or reemployment.	Plan participants whose benefits are suspended.	During the first month or first payroll period in which the withholding is to occur.[42]	DOL Reg. §2530.203-3.

38. *See* U.S. Dep't of Labor, *An Employee's Guide to Health Benefits COBRA* (Sep. 2016), https://www.dol.gov/sites/dolgov/files/legacy-files/ebsa/about-ebsa/our-activities/resource-center/publications/an-employees-guide-to-health-benefits-under-cobra.pdf.

39. ERISA §606(a)(2) through (4).

40. ERISA §105.

41. ERISA §105(a)(1).

42. *See* Labor Reg. §2530.203-3.

Document	What	To Whom	When	How
Notice of significant reduction in future benefit accruals	Notice if the plan is going to be amended so that there is going to be significant reduction in the rate of future benefit accruals or elimination or significant reduction in an early retirement benefit or retirement type subsidy.[43]	Plan participants and beneficiaries.	Not less than 45 days before the effective date of the plan amendment.[44]	ERISA § 204(h).
Domestic relations order (DRO) and qualified domestic relations order (QDRO) notices	The plan administrator must notify affected parties upon the receipt of a DRO and upon its determination as to whether the DRO is qualified.[45]	Participants and alternate payees.	Promptly upon receipt of the DRO and then determination must be made in a reasonable time.[46]	No form, see ERISA § 206(d)(3).
Notice of failure to meet minimum funding standards	Notification when a covered pension plan, otherwise required to make a contribution, fails to do by the 60th day after such payment or installment was due.[47]	Participants and beneficiaries.	Notice shall be made in a reasonable time as prescribed by the Secretary.[48]	ERISA § 101(d).

---

43. ERISA § 204(h)(1); I.R.C. § 4980F.

44. *Id.*

45. ERISA § 206(d)(3); Labor Reg. § 1056(d)(3).

46. *See also* U.S. Dep't of Labor, *QDROs: The Division of Retirement Benefits Through Qualified Domestic Relations Orders* (2014), https://www.dol.gov/sites/dolgov/files/ebsa/about-ebsa/our-activities/resource-center/publications/qdros.pdf.

47. ERISA § 101(d)(1). Note, this may not apply if a waiver is pending, *see also* ERISA § 101(d)(2).

48. *See* U.S. Dep't of Labor, *Reporting and Disclosure Guide for Employee Benefits Plans* (Sep. 2017), https://www.dol.gov/sites/dolgov/files/EBSA/about-ebsa/our-activities/resource-center/publications/reporting-and-disclosure-guide-for-employee-benefit-plans.pdf.

Document	What	To Whom	When	How
Joint and Survivor Notice	Explanation of the qualified joint and survivor annuity, including the right to waive, effect of election/revocation, and rights of the participant's spouse.	Plan participants.	Not less than 30 days, but not more than 180 days prior to the annuity starting date.[49]	Treas. Reg. §§ 1.4001(a)-20 and 1.417(e)-1(b)(2).
Preretirement Survivor Notice	Explanation of the preretirement survivor annuity, including the right to waiver or revocation, effect of waiver/revocation, and the rights of the participant's spouse.	Plan participants.	The later of (1) the beginning of the first day of the plan year in which participant attains age 32 and ending on the last day of the plan year in which the participant attains age 34, or (2) one year after the employee becomes a participant.[50]	Treas. Reg. §§ 1.401(a)-20, Q&A 35 and 1.417(e)-1(b)(2).
401(k) Safe Harbor Notice	Explanation of the safe harbor matching contribution formula under the plan, including other contributions available and conditions by which they may be made, type and amount of compensation that may be deferred, period for making elections, method for making contributions, the withdrawal and vesting provisions, and how to get additional information about the plan. The SECURE Act eliminated the safe harbor notice requirement with respect to nonelective 401(k) safe harbor plans.	Plan participants.	Between 30 and 90 days prior to the beginning of the plan year; for an employee who becomes eligible after the 90th day before the beginning of the plan year, notice is to be made no more than 90 days before the employee becomes eligible.	I.R.C. § 401(k)(12) and Treas. Reg. § 1.401(k)-3(d).

---

49. ERISA § 205(c).

50. Treas. Reg. §§ 1.401(a)-20, Q&A 35, and 1.417(e)-1(b)(2).

Document	What	To Whom	When	How
Automatic Enrollment Notice	Annual notice explaining how to opt out of or change the amount of deferrals, including investment of deferrals if there is no investment election made.[51]	Plan participants.	The initial notice is made between 30 and 90 days prior to the participant becoming eligible to participate. An annual notice is to be provided between 30 and 90 days prior to the beginning of the plan year.	ERISA §§404(c)(5)(B), 514(e)(3), and I.R.C. §401(k)(13)(E).
Default Investment Alternative Notice	Explanation as to how contributions will be invested in the absence of an investment election, including a description as to the right to direct investments, a description of the default investments, investment objectives, risk and return criteria, fees and expenses, and direction as to where participants may obtain investment advice.[52]	Plan participants.	At least 30 days prior to the date of plan eligibility or at least 30 days prior to the date of the first investment in a default investment alternative. Annually at least 30 days prior to the plan year.	DOL Reg. §2550.404c-5(c).

---

51. ERISA §§404(c)(5)(B), 514(e)(3); I.R.C. §401(k)(13)(E).
52. ERISA §404(c)(5)(B).

Document	What	To Whom	When	How
Funding-Based Limitation on Distributions Notice	For plans funded below 60%, notice of restrictions on shutdown benefits, lump sum distributions and frozen benefit accruals. For plans between 60% and 80% funded, notice of restriction on accelerated distributions.	Plan participants and beneficiaries.	Within 30 days after the plan is restricted.	ERISA § 101(d).
Annual Funding Notice	Notice regarding a defined benefit plan's assets, liabilities, and funding percentages for the current year and prior two years, including number of active and retired participants, the plan's funding policy and asset allocation, benefit changes, plan amendments and other events affecting plan liabilities, a summary of the PBGC termination rules and guarantees, and how to obtain an annual report.[53]	Plan participants, beneficiaries, unions, contributing employers to multi-employer plans, and the PBGC.	Within 120 days after the end of the plan year to which the notice relates. Small plans have until the time for filing the Form 5500.	DOL FAB 2009-01 (model notice).

---

53. ERISA §§ 101(f), 305(b)(3)(D).

Document	What	To Whom	When	How
Section 404(c) plan disclosures	When a pension plan provides for individual accounts and permits a participant or beneficiary to exercise control over the assets in his/her account, the participant or beneficiary must be provided with notice that he/she will be allowed to make investment decisions, and the plan administrator must provide the individual enough information to make an informed investment decision.[54]	Plan participants and beneficiaries receiving benefits.	Information should be provided before investment decisions are to be made and upon request.	See Labor Reg. § 2550.404c-1.
Notice of blackout period for individual account plans	Notice must be provided to participants of 404(c) plans when investment direction or diversification is to be suspended, limited, or restricted for any period of more than three consecutive business days (i.e., "blackout period").[55]	Participants and beneficiaries.	At least 30 days, but not more than 60 days, before blackout.[56]	See Labor Reg. § 2520.101-3.

---

54. ERISA § 404(c); Labor Reg. § 1104(c); *see also* Labor Reg. § 2550.404c-1.
55. ERISA § 101(i); Labor Reg. § 1021(i); *see also* Labor Reg. § 2520.101-3.
56. *Id.*

The DOL introduced a safe harbor in 2002, set forth in DOL Reg. § 2520.104b-1(c), whereby a plan administrator could use electronic mail to satisfy the delivery requirements of all information required to be furnished to participants, beneficiaries, and other individuals under Title I.[57] The two categories of individuals that could be recipients of electronic delivery included: (1) the "wired at work" group (i.e., participants who had access to the employer's or plan sponsor's electronic information system as an integral part of his or her duties at work) and (2) individuals who affirmatively consented to receive documents electronically. President Trump issued Executive Order 13847 in 2018 directing the DOL to review guidance to make retirement plan disclosures required under ERISA and the Code more understandable and useful, and to explore broader use of electronic delivery of such disclosures.[58] In response, the DOL proposed an additional safe harbor method for electronic delivery of participant notices under proposed regulations in 2019.[59] These regulations were finalized on May 27, 2020, effective as of July 27, 2020.[60] Read portions of these regulations in the Materials section. Consistent with the proposal, the DOL set forth an additional safe harbor, relying on a "notice and access" approach. Under this approach, the plan administrator may post disclosures on a website and inform participants with an electronic "notice of internet availability."[61] This safe harbor applies to *retirement plan* disclosure (not welfare plan disclosure) required under Title I, except for documents supplied only on request (which will continue to be provided via paper).[62] The regulations allow for the use of mobile apps, going beyond email. The new safe harbor applies to "covered individuals" (e.g., participants, beneficiaries, alternate payees) who are entitled to "covered documents" and who provide the employer, plan sponsor, or plan fiduciary with an electronic address (e.g., email address or cell phone number).[63] Alternatively, if the employer assigns an electronic address to the employee, he or she is deemed to have provided the electronic address.[64]

Prior to relying on the new safe harbor, the plan must provide a *paper* notice which must set forth:

- Notification that covered documents will be provided electronically to an electronic address;

- Identification of the electronic address that is to be used for that covered individual (a somewhat difficult requirement, as the notice will have to contain this individualized field);

---

57. Labor Reg. § 2520.104b-1(c).

58. Exec. Order No. 13,847, 83 FR 45321 (Aug. 31, 2018).

59. Prop. Labor Reg. § 2520.104b-31 (entitled "Alternative method for disclosure through electronic media — Notice and access").

60. Labor Reg. § 2520.101-3, 2520.104b-1, 2520.104b-31 (amended at 85 Fed. Reg. 31884 (May 27, 2020)).

61. Labor Reg. § 2520.104b-31(d).

62. Labor Reg. § 2520.104b-31(c).

63. Labor Reg. § 2520-104b-31(b)–(c).

64. Labor Reg. § 2520.104b-31(b). However, the employer-assigned electronic address must be used for employment purposes and not for the sole purposes of providing documents under the safe harbor.

- Instructions as to how to access the documents, including notification that the materials may not be available for more than a year, or if later, after it has been superseded by another document; and

- An explanation of the ability to request a paper copy of the document and the right to opt out of electronic disclosure.[65]

Thereafter, the administrator may furnish to each covered individual a notice of internet availability for each document when a disclosure is newly available on its website.[66] The notice of internet availability must contain the following information:

- A prominent statement (e.g., "Disclosure About Your Retirement Plan");

- A statement that reads, "Important information about your retirement plan is available at the website address below. Please review this information.";

- A brief description of the document;

- The internet website address (or hyperlink to such address) that is sufficiently specific to provide ready access to the document;

- A statement of the right to request and obtain a paper copy of the document and a statement of the right to opt out of receiving documents electronically that explains how to exercise that right;

- A cautionary statement that the covered document is not required to be available on the website for more than one year, or if later, after it is superseded by a subsequent document; and

- A telephone number to contact the administrator.[67]

As to the form and manner of furnishing the notice, it must be sent electronically; contain only the required content; be furnished separately from any other documents or disclosure (but there is an exception for combined notices); and be written in a manner reasonably expected to be understood by the average participant.[68]

The DOL mentions in the preamble of the proposed regulations the possibility of issuing a model notice of internet availability. Generally, the administrator is to provide a separate notice of internet availability for each required disclosure, but may issue a single combined notice for all or some of the most common documents (e.g., SPDs, covered documents that must be furnished annually, documents authorized by the DOL, and any applicable notice required by the Code).[69] The administrator will need to establish and maintain a website for disclosures and the final rules set forth standards which must be met.[70] The final rules added a new rule whereby the plan fiduciary must attempt to attain an electronic address from the covered individual upon a severance from employment.[71]

---

65. Labor Reg. § 2520.104b-31(g).
66. Labor Reg. § 2520.104b-31(d).
67. Labor Reg. § 2520.104b-31(d)(3).
68. Labor Reg. § 2520.104b-31(d)(4).
69. Labor Reg. § 2520.104b-31(i).
70. Labor Reg. § 2520.104b-31(e).
71. Labor Reg. § 2520.104b-31(h).

4. PBGC Reporting and Disclosure

Document Annual Reporting	What	To Whom	When	How
E-filing	Estimated flat-rate and variable premium payments	PBGC	15th day of the 10th full month following the end of the prior plan year.	Electronically.[72]
E-filing	Annual report regarding premiums due and the payment of premiums, based on reported information. All employers covered under ERISA §4021 are required to file even if no premiums are due for the filing year.[73]	PBGC	15th day of the 10th full calendar month following the end of the prior plan year.[74]	Electronically.[75]
Standard Termination[76]				
Notice of Intent to Terminate (NOIT)	Notifies participants and affected parties of the proposed termination and procedures.	Participants, beneficiaries, alternate payees, and union.	At least 60 days but not more than 90 days before the proposed termination date.[77]	See Form 500 Instructions, Appendix B "Model NOIT."

72. *See* www.pbgc.gov/prac/forms.html (provides links to all PBGC forms and instructions for filing).

73. *See* PBGC, *Comprehensive Premium Filing Instructions for 2020 Plan Years*, "Who Must File" (revised Mar. 5, 2020), https://www.pbgc.gov/sites/default/files/2020-premium-payment-instructions.pdf (an administrator may request a coverage determination letter if he/she is unsure if the plan is subject to PBGC reporting; however, this request does not extend the due date for premiums.).

74. *Id.* at "When to File."

75. Form 1 and premiums may be filed online at www.pbgc.gov at Online Premium Filing ("My PPA" Plan Administration Account). The PBGC plans to require electronic filing of premiums, beginning with large plans in 2006.

76. Plans that are sufficiently funded to provide all plan benefits may be voluntarily terminated in a standard termination.

77. *See* PBGC, *Standard Termination Filing Instructions, Form 500*, https://www.pbgc.gov/documents/500-instructions.pdf.

Document	What	To Whom	When	How
Standard Termination Notice	Notifies PBGC of termination date and plan data.	PBGC	On or before the 180th day after the proposed termination.	Form 500.
Notice of Plan Benefits (NOPB)	Provides affected parties with benefit details.	Participants, beneficiaries and alternate payees.	Not later than the time Form 500 is filed.	Information from Form 500.
Post-Distribution Certification	Certification by the Plan Administrator that all the plan assets have been distributed.	PBGC	Not later than 30 days after all plan benefits are distributed.	Form 501.
Missing Participants	Details participants and beneficiaries the plan administrator could not locate.	PBGC	See above.	Form MP-100.
Distress Termination[78]				
Distress Termination Notice of Intent to Terminate	Notifies PBGC of the intent to terminate the proposed termination date and sponsor(s) data.	PBGC	At least 60 days but not more than 90 days before the proposed termination date, and it may not be filed before the NOIT is filed with affected parties.[79]	Form 600.

78. A distress termination occurs when the plan does not have sufficient funds to pay all of the plan's outstanding benefits. In order to qualify for a distress termination, the contributing sponsor and each member of the contributing sponsors control group must fit into one of the following four categories: (1) Liquidating in bankruptcy or insolvency, (2) Reorganization in bankruptcy or insolvency proceedings with court approval of the termination, (3) Inability to pay debts when due and to continue in business unless distress termination occurs, and (4) Unreasonably burdensome pension cost due solely to a decline in employment. *See* PBGC, *Distress Termination Filing Instructions, Form 600*, https://www.pbgc.gov/sites/default/files/distress-terminations-instructions.pdf.

79. *Id.*

Document	What	To Whom	When	How
Distress Termination Notice	Notifies PBGC of termination date and plan data. Note: The plan will file participant information with the PBGC by the later of 120 days after the termination date or 30 days after receiving the determination from the PBGC regarding termination.[80]	PBGC	On or before the 120th day after the proposed termination.[81]	Form 601, Schedule EA-D.
Notice of Intent to Terminate to Affected Parties Other than PBGC ("NOIT")	Notifies participants and affected parties of the proposed termination and procedures.	Participants, beneficiaries, alternate payees, and union.	At least 60 days but not more than 90 days before the proposed termination date.[82]	See Form 600 Instructions, Appendix B "Model NOIT," Schedules P and F.
Post-Distribution Certification for Distress Termination	Certification by the plan administrator that all the plan assets have been distributed.	PBGC	Not later than 30 days after the last distribution date for any affected party.[83]	Form 602.
Missing Participants	Details participants and beneficiaries the plan administrator could not locate.	PBGC	See above.	Schedule MP, file with Form 602.

---

80. *Id.*
81. *Id.*
82. *Id.*
83. *Id.*

Document	What	To Whom	When	How
Other Reports				
Post-Event Notice of Reportable Events[84]	Information regarding plan events such as a failure to make required funding payment, changes in contributions, and other reportable events.	PBGC	Within 30 days after a plan administrator or contributing sponsor knows or has reason to know a reportable event has occurred.[85]	Form 10 must be filed electronically.[86]
Advance Notice of Reportable Events[87]	Information regarding plan events such as: changes in contributions, transfer of benefit liabilities, and other reportable events.	PBGC	Not later than 30 days prior to the reportable event.[88]	Form 10-Advance must be filed electronically.[89]

---

84. *See* ERISA § 4043; PBGC § 4043.1-10, 4043-20-35. Reportable events include five corporate events (i.e., extraordinary dividend; change in controlled group; insolvency or similar settlement; loan default; and liquidation) and six plan events (i.e., active participant reduction; distribution to a substantial owner; transfer of benefit liabilities, missed required contributions; application for a minimum funding waiver; and inability to pay benefits when due).

85. Form 10 instructions, When to File. *See* PBGC § 4043.61-68.

86. Form 10 instructions, How to File.

87. *See* ERISA § 4043.

88. Form 10—Advance Instructions, When to File. (Note if a plan files an advance report, then there is no obligation to file a post-event Form 10).

89. *Id.* at How to File.

Document	What	To Whom	When	How
Notice of Failure to Make Required Contribution[90]	Required when a plan sponsor has failed to make more than $1 million in contributions.	PBGC	Not later than 10 days after the due date of the required payment.[91]	Form 200 must be filed electronically.[92]
Annual Financial and Actuarial Information Reporting	Reporting required when a controlled group with a defined benefit plan had a funding target attainment percentage (FTAP) at the end of the prior plan year less than 80%, had a minimum funding waiver over $1 million, or sponsor subject to a lien for missed contributions.[93]	PBGC	Not later than 105 days after the end of the fiscal year.[94]	N/A

90. *See* ERISA § 302(f) and I.R.C. § 412(n).
91. Form 200, When to File.
92. *Id.* at How to File.
93. ERISA § 4010.
94. *See* PBGC, *Reporting Dates Under ERSIA § 4010*, http://www.pbgc.gov/prac/reporting-and-disclosure/4010-reporting.

5. Promotion of Lifetime Income Options

In an effort to promote the use of lifetime income streams of payment under defined contribution plans, the DOL in May 2013 issued an advance notice of proposed rule-making (ANPRM) per its statutory authority under ERISA § 105.[95] That section requires the distribution of periodic benefit statements, at least quarterly for participant-directed plans.[96] Under the proposal, the participant's benefit statement would include an estimated lifetime income stream of payment based on the current account balance (even though the participant had not yet attained the plan's normal retirement age) and projected account balance, using a given interest rate and mortality rate, at the participant's normal retirement age under the plan. Such annuities would be based on the joint lives of the participant and his or her spouse. The actuarial assumptions used to annuitize the account balance had to be set forth in the statement. Several safe harbors were provided at various rates that could be used. Those proposals were never finalized.

The SECURE Act now requires sponsors of defined contribution plans to provide an estimate of the amount of monthly annuity income the participant's account balance could produce in retirement (in a life annuity and joint and survivor annuity form).[97] Such disclosure must be on the participants' annual benefit statements. Plan fiduciaries will be protected from liability exposure if they rely on DOL assumptions and guidance. The Act mandates the DOL issue model lifetime income disclosures and prescribe actuarial assumptions to be used in converting an account balance into lifetime income stream equivalents. The new rules will be effective for benefit statements given more than 12 months after the latest of either the DOL's publication of an interim final rule (which would go into effect but allow the DOL to continue to take comments and make changes going forward) or publication of model disclosures and assumptions.[98]

6. Enforcement

The DOL has a cause of action under ERISA to obtain appropriate equitable relief for fiduciary violations,[99] to enjoin any act or practice, which violates any provision of Title I, or to obtain any other appropriate equitable relief to redress a violation or to enforce any provision of Title I. The SECURE Act increased penalties for failure to file certain information:

- The penalty for failure to file a Form 5500 has been increased to $250 per day (not to exceed $150,000);
- The penalty for failure to provide a required withholding notice has been increased to $100 per day (not to exceed $500,000 in penalties per year);

---

95. *See* Advance Notice of Proposed Rulemaking, 78 Fed. Reg. 26,727-01.
96. ERISA § 105.
97. SECURE § 203, amending ERISA § 105(a)(2).
98. For a discussion of the DOL's interim final rules, see Kathryn J. Kennedy's "Lifetime Income Disclosures," 48 Tax Mgmt Comp J. No. 9 (Sept. 4, 2020).
99. ERISA § 409.

- The penalty for failure to file a registration statement for deferred vested benefits or to file a required notification of change has increased to $10 per day (not to exceed $50,000 and $10,000, respectively).[100]

The Secretary of Labor has the authority to assess a civil penalty not exceeding $1,000 per day from the date of the plan administrator's failure or refusal to file an annual report.[101] ERISA imposes a criminal penalty on any person who willfully violates the provision of the reporting and disclosure requirements.[102]

A participant or beneficiary has a cause of action under ERISA to enforce his or her rights in order to obtain appropriate relief.[103] Such action can also result in a penalty of up to $100 per day (up to $1,000) for failing to respond to a timely request for information.[104] In some cases, the plan administrator may be personally liable for paying a fine if he or she fails to produce documents ordered by the Secretary within 30 days of the request.[105]

B. Materials

REGULATIONS FOR REPORTING AND DISCLOSURE

- 1. The authority citation for part 2520 continues to read as follows:

Authority: 29 U.S.C. 1021–1025, 1027, 1029–1031, 1059, 1134 and 1135; and Secretary of Labor's Order 1-2011 77 FR 1088 (Jan. 9, 2012). Sec. 2520.101-2 also issued under 29 U.S.C. 1132, 1181–1183, 1181 note, 1185, 1185a–b, 1191, and 1191a– c. Secs. 2520.102-3, 2520.104b-1 and 2520.104b-3 also issued under 29 U.S.C.1003, 1181–1183, 1181 note, 1185, 1185a–b, 1191, and 1191a–c. Secs. 2520.104b-1 and 2520.107 also issued under 26 U.S.C. 401 note, 111 Stat. 788. Sec. 2520.101-5 also issued under sec. 501 of Pub. L. 109-280, 120 Stat. 780, and sec. 105(a), Pub. L. 110-458, 122 Stat. 5092.

- 2. Amend § 2520.101-3 by revising paragraph (b)(3) to read as follows:

§ 2520.101-3 Notice of blackout periods under individual account plans.

* * * * *

(b) * * *

(3) Form and manner of furnishing notice. The notice required by paragraph (a) of this section shall be in writing and furnished to affected participants and beneficiaries in any manner consistent with the requirements of § 2520.104b-1 of this

---

100. SECURE §§ 402–403, effective after December 31, 2019.
101. ERISA § 502(c)(2).
102. *See* ERISA, Title I, Part 1, Subtitle B (reporting and disclosure requirements); *see also* ERISA § 501.
103. ERISA § 502(c).
104. ERISA § 502(c)(1).
105. ERISA § 502(c)(6).

chapter, including § 2520.104b-1(c) or § 2520.104b-31 of this chapter relating to the use of electronic media.

* * * * *

• 3. Amend § 2520.104b-1 by revising

paragraph (c)(1) introductory text and

adding paragraph (f) to read as follows:

§ 2520.104b-1 Disclosure.

* * * * *

(c) * * *

(1) Except as otherwise provided by applicable law, rule or regulation, including the alternative methods for disclosure through electronic media in paragraph (f) of this section, the administrator of an employee benefit plan furnishing documents through electronic media is deemed to satisfy the requirements of paragraph (b)(1) of this section with respect to an individual described in paragraph (c)(2) of this section if:

* * * * *

(f) Alternative disclosure through electronic media as an alternative to electronic media disclosure obligations in paragraph (c) of this section, the administrator of an employee benefit plan is deemed to satisfy the requirements of paragraph (b)(1) of this section, provided that the administrator complies with the obligations in 29 CFR 2520.104b-31.

• 4. Add § 2520.104b-31 to subpart F to read as follows:

§ 2520.104b-31 Alternative method for disclosure through electronic media — Notice-and-access.

(a) *Alternative method for disclosure through electronic media — Notice-and access.* As an alternative to § 2520.104b-1(c), the administrator of an employee benefit plan satisfies the general furnishing obligation in § 2520.104b-1(b)(1) with respect to covered individuals and covered documents, provided that the administrator complies with the notice, access, and other requirements of paragraphs (b) through (k) of this section, as applicable.

(b) *Covered individual.* For purposes of this section, a "covered individual" is a participant, beneficiary, or other individual entitled to covered documents and who — when he or she begins participating in the plan, as a condition of employment, or otherwise — provides the employer, plan sponsor, or administrator (or an appropriate designee of any of the foregoing) with an electronic address, such as an electronic mail ("email") address or internet-connected mobile computing-device (e.g., "smartphone") number, at which the covered individual may receive a written notice of internet availability, described in paragraph (d) of this section, or an email described in paragraph (k) of this section. Alternatively, if an electronic address is assigned by an employer to an employee for employment-related purposes that include but are not limited to the delivery of covered documents, the employee is treated as if he or she provided the electronic address.

(c) *Covered documents.* For purposes of this section, a "covered document" is:

(1) *Pension benefit plans.* In the case of an employee pension benefit plan, as defined in section 3(2) of the Act, any document or information that the administrator is required to furnish to participants and beneficiaries pursuant to Title I of the Act, except for any document or information that must be furnished only upon request.

(2) [Reserved]

(d) *Notice of internet availability*—(1) *General.* The administrator must furnish to each covered individual a notice of internet availability for each covered document in accordance with the requirements of this section.

(2) *Timing of notice of internet availability.* A notice of internet availability must be furnished at the time the covered document is made available on the website described in paragraph (e) of this section. However, if an administrator furnishes a combined notice of internet availability for more than one covered document, as permitted under paragraph (i) of this section, the requirements of this paragraph (d)(2) are treated as satisfied if the combined notice of internet availability is furnished each plan year, and, if the combined notice of internet availability was furnished in the prior plan year, no more than 14 months following the date the prior plan year's notice was furnished.

(3) *Content of notice of internet availability.* (i) A notice of internet availability furnished pursuant to this section must contain the information set forth in paragraphs (d)(3)(i)(A) through (H) of this section:

(A) A prominent statement—for example as a title, legend, or subject line—that reads: "Disclosure About Your Retirement Plan."

(B) A statement that reads: "Important information about your retirement plan is now available. Please review this information."

(C) An identification of the covered document by name (for example, a statement that reads: "your Quarterly Benefit Statement is now available") and a brief description of the covered document if identification only by name would not reasonably convey the nature of the covered document.

(D) The internet website address, or a hyperlink to such address, where the covered document is available. The website address or hyperlink must be sufficiently specific to provide ready access to the covered document and will satisfy this standard if it leads the covered individual either directly to the covered document or to a login page that provides, or immediately after a covered individual logs on provides, a prominent link to the covered document.

(E) A statement of the right to request and obtain a paper version of the covered document, free of charge, and an explanation of how to exercise this right.

(F) A statement of the right, free of charge, to opt out of electronic delivery and receive only paper versions of covered documents, and an explanation of how to exercise this right.

(G) A cautionary statement that the covered document is not required to be available on the website for more than one year or, if later, after it is superseded by a subsequent version of the covered document.

(H) A telephone number to contact the administrator or other designated representative of the plan.

(ii) A notice of internet availability furnished pursuant to this section may contain a statement as to whether action by the covered individual is invited or required in response to the covered document and how to take such action, or that no action is required, provided that such statement is not inaccurate or misleading.

(4) *Form and manner of furnishing notice of internet availability.* A notice of internet availability must:

(i) Be furnished electronically to the address referred to in paragraph (b) of this section;

(ii) Contain only the content specified in paragraph (d)(3) of this section, except that the administrator may include pictures, logos, or similar design elements, so long as the design is not inaccurate or misleading and the required content is clear;

(iii) Be furnished separately from any other documents or disclosures furnished to covered individuals, except as permitted under paragraph (i) of this section; and

(iv) Be written in a manner calculated to be understood by the average plan participant.

(e) *Standards for internet website.* (1) The administrator must ensure the existence of an internet website at which a covered individual is able to access covered documents.

(2) The administrator must take measures reasonably calculated to ensure that:

(i) The covered document is available on the website no later than the date on which the covered document must be furnished under the Act;

(ii) The covered document remains available on the website at least until the date that is one year after the date the covered document is made available on the website pursuant to paragraph (e)(2)(i) of this section or, if later, the date it is superseded by a subsequent version of the covered document;

(iii) The covered document is presented on the website in a manner calculated to be understood by the average plan participant;

(iv) The covered document is presented on the website in a widely available format or formats that are suitable to be both read online and printed clearly on paper;

(v) The covered document can be searched electronically by numbers, letters, or words; and

(vi) The covered document is presented on the website in a widely available format or formats that allow the covered document to be permanently retained in an electronic format that satisfies the requirements of paragraph (e)(2)(iv) of this section.

(3) The administrator must take measures reasonably calculated to ensure that the website protects the confidentiality of personal information relating to any covered individual.

(4) For purposes of this section, the term website means an internet website, or other internet or electronic-based information repository, such as a mobile application, to which covered individuals have been provided reasonable access.

(f) Right to copies of paper documents or to opt out of electronic delivery. (1) Upon request from a covered individual, the administrator must promptly furnish to such individual, free of charge, a paper copy of a covered document. Only one paper copy of any covered document must be provided free of charge under this section.

(2) Covered individuals must have the right, free of charge, to globally opt out of electronic delivery and receive only paper versions of covered documents. Upon request from a covered individual, the administrator must promptly comply with such an election.

(3) The administrator must establish and maintain reasonable procedures governing requests or elections under paragraphs (f)(1) and (2) of this section. The procedures are not reasonable if they contain any provision, or are administered in a way, that unduly inhibits or hampers the initiation or processing of a request or election.

(4) The system for furnishing a notice of internet availability must be designed to alert the administrator of a covered individual's invalid or inoperable electronic address. If the administrator is alerted that a covered individual's electronic address has become invalid or inoperable, such as if a notice of internet availability sent to that address is returned as undeliverable, the administrator must promptly take reasonable steps to cure the problem (for example, by furnishing a notice of internet availability to a valid and operable secondary electronic address that had been provided by the covered individual, if available, or obtaining a new valid and operable electronic address for the covered individual) or treat the covered individual as if he or she made an election under paragraph (f)(2) of this section. If the covered individual is treated as if he or she made an election under paragraph (f)(2) of this section, the administrator must furnish to the covered individual, as soon as is reasonably practicable, a paper version of the covered document identified in the undelivered notice of internet availability.

(g) *Initial notification of default electronic delivery and right to opt out.* The administrator must furnish to each individual, prior to the administrator's reliance on this section with respect to such individual, a notification on paper that covered documents will be furnished electronically to an electronic address; identification of the electronic address that will be used for the individual; any instructions necessary to access the covered documents; a cautionary statement that the covered document is not required to be available on the website for more than one year or, if later, after it is superseded by a subsequent version of the covered document; a statement of the right to request and obtain a paper version of a covered document, free of charge, and an explanation of how to exercise this right; and a statement of the right, free of charge, to opt out of electronic delivery and receive only paper versions of covered documents, and an explanation of how to exercise this right. A notification furnished pursuant to this paragraph (g) must be written in a manner calculated to be understood by the average plan participant.

(h) *Special rule for severance from employment.* At the time a covered individual who is an employee, and for whom an electronic address assigned by an employer pursuant to paragraph (b) of this section is used to furnish covered documents, severs from employment with the employer, the administrator must take measures reasonably calculated to ensure the continued accuracy and availability of such electronic address or to obtain a new electronic address that enables receipt of covered documents following the individual's severance from employment.

(i) *Special rule for annual combined notices of internet availability.* Notwithstanding the requirements in paragraphs (d)(4)(ii) and (iii) of this section, an administrator may furnish one notice of internet availability that incorporates or combines the content required by paragraph (d)(3) of this section with respect to one or more of the following:

(1) A summary plan description, as required pursuant to section 104(a) of the Act;

(2) Any covered document or information that must be furnished annually, rather than upon the occurrence of a particular event, and does not require action by a covered individual by a particular deadline;

(3) Any other covered document if authorized in writing by the Secretary of Labor, by regulation or otherwise, in compliance with section 110 of the Act; and

(4) Any applicable notice required by the Internal Revenue Code if authorized in writing by the Secretary of the Treasury.

(j) *Reasonable procedures for compliance.* The conditions of this section are satisfied, notwithstanding the fact that the covered documents described in paragraph (b) of this section are temporarily unavailable for a reasonable period of time in the manner required by this section due to technical maintenance or unforeseeable events or circumstances beyond the control of the administrator, provided that:

(1) The administrator has reasonable procedures in place to ensure that the covered documents are available in the manner required by this section; and

(2) The administrator takes prompt action to ensure that the covered documents become available in the manner required by this section as soon as practicable following the earlier of the time at which the administrator knows or reasonably should know that the covered documents are temporarily unavailable in the manner required by this section.

(k) *Alternative method for disclosure through email systems.* Notwithstanding any other provision of this section, an administrator satisfies the general furnishing obligation in §2520.104b-1(b)(1) by using an email address to furnish a covered document to a covered individual, provided that:

(1) The covered document is sent to a covered individual's email address, referred to in paragraph (b) of this section, no later than the date on which the covered document must be furnished under the Act.

(2) In lieu of furnishing a notice of internet availability pursuant to paragraph (d) of this section, the administrator sends an email pursuant to this paragraph (k) that:

(i) Includes the covered document in the body of the email or as an attachment;

(ii) Includes a subject line that reads: "Disclosure About Your Retirement Plan";

(iii) Includes the information described in paragraph (d)(3)(i)(C) of this section if the covered document is an attachment (identification or brief description of the covered document), paragraphs (d)(3)(i)(E) (statement of right to paper copy of covered document), (d)(3)(i)(F) (statement of right to opt out of electronic delivery), and (d)(3)(i)(H) (a telephone number) of this section; and

(iv) Complies with paragraph (d)(4)(iv) of this section (relating to readability).

(3) The covered document is:

(i) Written in a manner reasonably calculated to be understood by the average plan participant;

(ii) Presented in a widely-available format or formats that are suitable to be read online, printed clearly on paper, and permanently retained in an electronic format that satisfies the preceding requirements in this sentence; and

(iii) Searchable electronically by numbers, letters, or words.

(4) The administrator:

(i) Takes measures reasonably calculated to protect the confidentiality of personal information relating to the covered individual; and

(ii) Complies with paragraphs (f) (relating to copies of paper documents or the right to opt out); (g) (relating to the initial notification of default electronic delivery), except for the cautionary statement; and (h) (relating to severance from employment) of this section.

(l) *Dates; severability.* (1) This section is applicable July 27, 2020.

(2) If any provision of this section is held to be invalid or unenforceable by its terms, or as applied to any person or circumstance, or stayed pending further agency action, the provision shall be construed so as to continue to give the maximum effect to the provision permitted by law, unless such holding shall be one of invalidity or unenforceability, in which event the provision shall be severable from this section and shall not affect the remainder thereof.

Chapter 17

Roles of the Department of Labor and the Pension Benefit Guaranty Corporation

Reading Assignment: Visit the DOL's EBSA website at www.dol.gov/agencies/ebsa

ERISA § 512

Visit the PBGC's website at www.pbgc.gov

Class Discussion Questions: What are the various forms of guidance issued by the DOL regarding employee benefit plans?

Explain the differences between VFCP and DFVCP.

Why is the PBGC a federal corporation instead of a federal agency?

Overview

Which group within the DOL has jurisdiction over ERISA retirement and health and welfare benefit plans?

- the Employee Benefits Security Administration (EBSA)

What does the EBSA group do?

- they audit ERISA plans for both criminal and civil violations of reporting and disclosure and fiduciary issues (as well as the continuation and the portability and accountability in group health plans)

- they receive calls from plan participants and assist them in understanding their rights under ERISA

- they try to educate plan sponsors and fiduciaries of their obligations under ERISA

What forms of guidance does EBSA provide?

- as an executive agency, they interpret statutory provisions through regulations, field advisory opinions, and other promulgated guidance

- they have jurisdiction to grant individual transaction exemptions between an ERISA plan and a party in interest to proceed with the transaction even though it is statutorily prohibited (and they can extend that PT exemption to a whole class of parties in interest)

How does EBSA protect the rights provided to employees under ERISA?

- in some litigation, the Secretary of Labor has the authority to stand in the shoes of a disgruntled participant and actually use its full resources to be a party in civil litigation

- more often than not, however, EBSA can offer to file an *amicus curiae* brief in litigation to show its interpretation of the participant's legal arguments

How does EBSA ensure proper reporting and disclosure?

- EBSA has been designated as the single agency to receive the annual Form 5500 reporting form (and attachments), and once processed, shares the information with the IRS and PBGC

How does the PBGC protect the rights of employees under Title IV of ERISA?

- PBGC encourages the continuation and maintenance of private-sector defined benefit pension plans, provides timely and uninterrupted payment of pension benefits from underfunded defined benefit plans, and keeps pension insurance premiums at a minimum

- it is not funded by general tax revenues but instead collects insurance premiums from employers that sponsor insured pension plans, earns money from investments, and receives funds from pension plans it takes over

A. Organization of the DOL

According to the DOL, its mission is "[t]o foster, promote, and develop the welfare of the wage earners, job seekers, and retirees of the United States; improve working conditions; advance opportunities for profitable employment; and assure work-related benefits and rights."[1] It administers and enforces over 180 federal laws, covering about 10 million employers and 125 million workers. As Title I of ERISA amended 29 U.S.C., which is the federal labor statute, it is within the jurisdiction of the DOL, particularly the Employee Plans Security Administration (EPSA). EBSA also administers reporting requirements for continuation of healthcare provisions, required under the Comprehensive Omnibus Budget Reconciliation Act of 1985 (COBRA), and for the healthcare portability requirements on group plans under the Health Insurance Portability and Accountability Act (HIPAA).

EBSA oversees nearly 710,000 private retirement plans, 2.4 million health plans, and similar numbers of other welfare benefit plans, whose plans hold approximately $11.1 trillion in assets. It assists nearly 154 million workers, retirees, and their families with education and outreach. It balances proactive enforcement with compliance as-

---

1. *About Us*, U.S. Dep't of Labor, www.dol.gov./general/aboutdol.

sistance. It provides quality assistance to plan participants and beneficiaries and raises the knowledge level of this constituent base by giving them access to available plan documents that have been filed with the DOL.

The EBSA organizational chart consists of an Acting Assistant Secretary (Jeanne Wilson, as of the writing of this book), and three deputies: the Principal Deputy Assistant Secretary who oversees regulations and prohibited transaction exemptions; the Deputy Assistant Secretary of the National Office who oversees enforcement and outreach, education, and assistance; and the Deputy Assistant Secretary who oversees 10 regional offices throughout the United States.

ERISA § 512 calls for the establishment of an Advisory Council on Employee Welfare and Pension Benefit Plans, known as the ERISA Advisory Council. The duties of the council are to advise the secretary and submit recommendations regarding the Secretary's functions under ERISA. The council consists of 15 members, with three-year terms, representing employee organizations, employers, and the general public. The council meets at least four meetings each year, which are open to the public. It concludes each year by issuing a report to the assistant secretary.[2]

The author was a member of the ERISA Advisory Council from 2005 through 2007 when it reported on the following topics:

- Retirement Distributions and Options, and Health and Welfare Benefit Plans' Communications (2005 Report)

- Plan Assets, Exemptions and Cross-Trading, and Health Information Technology, and Prudent Investment Process (2006 Report)

- Financial Literacy of Plan Participants and the Role of the Employer, Fiduciary Responsibilities and Revenue Sharing Practices, and Participant Benefit Statements (2007 Report).[3]

As was true for the reports issued by the IRS' Advisory Committee (ACT), the reports by the ERISA Advisory Council contain a wealth of information as they generally provide history and context regarding the issues that are being addressed.

1. Enforcement

If a DOL agent uncovers a violation of ERISA's civil provisions (e.g., breach of fiduciary duty claim), EBSA will seek to obtain correction of the violation. The goal of EBSA is to promote voluntary compliance whenever possible. In the context of a breach of fiduciary duty claim, the correction may involve paying amounts to restore losses, disgorging profits, and paying penalty amounts, if applicable. The Deputy

---

2. The reports include a synopsis of the meetings and recommendations for the assistant secretary of EBSA. In consultation with the assistant secretary of EBSA, the ERISA Advisory Council selects germane, current issues that need solutions.

3. The ERISA Advisory Council's reports are available at https://www.dol.gov/agencies/ebsa/about-ebsa/about-us/erisa-advisory-council.

Assistant Secretary for National Office Operations (Timothy Hauser, as of the writing of this book) works with field agents to make opportunities available for the fiduciary to self-correct. In such cases, ESBA will not bring a civil lawsuit regarding the issue involved. If voluntary compliance is not achieved, EBSA may refer a case to its attorneys (through the Solicitor of Labor's Office) for litigation. ESBA keeps a yearly fact sheet showing its enforcement accomplishments.[4]

Civil Investigations

For the 2019 fiscal year, EBSA restored over $2.57 billion to employee benefit plans, participants, and beneficiaries: $2.02 billion in recoveries from enforcement action; $14.6 million from the Voluntary Fiduciary Correction Program; $33.2 million from the Abandoned Plan Program; and $510 million in monetary benefit recoveries from informal complaint resolutions. EBSA for the 2019 fiscal year closed 1,146 civil investigations with 770 (67%) of them resulting in monetary results for the plans or other corrective action. Examples of civil wrongdoing included:

- Failing to operate the plan prudently and for the exclusive benefit of participants and beneficiaries;
- Using plan assets to benefit certain related parties to the plan, such as the plan administrator, the plan sponsor, and parties related to these individuals;
- Failing to property value plan assets at their current fair market value or to hold plan assets in trust as required;
- Failing to follow the terms of the plan (unless it would not be consistent with ERISA);
- Failing to properly select and monitor service providers as required by the prudence standard;
- Taking any adverse action against an individual for exercising his or her rights under the plan (such as being fired, fined, or otherwise discriminated against); and
- Failure to comply with ERISA Part 7 and the Affordable Care Act (applicable to welfare plans only).[5]

Criminal Investigations

EBSA also conducts criminal investigations regarding employee benefit plans such as embezzlement, kickbacks, and false statements. Prosecution of these criminal violations is handled by the U.S. Attorney's Office.

Title 18 of the U.S. Criminal Code contains three statutes which address violations involving employee benefit plans:

---

4. The fact sheet for the fiscal year is available at https://www.dol.gov/sites/dolgov/files/EBSA/about-ebsa/our-activities/resource-center/fact-sheets/ebsa-monetary-results.pdf.
5. This list of examples of common civil violations is available at https://www.dol.gov/agencies/ebsa/about-ebsa/our-activities/enforcement.

- Theft or Embezzlement from Employee Benefit Plan (18 U.S.C. § 664);
- False Statements or Concealment of Facts in Relation to Documents Required by ERISA of 1974 (18 U.S.C. § 1027); and
- Offer, Acceptance, or Solicitation to Influence Operations of Employee Benefit Plan (18 U.S.C. § 1954).

ERISA also contains its own criminal provisions:

- § 411, Prohibition Against Certain Person Holding Certain Positions. Persons convicted of violations enumerated in § 411 are subject to a bar from holding plan positions or providing services to plans for up to 13 years;
- § 501, Willful Violation of Title I, Part 1;
- § 511, Coercive Interference; and
- § 519, Prohibition on False Statements and Representations. Persons shall not make false statements in connection with the marketing or sale of a Multiple Employer Welfare Arrangements (MEWA).

Decisions to seek criminal action turn on a number of factors, including:

- The egregiousness and magnitude of the violation;
- The desirability and likelihood of incarceration both as a deterrent and as a punishment; and
- Whether the case involves a prior ERISA violator.[6]

Voluntary Compliance

EBSA has two important voluntary compliance programs designed to encourage employers to comply with ERISA and self-correct certain mistakes/delinquencies. The programs entice employers into complying and self-reporting/correcting by providing protection from higher civil penalties, allowing employers to pay a voluntary reduced penalty, and in some cases, providing for an excise tax exemption. In order to qualify, the employer must have a plan subject to Title I of ERISA, and the DOL cannot have already taken action against the plan or the employer regarding the delinquency, including but not limited to a written notice by the Department identifying the problems.

Theses two voluntary compliance programs include the Voluntary Fiduciary Correction Program (VFCP) and the Delinquent Filer Voluntary Compliance Program (DFVCP). Each program has a different set of criteria for acceptance.

Voluntary Fiduciary Correction Program (VFCP)

Anyone who may be liable for fiduciary violations under ERISA may apply for relief under the VFCP assuming all the requirements of the program are met.[7] Since

---

6. A description of EBSA's criminal enforcement provisions is available at https://www.dol.gov/agencies/ebsa/about-ebsa/our-activities/enforcement.

7. U.S. Dep't of Labor, EBSA, *Fact Sheet: Voluntary Fiduciary Correction Program* (Dec. 2018), https://www.dol.gov/sites/dolgov/files/EBSA/about-ebsa/our-activities/resource-center/fact-sheets/

plan fiduciaries can be held personally liable for plan losses attributable to their breaches, it is imperative that they discover and correct problems as soon as possible. VFCP was updated in October of 2019 to expand the transactions eligible for correction, to add new correction methods, to simplify the method of calculating the correction amount, and to develop an online calculator to assist in determining correction amounts.[8]

The primary requirement of the program is that the transaction which violated ERISA must fall into one of 23 types of violations eligible for correction (e.g., below market interest rate loans with parties in interest, purchases of assets by plans from parties in interest, payment of dual compensation to plan fiduciaries, etc.).[9] For the 2019 fiscal year, EBSA received 1,600 applications for VFCP.

Participants in the VFCP need to satisfy four requirements to participate in the program:

- Identify any violations and determine whether they fall within the transactions covered by the VFCP;

- Follow the process for correcting specific violations;

- Calculate and restore to the plan any losses or profits with interest, and distribute any supplemental benefits to participants; and

- File a VFCP application with the EBSA regional office, including documentation of the corrective action taken. A model application form is now available.[10]

Delinquent Filer Voluntary Correction Program (DFVCP)

EBSA allows plans subject to Title I of ERISA to self-correct when they fail to file an annual report, in order to avoid potentially higher civil penalty assessments. For the 2019 fiscal year, EBSA received 20,088 annual reports through the DFVCP. The first condition for program eligibility is that EBSA has not yet contacted the employer to inform him or her that the annual report was not filed. The second condition is then to electronically file with EFAST2 a complete Form 5500 or, if eligible, Form 5500-SF, with any required schedules and attachments, for each year relief is requested.[11] The basic penalty under the program is $10 per day for delinquent filings, but there are maximum "per filing" caps and "per plan" caps.[12]

---

vfcp.pdf. The original program was introduced in 2002, and simplified and expanded in a 2006 Update Notice.

8. A fact sheet describing the October 2019 changes is https://www.dol.gov/sites/dolgov/files/EBSA/about-ebsa/our-activities/resource-center/faqs/vfcp.pdf.

9. U.S. Dep't of Labor, EBSA, *Correction Programs, Voluntary Fiduciary Correction Program*, http://www.dol.gov/agencies/ebsa/employers-and-advisers/plan-adminstrtion-and-compliance/correction-programs.

10. *Id.*

11. *See* U.S. Dep't of Labor, EBSA, *Fact Sheet: Delinquent Filer Voluntary Compliance Program* (Jan. 29, 2013), https://www.dol.gov/sites/dolgov/files/EBSA/about-ebsa/our-activities/resource-center/fact-sheets/dfvcp.pdf.

12. *Id.*

Informal Complaint Resolution

EBSA encourages workers who experience a problem with an employee benefit plan to contact them. It assists in finding lost or stolen pension benefits; denied health or disability benefits; COBRA issues; association health plans; and plan administration and compliance. For the 2019 fiscal year, EBSA's benefits advisors closed more than 166,000 inquiries and recovered $510 million in benefits on behalf of workers and their families through informal resolution of individual complaints. Many of these inquiries came through EBSA's toll-free number, 1-866-444-EBSA (3272), and its website, askebsa.dol.gov. Such inquiries often lead to enforcement actions. When EBSA becomes aware of frequent complaints regarding a particular plan, employer, or service provider, the matter is referred for investigation. For the 2019 fiscal year, EBSA opened 501 new investigations from benefits advisors' referrals.

Outreach and Education

EBSA organizes education and outreach events for workers, employers, plan officials, and members of Congress. Such events include assisting dislocated workers who are facing layoffs, educating employers of their obligations under ERISA, using the train-the-trainer approach to inform congressional staff of EBSA programs for their use in constituent services, and providing employees with information about their federal rights. For the 2019 fiscal year, 1,788 outreach events were held.

EBSA also reaches workers, retirees, employers, plan service providers, and the public through its printed materials and website at www.dol.gov/agencies/ebsa. English and Spanish language publications featuring participant and compliance assistance information are available through its toll-free numbers. In 2019, 376,991 publications were distributed, and 3.91 million visitors visited its website.

2. Guidance and Prohibited Transaction Exemptions

EBSA's Office of Regulations and Interpretations (directed by Joe Canary, as of the writing of this book) is responsible for carrying out the agency's regulatory agenda and interpretive activities. It is comprised of three divisions: the Division of Regulations, the Division of Fiduciary Interpretations, and the Division of Coverage, Reporting and Disclosure. The Division of Regulations is responsible for managing and implementing EBSA's regulatory priorities under Title I of ERISA and coordinating regulatory activities with other federal agencies (e.g., IRS, HHS, and the PBGC). The general interpretive responsibilities of the Office are allocated on a subject-matter basis between the Division of Fiduciary Interpretations (e.g., fiduciary responsibilities, prohibited transactions, qualified domestic relations orders, and qualified medical child support orders) and the Division of Coverage, Reporting, and Disclosure (e.g., coverage, reporting, disclosures, suspensions of benefits, preemptions, claims procedures).

As a regulatory department, the Department of Labor has the power to create federal regulations deemed necessary to implement and enforce labor-related laws and policies enacted by Congress. Similar to the Treasury's regulations, the DOL regulations have the full force and effect of law, unless they conflict with the labor statute.

Other types of technical guidance issued by EBSA include:

- *Field Assistance Bulletins (FAS):* These are written by the Office of Regulations and Interpretations to the Director of Enforcement and the Regional Directors to provide guidance in response to questions that have arisen in field operations.

- *Advisory Opinions:* These opinions are issued by the Office of Regulations and Interpretations, answering inquiries from individuals and organizations, which apply the law to a specific set of factors (e.g., advisory opinions) or which merely call attention to well established principles or interpretations (e.g., information letters).

- *Prohibited Transaction Exemptions:* Applications for processing requests for individual and class exemptions from ERISA's prohibited transaction provisions are made to the Office of Exemption Determinations. It is comprised of two divisions, the Division of Individual Exemptions and the Division of Class Exemptions. The Division of Individual Exemptions is staffed by a division chief and three teams of analysts, who examine individual exemption applications, prepare interpretive letters and DOL notices, and review petitions for good faith waivers of ERISA § 502(l) penalties. The Division of Class Exemptions is responsible for examining class exemptions applications, preparing DOL notices, reviewing petitions for good faith waivers of ERISA § 502(l) penalties, drafting advisory opinions and information letters regarding class exemptions, and handling special projects.

B. Organization of the PBGC

The PBGC is headed by a director (Gordon Hartogensis, as of the writing of this book) who is appointed by the President and confirmed by the Senate.[13] The Board of Directors consists of the Secretaries of Labor, Commerce, and Treasury, with the Secretary of Labor as Chair. In its mission statement, it states that the PBGC's purpose is to protect the retirement income of over 35 million American workers in private-sector defined benefit pension plans. It is not funded by general tax revenues but instead collects insurance premiums from employers that sponsor insured pension plans, earns money from investments, and receives funds from the pension plans it takes over. For the 2019 fiscal year, the PBGC paid for monthly retirement benefits, up to a guaranteed maximum,[14] for more than 932,000 retirees in more than 4,900

---

13. The PBGC is headed by a director, who reports to its board of directors. Previously, the PBGC's Board Chairman (the Secretary of Labor) appointed the director. Under PPA '06, Congress changed this, such that the PBGC's director is to be appointed by the President and confirmed by the Senate. *See* PPA '06 § 411(a)(1), amending ERISA § 4002(a).

14. As you will recall from Chapter 15, the PBGC does not insure all benefits from a defined benefit plan, but only those that are guaranteed. A guaranteed benefit must meet three criteria: (1) it must be nonforfeitable (which does not include those benefits that become nonforfeitable solely

single-employer plans that could not pay promised benefits. Including those who have not yet retired and participants in multi-employer plans receiving financial assistance, the PBGC is responsible for the current and future pensions of about 1.5 million people.

The PBGC is assisted by a seven-member advisory committee, appointed by the President of the United States to represent the interests of labor, employers, and the general public. This advisory committee provides advice on investment policy and on other matters related to the PBGC's mission.

The PBGC has a robust customer service plan to engage customers (e.g., participants) and practitioners. It provides multiple resources on its www.pbgc.gov website for finding insured and trusteed pension plans and locating lost pensions. One of its online transactional tools, MyPBA (My Pension Benefit Account), lets participants handle routing transactions (e.g., address changes, direct deposit changes). It provides newsletters and participates in industry events to educate the public.

Similar to the DOL, the PBGC issues regulations, notices, and opinion letters, and publishes the interest rate and mortality assumptions to be used in determining benefits from terminating single-employer defined benefit plans.

---

because of the plan's termination under the Code), (2) it must be a pension benefit, and (3) the participant must have been entitled to the benefit.

Section IV

Other Employee
Benefits Plans

While the focus of this textbook has been on retirement plans, especially qualified retirement plans, students should be aware of other types of employee benefits plans, namely executive compensation plans, health and welfare benefits plans, and Individual Retirement Accounts (IRAs). The rules governing these other types of employee benefits plans are complex; henceforth, these chapters provide a high overview regarding how these plans operate.

Chapter 18 examines executive compensation — its different forms and their treatment under the federal tax code. It also demonstrates how other federal law interact with executive compensation plans.

Chapter 19 provides the basics on health and welfare benefits plans. It lists the various types of welfare benefits plans and the federal tax treatment for each. It identifies how group health plans have evolved since the passage of the Affordable Care Act, as well as examining how other federal laws impact those plans.

Chapter 20 concludes with a review of Individual Retirement Accounts (IRAs). While such plans are not covered under Title I of ERISA, they are regulated under Title II of ERISA.

Chapter 18

Basics of Executive Compensation

Reading Assignment: ERISA § 4(b)(5), 201(2)

I.R.C. §§ 61(a)(1), 83, 162(a)(1), 162(m), 404(a)(5), 422, 451, 280G, 4960

Class Discussion Questions: Why is executive compensation so different than rank-and-file compensation?

How do executives benefit from golden parachute arrangements?

What are the types of nonqualified deferred compensation arrangements for executives?

Why do very few plans qualify as excess benefit plans?

What is a top hat plan for purposes of Title I of ERISA?

Distinguish between the various forms of equity compensation that can be given to an executive.

Overview

What are some ways to pay executives and other employees with current cash or cash-like compensation?

- there is generally no dollar limit cap on compensation; however, in order for the employer to deduct salary paid as a business expense, the salary must be "reasonable"—over the years, a five-factor test has been developed to determine reasonableness

- prior to 2018, in a publicly traded company, for the chief executive officer and next four most highly paid employees whose compensation is disclosed under SEC proxy statement rules, the employer's deduction for general compensation that is not "performance based" or "commission based" is limited to $1 million; TCJA deleted the two exceptions for performance based and commission based compensation

- golden parachutes:
  - some key executives will receive certain compensation in the future if there is a change in control of ownership in the employer
  - if this compensation is deemed a "parachute" payment, then, in addition to normal income taxes, the individual will need to pay a 20% excise tax on the "excess amount" (i.e., anything in excess of base salary), and the employer will lose its salary deduction on this amount
  - compensation will be deemed "parachute" payments if they are in excess of three times base salary
  - if a severance agreement is executed within one year prior to the change of control, then the severance payments could lose their protected status and be deemed a "parachute" payment (they are presumed to be parachute, and the employer would need to prove that it was a bona fide severance agreement with no advance knowledge of the eventual change of control)
  - similarly, payments made due to termination of employment within one year following the change in control will be assumed to be a "parachute" payment as well
  - a change in control means a change in the actual ownership or effective control, or a change in control of a substantial portion of the corporate assets
- corporate owned life insurance:
  - the employer can "loan" the employee enough money to pay the premiums for whole life insurance
  - to gain the best tax advantages, the employer will be repaid for the loan from the cash surrender value of the policy upon the payment of death benefits to the employee's estate (or upon cancellation of the policy)
  - the policies can just be general life insurance coverage or can be part of business succession planning
  - the IRS has changed its position on the proper taxation of split dollar life insurance, and the regulations need to be reviewed before a split dollar policy is drafted
- phantom stock plans:
  - unlike equity-based plans where actual ownership rights are transferred to employees, these plans will track certain predetermined stocks or indices and will pay the employee in cash the calculated gain which would have been realized if the employee were actually given such stocks or invested in such indices
  - employers can also promise income tax gross-ups, club memberships, housing, and other perks

What are some ways to pay executives in their retirement with deferred compensation?

- the employer generally maximizes the use of qualified plans for the broad cross-section of employees.
- then, in order to attract, retain, or reward certain favored employees, other plans are set up
- if structured properly, deferred compensation plans for executives will only be subject to minimal reporting and disclosure rules of ERISA
- since these plans are not subject to the minimum vesting and coverage requirements of ERISA, they can be offered to any executive, can offer discriminatory benefits in favor of any one executive or groups of executives, and the benefits can vest and accrue in any manner
- these plans are not subject to the advanced funding requirements of ERISA (in fact, in most instances, they must remain unfunded)
- since these generally represent one-on-one negotiations between the executive and the employer, they are generally enforceable under appropriate state contract laws rather than under the federal ERISA law; however, care must be taken because, if enough executives are offered similar deferred compensation plans, then a court might determine that, collectively, the agreements looks like a single ERISA plan, subject to all the rules of ERISA

How can retirement plans be structured?

- deferred compensation plans:
  - plans set up so that an employee can make an election before services are rendered (generally by the preceding December 31) to defer a portion of currently taxable compensation to be paid in a future year
  - generally, these plans are set up to complement a qualified 401(k) plan, thus allowing an avenue for employees to defer in excess of the annual deferral limit of $19,500 (the amount for 2020)—for example, if a highly paid employee wishes to defer $100,000 of compensation she would have otherwise earned, then the maximum amount (i.e., $19,500) will be deposited into the qualified 401(k) plan and the remainder (i.e., $80,500) will be credited under a non-qualified plan
  - however, since the excess deferrals are part of the employer's general assets (and not invested in a tax-exempt qualified trust), there is no guarantee that the employees will ever receive their non-qualified deferral promises and associated fund earnings
  - there are things that can be done to segregate these deferrals in special employer accounts or trusts, but once the employee no longer has a "substantial risk of forfeiture," then the benefits are immediately taxable to the employee, even if the benefits will not be paid until a future date under the terms of the plan or employment contract

- supplemental executive retirement plans (SERPs)
  - these will take the form of either a defined benefit plan or a defined contribution plan, where the employer will promise benefits either exclusively through a nonqualified deferred compensation plan or as a supplement to the qualified plan
- excess-only plans:
  - plans set up only to offer benefits lost in a qualified plan due to the benefit limitations imposed by the Code (i.e., I.R.C. §415 maximum benefits)—so the employer can provide allocations in excess of $57,000 (for 2020) per year in a defined contribution model or can pay distributions in excess of $230,000 (for 2020) per year in a defined benefit model
  - however, other limitations (like the $200,000 salary cap of I.R.C. §401(a)(17)) were added to the Code after ERISA was enacted; therefore, few plans meet the very specific definition of an excess-only plan
- top hat plans:
  - to be excluded from Parts 2, 3, and 4 of Title I of ERISA ("Participation and Vesting," "Funding," and "Fiduciary Responsibility," respectively), a plan, which is commonly referred to as a "top hat plan" must be "a plan which is unfunded and is maintained by an employer primarily for the purpose of providing deferred compensation for a select group of management or highly compensated employees"
  - these are unfunded plans (i.e., the assets accumulated to pay liabilities always remain part of the employer's general assets which can be attacked by their creditors)
  - many plans have been designed to be top hat plans to avoid the onerous rules of ERISA and qualified plans, but due to poor design or communication, some plans have been deemed by courts to fail the specific definition
- a "rabbi trust" is a very common type of funding vehicle where benefits are "funded" through a trust which can only pay benefits to such favored employees, but which can also pay assets to the employer's creditors pursuant to a court order (thus, keeping the plan unfunded)

How are executives taxed on benefits from nonqualified deferred compensation plans?

- the deferred compensation benefits have some tax advantages:
  - deferral of income taxation to the employee until there is no longer a substantial risk of forfeiture;
  - deduction by the employer at the same time the employee includes the amount in gross income; and
  - employer pays taxes on fund earnings because the plans are unfunded (i.e., the assets remain part of the general assets of the employer—they are not part of a tax-exempt trust like qualified retirement plan assets)

- in addition to the existing income tax regime, under I.R.C. §409A, the plan must be drafted to require the executive employee to make an irrevocable election before services are performed in connection with the deferred compensation to only receive the deferred compensation at a certain point in time or upon an event like death, disability, or change in control
  - the employee executive can make elections to further postpone benefits but cannot accelerate benefits
  - if the plan is not drafted properly, then the employee will pay income taxes as of the year of deferral, plus interest, plus a 20% penalty tax
  - the wording of I.R.C. §409A causes many unexpected benefits paid to executives to be covered by the statute, but there are some exceptions for short-term deferrals and properly structured severance pay

What are some ways to transfer ownership of the business to employees?

- actual ownership:
  - ownership generally means stock shares in an incorporated business, interest shares in a partnership, and membership units in a limited liability partnership or limited liability corporation; however, publicly traded businesses are generally corporations, with shares of stock traded on the open market
- stock options:
  - in order to encourage employees to perform as well as they are able to, the employer might want to give options to purchase shares of the unrestricted employer stock at a discount
  - the theory is to offer to the employees the right to purchase stock in the future at a reduced rate; thus, if all employees collectively perform well, then market price will rise over the next few years if and when the option is exercised, and the employees will purchase the stock at a discount
  - generally, the exercise price is the current market price—for example, if ABC, Inc., is trading today at $23 per share, then a 10-year option may be granted today to an individual that allows him or her to purchase one share of ABC, Inc., stock anytime in the next 10 years for $23 per share—if the stock is trading above $23 in the future, the employee will likely purchase the stock by using her own money; if it is trading below $23, then the option will likely not be exercised until it hopefully rebounds; and if the 10-year term expires, then the stock option is valueless
  - there are special securities law rules which require certain information for publicly traded employers to communicate stock option plans with the SEC and which exempt private companies from any registration
  - there are special tax rules on when and how the employee is taxed, and when the employer can take a corresponding deduction as a reasonable business expense

- additionally, there are special accounting rules on how a publicly traded employer needs to show the stock option on its financial statements
- incentive stock options (ISOs):
  - ISOs are plans, described at I.R.C. §422, which are offered to a broad cross-section of employees and which are approved by the shareholders
  - there are limits on the types, amounts, transferability, exercise period, and holding periods of options which can be offered, but the employees will only pay capital gains rates on the gain upon the exercise of the options (the employer gets no deduction)
  - these options are only available to employees
- nonqualified stock options:
  - any option which does not comply with the ISO rules
  - the employer is not limited in how to structure the options or in who they can be offered to (e.g., a select group of employees, members of the board of directors, independent contractors, attorneys, accountants, and other business advisors)
  - the individual will pay regular income taxes on the gain upon exercise, and the employer will get a corresponding deduction at that time
- stock appreciation rights:
  - ownership generally means stock shares in an incorporated business, interest shares in a partnership, and membership units in a limited liability partnership or corporation
  - however, publicly traded businesses are generally corporations, with shares of stock traded on the open market

How are benefits from nonqualified deferred compensation plans disclosed to the public in publicly traded companies?

- in the proxy statement of publicly traded companies:
  - all components of the compensation package (including the value of stock options granted) must be disclosed for the CEO, the CFO, and the three next highest paid executives
- in the corporate financial statements:
  - the value of all stock options granted during the year must be shown as an actual cost on the financial statements

A. Issues with Current Compensation for Executives

The topic of executive compensation is one that has dominated the press, particularly with respect to the disparity in levels between the chief executive officer (CEO) and the rank-and-file worker. Executive pay differs substantially from the typical pay package offered to hourly workers or salaried management and professionals because it is biased toward rewards for actual results in the company's productivity or company stock value. As such, executive pay is designed to reward company performance and align itself with shareholder value. This chapter demonstrates how Congress has attempted to use the tax code as a means of curbing the amount of pay and type of payment. While the tax code regulates executive compensation, it is also governed by ERISA, state and federal securities laws, and common law contract principles.

At the heart of executive compensation is the employment agreement signed between the executive and the employer. It contains provisions relating to salary, bonuses, equity compensation, severance, and nonqualified deferred compensation. It will generally set out the consequences and circumstances in which the executive can be terminated. An employer may limit the executive's post-employment conduct with non-compete clauses for a period of time.

1. Types of Executive Compensation

While the typical employee is paid a base pay (determined on an hourly or salaried basis), the typical executive's pay is structured to incentivize executives to achieve company performance consistent with increases in shareholder value. Thus, unlike most other employees, the majority of an executive's pay is contingent on performance (i.e., if the company or executive fails to perform, the executive is not paid).

Components of an executive's pay typically include:

- Base pay (e.g., annual salary amount paid regardless of performance);
- Short-term incentive pay, which is annual pay if the executive achieves specified company objectives or increases shareholder value (which means the value of the stock increased);
- Long-term incentive pay, which is salaried and payable over a longer period of time if the executive achieves specified company objectives or increases shareholder value (together, short-term and long-term incentive pay is referred to as "incentive pay");
- Stock options, which provide the executive with the right to purchase a fixed number of the company's shares of stock at a set price over a period of time (e.g., 10 years), where the price at which the option may be "exercised" is the price of the company's stock as of the date the options are granted. For example, A gets the right to purchase 100 shares of ABC stock at $50/share (today's price on the stock exchange) over the next 10 years; if the stock goes up in value to $75/share,

A buys the stock at $50 and has a gain of $25/share. Usually, the options must "vest" (e.g., held by A for five years before the option can be exercised);

- Restricted stock, which are actual grants of stock shares to the executives that have restrictions attached to the stock such as vesting periods or other performance requirements before the stock is owned by the executive;

- Stock appreciation rights (SARs), which are a type of equity-related compensation in which the executive receives pay that represents the increase in the company's stock price over a specified period of time. Like stock options, SARs have a strike price, a vesting period, and carry a certain term. For example, if a SAR of 500 units is granted when the current stock price is $30, with a three-year vesting period, and if the price of the stock has risen to $50, the SAR would pay the $20 increase times the number of units ($20 × 500 units = $10,000), in either cash or stock. SARs give a similar gain as a stock option, without having the company issue stock;

- Severance pay, which may include cash, acceleration of unvested stock options, and other benefits, paid to an executive when dismissed without cause. Golden parachute payments are severance payments awarded to senior executives due to a company merger or sale, usually because the executive's position is lost due to the change;

- Additional retirement benefits, which would supplement the retirement benefits an executive already accrues under the company's qualified retirement plans; and

- Executive perquisites which could include use of the company jet.[1]

2. Deductibility of Current Compensation

Under the federal income tax code, income tax is imposed on an annual basis (known as the tax year). Most individual taxpayers are on a calendar year tax year, whereas business entities may have different tax years for a variety of reasons (e.g., April 1 through March 31). The tax code also has timing rules to determine *when* an item becomes income and *when* an item of expense is deducted. For the most part, taxpayers will be economically advantaged by deferring taxable income, whereas business entities will be economically advantaged by accelerating tax deductions. The reason for this is "the time value of money"—the theory that money available at the present time is worth more than the identical sum in the future due to its potential earning capacity (e.g., $1,000 is worth only $1,000 today, but worth $1,285 five years from now if it earns 5%).[2]

Conversely, the IRS has an interest in accelerating the reporting and taxing of income and in deferring the reporting of a deduction to increase current tax revenues.

---

1. For a glossary of terms explaining the components of an executive's pay package, see *Glossary of Terms*, CENTER ON EXEC. COMP., https://execcomp.org/Basics/Glossary.

2. *See* Tony Armstrong, *Compound Interest Calculator*, NERDWALLET (Aug. 20, 2018), https://www.nerdwallet.com/banking/calculator/compound-interest-calculator.

I.R.C. §446(c) sets forth the *timing rules* for income and deductions—it does not set forth the rules as to whether an item is income or whether one has the right to claim a deduction—it just tells us *when* to report or when to deduct. The applicable sections of the Code—sections 61 and 162—tell us if an item is includable in income or deductible from gross income.

For the executive, I.R.C. §61(a)(1) states that gross income includes compensation for services, including fees, commissions, fringe benefits, and similar items.[3] I.R.C. §451(a) sets forth the general rule that an item of gross income is includable in the tax year in which it is *received* by the taxpayer.[4] The regulations interpret that to mean that an item is income at the time the compensation is actually or *constructively* received.[5] This means that an item is *constructively* received if "it is credited to his account, set apart for him, or otherwise made available so that he may draw upon it at any time."[6] Income is not constructively received if "the taxpayer's control of its receipt is subject to substantial limitations or restrictions."[7] Such doctrine prevents the taxpayer from determining on his or her own the tax year in which the income is reported. Thus, in the context of executive compensation, if any of his or her compensation is "subject to substantial limitations or restrictions," it becomes deferred compensation, and will be taxable in a future tax year when the limitations or restrictions lapse.

The Code does not impose a dollar limit on the amount of an executive's current compensation. But a business entity is limited by I.R.C. §162(a)(1) in that only "reasonable" compensation for services rendered is deductible.[8] The issue of reasonableness generally arises in the context of a closely held business that pays "compensation" to its executive/owner that is really a disguised dividend. The reason for this is that compensation is deductible by the small business but dividends are not, so classifying the payment as compensation would generate a deduction for the business. The Internal Revenue Manual takes into account 12 factors in determining reasonableness and is applied on a case-by-case basis. In contrast, the courts have considered as many as 21 factors, weighed differently to result in two basic approaches, resulting in a case-by-case analysis.[9]

A good example of how the courts have handled the issue is seen in the case of *Elliotts, Inc. v. Commissioner*, in which the court used a five-factor test in determining reasonableness that considered:

---

3. I.R.C. §61(a)(1).
4. I.R.C. §451(a).
5. Treas. Reg. §1.451-2(a).
6. *Id.*
7. *Id.*
8. I.R.C. §162(a)(1).
9. Under the multiple factor approach, many different factors are included but not limited to the employer's financial size, health, and complexity. Criticized as being too vague, other courts use another approach known as the independent investor perspective (which asks what would a hypothetical independent investor with no management role use to determine the reasonableness of the executive's compensation). The tax court has taken a middle-of-the-road approach of using multiple factors but through the lens of an independent investor. Recently, both the Sixth and Ninth Circuits reversed the tax court in its approach.

- The employee's role in the company, including his position, hours worked, and duties performed;
- A comparison of the employee's compensation with those paid by similar companies for similar services;
- The character and condition of the company, focusing on the company's size as indicated by its sales, net income, or capital value;
- The potential for any conflict of interest (i.e., whether some relationship exists between the taxpaying company and its employee which might permit the company to disguise nondeductible corporate distributions of income as salary expenditures deductible under section 162(a)(1));
- Whether there is evidence of an internal inconsistency in a company's treatment of payments to employees that may indicate that the payments go beyond reasonable compensation.[10]

Congress had used the tax code in the past to curb *how much* should be paid to executives and the *form of payment* (e.g., base pay, stock options, and deferred compensation), but often with unintended consequences. Normally, corporate governance issues (e.g., how much and the form of payment of compensation) fall within the province of states' traditional police powers. More recently, the avenue has shifted away from the tax code to other federal legislative and regulatory mandates (e.g., Sarbanes-Oxley, SEC disclosure rules, New York Stock Exchange rules, and Dodd Frank) to regulate what were otherwise perceived to be state corporate governance issues.

Congress attempted in 1993 to curb the *amount* of current executive compensation with the enactment of I.R.C. § 162(m).[11] That subsection capped an employer's deduction for an executive's current compensation at $1 million for publicly held corporations, but only for the chief executive officer (CEO) and the next four highest paid employees.[12] There were two notable exceptions to the deduction limit — the exception for performance-based pay and the exception for commission-based pay.[13] This obviously pushed executive compensation in favor of incentive compensation packages (e.g., tied to performance goals) once the salary of $1 million in cash had been received. The result was unintended consequences — the $1 million limit became the new "minimum wage" for CEOs and was cited as being "reasonable" for I.R.C. § 162(a)(1) purposes, regardless of the industry, size, or profitability.[14] But the change affected *how* executives would be compensated due to the exception for performance-based compensation. This led to the growth of stock options which are inherently performance-based, as the option holder is given the stock option at the stock's present

---

10. *See* Elliotts, Inc. v. Comm'r, 716 F.2d 1241, 1245–47 (9th Cir. 1983).

11. I.R.C. § 162(m).

12. *Id.*

13. I.R.C. § 162(m)(4)(B)–(C).

14. See the empirical data by Harris and Livingston indicating that I.R.C. § 162(m) has caused firms' executive compensation costs to increase. David G. Harris & Jane R. Livingstone, *Federal Tax Legislation as an Implicit Contracting Cost Benchmark: The Definition of Excessive Executive Compensation*, 77 ACCT. REV. 997, 1014 (2002).

value and will not realize any value from the option unless the share price of the stock increases or the company outperforms an industry benchmark. Back in 1993, only 35% of CEO pay was attributed to incentive pay, whereas it jumped to 61% by 2013.[15]

The performance-based exception of I.R.C. § 162(m)(4)(C) required the compensation to meet the following tests:

- The performance goals are determined by a compensation committee of the company's board of directors which is comprised solely of two or more outside directors (an outside director is someone on the board who is not an employee or shareholder of the company);

- The material terms under which the compensation is to be paid, including the performance goals, are disclosed to the shareholders and approved by a majority of votes; and

- Before any payment of compensation is made, the compensation committee certifies that the performance goals were met.[16]

These criteria proved easy to meet, allowing most CEOs and the next three most highly paid executives to receive a base compensation of $1 million and then performance-based compensation (such as stock options) tied to the growth of the company or specific performance goals (e.g., setting up a new office in a foreign company). For example, Enron had a pay-for-performance attitude and relied heavily on the use of stock options. After the Enron scandal occurred, the Joint Committee on Taxation prepared a report for Senators Baucus and Grassley of the Senate Finance Committee and noted that in 2000, total compensation for the 200 highest paid employees at Enron was $1.4 billion, of which $56.6 million was attributable to 14 bonuses, $1.06 billion was attributable to stock options, $131.7 million was attributable to restricted stock, and $172.6 million was attributable to other income, including base salary.[17] The Joint Committee on Taxation found that the compensation committee of the company's board of directors was simply a "rubber stamp" for management and that the goal of the $1 million deduction limitation in reducing excessive compensation had not been realized. It recommended repealing I.R.C. § 162(m) and using non-tax laws to affect executive compensation pay decisions.[18]

In the aftermath of the financial meltdown and subprime mortgage crisis of 2008, TARP imposed new limits on executive base pay and severance pay *for banks receiving public aid* through the Capital Purchase Program (CPP).[19] The I.R.C. § 162(m) limit was lowered to $500,000 from $1 million for any senior executive officer (SEO) (de-

---

15. *See Designing Executive Compensation Plans*, SHRM (Apr. 3, 2017), https://www.shrm.org/resourcesandtools/tools-and-samples/toolkits/pages/executivecompensationplans.aspx.

16. I.R.C. § 162(m)(4)(C)(i)–(iii).

17. *See* Staff of Joint Comm. on Taxation, *Report of Investigation of Enron Corporation and Related Entities Regarding Federal Tax and Compensation Issues, and Policy Recommendations: Volume I* (Feb. 2003), http://www.jct.gov/s-3-03-vol1.pdf.

18. *Id.*

19. The Capital Purchase Program was formed under TARP which was created by the Emergency Economic Stabilization Act of 2008 (EESA).

fined as the top five most highly paid executives whose compensation was subject to SEC proxy disclosure rules) for any year in which the employer received CPP funds. It also *eliminated* the exceptions for commission-based and performance-based compensation.[20]

The Affordable Care Act in 2010 lowered the I.R.C. § 162(m) limit to $500,000 for any covered *insurance company* (publicly traded or private) with respect to compensation paid to any employee (not just the CEO and the next three highest paid executives) and some independent contractors, including directors.[21] The deduction limit for insurance companies did not have an exception for performance-based compensation or commissions. It applied to current compensation, as well as compensation currently earned for which a deduction is deferred into the future (referred to as "deferred deduction remuneration").[22]

The Coronavirus Aid, Relief, and Economic Security Act (CARES Act) was created in response to business losses resulting from COVID-19, and it imposed limitations on executive compensation for employers who initiated a CARES Act loan or guarantee under the Title IV Exchange Stabilization Fund.[23] If the employer initiated such a loan, the employer would be unable to increase compensation for certain executives, beginning on the date the loan starts and ending one year after the loan or guarantee ends.[24]

As a result of the continuous whittling away of the deduction limit, the TCJA repealed the exceptions to I.R.C. § 162(m) altogether, placing a total cap on the amount a company can deduct for executive compensation at $1 million for a company's CEO, CFO, and other three most highly paid executives.[25] Thus, the $1 million annual deduction limit becomes much harder to avoid. This change is expected to have a major impact on compensation decisions going forward. It is likely to reduce the appeal of stock options, phantom stock options, and long-term incentive packages.

From the employer's perspective, the determination of whether compensation is to be paid currently or deferred into a future tax year is critical to complying with the federal tax rules and taking a deduction for current compensation.[26] Hence, the employer must decide when the compensation for services is to be paid and thus taxable to the executive. According to the constructive receipt rules, if current compensation is to be paid, it should be free of substantial limitations or restrictions. But if

---

20. EESA § 302(a) (which created the Troubled Asset Relief Program (TARP)).

21. PPACA § 9014(a), adding I.R.C. § 162(m)(6).

22. I.R.C. § 162(m)(6)(D).

23. CARES § 4004.

24. *Id.*, prohibiting employer from increasing the compensation of any officer or any employees whose total compensation exceeds $425,000, or from offering such employees severance pay, which exceeds twice the maximum total annual compensation received by that employee.

25. TCJA § 13601(a), effective for tax years beginning after December 31, 2017. TCJA also imposed a new excise tax for exempt organizations paying renumeration in excess of $1 million for certain "covered employees." TCJA § 13602(c), effective for tax years beginning after December 31, 2017.

26. *See* Rev. Rul. 2007-12, permitting a deferral of compensation for a brief time (2½ months) after the close of the tax year).

it is to be deferred, then the employer should decide how the compensation is to be deferred, whether through a qualified retirement plan, through a nonqualified retirement plan, or neither if it is part of an employment agreement that is not deemed to be a plan, fund, or program for purposes of ERISA (and therefore, exempt from ERISA). Not only are the tax consequences important to consider, but the employer must also be aware of the rules applicable under Title I of ERISA to see if the arrangement is a plan, fund, or program, and if so, whether it is exempt from ERISA.

As a review, remember that qualified retirement plans extend favorable tax advantages to both the employer and employee, but such plans must comply with the requirements of I.R.C. §401(a). The employer receives a current deduction for contributions made to the qualified trust, but the employees defer taxation of their vested account balances until actual distribution. While not-for-profit employers that sponsor an I.R.C. §401(a), 403(b), or 457(b) or (f) plan are not interested in any deductions, they will want to comply with the applicable code provisions to defer taxation for eligible participants.

An unfunded excess benefit plan for executives (to be defined later) can be structured to defer compensation not only for executives, but also for independent contractors or consultants, or outside members of the board of directors.[27] As such, they are subject to minimal reporting and disclosure rules under ERISA. An "unfunded deferred compensation plan maintained primarily for the purposes of providing deferred compensation for a select group of management or highly compensated employees" (known as a top hat plan) is exempt from ERISA's participation, vesting, and funding requirements.[28] To the extent the executive elects to defer some of his or her current compensation, that compensation becomes part of the employer's general assets, as it cannot be invested in a tax-exempt qualified trust. As such, there is no guarantee the executives will actually receive such funds and their related earnings. As we discussed in Chapter 2, employers sought to *fund* nonqualified deferred compensation promises through trusts, referred to as "rabbi trusts."[29] A rabbi trust is simply an irrevocable grantor trust providing executives with protection in the event the employer has a later change of heart or if there is a possible change of control such that the new owner would not honor the prior commitment. The intent behind the trust was to provide security to the executives that funds would be available to pay the promised deferred compensation in the event of a change of control whereby a new employer would not honor the prior commitment. To be exempt from taxation, the assets of the rabbi trust could be set aside or segregated for the purpose of only providing deferred compensation, provided such funds were available to the employer's

---

27. ERISA §4(b)(5) (where the term "excess benefit plan" is defined in ERISA §3(36)).
28. ERISA §201(2).
29. *See* Priv. Ltr. Rul. 81-13-107 (Dec. 31, 1980). The term "rabbi trust" was coined by the first IRS private letter ruling that addressed such funding vehicles. The private letter ruling was requested by a congregation seeking to set aside or segregate funds for the express purpose of satisfying its obligation to the rabbi under a deferred compensation plan. Employers cannot formally fund nonqualified deferred compensation arrangements without putting the executives' benefits at risk for taxation.

creditors in the event of bankruptcy or insolvency.[30] For tax purposes, the rabbi trust was deemed to be an employer grantor trust, and its income, losses, and deductions flowed back to the employer.[31]

Some deferred compensation plans are simply part of an employment agreement between the executive and the employer, negotiated upon hire or renewed over the term of the agreement, and so do not rise to the level of a "plan, fund, or program"; thus they are exempt from ERISA and enforceable under state contract law. But if the employer makes similar employment arrangements to defer compensation for enough executives, the collective group may be viewed by courts as a plan, fund, or program, and thus subject to parts of ERISA.

3. Other Cash-Like Benefits

Golden Parachutes: Due to the flurry of mergers and acquisitions of the 1980s, Congress enacted I.R.C. §§ 280G and 4999,[32] seeking to regulate the *type* of executive compensation (i.e., severance payments due to a corporate take-over) that could be deducted. The Code limited an employer's deduction for excessive severance packages (referred to as golden parachutes, as they were intended to provide a soft landing for executives who lost their jobs). Payments deemed to be "excessive" (i.e., in excess of three times the executive's base pay) and triggered under a "change in control" clause would be nondeductible to the employer under I.R.C. § 280G and subject to a 20% excise tax for the executive under I.R.C. § 4999. A change of control was defined as a change in the ownership or effective control of the corporation or change in a substantial portion of the assets of the corporation.[33] There was an exception for small business corporation (e.g., S corporations with fewer than 100 shareholders).[34] In the event the severance arrangement was negotiated within one year prior to the change of control, the employer had the burden of showing that it was a bona fide severance agreement with no actual knowledge of the eventual change of control in order to be exempt from the rule.[35]

Ironically, this tax legitimized the payment of golden parachutes, and parachute payments of three times the executive's base pay became the new industry standard.

---

30. Although funds set aside in a rabbi trust must be available to the employer's general creditors, the trust tends to afford executives a larger share of assets in bankruptcy or insolvency proceedings. *See* M Benefit Solutions, White Paper: Why Companies Use Rabbi Trusts 4 ("M Benefit Solutions has had several clients go through a bankruptcy and the existence of a rabbi trust, we believe, helped executives there to obtain payment of all or a large percentage of their nonqualified deferred compensation benefits. Whether they would have been able to obtain this result without an asset already set aside to make the benefit payments is difficult to say, but is less likely.").

31. I.R.C. §§ 671–77.

32. I.R.C. §§ 280G, 4999.

33. I.R.C. § 280G(b)(2)(A).

34. I.R.C. § 280G(b)(5).

35. I.R.C. § 280G(b)(2)(C).

Some employers "softened" the blow through the use of gross-ups (i.e., paying the executives the taxes plus the 20% excise tax when the payments became income). Employers in danger of a takeover felt compelled to offer larger parachute packages to compete, and executives were incentivized to welcome the takeover in order to receive the parachute package, instead of resisting take-overs.

TCJA enacted something comparable to I.R.C. §§ 162(m) and 280G by adding I.R.C. § 4960 applicable to *tax-exempt* organizations.[36] It imposes an excise tax on the amount of remuneration in excess of $1 million, plus any "excess parachute payment" paid by a covered tax-exempt organization to a "covered employee" (top five highest paid).[37] The excise tax is currently 21%, applicable for tax years beginning after December 31, 2017.

Corporate Owned Life Insurance: Corporate owned life insurance (COLI) products are another informal way for employers to fund nonqualified deferred compensation accounts. As mentioned earlier, employers cannot formally fund these arrangements without jeopardizing the executive's tax deferral. But the employer can informally fund them by setting aside funds to offset their nonqualified deferred compensation obligations. With a COLI, the employer purchases permanent life insurance (i.e., it builds up cash value) on the lives of current executives and former employees. The employer is the owner of the policy and the named beneficiary to receive the policy proceeds on the employee's death. Thus, the COLI policy is a general corporate asset, but the policy could be held within a rabbi trust.

The COLI has tax advantages for the employer. First, the increase in the cash value under the policy accrues tax-free while the policy remains in force. Second, the policy proceeds are tax-free to the employer upon the death of the insured. Third, before the policy matures, the employer can borrow against the cash value tax-free. Even if the policy is liquidated prior to the death of the insured, the employer has deferred taxes on the gains.

Some employers found COLIs to be such good tax saving tools that they purchased coverage on many non-key employees (referred to as janitor insurance) and left the policies in effect long after the employees terminated employment. This raised some state insurance law concerns, as someone purchasing life insurance on someone else needs to have an "insurable interest" in the life of the insured. While the employer may have an insurable interest on its key employees, it is unlikely to have an uninsurable interest on all of its employees. There were also employees' concerns that the employer had insurance on their lives and could collect the proceeds without any amounts going to their families.

---

36. TCJA § 13602(a).
37. I.R.C. § 4960(a).

PPA '06 attempted to curb the use of these arrangements. It is still possible for an employer to receive the policy proceeds tax-free, but now several conditions must be met:

- The individual insured whose death has resulted in a pay-out must have been employed by the employer within the 12 months before the time of his or her death, or must have been a director or highly compensated employee at the time the policy was issued;

- Prior to the purchase of the policy, the employer must notify the above individual of its intent to insure his or her life, the maximum face amount of the policy, and the fact that the proceeds will be paid to the employer;

- The above individual insured must have provided consent before the policy was issued, and if applicable, that consent must specifically allow the employer to continue the coverage after termination of employment.[38]

Phantom Stock Plans: In cases where the performance-based plan does not wish to confer actual ownership rights to the executives (as would be the case in a stock option plan), a phantom stock plan tracks the change in the stock shares (or other indices) and pays the gain that would have been realized if stock had actually been transferred. Such plans are similar to SARs, but they may also feature rights to dividends. These are typically used to compensate international executives.

B. Retirement Plans for Executives

1. Nonqualified Deferred Compensation (NQDC) Plans, Generally

In order to be competitive and attract top talent, the employer may wish to promise benefits to executives and officers, and independent contractors, over and above what it offers through a qualified retirement plan. The term "excess benefit" plan is used in ERISA § 4(b)(5) and is exempt from ERISA's coverage. An excess benefit plan is defined in ERISA § 3(36), as a plan maintained by an employer solely for the purpose of providing benefits to certain employees in excess of the limitations of I.R.C. § 415(b) (maximum limitations for defined benefit plans) and 415(c) (maximum limitations for defined contribution plans).

> **Example:** If a qualified defined contribution plan called for an allocation of 25% of an employee's compensation, and the employee's compensation was $200,000, back in 1974, the employee could not receive an allocation of [25% × $200,000] = $50,000, as the I.R.C. § 415(c) limitation was the lesser of

---

38. PPA '06 § 863(a), adding I.R.C. § 101(j).

[$25,000 (the dollar limit), (25% × $200,000 = $50,000)] = $25,000.[39] Hence, the employee could receive an allocation of $25,000 to the qualified defined contribution plan and an allocation of an additional $25,000 could be made under the nonqualified defined contribution plan.

When the dollar cap on the compensation limit from I.R.C. § 401(a)(17) was added back in 1989 to reduce what an executive could receive under a qualified plan, ERISA § 3(36) was **not** amended to redefine an excess benefit as one maintained by an employer solely for the purpose of providing benefits to certain employees in excess of both the limitations of I.R.C. §§ 415 and 401(a)(17). As a result, the reliance on ERISA's exclusion for an excess benefit plan became moot, as an executive wanted to be made whole because of both the I.R.C. §§ 415 and 401(a)(7) limitations, not just the I.R.C. § 415 limitation.

> **Example:** If the qualified defined contribution plan called for an allocation of 25% of compensation and an executive made $500,000, the maximum allocation would be [25% × $285,000 (the 2020 § 401(a)(17) limit)] = $71,250, which is further limited by the I.R.C. § 415(c) limit = lesser of [$57,000, 100% × $285,000] = $57,000. But the executive wants to receive 25% × $500,000 = $125,000 – $57,000 from the qualified plan and $68,000 from the nonqualified plan.

The advent of the compensation limit of I.R.C. § 401(a)(17) (in 1989, at $200,000), its drastic decline to $150,000 in 1994, and the drastic declines in the maximum limitations in I.R.C. § 415 in 1983, led to the rise of nonqualified deferred compensation plans for executives, known as supplemental executive retirement plans (SERPs), in order to make executives whole.

SERPs can be designed in many ways, but one of the most common is to simply mirror the qualified plan available to the executive and pay the "excess benefit" that the qualified plan cannot pay.

> **Example:** If the executive is covered under a qualified defined benefit plan with an NRB = [80% × FAE]/65/life only or J&S, subject to I.R.C. §§ 415(b) and 401(a)(17), and the executive retires in 2020 with FAE of $1 million, the maximum the qualified defined benefit plan can pay an unmarried executive is [80% × $280,000]/65/life only or $224,000/65/life; however, the executive wants to be made whole and receive the full [80% × $1 million]/65/life only or $800,000/65/life—thus the $224,000 annual amount will come from the qualified defined benefit plan, and the remaining $576,000 annual amount will come from the nonqualified defined benefit plan, such that he or she will receive $800,000 annually.

---

39. The percentage limitation in I.R.C. § 415(c) was originally 25% of the employee's compensation. The percentage limitation was increased from 25% to 100%, effective in 2002, as a result of EGTRRA '01 § 611(c).

Similarly, if the executive was covered under a qualified defined contribution plan which permitted him or her to annually defer [10% × compensation], with a 100% match, subject to I.R.C. §§ 415(c), 401(a)(17), and 402(g), the executive with compensation of $1 million could defer no more than $19,500 (for 2020, or $26,000 if age 55 or older), with an employer match of $19,500. However, the executive wants to be made whole and defer the full [10% × $1 million], with a 100% match, and defer $100,000, with a $100,000 employer match. This can be achieved by allocating $19,500 of the deferral to the qualified defined contribution plan, with a $19,500 matching contribution, and the remaining $80,500 to the nonqualified defined contribution plan, with an $80,500 employer matching contribution under such nonqualified plan.

The employer may offer a deferred compensation individual account plan that takes the form of a defined contribution plan but does not mirror the employer's qualified defined contribution plan. Such a plan may allow an executive to defer all or a portion of his or her base pay and short-term incentive pay (i.e., bonus) into this nonqualified vehicle, with or without matching employer contributions. The executive's deferrals must be elected prior to the calendar year in which the performance of services occurs in order to avoid current taxation. As will be discussed later in the chapter, I.R.C. § 409A was added to the Code in 2004 to place restrictions on when and how executives can defer income in order to avoid current taxation. These rules must be satisfied to avoid current taxation.

As noted earlier, all promises made to executives under a nonqualified deferred compensation arrangement must be "unfunded" and subject to the employer's creditors at all times. While the use of a rabbi trust affords some protection to executives, the trust must be subject to the employer's creditors to avoid current taxation.

2. Excess Benefit Plans and Top Hat Plans

As mentioned earlier, the use of excess benefit plans was popular after the passage of ERISA to supplement the benefits not otherwise provided through qualified retirement plans due to the limitations of I.R.C. § 415; however, when I.R.C. § 401(a)(17) was added to limit the amount of compensation that could be used in determining benefits, the definition of "excess benefit" plan under Title I was **not** amended to take into account that limitation. Nonetheless, executives wished to be made whole through a nonqualified retirement benefit plan for benefits not otherwise available to them because of both of the limitations of I.R.C. §§ 415 and 401(a)(17), and excess benefit plans are now moot.

For nonqualified deferred compensation plans that are not excess benefit plans, Title I provides an exclusion for Parts 2, 3, and 4 (i.e., participation, vesting, funding, and fiduciary rules) for plans that are "unfunded deferred compensation plans maintained primarily for the purposes of providing deferred compensation for a select group of management or highly compensated employees," which are referred to as "top hat" plans.[40] The employer must file with the DOL in order to receive an exemption from the reporting and disclosure rules. The nonqualified arrangement is unfunded if its assets are part of the employer's general assets that are available to their creditors. But there is very little DOL guidance as to what constitutes a top hat plan.[41] And there has been a considerable amount of litigation surrounding the criteria as to what it means to be a plan "primarily for the purpose of deferring compensation" and what it means to have a "select" group of management or highly compensated employees.[42]

3. Income Tax Rules for Executive Retirement Plans

After the Enron scandal in which executives were able to access funds from their nonqualified deferred compensation plans, Congress enacted I.R.C. §409A which placed draconian restrictions on the timing of when executives could defer income and when they could access such funds (i.e., distributions), effective as of January 1, 2005. The rules are extremely complex and entire books have been written to explain them; the description here is to simply summarize them in very general terms. The rules apply to any plan in which the executive has a legally binding right during the taxable year to compensation that is or may be paid in a later taxable year (i.e., deferred compensation), regardless of whether the compensation is the transfer of cash or property and whether it is vested or not.

The rules regulate nonqualified deferred compensation paid by a "service provider" (i.e., the employer of an employee, but also an employer who hires independent contractors) to a "service recipient" (i.e., an executive, but also independent contractors and outside board members) by imposing a 20% excise tax when certain design or operational rules are violated. I.R.C. §409A contains three broad restrictions on the timing of deferral elections, the timing of distributions, and prohibitions against the acceleration of distributions. As to the timing of deferral elections (i.e., an executive's deferral of current compensation), the initial deferral election must be made no later

---

40. ERISA §201(2).

41. The DOL has not issued regulations as to the category of "a select group of management or highly compensated employees." In Adv. Op. 90-14 (May 8, 1990), the DOL said that the category would be limited to "individuals [who] by virtue of their position or compensation level, have the ability to affect or substantially influence, through negotiation or otherwise, the design and operation of their deferred compensation plan, taking into consideration any risks attendant thereto, and, therefore, would not need the substantive rights and protections of [ERISA]." This certainly was not a bright line test.

42. See *Sikora v. UPMC*, 876 F.3d 110 (3d Cir. 2017), and *Alexander v. Brigham & Women's Physicians Org., Inc.*, 467 F. Supp. 2d 135 (D. Mass. 2006), which rejected as a factor whether the group of covered employees had bargaining power over the plan's design in its determination as to a "select group."

than the close of the executive's taxable year immediately preceding the service year. The election includes all decisions, whether made by the executive or the employer, as to the time or form of payment. Subsequent changes to elections of time and form of payment must be made at least 12 months prior to the scheduled payment and must defer payments for at least five years.

As to the timing of distributions under a nonqualified deferred compensation plan, they can only be paid upon the occurrence of one of six events:
- The executive's separation from service, but there is a six month delay in payment to key employees of public companies;
- The executive becoming disabled;
- The executive's death;
- A fixed time (or a fixed schedule) set forth under the plan at the date the deferral is made;
- A change in ownership or effective control of the employer, or a change in the ownership of a substantial portion of the employer's assets; and
- The occurrence of an unforeseeable emergency.

Acceleration of payments is generally prohibited. Penalties for noncompliance with the rules are: taxation of all deferred compensation for the tax year in which the compensation is not subject to a "substantial risk of forfeiture" and has not previously been included in gross income, accrued interest on the taxable amount, and a 20% excise penalty.

4. Limitations Based on Funding Targets in the Employer's Qualified Defined Benefit Plan

As discussed in Chapter 9, PPA '06 added new funding target rules for single-employer qualified defined benefit plans. It also created a new status of plans — called "at risk" plans — for which additional requirements relating to funding exist. But it also restricted employers of "at risk" qualified defined benefit plans from "funding" (i.e., setting aside assets in a trust or other arrangement) nonqualified deferred compensation arrangements.[43] Failure to comply results in inclusion of income under the nonqualified deferred compensation plan and a 20% penalty. The intent was to penalize the transfer of assets to a rabbi trust for highly paid executives at a time when the corporation's qualified plan covering the rank-and-file was underfunded.

---

43. PPA '06 § 116, adding I.R.C. § 409A(b)(3)(A).

C. Equity Benefits

Another important part of an executive's compensation package can be an equity interest in the employer, which is ownership in the employer either through company stock or partnership interest.

1. Stocks

Under securities law, stock of a corporation is a security and must be registered with the Securities Exchange Commission,[44] and if traded in a secondary market, will be subject to that market's trading rules.[45] When a normal investor purchases a company's stock, he or she obtains ownership and voting rights and can buy and sell his or her shares without restriction. If he or she eventually sells the stock for more than its purchase price, he or she receives a profit. Conversely, if he or she sells the stock at less than its purchase price, he or she realizes a loss.

If stock is issued to an executive as part of his or her compensation package, it is usually restricted. There may be a vesting period (e.g., need to hold the stock for 5 years), a performance metric (tied to the company' profitability, stock price, or some other goal established by the employer), and/or both. There generally are limitations as to how and when the stock can be sold, and how and when voting rights can be exercised.

2. Stock Options

Stock options provide the executive the right to purchase the employer's stock at a later date at a price set at the time the employer grants the option to the executive (known as the strike price), regardless of the market's actual price of the stock. The exercise price is generally the fair market value of the stock at the time of grant.

> **Example:** Executive A is given 100 options to buy the employer's stock at $5 (i.e., the strike price). If the stock increases in value to $10, the executive can lock in a $500 profit by exercising the option because it allows him or her to buy shares at $5 and sell them for $10 in the open market.

There are two types of stock option plans:

- *Incentive Stock Option (ISO) Plans:*[46] These options allow the employee the right to purchase stock at a price equal to or greater than the fair market value of the stock at the date of the grant. For example, the employer's stock is presently trading at $50/share, and the ISO provides the employee with the right to purchase shares at $50/share. There may be a dollar limit imposed, determined as

---

44. Securities Act of 1933.
45. Securities Exchange Act of 1934.
46. I.R.C. § 422.

of the date of grant (e.g., the executive may exercise up to $100,000 of shares each year). To qualify for special tax treatment, the following requirements must be met:

○ The employee does not realize income at the time of the grant or when the employee exercises his or her stock options while still employed by the employer. The employee gets favorable tax treatment if he or she holds the stock for one year after the date of exercise and does not sell the stock for two years after the date of grant. After meeting these holding periods, any profits will be taxed as capital gains, but with no corresponding deduction for the employer granting the option.[47]

○ The employer must grant the shares through a plan that was approved by the shareholders within 12 months of the date of the grant.

○ The employee must exercise the options 10 ten years of the date of the grant.

• *Nonqualified Stock Option (NQSO) Plans:* This stock option plan has less favorable tax treatment than ISOs. The employee is taxed at ordinary income tax rates (not capital gains rates) on the difference between the price that he or she purchases the stock and the fair market value of the stock on the date of exercise.[48] The employer may deduct the amount the employee takes in as income. The employee is ultimately taxed again upon the sale of the stock.

An employer granting stock options under either of these plans is required to register those options under the Securities Act of 1933.

D. Sarbanes-Oxley and Dodd-Frank Wall Street Reform and Consumer Protection Act

1. SEC Disclosures

In 2002, Sarbanes-Oxley was passed in response to the Enron scandal and widespread fraudulence in corporate financial reports, and it is regulated by the SEC.[49] It established the Public Company Accounting Oversight Board to oversee and supervise the accounting industry. The goal of the Act was to strengthen the independence and financial literacy of corporate boards of directors, and to make the CEO of the company personally responsible for errors in accounting audits. The Act is arranged into 11 titles, including the following key provisions of the Act:

• *Corporate Responsibility for Financial Reports:* The CEO and CFO must review all company financial reports to ensure that there are no misrepresentations.[50]

---

47. I.R.C. § 421.
48. Treas. Reg. § 1.83-7(a).
49. The Sarbanes-Oxley Act of 2002 was named after its sponsors, Senator Sarbanes, D-Md., and Congressman Oxley, R-Ohio. It is also referred to as Sarbox or SOX.
50. Sarbanes-Oxley Act of 2002 § 302.

They are responsible for having internal accounting controls and must report any deficiencies in such controls.

- *Clawbacks:* This provision permits the SEC to seek clawbacks (i.e., recoupment of an executive's excess incentive pay) if the company is required to restate previously issued financial statements as a result of the executive's misconduct.[51] This rule applies to excess incentive pay made to the CEO or CFO for 12 months prior to the financial restatement. Dodd-Frank supplemented these rules by requiring company disclosure of incentive pay policies which were tied to financial information and reporting.[52] It eliminated the "executive misconduct" caveat and required clawbacks if the company refiled an accounting restatement for any reason and applied this to incentive pay accrued by any current or former executive for the prior three years.

- *Disclosure in Periodic Reports:* All financial statements must be accurate and state material information. They must include all material off-balance sheet liabilities, obligations, and transactions.[53]

- *Management Assessment of Internal Controls:* The company must publish in its financial reports an Internal Control Report that sets forth the scope and adequacy of the company's internal control structure. Any deficiencies in these controls must be reported. The registered external auditors used to review the company's financial reports must attest to and report on the accuracy of management's assertion that internal accounting controls are in place, operational, and effective; if they find weaknesses in such controls, they must disclose them.[54]

- *Real Time Issuer Disclosure:* Companies must disclose to the public, on an urgent basis, any information concerning material changes to the company's financial condition or its operations.[55]

- *Criminal Penalties for Altering Documents:* This section sets forth penalties of fines and/or up to 20 years imprisonment for altering, destroying, mutilating, concealing, and/or falsifying records and documents with the intent to obstruct, impede, or alter a legal investigation.[56]

The SEC also requires disclosure for publicly traded companies listed on a national stock exchange in the United States to disclose remuneration for all directors as well as for the CEO, CFO, and the three other most highly paid officers.[57] Information

---

51. *Id.* at §304.
52. Dodd-Frank §954.
53. *Id.* at §401.
54. *Id.* at §404.
55. *Id.* at §409.
56. *Id.* at §802.
57. The particular rules for disclosure are set forth in the provisions of the SEC's Regulation S-K, specifically, Item 402 (Executive Compensation), Item 403 (Security Ownership), and Item 404 (Related Party Transactions). SEC §229.402-404 (2008).

about executive compensation and the company's executive compensation policies and practices can be found in: (1) the company's annual proxy statement, (2) the company's annual report on Form 10-K, and (3) registration statements filed by the company to register securities for sale to the public. The cornerstone of the SEC's required disclosure on executive compensation is the summary compensation table, which provides a comprehensive overview of the company's executive pay practices. It sets forth the total compensation paid to the CEO, CFO, and three other most highly paid executives for the past three fiscal years. It is followed by other tables that set forth narratives about grants of stock options and SARs, long-term incentive plan awards, deferred compensation, and employment contracts. The compensation discussion and analysis (CD&A) provides the narrative about the material components of the company's executive compensation programs. For a description of the SEC's final rule regarding enhanced proxy disclosure of executive compensation pay packages and policies, see the SEC's final rule on Proxy Disclosure Enhancements, available at https://www.sec.gov/rules/final/2009/33-9089.pdf.

2. Financial Statements

All publicly held companies whose shares are traded on a U.S. stock exchange must maintain and file financial statements (e.g., balance sheets, cash flow statements) with regulators (i.e., the SEC). One of these statements is the annual report, which assists investors in ascertaining the financial health of the company. Generally, a publicly traded company files both an annual report and a 10-K report to the SEC. The annual report is an abbreviated version of the 10-K report that has illustrations, a letter from the CEO, and an overview of the company's financials. The 10-K report is a more detailed report, available to the public on the SEC's website.

Financial statements of publicly held companies must be prepared in accordance with generally accepted accounting principles (GAAP), set forth by the Financial Accounting Standards Board (FASB). Initially, when a company granted a stock option, it was not reflected on the company's financial statements. The rationale was that the option did not involve a "cost" to the employer until the executive exercised the option and purchased the discounted stock share. FASB Statement n. 123(R), Share-Based Payment, reversed this rule, effective after June 15, 2005. Under the new rule, the stock option must be valued as of the grant date and shown as a current year cost on the financial statement.[58] Hence, stock options are no longer regarded as "free" to the company.

---

58. For a summary of Statement 123, visit FASB's website, https://www.fasb.org/summary/stsum123.shtml. The SEC recently relaxed the application of this rule for small businesses (e.g., start-ups), see SEC, *Exempt Offerings Pursuant to Compensatory Arrangements* (July 24, 2018), https://www.federalregister.gov/documents/2018/07/24/2018-15730/exempt-offerings-pursuant-to-compensatory-arrangements.

Chapter 19

Health and Welfare Benefit Plans

Reading Assignment: ERISA §§ 601–607, 701–713

I.R.C. §§ 79, 105, 106, 125, 127, 129, 132, 213, 223, 4980B, 9802

Class Discussion Questions: What are the different ways in which health care benefits can be delivered in the United States?

What individual and large employer mandates were imposed by the ACA?

What are the differences between an FSA, HSA, and HRA?

How can wellness programs violate various federal laws?

What was the goal of enacting COBRA?

What was the goal of enacting HIPAA?

Overview

How can an employer provide health benefits to employees (and possibly to their families)?

- medical care is the "diagnosis, cure, mitigation, treatment, or prevention of disease, or for the purpose of affecting any structure or function of the body"

- the employer can set aside reserves to reimburse medical expenses (self-funded) or can pay premiums to an insurer or medical services provider to pay for medical expenses incurred by employees, their spouses, and their dependents

- delivery of health benefits can generally be through

  ○ *fee-for-services plans* — each expense is reimbursed in full or in part; these plans may use preferred provider organizations whereby a lower out-of-pocket expense is charged for visiting such provider

  ○ *health maintenance organizations (HMOs)* — a group of doctors and medical staff (usually in a common building) provides all basic medical services

  ○ *high deductible health plans (HDHPs)* — these plans provide for a much higher deductible than traditional insurance plans, but premium costs are lower

    ◦ *consumer-driven health plans*—this describes a wide range of approaches that allow employees greater freedom in spending health care dollars up to a designated dollar amount and receiving full coverage for in-network preventive care

What were the mandates of the Affordable Care Act?

- the first set of initiatives prohibited lifetime dollar limits and restricted annual dollar limits on "essential health benefits", disallowed preexisting condition exclusions, expanded coverage under a parent's plan to include adult children up to age 26, and provided mandatory first dollar coverage of certain preventive care
- the second set of initiatives imposed new taxes to finance the expansion of health care coverage; many of these taxes subsequently have been repealed
- the third set of initiatives involved the individual mandate, the large employer mandate, the type of health coverage that could be offered on the ACA Exchanges, and expansion of the state-operated Medicaid program

What are some of the types of welfare benefit plans an employer can sponsor?

- here, the appropriate provision of the Internal Revenue Code dictates what needs to be included in the plan document (and how the plan must be administered) in order (1) for the employer to take an ordinary and necessary business deduction for paying for the cost of the benefits and (2) for employees to exclude all or a portion of the benefits received from gross income for both income and FICA tax purposes
- the most common are:
  - group term life insurance for employees with face amounts up to $50,000
  - educational assistance programs
  - dependent care assistance programs
  - adoption assistance programs
  - cafeteria plans
  - qualified transportation fringe benefits
  - other fringe benefits
    - a no-additional cost service
    - a qualified employee discount
    - a working condition fringe
    - a de minimis fringe
    - a qualified moving expense reimbursement

How can an employee pay any required out-of-pocket health benefit expenses on a tax-free basis?

- as the cost of providing health care continues to grow, employers are passing all, or a portion, of the cost to employees (known as cost-sharing)

- in addition to the actual group health plan, the employer can provide the following plans to help the employee pay for his or her share, and any family member's share, of out-of-pocket medical expenses not otherwise paid for by the plan on a pre-tax basis (but the cost will be included in the employee's Gross Income if the family member is not a spouse or dependent):
  - ○ flexible spending arrangements (FSAs)
    - the employer can allow employees to elect to contribute amounts through salary reduction to an FSA to pay medical expenses not paid for by the health plan
    - contributions to an FSA are limited to $2,750 (for 2020), indexed to inflation
    - employees are permitted to carry over up to $550 (for 2020) of unused FSA deferrals to the following year, but they must forfeit any unused amounts in excess of $550
  - ○ medical savings accounts (MSAs)
    - initially, only allowed for small employers (defined here as an employer that employed an average of 50 or fewer employees)
    - phased out of the law by 2007
    - replaced by health savings accounts (HSAs)
  - ○ health savings accounts (HSAs)
    - Congress added a statutory provision to allow employees to open an HSA at the bank or financial institution of their choice
    - HSAs can be funded by employee salary reduction contributions or employer contributions
    - The employee owns the account, so unused balances at the end of the year can be carried forward, and the employee keeps the account even if employment is terminated (hence, it is portable)
    - however, in order for the employee to be allowed to fund his or her HSA, the HSA must be tethered to a high deductible health plan (HDHP) (i.e., the employee must be enrolled in an HSA-eligible HDHP to be eligible to contribute to an HSA)
  - ○ health reimbursement arrangements (HRAs)
    - the employer sets up a notional account as part of its general assets, and credits the amount in an employee's account
    - similar to HSAs, unused balances at the end of the year can be carried forward
    - however, similar to cafeteria plans, once the individual's service is terminated, the employer can decide to retain all unused account balances (i.e., an HRA is not portable)

- HRAs can be used alongside a "group health plan" to pay for premiums and for medical expenses not otherwise paid for by the plan (e.g., amounts before the deductible is met or co-pays)
- The Cures Act added a new type of HRA, known as the QSEHRA, available to small businesses who do not offer a group health plan
- HRAs can also be used to purchase a health plan sold in the "individual" market (referred to as ICHRAs) on a tax-free basis, provided certain requirements are met (e.g., the employer cannot also offer a "group health plan" to a particular "class" of employees)

  ○ wellness programs

- the employer can have programs to encourage weight loss or smoking cessation, with the reward being a reduced share of the premium cost
- EEOC regulations came under fire and were vacated by the U.S. District Court for the District of Columbia

What are the COBRA rules that apply to group health plans?

- COBRA was enacted in 1985 so that terminated employees and their covered family members, who may lose coverage under a group health plan because of termination of employment, death, divorce, or other life events, may be able to continue coverage under the group health plans for themselves and their covered dependents for limited periods of time for essentially the cost of the full premiums (plus 2%)
- COBRA generally applies to an employer with 20 or more employees
- COBRA notices are one of the most important aspects of COBRA, and one of the aspects that is most litigated
  ○ basically, an initial notice informing the employee of his or her COBRA rights must be communicated upon employment, and then another notice must be given timely (within either 30 days or 60 days, depending on the reason) after a "qualifying event"
- generally, if the individual or any qualified beneficiary elects COBRA coverage within 60 days of a qualified event, then as long as premiums are properly paid to the employer, the COBRA coverage will continue for 18 months (or 36 months for some reasons)
- a "qualifying event" is defined, for the employee, as a voluntary or involuntary termination of employment for reasons other than gross misconduct or a reduction in the number of hours of employment
- for the qualified beneficiaries, "qualifying events" are defined to include death of the employee, divorce, or legal separation, or, for children and dependents, the loss of such status under the tax laws
- employers that fail to comply with COBRA may be assessed a penalty

What are the HIPAA rules that apply to group health plans?

- HIPAA was enacted in 1996 so that employees, and members of their families, who have a pre-existing medical condition will not suffer discrimination in future health coverage based on a factor that relates to the individual's health; with the enactment of the Affordable Care Act (ACA), both fully-insured and self-insured group health plans cannot deny a person coverage because of their pre-existing condition

- in addition, HIPAA imposes uniform standards for the electronic transfer of medical, billing, and other information used in the administrative and financial transactions between health care providers, group health plans, and health care clearinghouses; and also imposes new privacy safeguards on certain individually identifiable health information and medical records

- HIPAA generally applies to all group health plans with more than two employees

- HIPAA generally applies to all types of benefits offered, except for those specifically excluded under the statute (such as accidental death and dismemberment coverage)

- in regard to portability,

  ○ a preexisting condition refers to any physical or mental condition for which medical advice, diagnosis, care, or treatment was recommended or received before the enrollment date; as stated, the ACA eliminated the use of preexisting condition restrictions

- in regard to nondiscrimination and coverage,

  ○ pre-ACA group health plans could offer whatever benefits they wanted and could apply across-the-board limitations on the levels and types of benefits; however, HIPAA prohibits group health plans from discriminating in eligibility or enrollment based on health-related factors (such as health status, mental or physical medical condition, claims experience, receipt of health care, medical history, genetic information, evidence of insurability, or disability status) and cannot charge an individual a higher premium than is charged to similarly situated individuals

  ○ therefore, pre-ACA, group health plans could (1) exclude coverage for certain diseases or conditions, or certain treatments or drugs, and could (2) limit coverage to annual or lifetime limits and set deductibles, co-payments, and co-insurance—as long as they were applied uniformly and were not directed to any individual's health-related factors; with the enactment of the ACA, however, fully-insured and self-insured group health plans cannot impose annual and lifetime limits on certain benefits covered under the plan and must provide free coverage for certain preventive service, and "individual" and "small group" market plans must cover the "essential health benefits" (EHBs) (but fully-insured "large group" and self-funded plans are not required to cover EHBs)

- in regard to privacy,

- only certain people can see and use "protected health information" (PHI) (i.e., individually identifiable health information related to the past, present, or future physical or mental health or condition of an individual, including demographic information held by the health plan administrator) for specific purposes
- in all cases, only the minimum amount of PHI necessary can be used
- all covered entities (other group health plans, insurers, and HMOs) as well as any business associates (an agent that conducts business transactions on behalf of the plan or any person who provides legal, actuarial, accounting, consulting, data aggregation, management, administration, accreditation, or financial services involving disclosure of an individual's PHI) need to comply with the privacy regulations
- under the rules, the employer cannot use PHI from the group health plan to administer any other type of employee benefit program and is prohibited from using it for employment-related purposes (such as performance reviews, promotions, raises, and terminations)
- employers that fail to comply with HIPAA may be assessed a penalty

What other rules apply to group health plans?

- The Affordable Care Act (ACA) was enacted in 2010. The "coverage requirements" applicable to fully-insured and self-insured group health plans generally did not become effective until 2014 (although some of them became effective in 2011). Currently, all group health plans must: eliminate all pre-existing condition exclusions for all plan participants; stop imposing annual and lifetime limits on the "essential health benefits" (EHBs) covered under the plan; provide coverage for certain preventive health services with no cost-sharing; cover "adult children" up to age 26; stop rescinding coverage absent fraud or misrepresentation; include new internal and external appeals processes (and provide notice); allow participants a choice of primary care physician/pediatrician/OB/GYN; provide direct access to emergency services; refrain from establishing rules for eligibility based on, among other things, health status, medical condition, claims experience, medical history, or genetic information; limit the plan's cost-sharing to the maximum out-of-pocket limits for a high-deductible health plan defined under the health savings account (HSA) rules for 2014; eliminate waiting periods that exceed 90 days; cover the cost of clinical trial participation; provide participants with a summary of benefits and coverage; and provide annual reports describing the plan's quality-of-care provisions.

- The Genetic Information Nondiscrimination Act (GINA) was enacted in 2008 to expand upon the nondiscrimination protections included in HIPAA by negating the ability of a group health plan to base premiums for a plan or a group of similarly situated individuals on genetic information. It also revised HIPAA's privacy regulations to § 105 of Title I of GINA, which required HHS to revise the HIPAA privacy regulations to explain that genetic information is health information under those rules

- The Mental Health Parity and Addictions Equity Act (MHPAEA) was enacted in 1996 so that group health plans were prohibited from setting lower lifetime or annual dollar limits for mental health coverage than was set for the medical and surgical benefits for physical health (thus, although a group health plan is not required to offer mental health coverage, if it does, then the dollar limits for the mental health benefits provided cannot be lower than other limits—employers that fail to comply with MHPA may be assessed a penalty)

- The Newborn and Mother's Health Protection Act (NMHPA) was enacted in 1996 so that group health plans must allow mothers and newborns to remain in the hospital for at least 48 hours after vaginal birth (or 96 hours in the case of a cesarean delivery) and cannot apply pressure for an earlier release (employers that fail to comply with NMHPA may be assessed a penalty)

- The Women's Health and Cancer Rights Act (WHCRA) was enacted in 1996 so that group health plans that offer medical and surgical benefits for mastectomies must also offer benefits for reconstructive surgery of the removed breast, for symmetrical appearance of the other breast, and all prostheses and coverage of physical complications at all stages of the mastectomy (employers that fail to comply with MHPA may be assessed a penalty)

What are association health plans (AHPs)?

- *pathway #1 Association Health Plans (AHPs):* employers that are in a "bona fide group" under Department of Labor guidance may establish a group health plan, even though the employers are unrelated

- *pathway #2 AHPs:* employers in different industries, as well as self-employed individuals, may establish a group health plan under recent DOL guidance if they have requisite "control" over it; a district court recently vacated part of the regulations governing Pathway #2 AHPs

A. Introduction

For the typical rank-and-file employee, any part of the compensation package that is not paid in cash is generally a health or welfare benefit. ERISA defines a welfare benefit plan as a plan, fund, or program established or maintained by an employer or employee organization, or both, providing, through the purchase of insurance or otherwise, (1) medical, surgical, or hospital care or benefits or (2) benefits in the event of sickness, accident, disability, death, or unemployment, or vacation benefits, apprenticeship or other training programs, or day care centers, scholarship funds, or prepaid legal services.[1] The same discussion we had before as to who is an employer and who is an employee for purposes of Title I in the retirement plan context hold true for the welfare plan context. But there are three types of welfare benefit plans

---

1. ERISA § 3(1).

452 · 19 · HEALTH AND WELFARE BENEFIT PLANS

depending on the plan sponsor: (1) a single-employer welfare benefit plan; (2) a multi-employer welfare benefit plan; and (3) multiple-employer welfare arrangements (MEWAs), that now include association health plans (AHPs). There are a variety of rules that must be followed in the health and welfare benefit setting:

- Tax rules under the Code to provide a partial or full exclusion from income, depending on the type of benefit;
- ERISA rules under Title I; and
- Other laws, including:
  - Health Insurance Portability and Accountability Act (HIPAA) Administrative Simplification rules, amended by the Health Information Technology for Economic and Clinical Health (HITECH) Act and the Affordable Care Act (ACA)
  - Medicare Modernization Act of 2003 (MMA), establishing the Medicare Part D program;
  - Prohibition against discrimination based on one's disability with respect to the terms and conditions of employment (including compensation and fringe benefits) under the Americans with Disabilities Act (ADA);
  - Prohibitions against discrimination based on genetic information under ERISA through the Genetic Information Nondiscrimination Act (GINA);
  - Maintenance of health coverage while on leave for specified family and medical reasons through the Family and Medical Leave Act (FMLA)
  - Mental Health Parity and Addiction Equity Act (MHPAEA); and
  - The Affordable Care Act (ACA).

1. Health Benefits

a. National Health Care Insurance System

The United States national health care insurance system consists of four parts: the federal Medicare program, the federal Medicaid program, "individual" health insurance policies purchased by private individuals through an ACA Exchange or in a market sold outside of the Exchange, and employer-provided health care. The fourth is by far the largest part for employees under the age 65 and their families, covering roughly 160 million Americans.

The federal Medicare program covers all persons eligible for Social Security retirement benefits, guaranteeing health care coverage for persons age 65 and older. The Centers for Medicare and Medicaid Services (CMS, within the Department of Health and Human Services) administers Medicare.

Medicare itself has four parts:

- Part A (Hospital Insurance) which covers inpatient care in hospitals, skilled nursing facility care, hospice care, and some home health care;

- Part B (Medical Insurance) which covers services from doctors and other health care providers, outpatient care, home health care, durable medical equipment (e.g., wheelchairs), and preventive services (e.g., vaccines);

- Part C (Medicare Advantage Plans) which provides alternatives to coverage under Parts A and B (i.e., providing the same coverage as under Parts A and B, as well as additional coverage such as home health care, but administered by private insurers); and

- Part D (Prescription Drug Coverage) which covers the cost of prescription drugs. Part D plans are run by private insurance companies that follow the guidelines established by Medicare.

The federal Medicaid program is jointly administered and financed by the federal government and the states. Medicaid provides health care coverage to low-income persons, satisfying the criteria set forth in the person's state of domicile.

Employees under the age of 65 who do not qualify for Medicaid rely on obtaining coverage through their employer or the employer of their spouse, or if such coverage is unavailable, through the purchase of "individual" insurance through an ACA Exchange or in the market sold outside of the Exchange (known as the "unsubsidized" individual market).[2]

The largest group of employer-provided welfare plans is group health plans, which may be provided through a fully-insured plan or self-insured plan sponsored by the employer. If the employer self-insures the benefits, it may wish to set aside reserves on its balance sheet that will be available to reimburse providers or the employees for medical expenses. If the plan is insured with an insurance company (e.g., Blue Cross & Blue Shield), the employer will generally pay a portion of the premiums for accident and health insurance for personal injuries or sickness. The employee may also receive amounts from the insurer covering accident and health benefits. The group health plan may be prefunded or funded on a pay-as-you-go basis (i.e., the latter is referred to as unfunded). The definition of "medical care" used in the tax code, which serves as the basis for the employer's deduction and the employee's exclusion from income, is "the diagnosis, cure, mitigation, treatment, or prevention of disease, or for the purpose of affecting any structure or function of the body."[3]

If the group health plan is fully insured, the employee and the employer pay premiums to the insurer, which in turn pays under the policy amounts for medical care,

---

2. In a 2011 GAO Report, GAO-11-392, *Voluntary Health Insurance Enrollment: Private Health Insurance Coverage: Expert Views on Approaches to Encourage Voluntary Enrollment*, https://www.gao.gov/new.items/d11392r.pdf, it was reported that, of the nearly 265 million individuals in the United States under age 65 in 2009, more than 156 million (59%) received coverage through an employer-provided health plan and nearly 17 million (6.3%) received coverage from an insurer through the individual market. Another 56 million (21%) were covered through public programs such as Medicaid or other public programs.

3. I.R.C. § 213(d)(1).

which includes diagnosis, cure, mitigation, treatment, or prevention of disease. The employees generally share in a portion of that premium, paying more for family coverage (e.g., covering spouse and/or dependents) than for employee-only coverage (e.g., self-only coverage). Before the insurer pays for the full amount for medical care, there may be a deductible (e.g., first $500 or $1,000 of annual costs are the employee's responsibility, to guarantee that he or she has "skin in the game"), followed by a co-pay (i.e., fixed amount for the service, such as $10 for a prescription) and coinsurance (e.g., 20% of all costs after the deductible has been met are the employee's responsibility). The deductible, co-pays, and coinsurance are considered to be the employee's out-of-pocket costs (or cost-sharing), as he or she must pay for them. There also may be a maximum ceiling as to the employee's annual total out-of-pocket costs. For this purpose, only the deductible and co-insurance costs are considered out-of-pocket costs; the employee's premium for the health coverage and out-of-network (i.e., using a health care provider that is not in the plan's network of providers) costs are not.

> **Example:** The employee has an emergency room visit for his or her spouse that costs $10,500. The employee may be responsible for the first $500 in costs (the deductible) and 20% of the remaining $10,000 [20% of the remaining $10,000] = $2,000. If the employee gets a prescription filled after the emergency room visit, he or she may have a $10 co-pay when filing the prescription.

The delivery of health benefits can be fashioned into different categories, each with its own advantages and disadvantages:

- *Fee-for-Service Plan (Indemnity):* Such a plan reimburses medical providers based on the services provided to a covered employee. These are referred to as traditional insurance plans and are generally more costly than some consumer-driven health plans. These plans are of two types—with a preferred provider organization (PPO) and without a PPO. The PPO has contracted with the employer and/or insurer to received reduced fees, but the covered employee must use the PPO provider to take advantage of this reduction. PPOs may have a strong presence in a large urban environment, where there is competition for the providers' services.

- *Health Maintenance Organization (HMO):* This is a plan that provides care through a network of physicians and hospitals in a given geographical area (e.g., Chicago). The covered employee's eligibility to enroll in an HMO is determined by where he or she lives or works. HMOs limit the employee's out-of-pocket costs to relatively low amounts, but the employee must use the services of the doctor or medical group that works through the HMO. Some HMOs offer a Point of Service (POS) product where the employee can use providers who are not part of the HMO network, if his or her primary physician recommends a specialized medical doctor or procedure; however, the employee pays more for using these out-of-network providers in the form of higher deductibles and coinsurance.

- *High Deductible Health Plan (HDHP):* These plans provide the employee with a much higher deductible than traditional insurance plans (e.g., $1,400 for self-only coverage or $2,800 for family coverage, for 2020), but the monthly premium cost is much lower. The annual out-of-pocket costs (including deductibles and copayments) cannot exceed a dollar threshold ($6,900 for self-only coverage and $13,800 for family coverage, for 2020). These types of plans may be helpful to younger, healthy employees. As will be discussed later in this chapter, an HDHP can be combined with a health savings account (HSA), allowing the employee to pay for certain medical expenses with pre-tax dollars (funded through payroll employee salary reductions or employer dollars). Unspent dollars in the HSA roll over at the end of the year and are available for future health expenses.

- *Consumer-Driven Health Plan (CDHP):* This describes a wide range of approaches that provide the employee with greater freedom in spending health care dollars up to a designated dollar amount and receiving full coverage for in-network *preventive* care. The covered employee assumes much higher cost-sharing expenses after he or she has used up the designated amount. A CDHP is primarily paired with an HDHP and either an HSA or an HRA.

In deciding whether and how to provide group health insurance to its employees, an employer must consider several factors:

- Whether to self-fund or fully insure the benefits;

- Whether to pass along some of the costs to the employees;

- Whether to offer coverage to the employee's spouse and/or dependents (referred to as "family coverage");

- Whether to have the benefits coordinate with Medicare for individuals who are age 65 and older; and

- Whether to outsource the administration and operation of the plan to an insurer or a third party administrator.

2. Mandates of the Affordable Care Act

On March 23, 2010, President Obama signed into law the Patient Protection and Affordable Care Act (PPACA).[4] With a series of back-and-forth votes in both the House and Senate, the Health Care and Education Reconciliation Act of 2010 also became law. These two pieces of legislation together are referred to as the Affordable Care Act (ACA), which changed the landscape of health care in the United States for group health plans, individual insurance issuers, employers, and individuals.[5]

---

4. PPACA was originally enacted on March 23, 2010, and modified by the Health Care and Education Reconciliation Act of 2010 on March 30, 2010, and referred to as ACA.

5. The provisions of ACA generally appear in PHSA, but they also amended ERISA §715 and I.R.C. §9815.

The health care reforms under ACA came in the form of the following three major initiatives:

- The first set of initiatives included reforms effective on January 1, 2011:
    - prohibit lifetime dollar limits and restrict annual dollar limits on the "essential health benefits" (EHBs) covered under the plan (for example, a plan previously could set forth lifetime maximums of $100,000 such that all costs over that amount became the employee's responsibility);
    - disallow preexisting-conditions exclusions (previously, plans could reject, charge more, or refuse to pay for health benefits for a condition that the employee, spouse, or dependent had before coverage started) (this limit existed for children under 19, later extended to adults);
    - expand coverage under the parent's plan to include adult children up to age 26; and
    - implement mandatory first dollar coverage of certain preventive care (i.e., the plan must pay for these services even before the employee has met his or her deductible, and the participant cannot be required to pay a co-pay, coinsurance, or other cost-sharing amount).

- The second set of initiatives included new taxes to fund the expansion of health insurance coverage beginning in 2014:
    - A new tax of 3.8% on unearned income for individuals;
    - An increase in the Medicare tax of 0.9% for high-income individuals;
    - A higher threshold amount for deductions of medical expenses (from 7.5% to 10%);
    - A cap on the maximum annual contribution to a flexible spending account (FSA) ($2,500, adjusted to cost-of-living; $2,750 for 2020);
    - A three-year tax (2014–2016) on insured and self-funded group health plans to fund a temporary reinsurance program to lessen the impact of adverse selection in the individual insurance market;
    - A per participant "fee" to pay for comparative effectiveness research through the Patient-Centered Outcomes Research Institute;
    - An annual fee on health insurance providers (the so-called health insurance tax or HIT tax, which was fully repealed from the law at the end of 2019);
    - The "Cadillac tax," which was a 40% nondeductible excise tax on so-called "Cadillac" health insurance plans (which was fully repealed from the law at the end of 2019); and
    - A 2.3% excise tax on manufacturers of medical devices (which was fully repealed from the law at the end of 2019).[6]

---

6. *See* Further Consolidated Appropriations Act, 2020, Pub. L. No. 116-94, 133 Stat. 3095, Division N, § 501 (repeal of the medical device tax), § 502 (repeal of the annual fee on health insurance providers), and § 503 (repeal of the Cadillac tax).

- The third set of initiatives involved individual mandates, large employer mandates, creation of insurance marketplaces, and the expansion of Medicaid:

  ○ Individual taxpayers were required to have "minimum essential coverage" (including for his or her dependents) or face a tax penalty.[7] This penalty was referred to as a "shared responsibility payment" or "individual mandate." It was a combination of a flat dollar amount or an applicable percentage of income.[8] The Tax Cuts and Jobs Act of 2017 (TCJA) effectively repealed this tax penalty by zeroing out both the dollar amount and percentage of income penalties imposed by the individual mandate.[9]

  ○ Larger employers (i.e., employers with the equivalent of 50 full-time equivalent employees) are subject to tax penalties (known as the "employer mandate") if they fail to offer an employer-sponsored group health plan to their full-time employees, or if they offer a group health plan, but the coverage is not "affordable" or does not provide "minimum value."[10] TCJA made no changes to this employer mandate. Small employers were not subject to this mandate.

  ○ The ACA created insurance marketplaces (known as the "ACA exchanges") whereby individuals and small businesses on behalf of their employees (if they so desired) could purchase health insurance policies that provided "essential health benefits" (EHBs).[11] Tax credits may be used to reduce the cost of the premium for individuals and families not covered under an employer-sponsored plan and with incomes between 100% and 400 % of the federal poverty level.

  ○ The state-operated Medicaid program was to be expanded for all adults under age 65 with income up to 133% of the federal poverty level. This was to be funded through federal grants through 2016, decreasing thereafter. Under the law as originally enacted, states that failed to expand Medicaid properly

---

7. The requirement to have coverage (referred to as to the individual mandate) was challenged on constitutional grounds in *NFIB v. Sebelius*, 132 S. Ct. 2566 (2012), but upheld by the Supreme Court.

8. I.R.C. §5000A(c)(2).

9. TCJA §11081(a), amending I.R.C. §5000A(c).

10. I.R.C. §4980H. An employer-sponsored group health plan is "affordable" if the employee's cost of the lowest cost self-only plan does not exceed 9.86% of the employee's W-2 income or hourly rate of pay. An employer-sponsored group health plan provides "minimum value" if at least 60% of the cost of the benefits is covered under the plan (meaning 40 percent of the cost is borne by the plan participant).

11. See 45 C.F.R. §156.100, et seq. ("essential health benefits" (EHBs) must include 10 medical benefits and services, which are: ambulatory patient services (outpatient services); emergency services; hospitalization; maternity and newborn care; mental health and substance use disorder services, including behavioral treatment; prescription drugs; rehabilitative and habilitative services (those that help patients acquire, maintain, or improve skills necessary for daily functioning) and devices; laboratory services; preventive and wellness services and chronic disease management; and pediatric services, including oral and vision care). Congress explicitly exempted fully-insured large group plans and self-insured plans (of any size) from the requirement to cover the EHBs. As a result, only individual and small group market plans are required to cover the EHBs.

would have all federal Medicaid withheld in its entirety. The U.S. Supreme Court ruled that this portion of the law is optional to the states (meaning states can choose whether or not they want to expand Medicaid in accordance with the ACA).[12] As of 2020, 37 states and the District of Columbia have expanded Medicaid.

3. Group Medical and Dental Benefits

I.R.C. § 105(a) provides an exclusion from income for amounts received for sickness or injury from accident and health insurance that is paid for by the employer or that is attributable to the employer contributions that have not been included in the employee's gross income.[13] This includes amounts received for sickness or injury paid to the employee, his or her spouse, or dependents.

I.R.C. § 105(b) provides an exclusion from income for amounts paid to the employee directly or indirectly to reimburse him or her (or spouse or dependents) for expenses incurred for medical treatment, regardless of whether the payment was made by insurance or a noninsured health reimbursement plan.[14] If the medical benefits are self-insured by the employer, I.R.C. § 105(h) imposes a nondiscrimination test, such that highly compensated individuals will not qualify for the exclusion if benefits are discriminatory.[15]

Contributions made by an employer to pay for all or a portion of fully-insured or self-insured health insurance coverage for an employee and his or her spouse and dependents are excludable from gross income under I.R.C. § 106, which means these amounts are not taxable to the employee for income[16] and FICA[17] tax purposes.

4. Welfare Benefits

Welfare benefits generally include other non-cash benefits that are not health benefits but promote the welfare and well-being of the employee, his or her spouse, and

---

12. *NFIB v. Sebelius*, 132 S. Ct. 2566 (2012).

13. I.R.C. § 105(a). The Supreme Court held, in Bostock v. Calyton County, Slip Op. No. 17-1618 (June 15, 2020), that Title VII of the Civil Rights Act of 1964 which prohibits workplace discrimination based on sex extends to discrimination based on sexual orientation or gender identity. Thus, Title VII's protection for lesbian, gay, bisexual, transgender and queer (LGBTQ) individuals extends to employer-provided healthcare benefits.

14. I.R.C. § 105(b).

15. I.R.C. § 105(h).

16. Specifically, I.R.C. § 106(a) provides that employer-provided coverage under an "accident or health plan" is excludable from an employee's gross income. An accident or health plan is an arrangement for the payment of amounts to employees in the event of personal injury or sickness. Treas. Reg. § 1.105-5(a).

17. I.R.C. § 3121(a)(2)(B). Specifically, I.R.C. § 3121(a)(2)(B) provides that wages do not include amounts paid by an employer for insurance to provide payment for medical or hospitalization expenses in connection with sickness or accident disability.

dependents. They generally provide relief for events that are out of the control of the employee, spouse, or dependents (e.g., accident, disability, death). To promote them, Congress has granted preferential tax treatment to some of these welfare benefits:

- *Group Term Life Insurance*: I.R.C. § 79 provides a partial exclusion from gross income for employer-provided group term life insurance.[18] Term insurance provides death benefit protection for the insured, but has no cash value until death; in contrast, whole life insurance has a cash value build-up and thus, is more expensive. If the requirements of I.R.C. § 79 are met, the cost of the first $50,000 of group term life insurance is excluded from taxation. Cost of coverage in excess of $50,000 is taxable as a fringe benefit at the greater of (1) the cost under the uniform premium tables contained in the regulations or (2) the employer's actual cost. There are nondiscrimination rules under I.R.C. § 79 in order to qualify for the preferential tax treatment.[19] Employer-provided premiums for group term life insurance protection on an employee's life are generally deductible by the employer, assuming the employer is not the beneficiary of the policy and retains no incidents of ownership under the policy.

- *Educational Assistance Benefits*: I.R.C. § 127 provides a partial exclusion from gross income for educational assistance provided through an educational assistance program.[20] An educational assistance benefit is the amount paid by the employer for the employee's education if the education has a reasonable relationship to the employer's business or is required as part of the degree program. Such program cannot favor highly compensated employees, may not provide more than 5% of its annual benefits to shareholders or owners, may not allow employees to choose cash in lieu of the benefit, and must provide reasonable notice to all employee of its availability.[21] The maximum annual exclusion for educational assistance benefits is $5,250 per employee.[22]

- *Dependent Care Assistance Benefits*: I.R.C. § 129 provides a partial exclusion from gross income for dependent care assistance benefits provided by the employer through a qualified program.[23] The maximum exclusion is $5,000 per year ($2,500 per year if married filing individually). Such a program:

  ○ Must be a written plan for the exclusive benefit of employees;

  ○ Cannot discriminate in favor of highly compensated employees;

  ○ Must pay no more than 25% of its benefits to shareholders or owners;

---

18. I.R.C. § 79.

19. I.R.C. § 79(d)(2)(A).

20. I.R.C. § 127.

21. I.R.C. § 127(b).

22. I.R.C. § 127(a)(2). CARES § 2206 expands I.R.C. § 127 to permit employers to pay up to $5,250 per year for student loan payments made by the employer after March 27, 2020, and prior to January 1, 2021.

23. I.R.C. § 129.

○ Must provide reasonable notice to employees of its existence; and

○ Must deliver a statement of expenses.[24]

• *Cafeteria Plans*: Cafeteria plans are regulated by I.R.C. §125. They provide the employee with the choice of receiving cash or electing to receive certain welfare benefits or making a tax-deferred contribution to an employer-provided profit sharing plan.[25] If cash is not elected, the benefits offered are excluded from gross income. While a cafeteria plan is not subject to ERISA, its component plans will be. Such plans can range from extremely simple, offering only tax-free payments of medical premiums, to very complex, offering health care FSAs, dependent care FSAs, the ability to contribute to an HSA, adoption assistance, and a §401(k) component. The health care FSAs are subject to the dollar cap ($2,750 for 2020). These plans are limited to employees. The plan must be in writing and must contain: (1) a description of the benefits provided under the plan; (2) the period of coverage for each benefit provided under the plan; (3) the plan's eligibility rules; (4) the plan's rules for making elections or changing elections, including the period for which the elections are effective, and the rules about revoking elections; (5) the plan's provisions relating to contributions; and (6) the plan year.[26]

5. Miscellaneous Fringe Benefits

There are a variety of miscellaneous fringe benefits that are afforded a full or partial exclusion from gross income as a result of the rules of I.R.C. §132 and other Code provisions:

• *Achievement awards* are defined as tangible personal property (e.g., a watch) given to an employee as an award for either length or service or safety achievement. They do not include cash, cash equivalents, gift certificates, or other intangibles such as vacations, lodging, theatre tickets, or securities.[27]

• *Athletic facilities* can be made available by the employer to its employees if substantially all of the users of the facility are the employees, spouses, and dependents, and not outsiders.[28]

• *De minimis benefits* are property or services provided by the employer to the employee that have so little value that it would make accounting for these benefits unreasonable or impracticable. These benefits may be excluded from gross income, but cash is never excludable as a de minimis benefit.[29]

24. *Id.*
25. I.R.C. §125.
26. Treas. Reg. §1.125-1, Q&A-3.
27. I.R.C. §74(c).
28. I.R.C. §132(j)(4).
29. I.R.C. §132(e).

- *Employee discounts* are price reductions given by an employer to an employee on property or services offered to customers in the ordinary course of the employer's business. The value of the discount is excludable from gross income as long as the discount does not exceed (1) in the case of property, the gross profit percentage at which the property is being offered for sale to customers or (2) in the case of services, 20% of the price at which services are being offered to customers.[30]

- *Meals and/or lodging on business premises* may be excluded from an employee's wages if (1) the meals are furnished on the employer's business premises, (2) the lodging is furnished at the employer's place of work, (3) the lodging is for the convenience of the employer, and (4) the employee must accept the lodging as a condition of employment.[31]

- *Working condition fringe* is an employer-provided benefit that would have been deductible by the employee as a business expense if the employer had not provided it (e.g., reimbursement for business travel expenses).[32] Such amounts are excluded from the employee's gross income.

- *Moving expense reimbursements* were excluded from gross income if they were expenses that the employees could have deducted themselves but which were reimbursed by the employer. TCJA suspended this exclusion for years 2018 through 2025, except for members of the U.S. Armed Forces on active duty who move pursuant to military order.[33]

In addition, I.R.C. § 139 was added in the aftermath of the terrorist attacks of September 11, to allow for tax-free and non-reportable cash payments that qualify as "qualified disaster relief"[34] to be made to employees from the employer or from federal, state, or local governments or agencies. The intent was to provide tax-free financial assistance to individuals who suffered because of a natural disaster such as hurricanes and floods. "Qualified disaster relief" payments include amounts paid for rent, water, utilities, and other expenses of maintaining a household; travel expenses away from home; medical expenses that would be deductible under I.R.C. § 213; and child care expenses, all incurred in connection with a disaster.[35] A disaster includes not only one that results from a terroristic or military action but also federally declared disasters.[36]

---

30. I.R.C. § 132(c).

31. I.R.C. § 119.

32. I.R.C. § 132(d).

33. TCJA, § 11049(b), adding I.R.C. § 132(g).

34. I.R.C. § 139, as added to the Code by the Victims of Terrorism Tax Relief Act of 2001, Publ. L. No. 107-134, 115 Stat. 2427.

35. *See* Staff of Joint Comm. on Taxation, *Technical Explanation of the "Victims of Terrorism Tax Relief Act of 2001," as Passed by the House and Senate on December 20, 2001*, 107th Cong., 1st Sess. 16 (2001).

36. I.R.C. § 139(b). For I.R.C. § 139 to apply, the disaster must be a qualified federal disaster. President Trump declared the COVID-19 pandemic to be a national disaster under the Robert Stafford

B. Paying for Health and Welfare Benefits

1. Fully Insured or Self-Funded

Employer-provided group health plans can be funded in a variety of ways: fully insured; self-insured; or partially fully and self-insured. If the plan is fully insured, benefits are provided through an insurance company (e.g., Blue Cross & Blue Shield) or through an HMO. Premiums are paid by the employer through its general assets and by the employee through payroll salary reductions. If the plan is self-insured, the employer takes on the financial risk of paying for its employees' own health claims out of its general assets. Under a partially fully funded and partially self-insured plan, the employer and the insurance company take on different portions of the risk (e.g., the employer takes on a given dollar amount of risk that is funded through premiums, and the insurance company steps in for any catastrophic claims by offering stop-loss or reinsurance coverage). To the extent the plan is fully insured or partially insured, it will be subject to the state's insurance laws, which are not preempted by ERISA due to ERISA's preemption "savings clause."

2. Cost-Sharing with Employees

As medical costs have increased over the decades, more and more employers are requiring their employees to pay more for their own health coverage under the group health plan (known as cost-sharing).[37] Cost-sharing typically includes amounts an employee must pay out of his or her own pocket for medical care before the plan's deductible is met. Cost-sharing can also be in the form of out-of-pocket co-pays and co-insurance.

a. Subsidy for Employees

Large employers provide health benefits to be competitive in attracting top talent. Small businesses are less likely to provide health benefits due to theirs costs, but small employers also seek to attract and retain talented workers by offering health benefits. Large employers—due to the size of the insured group of employees—have better bargaining power in negotiating premium rates with insurers and medical costs with providers than small employers. Regardless, to promote the use of the group health plan, both large and small employers subsidize a portion of the cost of the health coverage. As reported by the Kaiser Family Foundation, in 2018, employers typically

---

Disaster Relief and Emergency Assistance Act. Under the IRS' interpretations of the declaration of a national disaster for other tax purposes, it appears COVID-19 would qualify for relief under I.R.C. § 139.

37. According to the 2011 GAO report, *supra* note 2, most employees participate in employer-provided group health plans, when made available, because employers typically subsidize a large share of employees' premiums and the premium contributions are tax-deductible.

paid 82% of the cost of self-only coverage and 71% of the cost of family coverage, resulting in large subsidies for employees.[38]

b. Subsidy for Employees' Spouse and Dependents

As mentioned before, the value of the group health coverage provided to an employee is excludable from his or her gross income, regardless of whether the coverage is self-only coverage or family coverage. Hence, covering one's spouse and/or dependents under an employer-provided group health plan does not result in any additional income. To the extent *non-family* members could be covered under the group health plan, the value of those benefits provided to the non-family member would be imputed income for the employee, as the Code does not grant an exclusion for such individuals. This was an issue prior to the Supreme Court's decision in *Obergefell v. Hodges*; before *Obergefell*, when an employee wished to cover his or her same-sex domestic partner under its employer-provided group health plan, the same-sex partner was not considered a spouse for federal tax purposes.[39]

c. Pre-Tax Funding Vehicles for Employees

Employers can make available pre-tax funding vehicles such that employees may pay the premiums, deductibles, co-pays, and coinsurance amounts with pre-tax dollars.

Flexible Spending Accounts

A flexible spending account (FSA) is a special type of cafeteria plan which reimburses employees for out-of-pocket medical expenses incurred by the employee, spouse, and/or dependent. The employee elects to have an amount withheld from his or her compensation (on a pre-tax basis) to be deposited into a health care FSA. Due to the constructive receipt rules, all amounts deferred under such an account that have not been used by year-end were required to be forfeited (referred to as the "use it or lose it" rule). But in recent years, the Service has allowed limited rollover of these funds (e.g., up to $550 of unused FSA amounts can be rolled over to the following year).[40] The ACA imposed a maximum cap on how much money an employee may contribute to their FSA. The contribution limit was set at $2,500, indexed to inflation (for 2020, the limit is $2,750).[41] These accounts can be very beneficial for individuals with chronic health problems, as they can better forecast their out-of-pocket expenses (e.g., someone with diabetes who needs daily insulin), but they are not as valuable for individuals who incur costs solely due to emergency care. As a result,

---

38. *See* Christina Merhar, *What Percent of Health Insurance Is Paid by Employers*, PeopleKeep (Nov. 8, 2018), https://www.peoplekeep.com/blog/what-percent-of-health-insurance-is-paid-for-employers.

39. *See* the discussion regarding same sex marriages in Chapter 2 for an overview of these issues.

40. *See* Notice 2013-71. *See* Notice 2020-33 (increasing the $500 limit to $550, effective for play years beginning in 2020).

41. CARES § 3702 allows patients to use FSAs for the purchase of over-the-counter medical products without a prescription from their doctor.

the latter group of individuals often uses the funds remaining in their account balances at the end of the year for non-essential medical expenses so as to avoid losing them. In addition, FSAs are not portable, and thus, unspent amounts will be forfeited when the employee terminates employment.

Medical Savings Accounts

In 1996, Congress launched a federal pilot program as part of HIPAA, establishing medical savings accounts (MSAs) to assist small businesses in offering some group health coverage. These were only available to employees of a small employer (50 or fewer employees) or self-employed individuals, who were covered under a high deductible health plan (HDHP). Initially, the HDHP was one that provided health coverage only after the individual paid an annual deductible of $1,500–$2,250 for single coverage and $3,000–$4,500 for family coverage.[42] Contributions to the MSA were deductible if they were made by the employee or excluded from gross income if they were made by the employer, but MSAs could not accept both employee and employer contributions. Distributions from the MSA to pay for medical expenses (e.g., to cover the deductible) were not includable in gross income. These accounts did not follow the use-it-or-lose-it doctrine, and amounts could accumulate over time. They furthered the goal of consumer-driven health care, but only a limited number of taxpayers established them. As they required *annual* congressional reauthorization, they were phased out in 2007.

Health Savings Accounts

MSAs were replaced by health savings accounts (HSAs) through the enactment of I.R.C. § 223.[43] These accounts, like the MSAs, must be coupled with an HDHP.[44] Unlike the MSAs, HSAs can be funded by the employee through pre-tax salary reduction deferrals **and** by the employer with tax deductible contributions. Contributions are limited to the lesser of the employee's deductible under the HDHP or a statutory amount,[45] and the contributions are not included in the employee's gross income. Medical expenses that are reimbursed from the account are also not included in the employee's gross income;[46] however, amounts withdrawn that are unrelated

---

42. *See* IRS Publication 969, *Health Savings Accounts and Other Tax-Favored Health Plans* (2004).

43. The Medicare Prescription Drug, Improvement, and Modernization Act of 2003, adding I.R.C. § 223.

44. An HDHP is a health plan that satisfies requirements under I.R.C. § 223(c)(2), which has strict requirements with respect to minimum deductibles and maximum out-of-pocket expenses. Normally, these limits would pose a hurdle for employers wishing to waive copays or cost sharing for COVID-19 testing and treatment. In Notice 2020-15, the IRS allows an HDHP to permit testing for and treatment of COVID-19 without a deductible, or with a deductible below the minimum deductible for an HDHP. CARES § 3701 amended I.R.C. § 223(c) to permit an HDHP to provide coverage with no deductible for telehealth services in an HDHP for plan years beginning on or before December 31, 2021.

45. For 2020, the HDHP annual deductible is at least $1,400 for single coverage and $2,800 for family coverage. HDHP in-network, out-of-pocket expense maximums cannot exceed $6,900 for single coverage and $13,800 for family coverage in 2020.

46. CARES § 3702 allows patients to use funds in HSAs for the purchase of over-the-counter medical products without a prescription from their doctor.

to a medical expense are subject to income tax and a 20% excise tax. HSAs are portable, meaning that the account stays with the employee if he or she changes employers. The income earned on an HSA also accrues tax-free for the employee.

Health Reimbursement Arrangements

A health reimbursement arrangement (HRA) is an IRS-approved program, funded solely with employer money, that may be used to reimburse employees for their out-of-pocket expenses. An HRA is not health insurance, but instead it is designed to provide "notional" accounts (funded through the employer's general assets) that the employer uses to reimburse employees up to a given maximum allowed amount, without any tax consequences to the employees. Unlike cafeteria plans, unused HRA balances at the end of the year can be carried forward. The employer receives a deduction for amounts actually reimbursed from the HRA. HRAs offered alongside a group health plan can be used to pay for the premiums of the plan or medical expenses not paid for by the plan (or both). This is primarily how HRAs are used.

The Cures Act of 2016 added a new type of HRA, known as the QSEHRA.[47] It is available only to businesses with fewer than 50 employees which do not offer a group health insurance policy. All full-time employees must be automatically eligible to participate, and the maximum amounts available can differ depending on whether or not the employee is "self-only" or has a family.[48] It must be funded solely by the employer. The amounts in one's account can roll over month to month or year to year, but the total reimbursements may not exceed the annual limits for the year. Initially the payments could not exceed $4,500 per year ($10,000 for family coverage).[49] HRAs do not have to be designed to be portable but can be available to the employee after he or she terminates employment.

On June 14, 2019, the Trump administration issued regulations allowing employers of *all* sizes to offer an HRA that can be used to purchase an "individual" market plan on a tax-free basis (referred to as "individual coverage HRA arrangements" or "ICHRAs"). According to the regulations, an employer cannot offer both a group health plan to a particular "class" of employees and an ICHRA. Instead, the employer must choose one or the other (i.e., choose to offer a group health plan or to offer an ICHRA to a particular "class" of employees, but not both).

The regulations create 10 "classes" of employees: (1) full-time employees, (2) part-time employees, (3) union employees, (4) seasonal employees, (5) foreign employees, (6) employees in a waiting period, (7) employees in different geographic locations (i.e., rating areas), (8) salaried employees, (9) non-salaried employees, and (10) temporary workers employed by a staffing firm.

So, for example, an employer could offer a group health plan to its full-time employee class and an ICHRA to its part-time, seasonal employee, and/or employees

---

47. Cures Act § 18001, adding I.R.C. § 9831.

48. For 2020, the annual contribution caps were $5,250 per self-only employee and $10,600 per employee with a family.

49. *See* Rev. Proc. 2019-44, announcing the 2020 limits of $5,250 and $10,600 (family coverage).

in a waiting period classes. An employer may also choose to offer a group health plan to its salaried employee class and an ICHRA to its non-salaried employee class.

No dollar limit is placed on the amount of money that can be set aside in an ICHRA; however, the contribution amount must be the same for all the employees in a particular class. An employer may vary the HRA contribution amount by age and family size but must provide the same contribution amount to all employees in the same class who are the same age and/or have the same family size. If certain requirements are met, the ICHRA would not be considered an ERISA-covered plan. An employer must meet certain notice requirements, and the employee must substantiate that they are covered under an individual market plan when requesting reimbursement from the ICHRA.

Wellness Programs

In addition to providing and subsidizing the cost of health care, employers can also establish workplace wellness programs, designed to promote better health by avoiding and controlling diseases for their employees, spouses, and dependents. Such wellness programs can be part of the employer's group health plan or a stand-alone plan. The plan can be designed to simply provide education regarding unhealthy lifestyles or to provide financial incentives for attaining certain health standards (e.g., achieving a given cholesterol level).

Depending on how they are structured, wellness plans may be subject to a myriad of federal laws:

- The Health Information Portability and Accountability Act (HIPAA), which prohibits group health plans from discriminating against participants and beneficiaries based on health factors (including health status, medical condition, claims experience, receipt of health care, medical history, genetic information, evidence of insurability, or disability);[50]

- The Americans with Disabilities Act (ADA), which prohibits discrimination against a qualified individual with a disability with respect to the terms and conditions of employment (including compensation and fringe benefits[51]) and requires reasonable accommodation unless to do so would impose an undue hardship;[52]

- The Genetic Information Nondiscrimination Act (GINA), which generally prohibits acquiring genetic information from employees unless the employer is offering *voluntary* health or genetic services to the employees or their family members;[53] and

---

50. HIPAA has amended § 401(a) of ERISA by adding § 702 to ERISA in 1996 and § 9802 to the Internal Revenue Code of 1986 (1996).

51. Equal Employment Opportunity Commission (EEOC) Prohibited Discrimination, EEOC § 1630.4(a) (2006) (prohibiting discrimination on the basis of disability against a qualified individual regarding fringe benefits available by virtue of employment, whether or not administered by the covered entity).

52. ADA, effective on July 26, 1992, for employers of 25 or more employees and on July 26, 1994, for employers with 15 or more workers.

53. GINA § 202(b)(2).

- The Internal Revenue Code (Code), which would exclude from gross income any medical care provided through an employer's wellness program due to I.R.C. § 106(a) and any medical care benefits provided by the program under I.R.C. § 105(b) but would not exclude from income any incentives or rewards payable from a wellness program unless they qualified under an exclusion under I.R.C. § 132.

These laws are regulated by different agencies — Department of Health and Human Services (HHS), Department of Labor, Department of the Treasury and IRS, and Equal Employment Opportunity Commission (EEOC) — which do not necessarily coordinate with one another to create a common set of standards applicable to wellness incentive programs. Thus, employers establishing and maintaining wellness programs have a myriad of rules to navigate to avoid violating these laws.

The issue that has caused the most complications under these laws is the use of financial incentives or rewards to incentivize the employee, spouse, and/or dependent to meet a specific standard related to his or her health (e.g., a reduction in the employee's premium if he or she stops smoking). Under the HIPAA rules, wellness programs are divided into two categories: (1) participatory wellness programs (where rewards are based only on the employee's involvement) and (2) health-contingent wellness programs (where the reward is attached to certain outcomes). There is generally no limit on financial incentives for participatory wellness programs, but the incentive or penalty is limited to 30% of the cost of the health insurance premium (or 50% for programs related to reduction in tobacco use) in health-contingent wellness programs. The ACA built upon the HIPAA rules and affirmed that employers could offer rewards or apply penalties under wellness programs provided they do not exceed 30% of the cost of the health plans.[54]

But ADA and GINA have different rules regarding discrimination in the context of employment. Under those laws, the EEOC finalized regulations in 2016 and affirmed the use of financial incentives or penalties in a wellness program so long as the incentive did not exceed 30% of the cost of self-only medical coverage.[55] The incentive portion of the regulations was challenged and vacated by the U.S. District Court for the District of Columbia, on the grounds that the EEOC had not sufficiently explained the reasoning for its interpretations of the ADA and GINA rules.[56] According to its regulatory agenda, the EEOC was planning to release new proposed rules regarding wellness programs in January 2020; it did not.

The lack of guidance from the EEOC during 2018 and 2019 left employers in a quandary. Basically, employers using financial incentives or penalties in their wellness programs had three options: (1) keep the financial incentive or penalty equal to 30% of the total cost of self-only group health plan coverage; (2) significantly reduce the

---

54. PHS Act § 2705(a)(9), as amended by ACA.
55. EEOC §§ 1630.14(d)(3)(i), 1635.8(b)(2)(iii)(A)–(D).
56. AARP v. EEOC, 292 F. Supp. 3d 238, 245 (D.D.C. 2017).

incentive or penalty below this 30% threshold; or (3) eliminate any incentive or penalty from the program.

C. ERISA Rules for Health and Welfare Benefits

Parts 6 and 7 of ERISA provide additional rules applicable to employer sponsored group health plans:

- The Consolidated Omnibus Budget and Reconciliation Act of 1985 (COBRA), adding ERISA §§ 601–609;

- HIPAA of 1996, adding ERISA §§ 701–734;

- The Newborns' and Mothers' Health Protection Act of 1996 (NMHPA), adding ERISA § 711;

- Mental Health Parity Act of 1996 (MHPA), adding ERISA § 712; and

- Women's Health and Cancer Rights Act of 1998 (WHCRA), adding ERISA § 713.

1. COBRA

Under the Code, medical benefit coverage for an employee and his or her family will end when employment ends, or when the spouse or dependent ceases to qualify for coverage under the plan.[57] COBRA protects certain persons by extending them the opportunity to continue coverage under the employer's group health plan, at their own expense, when certain qualifying events occur that would have otherwise caused them to lose coverage under the plan.[58]

COBRA's rules are set forth in ERISA §§ 601–609, with corresponding tax penalties under I.R.C. § 4980B for failure to comply with such rules. The COBRA provisions of ERISA and the Code apply to group health plans of private-sector employers, whereas the COBRA provisions of PHSA apply to group health plans of state and local governments.

The COBRA rules apply to group health plans (whether insured or self-funded), covering 20 or more employees, but only for health benefits (including dental) — not life or disability insurance.[59] A qualified beneficiary includes the employee, spouse, and dependent children.[60] A qualifying event includes: death, voluntary or involuntary termination of employment, reduction in hours causing a loss of coverage, divorce or legal separation, the covered employee becoming entitled to Medicare if that would cause loss of coverage, and cessation of the dependent child's coverage under the

---

57. I.R.C. § 4980B.
58. ERISA § 601(a).
59. ERISA § 601(b).
60. ERISA § 607(3).

terms of the plan (e.g., the dependent's age exceeds 26).[61] Additional qualifying events may include: strike or layoff, Family and Medical Leave Act (FMLA) leave, and certain events resulting in a loss of coverage that are not specifically listed as qualifying events (e.g., loss of coverage due to failure to remit premiums).[62]

While the statute states that the COBRA benefits that are continued must be identical to the coverage under the plan available to similarly situated non-COBRA beneficiaries, they do not have to be.[63] If coverage for non-COBRA beneficiaries has changed under the plan, coverage for qualified beneficiaries of COBRA must also be modified. If one of the employer's group health plans is being eliminated, the COBRA beneficiary must be allowed to elect from the remaining plans.[64]

Once the qualifying event has occurred, the qualified person must be given 60 days from that date to elect to continue health coverage.[65] For the qualified person to have made a proper election for coverage, there are strict notice requirements imposed on the employers.[66] In recent years, there has been a considerable amount of litigation involving failure to issue a proper notice.[67]

The duration of health coverage depends upon the qualifying event that triggered the loss and can range from 18 to 29 to 36 months.[68] The premium amount that the group health plan can charge the qualified beneficiary cannot exceed 102% of the cost of the plan.[69] COBRA coverage can terminate for a number of reasons: failure to make the required premium, the person becomes covered under another plan, the person becomes eligible for Medicare, the group health plan terminates, or coverage is terminated for cause (e.g., the person submits fraudulent claims).[70]

2. HIPAA

HIPAA was enacted for the following reasons: (1) to restrict group health plans and health insurers to exclude an individual from coverage due to preexisting conditions, and (2) to prohibit plans and issuers form conditioning plan enrollment based on certain heath status-related factors.[71] It did this by amending Part 7 of

---

61. ERISA § 603(1)–(6).

62. IRS Prop. Reg. § 1.162-26, Q&A-19; IRS Reg. § 54.4980B-10, Q&A-1(a); IRS Reg. § 54.4980B-4, Q&A-1(c).

63. ERISA § 602(1).

64. IRS Prop. Reg. § 1.162-26, Q&A-23.

65. ERISA § 605. A model election form is available at www.dol.gov/agencies/ebsa/laws-and-regulations/laws/cobra. Coverage will then be retroactive back to the date of the qualifying event. Failure to provide the notice results in a penalty.

66. ERISA § 606(a).

67. See Stacey C.S. Cerrone, Suzanne G. Odom, & Howard Shapiro, *COBRA Notice Litigation Mushrooms, Along with Settlements*, SHRM (Mar. 6, 2020), https://www.shrm.org/resourcesandtools/hr-topics/benefits/pages/cobra-notice-litigation-mushrooms-along-with-settlements.aspx.

68. ERISA § 602(2).

69. ERISA § 602(3).

70. ERISA § 602(2)(A)–(E).

71. ERISA §§ 701–702; I.R.C. §§ 9801–9802.

ERISA, applicable to group health plans with two or more participants who are current employees established by private employers, and enforcing such requirements through parallel sections in the Internal Revenue Code of 1986 ("the Code") § 9801 et seq.[72] If the group health coverage was *insured*, parallel provisions appeared in the PHS Act, which is applicable to health insurance offered under a group health plan with as few as one employee who is a current participant.[73]

Initially, group health plans and health issuers could exclude coverage for preexisting conditions for 12 months; ACA later eliminated the use of preexisting condition clauses altogether.[74] HIPAA also prohibited group health plans from discriminating against participants and beneficiaries based on health status and health statusrelated factors which included the following:

- Health status;
- Medical conditions (both physical and mental);
- Claims experience;
- Receipt of health care;
- Medical history;
- Genetic information;
- Evidence of insurability; and
- Disability.

On December 20, 2000, HHS issued final regulations under HIPAA guaranteeing individuals new *privacy* rights against disclosure of their health records.[75] The goal was to guarantee the security of medical records and other personal health information (PHI) maintained, used, or disclosed by covered entities. PHI referred to individually identifiable health information related to the past, present, or future physical or mental health or condition of an individual, including demographic information held by the health plan administrator. Covered entities included health care clearinghouses, health plans, and most health care providers. The regulations also restricted the use and release of medical records, by not allowing them to be used for purposes unrelated to health (e.g., used for performance reviews, promotions, raises, and terminations), without authorization from the individuals. There are civil and criminal penalties for noncompliance. HHS published final *security* rules under HIPAA in 2003, setting forth standards for protecting the confidentiality, integrity, and availability of electronically protected health insurance.[76]

The American Recovery and Reinvestment Act of 2009 included the Health Information Technology for Economic and Clinical Health Act (HITECH), which expanded

---

72. ERISA § 702; I.R.C. § 9802.
73. PHS § 2702.
74. ERISA § 701(a) and I.R.C. § 9801(d), later amended by ACA § 1201.
75. 45 C.F.R. parts 160, 162, and 164, as amended through February 16, 2006.
76. 45 C.F.R. parts 160, 162, and 164, as amended through February 20, 2003.

the privacy and security provisions of HIPAA. It established a wide range of notice requirements for covered entities and their business associates in the event a breach occurred (e.g., unauthorized acquisition, security, or privacy of medical information). It extended HIPAA obligations directly to business associates, which were third parties used by the covered entities to carry out their health care activities and functions. It also increased enforcement and penalties.

3. GINA

GINA was enacted in 2008, and amended ERISA, the PHS Act, the Code, and the Social Security Act (SSA) to prohibit discrimination in health coverage based on genetic information. GINA expanded the genetic information nondiscrimination protections included in HIPAA by not allowing group health plans to base premiums for a plan or a group of similarly situated individuals on genetic information.[77] It directed HHS to revise the HIPAA privacy regulations to clarify that genetic information is health information under that rule, and such information includes information not only about an individual's genetic tests but also the genetic tests of the individual's family members, the manifestation of a disease or disorder in family members, or any request for or receipt of genetic services, or participation in clinical research that includes genetic services by the individual or his or her family member.[78]

GINA imposed additional underwriting protections, limited the requests for or mandates of genetic tests, and restricted the collection of genetic information.[79] More specifically:

- GINA states that group health plans cannot adjust premiums for insured plans or contributions for self-insured plans based on genetic information of some members of the plans, but the plans could adjust premiums or contributions for the group as a whole based on diseases or disorders manifested by members of the group;[80]

- GINA prohibits plans from asking or requiring an individual to undergo a genetic test, but may request the results of a genetic test in order to determine claim payment;[81]

- GINA disallows plans from collecting genetic information (including family medical history) from an individual prior to or during their enrollment in the plan or at any time for underwriting purposes.[82] For this purpose, underwriting is defined broadly.

---

77. GINA §§ 101–104, applicable to group health plans, health insurance issuers in the group and individual markets, and issuers of Medicare supplemental policies.
78. GINA § 105.
79. GINA § 101(a) through (d).
80. GINA § 101(a)(3).
81. GINA § 101(c)(1).
82. GINA § 101(d)(1)–(3).

4. Newborns' and Mothers' Health Protection Act of 1996 (NMHPA)

This Act was enacted to ensure that the group health plan or the health insurer would not be able to discharge the mother or her newborn before 48 hours for vaginal delivery or 96 hours for Caesarian delivery.[83] Early discharge is available only by the joint agreement of the mother and the health care provider, but no inducements may be given for early discharge.

5. Mental Health Parity and Addiction Equity Act of 2008 (MHPAEA)

MHPAEA does not apply to group health plans sponsored by a small business (i.e., fewer than 50 employees) and does not require a group health plan to cover a particular mental health disorder or substance abuse disorder.[84] But if a plan does cover a particular mental health condition or a substance abuse disorder, the coverage must be in parity with (or better than) coverage of medical and surgical conditions in the same classifications. This parity includes the following classifications: network office visits, out-of-network office visits, network outpatient, out-of-network outpatient, network inpatient, out-of-network inpatient, emergency care, and prescription drugs. Coverage of a mental health condition or substance abuse disorder has to be reviewed for parity within each of these classifications with respect to financial requirements, quantitative treatment limits, and non-quantitative treatment limits.

6. Women's Health and Cancer Rights Act of 1998

The Women's Health and Cancer Rights Act of 1998 requires certain coverage for reconstructive surgery if the group health plan provides benefits for mastectomies.[85] This coverage includes reconstruction of a breast, other surgery and reconstruction to promote symmetrical appearance, and prostheses and coverage of physical complications. There may be no inducement for consenting to lesser care.

D. Association Health Plans

Under ERISA, group health plans may be offered by employers or employee organizations, and as such, are subject to ERISA's reporting, disclosure, and fiduciary rules. They are also subject to the ACA's health care coverage reforms as they are "a group health plan maintained by an employer." That definition makes it difficult for

---

83. ERISA §711.
84. ERISA §712.
85. ERISA §713.

unrelated employers to band together and form a group health plan, in order to achieve economies of scale and to leverage negotiating powers in setting costs.

However, ERISA does envision a multiple-employer welfare arrangement (MEWA), which is a welfare plan (including a medical or health care plan) covering employees of two or more unrelated employers.[86] If the MEWA were fully insured, it would be regulated under state insurance laws and ERISA. However, promoters of MEWAs attempted to avoid both federal and state regulation by claiming that the MEWA was not a "plan" (and therefore not subject to ERISA) and not an "insurance company" (and therefore not subject to state insurance regulation).[87] As a result, a number of these MEWAs were scams and left members with unpaid claims, as the MEWA went insolvent. Over the past 20 years, state and federal laws have been enacted to prevent any fraudulent activity, and the new regulatory environment has generally rooted out bad actors.

One type of MEWA that has been utilized by member-based organizations (e.g., a trade association or a chamber of commerce) is called an association health plan (AHP). An AHP must be established by a group of employers that qualify as a "bona fide group or association of employers" (known as a "bona fide group").

There are two types of AHPs that can be established by bona fide groups under the law—a Pathway #1 AHP and a Pathway #2 AHP. Each type of AHP, however, is governed by different rules.

A Pathway #1 AHP is governed by DOL advisory opinions that have been issued over the past 20 years. According to existing DOL guidance, a Pathway #1 AHP can only offer health coverage to employers in the same "industry" which have at least one common law employee.[88] In other words, a Pathway #1 AHP *cannot* offer coverage to self-employed individuals or a group of employers in different industries.

A Pathway #2 AHP is governed by DOL regulations that were issued on June 21, 2018.[89] According to these regulations, a Pathway #2 AHP is permitted to offer coverage to employers in different industries as well as self-employed individuals.

A group of employers and/or self-employed individuals sponsoring a Pathway #1 or Pathway #2 AHP will only be considered a bona fide group if the employer-members and/or self-employed individuals participating in the AHP have the requisite "control" over the AHP. Control is established if the employer-members and/or self-employed individuals have the ability to nominate and elect members of a board (e.g., a board of trustees or board of directors) that is established to operate and manage the AHP.

In March of 2019, the U.S. District Court for the District of Columbia vacated a portion of the DOL's regulations governing Pathway #2 AHPs.[90] The Department of

---

86. ERISA § 3(40)(A). These plans are not the same as a multi-employer plan because the arrangement is not set up pursuant to a collective bargaining agreement.

87. See *Donovan v. Dillingham*, 688 F.2d 1367 (11th Cir. 1982), where the operators of the MEWA argued the MEWA was not a plan subject to Title I of ERISA.

88. See DOL Adv. Op. 2008-07A; 2003-17A; 2001-04A.

89. Labor Reg. § 2510.3-3, -5; 83 Fed. Reg. 28,912 (June 21, 2018).

90. See *New York v. United States Dep't of Labor*, 363 F. Supp. 3d 109 (D.D.C. 2019).

Justice appealed the ruling, and oral arguments were heard on November 14, 2019, before a three-judge panel for the Court of Appeals for the District of Columbia. A ruling from the circuit court has yet to be rendered.

Despite the district court ruling vacating the DOL's regulations governing Pathway #2 AHPs, Pathway #1 AHPs are unaffected, which means that groups of employers in the same industry that offer health coverage to employer members with at least one common-law employee remain viable under the law.

Chapter 20

Individual Retirement Accounts

Reading Assignment:	ERISA § 201(6)
	I.R.C. §§ 219, 408, 408A, 4975
Class Discussion Questions:	Why is there so much money in IRAs?
	Who is a custodian?
	What is the difference between a traditional IRA and a Roth IRA?
	What is a "qualified distribution" for purposes of the Roth IRA rules?
	Why are the prohibited transaction rules applicable to IRAs?

Overview

What is a traditional IRA?

- IRAs can only have a bank, investment company, or other qualifying financial institution serve as custodian

- the contribution is a deduction from the individual's tax return (i.e., it's a pre-tax contribution) or a non-taxable rollover from a qualified plan

- individual taxpayers may deposit up to $5,000 (as adjusted for inflation, $6,000 in 2020) each year; however, the limit is phased out depending on the taxpayer's adjusted gross income or if an individual is a participant in a qualified retirement plan

- individuals age 50 or older can make additional "catch up" contributions of $1,000 (as adjusted for inflation) each year

- the money accumulates tax-free until withdrawn

- the individual pays taxes in the year distributed on contributions plus investment earnings actually received

- there will generally be a 10% penalty for withdrawals taken before attaining age 59½ (unless used for certain expenses like education or the purchase of a home — however, there are very specific rules for these qualified expenses)

- individuals must start taking out money at age 70½ (now age 72 due to changes made by the SECURE Act) and therefore cannot use it as a wealth transfer device

What is a Roth IRA?

- Roth IRAs can only have a bank, investment company, or other qualifying financial institution serve as custodian
- the contribution is made after it is included in the individual's gross income (i.e., it's an after-tax contribution) or is a non-taxable rollover from a Roth account in a qualified plan
- individual taxpayers may deposit up to $5,000 (as adjusted for inflation, $6,000 for 2020) each year into a Roth IRA; however, the limit is phased out depending on the taxpayer's adjusted gross income or if an individual is a participant in a qualified retirement plan
- individuals older than 50 can make additional "catch up" contributions of $1,000 (as adjusted for inflation) each year
- the money accumulates tax free until withdrawn
- the individual pays no taxes on any amounts received as long as he or she is older than 59½ and the money has been deposited for at least 5 years
- individuals do not need to start taking out money at age 70½ and therefore can use it as a wealth transfer device

A. Individual Savings

1. Overview

If an employee does not have access to an employer-provided retirement plan, the only tax-favored vehicle he or she can use is an individual retirement account (IRA) or an individual retirement annuity (IRA). The IRA model is a defined contribution plan which shifts investment risk and mortality risk to the individual taxpayer. It is created under I.R.C. § 408, and permits eligible taxpayers to make contributions without incurring taxes on the contributions and the subsequent interest/gains.[1] The maximum dollar amount and percentage allowed to be contributed on a tax-deductible basis is the lesser of $1,500 (as indexed, the dollar limit for 2020 is $6,000) or 100% of the taxpayer's compensation.[2] The percentage of compensation limit applicable to IRAs assures that no one can contribute in excess of their earned income in a given year.

These IRA limits are less than the maximum dollar and percentage amounts under an I.R.C. § 401(k) plan, which was the lesser of $40,000 (as indexed, the dollar limit

---

1. I.R.C. § 408.
2. I.R.C. § 219(b).

for 2020 is $57,000) or 100% of compensation.[3] Both IRAs and I.R.C. § 401(k) plans allow for catch-up contributions for taxpayers age 50 and over, but the dollar amounts are much different—for IRAs, the maximum dollar limit for catch-up contributions is $1,000, as indexed (the dollar limit for 2020 is $1,000), as compared to I.R.C. § 401(k) plans, whose maximum dollar limit for deferrals is $5,000, as indexed (the dollar limit for 2020 is $6,500).

Congress began to constrict the use of IRAs in 1986 so as to permit pre-tax contributions only for those employees who were not active participants in an employer-provided retirement plan and whose adjusted gross income fell below a given threshold (initially, $40,000 for a couple and $25,0000 for an individual).[4] IRAs were designed to have the contributions and interest accumulate tax-free until retirement; premature withdrawals would be subject to a 10% penalty tax, and distributions had to begin by age 70½.

Roth IRAs were named for Senator Roth of Delaware, Chairman of the Senate Finance Committee at the time. Contributions to these vehicles would not be deductible; however, all earnings would accumulate tax-free and upon withdrawal, all distributions would be tax-free—thereby providing a total exclusion from gross income on the total amount of earnings. The goal of Congress was to receive the tax revenue upfront, by taxing the contributions made to the Roth IRA, in exchange for the exclusion from gross income on the accumulation. Both types of IRAs—traditional and Roth— accept rollovers of monies from an employer-provided qualified retirement plan. Participants generally prefer to take their monies from a retirement account upon termination of employment, and a rollover of those funds to an IRA permits the former participant to consolidate retirement savings and to exercise greater control over the investment of such funds. Alternatively, an individual may create an individual retirement annuity issued by an insurance company in order to secure an annuity guarantee so as not to outlive one's savings.[5]

Whether an individual can deduct contributions made to a traditional IRA depends on the modified adjusted gross income (MAGI) of the individual and spouse and the individual's filing status. The various MAGI thresholds vary depending on whether the individual is also an active participant under any employer-provided retirement plan, whether the spouse is also an active participant under any employer-provided retirement plan, and whether the contribution is a deductible IRA contribution to a traditional IRA or a nondeductible IRA contribution to a Roth IRA. For example, if an individual wishes to make a deductible contribution to a traditional IRA, but he or she is also an active participant in an employer plan, the MAGI thresholds for mar-

---

3. EGTRAA '01, § 611(c), effective for 2002 through 2019, subsequently made permanent by PPA '06, § 811.

4. TRA '97 § 301(a)(1), amending I.R.C. § 219(g)(3)(B).

5. I.R.C. § 408(b). Such annuities have restrictions regarding the use of life insurance, nontransferability clauses, no fixed premiums, and maximum annual premiums.

ried persons filing a joint return for 2020 are $104,000 and $124,000. If the individual's MAGI is less than or equal to $104,000, he or she may make a full deductible contribution of $6,000 to a traditional IRA; if the individual's MAGI is greater than $124,000, he or she cannot make a deductible contribution to a traditional IRA; and if the individual's MAGI is $114,000 (the midpoint between $104,000 and $124,000), he or she can make a deductible contribution of $3,000 to a traditional IRA. The reduction in the maximum deductible IRA contribution within the phase-out MAGI region is proportional to the amount by which the MAGI exceeds the lower limit. Thus, if the individual in this example has a MAGI of $114,000, he or she could make a deductible contribution of $3,000 to the traditional IRA and a nondeductible contribution of $3,000 to the traditional IRA. Since only half of the $6,000 maximum annual IRA amount is eligible as a deductible contribution, he or she should consider whether to make the other $3,000 nondeductible contribution to a Roth IRA instead of a traditional IRA. However, the MAGI thresholds applicable to Roth IRAs are much higher, and the individual may or may not qualify to make a nondeductible contribution to the Roth IRA. As the 2020 MAGI thresholds applicable to Roth IRAs are $196,000 to $206,000 for married individuals filing jointly, the individual with MAGI of $114,000 would qualify to make a nondeductible contribution of $3,000 to the Roth IRA.

According to the Investment Company Institute, IRA funds consist of $11 trillion, as compared to $32.3 trillion in the overall U.S. retirement market, generally as a result of rolling monies from an employer-provided plan into an IRA.[6] Thus, IRAs represent a large share of an individual's retirement nest egg.

IRAs established by an individual are not subject to Title I of ERISA.[7]

---

6. *See, Frequently Asked Questions About Individual Retirement Accounts (IRAs)*, INVESTMENT CO. INST. (June 2020), https://www.ici.org/faqs/faq/Individual-Retirement-Accounts-(IRAs)-FAQs/ci.faqs_iras.print.

7. IRAs are exempt from Title I of ERISA, including the reporting and disclosure rules of Part 1, ERISA § 101(a); the participation, benefit accrual, and survivor annuity rules of Part 2, ERISA § 201(6); the funding rules of Part 3, ERISA 301(a)(7); and the fiduciary standards of Part 4, ERISA § 401(a). According to the DOL regulations, IRAs are generally not employee benefit plans and thus not subject to Title I of ERISA, unless they are sponsored by an employer who does more than facilitate the payroll deduction of contributions to an IRA. 29 C.F.R. § 2510.3-2(d)(1) provides that "(1) For purposes of Title I of the Act and this chapter, the terms 'employee pension benefit plan' and 'pension plan' shall not include an individual retirement account described in section 408(a) of the Code, an individual retirement annuity described in section 408(b) of the Internal Revenue Code of 1954 (hereinafter 'the Code') and an individual retirement bond described in section 409 of the Code, provided that — (i) No contributions are made by the employer or employee association; (ii) Participation is completely voluntary for employees or members; (iii) The sole involvement of the employer or employee organization is without endorsement to permit the sponsor to publicize the program to employees or members, to collect contributions through payroll deductions or dues checkoffs and to remit them to the sponsor; and (iv) The employer or employee organization receives no consideration in the form of cash or otherwise, other than reasonable compensation for services actually rendered in connection with payroll deductions or dues checkoffs."

2. Required Provisions for IRAs

There are a number of required provisions for an IRA to retain its tax status:

- The IRA assets must be fully vested at all times;[8]

- The IRA must have a written document setting forth the owner's legal rights and obligations, as well as the duties of those holding the IRA assets.[9] IRA assets must be held either by a trustee or a custodian. Custodians may be banks, trust companies, or other entities/persons approved by the IRS to serve as a custodian;

- The IRA must reside as a domestic trust or custodianship so that the U.S. federal courts have access to the funds should the trustee or custodian have to be removed;[10]

- The trust or custodial account must be established "for the exclusive benefit of an individual or his beneficiaries";[11]

- Non-rollover IRAs are subject to maximum annual contribution limits;[12]

- No contributions could be made after age 70½; however that limitation was repealed by SECURE Act;[13] and

- The IRA account balance cannot be used as security for a loan (i.e., pledging the IRA).[14]

Contributions must be in cash only and generally are deductible if made on or before the due date of the taxpayer's return (for example, the taxpayer can take a deduction for the 2020 calendar year if contributions are made no later than April 15, 2021).

The distribution rules for IRAs are similar to the ones applicable to qualified retirement plans. Generally, the individual pays taxes in the year of distribution on both the initial contributions and earnings on such amounts. There is 10% tax penalty for early distributions (i.e., before age 59½).[15] But there are exceptions to the premature penalty, for first-time home purchases and for certain medical expenses. The minimum

---

8. I.R.C. § 408(a)(4).

9. I.R.C. § 408(a); Treas. Reg. § 1.408-2(b). Normally a trustee is the owner of the trust, whereas the custodian merely holds the assets of the trust. But for IRA purposes, there is little difference. Banks generally serve as trustee for the IRA, whereas financial institutions generally serve as custodian. However, I.R.C. § 408(h) states that the IRA custodial account is to be treated as an IRA trust provided the assets are held by a bank, trust company, or other approved entity. Thus, the IRA custodian is to be treated as a trustee for all Code requirements.

10. I.R.C. § 408(a); Treas. Reg. § 1.408-2(b), -2(a).

11. I.R.C. § 408(a).

12. I.R.C. § 408(a)(1).

13. SECURE § 107, repealing I.R.C. § 219(e).

14. I.R.C. § 408(e)(4). This prohibition clearly applies when the IRA owner uses his or her IRA as security for a personal loan; what is unclear is whether it extends to pledging other assets of an IRA for a loan to another IRA.

15. I.R.C. § 72(t)(1).

distribution rules discussed in Chapter 10 apply to IRAs, but there is no exception for delayed retirement (i.e., the rules are delayed for non-5% owners until actual retirement), as the IRA owner owns 100% of the IRA and thus is always a 5% owner.

3. Custodian versus Trustee

IRAs (both traditional and Roth) can be established as a trust or a custodial account in the United States. The differences between a trust account and a custodial account are minor, but important. Both types of accounts hold the monies for the benefit of the owner, but a trustee has discretionary authority over the monies, whereas a custodian does not. The IRS regulates who can serve as a trustee or a custodian. Generally, banks, federally insured credit unions, life insurance companies, mutual fund companies, savings and loan associations, and investment brokerage firms may serve as either a trustee or a custodian for an IRA. Thus, the IRA owner will want to know which type of account he or she is opening, and the amount of investment authority to be conferred upon the trustee or custodian.

4. Rollovers

A rollover is a transaction in which the taxpayer takes funds from one IRA or other eligible retirement plan and moves them to another IRA or other eligible retirement plan. Under the tax rules, the taxpayer has a maximum of 60 days to put the funds into an IRA or other eligible retirement plan to avoid having the funds subject to taxation. Under the one-year hold rule, an individual gets only one rollover between IRAs per 12-month period.[16] The rollover must qualify as a tax-free rollover in order to avoid income tax liability and the tax penalty for early withdrawal. The annual contribution maximum limit does not apply to a rollover contribution. The bulk of the IRA assets come from these rollover transfers.

A rollover is in contrast to a transfer, whereby the assets of an IRA or other eligible retirement plan are transferred directly by the trustee to another IRA trustee, custodian, or annuity issuer (referred to as a trust-to-trust transfer). The advantages of doing a trust-to-trust transfer are that (1) there is no required federal income tax withholding, and thus the entire amount can be transferred, and (2) the transfer avoids the one-year waiting period applicable to IRA-to-IRA rollovers. The direct trust-to-trust transfer is the preferred route unless the taxpayer needs access to the funds for a short period of time and expects to make the transfer to an IRA or other eligible retirement plan within the 60-day period.

5. Roth IRAs

Roth IRAs are a creation of the TRA '97 and operate in the same fashion as a traditional IRA, other than that the contributions are not deductible, but all the "qual-

---

16. *See* IRS Announcement 2014-15.

ifying distributions" from the Roth IRA are tax free.[17] Other advantages attributable to Roth IRAs include being able to make contributions regardless of age and not being subject to the minimum distribution rules.

The maximum dollar and percentage limitations on annual dollar contributions made to the Roth IRA are the same as a traditional IRA, but they are phased out based on one's adjusted gross income; AGI income threshold numbers are larger than those used for traditional IRAs.

A "qualifying distribution" from a Roth IRA will not be taxable as gross income provided the payment or distribution is one that is *both* (1) made after five years and (2) made on account of the following reasons:

- Made on or after the date on which the individual attains age 59½;
- Made to a beneficiary or the estate on or after the death of the individual;
- Attributable to the individual becoming disabled; or
- Which is a qualified special purchase distribution (i.e., used to buy a first home or for qualified higher education expenses).[18]

The five-year period noted above begins on the first day of the individual's tax year for which the individual made a Roth IRA contribution (or the individual's spouse made a contribution to the Roth IRA established for the individual).

B. Prohibited Transaction Rules

1. Overview

I.R.C. § 4975 subjects IRAs to the Code's prohibited transaction rules which are set forth in that section.[19] Since Title I and the Code set forth comparable prohibited transaction rules, the DOL was granted jurisdiction over these rules through the Reorganization Act of 1978. Those rules generally prohibit the sale, lending, furnishing of goods or services, transfer of plan assets, dealing on one's own interest, and receipt of compensation for one's own benefit between the plan and a disqualified person.[20] The term "disqualified person" for Code purposes is generally the same as the term used to describe a "party-in-interest" person for Title I purposes; however, an employee who is a participant of the plan or account is not automatically a disqualified person for Code purposes.

2. Self-Directed IRAs

By definition, IRAs are self-directed accounts, as the IRA owner must select the account's investments. The term "self-directed" may mean different things to different

---

17. I.R.C. § 408A.
18. I.R.C. § 408A(2)(A).
19. I.R.C. § 4975.
20. I.R.C. § 4975(c).

people, but it generally refers to the IRA owner's ability to select investments for the IRA that *go beyond* the investment platform offered by the trustee or custodian. Due to factors regarding the financial markets in 2008, low interest rates, and mutual fund fees, IRA owners have begun to invest in less conventional, non-publicly traded assets (e.g., real estate, gold and silver, private equity). The decline in the financial markets during 2020 due to the Coronavirus will undoubtedly lead to IRA owners looking to other nonmarketable securities. Under the terms of many IRAs, the trustees and custodian routinely state that they will not review the merits or legality of a given investment under the IRA made by its owner. Thus, there is no oversight of the investments purchased, leaving the IRA owner to be responsible as to the legality of its investments. However, IRA owners may be unaware of investments that may run afoul of the prohibited transaction rules. The consequences of committing a prohibited transaction in the IRA context are dire, because it ceases to be an IRA retroactively as of the first day of the taxable year in which the prohibited transaction occurred.[21] Other parties (e.g., bank trustee or custodian) who have engaged in a prohibited transaction are subject to a 15% initial excise tax on the amount involved, plus the potential for another 100% excise tax if the transaction is not timely corrected.[22]

The GAO has done a number of reports on IRAs in recent years. In 2014, it noted concern over the use of mega IRAs and self-directed IRAs, recommending that the IRS keep data regarding IRA accounts that hold *nonmarketable securities*. The fear was that IRA owners were engaging in prohibited transactions when investing their IRA assets (for example, using one's IRA account to purchase a vacation home for the IRA owner's family). Beginning in 2015, the IRS began to require trustees and custodians of IRAs to report information about nonmarketable securities. The intent was to target audits of IRAs that may have been improperly valuing their assets and to assess the threat of prohibited transactions occurring. Another GAO Report in 2016 recommended to the IRS to do more educational training for IRA owners as to the potential danger in investing in nonmarketable securities.[23] A subsequent 2019 GAO report recommended the IRS and DOL collaborate to better educate the IRA owner community of the potential for disqualifying the IRA with nonmarketable securities.[24] This issue continues to be pervasive as IRA assets continue to grow in the U.S. marketplace.[25]

21. I.R.C. §§ 408(e)(2)(B), 408(d) (causing the entire distribution to be taxable under I.R.C. § 72, with possible excise taxes for premature distributions under I.R.C. § 72(t)).

22. I.R.C. § 4975(a), (b).

23. U.S. Gov't Accountability Office, GAO-15-16, *Individual Retirement Accounts: IRS Could Bolster Enforcement on Multimillion Dollar Accounts, but More Direction from Congress Is Needed* (2014), https://www.gao.gov/products/GAO-15-16.

24. U.S. Gov't Accountability Office, GAO-19-945, *Individual Retirement Accounts: Formalizing Labor's and IRS's Collaborative Efforts Could Strengthen Oversight of Prohibited Transactions* (2019), https://www.gao.gov/products/GAO-19-495.

25. *See* Kathryn J. Kennedy, *The Perils of Self-Directed IRAs, in* Marquette Benefits & Social Welfare L. Rev. (forthcoming 2020).

3. Fiduciary Rules

Professional investment advisers may receive commissions or fee-based compensation for investment services rendered to plans, including IRAs. Title I applies to employer plans and thus, would judge the services of a professional investment adviser according to ERISA's exclusive purpose rule, which requires any compensation paid to be reasonable. IRAs are not subject to Title I and thus, the exclusive purpose of Title I does not apply. Under the prohibited transaction rules, their compensation could not be related, directly or indirectly, to the selection of an investment choice made by the employer or a plan participant. Under the DOL's 1976 rules as to who is a fiduciary by virtue of rendering investment advice (the so-called "fiduciary investment advisor"), any recommendation by a professional investment adviser to a plan participant or beneficiary to take a distribution from the plan and roll it into an IRA was **not** investment advice.[26] The DOL attempted to change the definition of a fiduciary who renders investment advice and what constitutes investment advice in its 2016 final regulations.[27]

The 2016 regulations revoked the earlier five-part definition of a fiduciary who renders investment advice and replaced it with a much broader test. The new rules define a fiduciary investment advisor for purposes of ERISA § 3(21) as someone who (1) provides "covered advice" for a fee to a plan, participant, or beneficiary, or an IRA or IRA owner, and (2) either acknowledges himself or herself to be a fiduciary or provides advice under an agreement based on the investment needs of the participant or directs advice to the participant regarding the advisability of a particular investment or management decisions regarding securities.[28] "Covered advice" for this purpose included two different types of recommendations:

- Recommendations as to whether to acquire, hold, dispose, or change securities or other property, including whether to take a distribution of benefits from a plan and roll over such amounts into an IRA; and

- Recommendations with respect to the management of securities including the names of other persons who could provide advice or management services, whether to select a brokerage or advisory account arrangement, or whether, in what amount, and in what form, to what destination, rollovers from a plan or IRA are to be made.[29]

The DOL regulations attempted to broaden the net of persons who could be a fiduciary by virtue of rendering investment advice, and to expand the type of investment advice that could be considered "rendering investment advice." The DOL also used its authority under the Reorganization Act of 1978, which gave it jurisdiction over the prohibited transaction rules both in Title I and in the Code, to subject IRAs to

---

26. Labor Reg. § 2510.3-21(c)(1) (Oct. 31, 1975).
27. Labor Reg. § 2510.3-21 (Apr. 8, 2016).
28. Labor Reg. § 2510.3-21(a)(2).
29. *Id.*

these new rules. As IRAs are not employee benefit plans for purposes of Title I, the DOL normally would not have jurisdiction over those plans. However, IRAs are subject to the Code's prohibited transaction rules.

As part of the package, the DOL issued new prohibited transaction class exemptions, including the best interest contract (BIC) exemption.[30] The BIC exemption was intended to cover broker dealers and insurance agents rendering nondiscretionary investment advice to retirement investors in return for fees that were related to the selection of the investment option. Without such an exemption, any commissions received by those individuals would have been a prohibited transaction. It also expanded what types of recommendations made by a broker dealer or insurance agent constituted "investment advice" recommendations, thereby subjecting those individuals to ERISA's fiduciary standards. It also created for IRA owners private causes of actions in cases where advisers failed to abide by the BIC Exemption.

Needless to say, the DOL regulations and their related class exemptions met with resistance from the financial industry. The U.S. Court of Appeals for the Fifth Circuit vacated the DOL's fiduciary rules *in toto* (i.e., unless appealed, the entire rule would be invalid nationwide).[31] The court found that the DOL had exceeded its authority under ERISA to expand the definition of an investment advice fiduciary. The DOL allowed its right to appeal to expire and the Fifth Circuit declined to allow other parties to join the case. Hence its rule became final on June 21, 2018.[32] Thus, the original DOL fiduciary rules defining who is an investment advice fiduciary continue to apply. In May of 2018, the DOL issued a Field Assistant Bulletin providing temporary non-enforcement of the prohibited transaction exemption for investment advice fiduciaries who worked "diligently and in good faith" to comply with certain provisions of the Best Interest Contract Exemption.[33]

The DOL's fiduciary rule and exemptions would have directly impacted those individuals selling investment products and services to IRA owners.[34] By 2019, practitioners shifted their attention to the new Securities and Exchange Commission's final regulations regarding new fiduciary standards for broker-dealers and registered investment advisers providing investment advice to retail investors, including IRA owners, referred to as Regulation Best Interest.[35] On June 29, 2020, the DOL affirmed

---

30. Best Interest Contract Exemption, 81 Fed. Reg. 20946 (Apr. 8, 2016), and Class Exemption for Principal Transactions in Certain Assets Between Investment Advice Fiduciaries and Employee Benefit Plans, 81 Fed. Reg. 21089 (Apr. 8, 2016).

31. U.S. Chamber of Commerce v. DOL, 885 F.3d 360 (5th Cir. 2018).

32. U.S. Chamber of Commerce v. DOL, No. 17-10238 (5th Cir. May 2, 2018).

33. DOL Field Assistant Bulletin 2018-02, https://dol.gov/agencies/ebsa/employers-and-advisers/guidance/field-assistance-bulletins/2018-02 (May 18, 2018).

34. *See* U.S. Dep't of Labor, Adv. Op. 2005-23A, regarding the responsibility of a plan fiduciary when investment advice and services are provided to plan participants and beneficiaries by outside financial planners or advisers, in the context of self-directed definition contribution plans.

35. SEC, Press Release 2019-89, *Regulation Best Interest ("Regulation BI"), SEC Adopts Rules and Interpretations to Enhance Protections and Preserve Choice for Retail Investors in Their Relationships with Financial Professionals* (June 5, 2019), https://www.sec.gov/news/press-release/2019-89?utm_

that the 1975 regulation with its five-part test, has been reinstated. It also proposed a new class prohibited transaction exemption permitting the receipt of compensation when a fiduciary provided non-discretionary investment advice, invoking requirements of an impartial conduct standard, a best interest standard, and a reasonable compensation standard.[36]

---

source=Law+Alert+-+Reg+BI+-+6%2F7%2F19&utm_campaign=2%2F21%2F17+Newsletter&utm_medium=email.

36. *See* DOL Improving Investment Advice for Workers & Retirees, ZRIN 1210-ZA29, https://www.dol.gov/sites/dolgov/files/ebsa/laws-and-regulations/rules-and-regulations/proposed-regulations/investment-advice-fiduciaries/improving-investment-advice-for-workers-and-retirees.pdf (June 29, 2020).

About the Author

Kathryn J. Kennedy is a full Professor of Law and Director of the Graduate Programs in Taxation, the Graduate Programs in Employee Benefits Law, and the Graduate Programs in Estate Planning at UIC John Marshall Law School in Chicago. She received her B.S. from Drake University (with honors) and a J.D. from Northwestern University School of Law (*summa cum laude*). She practiced with the law firm of McDermott, Will & Emery in Chicago, IL. She is also a Fellow of the Society of Actuaries (FSA) and was a practicing actuary for CNA Insurance Company and Towers Perrin. She joined the faculty of UIC John Marshall Law School in 1996. Since that time, she developed the nation's only graduate programs in employee benefits law, now with a total of 20 different courses in employee benefits. Professor Kennedy writes and lectures on matters relating to tax and employee benefits law. Professor Kennedy has been a member of the IRS' Advisory Committee on Tax Exempt and Government Entities (the "ACT"), as well as a member of the U.S. Department of Labor's ERISA Advisory Council. She was awarded the ASPPA Educator of the Year Award. She was chair and vice chair of the Employee Benefits Committee of the ABA Section of Taxation. She has served on the Board of Governors of the American College of Employee Benefits Council (ACEBC). She has a more advanced textbook on the topic of employee benefits law entitled *Employee Benefits Law Qualification and ERISA Requirements*, 3d edition, published by Carolina Academic Press Graduate Tax Series.

Index

Pages with tables are indicated by a "t" following the page number.